HG2491 .R44 1988

Restructuring banking and
financial services in America

DATE DUE

OCT 1 0 1990			
MAR 20 02			

DEMCO 38-297

RESTRUCTURING BANKING & FINANCIAL SERVICES IN AMERICA

RESTRUCTURING BANKING & FINANCIAL SERVICES IN AMERICA

EDITED BY
WILLIAM S. HARAF
AND
ROSE MARIE KUSHMEIDER

AMERICAN ENTERPRISE INSTITUTE FOR PUBLIC POLICY RESEARCH
WASHINGTON, D.C.

Distributed by arrangement with

UPA, Inc.
4720 Boston Way
Lanham, Md. 20706

3 Henrietta Street
London WC2E 8LU England

Library of Congress Cataloging-in-Publication Data

Restructuring banking and financial services in America / William S.
  Haraf and Rose Marie Kushmeider, editors.
    p. cm. — (AEI studies ; 481)
  Bibliography: p.
  Includes index.
  ISBN 0-8447-3670-8 (alk. paper). ISBN 0-8447-3671-6 (pbk. : alk. paper)
    1. Banks and banking—United States. 2. Financial services industry—United States. I. Haraf, William S. II. Kushmeider, Rose Marie. III. Series.
  HG2491.R44 1988
  332. 1'0973—dc19   88-19720
                                                                   CIP

1 3 5 7 9 10 8 6 4 2

AEI Studies 481

© 1988 by the American Enterprise Institute for Public Policy Research, Washington, D.C. All rights reserved. No part of this publication may be used or reproduced in any manner whatsoever without permission in writing from the American Enterprise Institute except in the case of brief quotations embodied in news articles, critical articles, or reviews. The views expressed in the publications of the American Enterprise Institute are those of the authors and do not necessarily reflect the views of the staff, advisory panels, officers, or trustees of AEI.

"American Enterprise Institute" and (AEI) are registered service marks of the American Enterprise Institute for Public Policy Research.

Printed in the United States of America

Contents

	Foreword *Christopher C. DeMuth*	ix
	Preface *William S. Haraf*	xiii
	Contributors	xix
1	Redefining Financial Markets *William S. Haraf and Rose Marie Kushmeider*	1
	Recent Trends in the Financial Services Industry 2 Conclusions 26	
2	Financial Stability and the Federal Safety Net *Anna J. Schwartz*	34
	A History of Banking Difficulties 39 The Increase in Regulation after the Bank Failures of the 1930s 43 Deposit Insurance in an Era of Change 47 The Role of Monetary Authorities 50 Are Deregulation and Financial Stability Compatible? 53	
3	Regulating Bank Safety and Performance *George J. Benston and George G. Kaufman*	63
	Proposals for Changing the Present Bank Regulatory System 63 A Proposal for Timely Intervention and Reorganization of Banks 85	
	Commentary	100
	Paul M. Horvitz 100 *John H. Kareken* 104 *Stanley C. Silverberg* 108	

4 THE FUTURE FINANCIAL STRUCTURE: FEARS AND
POLICIES *Franklin R. Edwards* 113

    Regulation versus the Free Market 115
    Consolidation, Concentration, and Monopoly
        Power 116
    Are Banks Special? 121
    Noncompetitive Concerns 125
    The Law and Policy Governing
        Competition 134
    Summary and Recommendations 139
    Appendix A 141
    Appendix B 147

5 BANK HOLDING COMPANIES: STRUCTURE,
PERFORMANCE, AND REFORM *Anthony Saunders* 156

    The Unique or Special Functions of Banks 157
    The Costs and Benefits of Bank Affiliation with
        Holding Companies 163
    Alternative Bank Organizational Structures 190
    Conclusion 192

COMMENTARY 203

    Robert A. Eisenbeis 203
    Thomas F. Huertas 211

6 FINANCIAL DEREGULATION, MONETARY POLICY, AND
CENTRAL BANKING *Marvin Goodfriend and Robert G.
King* 216

    Monetary and Banking Policy 217
    Deregulation and Monetary Policy 218
    Deregulation and Banking Policy 225
    Systemwide Banking and Financial Market
        Crises 236
    Conclusion 243

COMMENTARY *Phillip Cagan* 254

7 PAYMENTS SYSTEM RISK AND PUBLIC POLICY *Mark J.
Flannery* 261

    Risks in the Payments System 263
    Contagious Failures and Payments System
        Risk 271

Controlling Daylight Overdrafts on
  Fedwire   273
Commercial Firms' Access to the Payments
  System   277
Some Related Issues for Further Research   280
Summary   282

COMMENTARY   *Edward C. Ettin*   288

8 The Future Structure of the Housing Finance System   *John C. Weicher*   296

The Development of the System   297
Inflation and the Disintegration of the
  Specialized System   301
The Problem of the FSLIC and the S&Ls   304
The Secondary Market Agencies   310
The System of the Future   322
Housing and the New System   325
Is Housing Special?   327

COMMENTARY   *Bert Ely*   337

9 How Market Forces Influence the Structure of Financial Regulation   *Edward J. Kane*   343

Regulatory Market Structure   345
Patterns of Adjustment in Regulatory Market
  Structure   352
Regulatory Benefits, Costs, and Profits   356
Differences in Performance Criteria and
  Managerial Incentives between Private and
  Governmental Regulators   360
Constraints on Effective Regulatory
  Burdens   362
Structural Arbitrage and Unintended Subsidies
  to Risk Bearing by Financial Institutions   364
International Competition among
  Regulators   366
Summary and Policy Implications   378

COMMENTARY   383

Kenneth A. McLean   383
Kenneth E. Scott   386

10	**INNOVATION, INSTITUTIONAL CHANGES, AND REGULATORY RESPONSE IN INTERNATIONAL FINANCIAL MARKETS** *David F. I. Folkerts-Landau and Donald J. Mathieson*	392
	Structural Change, Regulatory Policy, and Supervisory Practices 393
Evolution of International Financial Markets and Changes in Regulatory and Supervisory Policies 400
Issues Raised by Recent Developments 414
Appendix: Liberalization and Innovation 419	
	COMMENTARY *Richard J. Herring*	424
11	**PRINCIPAL POLICY CONCLUSIONS AND RECOMMENDATIONS OF THE FINANCIAL SERVICES REGULATION PROJECT** *William S. Haraf*	431
	Competition and Financial Structure 432
Deposit Insurance Reform 433
Monetary Policy, Central Banking, and the Payments System 435
The Housing Finance System 437
The Regulatory Structure and International Coordination 438
Conclusions 439	
	THE POLICY PROPOSALS IN THE AEI STUDIES *Allan H. Meltzer*	440
	General Comments 441
The Specific Recommendations 444	
	BIBLIOGRAPHY	449
	INDEX	483

Foreword

Financial markets have been the scene of revolutionary change in recent years, caused by more volatile economic conditions, the development of new technologies, and the opening of world capital markets. New financial services and new marketing methods have emerged and flourished alongside established services and suppliers. Firms accustomed to being sheltered from competition are learning to navigate in the gale. Consumers—from home buyers to pensioners to corporate takeover specialists—are making use of an array of financing alternatives unheard of fifteen years ago.

The statutes and regulations governing our financial markets have not kept pace with this change. These laws, largely dating from the 1930s and earlier, segment financial markets by "lines of business" (commercial banking, mortgage banking, investment banking, insurance, securities brokerage, and others) and by state and geographic region. They also insure customers against losses from some but not other kinds of financial services and supervise in varying detail the management of some but not other kinds of financial service suppliers.

The established system of regulation, government market allocation, and deposit insurance protection is straining under the forces of economic change and increased international competition. New financial services defy the received line-of-business and geographic boundaries. In part because of obsolete regulatory policies, the federal deposit insurance programs are under greater financial pressure than ever before. At the same time, new risks to the financial system have emerged, such as the risk of large-scale disruptions in the payments system, that the deposit insurance system is incapable of managing. As a result, the actions of the Federal Reserve have taken on increasing significance. The overriding goal of the established banking policies is to promote safety and soundness, even at some sacrifice in economic efficiency. But today one must ask whether these policies are not seriously harming the soundness as well as the efficiency of our financial infrastructure.

FOREWORD

In response to these problems, legislators and regulatory officials have proposed an array of financial policy reforms in recent years. Some would give market forces a greater role by eliminating many regulatory barriers to line-of-business and geographic expansion while at the same time attempting to place the government's deposit insurance and supervisory programs on a more businesslike basis. Other proposals would strengthen regulatory barriers, impose new public obligations on certain kinds of financial service suppliers, and transfer more of the risk of bank and savings and loan failures to taxpayers. In general, the studies collected in this volume argue strongly for the former approach—for a thorough relaxation of market barriers and for a more limited and focused role for deposit insurance and regulation. They do so, however, not out of a reflexive preference for deregulation but out of a careful evaluation of the benefits and costs of current policies in today's dynamic economic circumstances and a serious regard for the goal of maintaining a financial system that is "safe and sound" as well as economically efficient.

The studies presented in this volume are the fruits of a two-year research project on the regulation of financial markets sponsored by the American Enterprise Institute for Public Policy Research. The project was directed by William S. Haraf, J. E. Lundy Scholar at AEI, and supervised by Marvin Kosters, AEI's director of economic policy studies. It was assisted by a distinguished advisory committee of legal experts, economists, and prominent business executives from all segments of the financial services industry.

The studies were conducted and written by leading banking and finance scholars who met frequently as their work proceeded to share drafts of their research with one another and with the project's advisory committee. Their papers were presented at a major AEI conference in Washington, D.C., on November 16–17, 1987. The conference attracted a large group of senior legislators and regulatory officials, business executives, academics, and journalists.

The result is a collection of papers that are individually fresh and penetrating, that complement one another in subject and approach, and that make a landmark contribution to one of the most urgent policy debates of the day. Their publication could not have come at a more auspicious time.

As this volume is going to press, it appears increasingly likely that major changes to established financial service policies will be considered in an atmosphere of crisis brought about by the looming insolvency of the federal deposit insurance programs. This atmosphere may lead to panicky stop-gap measures, or it may lead to more fundamental, forward-looking reforms than would otherwise have been politically feasible. If the AEI studies presented here demonstrate nothing else, they show that the stakes for the future performance of America's financial sector are immense and that the immediate dilemmas of the deposit insurance programs cannot usefully be considered in isolation. We hope and expect that these studies will also make an important contribution to the substance of the policy debates and to the ultimate goal of a sounder and more efficient financial system.

CHRISTOPHER C. DEMUTH
President
American Enterprise Institute
for Public Policy Research

Preface

Important developments have recently taken place in financial markets and public policy. Despite a pledge in 1987 to rationalize financial industry regulation, Congress in 1988 appears stalemated in its attempt to compromise on a piecemeal approach to deregulation. Meanwhile, the condition of the savings and loan industry and its deposit insurer, the Federal Savings and Loan Insurance Corporation, has deteriorated substantially despite favorable economic conditions and a congressional recapitalization of the FSLIC in spring 1988. Important segments of the banking industry remain seriously undercapitalized. The European Community has agreed to significant new directives making Western Europe a single market for financial services by 1992, posing an important competitive challenge to U.S. financial markets. These developments have increased the urgency of a bold approach to financial restructuring and safety net reform. Taken together, the policy recommendations in this volume offer a comprehensive approach that can place the financial system on a sound and competitive footing for the coming decades.

The American Enterprise Institute's financial regulation project was stimulated by the recognition that the system of laws and regulations governing financial firms is outdated and in need of a fundamental restructuring. We engaged a team of leading scholars to conduct a comprehensive study of financial regulatory issues in order to develop a consistent and coherent approach to regulatory reform. In view of the complex interrelations among the issues, the scholars met regularly over a fourteen-month period to review and discuss their findings. The studies in this volume reflect the results of that research.

In planning the project, we consulted extensively with government officials, private sector representatives, and academic scholars. To provide for systematic advice and review while the project was under way, we established an advisory committee, originally chaired by Barber Conable, then a senior fellow at AEI, and later chaired by Herbert Stein. Consultations among the scholars, members of the

PREFACE

advisory committee, and others while the research was in progress contributed importantly to shaping and enriching the studies in this volume.

The studies examine the full range of financial regulatory issues: policy mechanisms to ensure financial stability; product-line and geographic regulation; corporate structure issues and holding company regulation; the federal government's role in the housing finance system; the influence of regulation on international competition; and the design of the regulatory structure. Some issues, such as deposit insurance reform and the role of the lender of last resort, have long histories. Others, such as management of payments system risks and international coordination of regulatory policies, are newer but becoming increasingly important.

In chapter 1, "Redefining Financial Markets," Rose Kushmeider and I examine some of the important changes that have occurred in financial markets over the past decade: the securitization of credit; the development of new financial products and services; a trend toward geographic expansion by financial services firms both nationally and internationally; the movement toward the integration of a range of financial services offerings within a single organization; important innovations in the payments system; and, finally, significant strains within the banking and thrift industries. This chapter sets the stage for the chapters that follow by considering the major forces at work, the problems posed by regulations that have not kept pace with these developments, and the appropriate direction for regulatory reform.

Chapters 2 and 3 are devoted to policies for ensuring financial stability. Responsibility for maintaining financial stability in the United States is shared between the deposit insurance system and the Federal Reserve in its role as lender of last resort and ultimate supplier of liquidity to the financial system. Indeed, deposit insurance was established in 1933 after the failure of monetary policy effectively to contain the financial crisis associated with the Great Depression. Today the rising number of problem and failed banks and thrifts, the proliferation of new financial instruments, the vulnerability of the payments system to disruptions of various kinds, the ability to transfer funds rapidly across national borders, and the reduced role of traditional financial intermediation have raised new concerns about safety net policies. In chapter 2, "Financial Stability and the Federal Safety Net," Anna Schwartz examines the roles of deposit insurance and the central bank in maintaining financial stability, focusing on the latter. She reviews the historical causes and consequences of financial crises in the United States and abroad to draw lessons for central bank policy.

Deeply rooted problems with the deposit insurance system are at the core of many concerns about the present regulatory system. In recent years policies on failure resolution, regulatory forbearance, and explicit extensions of coverage have expanded the level of deposit insurance protection. As a result, market disciplines have eroded, exacerbating the perverse incentives built into the system. In chapter 3, "Regulating Bank Safety and Performance," George Benston and George Kaufman critically examine the key problems with the present deposit insurance system and make some specific recommendations for improving its functioning.

Chapters 4 and 5 focus on the effect of regulation on efficiency, competition, and innovation in the financial industry. In chapter 4, "The Future Financial Structure: Fears and Policies," Franklin Edwards examines arguments against removing barriers to geographic expansion and to integration of financial services within a single firm. He evaluates the potential for unfair competitive practices and conflicts of interest and how best to address those problems. He also examines concerns over safety and soundness and concentration of economic and political power.

Depository firms have been uniquely subject to restrictions on corporate ownership and affiliations that have impeded the integration of banking with other financial and nonfinancial services. The potential benefits from integration in the form of synergies to producers and consumers could be substantial, but significant concerns have also been expressed. In chapter 5, "Bank Holding Companies: Structure, Performance, and Reform," Anthony Saunders examines the major issues posed by affiliations between depository firms and other financial and commercial enterprises, such as containing implicit subsidies from safety net policies, minimizing conflict-of-interest abuses, and protecting the payments system.

Monetary policy is conducted within a framework that includes reserve requirements, access to the discount window, examination and supervision, and interest rate controls. In chapter 6, "Financial Deregulation, Monetary Policy, and Central Banking," Marvin Goodfriend and Robert King argue that the Federal Reserve's banking policies are unnecessary for the conduct of monetary policy. These policies impose both direct costs and efficiency losses that are not justifiable on macroeconomic grounds. Goodfriend and King examine in particular the underlying rationale for public lending to individual firms through the discount window, and in so doing they raise important questions concerning the Federal Reserve's management of the discount window.

The system for making payments in the United States has been evolving rapidly in recent years. A surging volume of payments, especially over the electronic transfer systems, has raised new concerns. The Federal Reserve and users of private electronic transfer systems are exposed to substantial credit risk during the day under current arrangements. Concern over these exposures has led to a wide range of proposed changes in payments practices and has been used to justify restrictions on the activities of bank holding companies. Mark Flannery evaluates a range of proposed changes in the payments system and recommends measures for managing electronic payments system exposure in chapter 7, "Payments System Risk and Public Policy."

The United States has had a specialized housing finance system with pervasive government involvement since the 1930s. That system is now coming apart as a result of a number of pressures. The problems of the savings and loan industry and the recent bankruptcy of its deposit insurer, the FSLIC, have received considerable attention, but the role of the federally sponsored secondary mortgage market agencies also merits reassessment. In chapter 8, "The Future Structure of the Housing Finance System," John Weicher concludes that the FSLIC recapitalization passed by Congress is inadequate for the full scope of the savings and loan problem. He evaluates a range of options for coping with the near-term problem, including a merger with the Federal Deposit Insurance Corporation fund. Weicher also examines a range of proposals for the secondary mortgage agencies, including privatization. Finally, he examines the underlying rationales for government involvement in housing finance and considers the operation of a system with a diminished federal presence.

The regulatory system in the United States imposes a mixture of burdens and subsidies on regulated firms. Historically, changes in financial regulation have occurred as a result of market and political forces that have affected the magnitude of those burdens and subsidies and as a result of competition among regulators both in the United States and abroad. In chapter 9, "How Market Forces Influence the Structure of Financial Regulation," Edward Kane examines ways to improve the functioning of the regulatory system within a framework that incorporates the influence of both market forces and political and bureaucratic incentives.

Financial firms are increasingly competing in a global marketplace for financial services. This competition is taking place not only among private firms but also among regulatory systems as nations compete to attract a greater share of the international financial services market. Standards of leverage, accounting rules, levels of supervision, and the reach of government safety nets differ substantially around the world, but pressures for greater coordination of regulatory policies are developing as financial firms relocate their activities to favorable regulatory climates. In chapter 10, "Innovation, Institutional Changes, and Regulatory Response in International Financial Markets," David Folkerts-Landau and Donald Mathieson review international differences in regulatory policies and financial structures and the complex forces leading to change. They examine efforts to achieve greater coordination of regulatory policies and explore possibilities for improving the efficiency, stability, and integration of international financial markets.

Taken together these studies constitute a comprehensive review of financial services regulatory issues that is unique in its scope. Chapter 11, "Principal Policy Conclusions and Recommendations of the Financial Services Regulation Project," summarizes and synthesizes the major policy conclusions of the studies.

I am very grateful to the project authors and to members of the advisory committee for their individual and cooperative efforts in connection with this project. In addition, I thank Thomas Huertas, Fred Deming, John Hunnicutt, Milton Hudson, Michael Laub, Samuel Chase, and many others too numerous to mention for their help in various aspects of this project. I owe special thanks to Marvin Kosters for giving me the benefit of his insight and experience as the project progressed and to Rose Kushmeider, my research associate, for her efforts in bringing this project to fruition.

> WILLIAM S. HARAF
> J. E. Lundy Scholar and
> Director, Financial Markets Project
> American Enterprise Institute

Contributors

GEORGE J. BENSTON is the John H. Harland Professor of Finance, Accounting, and Economics, School of Business, and professor of economics, College of Arts and Sciences, at Emory University. He is also an honorary visiting professor at City University, London, and an invited lecturer, Law and Economic Center, George Mason University Law School. Dr. Benston has held numerous other teaching positions and has been a consultant to various public and private institutions. He is a trained C.P.A. and holds an M.B.A. from New York University and a Ph.D. from the University of Chicago.

PHILLIP CAGAN is a professor of economics at Columbia University and a visiting scholar at the American Enterprise Institute. He was a senior staff member of the Council of Economic Advisers and a member of the Advisory Committee on Monetary Statistics at the Federal Reserve Board. He has taught at several universities and is a research associate at the National Bureau of Economic Research. He is the author of five books and numerous articles on monetary policy, interest rates, inflation, and other economic topics. He holds a master's degree and a Ph.D. from the University of Chicago.

FRANKLIN R. EDWARDS is a professor and director of the Center for the Study of Futures Markets at Columbia University. His teaching and research interests include the regulation of financial markets and institutions, banking, and futures markets, and he has published widely in these areas. Dr. Edwards has also worked at the Federal Reserve Board and at the Office of the Comptroller of the Currency and consults on matters relating to antitrust law and regulation. He holds a Ph.D. from Harvard University and a J.D. from New York University Law School.

ROBERT A. EISENBEIS is the Wachovia Professor of Banking and coordinator of finance at the School of Business Administration at the University of North Carolina, Chapel Hill. A former senior deputy associate director of the Division of Research and Statistics at the Federal Reserve Board, Dr. Eisenbeis has written extensively in the area of banking. He received a master's degree and a Ph.D. from the University of Wisconsin.

BERT ELY is president of Ely & Company, Inc., a consulting firm to financial institutions. Specific projects with which Mr. Ely has been involved include an examination of the depositor protection process, historical studies of the banking system, and analyses of various aspects of current private and government deposit programs. He is currently examining how the structure of banking and financial services will be responding to technology and market-driven deregulation. Before forming his own consulting firm, Mr. Ely was chief financial officer of the Stuart McGuire Company and a senior consultant with Touche Ross & Company. Mr. Ely holds an M.B.A. from the Harvard Business School.

EDWARD C. ETTIN is deputy director of the Division of Research and Statistics of the Federal Reserve Board. With the board since 1964, he has served in various sections, including the Depository Institutions Deregulation Committee, the Federal Open Market Operations Committee, and the Office for Monetary and Financial Policy. Earlier, Mr. Ettin was an assistant professor of economics at Duke University. He received his Ph.D. from the University of Michigan.

MARK J. FLANNERY is professor of finance at the University of North Carolina, Chapel Hill. Previously, he was an assistant professor of finance at the Wharton School, University of Pennsylvania, and a research adviser at the Federal Reserve Bank of Philadelphia. In the field of banking he has written on bank profitability and capital, electronic funds transfer, and bank regulation. He is an associate editor of the *Journal of Finance*. Dr. Flannery received his master's degree and Ph.D. from Yale University.

DAVID F. I. FOLKERTS-LANDAU is a senior economist with the International Monetary Fund, where he is currently researching issues relating to the institutional evolution of international capital markets and the implications for pricing of credit, development finance, and financial regulation. Previously, he was an assistant professor at the University of Chicago and taught at Princeton University. He received his doctorate from Princeton University.

MARVIN GOODFRIEND is vice president and economist at the Federal Reserve Bank of Richmond and a visiting associate professor at the

University of Virginia. Previously, he was a visiting professor at the University of Rochester, a senior staff economist with the Council of Economic Advisers, and a visiting economist at the Federal Reserve Board. He is the author of *Monetary Policy in Practice* and an associate editor of the *Journal of Monetary Economics*. Dr. Goodfriend holds a master's degree and a Ph.D. from Brown University.

WILLIAM S. HARAF is the J. Edward Lundy Visiting Scholar and director of the Financial Markets Project at the American Enterprise Institute. Previously, he served as special assistant and as senior staff economist to the Council of Economic Advisers and has been a consultant to the World Bank. He is a contributing editor to *Regulation* magazine and the author of numerous articles on financial institutions and markets, macroeconomics, and monetary policy. Dr. Haraf has taught at Brown University. He received his Ph.D. from the University of Washington.

RICHARD J. HERRING is a professor of finance and director of the Program in International Banking and Finance at the Wharton School of the University of Pennsylvania. His research interests are banking and international finance, and he has written extensively in these areas. Dr. Herring has served as a consultant for the U.S. Department of the Treasury, the Federal Reserve Board, and the International Monetary Fund, as well as private corporations. He received his master's degree and Ph.D. from Princeton University.

PAUL M. HORVITZ is the Judge James A. Elkins Professor of Banking and Finance at the University of Houston. Formerly, he was a financial economist with the Federal Reserve Bank of Boston, senior economist at the Office of the Comptroller of the Currency, and assistant to the chairman of the Federal Deposit Insurance Corporation (FDIC). Dr. Horvitz has lectured at several universities and is the author of numerous books and articles on the financial system. He received his Ph.D. from the Massachusetts Institute of Technology.

THOMAS F. HUERTAS is assistant to the vice chairman for legal and external affairs at Citibank, where he is responsible for economic analysis of strategic and regulatory issues facing Citicorp. He is director of the Wall Street Planning Group, a research fellow at the Lehrman Institute, and a member of the Economic Advisory Committee of the American Bankers Association. Dr. Huertas holds a Ph.D. from the University of Chicago.

EDWARD J. KANE occupies the Everett D. Reese Chair of Banking and Monetary Economics at Ohio State University and is a research associate of the National Bureau of Economic Research. He has taught at several colleges and universities and has been a consultant to the FDIC, the Federal Reserve System, and several other government agencies. Dr. Kane is a former Guggenheim fellow and a past president of the American Finance Association. He received his Ph.D. from the Massachusetts Institute of Technology.

JOHN H. KAREKEN is a professor of banking and finance at the University of Minnesota, where he teaches financial management and regulation of depository institutions, international finance, and international banking. He has consulted on a variety of matters and was economic adviser to the president of the Federal Reserve Bank of Minneapolis. His publications include work in the theory of financial intermediaries, reform of deposit insurance, regulation of depository institutions, and international monetary reform. Dr. Kareken received his Ph.D. from the Massachusetts Institute of Technology.

GEORGE G. KAUFMAN is the John F. Smith Professor of Finance and Economics at Loyola University and is cochairperson of the Shadow Financial Regulatory Committee, a group of independent banking experts who analyze and comment on economic, legislative, and regulatory factors affecting the financial services industry. He has served as consultant to numerous government agencies and private firms, including the Federal Savings and Loan Insurance Corporation Task Force on Reappraising Federal Deposit Insurance, and has taught at several universities. Dr. Kaufman's research interests are financial economics, institutions and markets, and monetary policy. He received his Ph.D. from the University of Iowa.

ROBERT G. KING is a professor and chairman of the Department of Economics at the University of Rochester. His fields of interest are monetary and macroeconomic theory and applied econometrics and macroeconomics. He is the editor of the *Journal of Monetary Economics*. His Ph.D. is from Brown University.

ROSE MARIE KUSHMEIDER is a research associate with the Financial Markets Project at the American Enterprise Institute. She was previously a staff economist with a Washington, D.C., consulting firm specializing in regulatory and antitrust issues. Ms. Kushmeider is a doctoral candidate at the University of Maryland.

DONALD J. MATHIESON is chief of the Financial Studies Division of the International Monetary Fund. He is the author or coauthor of several articles on international capital markets. Dr. Mathieson has taught at Columbia University and California State University, Hayward. He holds a Ph.D. from Stanford University.

KENNETH A. MCLEAN has worked on Capitol Hill since 1967, serving with the exception of a brief stint as minority staff director of the Subcommittee on Labor, Health and Human Services, and Education, on the staff of the Senate Committee on Banking, Housing, and Urban Affairs. He is currently staff director of the committee under the chairmanship of Senator William Proxmire. Mr. McLean has worked on the Truth in Lending Act, the Monetary Control Act of 1980, and the Financial Services Competitive Equity Act. Mr. McLean is a graduate of the University of Iowa.

ALLAN H. MELTZER is the John M. Olin Professor of Political Economy and Public Policy at Carnegie-Mellon University. He has been a visiting professor at Harvard University, the University of Chicago, and the Austrian Institute for Advanced Study. He is a consultant to congressional committees, the president's cabinet, the Federal Reserve Board, and foreign central banks, among others. Dr. Meltzer's research and writing focus on the issue of money and capital markets. He is a founder and cochairman of the Shadow Open Market Committee. He holds a doctorate from the University of California, Los Angeles.

ANTHONY SAUNDERS is a professor of finance at the New York University Graduate School of Business Administration and a visiting scholar at the Federal Reserve Bank of Philadelphia. During 1984–1985 he was acting director of the Salomon Brothers Center for the Study of Financial Institutions at New York University. He is the editor of the Salomon Brothers Center Monograph Series in Finance and Economics. Dr. Saunders received his master's degree and Ph.D. from the London School of Economics.

ANNA J. SCHWARTZ is a research associate with the National Bureau of Economic Research and the 1987–1988 president of the Western Economic Association. In 1981–1982 she served as staff director of the U.S. Gold Commission. Dr. Schwartz is the author of numerous articles on monetary economics, which have recently been reprinted in *Money in Historical Perspective*. She has also collaborated with Milton Friedman on a series of studies, including *A Monetary History of the United States, 1867–1960*. Dr. Schwartz holds a Ph.D. from Columbia University.

CONTRIBUTORS

KENNETH E. SCOTT is the Ralph M. Parsons Professor of Law and Business at Stanford University, specializing in government regulation. He has served as chief deputy savings and loan commissioner of California and was general counsel of the Federal Home Loan Bank Board. Recently, Mr. Scott was a consultant with the Federal Reserve Board on the issue of the Glass-Steagall Act. He is coauthor or coeditor of two books on administrative law. He was chairman of the Banking Committee of the American Bar Association, Administrative Law Section. Mr. Scott holds a master's degree in political science from Princeton University and an L.L.B. from Stanford University.

STANLEY C. SILVERBERG is a consultant in banking, financial services, and economics. Previously, he was director of research at the Federal Deposit Insurance Corporation. While at the FDIC Dr. Silverberg played an active role in developing policy, especially in matters related to deposit insurance and the handling of failed banks and thrifts. He has also worked at the Department of the Treasury and taught at Yale University and George Washington University. Dr. Silverberg received his master's degree and Ph.D. from Yale University.

JOHN C. WEICHER holds the F. K. Weyerhaeuser Chair in Public Policy Research at the American Enterprise Institute. On leave from AEI during 1988, Dr. Weicher is serving as associate director for economic policy at the U.S. Office of Management and Budget. In 1981 he served as deputy staff director for the President's Commission on Housing, with primary staff responsibility for the interim report on subsidized housing. He has also served on the staff of the National Housing Policy Review and as chief economist and deputy assistant secretary for economic affairs at the U.S. Department of Housing and Urban Development. He has written widely on housing and domestic programs, including books on housing and on urban renewal. He has been a program director at the Urban Institute and a professor of economics at Ohio State University. He has a Ph.D. in economics from the University of Chicago.

Financial Markets Project Advisory Committee

Herbert Stein (Chairman)
Senior Fellow, American Enterprise Institute

Hans Angermueller
Vice Chairman, Citibank, N.A.

George J. Benston
Professor, Emory University

Stephen L. Brown
President and Chief Operating Officer
John Hancock Mutual Life Insurance Company

William Brown
Former Chairman and Chief Executive Officer
Bank of Boston Corporation

Barber Conable*
President, The World Bank

Richard Diehl
Chairman, Home Savings of America (H. F. Ahmanson)

David Feldman
Corporate Vice President for Investments
American Telephone and Telegraph Company

James Ford
Former Chairman, Ford Motor Credit Company

---

* Through June 1986.

Carter Golembe
Chairman, Golembe Associates Incorporated

Alan Greenspan**
Chairman, Board of Governors of the Federal Reserve System

John Hawke
Partner, Arnold and Porter

John Heimann
Vice Chairman, Merrill Lynch Capital Markets

Larry D. Horner
Chairman, Peat, Marwick, Main and Co.

Philip M. Knox
Greve, Clifford, Diepenbrock and Paras

David Marcus
Executive Vice President, New York Stock Exchange

Robert McCormick
President and Chief Executive Officer
Stillwater National Bank and Trust Company

Charles H. Morin
Partner, Dickstein, Shapiro and Morin

Tokuyuki Ono
Former Managing Director, Sumitomo Bank

John Rau
President, Exchange National Bank

Kenneth Scott
Professor, Stanford Law School

Donald Shackelford
Chairman, State Savings Company

** Through May 1987.

David Shute
Vice President and General Counsel
Sears Roebuck and Company

Howard Stein
Chairman and Chief Executive Officer
Dreyfus Corporation

Joel R. Wells, Jr.
President, SunTrust Banks, Inc.

Frank Zarb
Partner, Lazard Freres and Company

1
Redefining Financial Markets
William S. Haraf and Rose Marie Kushmeider

Financial markets facilitate the flow of funds between ultimate suppliers and ultimate users. They do so both directly through securities markets and indirectly through financial intermediaries. Financial markets also facilitate the exchange of assets within the economy. Ideally, financial markets should assist in channeling savings to their highest valued uses and in allocating specific risks to those willing and best able to bear them.

Financial firms provide services that can be generally grouped into four categories:

1. *Intermediation services.* Financial firms issue claims on themselves to fund their claims on others, thereby channeling cash from ultimate sources to ultimate users of funds.
2. *Transactions services.* Financial firms facilitate the transfer of claims between parties. These services range from simple check clearing, to securities brokerage, to complex transactions such as mergers and acquisitions.
3. *Financial advice.* Financial firms advise clients about the design of portfolios, cash management, financial structure, mergers and acquisitions, and the issuance of securities.
4. *Risk management.* Financial firms reallocate, diversify, and transform risks to which individuals and businesses are exposed.

Traditionally, financial firms have been classified according to the type of financial services they supply. Finance companies, for example, supply pure intermediation services, borrowing funds through securities markets to lend to others. The basic commercial banking function of accepting deposit liabilities to fund loans combines intermediation with the most basic of transactions services—payments services. Insurance companies offer intermediation services, financial advice, and risk management. The basic investment banking functions of underwriting and dealing securities combine both transactions services and financial advice. In reality, however, financial services define functions rather than firms. Although some firms do specialize, many now supply a wide range of services, sometimes through separate subsidiaries.

Over the years financial firms have adapted the services they provide to the changing requirements of the nonfinancial sector, to new technologies, to government intervention, and to changes in macroeconomic conditions. This has led to changes in the relative importance of existing financial products and to the development of new financial products and new methods of delivery. These developments, in turn, have blurred the sharp connection between financial products and industry segments. As the financial system continues to evolve, terms such as banking, insurance, and securities will increasingly be used to refer to specific services, not industries.

Recent Trends in the Financial Services Industry

Six broad categories of financial change have significantly affected the character of the financial services industry since the late 1970s: (1) the securitization of lending; (2) the development of new financial products and services; (3) an expansion of the geographic markets served by financial firms, both nationally and globally; (4) a growing number of mergers, acquisitions, and other affiliations both within the financial services industry and between financial and nonfinancial firms; (5) important new developments in the payments system; and (6) increasing financial strains among depository firms.

Securitization

A major development in financial markets around the world has been an explosion in the use of marketable securities. This phenomenon, known as securitization, has two dimensions. First, more borrowers are choosing to raise funds directly through the securities market rather than through financial intermediaries. Second, financial firms are increasingly involved in the process of creating, issuing, and distributing securities that represent ownership interests in other financial instruments or direct financial claims. Many observers believe the potential growth of securitized assets is enormous.

Corporate finance in the United States has been dramatically affected by the securitization process. For example, the commercial paper market, the primary substitute for short-term bank credit to corporate borrowers, grew from $13 billion in nonfinancial commercial paper outstanding in 1976 to $81 billion in 1987. Although the volume of short-term bank loans also grew, the relative importance of commercial paper as a short-term funding source over this period almost doubled.[1] Another aspect of the changing pattern of corporate finance has been the growth of the high-yield or "junk" bond market. By mid-1987 approximately $125 billion in high-yield bonds were outstanding.[2] Before 1982 companies lacking the credit standing to issue investment grade bonds were generally confined to borrowing through financial intermediaries.[3]

Whereas ten years ago only a small fraction of mortgage obligations were securitized, today the market for mortgage-backed securities is the largest of the securitized markets. By the third quarter of 1987, mortgage-backed securities outstanding exceeded $640 billion, over one-fifth of the total value of all mortgage claims. Since 1982, mortgage-backed securities have accounted for 60 percent of the growth in mortgage debt.[4] The sale of other asset-backed obligations—debt instruments that are claims against a pool of assets such as automobiles, credit card receivables, or leases—only began in 1985. Yet in just two years the amount of these securities outstanding had risen to almost $12 billion.[5] At the end of 1986, GMAC was the largest issuer of nonmortgage asset-backed obligations, with $8 billion outstanding.

Accompanying securitization has been a rapid expansion of the market for outright sales of loans, through participations and syndications. Loan sales grew from about $27 billion in the second quarter of 1983 to $115 billion in the first quarter of 1987.[6] Money center banks in particular are important originators of loans in this market, selling loans to pension funds, foreign banks, and smaller domestic banks.

The Causes of Securitization. Several factors account for the increased attractiveness of securities markets:

• Dramatic declines in transactions costs brought about by tremendous improvements in computer and communications technology have made it cheaper to collect and disseminate information. These lower costs have reduced the traditional comparative advantage of banks in information management and have contributed to an enormous expansion of securities trading volumes.[7]

• Greater volatility in the economy and of asset prices has increased the demand for the additional liquidity and risk management capabilities that securitization provides.

• The institutionalization of savings through insurance products, pension plans, and mutual funds has reduced the demand for intermediation services. Professional portfolio managers are less dependent upon other intermediaries for risk management and financial advice. Capital market instruments that are standardized, rated, and liquid afford portfolio managers greater flexibility and opportunities to earn higher returns.

• Developments in financial theory have led to sophisticated asset-liability management systems and techniques for pricing complex financial instruments.

• Regulatory changes, such as passage of SEC Rule 415 (shelf registration) in April 1982, have reduced the relative cost of issuing securities.[8] The efforts of government agencies such as the Federal Home Loan Mortgage Corporation (Freddie Mac) and the Federal National Mortgage Association (Fannie Mae) in the mid-1970s to standardize loan applications and appraisal reports and to introduce uniform security instruments greatly aided in the securitization of the mortgage market.

• Rising deposit insurance premiums, lower credit ratings on the debt instruments of banking organizations, and a higher opportunity cost of non-interest-bearing reserves may have raised the cost of borrowing through depository firms as compared with securities markets.

The Consequences of Securitization. Securitization has had a profound effect on financial markets. It has broadened the choices available to borrowers and lenders, it has increased liquidity, and it has provided new opportunities to diversify and tailor risk exposures.

Securitization has provided investment bankers with a direct way of challenging the position of commercial banks in the credit markets and has given commercial banks the impetus to expand their securities activities. Although commercial banks continue to be the chief source of short-term financing to corporate customers, certain categories of corporate lending have declined as a result of securitization. Money center banks have been particularly affected as well-known corporate customers with strong credit ratings, traditionally their strongest customers, have moved to the securities markets. Between 1975 and 1985, the commercial and industrial loans (C&I loans) of the nine largest banks declined from 25 to 15 percent of one broad measure of short-term credit extended to nonfinancial businesses.[9]

Commercial banks and savings and loans in all size ranges have transformed their businesses by focusing resources on the origination, distribution, servicing, and trading of obligations, rather than traditional portfolio lending.[10] Some S&Ls, in particular, have used securitization to reduce the volume of mortgages on their books and to focus their efforts on mortgage servicing and origination.[11] Of the $150 billion in mortgages that thrifts originated in 1985, only $57 billion were added to their own portfolios.[12] Many, however, hold mortgage-backed securities.

Securities firms have also aggressively expanded their role in financial markets. In addition to acting as underwriters and financial advisers, they are increasingly serving as direct commercial lenders providing bridge financing for mergers, acquisitions, and leveraged buyouts in competition with commercial banks.[13] Securities firms also trade for their own account and make markets in securities that have experienced rapidly increasing transactions volumes. As a result, the total assets held by securities firms have increased substantially. In 1985 alone, total assets increased 45 percent to $456 billion.[14]

Because of the growing volume of transactions handled by securities firms, investment banking requires greater amounts of capital than it did a decade ago. This has led to a significant consolidation of the industry and to a number of public and private equity offerings to outsiders.[15] Still, the securities industry is more highly leveraged than the commercial banking industry. For wholesale investment banks the equity-to-asset ratio averaged under 3 percent in 1986, while the equity-to-capital asset ratio of the largest commercial banks averaged over 5 percent.[16]

Securitization and the Separation of Commercial and Investment Banking. Increased securitization has renewed the debate over the value of separating commercial and investment banking. Until the 1930s, state and national banks engaged in securities underwriting and dealing, sometimes through affiliates. The wave of bank failures of the early 1930s and the belief by some that these failures were related to securities speculation by the banking industry led Congress to enact the Glass-Steagall Act as part of the Banking Act of 1933. The Glass-Steagall Act was designed to separate commercial and investment banking by barring Federal Reserve member banks from underwriting or dealing in most securities and barring securities firms from accepting deposits. The separation was intended to be incomplete from the start, however, and over time it has become even less well defined.

On balance, Glass-Steagall and more recently the Bank Holding Company Act have probably limited the securities activities of commercial banking organizations to a greater extent than the intermediation activities of investment banks. Nonetheless, commercial banking organizations are engaged in a growing range of securities activities, and securities firms are providing traditional banking services. Indeed, the combination of investment and commercial banking services, sometimes known as merchant banking, has become the focal point of competition between commercial banking organizations and securities firms.

Commercial banks have expanded their securities activities through a variety of channels. Bank holding companies engage in securities activities outside the United States, including the underwriting of securities issued by U.S. firms in overseas markets. In the first half of 1987 two subsidiaries of U.S. bank holding companies were among the top twenty-five managers of Eurobond underwritings.[17] At the end of 1986, thirty-eight subsidiaries of U.S. banks and bank holding companies were primarily engaged in securities activities abroad.[18]

Commercial banks have also expanded their domestic activity in areas not prohibited by Glass-Steagall.[19] They now place commercial paper, underwrite general obligation government securities, offer discount brokerage services, and buy and sell a variety of securities such as options and futures, which were never envisioned when Glass-Steagall became law. Commercial banks are also ranked among the largest participants in the private placement market, selling a wide range of securities, such as corporate debt and equity, asset-backed securities, and lease financing, to investors such as insurance companies.[20]

The meaning of the Glass-Steagall Act is now being thoroughly reexamined by regulators and the courts. For example, the act prohibits affiliates of member banks from being "engaged principally" in specified securities activities. In controversial decisions in early 1987 the Federal Reserve approved the applications of several bank holding companies to engage in limited securities activities through subsidiaries not "principally engaged" in these activities.[21] The legality of the Federal Reserve's decisions was challenged in the courts and subsequently upheld by a U.S. court of appeals. When the Supreme Court declined to review the case in June 1988, a path was cleared for bank holding companies to conduct limited securities activities.

Prohibitions against bank securities activities apply only to banks that are members of the Federal Reserve System, and not to state-chartered nonmember banks. As of April 1987, only a small number of state nonmember banks had securities subsidiaries, but a recent court decision and changes in state laws have led a number of banking organizations to convert banks to state-chartered institutions in order to conduct securities activities through subsidiaries.[22]

Finally, securities firms, insurance companies, and diversified nonbank financial firms offer banking services through limited-service or "nonbank" banks.[23] The largest, Boston Safe Deposit & Trust, owned by Shearson/American Express, had $8.3 billion in assets as of

March 31, 1987. Merrill Lynch, Bear Stearns, Dreyfus, Drexel Burnham Lambert, and many other securities firms also own limited-service banks.[24] Altogether, the size and range of services offered by these firms makes them formidable competitors of commercial banks.

Sentiment in favor of removing Glass-Steagall barriers is growing. In March 1988, the U.S. Senate passed a bill to repeal large sections of Glass-Steagall. The changes would allow organizations to conduct commercial and investment banking activities in separately capitalized affiliates within a common holding company structure.

New Products and Services

Financial market participants have been extraordinarily active in developing and utilizing a wide variety of new financial products and services.

Beginning in the 1960s, the combination of rising interest rates and binding interest rate ceilings on domestic deposit accounts led to innovations such as negotiable certificates of deposit (CDs), overnight and term Eurodollars, and overnight and term repurchase agreements (RPs) and later to sweep accounts and money market mutual funds. Financial innovation accelerated in the late 1970s as inflation and interest and exchange rate volatility led to new products to control risk and offer higher rates of return. Products such as floating rate bonds, convertible bonds, zero-coupon bonds, and bill and bond futures contracts expanded the range of options for coping with interest rate risk. Inflation risk also led many households to turn away from traditional cash-value life insurance as a means of saving in the 1970s. Terminations of and loans against existing policies increased while sales of new policies slowed. Insurance companies introduced major new products such as variable life and universal life policies, offering current market rates on the savings portion of the policy. In 1985 these policies accounted for 42 percent of new premiums on life insurance sales.[25] Health insurance and annuity offerings have also expanded. By 1985 these activities accounted for over 60 percent of life insurance companies' premium receipts.[26]

For banks and thrifts the late 1970s were a period of increasing challenges by nondepository firms. Between 1979 and 1982, for example, money market mutual funds grew by $170 billion as short-term interest rates approached the double-digit range for the first time in the postwar period. By the end of 1987 these funds controlled $310 billion in assets. Congress passed the Depository Institutions Deregulation and Monetary Control Act of 1980, which phased out interest rate ceilings on time and savings accounts, and the Garn–St

Germain Act of 1982, which authorized negotiable order of withdrawal (NOW), SuperNOW, and money market deposit accounts, to enhance the ability of depository firms to compete with these fast-growing funds. Between 1980 and 1986 the sum of NOWs, money market deposit accounts, savings, and small time deposits grew from 26 percent to 38 percent of commercial bank assets.[27] Depository firms continue to seek new ways to attract customers. In spring 1987, for example, the Chase Manhattan Bank introduced a deposit account with a return tied to the performance of Standard & Poor's 500-stock index.

Many of the fastest growing new products do not generate balance-sheet entries. Collectively, they are referred to as "off-balance-sheet activities." Commercial banks, especially large money center banks, have been active in developing and marketing these new products and services to reduce their emphasis on traditional portfolio lending. The percentage of bank income generated by such activity has significantly increased in recent years.[28] Other financial firms, such as securities firms and insurance companies, have expanded their off-balance-sheet activities also, but the extent of their involvement is not as well known.[29]

Off-balance-sheet activities can be divided into two categories—those creating contingent claims on the issuer and those providing a service for a fee. The most important and fastest growing new products fall within the contingent claim category. This category includes investment-related activities such as futures and forward contracts, swaps, caps, and various option contracts and financial guarantees such as standby letters of credit (SLCs) and a variety of loan commitments.[30] Table 1–1 shows the very rapid growth in the dollar volume of selected off-balance-sheet activities at commercial banks.[31]

One fast-growing category of off-balance-sheet activity not reported in table 1–1 is interest rate and currency swaps. Commercial banks, investment banks, and insurance companies arrange swaps between parties, provide guarantees, and act as dealers—making secondary markets in these agreements. Over $180 billion in interest rate swaps existed in 1985; by the third quarter of 1987 there were over $600 billion.[32] About one-half of 1985's Eurobond offerings included swap arrangements.[33]

Causes of Product Innovation. Product innovations, both on and off the balance sheet, have resulted from many of the same forces that have led to securitization—more volatile economic conditions, technological breakthroughs, and regulation. These forces have encouraged the development of new financial products to provide greater

TABLE 1–1
SELECTED OFF-BALANCE-SHEET ACTIVITY
OF COMMERCIAL BANKS, 1980–1987
(billions of dollars)

Year	Standby Letters of Credit	Loan Commitments	Foreign Exchange Transactions	Other[a]
1980	47	n.a.	177	n.a.
1981	72	n.a.	189	n.a.
1982	100	n.a.	215	n.a.
1983	120	432	464	n.a.
1984	146	496	584	81
1985	175	531	735	121
1986	170	572	893	n.a.
1987[b]	168	595	1,558	n.a.

NOTE: n.a. = not available.
a. Includes commitments to purchase or sell futures and forward contracts, securities when issued, and standby contracts and other option arrangements.
b. Preliminary; annualized as of the third quarter 1987.
SOURCES: James Chessen, "Third-Quarter Update: Bank Off-Balance-Sheet Activity," *Federal Deposit Insurance Corporation Regulatory Review* (November/December 1987), p. 4; and *Statistical Information on the Financial Services Industry*, p. 187.

liquidity, transfer risk, tap new sources of credit or equity, and evade or reduce the cost of regulation.

A wide range of new innovations for transferring price risk such as financial futures, options, caps, and swap contracts were designed to enhance possibilities for hedging interest or exchange rate exposures. The increased emphasis on variable-rate lending and variable-rate deposit accounts is also a result of these forces. Many financial innovations would not have been profitable or feasible without advances in technology, which have dramatically improved communications and data processing capabilities and have enhanced capabilities for managing complex risk exposures. Finally, many financial innovations were designed to circumvent regulations such as binding interest rate ceilings on depository firms. In addition, capital requirements, reserve requirements, and deposit insurance premiums, which affect the cost and profitability of deposit intermediation, give depository firms an incentive to increase off-balance-sheet activity and to utilize nondeposit liabilities. Numerous innovations would have been unnecessary or their cost of development reduced if regulations had not prohibited more direct responses to changing economic conditions.

The Consequences of Product Innovation. Product innovation has brought a broader range of choices and, in the process, has altered the portfolio composition of firms and households. For both groups the unbundling and explicit pricing of products and services have been key elements in this process.

Since the early 1970s the composition of corporate liquid assets has shifted away from demand deposits and currency to time deposits and commercial paper.[34] A decline in compensating balance requirements, the growth of cash management services such as lockboxes, remote disbursement, and controlled disbursement, and the development of shorter-term CDs with active secondary markets have made this possible. Innovative bond products such as bonds with warrants and bonds with put options have permitted corporations to borrow over the long term while offering investors some protection from interest rate and credit exposures.

Households have benefited from the advent of nationwide bank credit cards; automated teller machines (ATMs); direct deposit; universal life insurance; discount brokerage; a plethora of mutual funds including money market, tax-exempt, and international mutual funds; and a host of close substitutes for demand and savings deposits. One result of this innovation can be seen in the increasing amount of household assets that are professionally managed. Households' holding of intermediated assets grew from 50 percent of their financial assets in 1952 to 60 percent in 1985 while their direct holdings of securities dropped.[35] This pooling of financial capital into professionally managed funds and their growing influence in financial markets have been termed the institutionalization of savings.

Innovations that generate credit and equity have helped to broaden and deepen capital markets. The growth of the market for high-yield bonds, letters of credit, commitments, financial futures, options, and swaps, as well as other innovations has accompanied and probably facilitated an increased demand for credit from consumers, businesses, and government. Between 1980 and 1986 every major sector of the U.S. economy increased its use of borrowed funds. The ratio of the debt of all nonfinancial borrowers to gross national product increased from 137.7 percent to 179.5 percent over this period.[36]

Issues in Product Innovation. The growth of off-balance-sheet products, coupled with the perception of increased risk taking and reduced liquidity at commercial banks, has led bank regulators to propose establishing minimum capital standards based on risk.[37] In December 1987, an international committee of bank regulators from twelve major industrialized nations proposed guidelines relating a bank's capital to the risk profile of its assets, including those off the balance sheet. The guidelines are intended to eliminate the distortions in the incentives to hold liquid assets, to make risky loans, and to expand off-balance-sheet activities that are present when minimum capital standards are a fixed percentage of bank assets. The proposed standard requires banks to hold capital in proportion to a weighted sum of exposures both on and off the balance sheet with higher-risk activities assigned a higher weight. Items such as Treasury bills that involve little risk receive low weights, while items with higher risks, such as commercial loans or off-balance-sheet loan guarantees, are assigned higher weights.

Whether this will lead to improvements in safety and soundness, however, is unclear. To the extent that a weighting scheme does not reflect the true risk exposure from a bank's potential activities, it may affect portfolio choices without affecting risk taking. The proposed capital standard applies a crude weighting scheme to broad categories of bank activities and does not take into account the effects of portfolio diversification on risk. As a result, it is not clearly preferable to an unweighted standard. The problem of excessive risk taking by depository institutions and a range of potential policy solutions are discussed by George Benston and George Kaufman in chapter 3 in this volume.

Geographic Market Expansion

National Market Expansion. Despite a complex set of federal and state laws governing the expansion of depository firms into new geographic markets, the marketing of financial services to households and small businesses is increasingly being conducted on a nationwide basis. A national market for corporate and institutional clients has existed since the mid-1960s, but now even the market for traditional banking services such as deposit taking and consumer lending has become national in scope.

State branching restrictions, the McFadden Act, the Banking Act of 1933, and the Bank Holding Company Act have restricted the geographic markets of commercial banks and their holding companies. By contrast, insurance companies, finance companies, and securities firms have, for the most part, offered services nationwide. As a result, the markets for many banking services tended to be local rather than national. This is changing. Legislation at the state and federal levels, technological changes, and innovation strategies are allowing depository firms to expand both intrastate and interstate. Depository firms have circumvented branching prohibitions by using holding companies, ATMs, and bank by mail or by operating limited-service affiliates such as nonbank banks, finance companies, mortgage banking firms, credit card operations, loan production offices, and Edge Act offices in geographic areas where they cannot establish regular branches.

Geographic expansion by financial firms has been facilitated by technological advances that have reduced the costs of managing multi-office firms. Depository firms operating in local markets are increasingly affected by competition from other financial services providers. Cash management, money market mutual funds, and other banklike services offered by securities and insurance firms on a nationwide basis grew rapidly beginning in the late 1970s when interest rate ceilings on bank and thrift deposit accounts became binding. More recently, financial affiliates of some retail and industrial firms have been aggressively offering financial services, including many banking services, nationwide.

Rising numbers of bank and thrift insolvencies and ad hoc entry by out-of-state banks and nonbanks have induced a number of states to pass legislation relaxing restrictions on interstate banking. Currently forty-four states and the District of Columbia allow some form of interstate banking.[38] Twenty-seven states and the District of Columbia have passed reciprocal laws that allow interstate banking on a regional level while excluding money center banks. A Supreme Court ruling in June 1985 upheld their legality. The 1982 Garn–St Germain Depository Institutions Act authorized interstate acquisition of failed and failing banks and thrifts on a temporary basis. The Competitive Equality Banking Act of 1987 permanently extended this authority. By December 1986, one bank and fifty-five thrifts had been acquired by or merged with out-of-state entities under this emergency power.[39]

Issues Posed by National Market Expansion. *Concentration.* Since the establishment of the First Bank of the United States in 1791, the issue of concentration has been a concern. Fears of excessive concentration and market power led to laws restricting interstate banking and led some states to establish systems of many small unit banks while efficiency considerations led other states to support systems of larger branch banks. As a result of these differences, the United States has operated under a dual system of unit and branch banking with restrictions on interstate banking. Economic and technological changes are now fostering a rethinking of our banking structure.

Over 5,000 commercial bank mergers and acquisitions have taken place over the past two decades, and large new regional banking organizations have emerged; yet the number of banks remains around 14,000 as new banks continue to be chartered.[40] In chapter 4, Franklin Edwards argues that fears of excessive concentration resulting from a consolidation of the financial services industry are misplaced. A substantial consolidation in the number of firms operating nationally can be consistent with increasing competition in local markets. To date, concentration in local banking markets has not increased.[41] Moreover, out-of-state entry does not seem to be threatening small banks. In states where both large and small banks compete, there is evidence that small banks are able to compete successfully.[42]

The flow of funds. Laws restricting geographic expansion of depository firms were intended to increase the availability of loans in local communities and to preserve local ownership and management. A common argument supporting geographic restrictions is that they prevent deposit funds from flowing out of local communities into large urban areas. In other words, geographic restrictions create localized capital markets.

Many banks in rural communities, however, buy and sell deposit funds in the federal funds market every day.[43] They also actively advertise for deposits through deposit brokers, toll-free telephone numbers, and bank by mail. On the asset side, smaller banks both buy and sell loans and loan participations. Rural banks are often net sellers of loans. Before its failure in 1982, the Penn Square Bank of Oklahoma sold billions of dollars in loans to many U.S. banks, including Continental Illinois and Seattle First.

This flow of funds between rural and urban areas occurs despite branching restrictions. Moreover, some states have explicitly recognized the benefits of these flows. In 1975 Maine became the first state to open its door to interstate banking, largely to attract new capital into the state.[44] Since then, a number of largely rural states such as Alaska have done the same.

International Market Expansion. Capital markets around the world are becoming increasingly integrated and international in character. Although financial service firms have been involved in activities outside their home countries for hundreds of years, financial service competition has been globalized to an extraordinary degree recently.

The globalization of financial services competition is broadly based across financial firms. Commercial banks, insurance companies, and securities firms are all participating in this expansion. As barriers to international capital flows continue to weaken, opportunities for investment expand, and capital market efficiency should increase worldwide.

The expansion of international banking activity is one aspect of the globalization of financial markets. One measure of this activity is the volume of Eurocurrency deposits.[45] Between 1970 and early 1987 total gross Eurocurrency deposits climbed from $110 billion to over $3,800 billion.[46] Between 1975 and 1985 the number of foreign-owned bank offices operating in the United States grew from 186 to 605, and the number of U.S. banks with offices abroad grew from 126 banks with 762 branches to 163 banks with 967 branches.[47] The assets controlled by foreign-owned banks also grew, from less than 6 percent of the total assets of banking offices in the United States in 1970 to almost 20 percent by 1986.[48] In many European countries the percentage of assets controlled by foreign-owned banks is substantially greater.[49]

Securitization has affected international markets as well as the U.S. domestic market. Since 1980 the composition of new international credit has shifted from syndicated bank loans to securitized assets. Between 1980 and 1986 international bond issues increased from $39 billion to $225 billion while syndicated bank loans fell from $97 billion to $38 billion.[50] About 25 percent of all American corporate debt was issued abroad in 1985.[51] New instruments such as floating-rate notes (FRNs), note issuance facilities (NIFs), swaps, and Euro–commercial paper have also grown rapidly.[52] The growth of the Euromarkets slowed in 1987, however. By midyear, a falling dollar and an increasing spread between U.S. interest rates and Eurobond rates were causing a decline in new Eurobond issues. That decline has persisted through 1988.[53]

The growth of the Euroequities market is another aspect of the globalization of financial markets. Uncertainties about the distribution of world economic growth and the growing importance of institutional investors in the equity markets have increased interest in international diversification of equity holdings. As a result, more equity trading is taking place away from the home market. Investment bankers are expanding equity markets by selling new issues worldwide, while secondary trading for large, well-known corporations is occurring both in established overseas exchanges and through over-the-counter markets. Between 1984 and 1987 the number of stocks traded daily outside the home country increased from 236 to 493.[54]

With the growth in international competition has come the tendency to compare firms across borders. Historically, U.S. banks and financial firms have dominated these rankings; in recent years, however, Japanese firms have moved to the top positions. The true competitiveness of financial firms is difficult, if not impossible, to measure, though, because of fluctuations in exchange rates and differences in accounting practices, regulatory regimes, and domestic savings rates.

Causes and Consequences of International Market Expansion. The movement toward a global financial market first accelerated in the 1960s with the development of the Eurodollar market. Rapid growth of international trade in relation to world output provided an inducement for financial firms to open branches and subsidiaries to serve their traditional customers overseas. Over time, they began to compete for local business with the domestic financial firms of the country in which they were located.

In the early 1970s, the move to flexible exchange rates, OPEC-induced oil price increases (and the accompanying recycling of "petrodollars"), and improvements and reductions in the cost of telecommunications and data processing stimulated growth of international financial markets. In recent years, large, persistent trade imbalances and a growing interest in international diversification have contributed to expansion of overseas markets.

Growth of international banking has also been encouraged by regulations such as reserve requirements, interest rate ceilings, deposit insurance premiums, and restrictions on activities in domestic markets. In the 1960s, foreign branches of U.S. banks were important sources of funds during disintermediation episodes. Overseas lending operations were also encouraged by controls on foreign borrowing of dollars in the United States and by restrictions on activities and geographic markets that limited domestic growth and profitability. Recently, for example, commercial banks have used foreign affiliates to engage in securities underwriting and dealing and various insurance activities.[55]

Issues Raised by International Financial Activity. Growing international financial activity raises several questions of public policy. One concerns the location of financial activity—does it take place in New York, London, or Tokyo? Another concerns the nationality of the firms engaging in the activity—are they U.S., British, or Japanese? Yet another has to do with the currency denomination—are the transactions in dollars, pounds, or yen?

Job creation, physical investment, and the efficiency of local capital markets are all affected by regulations influencing the location of financial activity. The competitiveness of U.S. firms operating within the United States and overseas is also affected by domestic and foreign regulations. The depth and integrity of dollar-denominated securities markets and the willingness of foreign investors to hold dollar-denominated assets depend importantly on public confidence in the Federal Reserve's ability to maintain macroeconomic and financial stability in the United States.

Differences in activity regulations, capital requirements, tax burdens, and levels of supervision of financial firms around the world also affect their competitiveness. Some have moved activities overseas, not only to serve new markets, but also to locate their activities in favorable regulatory and tax jurisdictions. In response, competition has increased among regulators. The "big bang" deregulation (that is, deregulation of the securities markets) in London was a conscious effort by the United Kingdom to capture a larger share of the fast-growing international market for financial services. Japan and other countries are now adapting their regulations to make their banking and capital markets more competitive as well. Chapter 10 describes in greater detail how these forces have affected international financial markets.

Regulatory authorities around the world have expressed growing concern over the lack of international policy coordination. As mentioned in the section "Issues in Product Innovation," efforts are under way to establish a common standard for banks in many of the industrialized countries. It remains to be seen, however, whether broader coordination will be possible. Chapter 10, by David Folkerts-Landau and Donald Mathieson, examines efforts to achieve greater international coordination and integration of international financial markets. Chapter 9, by Edward Kane, discusses the implications of competition between and among regulators and the regulated around the world.

Mergers, Acquisitions, Affiliations, and the Integration of Financial Services

Since the late 1970s mergers, acquisitions, and de novo establishment of financial affiliates and subsidiaries have been used by financial firms to integrate a full range of financial services. In addition, retailers and industrial-based companies, many of which have provided financial services for decades, have used mergers and acquisitions to integrate financial services offerings more fully with their other lines of business. Mergers and acquisitions within industry groups have also increased.

Causes and Consequences of Financial Firm Affiliations. Unlike other financial service firms, the ownership of most deposit-taking firms and the activities of their affiliates are subject to regulation. The Bank Holding Company Act (BHCA) limits the activities of corporations owning banks to those that the Federal Reserve Board determines are closely related to banking. Corporations owning commercial banks are thus prohibited from owning or acquiring firms offering other financial and nonfinancial products and services, and firms selling such products and services are prohibited from owning commercial banks. Similarly, the Savings and Loan Holding Company Act (SLHCA) restricts companies owning two or more savings and loan associations to activities permitted by the Federal Home Loan Bank Board.[56]

These laws, however, have not completely separated banking from other financial and nonfinancial services. Before March 1987, the BHCA defined a bank as an organization that both took demand deposits and made commercial loans. Corporations owning banks that were not engaged in both activities were not subject to the act or, therefore, to Federal Reserve oversight. Such banks have come to be known as limited-service or nonbank banks. The Competitive Equality Banking Act of 1987 closed the nonbank bank loophole by redefining the term "bank" in the BHCA to include all banks offering FDIC-insured deposits and all non-FDIC-insured institutions offering demand deposits or transactions accounts and making commercial loans. Existing limited-service banks were "grandfathered" but are subject to growth rate restrictions.

Companies owning a single savings and loan association (unitary savings and loan holding companies) are also not subject to limitations on their activities and affiliations. Indeed the Competitive Equality Banking Act of 1987 for the first time explicitly permits securities firms to acquire S&Ls. Moreover, the law has never restricted the ability of individuals directly to own or control depository firms along with other business interests.

The BHCA and the SLHCA are the principal obstacles to firms interested in offering banking services along with other products and services. Nonetheless, many retail, industrial, and financial firms operate grandfathered limited-service banks or a single thrift. As of February 1987, approximately 170 nonbank banks were in operation.[57] They are owned by such firms as Merrill Lynch, Dreyfus, J. C. Penney, Sears Roebuck, American Express, Control Data, and John Hancock. Bank holding companies also operate limited-service banks in states where they are prohibited from engaging in full-service commercial banking. In addition, firms such as Ford, Sears Roebuck, ITT, and Weyerhaeuser now own S&Ls.

Some retail-based firms use financial affiliates to compete in consumer-oriented product lines, offering banking services such as deposit taking, consumer loans, and mortgages along with insurance, mutual funds, and securities brokerage, activities in which banks cannot engage. Through their extensive networks of stores they can offer these products nationally to established customer bases. Sears Roebuck is perhaps the most prominent example of a retailer that has greatly expanded its financial services offerings. Three-quarters of the U.S. public visited a Sears store in 1984; more than 60 million people hold Sears credit cards.[58] At the end of 1983, Sears had almost 3,000 separate offices for its financial affiliates. Sears has successfully used this marketing network to become a leader in providing one-stop financial shopping.

Other retailers are teaming up with financial firms to offer financial services on their premises. Major grocery store chains, for example, have allowed banks and S&Ls to install ATMs in their stores. First Nationwide Bank, owned by the Ford Motor company, has established minibranches in K-Mart stores around the country. For banks and S&Ls, this is an inexpensive alternative to stand-alone branches.

Subsidiaries of industrial-based companies have generally provided financial services to households and businesses as an extension of their parents' primary line of business, but some have expanded their service offerings. These subsidiaries are strong competitors in some segments of the financial services market. General Motors, Ford, and Chrysler, for example, have owned captive finance companies for many years. In 1980 commercial banks supplied 53 percent of automobile financing; finance companies, dominated by the captive automobile finance companies, supplied 29 percent. By 1986 the finance companies' share of the market had increased to 38 percent, while the commercial banks' share had declined to 41 percent.[59] In 1985 five of the ten largest mortgage servicers were nonbank firms; GMAC Mortgage topped the list with more than $20 billion in mortgage volume.[60] The General Electric Corporation now manages numerous subsidiaries providing investment banking services; consumer, commercial, and industrial loans; equipment leasing; various types of insurance; limited partnerships in real estate syndications; and other activities. Other industrial-based firms with active financial services subsidiaries include ITT, Greyhound, and Xerox.

Financial firms have also organized to offer a full range of financial services. American Express is perhaps the preeminent example of a diversified financial holding company. It offers insurance products through Fireman's Fund and securities brokerage and underwriting services through Shearson Lehman Hutton, and it provides a variety of banking services in the United States and abroad through its limited-service banks. Other examples of diversified financial firms include John Hancock, which owns the securities firm Tucker Anthony and a nonbank bank, First Signature Bank & Trust Company; and Merrill Lynch, which in addition to its securities activities offers insurance services and operates the Merrill Lynch Bank & Trust Company, a nonbank bank. These firms compete directly with banks and thrifts in deposit taking and consumer lending while offering a broad range of other financial services through separate subsidiaries. They have nationwide distribution networks and large customer bases. Based on deposits in its cash management account alone, Merrill Lynch would rank as the eleventh largest bank in the United States.[61]

Foreign financial firms have established affiliations with U.S. financial firms as well. In 1986 Sumitomo Bank, which already owns a U.S. commercial bank, agreed to invest $500 million in Goldman Sachs in exchange for a limited partnership and a share in Goldman's profits. Whether large U.S. commercial banks could legally make the same type of investment is unclear.[62] Sumitomo has more recently received permission to affiliate with Security Pacific to offer investment advice to customers in the United States and Japan.[63]

Issues Posed by Affiliations among Financial Services Firms. Financial firm affiliations have given rise to intense debate over the desirability of separating banking from other financial services and from commerce. The debate focuses on two questions—whether banks are special and whether banking can be insulated from other financial and nonfinancial functions within subsidiaries or a holding company structure in such a way as to protect the safety and soundness of the bank while preserving opportunities for economic synergies.

The question of bank specialness focuses on whether banks provide a unique set of services that distinguishes them from other firms and that justifies strict separation between banking and other services.[64] In recent years, the inherent specialness of banks has been called into question. Anthony Saunders reviews this debate in chapter 5.

The question of whether banking can be insulated from other financial and nonfinancial functions is part of the broader question of how to ensure safety and soundness in the banking system. Some proponents of bank specialness argue that limits need to be placed on the ownership, affiliates, and subsidiaries of banks as well as on banks themselves. They believe it is not possible to insulate a bank effectively from potential risks posed by affiliates and subsidiaries and that the social cost of bank failures justifies strict limitations. Another concern is the expanded potential for conflicts of interest when bank holding companies have broad powers.

Current laws and regulations provide a substantial degree of insulation of a bank from its affiliates. A bank can lend no more than 10 percent of its capital to an affiliate and no more than 20 percent of its capital to all affiliates taken together. These loans must be fully collateralized. Other types of transactions such as loan guarantees and asset purchases are also subject to strict limitations. The Competitive Equality Banking Act of 1987 strengthened bank insulation provisions by requiring bank holding companies to engage in transactions on terms and under circumstances that are substantially the same or as favorable to the bank or its subsidiary as those prevailing at the time for comparable transactions with unrelated parties. A recent report produced by the Federal Deposit Insurance Corporation concludes that adequate insulation can be achieved with only minor changes in regulations. Nonetheless, the controversy over bank separateness within a holding company structure is of long standing and is currently a central part of the debate over restructuring financial regulation.[65]

The possibility of unfair competition resulting from implicit subsidies from federal guarantees, predatory pricing, or tying is another concern. One argument is that deposit insurance confers an implicit subsidy that banks can use to underprice competitors in the provision of other services. Another argument is that predatory pricing and tying can be profitable if bank holding companies gain monopoly power that they can extend to other products or services.

The potential benefits to be gained from integrating banking with other financial and nonfinancial services must be weighed against these safety and soundness and competitive concerns in evaluating financial structure issues. Eliminating barriers to the integration of banking services with other lines of business would promote competition and allow the most efficient producers to serve markets. Potential economies of scale and scope could be realized. Blanket restrictions on affiliations eliminate these opportunities for improved economic efficiency. Both Anthony Saunders and Franklin Edwards evaluate these arguments in their chapters in this volume.

The Payments System

The system for making payments in the United States has evolved in response to a number of forces. In recent years, very rapid growth in the volume of payments, particularly over the wire transfer systems, and an expansion in the range of firms with access to the payments system, either directly or through affiliates, have raised new public policy concerns.

The Evolution of the Payments System. The volume of payments is enormous—$154 trillion was debited to demand deposit accounts alone in 1985. Payments are made through a variety of mechanisms. The largest number of payments are probably made with currency, but these have the smallest total dollar value. Checks, credit cards, and direct transfers through automated clearinghouses account for a large number of payments with an aggregate value of approximately $75 billion per day.[66] In terms of value, however, wire or electronic transfers now dominate. Daily payments using wire transfers routinely exceed $1 trillion.[67] Although thousands of banks and thrifts have access to wire transfer systems, a relatively small number of money center banks account for a large percentage of the total volume.

Until recently, deposit accounts at commercial banks provided virtually the only means of access to the payments system. Beginning in the late 1970s, however, money market mutual funds, which provided customers with access to funds on demand and the transfer of funds by wire and by check, grew rapidly. Brokerage firms began to offer cash management accounts combining the money market fund with a broader ability to write checks and carry out other financial transactions. Although payments against these funds were made through zero-balance accounts at commercial banks, banks were left with a reduced role. Congress passed the Depository Institutions Deregulation and Monetary Control Act of 1980 and the Garn–St Germain Act of 1982 partly in response to the loss of funds by commercial banks and thrifts to these new competitors. These acts substantially deregulated deposit interest rates and integrated thrifts into the payments system by granting them authority to offer checking and NOW accounts and access to Federal Reserve services such as check clearing and the Fedwire.

Issues Raised by the Evolution of the Payments System. All payments transactions entail various risks to participants, including the risks of fraud and human error, but the main concern is the credit risk that results from gaps in the timing between making and receiving payments. While these timing gaps are shorter for wire transfers than for most other means of payment, wire transfer exposures have become a major public policy concern because the dollar amounts are so large. The problem of credit risk is not as great in the check clearing system, where the bilateral exposures are smaller and where the allocation of risk is well established in the law and well understood by participants. The allocation of risk in the private electronic transfer systems is less settled.

The two major wire transfer systems in the United States are Fedwire and the Clearing House Interbank Payments System (CHIPS).[68] Users of CHIPS, a private payments network handling both domestic and international transactions, exchange provisional payments messages during the day. Payments become final at the end of the day when the net positions of the participants are settled through their accounts with the Federal Reserve. By contrast, payments made over the Federal Reserve System's Fedwire are final when they are made.

Credit risk arises in the wire transfer systems because over both Fedwire and CHIPS banks can send more funds than they have on hand at the time of the transaction. This practice results in an intraday extension of credit, known as a daylight overdraft, either from the Federal Reserve over Fedwire or from other banks over CHIPS. At times, the total value of these overdrafts has exceeded $100 billion.[69]

The main public policy concern with the operation of a net settlement system like CHIPS is systemic risk. If a bank is incapable of settling its overdrafts at the end of the day, other banks that have extended it credit may, in turn, be unable to fulfill their commitments, creating ripple effects that could lead to widespread bank failures and a potential crisis. Since CHIPS serves as an international clearinghouse, even a foreign bank failure could significantly disrupt the domestic payments system. The main public policy concern with Fedwire is the exposure of public funds to credit risk.

Until recently, the Federal Reserve did little to control its daylight overdraft exposure. Now it has a system of bilateral ceilings, or caps, in place that limit overdrafts to a multiple of a bank's capital. The system depends on a self-evaluation of a bank's ability to monitor and control risk. It still leaves the Federal Reserve substantially exposed. A variety of proposals have been offered in recent years to eliminate or reduce credit risk problems over the wire transfer systems. Mark Flannery analyzes these proposals in chapter 7.

The integrity of the payments system has also been an issue in the broader debate about our financial structure and the regulation of bank holding companies. Former Federal Reserve Chairman Paul Volcker and others within the Federal Reserve have expressed serious reservations about affiliations between banks, thrifts, and other financial and commercial enterprises, in part because they believe these affiliations may jeopardize the integrity of the payments system. This is controversial. Others argue that the risks to the payments system from affiliate relationships can be controlled by restrictions on bank extensions of credit to nonbank affiliates and on other interaffiliate transactions such as already exist under current regulation. Both Mark

Flannery (in chapter 7) and Anthony Saunders (in chapter 5) evaluate these arguments.

FINANCIAL STRAINS

The rapid pace of change in financial markets has been accompanied by record numbers of problem and failed commercial banks and thrifts. This has opened debate over the best approach for maintaining a safe and sound financial system.

For over forty years after its establishment, the federal deposit insurance system was deemed an unqualified success. Between 1940 and 1980, few banks failed—generally fewer than ten per year. By 1980, however, stresses in the system began to appear. In 1983, 45 banks failed, more than in any year since 1940. Since then the annual number of failed banks has steadily increased; in 1987, 184 banks, or over 1 percent of all commercial banks, failed.[70] The number of banks officially classified as problem banks has also risen sharply. By year-end 1987, 1,575 banks, more than 10 percent of all banks, were officially classified as problem banks, up from 196 in 1981.[71]

The savings and loan industry has experienced even greater problems. Approximately one-third of all S&Ls failed or were merged out of existence between 1982 and 1987. At the end of 1987, over 500 insolvent S&Ls continued in operation.[72] These S&Ls remain open principally because the Federal Savings and Loan Insurance Corporation (FSLIC) does not have the funds to close them. Almost 600 additional S&Ls are operating with limited regulatory net worth below 3 percent.[73]

Like the problems at S&Ls, the problems of the FSLIC are severe. From 1981 through 1986, it provided almost $7 billion in open assistance to FSLIC-insured firms. In March 1987, the General Accounting Office concluded that the FSLIC was insolvent.[74] The Competitive Equality Banking Act of 1987 recapitalized the FSLIC by permitting it to sell $10.8 billion in bonds. Still, the FSLIC's cash resources remain low. After large cash payouts to two insolvent S&Ls in June 1988, its cash on hand amounted to only $1.9 billion.[75] Estimates of the cost of closing all the insolvent S&Ls in operation vary widely but are generally substantially in excess of the funds that will become available to the FSLIC over the next few years. The Federal Home Loan Bank Board estimates it would cost $221 billion.[76] As a result, many insolvent S&Ls will be permitted to remain in operation indefinitely and will probably continue to incur losses.[77] This problem is explored in greater detail in chapter 8 by John Weicher.

Although the FDIC is much better capitalized than the FSLIC, it also faces the strain of a rising number of problem banks.[78] Moreover, because it insures very large firms with assets many times the size of the fund, its exposure in the event of a single large failure is great. The rescue of Continental Illinois, with $41 billion in assets, cost the FDIC an estimated $4.5 billion and involved unprecedented guarantees to holding company creditors. Many believe that the ultimate cost to the FDIC of resolving the problems of First Republic Bank Corporation in Texas will exceed the cost of the Continental Illinois bailout.

Causes of Financial Strains. Volatile credit markets and macro-economic conditions have contributed to financial strains. Many of today's problems among commercial banks and thrifts are the result of the cycle of inflation and disinflation that began in the 1970s and the accompanying volatility of interest rates and real returns. Savings and loans, which typically financed long-term fixed-rate mortgages with short-term deposits, were particularly affected. In chapter 2 Anna Schwartz discusses the critical role of price stability in fostering a safe and sound financial system.

The mid-1980s have also been characterized by large disparities in regional economic performance. Sharp declines in energy and agricultural prices led to widespread problems among banks and thrifts in states where these industries dominate the local economies. Since 1985 the number of bank and thrift failures in states such as Nebraska, Texas, and Oklahoma has doubled.[79] Increasing competition and innovation in financial markets have brought strains to the financial system too. Some firms that had previously been protected from competition did not have the management expertise to survive in an increasingly complex, volatile, and competitive market.

Regulations have also contributed to financial strains. Banks and thrifts have been subject to substantial restrictions on their products, activities, and markets as a heritage of depression-era legislation. These restrictions have inhibited diversification across regions and products and limited depository firms' ability to adapt to changing market conditions and technology.

Finally, the deposit insurance system as it is currently structured may not provide sufficient incentives to control risk taking. Because depositors, borrowers, and the deposit insurance agencies are not compensated for risk bearing, the financial rewards for bearing risk go to a firm's owners. This provides an incentive for banks and thrifts to take on more risk than they otherwise would. This problem has been compounded in recent years as bank and thrift failures have been resolved in ways that protect even large depositors and other creditors, diminishing the incentives of sophisticated outsiders to monitor bank and thrift practices. Even more seriously, book-value accounting standards and the practice of regulatory forbearance have permitted banks and thrifts to operate with little or no economic net worth. Managers and owners have had little or nothing to lose by gambling in an effort to restore solvency. The irony is that these incentive problems may be undermining the goal of financial stability that deposit insurance was designed to maintain.[80]

The Consequences of Continuing Financial Strains. As the number of unresolved failed and problem banks and thrifts has increased, two problems have intensified. First, deposit insurance has permitted insolvent and nearly insolvent banks and thrifts to continue to attract funds. By offering higher yields on deposit accounts, some have bid for funds nationwide using deposit brokers and direct advertising in an attempt to grow their way out of their problems. Healthy, well-capitalized firms must compete with these firms for deposits. Second, the increasing number of firms operating with little or no capital greatly exacerbates the incentives for excessive risk taking, in turn increasing the exposure of the deposit insurance agencies and ultimately federal taxpayers to losses.

Regulatory forbearance has become a common practice. The Competitive Equality Banking Act of 1987 requires the Federal Home Loan Bank Board to forbear against thrifts with regulatory net worth of more than 0.5 percent and whose low capital can be attributable to adverse economic conditions. In some cases even S&Ls with net worth of less than 0.5 percent are eligible for forbearance. Since regulatory capital often overstates the market value of capital by a large margin, these provisions ensure that a substantial number of firms will continue to operate with effectively no equity funds at risk.

Banks and thrifts have historically been the focus of public policies to maintain financial stability. The Federal Reserve Act of 1913, the Banking Act of 1933, and an extensive examination and supervisory apparatus have provided the basis for the federal financial "safety net." Fears of runs by depositors, a collapse of the banking system, and economic distress are used to justify deposit insurance and concomitantly many banking regulations, but the role of deposit insurance in protecting financial stability is controversial. In chapter 3 George Benston and George Kaufman provide a comprehensive discussion of deposit insurance and the federal safety net and propose reforms designed to minimize the perverse incentive problem and place the deposit insurance system on a sounder footing.

Conclusions

This chapter has described some of the sweeping changes in financial markets in recent years. There is broad agreement on the major contributing forces: more volatile economic conditions and financial asset prices, technological change, increased interdependence among nations, and regulation.

Macroeconomic volatility has provided a powerful impetus for change. The cycle of inflation and disinflation that began in the mid-1970s, and the accompanying volatility of interest rates and real returns, produced lasting effects on financial markets. Depository firms, operating under interest rate controls and sometimes with significant maturity mismatches, were particularly affected. The financial products and services that have grown most rapidly are those that provide greater liquidity and improved hedging possibilities or facilitate international diversification.

The effect of technological change has also been profound. Quantum advances in telecommunications and computer technology have led to breakthroughs in the collection, organization, and transmission of information. Financial services firms are largely information managers—providing, storing, and communicating information. These breakthroughs have created new opportunities for efficiently combining a broad range of financial services, developing new products, and expanding into new markets.

The globalization of financial markets has introduced an important new element of competition. Branches and affiliates of foreign financial firms are now important competitors of U.S. firms within the United States and around the world. Indeed, by some measures, U.S. financial services firms have lost their position as the leading international suppliers of financial services.

Finally, public policies have played an important role in the evolution of the financial services industry through laws and regulations affecting the scope and cost of operation of financial firms. The incidence, effectiveness, and costs of financial regulation, however, fall unevenly on financial firms. Some are highly regulated, while others, providing similar services, are not. As a result, the intended effects of regulations have often been eroded by competitive pressures for efficiency and innovation. This chapter has illustrated the variety of ways that the private financial system has responded to profit opportunities created by legal and regulatory constraints on prices and activities.

In evaluating proposals for restructuring financial regulation, it is important to bear in mind these competitive constraints on what can usefully be accomplished by regulation. Regulation, more often than restraining competition, has over time simply forced it into new channels, in the process distorting resource allocation and imposing unnecessary costs on consumers, shareholders, and taxpayers.

The purposes of financial markets are to channel savings to their highest valued uses, provide liquidity, and allocate risk. Government's role should be to ensure the efficient and fair undertaking of these functions and to prevent financial market participants themselves from becoming a source of disturbances to the economy. The chapters that follow evaluate how well existing regulations fulfill this essential role and, where they fall short, develop proposals for reform.

Notes

1. In 1976 nonfinancial commercial paper amounted to 7 percent of short-term commercial borrowing measured as the sum of nonfinancial commercial paper and commercial and industrial loans. By 1987 the market had grown to 13 percent of total short-term commercial borrowing. *Federal Reserve Bulletin* (April 1988), p. A23.

2. Christopher Wood, "Wall Street: Halfway There," *Economist*, July 11, 1987, pp. 8, 13. For an in-depth discussion see Jan Loeys, "Low-Grade Bonds: A Growing Source of Corporate Funding," *Federal Reserve Bank of Philadelphia Business Review* (November/December 1986), pp. 3–12. The recent growth of this market is largely the result of efforts by Drexel Burnham Lambert, which began underwriting and making a secondary market in original-issue, high-yield bonds on a large scale in 1982.

3. Only 700 public companies in the United States, a small fraction of publicly traded companies, qualify to issue investment grade bonds. See Roderick Oram, "Wall Street's Money Spinners," *Banker* (March 1987), p. 34.

4. *Federal Reserve Bulletin* (January 1988), p. A39; and Stuart A. Gabriel, "Housing and Mortgage Markets: The Post-1982 Expansion," *Federal Reserve Bulletin* (December 1987), p. 900.

5. Christopher Farrell and Ellyn E. Spragins, "Making More Debt Do Double Duty," *Business Week*, March 30, 1987, p. 67.

6. Sean Becketti and Charles S. Morris, "Loan Sales: Another Step in the Evolution of the Short Term Credit Market," *Federal Reserve Bank of Kansas City Economic Review* (November 1987), p. 26. See also George Pennacchi, "Loan Sales and the Cost of Bank Capital" (Paper presented at the conference "Asset Securitization and Off-Balance Sheet Banking," Chicago, Illinois, January 1987), p. 1. Loan sales are reported in the Consolidated Reports of Condition and Income filed with the FDIC.

7. The number of shares traded on the New York Stock Exchange in all of 1960 was exceeded in just the first six trading days of 1987. The New York Stock Exchange is, in turn, dwarfed in terms of the dollar volume of transactions by the Treasury securities market and the Euromarkets. See *Federal*

Reserve Bulletin (July 1987), p. A31; and James J. Balazsy, "The Government Securities Market and Proposed Regulations," *Federal Reserve Bank of Cleveland Economic Commentary,* April 1, 1986, pp. 1–4.

8. Shelf registration allows a firm to register a volume of securities that do not have to be sold immediately but rather can be sold over a period of time as funds are needed and as economic conditions become relatively favorable.

9. See testimony of Paul A. Volcker, U.S. Congress, House of Representatives, Subcommittee on Commerce, Consumer, and Monetary Affairs of the Committee on Government Operations, 99th Congress, 2d session, June 11, 1986, p. 34.

10. For further discussion see Edward J. Frydl, "The Challenge of Financial Change," *Federal Reserve Bank of New York Annual Report,* 1985.

11. Ibid.; and William C. Freund, "The Securities Industry in the Financial Services Marketplace: A Review of Dynamic Trends," Center for Applied Research, Pace University, Working Paper no. 61 (September 1986), p. 67.

12. Savings and loan associations, mutual savings banks (savings banks), and credit unions are collectively known as thrifts. *1986 National Fact Book of Savings Institutions* (Washington, D.C.: National Council of Savings Institutions), p. 4.

13. In 1986 Merrill Lynch and First Boston each extended loans of almost $2 billion to a single client to finance takeover attempts. Loans of this size would exceed the lending limits imposed on even the largest U.S. commercial banks.

14. Association of Bank Holding Companies, *A Financial Services Industry Handbook* (Washington, D.C.: Association of Bank Holding Companies, 1987), p. VII-1.

15. This is discussed further in the section "Causes and Consequences of Financial Firm Affiliations" in this chapter.

16. Wood, "Wall Street: Halfway There," p. 8; and Ross Waldrop, "Commercial Bank Performance in 1986," *Federal Deposit Insurance Corporation Banking and Economic Review* (March–April 1987), p. 15.

17. "Global Financing Guide," *Euromoney* (September 1987,) p. 228.

18. This is the number of foreign subsidiaries with over $100 million in assets that report investment/merchant banking or securities brokerage or dealing as their principal activity. This information was obtained from James Houpt of the Board of Governors on April 6, 1988.

19. Bankers Trust received permission from the Federal Reserve to place commercial paper in December 1986 after a federal appeals court ruled that commercial paper placement activities did not violate Glass-Steagall restrictions. See "Fed Slates Hearings on BHC Securities Proposals, Approves Bankers Trust Plan," *Banking Report,* January 5, 1987, pp. 3–6.

20. David Neustadt, "Banks Encroach on Wall Street's Turf," *American Banker,* April 4, 1988.

21. See "Fed Slates Hearings on BHC Securities Proposals," p. 3; "Fed Says Chase Subsidiary May Underwrite and Deal in Commercial Paper as Principal," *Banking Report,* March 23, 1987, p. 497; "Fed Approves Underwriting Applications of J. P. Morgan, Citicorp, Bankers Trust," *Banking Report,* May 4,

1987, pp. 789–90; and "Fed Allows Bank Holding Firms to Enter Securities Business," *Washington Post*, May 1, 1987. To date these activities include underwriting and dealing in municipal revenue bonds, mortgage-related securities, commercial paper, and securities backed by consumer-related receivables.

22. See "FDIC Rules Permitting Nonmember Banks to Have Securities Affiliates Upheld," *Banking Report*, April 13, 1987, p. 691; and "Citicorp Seeks State Charter for Subsidiary," *American Banker*, April 21, 1987, p. 1.

23. For a further discussion of nonbank banks see the section in this chapter, "Mergers, Acquisitions, Affiliations, and the Integration of Financial Activity."

24. See the Federal Deposit Insurance Corporation Staff Study, "Mandate for Change: Restructuring the Banking Industry," August 1987, p. 25.

25. Timothy Curry and Mark Warshawsky, "Life Insurance Companies in a Changing Environment," *Federal Reserve Bulletin* (July 1986), p. 452.

26. Association of Bank Holding Companies, *A Financial Services Industry Handbook*, p. V-20.

27. Deborah J. Danker and Mary M. McLaughlin, "The Profitability of U.S.-Chartered Insured Commercial Banks in 1986," *Federal Reserve Bulletin* (July 1987), p. 544.

28. In 1985 the noninterest income of money center bank holding companies was approximately 40 percent of total operating income; in 1980 this figure was just 28 percent. Noninterest income includes trading account and foreign exchange profits, trust fees, service charges on deposits, fees and commissions on loans, letters of credit, and acceptances and business service fees. See Federal Reserve Bank of New York, *Recent Trends in Commercial Bank Profitability: A Staff Study* (New York: Federal Reserve Bank of New York, 1986), p. 231.

29. Commercial banks are required to report, by category, on Schedule L of the Call Report their off-balance-sheet activity; no such requirement exists for other financial firms.

30. SLCs are loan guarantees that can reduce a customer's borrowing cost by substituting the credit rating of the guarantor for that of the borrower in exchange for a fee. Instead of carrying a loan on the books, SLCs allow a bank to avoid an FDIC assessment, capital requirements, and reserve requirements. Loan commitments are binding promises to make future loans at the customer's demand for a fixed period. Interest rate swaps are agreements to exchange streams of interest payments with different time and risk characteristics but equivalent present values. Currency swaps are similar except that parties swap loans denominated in different currencies.

31. James Chessen, "Off-Balance-Sheet Activity: A Growing Concern?" *Federal Deposit Insurance Corporation Regulatory Review* (May 1986), p. 2.

32. See James Chessen, "Third-Quarter Update: Bank Off-Balance-Sheet Activity," *Federal Deposit Insurance Corporation Regulatory Review* (November/ December 1987), p. 4; and "Interest-Rate Swap Market Rose to $313 Billion in '86," *Wall Street Journal*, May 5, 1987.

33. John Shad, "Regulators Must Help Improve International Securities

Markets," *Financier* (August 1986), p. 53.

34. John F. Wilson, Elizabeth M. Folger, James L. Freund, and Guido E. vanderVen, "Major Borrowing and Lending Trends in the U.S. Economy, 1981–1985," *Federal Reserve Bulletin* (August 1986), pp. 520–21.

35. Data are from the Board of Governors of the Federal Reserve System, Flow of Funds Reports.

36. *Federal Reserve Bulletin* (December 1987), pp. A13, A51.

37. For a further discussion see Peter Norman, "Ways to Boost Global Banking Stability Proposed by 12 Industrialized Nations," *Wall Street Journal*, December 11, 1987; James Chessen, "Risk-based Capital Comes to the Fore," *Issues in Bank Regulation* (Spring 1987), pp. 3–15; and Janice M. Moulton, "New Guidelines for Bank Capital: An Attempt to Regulate Risk," *Federal Reserve Bank of Philadelphia Business Review* (July/August 1987), pp. 19–33.

38. "A Look at Laws Granting Interstate Powers to Banks," *American Banker*, June 14, 1988. See also Paul Calem, "Interstate Bank Mergers and Competition in Banking," *Federal Reserve Bank of Philadelphia Business Review* (January/February 1987), pp. 4–5.

39. Data from Federal Home Loan Bank Board press releases on FSLIC mergers and acquisitions, and *American Banker*, December 5, 1986.

40. By contrast, there has been a substantial consolidation of savings and loans, from 5,000 to 3,700 between 1975 and 1985. See Arnold Heggestad, "Fundamentals of Mergers and Acquisitions," in Richard C. Aspinwall and Robert A. Eisenbeis, eds., *Handbook for Banking Strategy* (New York: John Wiley and Sons, 1985), p. 704.

41. Donald T. Savage, "Interstate Banking Developments," *Federal Reserve Bulletin* (February 1987), p. 91.

42. See Stephen Rhoades and Donald T. Savage, "Can Small Banks Compete?" *Bankers Magazine* (January/February 1981); and B. Frank King, "Upstate New York: Tough Market for City Banks," *Federal Reserve Bank of Atlanta Economic Review* (June/July 1985).

43. See Linda Allen and Anthony Saunders, "The Large-Small Bank Dichotomy in the Federal Funds Market," *Journal of Banking and Finance*, vol. 10 (June 1986), pp. 219–30.

44. Savage, "Interstate Banking Developments," p. 80.

45. The Eurocurrency market is a market for bank deposits and short-term bank loans denominated in a currency other than the currency unit of the nation where the firm is located. The volume of Eurocurrency deposits underestimates the extent of international banking activity, however, since claims held or liabilities owed by foreigners denominated in domestic currencies are omitted from these totals. For further discussion, see Ralph C. Bryant, *International Financial Intermediation: Issues for Analysis and Public Policy* (Washington, D.C.: Brookings Institution, 1986), chap. 3.

46. Bank for International Settlements, *Recent Developments in the Economic Analysis of the Euro-Markets* (Basel, Switzerland: Bank for International Settlements, 1982); and Robert R. Dince, " 'Panama Hattie' Revival: A Grim Comedy for U.S. Banks," *American Banker*, March 16, 1988. A substantial amount of international banking activity involves interbank lending rather than direct

intermediation in domestic markets. Net international bank lending, omitting large interbank claims, is just over one-half the gross Eurocurrency market—$1,485 billion in 1985. Bryant, chap. 3.

47. Michael R. Darby, "The Internationalization of American Banking and Finance: Structure, Risk, and World Interest Rates," *Journal of International Money and Finance* (December 1986), tables 1 and 3; *Board of Governors Annual Report*, 1985; Statement by E. Gerald Corrigan before the Committee on the Budget, U.S. Senate, May 6, 1987, reported in the *Federal Reserve Bulletin* (July 1987), p. 571. See also Bank for International Settlements, *Recent Innovations in International Banking* (Basel, Switzerland: Bank for International Settlements, 1986), p. 151.

48. This number is somewhat inflated since some foreign banks book most of their Western Hemisphere loans in U.S. offices. See statement by E. Gerald Corrigan before the Committee on the Budget, U.S. Senate, May 6, 1987.

49. Bank for International Settlements, *Recent Innovations in International Banking*, p. 152.

50. See Merrill Stevenson, "International Banking: A Game of Skill as Well," *Economist*, March 21, 1987, p. 4; and *Bank for International Settlements Annual Report*, March 1987, p. 108. The $38 billion of syndicated bank loans for 1986 is a sharp reversal of the downward trend that saw these loans reach a low of $21 billion in 1985.

51. Wood, "Wall Street: Halfway There," p. 25.

52. NIFs are commitments by a bank to purchase or provide standby credit to a borrower issuing short-term paper in its own name.

53. "The Markets Discover Eurobondage," *Economist*, November 7, 1987, pp. 83–84; and Matthew Winkler, "Eurobond Market Sags, Crimping High Finance and Also High Living" *Wall Street Journal*, March 29, 1988.

54. "The Corporate List," *Euromoney* (May 1987,) pp. 187–222.

55. Robert Z. Aliber, "International Banking: A Survey," *Journal of Money, Credit and Banking*, vol. 16, no. 4 (November 1984, pt. 2), p. 669. See also the section "Securitization and the Separation of Commercial and Investment Banking."

56. See Carter H. Golembe and David S. Holland, *Federal Regulation of Banking 1986–87* (Washington, D.C.: Golembe Associates, 1986), chap. 10.

57. Data obtained from the FDIC.

58. Caroline E. Mayer, "Sears Unveils New Credit Card," *Washington Post*, April 25, 1985.

59. *Federal Reserve Bulletin* (July 1987,) p. A40.

60. American Bankers Association, *Statistical Information on the Financial Services Industry* (Washington, D.C., 1987), p. 18.

61. "Bank Regulators Call for Glass-Steagall Revisions and New Bank Securities Powers," *Washington Financial Reports*, April 28, 1986, p. 653.

62. Susan Warfel, "U.S. Banks May Need New Laws to Copy Sumitomo," *Investor's Daily*, August 11, 1986.

63. "Fed Lets Sumitomo Open U.S. Bank despite Failure to Meet U.S. Capital Standards," *Banking Report*, July 20, 1987, pp. 87–88.

64. This set of services is discussed in E. Gerald Corrigan, "Are Banks

Special?" *Federal Reserve Bank of Minneapolis Annual Report* (1982). For a further discussion of the uniqueness of banks see also E. Gerald Corrigan, "Financial Market Structure: A Longer View," *Federal Reserve Bank of New York Annual Report*, 1986; the conference volume *The Search for Financial Stability: The Past Fifty Years* (San Francisco: Federal Reserve Bank of San Francisco, 1985) has several articles that debate aspects and implications of bank specialness.

65. See Saunders, "Bank Holding Companies: Structure, Performance, and Reform," chapter 5 in this volume; Corrigan, "Financial Market Structure: A Longer View"; and Samuel Chase and Donn L. Waage, "Corporate Separateness as a Tool of Bank Regulation" (unpublished, 1983). See also Flannery, "Public Policy Aspects of the U.S. Payments System"; Federal Deposit Insurance Corporation Staff Study, "Mandate for Change: Restructuring the Banking Industry," August 1987; Thomas Huertas, "Redesigning Regulation: The Future of Finance in the United States" (Paper prepared for Federal Reserve Bank of Kansas City Symposium on Restructuring the Financial System, Jackson Hole, Wyoming, August 1987); Robert E. Litan, *What Should Banks Do?* (Washington, D.C.: Brookings Institution, 1987); and John H. Kareken, "Federal Bank Regulatory Policy," *Journal of Business* (January 1986), pp. 3–48.

66. E. J. Stevens, "Reducing Risk in Wire Transfer Systems," *Federal Reserve Bank of Cleveland Economic Review*, (2d Quarter 1986), p. 17.

67. Corrigan, "Financial Market Structure: A Longer View," p. 15.

68. CHIPS is owned and operated by the New York Clearing House.

69. Corrigan, "Financial Market Structure: A Longer View," p. 17.

70. "1987 Bank Failures Set Post-Depression Record," *Washington Post*, January 6, 1988.

71. "Banks Expected to Have Another Turbulent Year," *Washington Post*, January 24, 1988.

72. "FSLIC's Negative Net Worth Expanded in '87 to $11.6 Billion from $6.3 Billion," *Wall Street Journal*, April 19, 1988; and Deano Hagermand and Gregory Gajewski, "Patterns of Financial Institution Failures: Some Thoughts on Policy Implications," *Federal Deposit Insurance Corporation Banking and Economic Review* (May/June 1987), p. 8.

73. "GAO Estimates FSLIC Ran Out of Money in 1986, Incurred $3 Billion Deficit," *Banking Report*, March 9, 1987, p. 422.

74. Ibid.

75. Jim McTague, "Queue Forms for FSLIC's Biggest Payout," *American Banker*, June 7, 1988.

76. Private analysts estimate the cost to be much higher—between $40 billion and $60 billion. See "FSLIC's Negative Net Worth Expanded."

77. For a discussion of the recapitalization of the FSLIC fund, see the comments by Lawrence White in "FHLBB Member Appeals to Thrift Industry to Support Higher FSLIC Funding Level," *Banking Report*, June 29, 1987, pp. 1108–9.

78. At the end of 1987 the FDIC fund totaled $18.2 billion, covering approximately 1.1 percent of insured deposits. "FDIC Posts 1987 Surplus Amounting to $50 Million," *Washington Post*, February 3, 1988.

79. American Bankers Association, *Statistical Information on the Financial Services Industry,* p. 63.

80. See William S. Haraf, "Maintaining Financial Stability: Financial Strains and Public Policy," in Phillip Cagan, ed., *Contemporary Economic Problems: Deficits, Taxes, and Economic Adjustments* (Washington, D.C.: American Enterprise Institute, 1987).

2
Financial Stability and the Federal Safety Net

Anna J. Schwartz

The model on which the quest for financial stability was based during the preceding half century regarded banks as imprudent risk takers, vulnerable to the tendency for a run at one bank to lead to runs at other banks. I believe that model, a conception of the New Deal, was flawed. Banks were hemmed in by regulations that limited entry into the industry, the services they were authorized to offer, the prices they could pay and charge, and the geographical areas where they could operate. Because the regulations protected the monopoly position of existing banks and inhibited effective competition, the banks initially were comfortable with the New Deal approach.

Events have overtaken that model, and it cannot be restored. The fallacy underlying the model was its emphasis on inherent instability in triggering bank difficulties. Banks, however, are no more prone to imprudence than nonfinancial firms. Mismanagement and fraud occur from time to time, but there is no evidence that they are more widespread than in industry in general. Moreover, individual bank insolvency need not have contagious effects on other solvent institutions. In most cases of individual bank failures in this country and elsewhere runs have not occurred. The clearest example is the relative absence of runs during the 1920s in the United States, despite numerous bank insolvencies throughout the decade.[1] In the rare instances when runs ignited panics during the past two centuries, institutions did not exist or authorities were unschooled in the practices that prevent such a development, and the private sector had reason to doubt the dependability of preventive arrangements.

In the case of depository institutions, it is the government's responsibility to protect the functioning of the transactions and payments mechanism that they operate. The tripartite safety net in the present model for financial stability—consisting of deposit insurance, a lender of last resort, and regulation—relies on regulation to reduce the risk to the payments mechanism. It calls on a lender of last resort to inject funds into the banking system to preclude panics in which it is assumed that depositors shift from deposits to currency. Had there been no banking panics in the United States from 1930 to 1933, deposit insurance as a device to protect the circulating medium would have been redundant. Because of this historical accident, federal deposit insurance was adopted to serve that purpose. Deposit insurance, however, is not essential to prevent panics, given a reliable lender of last resort.

The model that I propose assigns major responsibility for financial stability to monetary authorities to ensure the basic prerequisite of price level stability. The model provides for an organization and the deregulation of the depository intermediary structure to encourage market efficiency with selected safeguards against excessive risk taking. Depository intermediaries would be free to establish firms where they chose, to pay whatever interest is required to obtain funds, and to offer a variety of services anywhere in this country and internationally where their presence is welcome. Possible restraints on their activities, including off-balance-sheet activities, might be capital requirements, marking assets to market, provision of information to authorities, and double liability for shareholders. Except for double liability, these are precisely the restraints on the activities of discount houses in the United Kingdom, which mark to market every night. The intent of the restraints would be to shift risks of depository intermediation to shareholders from the government safety net. The cumbersome existing regulatory framework might be streamlined in one agency covering all depository intermediaries.[2] The lender of last resort would operate only under extraordinary conditions of a panic that led depositors to shift to currency rather than to redeposit their funds in another institution. The aim of deposit insurance, which could be privately administered, would be to provide depositors and creditors in reorganized or closed institutions with immediate access to the full value of their deposits or their claims.

To realize the foregoing proposal, a blueprint for the transition from the present situation is required. It should address the resolution of the problems of a growing sick list of banks and savings and loan institutions as well as the pace of deregulation of the existing restrictions on deposit intermediary activities and the reshaping of the elements of the existing safety net.

This chapter addresses these points in detail. First it examines historical antecedents of current banking difficulties in this country and worldwide. Bank failures occurred in a variety of circumstances, the causes including fraud, mismanagement, banking structure, and relative price change or general price level instability. In some years of bank failures, there were runs but no panics. Panics sometimes occurred in conditions of general price level instability, but most countries had learned by the end of the nineteenth century what actions were necessary to prevent panics.

The next section deals with misconceptions about bank operations in the 1920s and the bank failure record of 1930–1933 that promoted the regulatory provisions subsequently imposed on U.S. depository institutions. The section also explains why the efforts to limit intermediary competitive behavior broke down. Price level instability led to interest rate instability. Financial innovations—a response to interest rate instability and regulation—in combination with technology contributed to the unraveling of the skein of regulatory controls.

The section on deposit insurance notes that until the recent wave of depository insolvencies, federal deposit insurance was widely acclaimed as the greatest success of the New Deal. Now the need for reform of the program is generally accepted, although there is no agreement on the details. The factors that have been undermining deposit insurance are explored, principally price level instability during the past two decades. In addition, the section gives some attention to why other countries that had felt no need for such a program adopted some form of deposit insurance, beginning in the late 1960s. Deposit insurance may be desirable even if contagious effects of bank runs are precluded by an effective lender of last resort.

A discussion of the role of monetary authorities in the current financial setting explores ways of achieving price stability, since it is the prerequisite for good economic and financial performance over a sustained period. There is no well-understood prescription to achieve price stability other than limited growth of the monetary base that the authorities alone determine. A quantitative measure of price stability averaged over some medium-term period needs to be adopted by legislation or in some other binding requirement imposed on them.

The authorities should be held accountable for the actual price level outcome. In addition, the authorities remain the ultimate source of liquidity for the financial system. It is a mistake for them to imagine threats of contagion that would damage the financial system generally whenever a large financial institution for good reason loses the confidence of its depositors and creditors, and even more so if the troubled institution is a nonfinancial firm. Shifts of funds from one intermediary to another in which depositors and creditors have greater confidence should not be the occasion for intervention by generous provision of liquidity either to the specific firm or to the market in general. Such intervention contributes to moral hazard and reduces the effectiveness of monetary policy.

Finally, the chapter asks whether financial stability can be attained in a deregulated financial environment once the transition from the present situation is concluded. In the transition, unsettled conditions that hang over the U.S. financial system must be dealt with: the problems of a growing list of sick commercial banks and savings and loan institutions; the progressive liberalization of the range of activities that depositories have been seeking and assignment of compatible regulatory functions to the agencies that supervise the institutions; and reform of the federal deposit insurance system.

Banks around the world have made innovative responses to three sources of change in their environment. One source has been technological advancement, which has made possible continuous calculation of the value of the portfolio backing new financial assets. A second has been change in the types of financial services demanded, such as the rise of multinational lending to accommodate large multinational corporations and syndicated lending to accommodate demand for large-scale loans. A third has been the incentive to bypass regulation. At least the first two sources of change will persist even when regulatory restrictions no longer promote banking innovations.

Despite all the changes in bank balance sheets and their off-balance-sheet activities that innovations have led to, banks still perform traditional functions as providers of payments, intermediary, and risk-sharing services. Some of the changes in banking and financial markets, such as financial futures and interest rate and currency swaps, have the potential to reduce risk. In the event of a liquidity panic, the private sector's confidence that the lender of last resort can be relied upon to provide emergency funds to the financial system will still be important.

But even if each asset acquired by depository intermediaries appeared to be liquid and safe, all such assets in the aggregate would not automatically also be liquid and safe. To a large extent financial stability depends on factors beyond the control of an individual intermediary or of all intermediaries as a class. These factors include monetary authority actions that do not destabilize the price level and real economic activity. Given a stable monetary environment, price level stability will follow. In such an environment, a deregulated financial system, besides producing a socially optimum allocation of resources in banking with lower costs and prices for banking services, will be compatible with financial stability. Without a stable monetary environment there cannot be financial stability, and a deregulated financial system will come to grief.

TABLE 2-1
INCIDENCE OF BANKING PANICS IN SEVENTEEN COUNTRIES, 1790–1929

Years with Panics	United States (1790)	Great Britain (1790)	France (1841)	Germany (1853)	Austria (1867)	Russia (1890)	Sweden (1890)	Netherlands (1890)
1793	√	√						
1797	√	√						
1810	√	√						
1815	√							
1819	√							
1825	√	√						
1833	√							
1837	√	√						
1839	√							
1847	√	√	√					
1857	√	√	√	√				
1864			√					
1866		√						
1869						√		
1873	√			√	√			
1882			√					
1891								
1893	√							
1897								
1899							√	
1900								
1901								
1907	√						√	
1913					√			
1914						√		√
1921								
1927								
Total	14	8	4	2	3	2	1	1

NOTE: The year in parentheses under the name of each country refers to the year that annals for it first became available.
SOURCE: W. L. Thorp, *Business Annals* (New York: National Bureau of Economic Research, 1926), pp. 75–87. The 1927 panic in Japan was related to disclosure of the volume of "earthquake" bills in bank portfolios (issued after the September 1, 1923, Tokyo earthquake) with government guarantees against loss only up to a ceiling figure. Actions of the Bank of Japan, in response to legislation authorizing it to make special and extraordinary advances for a year to the banks, with government guarantees of indemnity against losses, ended the crisis. For a discussion of the 1927 panic in Japan, see G. M. Taoka, "The Role of the Bank of Japan in the Administration of the Economic and Financial Controls of the Government during National Emer-

TABLE 2–1 (continued)

Years with Panics	Italy (1890)	Argentina (1890)	Brazil (1890)	Canada (1890)	South Africa (1890)	Australia (1890)	India (1890)	Japan (1890)	China (1890)
1891	√	√							
1893	√					√			
1897			√						
1899									
1900			√						
1901								√	
1907								√	
1913									
1914	√	√							
1921	√								
1927								√	
Total	4	2	2	0	0	1	0	3	0

gencies, with Special Emphasis on the Sino-Japanese War and the World War II Periods."

A History of Banking Difficulties

In seventeen countries the annals of banking have been punctuated by many years of individual bank failures (see table 2–1). The record covers nearly two centuries in the United States and Great Britain, nearly a century in a dozen other countries; in the three remaining ones, the coverage is between the two extremes.

It is noteworthy that the failure rate of banks is lower than that of nonbanking firms. The reason for concern about bank failures is not that they cause capital losses to both their owners and creditors, just as failures of nonbanking firms do. The main reason for concern about widespread bank failures is that they may degenerate into banking panics that produce a drastic decline of the money stock with disastrous effects on economic activity (see note 1). What does the historical record show with respect to the incidence of banking panics?

In contrast to the frequency of bank failures, before 1930 banking panics—in which all depositors attempted to withdraw their deposits in currency—were uncommon. Of the seventeen countries listed in table 2–1, the United States experienced the greatest number of years of panic—a total of fourteen. The runner-up was Great Britain with eight years of panic between 1793 and 1866. No British banking panic has occurred since then. Four banking panics occurred in France, between 1847 and 1882, and also in Italy, between 1891 and 1921. Austria and Japan each had three banking panics and seven countries one or two each. None are recorded in Canada, South Africa, India, or China before 1930, though banks occasionally failed in each of those countries.

Table 2–1 ends in 1929. The three banking panics that followed in 1930–1933 in the United States were unique occurrences in the world. Banking panics in Austria and Germany in May and June 1931, respectively, were not comparable to the breakdown of the domestic payments system in the United States. The continental European panics were a response to the depletion of the countries' international reserves, triggered by withdrawals of foreign balances. "It was a run on the entire banking system of a country," according to R. G. Hawtrey.[3] The continental European developments in turn triggered withdrawals of sterling balances from the Bank of England and the London money market in August and September 1931, culminating in Britain's suspension of convertibility into gold. Japan followed suit in December 1931. In neither country, however, did a banking panic occur.

The post–World War II period under the Bretton Woods system was punctuated by exchange rate crises in Canada, Italy, France, and Britain, but no banking panics. After the collapse of Bretton Woods, bank failures occurred in 1973–1974 in the United Kingdom, West Germany, and the United States, but no panics. A run is said to have occurred in connection with the scandal of the Banco Ambrosiano in Italy, but it was not permitted to spread to other institutions. In the United States the number of insured commercial bank failures in the 1980s has increased from low double digits to triple digits and in the late 1980s is still rising. Until the problem of Continental Illinois surfaced in 1984, bank failures had not been associated with runs. Although the run on Continental Illinois did not involve a shift from deposits to currency, the 1985 runs on state-insured savings and loan associations did. I discuss misconceptions related to these runs in the section on the role of monetary authorities.

Clearly, bank failures do not betoken either runs or the onset of panics. Bank failures have occurred in a variety of circumstances.[4] Typical causes were inexperienced management and fraud. Banking structure also figured in the causes of bank failure. A small undercapitalized unit bank with an undiversified portfolio was more likely to fail than a large multibranch bank. Nevertheless, multibranch banks failed in Canada between 1905 and 1923 owing to mismanagement and dishonesty at head offices rather than at branches.[5]

More significant than these internal causes of failure were the impact of relative price change affecting a particular industry or region and imperfectly diversified portfolios of local banks. Relative price change might occur in response to real shocks in a particular market—the Florida real estate boom of 1926, for example—but usually relative price swings were offshoots of general price level instability. An example of relative price change that was induced by general price level instability was the World War I and postwar rise of land, wheat, and corn prices and their subsequent collapse. That collapse was the principal cause of banking failures in U.S. farm states from 1921 to 1929. Another example of relative price change induced by general price level instability was the rise in the 1970s in prices of energy, land, real estate, and farm crops and their collapse in the 1980s. That collapse was the antecedent of the farm and energy regional banking failures in the 1980s and of the loan losses of banks that extended loans to less-developed countries. In contrast to general price level instability, relative price level instability leads to localized financial distress without damaging the overall financial structure or the aggregate economy.[6]

The effects of general price level instability are more widespread. Apart from inducing interest rate instability, it also distorts perceptions of credit and interest rate risk on both the upswings and the downswings of price movements, contributing to euphoric decisions by banks in the one case and inhibiting intermediation in the other. General price level instability was the principal cause of bank failures in the early 1890s (in Australia, Germany, and Italy), after World War I (in Austria, Belgium, Denmark, Italy, Japan, Norway, South Africa, and Sweden), and since the 1970s.[7] The asset portfolio might have been distributed across low-risk asset types, as judged by the initial economic environment, particularly one that fostered inflation. A reversal of inflationary developments in selected markets or in general could dramatically increase the riskiness of the banks' assets and lead to insolvencies. Ex post, the evaluation of the quality of the assets would differ from the ex ante evaluation.

Some U.S. banks failed in the years before 1930, and there were runs but no panics. The banks experiencing runs were either quickly closed or else relieved of their embarrassment by emergency assistance. Panics sometimes occurred when runs on banks were fomented by the effects on their assets of general price level instability. By the end of the nineteenth century, however, most countries had learned how to prevent panics. When banks became targets of suspicion by depositors, monetary authorities learned to demonstrate readiness to meet all demands of sound debtors for loans and of depositors for cash. A lender of last resort could avert a banking panic by signaling to market participants in a timely and predictable way its readiness to make available an augmented supply of funds. The funds might have been inflows from abroad—attracted by higher domestic than foreign interest rates—or emergency issues of domestic currency. The availability of the supply was sufficient to allay alarm, so that the funds might never have been drawn on. In some cases, orderly liquidation of troubled institutions, with a guarantee against loss by the liquidator, isolated the problem so that it did not spread to other institutions.[8]

As noted, Britain had learned the lesson by 1866. By contrast, the United States experienced a banking panic in 1873 because no institutional framework was immediately available to deal with a surge of demand for high-powered money by the public and banks. Belatedly, the crisis was alleviated by the issue against collateral of clearinghouse loan certificates for use in the settlement of clearing balances and by U.S. Treasury redemption with greenbacks of outstanding government debt.

Yet in 1893 the issue of loan certificates did not cut short a banking panic. One possible explanation is that the individual banks with the bulk of bankers' deposits had reserve deficiencies even though aggregate reserves of the banks were adequate. A more persuasive explanation is that rumors of refusal of banks to convert deposits into cash incited the panic. A misinformed public can nullify the beneficial effects of actions designed to avert panic.

In 1907 the right actions to quell a panic were taken, but too late to be effective. Assistance to troubled trust companies was granted slowly and without dramatic effect. The runs on the trust companies depleted the cash of the New York clearinghouse banks, which were also shipping currency to interior banks and paying it out over their counters to their own frightened depositors. Had the clearinghouse at this point issued loan certificates to enable banks to extend loans more freely to borrowers and also to prevent the weakening of particular banks with unfavorable clearinghouse balances, loss of confidence—displayed less by the public than by country banks (reminiscent of the nervous interbank depositors of Continental Illinois)—might have been calmed. The banks, however, believed that an issue of clearinghouse loan certificates would cause restriction of payments. When country banks demanded currency for funds on deposit or on call in New York, the New York clearinghouse belatedly issued loan certificates and immediately restricted the convertibility of deposits into currency.

As is well known, the panic of 1907 led to the far-reaching reform of the monetary system by creating the Federal Reserve System. The official lender of last resort had no institutional memory of the practices to forestall panic behavior. It did not act from 1930 to 1933 to stem the intensifying failure of banks with a steeply declining price level and the destruction of the payments system as panic followed panic.

The historical record supports the contention that bank failures were not synonymous with runs and did not lead to a loss of confidence in the banking system. Though isolated runs occurred, they were not contagious when a dependable lender of last resort existed.

The Increase in Regulation after the Bank Failures of the 1930s

The verdict of the New Deal on commercial banks in the 1920s was that they lent recklessly to speculative ventures, paving the way for the Great Depression. Competitive behavior by banks, it was held, fostered risk taking. The conclusion was that greater federal control over the commercial banking system was required, with the policy objective of restraining competition. In addition to banks, other depository intermediaries were subjected to extensive federal supervision, particularly savings and loan institutions that had been hard hit after 1929. Mutual savings banks and credit unions had done well during the 1930s, but were not therefore exempted from federal concern. In the decades since the 1930s, changes in regulations have proliferated. Subsequent events challenged the presuppositions of the New Deal regulatory compulsion, and the edifice of regulation it erected has been crumbling.

New Deal regulations applied to the establishment of banks, the services banks and other depository intermediaries were authorized to offer, the prices they could pay and charge, and the geographical areas where they could operate.

Regulations governing entry into the depository intermediary industry have a long history. Yet for nearly a century before the New Deal, freedom in chartering prevailed.[9] The failure rate since the 1920s was interpreted as indicating widespread overbanking. Rigid control of the establishment of new banks was the answer, continuing until the comptroller of the currency for a time in the 1960s changed the policy to allow liberal chartering. Control of entry stifled competition.[10] The possibility that a new bank might injure an existing bank was an argument to deny a charter. Public regulation and private industry associations supported the immediate interests of existing banks. More recently, the chartering of nonbank banks by the comptroller of the currency, despite the opposition of the Federal Reserve, has increased competition among depository intermediaries and between them and other financial and nonfinancial firms offering financial intermediary services. Competitive pressures from those seeking entry and conflicts among regulators over protecting the value of existing charters have eroded the barriers regulation originally established.

Regulations also were introduced to control the character of bank assets. The stock market crash and bank failures were linked to bank underwriting activities.[11] The Glass-Steagall Act terminated commercial bank underwriting of corporate bonds and restricted bank underwriting to U.S. government securities and general obligation state and municipal securities. The growth of consumer credit and the availability of lenient housing and other mortgage credit terms in the 1920s were deemed unsound. Rather than permitting markets to determine the allocation of credit and the level of interest rates, regulations limited the amount and terms of mortgage loans and enforced other investment restrictions.

Since 1968 commercial banks have been adroit in finding ways to circumvent Glass-Steagall restrictions that regulators and courts have approved. They can underwrite, distribute, and trade municipal revenue bonds, participate in private placements of corporate securities, and participate in underwriting and distributing U.S. corporate securities in the Eurobond market.[12] Commercial banks continue to seek ways to enlarge their securities activities without limiting their status as banks. Investment companies have been acquiring access to banking activities through affiliation with nonbank banks and savings and loan associations. The latter in turn have been authorized to acquire commercial and consumer loans, with relaxed limitations on the percentages of total assets allowed to be held in these forms. The intent of these new asset powers may not have been to increase competition in the markets that were opened to thrifts (the intent was to improve diversification of thrift portfolios), but the effect has been procompetitive.

Of the regulations introduced by the New Deal, the ones with the most unforeseen consequences were the prohibition of payment of interest on demand deposits and the imposition of maximum rates of interest payable on commercial bank time and savings deposits. Mutual savings bank and thrift deposits were exempt from the ceilings until the fall of 1966.

The prohibition of interest payments reflected the view that payment of interest on demand deposits fostered "destructive" competition among banks, encouraging them to operate on a low margin of reserves and, in order to earn income to pay the interest, to undertake risky loan and investment operations.[13] The risky ventures were taken to be the participation of banks as direct lenders and as agents for others in the stock market boom. In addition, the prohibition was intended to deter country banks from holding balances with correspondent banks and so promote local lending. Seasonal movements of interbank balances were also believed to affect adversely the stability of portfolios of money market banks. The prohibition was nothing other than a governmentally enforced price-fixing agreement. Until the mid-1950s, in conditions of low market interest rates and low rates of earnings on bank assets, the fixed price of zero that was payable on demand deposits was above the market price since banks imposed service charges.

Given the initial conditions, the banks welcomed the prohibition. As market interest rose, commercial banks began to offer services and gifts as a substitute for money interest payments prohibited on demand deposits. By 1970, however, other depository intermediaries were taking overt steps to evade the prohibition by making savings accounts on which interest was paid accessible by check. In succeeding years, the broadening by federal law of power to issue negotiable order of withdrawal (NOW) accounts in selected states, the installation of automatic terminal facilities by savings and loan associations, the provision of share drafts by credit unions, the provision by money market mutual funds of withdrawals by check, and the authorization by the Federal Reserve of automatic transfer services at commercial banks finally compelled congressional action to legalize the issuing in January 1981 of nationwide NOW accounts. Households were thereby explicitly freed from the prohibition of interest payments on checking accounts. The prohibition continues nominally in force for business demand deposit accounts. It is nominal since sweep accounts and overnight repurchase agreements permit firms to maintain virtually zero demand deposits. Market forces overwhelmed regulation.

The New Deal regulation setting maximum interest rates on commercial bank time and savings deposits also succumbed to market forces. The regulation was intended to limit competition among banks and increase bank profitability. Initially, with market interest rates and the interest rate banks paid below the ceiling, they welcomed the legal limitation. After World War II until 1966, market rates were infrequently above ceiling rates, and when that happened, ceiling rates were raised. In 1966, interest rate ceilings were imposed on mutual savings banks and thrifts at a level 75 to 100 basis points above those that applied to commercial banks (in 1970 reduced to 50 basis points, and in 1973 to 25 basis points). Thereafter, ceiling rates on some categories of time and savings deposits were deliberately set below market interest rates in the belief that competition for deposits between commercial banks and the other intermediaries was a cause of rising interest rates and that more mortgage credit would be available if the other intermediaries could be freed from the competition. It was expected that depositors would shift their accounts from commercial banks to the other classes of institutions. Since deposits at the latter slowed when market interest rates rose relative to the ceilings, changes in the availability of mortgage credit were destabilizing to residential construction, the objective of regulatory solicitude. The discriminatory consequences of the regulatory apparatus were plain: large savers could shift to money market securities paying market rates whereas small savers were stuck with the ceiling rates. In the 1970s, ceiling rates were removed from large time deposits, and floating ceiling rates tied to market interest rates were authorized for other categories. This process continued under the Depository Institutions Deregulation and Monetary Control Act of 1980 (Public Law 96-221) until March 1986, when all interest rate ceilings were eliminated, except for the zero rate on demand deposits.

None of the original objectives of interest rate ceilings was achieved. The extension of the ceilings in 1966 did not achieve a stable supply of mortgage credit. It distorted the growth of deposits at the intermediaries relative to each other and relative to securities paying market interest rates. The distinctions that originally existed among the four types of depository intermediaries were blurred by the time the ceilings had been phased out. Their loan rates rose more than would have been necessary had the intermediaries been free to pay the rates the market required to be paid on deposits.

The New Deal left no mark on laws governing the number and types of branches that intermediaries might have and the services these branches might provide. If the New Deal's objective was financial stability, nationwide branch banking would have been a more direct way to achieve it.[14] The existing arrangement of branching laws, however, served to control banking structure.[15] Other New Deal regulations had similar effects. The regulatory framework described above prevented banks from behaving in ways that would interfere with the existing structure. Nevertheless, the existing structure did not represent the interests of large metropolitan banks as much as it did those of banks in the suburbs and rural areas. Bank mergers and absorptions by the large city banks indicated their drive to change the structure. Smaller banks sought to slow down their absorption by metropolitan banks. A provision of the Federal Deposit Insurance Act required approval of some mergers by regulatory agencies. It was amended in 1960 to broaden the requirement for regulatory approval, "taking into consideration the effect of the transaction on competition."[16]

The bank holding company as an organizational form was another device to organize branches throughout the country offering all services except deposits.[17] Regulation of bank holding companies was included in the Banking Act of 1933, but not until 1956 was an effort to extend the legislation achieved. The Federal Reserve was given authority to supervise bank holding companies, to approve their acquisition of additional banks, and to allow or deny nonbank activities. A one-bank holding company, exempt from regulation until 1970, was useful until that year to evade ceiling interest rates on deposits, since the holding company could sell debt instruments without that limitation and also not be subject to assessment for deposit insurance.

Regulations designed to rigidify the banking structure and to inhibit competition have been changing in ways that erode geographical restrictions on banking. Automated teller machines permit deposit and withdrawal across states. Mergers across state lines to save troubled thrifts have been authorized by the Garn–St Germain Depository Institutions Act of 1982. Bank holding companies undertake many different types of activities across state lines. Stock brokerages offer checking accounts nationwide.

The U.S. banking structure may never resemble the highly concentrated banking systems of Britain, France, and Germany, but a new structure here is clearly inevitable. Efforts to limit intermediary competitive behavior have broken down. Interest rate instability as a consequence of price level instability spawned financial innovations that have frustrated regulation, and technological advancement has served the same end.

Deposit Insurance in an Era of Change

Deposit insurance is now divided among three agencies: the FDIC for deposits in commercial banks and mutual savings banks; the FSLIC for deposits in savings and loan associations and mutual savings banks that shifted from 1980 on from individual state charters to federal charters granted by the Federal Home Loan Bank Board; and Federal Share Insurance supplied by the National Credit Union Administration for credit union deposits.

For a long time after the 1930s, deposit insurance was hailed as the outstanding reform of the New Deal. Federal deposit insurance had been accompanied by a dramatic decline in commercial bank failures and in losses borne by depositors in banks that failed. Deposit insurance seemed clearly to have succeeded in preventing banking panics by removing the reason for runs—loss of confidence in the ability to convert deposits into currency. The existence of deposit insurance reduced if it did not eliminate the need for a lender of last resort to respond to fears of small depositors that they would be unable to realize on their deposits if banks should experience financial difficulties. Over the same period, other industrialized countries that had never adopted deposit insurance experienced a similar absence of runs and bank failures.

The perception of a banking system free of problem institutions in the United States and in other countries was altered by a rash of failures in the mid-1970s and mid-1980s. Two questions arise. What accounts for the relatively failure-free financial system, whether or not a deposit insurance scheme existed, in the earlier period? Why have financial systems in the more recent period been more or less plagued by financial intermediary insolvencies, if not also by runs?

My answer to the first question is that a relatively stable world price level before the 1960s promoted sound banking. In the United States deposit insurance was given the credit for the result. In countries without deposit insurance sound banking was also the rule in conditions of a relatively stable price level.

How does price stability contribute to sound banking? In credit analysis, decisions to limit bank risk are based on the value of collateral in secured loans and on projections of the ratio of a borrower's current assets to his current liabilities in unsecured loans of working capital. The maintenance of price stability is an implicit assumption on which the estimate of a borrower's balance sheet ratios or the valuation of collateral is based. Standards of loan evaluation can be preserved under conditions of price stability, and unexpected price change can invalidate the assumption underlying the loan. The same consideration underlies the management of a bank's bond portfolio. With suitable diversification of the total portfolio, a bank can keep risk low.

The argument could be advanced that it was not price stability but the restrictions on assets and banking structure that produced sound banking until the 1970s. If that were so, countries without such restrictions should not have enjoyed sound banking during those years. That is not the case, however. In Germany, for example, banks have a central role in the credit and capital markets and make long-term capital loans to companies on whose boards bankers serve as directors. As long as there was price stability, German banks' fixed-rate long-term loans to industry posed no problem. When interest rates rose during the 1970s, however, the German banks' refinancing costs rose and exceeded the interest earned.

My answer to the question why financial systems have been plagued by insolvencies is that since the late 1960s, price instability, marked by inflationary surges until the 1980s and by disinflationary plunges since then, accounts not only for the problems of financial institutions here and abroad but also for the attendant plight of the U.S. deposit insurance agencies. In this setting, banking risk has increased. Fraud and mismanagement are more likely to gain ground in conditions of price variability, and institutions of unimpeachable standards of risk management may make judgments that later turn out to be mistaken, if not disastrous.

In the postwar period when the inflation rate was low, the economy stable, and the bank failure rate low, the fixed-rate premium for insurance coverage charged by the deposit insurance agencies and the manner in which they settled failures aroused no concern about the incentive effects of deposit insurance. Currently, they are the center of the discussion about the need for reform. In the unstable economy since the 1970s, with high and variable inflation rates, the agencies have functioned in ways that compound the problems of financial intermediaries, including protecting some intermediaries that have acted and continue to act irresponsibly.

The current situation invites reexamination of what the safety net is designed to accomplish. The safety net exists to preclude banking panics, not bank failures. To protect depositors without shifting the risks of intermediaries to the insurance agencies and ultimately to the taxpayers, insolvent intermediaries should be closed promptly when net worth on a market-value accounting basis declines to zero.[18] To obviate concerns that a failure will result in runs on other solvent institutions, the lender of last resort should provide them with adequate liquidity so that reserves in the banking system remain at a level that does not shrink the money supply. Regulation should ensure that risk is borne by equity owners of the intermediaries.

The safety net has not been functioning in this manner. Intermediary risks have been assumed by the insurance agencies. Although the most troubled intermediaries have been liquidated or merged and in the case of Continental Illinois nationalized, the number of institutions that on a market-value accounting basis would be judged insolvent has been growing apace. The deposit insurance agencies have kept such institutions operating because of the drain on their resources that closing them would entail. As the costs of closing or merging troubled intermediaries have risen, the adequacy of the reserves of the insurance agencies remains unsettled.

Runs are not conspicuous among the reasons nine countries adopted compulsory deposit insurance schemes—two in the early

1960s, seven since the late 1960s.[19] The problems brought on by failures of some institutions apparently led regulators to conclude that depositor protection required insurance provisions. In general, the motivation appears to have been to recompense depositors in failed institutions.[20]

None of the deposit insurance schemes other countries have adopted is as unlimited as the present U.S. system. Regularizing the machinery to pay off depositors to the extent possible from liquidations of failed institutions seems to be the objective of deposit insurance, not the prevention of runs. A deposit insurance fund to settle claims quickly is reason enough for supporting an insurance scheme. It is also politically appealing.

Deposit insurance in this country is now widely criticized because the premiums are not risk related and so provide incentives to insured institutions to invest in risky projects and contribute to economic inefficiency by the subsidy to the borrowers. Proposals to reform the system include establishing risk-related premiums, privatizing deposit insurance, reducing the coverage of deposit insurance, and tightening capital requirements for the insured. There is, however, no agreement on the specific reforms to adopt.

Just as failure by the Federal Reserve in 1930–1933 to act as an effective lender of last resort led to deposit insurance, failure by the Federal Reserve in the past two decades to deliver price stability has contributed to undermining the deposit insurance system.[21]

The Role of Monetary Authorities

Given that price level stability is essential for financial stability, it falls to the Federal Reserve System, which is clearly responsible for monetary policy, to choose noninflationary policies. The Federal Reserve's present mandate is currently broader than dedication exclusively to price level stability. The Employment Act of 1946 (Public Law 79-304), the Humphrey-Hawkins Full Employment and Balanced Growth Act of 1978 (Public Law 95-523), and the Federal Reserve's own statement of its purposes and functions encompass at least four objectives of monetary policy: economic stability and growth, a high level of employment, stability in the purchasing power of the dollar, and reasonable balance in transactions with foreign countries. Taking account of the U.S. balance of payments means that the Federal Reserve has some opinion about the appropriate level of the exchange rate of the dollar.

The targets that the Federal Reserve sets for itself or that government economic policy imposes on it may be rhetorical in some degree.

It is not clear that the Federal Reserve has authority to intervene in the foreign exchange market unless deputized by the Treasury Department. Multiple targets, however, pose the problem of inconsistency. Efforts to maintain the exchange value of the dollar at a given level may require money supply growth rates and interest rate changes that have undesired effects on private investment and the level of unemployment. Since the mid-1960s the Federal Reserve has altered money growth rates first to lower the unemployment rate at the cost of a higher inflation rate and subsequently to lower the inflation rate at the cost of a higher unemployment rate. No lasting gains accrued from these temporary shifts in monetary policy. The lesson that the Federal Reserve cannot determine the long-run level of the unemployment rate should have been learned from that experience. The Federal Reserve, however, can work to achieve price stability.

For the Federal Reserve to abjure actions in areas it has regarded as its preserve will require that it adjust its conception of its proper role. The legislation that now governs the Federal Reserve will also require modification to define explicitly that its only objective should be achieving price stability. Some constraint needs to be placed on its ability to create the monetary base. Economists do not have a good enough understanding of the timing relations between monetary growth rates and the price level to do better than specify limited growth of the monetary base as the Federal Reserve's responsibility in its effort to achieve price level stability. A quantitative range that would qualify as "limited growth" of the monetary base might be imposed. In any event, the Federal Reserve should be held accountable for failure to operate within those limits.

In addition to its short-run actions to reduce the unemployment rate or lower the inflation rate, the Federal Reserve has displayed rash concern since 1970 that lender-of-last-resort intervention was called for whenever the market became aware of the insolvency of major financial or nonfinancial institutions.

The runs on Continental Illinois in 1984 and on savings and loan associations in 1985 in Ohio and Maryland apparently revived regulators' fear that financial panic is an ever-present contingency to be guarded against. The actions taken to rescue Continental Illinois imply that any less comprehensive response would have brought on contagion. Is this a valid assessment? The failure of Home State Savings in Ohio, it is clear, need not have resulted in runs on the state's savings and loan associations had authorities acted promptly to assure depositors that all their demands for cash would be met.[22]

If Continental Illinois had been closed as insolvent before its net worth turned negative, the institutions, foreign bank depositors, and creditors who ran on it would have redeposited their withdrawals in other institutions or bought financial assets to replace the certificates of deposit Continental had issued that they were no longer willing to buy. Even if some of the interbank depositors that held as much as half their equity in uninsured deposits at Continental had obtained only a fraction of their claims immediately upon the closing, they would ultimately have recovered after the liquidating of Continental the full nominal value of their claims. The market would have known that the claimants on Continental were not in jeopardy. Even if closing Continental had led to runs on the interbank depositors—ostensibly the reason for keeping Continental in operation—the lenders of last resort in the nations concerned could have provided adequate liquidity to their markets to tide the banks over if the Continental deposits were their only problem. Fear of panic alone should not determine the decision by a regulator to close an insolvent institution. The main point, however, is that a lender of last resort can nip a panic in the bud.

If this view is correct, it is a curiosity that the recent instability of intermediaries has stimulated the construction of models that highlight bank runs as a quintessential feature of a fractional reserve banking system. According to one model, runs need not depend on any loss in value of the assets that underlie fixed-claim deposits. They can occur even on a sound bank if the cost of liquidating assets reduces the value of the loan portfolio. A model of recurrent banking panics, however, is not compatible with the absence of runs and panic in the United Kingdom since 1866.[23] Moreover, the models all assume that runs involve conversion of deposits into currency. In the Continental Illinois run, no such conversion occurred. Depositors ran from a bank that was perceived to be troubled to untroubled banks or to safe securities. The effect on money supply was not an aspect of the run in the case.[24] The conclusion that "federally sponsored deposit insurance has been the most (the only?) effective device for preventing runs" is wrong.[25] An effective lender of last resort can also prevent runs. To quote Walter Bagehot on the science of political economy: "Those who are conversant with its abstractions are usually without a true contact with its facts."[26]

It is, nevertheless, important for central banks to be informed about their role as lender of last resort if an unusual constellation of events should ignite panic. That condition apparently arose the day after the stock market crash in October 1987, and the Federal Reserve correctly announced that it would lend freely, as it did for a brief period. In recent years, however, the role of lender of last resort has been exercised when it was gratuitously inferred that panic would result if, for example, a large industrial firm or a municipality were permitted to declare bankruptcy. A passive lender of last resort is not desirable, but no more so is a hyperactive one, pouring funds into the market when the occasion for doing so forecloses the adoption of fundamental solutions.

A Federal Reserve System that was able to maintain price level stability would also incidentally minimize the need for lender-of-last-resort intervention.[27] The breeding ground for panic has historically been price level instability, which led to bank failures and unreliable performance by the lender of last resort.

Are Deregulation and Financial Stability Compatible?

As the world financial systems have evolved from closely controlled to increasingly competitive, some observers express concern that an unregulated system will accept too high a level of risk. Because the financial instruments and the activities that depository institutions have innovated are novel, no record is yet available of the risk institutions are exposed to by these developments. There is an undercurrent of unease about bank safety and, in this country, about the role of deposit insurance in promoting risk taking. If bank failures occur, resulting bank runs could undermine the payments system. The argument for reregulation is that it will prevent the banking system from taking on too high a level of risk. Emphasis is placed on a failure-proof and run-proof financial system.

Since the U.S. experience of 1930–1933, economists and policy makers have feared that a banking panic of similar consequence might recur.[28] But experience teaches that it need not. The knowledge of how to prevent a panic has been available for well over a century. A loss of confidence in the convertibility of deposits into currency does not need to gather force, and no arcane procedures are required to buoy up a nonbank public or a banking community beset by doubts about the retrievability of its deposits. The U.S. response to panic in 1930–1933 was unique.

Indeed, there is an anachronistic aspect to the hypersensitivity to the possibility of panic. The assumption of a flight to currency on which panic conditions were based in the past is not compelling in present-day circumstances. Depositors might move from one institution perceived to be unsound to another perceived to be sound or switch from deposits to safe securities, but the consequences of such shifts are no threat to the payments system.[29]

If the apprehension of panic should be laid to rest, is the fear of bank runs as a result of failure or rumors equally overdone? The historical record supports the contention that, though isolated runs occurred, they were not contagious when a dependable lender of last resort existed. Bank failures were not synonymous with runs and did not lead to a loss of confidence in the banking system.

Is it true that unregulated banks operate at excessive risk levels? Perhaps they do with existing deposit insurance incentives, but would it be true when the risk is borne by owners and managers of institutions? Capital requirements, marking assets to market, provision of information to authorities, and double liability for stockholders are a possible set of restraints on the conduct of owners and managers.[30] Whatever risks the institutions were prepared to undertake, whether the activities were on or off balance sheets, the mistakes would be borne by the owners, not the deposit insurance agencies.

Picture a world in which owners and managers of depository institutions are free to choose any assets yielding the highest return as they judge it and to pay whatever price for funds they deem reasonable. They would know that mistakes that wipe out capital and reserves would prompt the immediate closing or reorganization of the institution, and stockholders might be liable for an assessment equal to their equity. Depositors and creditors under these arrangements would be fully protected, and the deposit insurance agency could operate without concern for its reserves. Failures of institutions would not precipitate runs. The lender of last resort would not need to anticipate panics. Regulatory agencies, if the separate ones that now exist were not merged, would function under changed circumstances, concerned with market-value accounting, capital adequacy, and the information required from the institutions they supervise. They would no longer monitor the activities institutions engaged in. Would not such a system yield financial stability?

Those who regard banks as inherently unstable will dismiss it. They see a recurring historical pattern in which many bankers "lose sight of conventional and conservative standards of asset management" and are then caught short when booms collapse.[31] Inherent instability resides in economic agents for proponents of this view. These proponents may refer to actions by the Federal Reserve but establish no connection between monetary policy and the conditions in which economic agents make decisions.

The critical condition that will determine the safety and soundness of financial institutions in the future, as it has in the past, is the price level environment in which they operate. Under our existing monetary system, banks make contracts when they have no way of knowing whether the price level or the inflation rate that they expect will be realized. The monetary authorities make no commitment to maintain any particular price level or rate of inflation. Yet to the extent bank contracts stipulate fixed rates of future money payments to others and from others, they have arbitrary consequences when the price level or inflation rate turns out to be greater or less than anticipated.

Stabilizing the price level will do more for financial stability than reforming deposit insurance or reregulating. The problem is that in the present fiat-money regimes worldwide, monetary authorities operate with no formal constraints. The ships have no rudders. We appear to be in a transition period in which the economy is adjusting to a reduction in inflation rates (with underlying fears of a potential resurgence of inflation) and to new types of financial assets in all the industrialized countries.

Tomorrow's money, like today's money, will be a combination of currency, fixed-value deposits, and money market funds—whether transferred electronically or by pieces of paper will make no difference. As long as currency issues are the base of the system and the transfer of money market funds requires drawing on a depository intermediary account, monetary authorities that issue the base can retain control.

A stable price level will not eliminate business cycle fluctuations but will substantially reduce their amplitude. Some risk in financial, as in nonfinancial, operations is therefore unavoidable, particularly if borrowers have interrelated debt structures.

Price level stability is a responsibility of monetary authorities. If monetary authorities cannot deliver predictable price level stability, financial stability may not be achievable. If price level instability is the outlook for the future, troubled depository institutions, whether deregulated or reregulated, will be one of the costs.

Notes

1. A widespread demand by depositors for immediate conversion of their deposits into currency is termed a bank run. In a fractional reserve banking system, drains of currency from banks reduce their reserves and result in a multiple contraction of deposits that reduces the stock of money. A run on an individual bank need not lead to its insolvency. A run can be halted and confidence in the bank restored by a demonstration that an ample supply of currency is available to satisfy all depositor demands. A run that spreads from one bank to other solvent banks because of a loss of confidence in the banking system is termed a banking panic. Only if additional currency and reserves are provided to the banking system can the damaging effects on the aggregate money stock of a panic be avoided.

On the infrequency of bank runs relative to bank failures, see the account the comptroller of the currency gave of national bank failures during the year ended October 31, 1921:

> Of the 34 banks placed in charge of receivers since October 31, 1920, 4 were closed on account of runs; 5 on account of injudicious banking; 1 on account of forgeries and embezzlement; 10 on account of the inability to realize on loans; 1 on account of robbery and the burning of the bank; 1 on account of the inability to realize on loans and the failure of stockholders to pay balance due on capital; 1 on account of defalcations by cashier; 1 on account of the stockholders' failing to vote to place the bank in liquidation after the sale of the assets; 1 wrecked by president; 5 on account of fraudulent management; 1 wrecked by assistant cashier; 1 on account of depreciation of securities; 1 on account of injudicious banking and depreciation of securities; 1 on account of fraudulent management, injudicious bank investment in real estate mortgages, and depreciation of securities. (U.S. Comptroller of the Currency, *Annual Report*, 1922, p. 91).

There were 8,179 national banks in operation on October 31, 1921.

In 1922, 31 national banks failed, with runs on only three. In 1923, 52 banks failed, with runs on only three. In 1924, 138 banks failed, with runs on only six. In 1925, 98 banks failed, and runs are not mentioned as causes of failure. In the remaining years of the decade there is no reference to runs in connection with bank failures.

In a recent paper on what happened in China in the 1930s, Brandt and Sargent note, "although there were numerous bank failures, there was no widespread panic or sequence of bank runs." The Chinese evidence is not unique among countries other than the United States. See L. Brandt and T. J. Sargent, "Interpreting New Evidence about China and U.S. Silver Purchases," unpublished manuscript, 1986, p. 5.

2. Objections to a single regulatory agency have been advanced in the context of the existing differentiation of types of depository institutions and the existing network of restrictions on the geographic scope and types of financial services they are authorized to offer. One objection, given existing institutional arrangements, is that the short-run horizon of a monopoly regulator would lead to maximization of his private interests but not to maximization of social values. I doubt that the objection would hold for the reformed financial system that I envisage. There would be no need for regulators matched to different types of intermediaries. All intermediaries would be unrestricted with respect to the services they offer. The functions of a redesigned regulator in a reformed financial system would differ radically from those currently exercised by existing regulators.

3. R. G. Hawtrey, *The Art of Central Banking*, 2d ed. [1932] (London: Frank Cass, 1962).

4. On causes of bank failures, see M. J. Flannery and J. M. Guttentag, "Problem Banks: Examination, Identification, and Supervision," in L. Lapidus et al., *State and Federal Regulation of Commercial Banks*, vol. 2, *Appraising the System: Significant Activities and Issues, Examination Studies* (Washington, D.C.:

FDIC Task Force on State and Federal Regulation of Commercial Banks, 1980); and U.S. Comptroller of the Currency, *Annual Reports*, 1921–1929 and 1931–1936 (Washington, D.C., 1922–1930 and 1932–1937).

5. H. P. Willis and B. H. Beckhart, eds., *Foreign Banking Systems* (New York: Holt, 1929).

6. On the relation of relative price variability to the rate of general price level change, see S. Domberger, "Relative Price Variability and Inflation," *Journal of Political Economy*, vol. 95 (June 1987), pp. 547–66, and the references cited therein.

7. Willis and Beckhart, *Foreign Banking Systems*, pp. 278–79, 514, 881, 1008, 1055–56; Thorp, *Business Annals*, pp. 211, 232, 268, 274; 323, 349. For bank failures in Japan, 1920–1921, see also Taoka, "The Role of the Bank of Japan," p. 53.

8. In 1905 the Chicago Clearing House liquidated three Chicago banks that failed, absorbing any loss to the banks' depositors. See Eugene A. White, *The Regulation and Reform of the American Banking System, 1900–1929* (Princeton, N.J.: Princeton University Press, 1983), p. 80.

9. Chartering agencies also have authority to close depository institutions. That the chartering agencies do not always exercise that facet of their authority promptly did not become an issue until the recent wave of sick institutions that continue to operate despite their insolvency on market-value accounting principles.

10. On the effects of limiting entry into banking, see S. Peltzman, "Entry into Banking," *Journal of Law and Economics*, vol. 8 (October 1965), pp. 11–50.

11. See Eugene A. White, "Before the Glass-Steagall Act: An Analysis of the Investment Banking Activities of National Banks," *Explorations in Economic History*, vol. 23 (1986), pp. 33–55, for a study based on 1931 data, showing that security affiliates did not increase the probability of bank failure, did not produce dangerous swings in earnings, and did not endanger commercial bank solvency or liquidity.

12. G. G. Kaufman, "The Securities Activities of Commercial Banks," in R. Aspinwall and R. Eisenbeis, eds., *The Banking Handbook* (New York: Wiley, 1984).

13. The inadequacy of the argument for interest rate control is analyzed in Albert M. Cox, Jr., "Regulation of Interest on Bank Deposits," *Michigan Business Studies*, vol. 17, no. 4; and George J. Benston, "Interest Payments on Demand Deposits and Bank Investment Behavior," *Journal of Political Economy*, vol. 72 (October 1964), pp. 431–49.

14. In 1925 only 2.5 percent of all banks were banks with branches, and 10.5 percent of all offices were branch offices. White finds a significant (but low) negative correlation in 1925 between bank failures and two measures of branching. In six states in which branching was permitted in 1927, the failure rate was considerably lower than in the remaining states. See Eugene A. White, "State-sponsored Insurance of Bank Deposits in the United States, 1907–1929," *Journal of Economic History*, vol. 41 (September 1981), pp. 537–57.

15. Ibid. White links the establishment of state-sponsored insurance of bank deposits in 1907–1929 to those states where small unit banks were

dominant. In other states, where branch banking was permissible, the banking structure provided self-insurance.

16. *Federal Reserve Bulletin*, vol. 46, no. 6 (June 1960), p. 611.

17. See "Bank Holding Companies: Structure, Performance, and Reform" by Anthony Saunders, in this volume, on the effect of circumventing restrictions in motivating the formation of bank holding companies.

18. An analysis of this recommendation is available in "Regulating Bank Safety and Performance" by George J. Benston and George G. Kaufman in this volume.

19. A reference to runs as a prelude to the establishment of deposit insurance appears in the discussion of the Lebanese scheme. In 1966 a run on the largest bank in Lebanon had contagious effects on fifteen smaller Lebanese banks, which collapsed when depositors switched to larger foreign banks. In the case of the Philippines, reference is made to the extension of assistance to banks in difficulties in 1970 by the Philippine Deposit Insurance Corporation to stem runs on apparently rural banks. See I. S. McCarthy, "Deposit Insurance: A Survey" (IMF, 1979, mimeo).

In Canada the introduction of deposit insurance in 1967 followed a bank run on a sound institution, although prevention of bank runs was not the main focus of the legislation (Canada, *Commons Debates*, February 3, 1967, p. 12621). In 1965 the failure of an acceptance finance company led the Bank of Canada to add to the cash reserves of the chartered banks to avoid liquidity difficulties in the financial markets (Bank of Canada, *Annual Report*, 1965, p. 7).

20. Before a deposit insurance scheme was launched in the United Kingdom in 1982, the Bank of England in 1973 with the participation of English and Scottish clearing banks contributed an amount estimated at upwards of £150 million (no comprehensive estimate is available) to rescue twenty-six troubled small banks involved in speculative property ventures. They were originally believed to be solvent, but many turned out not to be. Receivers were appointed for the latter, so the assistance in effect provided deposit insurance. See M. I. Reid, *The Secondary Banking Crisis, 1973–75: The Inside Story of Britain's Biggest Banking Upheaval* (London: Macmillan, 1982).

21. Would deposit insurance have been unscathed had price stability persisted? One can speculate that the pace of financial innovation would have been slower in the absence of inflation and high interest rates. International banking markets would, nevertheless, probably have developed given U.S. interest rate ceilings and reserve requirements, as would the Eurobond market given the interest equalization tax. Had there been no inflation, however, the oil cartel might not have succeeded in boosting oil prices in 1973–1974 and 1979–1980 with the resultant large imbalances in international payments and growth in international banking activity. If interest rates had not risen astronomically in the late 1970s, nonbank intermediaries might not have created money market accounts carrying market interest rates in competition with banks and thrifts subject to interest rate ceilings. De facto deregulation that has occurred might have been slowed. Had disinflation not characterized price behavior worldwide in the 1980s, risks of financial transactions might

have been lower. Technological advances in communications and data processing would have occurred in any event. These changes have made possible hedging against adverse changes in interest or exchange rates. These counterfactual speculations suggest that there may have been a less stressful outcome for intermediaries and the insurance agencies had price stability prevailed.

22. The following comment on the spread of the run supports this statement: "At the peak of the runs on ODGF [Ohio Deposit Guarantee Fund]-insured institutions (March 11–14), it was not clear to the general public whether the state would or would not reimburse depositors' losses, because state officials stopped short of making outright commitments of state resources to protect depositors from loss." Federal Reserve Bank of Cleveland, *Annual Report*, 1985, p. 17. See also E. J. Kane, "Who Should Learn What from the Failure and Delayed Bailout of the ODGF?" National Bureau of Economic Research, Working Paper no. 2260, 1987.

23. J. Bryant, "Bank Collapse and Depression," *Journal of Money, Credit, and Banking*, vol. 13, no. 4 (November 1981), pp. 454–64.

24. G. G. Kaufman, "The Truth about Bank Runs," Federal Reserve Bank of Chicago, SM-87-3.

25. D. W. Diamond and P. H. Dybvig, "Bank Runs, Deposit Insurance, and Liquidity," *Journal of Political Economy*, vol. 91 (June 1983), pp. 401–19.

26. Walter Bagehot, *The Works of Walter Bagehot*, vol. 5, *Economic Studies*, ed. Forrest Morgan (Hartford, Conn.: Travelers Insurance Company, [1876] 1889).

27. In the history of thought concerning the need for a lender of last resort, writers did not directly link that role and price level instability.

Francis Baring, discussing the error of directors of the Bank of England in curtailing discounts during the panic of 1793, wrote, "In such cases the Bank are not an intermediate body, or power; there is no resource on their refusal, for they are the *dernier resort*," but he did not note any connection between price instability, 1790–1793, and the banks' dependence on the Bank of England. See Sir Francis Baring, *Observations on the Establishment of the Bank of England and the Paper Circulation of the Country* (New York: Augustus M. Kelley, [1797]1967).

Henry Thornton also emphasized the necessity for a lender of last resort. The price level instability associated with the Napoleonic Wars during his lifetime was possibly an implicit condition for his recommendation. Bagehot believed banks were prudent but vulnerable to runs and hence provided a well-argued case for a lender of last resort. If monetary stability has primacy over the lender-of-last-resort function as a condition for financial stability, why did Bagehot emphasize the latter and not the former? It will be recalled that Bagehot regarded a competitive banking system as the best arrangement for financial stability, but deemed it impractical to restore such a system given the monopoly position that the Bank of England had attained. Under those circumstances, an effective lender of last resort was his second-best solution. See Henry Thornton, *An Enquiry into the Nature and Effects of the Paper Credit of Great Britain*, edited with an Introduction by F. A. Hayek (London: Allen and

Unwin, [1802] 1939), pp. 182–89; and Walter Bagehot, *Lombard Street* (New York: Scribner's, [1873] 1902), pp. 66–69.

Hawtrey, a twentieth-century contributor to the importance of a lender of last resort, was influenced by the drains on international reserves in 1931. Hence he advocated the creation of an international lender of last resort. He was certainly familiar with unstable price behavior during the period but did not develop propositions that related that behavior to the need for a lender of last resort. See Hawtrey, *The Art of Central Banking*.

28. The governor of the Bank of England explained the bank's motives in rescuing fringe banks in 1973–1975 to a House of Commons Select Committee (see Reid, *The Secondary Banking Crisis*, p. 18):

> We had as our purpose protecting depositors, and the purpose of protecting depositors was simply to avoid a widening circle of collapse through the contagion of fear. . . . The danger was real and, of course, we had seen it in the past. We saw it, for example, rage through the American banking system in the early 1930s, when hundreds of banks were closed and finally a total closedown of the banking system was involved.

29. It has been argued that a bank run or panic that involves a massive shift of deposits from one part of the banking system to another is as destructive as a flight to cash (C. A. E. Goodhart, "Why Do We Need a Central Bank?" n.d., mimeo.). The reasoning is that "it is the collapse of the borrowing relationship, as failing banks call in loans, leaving borrowers without the ability to replace the money at all easily or reasonably quickly, that is at least as responsible as the loss of depositors' wealth for the resulting dislocation." The argument is contrived. The assumed special relationship between bank and borrower and the cost to the bank of obtaining information known privately only to the borrower are said to inhibit establishing a new relationship. Many borrowers, however, have relationships not just with one source of funds—a bank, an insurance company, or a factor who lends money to producers and dealers on the security of accounts receivable—but with several of each. More important, banks to which deposits have been transferred are surely eager to invest the funds. Why borrowers of good standing would not find a responsive lender in the circumstances is not obvious. Finally, although "failing banks" are the ones described as losing deposits and calling in loans, the prescription for the case in question is: "What a Central Bank has to do is to recycle back to the original banks any large and destabilising movement of funds." The defense for this conclusion is that Bagehot was wrong to suggest that "only banks with liquidity problems and not with solvency problems, should be supported." Should all insolvent U.S. institutions be propped up, in accordance with this view? In the United Kingdom, the twenty-six troubled fringe banks that were given assistance in 1973–1975 were initially believed to be solvent. Would the Bank of England and the clearing banks have been willing to help them had their insolvency been known? See G. J. Benston and G. G. Kaufman, "Risks and Failures in Banking: Overview, History, and Evaluation," in G. G. Kaufman and R. C. Kormendi, eds., *Deregulating Finan-*

cial Services (Cambridge, Mass.: Ballinger Publishing Co., 1986); see also note 20.

30. Double liability for bank shareholders would be an option for recapitalization of an intermediary with vanishing net worth.

Double liability for bank shareholders had a long history in the United States, predating the Civil War in some states (Davis R. Dewey, *State Banking before the Civil War*, National Monetary Commission, 61st Congress, 2d sess., Sen. Doc. 581, Washington, D.C., 1910, pp. 117–20). The National Bank Act of 1864, section 12 (12USC63), imposed double liability on national bank shareholders. During the pre–World War I national bank period, in twenty-six states state commercial bank shareholders were subject to double liability; in one state, the decision was voluntary; in another, probably required; in eight states, it was not (S. A. Welldon, *Digest of State Banking Statutes*, National Monetary Commission, 61st Congress, 2d sess., Sen. Doc. 353, Washington, D.C., 1910). In the remaining states the statute was silent on the question. Section 5151 of the Revised Statutes applicable to banking repeated section 12 of the National Bank Act of 1864, on the basis of which double liability was imposed on shareholders of national banks that became members of the Federal Reserve System. State banks or trust companies that became members of the Federal Reserve System, however, were not subject to section 5151 of the Revised Statutes, although they were subject to double liability if there was such a provision in the state that chartered them (*Federal Reserve Bulletin*, September 1915, p. 273). On the other hand, the member bank shareholders of every Federal Reserve Bank were subject to double liability for the amount of their subscription to the stock of the Federal Reserve Bank. By 1933 the double liability provision existed in some states on some classes of bank shares but was nonexistent on other classes and in other states. The provisions were either constitutional or statutory (T. P. Cramer, Jr., "Double Liability (A Nationwide Survey)," *Banking*, vol. 28 (May 1936), p. 84).

The beginning of the repeal of the provision apparently dates from the Banking Act of 1933 (Public Law 73-66), section 22, which eliminated the additional liability on national bank shares issued after the date of the act. The Banking Act of 1935 (Public Law 74-305), section 304, terminated double liability on previously issued national bank stock on July 1, 1937. Some states repealed provisions for double liability between 1933 and 1937. To seal the termination of the provision in both the Banking Act of 1935 and the Federal Reserve Act, the act of September 8, 1959 (Public Law 86-230), section 7, made it explicit.

Despite the longevity of the provision, I have seen no economic analysis of its effect on the demand for bank equity. Possibly the provision was not strictly enforced. If it had been, one would expect that the yield on bank equity would be equalized with that on equity in other industries by either higher earnings or tax advantages. It does not appear that double liability limited bank capitalization. It has been noted that capital ratios at the turn of the century were close to 25 percent (Kaufman, "The Truth about Bank Runs," p. 13).

Some estimates of collections from assessments are available. The comptroller of the currency reported that stockholders of the 1,371 national banks fully liquidated from 1865 to the year ending October 31, 1935, paid in 50 percent of the stock assessments levied. The proportion of assessments collected by a sample of state banks averaged 46 percent (Cramer, "Double Liability," p. 4). It has been noted that a major barrier to fuller collections was the difficulty of pursuing nonresident stockholders in states where failed banks were located. The verdict that double liability failed to provide protection to depositors must have been based largely on the experience of 1930–1933. One source notes that three states repealed double liability on stock in banks that became members of the FDIC. The introduction of federal deposit insurance may well have denigrated the effectiveness of double liability in providing incentives for shareholders to monitor bank management.

31. C. P. Kindleberger, "Bank Failures: The 1930s and the 1980s" (Paper prepared for the Federal Reserve Bank of San Francisco Conference, "The Search for Financial Stability: The Last Fifty Years," 1985), p. 28.

3
Regulating Bank Safety and Performance

George J. Benston and George G. Kaufman

It is generally agreed that an efficient financial system is a prerequisite for an efficient developed economy. Because of the perceived importance for the other sectors of the economy of breakdowns in the financial system, the possible instability of the financial sector, as evidenced by the dramatic decline in the profitability of depository institutions (collectively referred to as banks) and the sharp jump both in the number of failures and in the costs of their resolution, is an important public policy concern. This is not the first time in history, either in the United States or elsewhere, that financial sector instability has been the focus of public attention. Indeed, during almost every one of the many actual or perceived financial crises in world history, legislation and regulation have been proposed and frequently enacted that purported to strengthen the system and prevent recurrence. Unfortunately, some of the regulations adopted to reduce financial instability have contributed to its increase in later years. We analyze a number of recent proposals for stabilizing the banking system and develop an alternative policy option to improve both the safety and the performance of the banking system at minimum cost and disruption.[1]

Proposals for Changing the Present Bank Regulatory System

In this section we enumerate and evaluate the costs and benefits of the more credible market-oriented proposals that have been suggested for increasing the safety and efficiency of the banking system. These include abolition of federal deposit insurance, reform of federal deposit insurance coverage and premium charges, risk-related capital requirements, the narrow bank proposal, and reorganization of banks before their economic capital becomes negative. Several of the proposals are not mutually exclusive. We do not consider proposals that would reimpose the regulations that were recently removed or liberalized since they have been found to be counterproductive.

Abolition of Federal Deposit Insurance. Because the current structure of federal deposit insurance is frequently identified as the major cause of the increased instability in the banking system through its encouragement of increased risk taking, elimination of federal deposit insurance has been proposed.[2] In a world without federal deposit insurance, banks would be subject to considerably greater market discipline from all depositors, shareholders, and private insurance companies if they chose to insure their deposits. As a result banks would be likely to assume less portfolio risk and maintain higher capital-to-asset ratios.[3] In effect, this would be a return to the period before the Federal Deposit Insurance Corporation (FDIC) was established.

Proponents of this proposal argue that none of the major reasons for introducing federal deposit insurance in 1933 remain valid today. These include protection against a collapse of the money supply and payments system, protection of small depositors, and protection of unit banking. Except in a few periods, bank failures neither were very frequent nor ignited the failure of other banks or a local or national economic downturn. Runs on individual banks led primarily to redeposits at other banks, and bank failures did not either permanently reduce the supply of banking services to a community or depress the local economy more than the failure of any other firm of comparable size.

The few periods in which bank failures did contribute significantly to national financial and economic instability were characterized by a loss of confidence in all banks and attempts to convert bank deposits into currency. Thus reserves were drained from the banking system, causing multiple contractions in money and credit. Except in the 1929–1933 period, the adverse effects were short-lived. The banks acted in common, generally through the major clearinghouses and temporary suspensions of convertibility of deposits into currency, to provide time for the orderly sale of assets and the restoration of depositors' confidence. But dissatisfaction with the ad hoc and questionable legality of these actions led to the establishment of the Federal Reserve System in 1913 to protect against reductions in aggregate bank reserves.[4]

Unfortunately, for whatever reasons, the Federal Reserve did not offset the currency drain in 1929–1933, and the private structure was not permitted to act as before. The results were disastrous but unique to that period. The crisis led to a loss of faith in the Federal Reserve

System's ability to perform its lender-of-last-resort function appropriately and to the establishment of the FDIC and the Federal Savings and Loan Insurance Corporation (FSLIC) as supplements, if not replacements.

Later evidence has clearly demonstrated that the Federal Reserve could have then and can now offset any reserve drain through open-market operations or the discount window.[5] If it had done so in 1929–1933, federal deposit insurance would not have been enacted. Proponents of eliminating it believe that the Federal Reserve has learned its lesson and can be counted on to operate rationally in the future. Any perceived supplementary need for deposit insurance would be fulfilled either by private insurance companies or by a system of self-insurance and mutual guarantees by the banks themselves.[6] Small depositors could also protect themselves against both default and price risks by purchasing short-term Treasury securities or money market funds, which provide transactions services similar to bank deposits.

Finally, small unit banks no longer need to be protected. Indeed, the liberalization of state branching and holding company acquisition regulations has been more damaging to the preservation of unit banking (assuming that this is or ought still to be a goal) than the removal of deposit insurance would be and suggests that unit banking is no longer the policy concern it was in the 1930s.

Opponents of the elimination of federal deposit insurance argue that it is necessary for a number of reasons. Some are not confident that the Federal Reserve can be counted on with absolute certainty to prevent a decline in aggregate bank reserves. While the risk of theft and the necessity of transferring funds by check do not permit large depositors to convert their funds to currency, a large number of people with small deposits might find it feasible and desirable to hold currency rather than deposits or alternative safe securities or deposit-like investments. In the absence of offsetting actions by the Federal Reserve, the result might be a multiple contraction in the money supply with all the accompanying undesirable effects for the economy as a whole. Consequently, they prefer an automatic mechanism or rule, to which they liken the FDIC, to human discretion and fallibility.

Others believe that the private sector cannot protect itself against system runs and bank failures and that any attempt to do so would require a federal program of support for the insurance companies rather than the banks. Thus there would be only a rearrangement rather than an elimination of existing guarantees.

Some also argue that private insurance companies would not be given the legal authority to reorganize individual economically insolvent institutions in as timely a fashion as the federal agencies could, if they so wished, and thus private insurers would experience or expect large losses, which would require large insurance premiums.[7] Moreover, because private insurance companies—even those that have the blessing and moral support of the state, such as those in Ohio and Maryland—can become insolvent, depositors would not have absolute faith in the protection of their deposits and might run to currency at times of uncertainty.

Finally, even some of those who would prefer to have private deposit insurance substituted for federal insurance doubt that federal insurance could be repealed, de facto or de jure. They believe that even if federal deposit insurance were withdrawn, the failure of a bank that caused substantial losses to many depositors would be followed by a federal government bail-out. This expectation is supported by a large amount of experience. Examples include the payment to depositors in the Home State Savings Bank of Cincinnati even though the state of Ohio had no legal obligation to make such payments. Canada paid off all depositors in two regional banks that failed, even though deposit insurance covered them only to $60,000 Canadian. The Bank of England bailed out the depositors in Johnson Matthey, even though they were not obligated to do so. Hence, even if it were politically possible to remove de jure federal deposit insurance, it is very unlikely that depositors would not, in fact, be insured.

Because we do not believe that federal deposit insurance can be replaced entirely with private or no insurance, we agree with those who look for reform of the system rather than for its abolition.

Reform of Federal Deposit Insurance. Proposals for reform of federal deposit insurance focus on changes that reduce the moral hazard problems inherent in the current structure and are modeled on the structure developed by private insurance companies in their operations.

Co-insurance. Private insurers frequently try to reduce moral hazard problems through co-insurance, so that the insured and the insurer share in some proportion of the covered loss. The proportions differ and may include (1) a *deductible,* in which the insured pays 100 percent of the first X dollars of loss and the insurer alone or in some combination with the insured pays the remainder; (2) a *cap,* in which the insurer pays up to X dollars of the loss and the insured alone or in some combination with the insurer pays the remainder; and (3) *fixed proportional sharing,* in which the insured and insurer share in the total amount of the loss in a given proportion, such as 50–50, or 20–80.

Indeed, the FDIC program enacted in 1933 and scheduled to go into effect on July 1, 1934, to succeed the temporary program adopted on January 1, 1934, included such provisions. The plan provided for 100 percent insurance of the first $10,000, 75 percent of the next $40,000, and 50 percent of all deposit amounts above $50,000. This plan was never put into effect.[8]

Opponents of co-insurance reforms argue that such changes would not affect the system greatly. The current de jure structure is already co-insurance; the insurer pays 100 percent of the first $100,000, and the insured pays 100 percent of the remaining loss. The question then becomes, What is the appropriate cap? Moreover, regardless of the de jure structure, unless the deposit insurance agencies were willing to abide by the de jure limits, de facto insurance coverage would continue to be close to 100 percent.

Maximum coverage. The maximum coverage per account significantly affects the degree of aggregate market discipline applied by depositors. The lower the maximum, the higher the number of depositors and amount of dollars that are at risk, and the more depositors have incentives to monitor the activities of banks. Moreover, the lower the maximum amount of coverage, the more difficult and costly it is to divide large amounts into an equivalent dollar amount of smaller fully insured deposit packages.

When FDIC coverage was introduced on January 1, 1934, the maximum coverage per private account was only $2,500. It was increased to $5,000 six months later, $10,000 in 1950, $15,000 in 1966, $20,000 in 1969, $40,000 in 1975, and $100,000 in 1980. This fortyfold increase is considerably greater than the sevenfold increase in the general price level over the same period. Thus de jure protection has been given to increasingly larger "small" depositors but at the cost of greater risk taking by banks and potential losses to the insurance funds. In light of this greater-than-inflation-adjusted increase and the ready availability of safe deposit-like outlets for these depositors, a significant rollback of the coverage to $50,000 or even less should reduce the moral hazard problems significantly and make raising funds quickly considerably more difficult for risk-prone banks at little, if any, cost to small depositors or protection of the money supply. Even if the amount per account were not reduced, deposit insurance could be limited to a total of $100,000 per depositor in all insured banks combined.[9] Thus, if a bank failed, a depositor who wanted to be paid would have to file a sworn statement giving the amount of insured deposits at all banks at the time of the failure. Deposits in the failed bank would be covered only to the extent that the depositor's funds in other insured banks totaled less than $100,000. Similarly, a lifetime $100,000 maximum per depositor has been proposed.

Arguments against a significant reduction in insurance coverage focus on political infeasibility, inconvenience to small depositors, greater individual and social costs of depositors' credit evaluations of banks, and the expectation that legislators would act to bail out de jure uninsured depositors if the losses were sufficiently widespread or if sufficiently powerful depositors were affected.

Risk-sensitive insurance premiums. The reform most widely proposed for the longest time is to replace the premium structure of a flat percentage of total domestic deposits with premiums scaled to the risk of loss assumed by the bank. Risk-sensitive premiums are charged for almost all kinds of insurance offered by private insurers, such as life, accident, fire, and automobile insurance. Private companies attempt to match their premiums to the actuarially computed fair value of the potential loss. Because the probability of loss is related to the risk assumed by the insured, the greater the risk, the higher the premium. Risk-related premiums serve not only to protect the insurance company but also to affect the behavior of the insured. The higher the premium, the more costly the activity, and the less likely is the insured to engage in it. In this way the insurance company can control its risk exposure.

Because all insurance companies, private or public, have an incentive to minimize their losses, they all attempt to control the risks assumed by the insured and relate their premiums to risk, either explicitly or implicitly. The use of flat percentage premiums forces the federal insurance agencies to rely on implicit risk-related insurance premiums in the form of regulations, capital requirements, and enforcement penalties.[10] Regulations restrict permissible activities, permissible numbers of banks and banking offices, geographical location, and prices paid and offered.

As the experience of recent years clearly demonstrates, the regulations have been highly inefficient and costly to both the banks and society. In addition, the recent evidence suggests that the insurance agencies have not been very successful in controlling bank risks through regulation, particularly for failing banks. Enforcement penalties, which by definition are ex post, have also failed to halt risk taking at risk-prone banks.[11] Thus explicit risk-related premiums are preferred.

Establishing risk-related insurance premiums is not easy. A large body of recent literature has considered the problem without devising an operational way of determining the premiums.[12] Most proponents of risk-based premiums recognize that risk should be measured with respect to market prices rather than accounting numbers. Thus, at least for regulatory purposes, book-value accounting would be replaced with market- or current-value accounting for both on- and off-balance-sheet accounts. Just how market-value accounting is to be done is generally not specified.

Some opponents of risk-based deposit insurance emphasize the difficulties of applying such accounting in practice, in particular of evaluating nonmarketable assets and good will for purposes of determining the premiums. This argument appears to be based on a reluctance to accept market values in principle rather than on a careful benefit-cost analysis. It is ironic that some bankers attempt to estimate the market value of their customers' equity but are unwilling to have an insurance agency evaluate their own market value. If federal deposit insurance were to be replaced by private deposit insurance, it is highly unlikely that the private firms would be willing to underwrite the insurance if they were not able to employ risk-related premiums based on market-value accounting.

The pros and cons of market-value accounting are discussed later in this chapter, where we describe an operational procedure. Nevertheless, implementation of market-value accounting is not a sufficient reason for rejecting risk-based premiums. Indeed, some proponents of risk-related premiums prefer nonmarket measures, such as reported balance sheet data and bank examination ratings. They argue that these numbers are preferable to market-determined values because they are both easy to obtain and less subject to dispute. These numbers can be supplemented with readily available market information and with internal data obtained by bank examiners. Since all banks are already being examined, the system would not require the installation of new and potentially costly monitoring systems.

Opponents note, however, that explicit risk-related insurance premiums are not necessary because the insurance agency would suffer no losses if it could reorganize a bank before the market value of its net worth fell to zero. Knowledge about the riskiness with which a bank is operated would be required by the agency only to determine the extent to which the bank must be monitored. For this purpose much less precision in estimating risks would be needed than would be required for establishing insurance premiums. The premiums charged should be related to the costs of monitoring and the perceived costs of more timely failure resolution.

To the extent that monitoring costs are related to the risk exposure of banks, risk could, however, serve as a surrogate for monitoring costs and thus be a basis for setting premiums. Additional premium amounts would be required to cover losses that result from an optimal trade-off between the cost of monitoring and supervision and expected losses, insufficient and ineffective monitoring by the insurance agencies, the inherent inability of any agency to uncover all fraud, extreme bad luck, the inability of the agency to measure economic net worth accurately, and political pressure that prevents the agencies from reorganizing banks before their net worth becomes negative.

Some analysts oppose activity-specific risk-related deposit insurance premium plans because the risk imposed on the insurance agency is related to a bank's total portfolio and operations rather than to its individual assets, liabilities, and activities. Relating the insurance premium to individual assets or liabilities thus not only will not provide a valid measure of risk but might result in the taking of more rather than less risk. For example, real estate investments alone might be more risky than traditional bank loans and investments in that the cash flows from real estate holdings and their market values might be more variable and hence have a higher probability of being negative at some time. But the cash flows from real estate might be imperfectly or even negatively correlated with cash flows from bank loans. Hence the risk a bank offers to the insurance agency might be lower if it held both real estate and bank loans than if it held only the loans.[13] The optimal combination of assets and liabilities need not be stable and is not readily determined by a formula or a banking supervisor. Moreover, ex ante projections of cash flows and risk may be more difficult to obtain from ex post evidence in banking than elsewhere. Would loans to Mexico and Brazil have been considered as risky in 1978 as in 1985 or interest rate mismatches as risky in 1965 as in 1982?

Risk-related insurance premiums would also give banking regulators considerable power to direct banks toward and away from specific kinds of investments and activities. For example, in the past bank examiners have objected to banks' making loans to inner-city borrowers and mortgages to integrated housing projects on the grounds that these investments were too risky. Such a premium structure may be used as a means of credit allocation, particularly if there is no competition among the federal insurance agencies, so that the risk premiums assessed may differ from their market-determined values.[14]

Perhaps most important, opponents of risk-related premiums doubt that they would dissuade risk-prone bankers from taking risks that are excessive from the point of view of the insurance agency. The premiums would have to be sufficiently high that the net returns from excessively risky behavior were less than the returns from acceptable behavior. In the absence of effective monitoring and co-insurance (such as capital requirements), the required premiums would have to be so high that only a banker who expected to get very high gross returns from risk taking would be willing to pay. Thus the insurance agency would suffer from adverse selection. And if monitoring were efficient, there would be no need for risk-based premiums.[15]

Risk-related Capital Requirements. Regulators have always been concerned with bank capital. Even in earlier periods of more or less "free banking," minimum capital requirements existed for new bank charters, and examiners evaluated the amount and adequacy of the capital of existing banks. Minimum capital requirements for bank charters are explicitly included in the National Bank Act and in many state banking statutes. Capital provides a cushion to protect both depositors and the deposit insurance agencies from losses. The larger the amount of capital, the less likely are losses of a given magnitude to wipe out the bank's capital and impose losses on depositors and the insurance agencies. A firm that has 100 percent capital, such as a money market or other mutual fund, can never become insolvent by definition.

Although bank capital ratios appear always to have been below capital ratios in other industries, the magnitude of the difference has widened since federal deposit insurance was enacted. At the beginning of the twentieth century, bank capital-to-asset ratios were about 20 percent. In 1930 they averaged about 15 percent. But those ratios understate the protection to depositors, since shareholders of all national banks and of state-chartered banks in many states were subject to double liability up to the par value of their investments. After federal deposit insurance was introduced, capital ratios declined, and double liability was discontinued. Capital-to-asset ratios for all commercial banks now average about 7 percent. In contrast, they average about 20 percent for major life insurance and property insurance firms, 11 percent for diversified insurance firms, 45 percent for all manufacturing firms, 37 percent for mining firms, and 34 percent for firms in wholesale and retail trade.

Until the 1970s bank examiners formally evaluated the adequacy of a bank's capital in relation to the assigned risk values of the bank's asset portfolios and combination of deposits. Around 1970 this approach was abandoned as unnecessary because the rate of bank failures had declined so far that concern about capital almost disappeared. In this period bank capital ratios declined, and the regulatory agencies found they had little legal power to enforce capital standards. In the mid-1970s, when the number of bank failures, including failures of some larger banks, increased and bank profitability started to decline, concern about capital standards reappeared. But it was not until the International Lending Supervision Act of 1983 that bank regulators were given legal authority to enforce capital standards.

In 1987 U.S. bank regulators formalized and issued for public comment a proposal for uniform risk-based capital standards, which they developed jointly with their counterparts in the United Kingdom. In 1988 the United States, the United Kingdom, and ten other nations joined in a similar proposal issued by the Bank for International Settlements Committee on Banking Regulations and Supervisory Practices. Among other objectives the "measure . . . attempts to . . . temper disincentives inherent in the existing capital requirements to hold low risk, relatively liquid assets."[16] Thus the objective of the structure is the same as that of risk-based deposit insurance premiums. The proposal includes provision for off- as well as on-balance-sheet accounts and thus differs from current capital regulations, which consider only on-balance-sheet accounts. Proponents prefer it because it builds on a base of capital regulation that is already in place and does not involve the out-of-pocket costs that insurance premiums would.

Critics of the proposal object to it on several grounds.[17] It appears to involve only a reshuffling of the existing capital in the industry among the individual banks, which would have little effect on bank safety generally, since banks tend to be undercapitalized. The proposal's details are seriously flawed in several important respects. First, capital would be valued on a historical book basis rather than at economic market values. Consequently, there would be an imperfect measured relationship between risk and capital that would be manipulable by a risk-seeking banker.

Second, the risk weights to be used are based on unjustified, apparently subjectively determined, criteria (see table 3–1) rather than on market valuations of risk. For example, a ten-year fixed-interest U.S. government obligation is subject to considerably more interest rate risk than a five-year obligation or a variable-interest ten-year obligation; yet all would be subject to a 10 percent capital requirement. What reason is there to believe that a twenty-year Treasury security is one-half as risky as a two-year municipal general obligation bond (10 percent versus 20 percent) or one-fifth as risky as a two-year municipal revenue bond (10 percent versus 50 percent), regardless of the credit quality of the last two kinds of securities? Are residential

TABLE 3–1
SUMMARY OF U.S. REGULATORY AGENCIES' PROPOSED GUIDELINES
FOR RISK-BASED CAPITAL FOR ON-BALANCE-SHEET ASSETS
OF COMMERCIAL BANKS

Zero Percent Risk Weight
- Cash
- Balances at Federal Reserve
- U.S. government securities with remaining maturity of ninety-one days or less

10 Percent Risk Weight
- U.S. government securities with remaining maturity of greater than ninety-one days
- That portion of assets guaranteed or collateralized by current market value of securities issued by U.S. government

20 Percent Risk Weight
- Claims on domestic depository institutions
- Claims on foreign banks with original maturity of one year or less
- Cash items in the process of collection
- Claims on U.S. government–sponsored agencies or portion of assets guaranteed or collateralized by current market value of securities issued by U.S. government–sponsored agencies
- General obligation bonds issued by state and local governments or portion of claims guaranteed by such governments
- Claims on official multilending institutions of which U.S. government is a member

50 Percent Risk Weight
- Revenue bonds issued by state and local governments for own use
- Credit equivalent of interest rate and foreign exchange contracts that do not qualify for lower risk category

100 Percent Risk Weight
- Commercial and residential mortgages
- Claims on foreign banks with original maturity exceeding one year
- Nonlocal currency claims on foreign central banks
- Municipal industrial revenue and similar bonds
- Claims on foreign and domestic government-owned commercial enterprises
- All other claims not specifically included in lower risk category

SOURCE: Adapted from Comptroller of the Currency, News Release 88-14, March 1, 1988, app. A, pp. 13–17.

mortgages twice as risky (100 percent versus 50 percent) as long-term municipal revenue bonds? Is a loan to Poland or Brazil as risky as a loan to IBM or an easily monitored broker's loan? All are classified as

100 percent risk weights. Do equal amounts of funds invested in consumer loans and in commercial loans to an oil prospector or to the government of Peru present equal risks?

Third, the effect on risk of various combinations of assets and liabilities is ignored. In particular, there is considerable room and incentive, both among and within risk classes, for reshuffling to increase risk without increasing capital requirements.

Fourth, the risk of the bank is incorrectly measured. Interest rate risk cannot be gauged by referring only to individual asset or liability accounts. The actual interest rate risk exposure of a bank is determined by the accounts on the two sides of the balance sheet considered together. By focusing only on individual accounts, the proposal gives no recognition to the risk-reducing characteristics of portfolio diversification. Appropriate weights should measure the marginal contribution of each account to overall portfolio risk. (Note that each of these criticisms could apply equally well to similarly poorly designed schemes for risk-based deposit insurance premiums.)

Narrow "Fail-Safe" Bank. Another proposal is to construct supposedly "fail-safe" or narrow banks that can provide the basic banking product—transaction balances or money supply—that the government perceives as having important safety concerns and as justifying intense regulation. All other bank activities would be placed in another institution, the safety of which would concern the government no more or less than that of nonbanking firms. That institution could be independent or an affiliate of a diversified financial holding company that also owned the narrow bank. If successful, this proposal would greatly reduce government risk regulation and permit bank holding companies to engage in a broader range of financial and nonfinancial activities than are currently permitted or would be permitted to bank holding companies that chose not to house the transaction deposit business in a narrow bank affiliate. Although the plan was initially appealing, careful consideration has revealed serious flaws that have reduced its popularity considerably.

As initially proposed, the fail-safe bank would hold only securities that were riskless with respect to both default and interest rate changes. That is, its investments would be restricted essentially to short-term Treasury and federal agency securities. Federal deposit insurance would seem to be no longer necessary, but depositors might bear losses from fraud and operations mismanagement. Hence deposit insurance and monitoring might have to be retained.

Because the proposed investment restrictions are unlikely to permit the bank to earn sufficient revenues to cover operating costs, fees would probably have to be charged and interest paid only on the largest balances. Other institutions, then, including affiliates in the same holding company, would have an incentive to develop transaction balance substitutes that could be offered at lower fees or higher interest rates. A shift of funds to those institutions would reduce the relative importance of the narrow banks and increase the concern of the government for the safety of the institutions offering alternative transaction deposits. Thus little would have been gained at the cost of developing new institutional arrangements.

To combat such potential shifts from the narrow banks, proponents of the proposal have progressively broadened the narrow permissible investment opportunities to securities such as commercial paper and long-term Treasury securities, which would subject the banks to credit and interest rate risk. Because banks holding those assets would no longer be fail-safe, federal deposit insurance would be required. Once the narrow bank is allowed to hold securities that entail some risk, where is the line to be drawn? It was a simple step to expand the proposed investment powers of the narrow bank to include all assets that have a reasonable secondary market and that could be valued at current market prices.[18] Capital standards could be introduced that were commensurate with the risk assumed by the bank. As the proposed bank's powers continued to be expanded, it would resemble today's broad bank except that its assets and liabilities would be valued at market prices. Unless timely reorganization procedures were introduced simultaneously, today's problems would not be solved.

Reorganization before Economic Capital Becomes Negative. *The advantages of timely reorganization.* The major failing of all these reform proposals is their inability to resolve economic insolvencies effectively and costlessly. Recent evidence has made it clear that the largest losses to the federal insurance agencies and uninsured depositors have occurred from delayed resolution of failures.[19] The delay has permitted insolvent banks to continue to generate losses and place larger bets using the funds of others and has signaled to other solvent institutions that the penalty for insolvency may not be as great as it is generally perceived to be. This has encouraged banks to take greater risks. Regardless of how insurance premiums, capital standards, or investment powers are structured, unless failures are resolved in a timely fashion, the banking structure will continue to impose unnecessary risks and costs on the economy. If depository institutions were reorganized (recapitalized, sold, merged, or, as a last resort, liquidated) before the market value of their capital (net worth and subordinated liabilities) declined to zero, the incentives for excessive risk taking by their managers and owners would be greatly reduced, and any subsidies involved in the provision of the insurance would be eliminated.[20]

Timely reorganization offers four significant bonuses that may increase its attractiveness and thereby promote its adoption. One, except in cases of major fraud, effective elimination of losses from bank failures would reduce the need for insurance premiums other than to pay the FDIC's and FSLIC's operational expenses, including improved and more frequent monitoring of insured institutions and the development of useful market-value accounting systems. Quicker action by the insurance agency would also reduce the opportunity for uninsured creditors to transform their unsecured claims into secured claims and thus increase the loss to the insurance agency.

Two, since uninsured depositors would probably experience smaller losses, if any, they would be less likely to run on their banks when they received unfavorable news. This would reduce potential disruption of other institutions and the economy as a whole.

Three, if the authorities would reorganize a bank expeditiously before it became economically insolvent, there would be little justification for regulating or legislating the activities in which banks may or may not engage on the basis of risk. Restrictions would have to be based on other considerations, such as concern about excess concentration, assumptions about conflicts of interest, the undesirability of bringing an activity under the surveillance of bank regulators, or demands to restrict competition among and by banks. In the absence of such considerations, the amount of risk a bank wished to assume and which products and services it would provide could be decided by its own managers, who might be expected to be sensitive to the penalties of failure. Decisions to take portfolio risk, then, would tend to be made in the belief that the bank's capital was sufficient rather than in the belief that the insurance agency would cover the losses. Greater risk would be undertaken only with greater capital.

Four, all failed banks and their depositors would be treated equally. Uninsured depositors at large failed banks are now reimbursed in full regardless of a bank's condition, while those at smaller failed banks are frequently assessed losses related to the market value of their banks' assets. This policy has important inequitable competitive implications that are severely disadvantageous to smaller banks. Timely reorganization, by effectively eliminating depositors' losses, would permit more equal treatment of banks regardless of their size or location or the nature of their business. No bank would be "too large to fail," and the authorities would not need to be reluctant to reorganize a bank for fear of touching off runs at other banks.

As a result of the lower premium costs to banks, the greater freedom from regulation of banks' risks and activities, and greater equity in treating banks in similar financial predicaments, timely reorganization should be much less costly than the narrow bank proposal. It should also be more efficient and attract less opposition than either risk-sensitive insurance premiums or sharp reductions in insurance coverage and be more effective than risk-sensitive capital requirements.

Timely reorganization also offers considerable advantages to public policy makers. Policy makers must have the resolve to apply the available remedies at the de jure specified point without exception. But at least part of the reason for the current banking situation is a reluctance of policy makers to apply the available remedies on a timely basis. Thus de facto deposit insurance coverage frequently exceeds de jure coverage, and bank capital is permitted to decline below established minimum standards and even become negative for many troubled institutions under "forbearance" programs.[21] This occurs because the utility function of public policy makers includes many variables other than economic efficiency, such as compassion and susceptibility to pressure from directly affected parties. To remain in office, whether elected or appointed, policy makers must balance various objectives. These include losses on what the public has come to assume are "riskless" securities, such as bank deposits, whether or not they are federally insured. They are also concerned with the loss of jobs and disruptions in the payments system and credit availability in their geographical or political districts. Losses to bank owners might be a concern as well.

Under current procedures bank failures might result in losses to depositors and are widely perceived to result in the loss of jobs, the interruption of financial relations, and the threat of severe spillover to other banks and sectors. The first consequence occurs only if failure resolution and reorganization are delayed, and the three other consequences are highly unlikely. Failed banks are generally sold or merged, with the preservation of most of the banks' services and the employees' positions, or, if liquidated, are replaced by other banks if the demand for banking services is warranted.

How, then, could policy makers be motivated to accept and stick with efficient remedies? The theory of public choice suggests that their self-interest must be appealed to.[22] A policy structure that minimizes the possibility of loss to depositors, loss of jobs by constituents, disruption of the payments mechanism, and domino effects on other banks and businesses at a low cost to taxpayers and other banks should have strong political appeal to policy makers. If timely failure resolution were adopted, the primary losers would be shareholders, holders of subordinated debentures, and senior management. Policy makers have generally been willing to permit losses to these parties while protecting others who have perceived themselves to be less at risk. By restricting losses primarily to not-to-be-protected parties, timely bank failure resolution and reorganization would result in less pressure on the authorities than imposed either by the current structure or by most other proposed reforms.

The same advantages should accrue to bank regulators. Moreover, because under the proposal any losses to depositors and the community would be small, bank failures should no longer be a major blot on their records. Thus the regulators should be more willing both to recognize bank failures officially and to avoid implementing inefficient and costly means of preventing them.

The application of timely reorganization rules requires the measurement of capital and the receipt by the authorities of timely and sufficiently accurate information on an institution's capital. These reorganization rules should also be able to deal effectively with fraud and gross mismanagement, which are the primary causes of bank failures and large losses to the deposit insurance agencies.

The measurement of economic capital—market-value accounting. The application of timely reorganization rules would be enhanced by the measurement of capital in terms of economic market values rather than generally accepted or other accounting principles. Banks and most other firms keep their books and render their financial reports on the basis of generally accepted accounting principles (GAAP) or regulatory accounting principles (RAP), when these are prescribed, for example, by the Federal Home Loan Bank Board. Unfortunately, these accounting methods do not provide measurements of the economic market values that are clearly needed for the deposit insurance agency to determine when reorganization is required.[23] Indeed, traditional accounting was not designed to measure nor, on the whole, does it measure economic market values. Moreover, there is strong reluctance among some parties in banking and elsewhere to accept the "vagaries" of the marketplace as the true valuation of a security or a firm rather than the evaluation of the owners or other experts.

The importance of measuring capital by market value rather than book value has been clearly demonstrated in a recent Federal Reserve study. It reported that while in book-value terms the capital-to-asset ratio of the twenty-five largest bank holding companies in the United States declined from 8 percent in 1960 to 4 percent in the late 1970s before increasing again to near 5 percent in 1986, in market-value terms the ratio fell twice as sharply, from 12 percent to 3 percent in 1980, before reversing.[24] The market value of capital consistently exceeded book value from the early 1950s to the mid-1970s, but it consistently fell short of book value from the mid-1970s through 1986. In the first period, when bank failures were low, the reported data understated the shareholders' investment in the banks. In the second period, when bank failures began to increase, the reported data overstated the shareholders' investment. This pattern is consistent with the hypothesized inverse relationship between the amount of bank capital and a bank's incentive for risk taking. It appears that the regulators may have badly underestimated the true decline in bank capital in the 1960s and early 1970s and devoted insufficient resources to controlling risk.

The use of market-value accounting should improve the regulators' ability to evaluate the condition of the banks and respond more quickly to changes in market forces. In addition, if market-value accounting were adopted for banks' public reports, as well as for internal and regulatory reporting, regulators would be subjected to a form of market discipline, since their actions could be more effectively evaluated by others.

Fortunately, market-value accounting is much more feasible and inexpensive for financial institutions to adopt than for most other enterprises. Unlike nonfinancial firms, banks have relatively small investments in assets for which current market values are difficult to measure. Such assets include land, buildings, equipment, patents and trademarks, advertising, and work-in-process inventory. These assets are often not traded in the market, in part because they are specific to an enterprise. Hence their economic values are difficult to obtain. Nevertheless, the following review of the principal items on a bank's balance sheet illustrates how satisfactory economic market values can be obtained for banks.

Liabilities—on balance sheet. Bank payables and deposit liabilities (checking, time, and savings accounts and short-term certificates of deposit) tend to be stated at or very near current market values. The sole important exception is fixed-interest long-term obligations when market interest rates have changed. If these obligations are traded in the market, their current values can be determined directly. Even if they are not negotiable or traded, their present values can be determined. Because they would be riskless under the present proposal, their economic value can be measured simply by discounting them by the present market rate of interest on currently issued similar obligations. On the whole, the liabilities side of the recorded balance sheet presents few problems for market-value accounting.

Liabilities—off balance sheet. Banks often issue letters of credit and guarantee loans, thereby assuming liabilities that are contingent on the nonperformance of a customer. In effect, the bank has an asset—the right to collect from a customer that does not meet its obligations to a third party as promised. It also has a liability—a promise to pay the third party if the bank's customer does not perform as promised. With respect to a capital requirement, there should be no difference between such a contingent liability and asset and an on-balance-sheet liability and asset. For on-balance-sheet accounts, the total nominal amount is recorded, regardless of the extent of the risk exposure, if any, of the institution. Hence the liability or asset would be stated at the amount for which the bank was contingently liable or a beneficiary, thereby increasing both assets and liabilities. (If the obligation could come due only at a future date, its present value would be the amount stated.) Thus on- and off-balance-sheet activities would be treated consistently.

Assets—marketable securities. The market values of a bank's marketable and fixed-interest securities (including equities) can easily be obtained. Where fixed-interest securities are not regularly traded, their present values can be determined as described above for fixed-interest liabilities. (The procedure for estimating the market value of nontraded securities is discussed below.)

Assets—loans. The realizable value of loans is now estimated by banks. The estimates are attested to by certified public accountants for all insured savings and loan associations and for banks subject to the securities acts of 1933 and 1934. The estimates are close, but not equal, to market values, since future expected payments are not discounted to obtain present values. Nor are changes in market rates of interest on asset values accounted for. But such changes are not a serious problem when assets carry interest rates that vary with market rates or are short term so that they are repriced before interest rates change radically (as is the case for most commercial loans and many mortgages). Where institutions hold duration-balanced portfolios or have hedged interest rate risk, the problem is obviated. The remaining situations can be estimated by reference to market prices on such obligations as mortgage-backed bonds.

Furthermore, an increasing proportion of bank loans are being packaged into marketable obligations and securitized. These include mortgages, automobile and other consumer loans, and even poor-quality foreign loans. The value of these and similar loans can be determined by reference to the market rates at which securitized loans trade. In addition, the economic value of loans to large businesses can be approximated by reference to traded securities, such as commercial paper and bonds, that are issued by those businesses. Alternatively, the debt of large companies and countries might be valued centrally by a government agency or private rating bureau, such as Moody's or Standard and Poor's, and the values used by all banks.

Assets—nonmarketed or nontraded investments. Banks also hold nonmarketable investments, such as real estate, and nontraded securities, such as bonds and stock in nonlisted companies. These assets would have to be valued by independent appraisers. Obviously the valuations of such assets would be subject to error, and the probity of the appraisers, who would be hired by the banks, should be questioned. Later in the paper we offer a means by which this problem can be handled satisfactorily, at least from the point of view of the deposit insurance agency.

Assets—investments in subsidiaries. A bank may choose to conduct some of its activities in a wholly or partially owned subsidiary. In this event the bank has an asset for which a market value must be obtained. Since the shares of the subsidiary are unlikely to be traded, market-value accounting would have to be applied to the balance sheet of the subsidiary unless the bank and the deposit insurance agency were willing to accept the subsidiary's book value or a partial revaluation at market as a lower bound. Since the bank is likely to be directly or indirectly liable for the debts of the subsidiary and it is very difficult to monitor or prevent transfers of resources between a bank and its subsidiary, subsidiary liabilities and assets would have to be consolidated with the bank's balance sheet numbers.

Assets—operating equipment, buildings, and the like. The market values of many long-term fixed assets may be determined from their replacement cost, where replacement is defined by the services derived from the assets. These values might be obtained from the new or used asset market or from engineering appraisals, although these numbers are often expensive to determine and are inexact, particularly when the assets are rarely traded. Because GAAP require accountants to record assets at the lower of cost or market, this evaluation is not required unless a bank wants to demonstrate that its capital is greater than it appears to be. In that event it would have to present appraisals that were accepted by the deposit insurance agency.

Assets—good will and other unrecorded intangible assets. Good will and most other intangibles (such as personnel training, computer software, organization costs, patents, and the value of core deposits) are not recorded on a bank's or other firm's financial statements unless they are purchased in the market directly or as a consequence of a merger or acquisition. Banks can rarely sell such assets separately from the entire organization. (An exception might be computer software packages.) Nor are similar assets often traded in the market. While the market value of a bank's stock less the economic value of its assets less liabilities can provide an estimate of the market value of intangibles, this method is not satisfactory for two reasons. First, most banks' shares are not actively traded. Second, the market value of a bank's equity reflects the value of underpriced deposit insurance—hence the stock market value cannot be used directly as a means of determining the bank's capital for purposes of eliminating or reducing the risk to the deposit insurance agency. If it could be so used, the stock market value would be a sufficient measure. Hence the measured economic value of bank equity will tend to be understated by the value of unrecorded intangibles. From the point of view of the deposit insurance agency, this is no worse than the present system of accounting.

Where good will was recorded as a result of an acquisition or other market transaction, it should not be included as an asset, for two reasons. First, stating the bank's other assets at market values would account for the portion of good will that reflects the difference between the market and book values of the acquired organization. Second, relatively less capital would be required of banks that grew by acquisition and merger than of banks that grew internally if the former could include good will in their assets and therefore in their capital. There is no justification for this bias.

An important concern about market-value accounting is the extent to which the banking authorities can rely on the figures. This problem could be almost entirely eliminated if the following proposal were adopted. All insured banks should have their accounts audited annually by certified public accountants (CPAs) acceptable to the authorities.[25] The CPAs would be charged with attesting to the numbers reported as being no greater than current market values on the statement date. If they were unsure of the amounts, they could attest to lower numbers or could refuse to give an unqualified opinion. Thus a bank would have to put up additional capital if it wanted to invest in assets of undeterminable value, since its stated capital would be reduced to an amount that its independent public accountants certified as being no greater than market value. Because their reputations and fortunes are at stake, CPAs have a strong incentive to be conservative. (As partnerships CPAs can be sued jointly and severally to the extent of their personal wealth.)[26] Furthermore, the cost of determining attestable market values, that is, the appraisers' and CPAs' fees, would be borne by the banks that made the investments. This is a form of risk-related insurance premium.

Supervisory monitoring of capital and banking operations. For purposes of frequent and timely monitoring, detailed quarterly statements using market values for marketable assets and book values for others would be required. These would be supplemented by more aggregated monthly reports for all banks and weekly reports for larger banks. The data reported should be confirmed by periodic and surprise audits or attestations by CPAs.

Computerization would permit rapid scanning of such reports for supervisory purposes. In the interim, changes in the values of traded assets could be obtained from market prices. Except for fraud, losses in nontraded assets generally occur only slowly and should be detectable from the periodic reports. In addition, information on potential risk-taking institutions could be obtained weekly from advertised deposit rates compiled by private services.

An insufficiently well diversified or excessively concentrated portfolio can result in sudden depletion of a bank's capital if prices change greatly. For example, stock prices fell by nearly 25 percent on October 19, 1987. Similarly, the sharp decline in energy and farm prices in the early 1980s resulted in sharp declines in the value of loans to borrowers in these sectors. Such portfolios could be observed, however, from the reports rendered by banks and from confirming field examinations. These situations should be closely monitored. The cease-and-desist powers now held by the supervisory authorities can be used to control situations that pose an immediate danger to the insurance fund.

Fraud and gross mismanagement. The largest losses absorbed by the deposit insurance funds have been a result of fraud and gross mismanagement.[27] Fraud is a particularly important problem because it is difficult to detect until it is too late. Furthermore, the incentives for bank managers and owners to engage in fraud or gross mismanagement are unlikely to be sufficiently affected by higher insurance premiums, higher capital requirements, or even prompt reorganization rules, either because they expect to steal or otherwise gain much more than they might lose or because their incompetence is so great that they cannot understand the nature of the risks they are taking.

Two methods can be employed to deal with fraud and gross mismanagement. One is to continue the present practice of field examinations and supervision. These procedures could be improved, however, by being directed specifically to the prompt detection of fraud and gross mismanagement rather than to a general review of a bank's operations. For this purpose more frequent reporting, the use of available public information, such as deposit rates paid and loan rates charged, and the use of statistical early warning models to direct field examinations to banks that are likely to be serious problems could reduce the cost and improve the effectiveness of supervision.

The second method is for the authorities to rely more on the annual reports attested to by CPAs. CPAs have incentives to attest correctly to accounting numbers. Futhermore, they could be explicitly charged with an obligation to report any serious weaknesses in a bank's internal controls and other problems directly to the banking authorities, as has been proposed in the United Kingdom.[28] The two methods can, of course, be used in combination.

Conclusion. Several of the proposals for change have features that are desirable and practical, both operationally and politically, but some do not. Abolition of federal deposit insurance is not desirable because we do not believe that it is politically feasible. Nor do we believe that the federal government could refrain from bailing out depositors if more than a few banks should fail. Thus we would have de facto deposit insurance without the benefits of federal responsibility for controlling moral hazard. Moreover, we need to protect small depositors, not so much for their own sake as for the sake of maintaining the aggregate money supply by not encouraging a run to currency. Private insurance is unlikely to instill the confidence to eliminate this possibility altogether.

We also find that the narrow bank proposal is not feasible in a form that is effective or desirable in a form that is feasible. To be economically feasible, the narrow bank would have to hold assets that would make it similar to ordinary banks, with similar problems. To the extent that its asset holdings were limited to "safe" assets, it would suffer the economic cost of inefficiency. Furthermore, alternative reforms can offer the benefits of the narrow bank without its limitations.

Reduction of deposit insurance coverage to some lower amount per account would be desirable to increase monitoring by depositors. But it is not clear whether this change is politically feasible. Furthermore, to the extent that demand depositors are not insured, they have both the incentive and the ability to run. While bankers' fear of runs is desirable for providing them with incentives to be responsive to depositors' concerns, the banking authorities now appear unwilling to allow a very large bank to suffer a run. Risk-related deposit insurance premiums would be desirable, but they do not appear to be operationally feasible quickly enough to deal with the problem at hand. Risk-related capital requirements suffer from similar operational difficulties. Indeed, the scheme proposed by the banking authorities has some important and obvious limitations. In addition, it does not increase the economic capital base of the industry and is therefore not likely to reduce overall risk greatly.

We believe that the last alternative discussed—reorganization before economic capital becomes negative—is both desirable and operational. Although it might lead at least initially to the formal recognition of more bank failures, it would not reduce the provision of banking services to customers. The scheme offers the advantages of reducing the costs of deposit insurance to the cost of monitoring plus losses that are not worth preventing or that cannot be prevented. It would virtually eliminate the moral hazard from deposit insurance because bank managers and owners would be playing only with their own funds and bearing almost all the costs of failure. There would be little reason to regulate banks' operations for purposes of risk control.

Other advantages include equal treatment of banks of all sizes. Fraud and gross mismanagement could be reduced more efficiently by greater reliance on CPAs, monitoring by the authorities of more frequently received information, and prompt reorganization of insolvent banks. Because the scheme is enhanced by the use of economic market-value accounting, we have suggested how this procedure could be satisfactorily implemented. Finally, the suggested reform appears to be feasible because it offers several advantages to public policy makers that the alternative proposals do not.

A Proposal for Timely Intervention and Reorganization of Banks

The Optimal Capital Requirement. Because losses can occur quickly or remain undetected until after a bank becomes insolvent, the optimal amount of required capital is clearly greater than zero, and the authorities must intervene and reorganize a bank before it becomes economically insolvent. Because the larger the amount of capital required, the greater the incentive of bank managers and owners not to take excessive risks, the capital requirement should be relatively high.[29]

A capital requirement for banks is a requirement of a specified amount of subordinated debt and equity that, if measured by economic market values, is available to absorb asset losses before they must be met from the deposit insurance funds and uninsured depositors. "Subordinated" refers to the claims of the federal deposit insurance agencies on the assets of the bank. Uninsured deposits have an equal pro rata claim with the federal deposit insurance agency in case of legal insolvency. The capital requirement is usually expressed as a percentage of assets.

An optimal capital requirement should protect the deposit insurance agencies adequately but not impose excessive costs on the insured institutions. As the following analysis demonstrates, a higher requirement is preferable to a lower one. A higher capital ratio would reduce not only the probability and magnitude of losses to the insurance agencies but also their need to monitor banks as frequently and carefully as otherwise. Because the benefits of higher capital ratios to the insurance agency are obvious, we focus our examination on the costs and benefits of such ratios to banks.

As is well known from finance theory, the relative amounts of debt and equity are unimportant and have no economic consequences for the firm, with the following exceptions: (1) since interest payments on debt are a tax-deductible expense and dividend payments and retained earnings on equity are not, debt is preferred to equity, *ceteris paribus;* (2) since bankruptcy costs are more likely to be incurred and monitoring costs are higher when equity is relatively lower, equity is preferred to debt, *ceteris paribus;* and (3) for banks, insured debt is preferred to uninsured debt or equity when deposit insurance premiums are less than the benefit of the insurance to the institution, as is now the situation for many banks. This last advantage is precisely what we want to remove, and the second factor argues for more capital. Therefore, from the viewpoint of public policy, we need be concerned only with the first factor.

The tax advantage of debt could be obtained to the same extent by banks as by other firms if they were permitted to count as capital subordinated (unquestionably de facto as well as de jure uninsured) debentures that are junior to the claims of the insurance agencies, cannot be redeemed before the authorities can force a reorganization of the bank, and cannot block that reorganization. To prevent flights of these funds from occurring, the debentures must not be redeemable by the bank before the authorities can intervene to reorganize the institution.

The banking authorities have severely limited the extent to which banks may meet their capital requirements with subordinated debt. This limitation appears based on a belief that debt holders do not exercise as great a monitoring function over bank operations as equity holders and that, unless perpetual, debt capital may be withdrawn at maturity and thus is not as permanent as equity capital. But neither of these conclusions is valid. If the debt holders' claims are subordinate to those of other creditors (including the deposit insurance agencies) and if they cannot remove their funds when a bank experiences difficulties, they bear the cost of a bank's failure. Hence, as is the situation for bondholders generally, they have an incentive to monitor the risks taken by the equity holders and will insist on a return that compensates them for the risk they are assuming. Equity holders, then, have a concomitant incentive to reduce risk to the bondholders (and hence a cost to the equity holders) by altering the bank's operations or by increasing their capital (equity) investments. Moreover, debt need not be permanent to achieve this result. It must only be restricted so that it cannot be redeemed before the authorities can act. Thus it will bear potential losses and protect the insurance fund. From the viewpoint of the banking authorities, it should not matter how much of a bank's capital is in the form of equity or subordinated debt. It all serves the same function.

Indeed, subordinated debt capital offers several banking and supervisory advantages over equity capital. First, smaller banks may be loath to sell equities either because the price they could receive for minority stock in a closely held bank would be low or because the owners do not want to dilute their control. They might find the cost of selling relatively small amounts of stock high. Subordinated debentures, on the other hand, could be offered to investors in their communities—in effect, they would simply be selling explicitly uninsured time deposits to people who are likely to have knowledge about how the bank is operated and the ability to monitor its operations.

Second, if the debentures were traded, the yields determined by the secondary market could give the authorities an early warning about the risks undertaken by the bank. Even if the debentures were not actively traded on secondary markets, any difficulties a bank might have in marketing its new debentures on the primary market as the old ones became due would provide timely information to the supervising authorities. Such signals could best be obtained if banks were required to hold debentures with evenly spaced maturity dates. For example, a rule might be that no less than 5 percent or more than 10 percent of the debentures might mature in any one year.[30] Indeed, theoretical analysis suggests that, unlike long-term debt, short-term debt that forces a bank to the marketplace frequently to refinance and thereby pass the market test reduces the shareholders' ability to undertake risky investments benefiting themselves at the expense of the bank's bondholders.[31]

An additional concern about imposing capital requirements on banks is that the amount of capital required to be invested might be more than the banking system could use efficiently. This result could occur if banks were required to invest in a limited subset of assets, such as U.S. Treasury obligations, or in physical assets that were limited to producing goods subject to limited demand. This concern would be largely eliminated, however, by the removal of limitations on the assets in which banks might invest. At the extreme, however, a very high capital requirement might result in a misallocation of resources if bankers had a comparative disadvantage in using the funds they were required to obtain from investors.

Thus, with the asset constraint removed, the capital requirement should and could err on the side of too much rather than too little capital. Too high a requirement serves largely to reduce to zero the benefit to risk preferrers of underpriced deposit insurance; too low a requirement increases the moral hazard cost of deposit insurance.

The Measurement of Capital. Economic capital is the difference between total assets measured at no more than market values and total liabilities measured at no less than market values less subordinated debentures serving as capital.[32] The market values reported are to be attested to by a certified public accountant whom the deposit insurance agency does not disapprove. Contingent (off-balance-sheet) assets and liabilities must be added to total liabilities and total assets. The documents to which these liabilities refer must state explicitly that they are not covered by federal deposit insurance. The liabilities would not be counted as capital, however, because they could be withdrawn quickly.

A bank's investments in subsidiaries would be measured at their net asset values when the bank had no liability for the subsidiaries' debts and this fact was verified by the bank's CPA. If the bank were directly or contingently liable for the subsidiaries' debts, subsidiary assets and liabilities must be consolidated with those of the parent bank. The consequence of the rules with respect to contingent and subsidiary liabilities would be to increase required capital, since the requirement is stated as a percentage of total assets. The allowance (reserve) for loan losses is sometimes considered a part of capital on the assumption that it is overstated. Before the federal tax code was changed in 1986, banks could deduct from their taxable income an amount for loan losses larger than the losses they anticipated. This overstated their allowance for loan losses. Consequently, the overstatement could appropriately be considered capital. GAAP and current tax regulations, however, require that the allowance reflect the expected amount of loans that will not be collected. Hence the loan loss allowance should be considered the amount necessary to reduce "loans receivable" net realizable (present) value, and the allowance should be recorded as an asset contra account.

Banks That Are Subsidiaries of Holding Companies or Other Corporations or That Are Not Diversely Owned. There is no reason for the authorities to examine or to be concerned with the management decisions of the owners of banks, including holding companies, as long as the banks have adequate capital and there are controls against self-dealing and fraud. Self-dealing can occur when any bank offers less-than-market prices to its owners or their interests. Fraud against the federal deposit agency can occur when a bank that is in danger of becoming insolvent transfers funds to avoid the claims of creditors, including the deposit insurance agency. These possibilities constitute potentially important dangers to deposit insurance. Consequently, banks owned by controlling interests must be monitored more closely than those that are diversely owned, and transfers (loans, dividends, and payments for services) between the bank and the owners' other interests may be restricted.

Holding company ownership of banks presents less risk to the insurance funds than ownership by controlling individuals. Individual owners generally have greater incentives than corporate executives to divert bank funds to their own projects and to other uses because the owners benefit personally and directly. In addition, it is difficult for the banking supervisors to identify the interests of the owners, in contrast to readily available information about holding company subsidiaries.

Holding companies are subject to Sections 23A and 23B (added by the Banking Act of 1987) of the Federal Reserve Act, which limit the extent to which funds can be upstreamed from the bank to its holding company or other affiliates.[33] Similar restrictions should be applied to all transfers between a bank with insured deposits and enterprises in which the bank's managers and owners have a substantial interest, say, more than 10 percent of the stock.

With monitoring and restrictions on funds transfers in place, the capital requirement would be applied only against the commercial bank, including its subsidiaries, not the holding company or other owner. The holding company's capital requirement would be determined by market forces since it would not be the recipient of federal deposit insurance, nor would the safety and soundness of its nonbanking activities be of concern to the government.

The managers or owners of the bank might believe it more efficient to include all affiliates within the same organization that offers federally insured deposits. This would pose no special problem; the capital and supervision requirement would then apply to the entire organization. The measurement of assets, liabilities, and capital would be the same as described above.

If the bank and its parent had the same or similar names, the deposit insurance authorities might fear confusion by the public about which was the insured bank. This possibility could be reduced or avoided by requiring the parent to state clearly in writing on each security that it was not a federally insured bank and that its obligations were not covered by deposit insurance. Nor would the bank be permitted to guarantee the obligations of its affiliates.

In addition, timely insolvency intervention would remove any subsidy associated with the provision of deposit insurance. It would remove any ability of insured banks to shift the benefits of underpriced insurance to other product lines or to its affiliates to gain competitive advantages, assuming that such cross-subsidization occurred.

Reorganization Rules. The capital required should be sufficiently high to absorb almost all probable reduction in net asset values. As already discussed, banks do not bear costs from an overhigh requirement (excluding the loss of the deposit insurance subsidy) unless the requirement is so high as to prevent them from holding an optimal portfolio of assets. For commercial banks, we suggest the reorganization rules shown in table 3–2. The precise values of the capital ratios at each level, or tranche, are illustrative.

The values shown in the table are likely to be on the low side and may need to be revised upward in light of the considerably higher bank capital ratios that existed before the introduction of the FDIC in 1934, the considerably higher capital ratios that exist in almost all other industries, and the relatively low cost of capital to banks when subordinated debt is included. The primary criterion is that the capital ratios be high enough to minimize the possibility of loss to the insurance agency for any reason other than massive fraud but not so high as to discourage capital investment in banking. Thus the tranche ratios need to be related to the historical and projected variability in the value of the institutions' portfolios and to the ability of the regulators to monitor performance accurately and in a timely way.

Application of the proposed capital requirements would, of course, require a transition period. The current values were selected in part because they conform to the present capital standards of the commercial bank regulatory agencies, although they are stated in market-value rather than book-value terms. Although market value of

TABLE 3–2
Illustrative Reorganization Rules for Federally Insured Commercial Banks
(capital-to-asset ratio, all accounts valued at market)

10 Percent or Greater	6–9.9 Percent	3–5.9 Percent	Under 3 Percent
No problem—minimum regulation and supervision; subject only to general reporting and examination requirements; all intra–holding company transfers must be fully disclosed and fraud provisions strictly enforced	Potential problem—more intensive regulatory supervision and monitoring; regulatory agency discretion to reduce or suspend dividend payments and upstream or downstream payments to parent or affiliates	Problem—intensive regulatory supervision and monitoring; mandatory suspension of dividend payments, interest payments on and redemption of maturing subordinated debt, and outflow of funds to parent or affiliate	Reorganization—mandatory recapitalization, sale, merger, or liquidation by federal insurance agency in orderly fashion; may require formation of "bridge" institution or "trusteeship" by insurance agency for no more than two years; non-deposit funds distributed up to ninety days before to be recovered

equity may exceed book value, as a general principle the tranche ranges in book-value terms should be increased, for example by three percentage points. Banks could be provided with a choice about which set of accounting rules they wish to use. The lower market-value ratios might provide banks with an incentive to move quickly to such an accounting system.

It is important that dividends, interest payments on subordinated debentures, and fund outflows to a parent or affiliates could be suspended by the insurance agency if the market value of a bank's capital declined below, say, 10 percent of its assets on a market-value basis and must be suspended if the capital ratio fell below, say, 6 percent. Indeed, with some exceptions, banks are now permitted to pay dividends only if their capital ratios exceed the regulators' minimum standards and are limited to their current and previous years' earnings. These limitations are necessary because, unlike other firms, banks that offer federally insured deposits can obtain funds regardless of their solvency. The suspension of interest payments would give the debenture holders the right to force a reorganization of the bank. Thus, in all except the extreme circumstance, when the market value of a bank's capital declined substantially and precipitously, the deposit insurance agencies would not have to reorganize a bank—the reorganization would already have been undertaken by the subordinated debenture holders.

Current owners of banks could always maintain their ownership by providing sufficient capital. But when, on the basis of quarterly or more frequent monitoring, the market-value capital-to-asset ratio of a bank declined to, say, 3 percent or below (tranche 4 in our illustrative reorganization rules), ownership of the bank would be automatically transferred to the FDIC or the FSLIC. This would occur if the owners, who might reasonably be assumed to know more about the true condition of the bank than the regulators, believed that the bank was not worth the investment of the necessary additional capital. The FDIC or the FSLIC would then attempt to sell or merge the bank. Only as a last resort would it liquidate the bank. This process would not constitute expropriation of shareowners' property, even though their investment in the bank might not be fully exhausted. Current shareholders would be given first choice to recapitalize their institutions. If they failed to do so, the proceeds to the FDIC or the FSLIC from sale or liquidation net of prior claims would be passed through to the previous owners. They would thus receive the fair market value of their investment in the bank.

To provide sufficient time for the FDIC to accomplish its task efficiently, it might be necessary for the agency to operate the very largest banks temporarily in a bridge or trustee relationship for a few weeks, but no longer than for, say, two years. Authority for the insurance agencies to establish such arrangements was included in the Banking Act of 1987. In addition, as in the bankruptcy law for nonbank firms, nondeposit funds distributed by the bank up to ninety days before the date the reorganization tranche is breached are to be recovered by the FDIC or the FSLIC.

The proposed reorganization scheme is different from that commonly applied to nonbank firms and may appear to be more stringent. A nonbank firm is generally declared involuntarily bankrupt and remedies for creditors are started when it fails to pay a major scheduled payment on time and in full. Economic insolvency per se is not generally considered sufficient grounds for creditors to file for involuntary bankruptcy and request remedies, although it may be for voluntary bankruptcy.[34] Thus nonbank firms may be permitted some time to continue to operate after they become economically insolvent.

More timely failure resolution is required for banks, however, because federal deposit insurance makes it possible for them to continue operations even after they become economically insolvent. Unlike creditors of noninsured firms, depositors would continue to advance funds to banks as long as they could look to an insurance agency believed immune to failure. In the absence of federal deposit insurance, insured depositors would assess the economic solvency of a bank much as creditors assess the solvency of any firm and would remove their funds in runs if they believed the bank to be insolvent. This would quickly cause the bank to miss a payment and result in involuntary bankruptcy. Thus timely failure resolution based on market valuations is simply a replication by the deposit insurance agency of the situation that faces insolvent noninsured firms.

Evidence that more timely closure reduces losses to deposit insurance agencies and to other creditors is quite strong. Until recently the FDIC closed banks reasonably quickly after it became evident that the market value of their assets had declined below that of their liabilities and, except in cases of major fraud, experienced minor if any losses.[35] In the absence of major fraud, the market values of banks are unlikely to decline abruptly. Rather, they will generally deteriorate slowly and can be monitored reasonably accurately. Through 1931 estimated losses at failed and swiftly closed national banks were ten cents on the dollar, compared with ninety cents on the dollar at nonfinancial firms.[36] In comparison, a recent study of defaulted corporate bonds estimated that the immediate loss in market bond values from 1974 through 1984 was about 60 percent.[37] This is consistent with the loss ratios estimated for the 1900–1943 period.[38]

Losses to creditors primarily reflect the delay in initiating involuntary bankruptcy procedures for nonfinancial firms. Losses to bank creditors may reasonably be expected to be reduced even further under the proposed capital scheme. As a bank's capital declined through the successively lower strata of capital tranches, progressively stricter monitoring and supervision by the regulatory agency would be automatically triggered. Such a scenario should result in "soft landings" since bad news surprises would be less likely.

Moreover, most other kinds of financial firms and almost all kinds of nonfinancial firms are forced by the marketplace to hold higher ratios of capital to assets. Thus speedier failure resolution would be necessary if banks were permitted to hold lower capital. Banks could, of course, hold higher capital voluntarily to reduce the probability of their being reorganized when losses are larger than expected.

As more timely failure intervention when a bank's capital is still positive would greatly reduce potential losses to depositors, the need for federal deposit insurance would be diminished. The need would not be removed altogether, however. Depositors could still suffer losses from a sufficiently large fraud or other large declines in market asset values between monitoring periods. As a result, small depositors might still lose faith in all banks and shift their funds to currency, and this action might not be appropriately offset by the Federal Reserve. Federal deposit insurance coverage per account, however, could be reduced or limited to a maximum per deposit at all insured banks. Additional insurance could be supplied privately if demanded by depositors.

Summary of the Advantages of the Proposal. The proposed capital rules offer the following advantages:

• The system would be voluntary in exchange for federal deposit insurance. Because the capital rules would apply only to the incorporated entity providing federally insured deposits, institutions would be free to determine their own structure. They could offer non-federally insured deposits and avoid these requirements. In that event they would have to disclose clearly that the deposits were not covered by federal insurance.

• Losses to the federal deposit insurance agencies (and, therefore, to banks and ultimately to the taxpayer) would be minimized, since banks would be recapitalized before their economic capital became negative. Deposit insurance premiums could thus be considerably reduced.

• Regulation of bank activities would be minimized. Because there would be only minor losses, if any, to the deposit insurance agency, there would be no justification for bank regulation based on solvency considerations by authorities other than the federal deposit insurance agencies. Those agencies would be responsible primarily for monitoring the reporting and capital requirements and for supervising banks that did not meet the requirements or that appeared to be operated recklessly or fraudulently. Indeed, they could better target their energies and limited resources to those banks that posed the greatest threat to the insurance funds. Since banks satisfying the capital requirements would be primarily risking loss of their own funds, there would be no need to restrict their activities. At least with respect to risk, they might engage in any financial or nonfinancial activity that could be monitored reasonably accurately and to whose market values recognized CPA firms were willing to attest.

• Banks could be run more efficiently and could serve the public better, because operating and product decisions would be made by bank managers rather than by regulators. Furthermore, banks could take advantage of synergies to produce products and services at lower cost to consumers if they were permitted to conduct activities within the bank, rather than only through affiliates, subject to the proposed capital requirements and reorganization rules.

- Banks of all sizes and characteristics in the same financial condition would be treated equally. No bank would be "too large or too special to fail."
- Banks would be subject to increased market discipline not only from subordinated debt holders but also from shareholders, who would not get second or more chances to recoup their losses when the economic value of their investments disappeared; from managers, who might lose their positions faster when their banks became insolvent; and possibly from uninsured depositors, who might experience losses if actual net worth at the time of reorganization was much below perceived net worth. The market discipline would resemble that in a noninsured environment. Because, except under conditions of fraud or highly unusual movements in marketplaces, net worth would not become zero or negative, the tendency to make high-risk end runs or take last-chance plunges would be significantly reduced. The frequency of both bank runs and bank failures should be greatly reduced.
- The proposal is not as radical as it might first appear. Mandatory reorganization when capital requirements were violated existed under the National Bank Act and was enforced until the Great Depression and the introduction of federal deposit insurance.[39] More recently support for a similar proposal was voiced by Acting Comptroller of the Currency H. Joe Selby in testimony before Congress in 1985. He suggested that

> a policy could be adopted that any time a bank's capital falls below 3 percent (the level at which the FDIC generally considers termination of deposit insurance), the primary supervisor would be given the authority to require the owners to seek a merger partner or to liquidate the bank. Alternatively, a conservator could be appointed by the primary authority to exercise the full range of powers possessed by bank management, including the sale of the bank.[40]

Moreover, such a rule was recently adopted by the Federal Home Loan Bank Board, which has incorporated a "prenuptial" clause in some of its agreements with buyers of failed savings and loan associations, by which the FSLIC will automatically reclaim the institution if the new owners permit its capital to fall below a specified small but positive percentage of its liabilities. A representative of a large commercial bank has noted that

> to the extent that there is a problem with deposit insurance, that problem arises from the failure resolution policies pursued by the FDIC and other bank regulators. Reforming the deposit insurance system therefore requires reforming bank failure resolution policies so that banks are closed as they become insolvent; nothing more and nothing less will solve the problem.[41]

Thus our suggested reorganization rule provides an operational means of extending the pragmatic response of some banking authorities to the problems they have been facing. Further research is required to establish the precise values of the optimal capital tranches, the schedule for implementing market-value reporting and monitoring (which have recently been proposed by the Financial Accounting Standards Board), and the particulars of the reorganization procedures and the transition process.

Notes

1. A review and evaluation of the reasons for regulating banks appears in George J. Benston and George G. Kaufman, "The Costs of Bank Failure: Overview, History, and Evaluation," in George G. Kaufman and Roger C. Kormendi, eds., *Deregulating Financial Services: Public Policy in Flux* (Cambridge, Mass.: Ballinger Publishing Co., 1986), pp. 49–77; and George J. Benston and George G. Kaufman, "Risk and Solvency Regulation of Depository Institutions: Past Policies and Current Options," Monograph Series on Finance and Economics, Salomon Center, New York University Graduate School of Business Administration, 1988.

2. Bert Ely, "Yes—Private Sector Depositor Protection Is a Viable Alternative to Federal Deposit Insurance," in *Proceedings of a Conference on Bank Structure and Competition*, Federal Reserve Bank of Chicago, 1985, pp. 338–53; and Catherine England, "A Proposal for Introducing Private Deposit Insurance," ibid., pp. 316–37.

3. Catherine England, "Agency Problems and the Banking Firm: A Theory of Unregulated Banking," in Catherine England and Thomas F. Huertas, eds., *The Financial Services Revolution: Policy Directions for the Future* (Boston: Kluwer Academic, 1988); Kevin Dowd, "Automatic Stabilizing Mechanisms under Free Banking," Working Paper, University of Sheffield, England, January 1987; and Kevin Dowd, "Some Lessons from the Recent Canadian Failures," in George G. Kaufman, ed., *Research in Financial Services: Private and Public Policy* (Greenwich, Conn.: JAI Press, forthcoming).

4. Richard H. Timberlake, Jr., "The Central Banking Role of Clearing House Associations," *Journal of Money, Credit, and Banking* (February 1984), pp.

1–15; and Gary Gorton, "Clearing Houses and the Origin of Central Banking in the United States," *Journal of Economic History* (June 1985), pp. 277–83.

5. See the chapters by Anna J. Schwartz and by Marvin Goodfriend and Robert G. King in this volume.

6. England, "Agency Problems"; and Ely, "Yes—Private Sector Depositor Protection."

7. Paul M. Horvitz, "The Case against Risk-related Deposit Insurance Premiums," *Housing Finance Review* (July 1983), pp. 253–63; Paul M. Horvitz, "A Reconsideration of the Role of Bank Examination," *Journal of Money, Credit, and Banking* (November 1980, pt. 1), pp. 654–59; Gerald O. Bierwag and George G. Kaufman, "A Proposal for Federal Deposit Insurance with Risk-sensitive Premiums," Staff Memoranda, 83-3, Federal Reserve Bank of Chicago (March 1983); and Federal Home Loan Bank Board, *Agenda for Reform* (Washington, D.C., March 1983).

8. Federal Deposit Insurance Corporation, *The First Fifty Years* (Washington, D.C., 1984).

9. George J. Benston, "Deposit Insurance and Bank Failures," *Federal Reserve Bank of Atlanta Economic Review* (March 1983), pp. 4–17.

10. George J. Benston, Robert A. Eisenbeis, Paul M. Horvitz, Edward J. Kane, and George G. Kaufman, *Perspectives on Safe and Sound Banking* (Cambridge, Mass.: Ballinger Publishing Co., 1986), chap. 9.

11. Ibid., chap. 10.

12. Edward J. Kane, *The Gathering Crisis in Deposit Insurance* (Cambridge, Mass.: MIT Press, 1985); Federal Deposit Insurance Corporation, *Deposit Insurance in a Changing Environment* (Washington, D.C., 1983); Federal Home Loan Bank Board, *Agenda for Reform*; Bierwag and Kaufman, "Proposal for Federal Deposit Insurance"; and Benston et al., *Perspectives on Safe and Sound Banking*.

13. See George J. Benston, *An Analysis of the Causes of Savings and Loan Failures*, Monograph Series in Finance and Economics, Salomon Center, New York University Graduate School of Business Administration, 1985—4/5 (1985), for a study of savings and loan associations that finds higher total returns and slightly lower variance of total returns associated with higher levels of direct investments.

14. Benston et al., *Perspectives on Safe and Sound Banking*.

15. Horvitz, "Case against Risk-related Deposit Insurance."

16. Comptroller of the Currency, "Minimum Capital Ratios: Risk-based Capital Ratios," News Release, March 25, 1986; Comptroller of the Currency, News Release, March 1, 1988; Federal Deposit Insurance Corporation, "Statement of Policy on Principles of Capital Forbearance for Banks with Concentrations in Agriculture and Oil and Gas" (March 27, 1986); and Board of Governors of the Federal Reserve System, "Capital Maintenance: Supplemental Adjusted Capital Guidelines," Press Release (January 24, 1986).

17. Shadow Financial Regulatory Committee, "Statement on Regulatory Proposals for Risk-related Capital Standards" (May 18, 1987).

18. Thomas F. Huertas and Rachel Strauber, "An Analysis of Alternative Proposals for Deposit Insurance Reform," subcommittee of the Committee on

Government Operations, *Structure and Regulation of Financial Firms and Holding Companies (Part 3): Hearings,* U.S. House of Representatives, 99th Congress, 2d session, December 17 and 18, 1986, pp. 390–463.

19. Horvitz, "Case against Risk-related Deposit Insurance"; Benston et al., *Perspectives on Safe and Sound Banking,* chap. 4; U.S. General Accounting Office, *Thrift Industry: Forbearance for Troubled Institutions, 1982–1986* (Washington, D.C., May 1987); U.S. General Accounting Office, *Thrift Industry: The Management Consignment Program* (Washington, D.C., September 1987); and James R. Barth, Dan Brumbaugh, Jr., and Daniel Sauerhaft, "Failure Costs of Government-regulated Financial Firms: The Case of Thrift Institutions," Research Working Paper no. 123, Federal Home Loan Bank Board, Washington, D.C., October 1986.

20. George G. Kaufman, "The Truth about Bank Runs," in England and Huertas, *The Financial Services Revolution;* George G. Kaufman, "Bank Runs: Cause, Benefits, and Costs," *Cato Journal* (January 1988); Barbara A. Bennett, "Bank Regulation and Deposit Insurance: Controlling the FDIC's Losses," *Federal Reserve Bank of San Francisco Economic Review* (Spring 1984), pp. 16–30; David H. Pyle, "Deregulation and Deposit Insurance Reform," *Federal Reserve Bank of San Francisco Economic Review* (Spring 1984), pp. 5–15; and Bierwag and Kaufman, "Proposal for Federal Deposit Insurance."

21. Federal Deposit Insurance Corporation, "Statement of Policy on Principles"; and Comptroller of the Currency, "Capital Forbearance Policies," News Release, March 28, 1986.

22. See the chapter by Edward J. Kane in this volume.

23. Benston et al., *Perspectives on Safe and Sound Banking,* chap. 8; and George J. Benston, "Accounting Numbers and Economic Values," *Antitrust Bulletin* (Spring 1982), pp. 161–215.

24. Michael C. Keeley and Frederick T. Furlong, "A Deposit Insurance Puzzle," *Weekly Letter* (Federal Reserve Bank of San Francisco), July 3, 1987.

25. If a CPA is unacceptable to the banking authorities on the basis of insufficient capital, reputation, or so on, they can request that a firm acceptable to them be engaged in addition. This procedure has recently been proposed to the British Parliament by the government.

26. For a complete analysis of the incentives faced by public accountants, see George J. Benston, "The Market for Public Accounting Services: Demand, Supply, and Regulation," *Journal of Accounting and Public Policy* (Spring 1985), pp. 33–79.

27. Benston et al., *Perspectives on Safe and Sound Banking,* chap. 10.

28. Germany and Switzerland rely on independent public accountants for bank examinations and reports.

29. Some bankers and economists have argued that higher capital requirements may actually encourage institutions to increase their risk taking to offset the higher cost of capital. See Michael Koehn and Anthony M. Santomero, "Regulation of Bank Capital and Portfolio Risk," *Journal of Finance* (December 1980), pp. 1235–44. As we demonstrate later, however, if subordinated debt were permitted to serve as capital to supplement equity, there need not be an increase in the cost of capital and thus no need to attempt to

increase returns. Moreover, these studies implicitly assume that all funds are de facto if not de jure insured and do not scale a bank's borrowing costs or deposit insurance premiums to its risk exposure. If they did, the results would differ. See Frederick T. Furlong and Michael C. Keeley, "Bank Capital Regulation and Asset Risk," *Federal Reserve Bank of San Francisco Economic Review* (Spring 1987), pp. 20–40. See also Stuart C. Myers, "Determinants of Corporate Borrowing," *Journal of Financial Economics* (November 1977), pp. 147–75; and Michael C. Jensen and William H. Meckling, "Theory of the Firm: Managerial Behavior, Agency Costs, and Ownership Structure," *Journal of Financial Economics* (October 1976), pp. 305–60.

30. Benston et al., *Perspectives on Safe and Sound Banking*, chap. 7.

31. Myers, "Determinants of Corporate Borrowing"; and George G. Pennachi, "Market Discipline, Information Disclosure, and Uninsured Deposits," in *Proceedings of a Conference on Bank Structure and Competition*, 1988.

32. If collateral were pledged to such debt, the lesser of the pledged assets or the debt would be excluded from the computation of the bank's capital ratio.

33. Benston et al., *Perspectives on Safe and Sound Banking*; Thomas F. Huertas, "Redesigning Regulation: The Future of Finance in the United States," in *Restructuring the Financial System*, a symposium sponsored by the Federal Reserve Bank of Kansas City, August 1987; Chase, Laub & Co., *Insulating Banks from Risks Run by Nonbank Affiliates* (Washington, D.C., October 1987); and Robert L. Clarke, "Statement" before the Subcommittee on Financial Institutions Supervision, Regulation, and Insurance of the Committee on Banking, Finance, and Urban Affairs, U.S. House of Representatives, October 28, 1987. See also the chapter by Anthony Saunders in this volume.

34. Benjamin Weintraub and Alan N. Resnick, *Bankruptcy Law Manual* (Boston: Warren, Gorham, and Lamont, 1986).

35. Benston et al., *Perspectives on Safe and Sound Banking*; Horvitz, "Case against Risk-related Deposit Insurance."

36. Joseph S. Lawrence, "What Is the Average Recovery of Depositors?" *American Bankers Association Journal* (February 1931), pp. 655–56, 722–23.

37. Edward I. Altman and Scott A. Nammacher, *Investing in Junk Bonds* (New York: John Wiley, 1987).

38. W. Braddock Hickman, *Bond Quality and Investor Experience* (Princeton, N.J.: Princeton University Press, 1958).

39. Cyril B. Upham and Edward Lamke, *Closed and Distressed Banks* (Washington, D.C.: Brookings Institution, 1934).

40. H. Joe Selby, "Statement" before the Committee on Banking, Housing, and Urban Affairs, U.S. Senate, July 23, 1985, p. 23.

41. Huertas and Strauber, "Analysis of Alternative Proposals," p. 406.

Commentary

Paul M. Horvitz

Economists, bankers, and public officials have been concerned about safety and soundness in banking for many years. Literally hundreds of policy proposals have been advanced, and many have been tried. Some have argued for a completely free, unregulated banking system, while others would opt for a system in which banks would be so tightly regulated that they could do nothing more than handle deposits. There have been many shifts in expert opinion. At one time 100 percent reserve banking was viewed as a crank scheme, and now, in a somewhat different reincarnation, it is getting serious consideration. Academic economists have long advocated risk-related premiums for the federal deposit insurance systems, but as bankers and the agencies began to take these proposals seriously, some economists began to have second thoughts about the wisdom of such a system. More basically, there has been a change in perception about deposit insurance itself. As Anna Schwartz notes, "For a long time after the 1930s, deposit insurance was hailed as the outstanding reform of the New Deal." In fact, it was so hailed by Friedman and Schwartz. But now Schwartz, at least, has changed her mind.

Over the past few years a great deal of substantive work has been done on these issues. Clearly, the state of the economy has stimulated this effort—there would be less interest in bank solvency if we were experiencing ten bank failures a year (as we did in the 1960s and 1970s) rather than 150–200. It is not remarkable, then, that the volume of research in this area has increased. The research includes sophisticated empirical work and careful historical research. Historical studies are of crucial importance because much of existing law and regulation was based on interpretation (often misinterpretation) of our history. What is remarkable about the study of banking stability is that we seem to be coming closer to a consensus on the major elements of appropriate public policy.

I may be overreacting to my agreement with the analysis of George Benston and George Kaufman. I have worked with both of them over the years, and it may be presumptuous to say that because we agree, that makes a national consensus. But the basis for my conclusion goes beyond that, as Anna Schwartz's policy proposals are in perfect agreement as well.

One potential area of disagreement is the question of how serious the problem is. Benston and Kaufman say "the system is not working!" I disagree with that, or at least I disagree with the exclamation point. It is my view that the system is working pretty well and that relatively modest changes in the system can solve the problem. Our disagreement on this is more apparent than real, however. The view that the system is not working is more relevant to the savings and loan industry than to the banking industry. Benston and Kaufman note that they refer to depository institutions collectively as banks. Perhaps because of this wording convenience, they fail to point out the significant differences in the regulation and insurance of banks and savings and loan associations. In particular, the operations of the FDIC have been very much closer to the policies they advocate than those of the FSLIC. Those policies represent only modest changes from accepted FDIC policies. In fact, it is reasonable to conclude that the reason the FDIC is in so much better shape than the FSLIC is precisely because of its closer adherence to those policies. This consideration provides significant empirical support for the policies they advocate. Benston and Kaufman seem to be aware of this, as they state at the very end of the paper that their proposal "is not as radical as it might first appear."

It might be noted that even some of those who advocate revolutionary change in financial structure do not necessarily believe that the system is not working. In particular, such advocates of narrow banking as Robert Litan and John Kareken have other considerations in mind. Litan's policy proposal is an attempt to resolve debate on the issue of appropriate activities for commercial banks rather than a response to a breakdown of the system. Kareken's exploration of narrow banking is an attempt to demonstrate that if perfectly safe transaction balances are an appropriate social objective, that objective can be achieved without the need for an elaborate regulatory framework.

The consensus on policy proposals consists of several elements, some of which were unrecognized just a few years ago. There is consensus that deposit insurance is not an essential prerequisite to a stable financial system. As Anna Schwartz notes, "Deposit insurance . . . is not essential to prevent panics, given a reliable lender of last resort." Other work of Anna Schwartz and George Kaufman shows that, while bank runs have always been with us, "flights to currency" have been rare. There is little evidence of runs' bringing down a bank that was solvent to begin with. Such an event can be prevented by a

COMMENTARY

central bank willing to make collateralized loans so that the bank is not forced to liquidate assets at "fire sale" prices.

It is also clear that deposit insurance can adversely affect bank safety and soundness through its effects on incentives and on market discipline.

Further, systems can be designed to provide a perfectly safe depository and payments system without either deposit insurance or a central bank, as shown by the proposals of Robert Litan, John Kareken, John Mingo, and others, as well as by the work of Merrill and Lynch.

Nevertheless, there is consensus that deposit insurance is a useful part of the financial structure (Benston and Kaufman point out the shortcomings of the narrow-bank proposals, and bank runs have costs even if they are not flights to currency that affect the money supply). We are left with general agreement that deposit insurance should be reformed or redesigned rather than eliminated. And Benston and Kaufman have correctly pointed out what elements of deposit insurance need change.

There is agreement that optimal closure policy is a crucial element in the supervisory system. This rather obvious point does not appear in the older deposit insurance literature. It is a key element of difference between the FDIC and the FSLIC that largely explains the difference in their current financial condition. The FDIC has generally attempted to close banks when they become insolvent and has generally been successful in doing so. It has failed to do so when fraud has been involved and the insolvency has thus not been detected promptly. Thus the FDIC has suffered large losses (relative to the size of the bank) in such cases as U.S. National Bank of San Diego, Penn Square Bank in Oklahoma, and the Butcher banks in Tennessee, but smaller losses in Continental Illinois, First Pennsylvania, and Franklin National Bank. Even under its current "forbearance" policy, the FDIC claims that insolvent banks will not be allowed to continue to operate.

The FSLIC, in contrast, has generally allowed insolvent institutions to continue in business when the insolvency has resulted from interest rate movements rather than credit losses. (In recent years, of course, the FSLIC has allowed many insolvent institutions to continue simply because it lacked the funds to close them. But everyone recognizes that, and no argument of principle is involved—only lack of principal.) Once an institution is insolvent, normal risk aversion disappears, and everyone becomes a risk seeker. On average, losses will become larger. Benston and Kaufman present a workable plan for closure policy that protects the insurance fund without unfairly confiscating the property of bank owners.

Optimum closure policy depends on a good monitoring system. A good monitoring system *requires* information on market values of assets and liabilities. This is a stronger statement than Benston and Kaufman make. Again, I believe that we have reached a consensus among economists that market-value accounting is essential, though that consensus does not extend to bankers or accountants. Much of the argument turns on workability and the difficulty of change rather than the substance of the issue. The Benston-Kaufman paper makes the best case I have seen for the feasibility of market-value accounting. Here also, the better condition of the FDIC as compared with the FSLIC rests in part on a monitoring system that is closer to being market-value-based than that of the FSLIC. The FDIC does calculate the market value of the securities portfolio, and long-term loans are a smaller fraction of total assets of banks than of savings and loans.

No one claims that monitoring can be perfect, and hence closure policy cannot be perfect. Some buffer or cushion must therefore exist to protect the deposit insurance system. A meaningful capital requirement is essential. No one knows precisely how high the capital requirement should be, but there is agreement among economists (though certainly not among bankers) that capital requirements can be significantly increased with little social or even private cost. Once again, bank capital requirements have been higher than those imposed on savings and loans.

There is room for argument about how high capital should be, or its precise form. Should subordinated debt count or be encouraged? Is double liability a workable option? I have argued in favor of much greater use of subordinated debt as a desirable form of capital. In addition to the considerations advanced by Benston and Kaufman, the option of subordinated debt is useful to those bankers who do not accept the conclusions of Modigliani and Miller about the irrelevance of capital structure. Further, even for those who want banks capitalized with clean, pure equity only, the opportunity to use debt at the holding company level allows the injection of equity at the bank level. Finally, Anna Schwartz includes a good analysis of double liability. Although I am somewhat skeptical of the feasibility of this approach, she presents a convincing case.

Because of my earlier work with both Benston and Kaufman, it may not be surprising that I agree with their policy conclusions. But note how closely Schwartz's conclusions fit: the only constraints she would put on bank operations are "capital requirements, marking assets to market, provision of information to authorities, and double liability for shareholders." My view that these are relatively modest changes from existing policies is supported by her comment, "Except

COMMENTARY

for double liability, these are precisely the restraints on the activities of discount houses in the United Kingdom." She later adds the recommendation that "insolvent intermediaries should be closed promptly when net worth on a market-value accounting basis declines to zero."

It is important to recognize what this consensus does *not* require. Risk-related deposit insurance premiums, though helpful in promoting equity and risk-avoiding incentives, are not essential to bank soundness. The same is true of risk-related capital requirements. (A good case can be made for capital requirements that would be based on the expected volatility of earnings from the overall portfolio, but that is quite different from the current proposals by the regulatory agencies.) Limitations on allowable activities cannot be justified by this approach, except insofar as they make monitoring conditions more difficult. We may choose to restrict bank activities because of concern about concentration of economic power, or out of a desire to protect insurance agents and realtors from competition, but not out of a need to protect the stability of the financial system. This also suggests that the intense current debate about the *location* of new bank powers—in the bank, a subsidiary of the bank, or a holding company affiliate—is irrelevant. Moreover, establishing the proper level of deposit insurance coverage—increasing it to 100 percent, or decreasing it to $20,000 or $40,000—is not important since depositors will not be exposed to serious risk of loss in any case.

We are still a long way from implementing the necessary reforms, and there are important vested interests that will make that task difficult. It is remarkable, however, how far we have come in recent years in identifying the route to be taken. This research project and others, including those undertaken by the insurance agencies, deserve a great deal of credit, as do the individual authors of these papers.

John H. Kareken

In commenting on the paper by Anna Schwartz, I concentrate on the policy she advocates for ensuring a smoothly functioning payments process. I argue that the policy will not produce the result she wants and, more particularly, that counting on the Federal Reserve for near-term price stability is naive. In commenting on the paper by George Benston and George Kaufman, I concentrate on the policy that they advocate and argue that it too is impractical and, hence, not to be implemented. What Benston and Kaufman urge, "timely reorganization" of depository institutions doomed to insolvency, is more a dream than anything else.

Financial Stability and the Federal Safety Net

For Schwartz, there is financial stability when, though there may be the occasional failure, most depository institutions are safe and sound. And for her, price stability is necessary for financial stability. Evidently, it matters not whether depository institutions are regulated as they were before, say, 1980, or as she would like to see them regulated (almost not at all) or whether the deposits (liabilities) of depository institutions are insured by the federal government. Schwartz says that without price stability, even tightly regulated depository institutions, the deposits of which are insured by the federal government, will not long remain safe and sound. In support of that assertion, she notes that failures of U.S. depository institutions began to mount only after the relative price stability of the early postwar period had become a past glory.

It seems clear, though, that what Schwartz should have made necessary for financial stability is not price stability but rather a predictable average of prices. The fate of a loan depends on whether the lender or borrower is surprised by what happens to relative prices, not on how those prices change. I suspect that Schwartz will agree, for she tells us that an "unexpected price change can invalidate the assumption underlying [a] loan."

It also seems clear that financial stability requires more than the average of prices changing as expected. All prices have to change as expected. Schwartz acknowledges that, if not in so many words. Why did so many agricultural area banks fail in the years immediately after World War I? Her explanation, doubtless right, is a surprise change in relative prices. And why in recent years have so many Texas banks and S&Ls gotten into deep trouble? Her explanation, also doubtless right, is a surprise change in relative prices.

According to Schwartz, history tells us that if the average of prices does not change, then, with probability near to unity, relative prices will not change. To an extent, I disagree. Is the observed sudden and sharp change in relative prices to be explained by a change in the average of prices? But in either event, whether the right answer to that question is yes or no, it is apparent why Schwartz makes a stable average of prices necessary for financial stability. She does, however, concede that a change in relative prices may be caused by a real shock or surprise and so, having no use for federal deposit insurance, cannot casually dismiss a local financial panic's being produced by such a shock. With some small probability the local panic becomes a national panic.

Schwartz would have the Federal Reserve keep the monetary base within realistically narrow bounds around some growth path. I cannot myself see our monetary authority even trying to do that. To be sure, the Federal Reserve's enabling legislation might be rewritten. But the historical record provides no assurance that a steadily increasing monetary base yields price stability, except perhaps on average over a long period of time. The historical record does not assure us of the virtual constancy of prices, nor therefore that a steadily increasing monetary base would make fear of a financial panic unnecessary.

Schwartz believes that a willing expert lender of last resort is sufficient for a panic-free history. To quote her: "a lender of last resort can nip a panic in the bud." But, then, we have to wonder why, if she believes that, Schwartz did not offer us an exceedingly brief paper. If a willing expert lender of last resort can always keep panicky depositors from doing harm, what more needs to be said? A lender-of-last-resort operation can cause a blip in the monetary base, and for that reason Schwartz may want the U.S. lender of last resort, the Federal Reserve, to be relied on as little as possible.

A keen student of the monetary history of the United States, Schwartz knows very well that the Federal Reserve has on occasion failed the U.S. public. That is why she would have the Federal Reserve's enabling legislation rewritten to make its officialdom made accountable. Whether of the Federal Reserve or in what the rewriting of a statute can accomplish, Schwartz is more trusting than I. It is almost beyond belief that our monetary authority, if confronted at some time in the future by an incipient panic, will once again sit on its collective hands. But it is not necessary to trust to the willingness and expertise of the Federal Reserve; and partly because it has been, if anything, too quick to the rescue, I would rather not.

Regulating Bank Safety and Performance

I turn now to the policy for financial stability advocated by Benston and Kaufman but first formulated by Paul Horvitz.

For Benston and Kaufman the reorganization of a depository institution doomed to fail or that has in effect already failed is "timely" if it happens before that institution's net worth, valued at market, has decreased to zero. But timely reorganization, arguably a confiscation of private property, could then be illegal. Benston and Kaufman seem not to have considered the possibility and so may have a little more work to do.

I suspect that advocating timely reorganization amounts to pushing for yet another way of enriching lawyers. For one thing, establishing generally acceptable market values for loans will not be quite as easy as Benston and Kaufman seem to think. More generally, it is easy at far remove to say that a depository institution has in effect already failed. Convincing real world shareholders of that may in some instances be rather difficult. There have already been quite a few legal challenges to FDIC and FHLBB closings, and it would thus seem a reasonable guess that if our deposit-insuring agencies go to timely reorganizations, then our courts will be even busier than they are at present.

Amazingly, Benston and Kaufman claim that even with what in theory is poorly priced deposit insurance, it will be possible, once the FDIC and the FHLBB have committed to timely reorganizations, to do away with virtually all restrictions on the portfolio choices of depository institutions. That amounts to claiming that however many depository institutions have failed, the insuring agencies can cope, that they have been blessed with miracle resources. Imagine that with all portfolio restrictions removed, virtually all depository institutions become extremely risky. Then when a surprise comes along a great many of the institutions become marked for failure. The question is the obvious one: Can all of the failed institutions be reorganized so quickly that there is no expenditure of insurance funds? On yet another count, then, the policy advocated by Benston and Kaufman appears less workable than they would have us believe.

By implication, Benston and Kaufman deny that with a risk-independent deposit insurance premium the typical depository institution will want to be as risky as possible. Imagine having the government remove all restrictions on the portfolio choices of depository institutions. If the FDIC and the FHLBB were doing timely reorganizations, then, according to Benston and Kaufman, the typical depository institution would maintain whatever capital is appropriate to its risk. Allegedly, the explanation is senior management's fear of failure. But why that fear? There is only one plausible way of accounting for it: for senior management, failure means the loss of comfortable jobs. So Benston and Kaufman get a depository institution that is well behaved even though its deposit insurance premium is risk-independent by assuming that senior management disregards the interest of shareholders. To put the point another way, they get a workable timely reorganization policy by making a most doubtful assumption.

Then, too, Benston and Kaufman rely on a proposition that in general has been shown to be false: that the probability that a depository institution will fail decreases as its equity capital increases. The probability of failure decreases only if the depository institution is subject to particular restrictions, to restrictions that in effect make the distribution of portfolio payoffs dependent on equity capital.

To repeat the essential point, the policy advocated by Benston and Kaufman is not nearly as practical or workable as they make out. It could be made to appear more practical, for they make no mention of on-line monitoring. As far as I know, no agency with responsibility for regulating depository institutions is at present capable of such monitoring, even though it has been technologically possible for some time. That all of the regulatory agencies are still in the dark ages does not, however, justify their remaining there. And on-line monitoring is fundamental. Having a look at each depository institution only every three or six months will not deliver zero losses for the FDIC and the FHLBB, and the alternative to on-line monitoring is a ridiculously large examination force.

Benston and Kaufman would have been justified in simply assuming on-line monitoring. Our regulatory agencies, state as well as federal, can be made to shape up. But as I said earlier, reorganizing a depository institution with net worth that valued at market is positive may be illegal. And we have to count on a far from insignificant number of timely reorganizations being challenged in court. Finally, it is not right, despite what Benston and Kaufman say, that once the responsible agencies have begun making timely reorganizations, there will be no risk in removing all restrictions on the portfolio choice of depository institutions.

Stanley C. Silverberg

George Benston and George Kaufman are concerned about the role that deposit insurance apparently has played in encouraging excessive risk taking by some banks and thrifts. That problem has been exacerbated by regulators who have allowed insolvent institutions to remain open, thereby increasing losses of the deposit insurance funds while putting cost and other pressures on solvent institutions and the system generally. Benston and Kaufman explore the various remedies to lessen the problem: eliminating deposit insurance altogether; reducing de facto insurance coverage; implementing variable rate insurance premiums; imposing risk-based capital requirements; and restricting what banks can do. They conclude that the last has a perverse effect and that the other options are likely neither to work nor to be politically feasible.

Their solution is to recommend earlier reorganization of banks, before they reach insolvency. They would impose high capital requirements (they suggest 10 percent), impose sanctions on banks that fall below some level (6 percent), and move to reorganize banks if they get below 3 percent. This combination of policies, they maintain, would limit losses of the deposit insurance funds, eliminate excessive risk taking by insured institutions, and reduce supervisory tampering with market behavior.

Subordinated debt would be permitted to satisfy a greater share of bank capital requirements. Capital would be determined by valuing bank assets and liabilities at market values in those areas where market values can be readily determined. There would be no restrictions on the leverage of bank holding companies, except those imposed by the market.

In the real world, some of what Benston and Kaufman advocate would be more difficult to implement than they suggest, and the cost and failure reductions would be less dramatic. And once we start making many compromises with their proposal, we may end up with a system that does not differ very much from the system that now exists for commercial banks. I focus most of my comments on some practical implementation issues and on a few areas where I differ with Benston and Kaufman. In my final comment I suggest how deposit insurance coverage might fit into the picture.

I generally agree with the thrust of Benston and Kaufman's policy recommendations. They are very similar to policies advocated by the FDIC a few years ago—higher capital requirements accompanied by greater tolerance of subordinated debt as the best approach to dealing with deposit insurance problems.

Measurement Problem. In trying to measure assets and liabilities more accurately, Benston and Kaufman focus on the easy stuff. The hard part is nonperforming loans, those expected to move into that category, and other real estate. Is a portfolio of nonperforming commercial real estate loans in Texas worth eighty cents on the dollar or twenty cents? That can make a big difference in solvency calculations.

Most failed banks would show up as insolvent far sooner if nonperforming loans were subtracted from book capital. The risk-based capital exercise ignored the nonperforming loan issue altogether. Currently, supervisors use rules of thumb based on examination reports, and though these are imperfect, they are clearly better than ignoring the problem.

Apparently, Benston and Kaufman would rely heavily on outside audits to deal with valuing problem assets. It is not my impression that auditors have been more aggressive than bank examiners in writing down loan values. I believe that in each of the specific large bank failures cited by Benston and Kaufman where fraud and mismanagement were said to be so important, outside auditors did not contribute significantly to uncovering problems (and that is probably an understatement).

I am uncomfortable with Benston and Kaufman's ignoring intangible values and market valuation altogether. Because some banks can deliver product more cheaply and profitably than others, their value may exceed their balance sheet net worth. In a world where capital requirements are very high for insured institutions and closings occur before insolvency, I doubt that the proposition that deposit insurance is underpriced would go unchallenged.

Private Sector Solution. Raising the threshold at which sanctions take effect is one of the best features of this proposal. It would put pressure on bank management to do something positive while a bank is still solvent and has reasonable options (I have seen a number of cease-and-desist orders that, translated into English, say stop being insolvent). Too often bank managements and directors are unwilling to recapitalize or merge on terms that appear to be unfavorable to shareholders, even when a bank is facing serious difficulty. Ultimately, shareholders end up with less or nothing. If sanctions and demands for corrective action come early enough, a larger share of problem situations would be handled as recapitalizations or unassisted mergers. Unfortunately, it is difficult to raise the threshold for sanctions and to follow through and force bank closings when so many depository institutions face difficulties.

Phase-in Problem. It would also be extremely difficult to implement much higher capital requirements when so many institutions could not meet them. Benston and Kaufman recognize the need for some phase-in. Even as an announced future policy it could pose some problems. In looking for recapitalization solutions today for over 1,500 problem banks, it may be difficult to encourage acquisitions of banks or bank stocks if it is known that capital requirements will be raised substantially in the future. It is this problem, I think, that caused the FDIC proposal to fail.

Subordinated debt can serve as a safety valve to allow the well-run bank to prevent high capital requirements from raising the cost of capital appreciably. But subordinated debt (and holding company debt placed in the bank as equity) will not help weaker institutions that have difficulty raising equity. Benston and Kaufman suggest that those institutions should not survive. That suggestion poses problems, however, because so many institutions would be affected.

What about savings and loans? I cannot imagine implementing the Benston and Kaufman proposal for banks and *not* for S&Ls (I believe that bank problems and closings have been only marginally affected by deposit insurance and forbearance, whereas those are probably the principal causes of the S&L problem). Will it be possible to find purchasers for failing S&Ls if they are told that sometime in the future capital requirements will be 10 percent—after subtracting good will?

Permissible Activities. Benston and Kaufman imply that with high capital requirements and frequent review there should be no restrictions on what banks can do. I am not sure how far they intend to go. Are we talking about nonfinancial activities within the bank? I do not care if a bowling alley or steel mill owns a bank, but I do think 10 percent capital requirements are low if bowling alleys or steel mills can be part of a bank's assets, and I do not think it is appropriate to expect bank examiners to value them. If banks are restricted to financial assets and services, then capital requirements *can* be set too high, perhaps resulting in a smaller banking system with bigger spreads and more expensive services.

On Closing Banks Quickly—Historical Experience. I agree that banks probably have not been closed quickly enough in recent years, although the cases cited by Benston and Kaufman in their paper are not appropriate examples. Slower closings have probably increased FDIC losses, though some of those losses are merely a statistical phenomenon—when a troubled bank shrinks, losses become a higher share of remaining assets and deposits. Banks that suffered some big losses caused by fraud would have been closed sooner if the facts had been known sooner. I know of no individual situation, however, where losses were dramatically increased because bank regulators knowingly allowed an insolvent bank to remain open. I can cite a number of examples where forbearance, interest rate changes, and luck dramatically reduced FDIC losses. And I can cite two instances in which I believe open bank assistance that should not have been given saved a lot of money for the FDIC. I believe Benston and Kaufman are correct in advocating earlier closings. In the long run, failures would probably be averted and costs saved. But FDIC experience in this area is not one-sided.

COMMENTARY

What about Deposit Insurance? Benston and Kaufman indicate that depositors of large and small banks should be treated similarly in bank failures, but they do not indicate whether insurance coverage should be changed or whether failures should be handled as payoffs or purchase and assumptions (a transaction in which the FDIC underwrites the assumption of several creditor obligations of a failed bank by another institution). If the capital policies they advocate are pursued, eventually there will be fewer depositor losses, so the issue will not matter so much. I agree that uniformity is desirable, that the present mix of policies sometimes is unfair to particular depositors or creditors. I also believe the so-called cost test is a sham that should be eliminated. (This is a process whereby the FDIC attempts to select the least costly method of handling a failing bank.) We can treat all failures as deposit transfers under existing or revised insurance limits (with and without depositor preference), or we can go to 100 percent deposit insurance and treat all failures as deposit transfers. I am not sure which is the better alternative, although I currently lean toward 100 percent deposit insurance coverage.

I believe that 100 percent insurance coverage for all deposits would actually reduce FDIC losses and increase creditor discipline compared with the policies that are pursued under existing statutes. All failures would be handled as deposit transfers so that nondeposit creditors and contingent claimants would share losses with the FDIC in *all* failures. The treatment of depositors and creditors in failed banks would be unaffected by the size or location of the failed institution. It would be extremely important, however, that capital requirements (whether they are 6 percent, 10 percent, or whatever) be rigorously enforced to curb those inclined to gamble using fully insured deposits.

4
The Future Financial Structure: Fears and Policies

Franklin R. Edwards

The structure of the U.S. financial system is undergoing tremendous change. Although this change is only in its early stages, its direction seems clear: the elimination of geographic and product constraints that in the past have prevented open and unfettered competition among all financial institutions.

Many view with alarm the prospect of unrestrained competition in financial markets. They fear that, rather than increasing the permanent state of competition, increased competitive rivalry will ultimately lead to a less competitive and efficient financial structure. They argue that after the structural turmoil plays itself out, the result will be a highly concentrated financial structure, in which only very large, highly diversified, and internationally integrated institutions can survive. With fewer and larger institutions, it is argued, competition will give way to oligopolistic markets, leaving lenders, borrowers, and consumers of financial services worse off than they are now.

This paper describes and analyzes this concern as well as others stemming from the feared structural changes. In particular, I examine the allegations that a financial structure of the kind that I envision, one with fewer and larger financial institutions, will be less competitive, will pose greater risks to the soundness of the financial system, will result in unfair competitive practices, will adversely affect the allocation of credit, or will confer undue political power on large financial institutions. In addition, I discuss regulatory and antitrust laws currently applicable to financial institutions and make recommendations on future policies on competition.

I want to thank the members of the SFRC project as well as the AEI Advisory Committee members for their helpful comments. Special thanks are due to Bill Haraf, the project director, and to Fred Deming. I alone, of course, am responsible for all errors and omissions.

The fear of large financial institutions, and of financial concentration, while not unique to the United States, is deeply embedded in this country. Both our political and our economic heritages extol the virtues of independence, smallness, and atomistically competitive markets, particularly with respect to banks. It is not surprising, therefore, that many are concerned that current developments are driving us away from these tested ideals.

The structural changes now under way stem directly from advances in information and data processing technologies, which make it attractive for financial institutions to operate as multiproduct service centers over large geographical areas. The amount of institutional capital needed to participate in many markets today also makes large size desirable. In addition, while this notion is difficult to verify, economies of both scale and scope appear to have increased in recent years and are likely to increase further in the future.

At the same time the regulatory restrictions that in the past have fostered and maintained an artificial (or non-market-determined) financial structure are giving way. Thousands of small, inefficient banks and thrift institutions have been able to survive only because of prohibitions on the ability of banks to branch both intrastate and interstate. Without these prohibitions, many institutions would either disappear or be absorbed by larger institutions (as branch offices). Similarly, product restrictions have kept alive many specialized financial institutions that otherwise would have been driven out. It is difficult to see a unique role in the future for the thousands of specialized consumer and mortgage lending institutions that we now have. I expect many of these to disappear as independent entities, although there will probably always be a place for specialized firms that offer superior service to a selected clientele. It is not possible to forecast just how many financial institutions will remain, how big they will be, what products they will offer, and what the size distribution of these firms will be. I have no doubt, however, that there will be fewer institutions in the future. It is also clear that with the globalization of financial markets U.S. financial institutions will have to compete directly with very large foreign institutions. (See, for example, appendix A, table A-9.) Thus, although it is too early to make a firm prediction about how our financial structure will look in the year 2000, it seems likely that we will have fewer and larger institutions.

Without knowing the precise contours of the future financial structure, we cannot say with certainty which of the fears about "bigness" need to be addressed. The future financial structure will depend to some extent upon which of the current regulations are eliminated and which are kept. For purposes of this paper, I assume that restrictions on interstate banking (or branching) will be completely eliminated and that financial institutions (including banks) will be able to provide, either directly or indirectly, a full range of financial products and services. In the absence of these restrictions market forces will be the primary determinant of our financial structure.

These assumptions do not seem unrealistic in view of the changes occurring in bank holding company laws, the erosion of barriers separating banking and commerce, and the increasing openness of states to branching and to interstate banking. By examining the structural implications of this kind of nationwide banking, I analyze what I believe to be the worst fears of those alarmed by recent developments. My objective here is to separate truth from fiction and to elucidate the bases for the concerns generated by the continuing structural evolution.

Regulation versus the Free Market

Even before examining the key arguments in the dispute, we must ask the fundamental question whether (or when) regulation should be used to interfere with the natural and competitive evolution of the financial structure. The wave of consolidation we are witnessing in financial services is clearly motivated by the desire of firms to survive or to strengthen their position for the future. Managers of financial institutions obviously see advantages to size and to the ability to provide a wide range of products over an extended geographical area.

Past studies of bank costs have generally not provided evidence of significant economies of scale in banking, although they do not find evidence of significant diseconomies either. These studies, however, rely on past data and therefore do not reflect recent changes in information and data-processing technologies, which have substantially changed the cost structures of financial institutions. In addition, the studies do not adequately measure the benefits of greater geographical, product, and country diversification and do not capture the financial and fund-raising capabilities of large size, all of which are difficult to capture and measure in a statistical cost analysis.

It is apparent that competition in financial markets is keener now than at any time since the 1920s. The present consolidation hardly seems a threat to the viability of this competition, at least in the near future. Both bank regulators and antitrust authorities have implicitly recognized this fact by challenging very few of the proposed mergers between financial institutions. The Department of Justice has also recently liberalized the merger guidelines applicable to banks in recognition of the increased competition in financial markets.

What justification, then, is there for government to intervene to alter or stop the continuing structural evolution? Two arguments come to mind. First, intervention at some point may be justified to prevent the development of monopoly power. Second, and less clear, intervention may be justifiable if large size *by itself* carries with it undesirable features. Although many do not object to large firms in general, they single out large banks as especially worrisome. This paper addresses both concerns: the fear of monopoly power and the contention that large banks (and possibly any large financial institution) should be treated differently from other large firms.

The paper does not attempt to assess the costs of regulation. An extensive literature demonstrates that government intervention (or regulation) is not without cost. With respect to financial markets in particular, the perverse allocation and managerial effects attributable to regulation have been amply shown.[1]

A restrictive merger policy, for example, may inadvertently protect inefficient firms from "hostile takeovers" that may enhance efficiency. Past regulation has made it nearly impossible to effect such a takeover of banks and other depository institutions. Thus, in developing an appropriate "competition policy," it is important to balance the potential benefits of such a policy against both the direct and the indirect costs that may accompany this policy. Too often these are overlooked in formulating a regulation to meet a perceived short-run threat.

Consolidation, Concentration, and Monopoly Power

The fear that the current wave of consolidation and bankruptcy will lead to excessive concentration and, as a consequence, to less competitive markets rests in large part upon a misunderstanding of what concentration is and how it affects competition.

Measuring Concentration. The measure of concentration germane to market competition is the degree of concentration in the relevant market—the relevant geographic and product market. Incorrectly measured, or measured for the wrong market, concentration becomes a meaningless concept. In theory, the level of concentration represents the competitive structure of a market—for example, the number and size distribution of competitors.[2] An essential element in making concentration a useful measure of competition, however, is to define the relevant market correctly.

Equally important is entry or how we treat the threat of entry into the relevant market, once defined. If entry into (and exit from) the relevant market were costless, even a single ("monopoly") firm would not have monopoly power in that market. If the firm were to raise its prices in an attempt to earn monopoly profits, new competitors would arrive on the scene and undercut its prices, forcing the firm to lower its prices to competitive levels.[3] If entry and exit are not costless (or there are entry barriers), concentration becomes more meaningful as a measure of market power. The higher the entry barriers are, the more likely it is that the level of concentration will give an accurate picture of the state of competition.[4]

Thus, for concentration to have any meaning, two essential elements must be present: the relevant market must be defined correctly and barriers to entry into that market must be accurately assessed.

Fear of Increased Concentration. Misunderstanding of these two factors has led to an unwarranted fear that the recent (and threatened) consolidation wave will raise concentration and diminish competition in banking and financial markets. A common mind-set is to view what is happening in financial markets from both a "traditional industry" perspective and a nationwide perspective. As consolidation occurs and the number of financial firms diminishes, it is often assumed that "concentration" in the United States as a whole will increase. A commonly used (but not very enlightening) measure of such concentration is the percentage of total bank deposits held by the ten largest banking organizations. This is now about 17 percent.[5] Will this figure rise or fall in the future, and should we be concerned?

If the entire country is deemed to be a relevant financial market, two factors need to be recognized. First, a concentration ratio of ten banks holding less than 20 percent of the banking market is a *low* level of concentration, not a high level. It implies vigorous competition, not monopoly. Second, it is not obvious that nationwide concentration will rise as a result of the financial revolution. It has, in fact, fallen since 1933. In addition, as "banking" is redefined, or as nonbanks (such as securities firms) compete more directly with banks, concentration is likely to fall rather than rise. The inclusion of large insurance companies (like Prudential) and securities firms (like Merrill Lynch) in any measure of concentration will reduce concentration.[6] Large foreign banks and financial institutions also are invading the United States at an unprecedented rate, further diluting concentration. In 1970, seven of the ten largest banks in the world were U.S. banks. In 1986, only two U.S. banks were among the top ten; five of the ten largest were Japanese.[7] Further, only one of the next largest fifteen banks is American. Thus, the fear that concentration will increase and that competition will diminish nationally seems both unwarranted and premature.

Another concern is that concentration will rise in local markets, such as in states and cities. Assuming this were to occur, is there reason for concern? Technological and market developments have redefined the boundaries of banking and financial markets. Electronic banking, computer information capabilities, automated tellers, credit cards, asset securitization, and the erosion of legal barriers have made traditional local market definitions old-fashioned. Concentration measured in the context of an irrelevant market is meaningless.

Even if traditional (local) market definitions were considered appropriate, concentration in such markets does not have the significance it once did. In past years local markets were more often than not insulated from outside competition by restrictive branching and holding company laws and by strict product delineations between different kinds of financial institutions. This is no longer the case. Most banking services, or perhaps all, depending upon how one classifies them, are now available at nonbank financial institutions, and most geographical restrictions have been or are being dismantled. In other words, the major entry barriers that used to exist no longer do. Entry into local markets is not the costly affair it once was. Indeed, entry costs in financial markets seem low in comparison with those in other industries. Thus, in the presence of low entry barriers, measures of concentration tell us very little about the state of competition. High concentration could very well be consistent with a high degree of competition because of the real and constant threat of entry.

A simple example may make this even clearer. Let us take banking. Regulatory authorities have in the past defined relevant banking markets quite narrowly. Commercial banks were viewed as unique; they provided a unique product: "commercial banking services." The rationale that underlay this approach was that banks alone provided both demand (or transaction) deposits and business loans. Taken together, these created a unique financial service. Thus, only other commercial banks could be considered competitors. Nonbank financial institutions were irrelevant in an assessment of the effects of a proposed merger between two banks.

The geographical scope of banking was also constrained to local areas. Branching and holding company regulations prevented banks located outside the local area from coming into the market. Thus, in nonbranching states (and perhaps in states with limited branching), the relevant geographical banking market was commonly defined to be either the local town (or city) or, at most, the county. In "statewide" branching states the market was expanded somewhat.

With banking markets defined in this way potential competitors and potential competition had little role. Only banks were viewed as competitors, and all competing banks were already included in the market. Potential competitors were excluded absolutely by legal barriers. We might say that entry barriers were infinitely high. Under these restrictive entry conditions, the level of concentration in the local market was a meaningful index of the state of competition.

Circumstances have clearly changed. Many financial institutions other than banks offer either transaction (deposit) accounts or business loans or both. Savings institutions, for example, compete actively for transaction balances and sometimes for business loan customers as well. Brokerage firms with their cash management accounts constitute another competitive alternative. Credit and debt cards have replaced the traditional checking account in many transactions. Further, automated teller machines (ATMs) in conjunction with "banking" cards have made it easier for institutions outside a local area to have an effective competitive presence in a given locality, and branching restrictions have been eroded to the point where entry from outside the area is again a matter of economics rather than legal barriers. Finally, in the 1950s, checking accounts constituted from 60 to 70 percent of banks' funds. Today they constitute just a little over 20 percent.

Business loans are also no longer the exclusive province of commercial banks. A remarkable development has been the explosive growth of the commercial paper and the corporate bond markets, both of which are substitutes for commercial bank business loans. Commercial paper issued by nonfinancial businesses and finance companies, for example, has increased from $4.5 billion in 1960 to almost $250 billion today. In addition, finance companies have become independent and viable competitors in the business loan market. At one time dependent upon banks for much of their funding, they now rely almost exclusively on securities markets. Foreign banks, and their agencies and branches, have also become aggressive competitors for business loans. From 1970 to 1986 U.S. banks' share of total loans to businesses fell from 81 percent to 65 percent.

In the future nonbank financial firms will probably be able to compete directly with commercial banks in any product line that banks offer. For example, Merrill Lynch now offers the small businessman a form of interest-bearing checking account combined with a line of credit, investment advice, retirement planning, and insurance. The development of sophisticated and deep securities markets, together with innovative financing arrangements, has made major financial firms (and even nonfinancial firms) potential competitors with traditional financial intermediaries such as banks.

Thus, the concept of a banking market as a local community with no competitors other than full-service commercial banks is no longer realistic. Both the relevant product and the relevant geographic markets must be redefined to reflect current market realities, and potential competition must be elevated to a significant role in an analytical assessment of the state of banking competition. Easy generalizations about relevant markets are no longer possible: markets must be defined case by case, based on the facts and circumstances of the case. Finally, concentration ratios, as indexes of the state of competition, must be carefully defined to include all competitors (not only banks) and must be interpreted in the context of entry barriers and potential competitors.

It is not, in any case, clear that concentration correctly measured will rise in local banking and financial markets. No evidence suggests that this has in general happened in the past twenty years.[8] In addition, it is easy to imagine that, even if we were left with some very large financial institutions in the United States, local markets would still contain more financial institutions in the future than they do now. The "minimum efficient size" of a branch office of a large nationwide institution is almost certainly less than for an independent bank.[9] A local market of a given size, therefore, could support a larger number of competitors, which are themselves part of larger nationwide institutions.

In summary, the current consolidation movement in financial markets does not foretell a lessening of competition. Although it is certainly true that the total number of banks and other financial institutions operating in the United States will decline, the relevant signs of competition are unlikely to deteriorate. Concentration in *relevant* markets is unlikely to rise and may even fall; and entry barriers will be lower than ever. Further, antitrust laws and other competitive policy guidelines can still be used to maintain a competitive environment. Thus, those who fear that rising concentration will lead to monopolistic financial markets are either focusing on meaningless measures (or concepts) of concentration or are misconstruing the nature of the competitive process now under way in banking and financial markets.

Are Banks Special?

In addition to the fear of increased concentration, there has always been concern that banking in combination with other financial services (or commercial activities) will result in "unfair competition." Banking conglomerates, it is argued, enjoy unfair competitive advantages that can be used to reduce market competition.[10]

This argument has two aspects. First, do banks, because of the explicit and implicit guarantees given to their creditors by the government (such as deposit insurance), enjoy competitive advantages over other financial institutions? Can they, for example, raise funds at lower cost? Second, are some bank services (or products) so rare that they enable banks to extend their monopoly power over these products to other products, through, in particular, tying arrangements and predatory pricing strategies?

Federal Guarantees and a Level Playing Field. Federal guarantees cannot be discussed without first specifying the kind of financial structure we assume will exist in the future. My assumption is that the financial firm of the future will conduct a banking business as well as many other financial businesses (securities, insurance, and the like). It will not, however, be a one-way street. If banks enter the securities business, securities firms will presumably be allowed to enter banking. In this scenario, all financial institutions will have equal access to federal guarantees, thus eliminating the issue of unfair competitive advantage.

In the absence of equal access to federal guarantees, an "equal competition" issue may arise, although its definition, measurement, and potential significance are debatable. To begin with, the competitive advantage may be relatively minor.[11] Second, institutions that receive federal guarantees (such as deposit insurance) may also have a heavier regulatory burden, which may outweigh any cost advantage associated with such guarantees. Last, while some institutions could be disadvantaged, overall market competition should not suffer. Competitors may be injured, but not competition. New competitors will merely replace old competitors. If, for example, banks enjoyed a cost advantage over securities firms, they would simply replace securities firms. Alternatively, if securities firms enjoyed the advantage, they would supplant banks. Firms would suffer but not competition, since many competitors would remain.

The issue, therefore, is really fairness rather than competition. Defining and constructing a "level playing field" is probably impossible under our existing maze of regulations. As a consequence, a fairness argument can be used to justify almost any kind of government intervention. The only sure solution is to adopt a regulatory structure that ensures equal access to all competing institutions, whether they are banks, savings institutions, securities firms, or insurance companies.

Unfair Competitive Practices. It is sometimes argued that banks might use predatory pricing tactics and various tying arrangements to restrain competition in nonbank markets. More specifically, some allege that banks will use the competitive leverage that certain banking products purport to bestow upon them to extend their market power to other products over which they would otherwise have no control. Thus, the argument goes, allowing banks to sell nonbanking products or to combine with nonbank financial institutions would lessen competition in associated nonbanking markets.

This concern stems from a misunderstanding of the conditions under which such tactics could actually reduce competition. A common misconception is that tying arrangements and predatory pricing are always harmful or that they always exert a restraint on competition. This is wrong. Careful analysis demonstrates that only under rather exceptional circumstances will these tactics diminish competition.

Tying arrangements. A tie-in sale is a form of marketing in which a seller insists on selling two distinct products or services as a package. A supermarket, for example, that will sell flour to consumers only if they also buy sugar is engaged in tying.[12]

The fear that banks will use tying as a device to reduce competition in financial service markets has long been embedded in our legislative and regulatory thinking. As early as 1969, when the bank holding company movement was in its early stages, the House Committee on Banking and Currency stated:

> Because many large and small businesses, as well as individuals, depend on bank credit for their economic existence, bank subsidiaries of one-bank holding companies are in a position to insist or "strongly suggest" that if the borrower wants continued access to bank credit, it should also use the services of the holding company's other subsidiaries. These services might include insurance, equipment leasing, property management, accounting, computing, investment and travel services, or any other business the holding company might decide to undertake. This would create unfair competition for non-bank related competitors of these subsidiaries and could in the long run substantially reduce or eliminate

competition in many businesses to the detriment of the public interest.[13]

A similar alarm was also sounded by the chairman of the Federal Reserve Board at that time: "Another safeguard that should accompany expansion of bank holding company activities is a prohibition against so-called 'tie-in' arrangements."[14] These warnings ultimately found expression in section 106 of the 1970 Bank Holding Company Act, which expressly prohibits coerced joint sales.[15]

The ability of a tying seller to restrain competition—either by reducing the number of competitors in the tied-product market or by raising entry barriers into that market—depends on a number of market factors. First and most important, the tying seller must have sufficient economic power with respect to the tying product to restrain appreciably free competition in the market for the tied product.[16] Without "control or dominance over the tying product," the seller could not use the tying product as "an effectual weapon to pressure buyers into taking the tied item," so that any restraint of trade would be "insignificant."[17]

Second, the market circumstances must be such that the monopolistic tying seller can extend his monopoly power to (or acquire additional market power in) the tied-product market. Economic analysis suggests that the ability to do this will depend upon the following: (1) the shape of the monopolist's long-run average cost curve for producing the tied product; (2) the minimum efficient size of plant relative to the size of the market for the tied product; (3) the number of competitors in the tied-product market before the tie-in; and (4) the proportion of the tied-product market that the monopolist can foreclose with a tying arrangement.

To see the importance of these factors, consider the following. Suppose that there are absolutely no economies of scale in producing the tied product (B) and that our monopolist (M) is able to foreclose the "entire" market by tying B to A (the tying product). Thus, assume that everyone who buys B also buys A. If new firms are able to enter the market for B at a small volume of sales but with long-run costs similar to those of M, M can never establish additional monopoly power over B. As soon as M tries to charge the buyers of B a higher price than the combination of A and B is worth to them, some buyers of B will stop purchasing A from M and look to other sellers for a lower price on B, establishing an incentive for firms to enter the market. Since the absence of economies of scale permits entry at a small volume, entry will materialize quickly. Thus, the tying arrangement will not have an adverse welfare effect.

Even in the absence of economies of scale, however, it is possible that the ability to foreclose the entire market for *B* may result in higher entry barriers. Potential entrants will have to contend with the possibility that *M* may reduce the price of *B* to a point where he can again foreclose the entire market, forcing the new entrants to exit the market. If potential entrants evaluate this risk as high, *M* may be able to sell *B* at a higher price and still not provoke entry. In other words, the entry-forestalling price will be higher than it would be if *M* did not have the capability of foreclosing the entire market. Under these conditions the consumers of *B* will be worse off.

It is clear that the competitive effects of a tie-in sale depend upon the particular conditions that exist in the market at the time. One generalization, however, can be made. If many firms either produce or are able to produce both *A* and *B* and there are low entry barriers into the markets for *A* and *B* when sold jointly (or when tied), no producer can for long earn monopoly rents by tying *A* and *B* together. New entrants will prevent that from occurring. In the emerging financial markets, many institutions are likely to be capable of entering two or more markets simultaneously. Thus it is questionable whether, as a general proposition, tying arrangements will adversely affect competition.

Before the recent evolution in financial markets, the argument that banks might possess significant market power over certain traditional banking products and services, such as business credit, had some basis. Today there are a number of alternatives for these banking products. As a consequence, banks are even less likely today than in the past to have the requisite market power (over the tying product) to implement a destructive tying arrangement.

Predatory pricing. Another concern is that banks might use their (monopoly) profits from certain services to sell other services at "below-cost" prices, thereby driving competitors from the other market and lessening competition. As defined in *Cargill Inc. et al.* v. *Monfort of Colorado,* predatory pricing is "pricing below an appropriate measure of cost for the purpose of eliminating competitors in the short run and reducing competition in the long run."[18] The fear is that banks will use supracompetitive profits from products for which they allegedly possess monopoly power to cross-subsidize other products, driving competitors from that market and ultimately creating still another monopoly position.

Two factors must be present for this result to occur: first, the "predator" must possess monopoly power in at least some markets; and, second, the "predator" must have a reasonable expectation of recovering more than its initial losses (from cross-subsidizing another product) in the form of later monopoly profits. Neither of these factors is likely to be present in today's financial markets or in the financial structure I envision in the future. First, banks no longer possess monopoly power over traditional banking products, and competition in all product lines is quite intense. Second, in today's markets (and in the future) monopoly pricing should breed quick entry by new competitors eager to share in the excess profits. A rational, profit-maximizing predator, therefore, could not expect to maintain its monopoly position long enough to recoup its initial losses. Furthermore, its ability to harvest additional profits is even more unlikely. Not surprisingly, commentators agree "that predatory pricing schemes are rarely tried, and even more rarely successful."[19]

Thus, predatory pricing should not be viewed as a serious obstacle to the affiliation of banks with other financial institutions or to the proliferation of branching. Although predatory pricing schemes are a possibility, they are unlikely to succeed in lessening competition.

In summary, nothing special about banks or financial institutions makes unfair competitive schemes of greater concern than they are in any other industry or market. To the extent that strategies like tie-in sales and predatory pricing pose a competitive threat to financial markets, they should be subject to the same antitrust scrutiny that would apply to such activities in any other industry.

Noncompetitive Concerns

A number of additional, noncompetitive concerns commonly surface in a debate about the merits of "concentration" or "firm size" in financial markets. They fall into four general categories: conflicts of interest, the safety and soundness of the financial system, the potential political power of large financial institutions, and the allocation of credit among competing interests. In general, these concerns focus more on scale than on concentration; and, while they have all been narrowly directed at banks at one time or another, they are broadly applicable to all kinds of financial institutions.

Conflicts of Interest. Conflicts of interest occur when there are two or more competing interests present and the person or firm making a decision affecting those interests has a larger stake in one of the interests than in the other but is expected, indeed required, to serve each interest equitably, regardless of his or its own stake.

Conflicts, so defined, are pervasive: they are not unique to financial institutions or to banks in particular. Nevertheless, since financial institutions, especially banks, are seen as having a higher order of fiduciary responsibility than other firms, conflicts have always been a controversial issue in the financial area.

This issue has several dimensions, which must be carefully distinguished. Much of the controversy relates to the type of organization of the firm: for example, a holding company versus a single, integrated company. It is often argued that holding companies are subject to conflicts of interest because of the differing capital structures of their affiliates and subsidiaries. The essence of this debate is whether these conflicts (and incentives) can or cannot be adequately controlled by regulation. Unfortunately, the proponents of the alternative positions support their views with little more than their own judgments about the ability of regulators to monitor and control such conflicts.

Will the current structural evolution, by increasing the size of financial institutions, increase the conflicts problem, either by decreasing competition or by decreasing the information available to the customers or the debt holders of banks and other financial institutions? It is generally recognized that in the absence of competitive and information imperfections conflicts cannot disadvantage customers or debt holders. It seems unlikely that large size by itself will exaggerate whatever imperfections already exist. In fact, serious conflicts may be more common in small institutions than in large institutions. The predominant form of organizational structure among large financial institutions today is the holding company, in which the parent owns all (or the vast majority) of the subsidiaries. This can be contrasted with our historical financial structure, populated by small local institutions, in which owners (or managers) often had personal equity interests in the business activities of their customers. Under these conditions, the incentive to favor one set of customers to the detriment of others is strong. That incentive is considerably muted if the institution itself has total ownership of all its subsidiaries and does not have equity interests in its customers' businesses. Large size, therefore, may result in fewer potential conflicts than exist in smaller financial institutions.

In addition, discriminatory treatment of certain interests (or customers) by managers implicitly assumes that these interests are not in a position to know what is happening to them—that they cannot monitor the institution effectively. Large institutions, to the extent that they discriminate at all, are likely to do so between different kinds of interests (or types of customers) and not between *individual* customers. It would be bureaucratically cumbersome to discriminate any other way. Thus, if any customers within a group can monitor the institution effectively, all customers within that group will be protected. This together with the current trend toward making more information available about all aspects of financial institutions' activities provides a significant check on abusive managerial behavior.

Increased competition is another check on managerial behavior. If customers have alternatives, they will go elsewhere if not fairly treated. The current structural evolution will increase competition, providing a more effective check on managerial abuses. Abusive behavior is a luxury that competitive firms cannot long afford. Thus, there is little reason to think that larger firm size in financial markets will increase the problems commonly associated with conflicts of interest. Indeed, the reverse is more likely.[20]

Safety and Soundness. Another consideration, more often directed at banks than at nonbank financial institutions, is the "safety and soundness" of the financial system. Will a system of predominantly large banks be more or less susceptible to instability than the present one? Or, alternatively, must our present regulatory structure for maintaining financial soundness be altered to accommodate a system of large banks?

The first question is whether large banks are more or less prone to insolvency. We would expect them to be less vulnerable to insolvency. Large banks are more diversified, have better access to capital markets, and, in general, are probably better managed. Thus the probability of failure for a large bank should be less than for a small bank.

A structure of large banks, however, may pose additional concerns. Interdependence among large banks, it is feared, may cause the failure of one to precipitate the failure of others, so that the failure of a single large bank may expose the federal deposit insurance system to greater risk of insolvency.[21]

Some who harbor this concern cite the law of large numbers for support. This law states that as the number of exposure units (such as banks) increases, the more certain it is that actual loss experience will equal the probable (or the expected) loss experience. Hence, insurance risk (or uncertainty) will increase as the number of exposure units decreases. Under certain assumptions, such risk can be shown to vary inversely with the square root of the number of banks.

The law of large numbers requires that certain key assumptions be met before its implications are valid. First, the probability of bankruptcy is assumed to be the same for all banks; second, bank insolvencies are assumed to be completely independent of one another; and, third, all units are assumed to be of identical size. None of these assumptions is valid for banking: large banks should have a lower probability of insolvency, interdependence is likely, and there is obviously a size disparity among banks. Standard insurance theory, therefore, cannot be used to determine whether a system of large banks poses a greater threat to financial soundness.

Another concern is that market discipline will be undermined because regulators may not allow a large bank to fail. But bank failures need not mean market disruption or even customer inconvenience. They can be accomplished by simply replacing old owners with new owners. The losses can be borne entirely by the old owners if regulators act in a timely fashion, "closing" banks before the market value of their equity is less than zero. The restructuring of large banks does not pose any special problems.[22]

Finally, a historical comparison among countries suggests that the U.S. financial structure has been more susceptible to financial panics (or "bank runs") than have other countries' financial systems.[23] Since the financial structures of other countries are characterized by relatively fewer and larger banks (in contrast to the U.S. system of thousands of small, independent banks), this suggests that a system of large banks may be less vulnerable to insolvency and instability. A structure characterized by large banks and financial institutions, however, makes it more urgent that we rethink the current deposit insurance system. A flat premium structure, together with the current policy of de jure less-than-full deposit insurance but de facto full coverage, seems dangerously inappropriate. A world populated by large financial institutions may also require a more active central bank lender-of-last-resort policy. We need to determine the ramifications of such a policy.

Political Power. The fear that large financial institutions operating in concentrated markets may be able to exercise substantial political power has kept many from enthusiastically endorsing the current financial evolution. This concern stems from the belief that large firms have disproportionate political power (relative to smaller competitors) and that high concentration facilitates the exercise of such power.

Large size, however, must be distinguished from concentration. Large firms can exist in markets without necessitating high concentration, and high concentration can occur without necessitating large firms. Thus, the theory used to analyze the political influence of large firms need not be the same as that used to explore the relationship of concentration to political power.

The general issue of the relationship between firm size and political power does not seem particularly germane to the changes taking place in financial markets. First, there are already very large firms outside banking and finance (such as IBM and Exxon). The "bigness" issue is not unique to banking or financial markets. With respect to political influence, there would seem to be little difference between a large bank and either a large manufacturing firm or a large insurance company. Second, while we can expect existing financial institutions to become even larger, the size distribution of banks and other financial firms in the future will probably be less skewed than at present. This may work to neutralize (or offset) any disproportionate political power that large institutions may have.

Do firms in concentrated markets exercise greater political power? The view that they do rests on two premises. First, firms in concentrated markets may have greater (monopoly) profits. If the managers of these firms have discretionary authority—perhaps because stockholders either have difficulty monitoring management or must bear significant costs to do so—they may elect to use some of the firm's profits to obtain political influence. Indeed, stockholders might even approve of such activity if it increased profits. Thus, in its most simplistic form, firms in concentrated markets are viewed as simply having disproportionately more resources to employ to win political concessions.

The second premise rests on a "transaction cost" argument: in concentrated markets there are fewer firms with more homogeneous interests; so it costs less to organize a political campaign. The costs of having to bring together many firms with diverse interests is avoided. If both the average and the marginal costs of a given political action are less, it stands to reason that the marginal (net) benefit of such action for a given total resource expenditure will increase. Thus, firms may choose to spend more on political action and less on something else. The result may be that they have greater political influence.

This view has found credence in the literature of political economy. For example, Vogel argues that

> companies in concentrated industries do appear to enjoy an important advantage: firms in these industries are more readily able to perceive their political interests and can more easily communicate with each other. To the extent that firms in more concentrated industries are often relatively large, this advantage is reinforced: larger firms are more able to monitor political developments, analyze and document the impacts of various public policies, and support a Washington office than are smaller firms. While this does not automatically translate into political power, it certainly constitutes a necessary condition for its exercise.[24]

THE FUTURE FINANCIAL STRUCTURE

In addition, fragmented or unconcentrated markets may be subject to free-rider problems. An individual company may be unwilling to put substantial time, effort, and money into a political campaign for fear that others will not do the same.

This view is not without its dissenters. In discussing the political power of the 200 largest corporations, L. E. Birdzell takes the contrary position:

> The argument that conglomerates represent a political power threat is . . . difficult to take seriously. A large concentration of wealth undoubtedly has a substantial political capability if it can lawfully be applied to political purposes, as illustrated by the successful political use of Rockefeller and Kennedy fortunes. The fatal problem with similar political use of corporate concentrations of wealth is that they cannot lawfully be applied to political uses, even if stockholders could be induced to agree on common political objectives and the business organization could survive the necessary diversion of effort. Salaried corporate managers are probably not as rich a potential source of political contributions as oil lessors, owners of automobile dealerships, and other entrepreneurs with substantial personal fortunes. And corporate management is rarely able to deliver the votes even of corporate stockholders, let alone employees, dealers or suppliers. The Automobile Dealers Day-in-Court Act is eloquent testimony to the comparative political power of some very large corporations on the one hand and a group of "small" businessmen on the other.[25]

In a study of special interest legislation, Richard Posner also concludes that large corporations have no more influence in the political process than small firms:

> The fact that a great deal of legislation appears to be designed to protect firms against competition . . . provides the basis for a serious criticism of our political system and, perhaps, more broadly, of the role which we allow "interest groups" to play in shaping public policy. It does not suggest a basis for a criticism of large corporations as such. The subordination of consumer to producer interests in the production of legislation seems quite independent of the size of the individual firms involved. We observe as much protective legislation in small business industries, such as agriculture, textiles, and trucking, as in large—perhaps more. We observe much protective legislation in industries where production is carried on by individuals rather than by firms—unionized trades

(barbering, plumbing, pharmacy) and regulated professions such as medicine are more important examples.[26]

With respect to the financial services industry in particular, some of the assumptions that underlie the argument that large firms will have disproportionate political influence may not be correct. To begin with, the current structural evolution is likely to increase competition by lowering entry barriers into all markets. Thus there will be less "discretionary" profits in the future to support political activities—political influence may diminish, not increase. Second, to the extent that concentration contributes to "efficiency" of political action, that may not necessarily be bad. In a democratic (indeed, any) society, political action and influence are a fact of life. It is not clear that, if large firms are a more effective vehicle for political action, the result will be a worse "social contract." There are large firms in other industries, large unions, and many large influential organizations that represent otherwise small economic interests.

There is, in addition, little empirical evidence to suggest that large banks have wielded disproportionate political power in the past.[27] The few studies of which I am aware fail to find a relationship between bank size, concentration, and political influence. For example, John Rose tests the hypothesis that domination of a state by a few banks may enable such banks to get laws passed that are favorable to themselves. He could find no relationship between state banking concentration and the votes of state senators on a bill to delay the introduction of nationwide negotiable order of withdrawal (NOW) accounts, however.[28]

In another study Linda Edwards and I investigated the relationship of both concentration and firm size to (regional) statutory interest rate ceilings on consumer loans.[29] A wide disparity of rate ceilings exists among states. The ceilings vary from a low of 10 percent to over 40 percent. We attempted to determine if rate ceilings were higher in states with a higher concentration among finance companies (the beneficiaries of high rate ceilings) or were lower in states with a greater number of finance companies. The results revealed no relationship between the level of states' rate ceilings and either concentration or number of firms.

Thus, there is no evidence that the structural evolution in financial markets will allow banks and other financial institutions to acquire unacceptable political power. Further, to the extent that an issue of political power exists, there is no reason to single out banks and financial institutions for special treatment. In this respect financial institutions are no different from other firms in other markets. They too can acquire and use political power. If a policy is needed to control the political power exercised by large firms or by firms in concentrated markets, this policy should have universal application: it should apply to all firms in all markets and not only to banks and financial institutions.

Credit Allocation. It has been alleged that a more concentrated financial structure will result in an undesirable reallocation of credit. For example, in a recent letter to the *Washington Post*, Senator William Proxmire, chairman of the Committee on Banking, Housing, and Urban Affairs, says:

> Separating banking and commerce has fostered a vibrant economy based on small business. Small banks lend almost exclusively to small businesses, which account for 85 percent of job creation. (Only 13 percent of a large bank's loan portfolio is with small businesses.) When banking and commerce are mixed, the result is a higher concentrated industry dominated by huge companies.[30]

This statement typifies the confusion surrounding the issue of credit allocation. First, it presumes that the consolidation of financial institutions into larger entities will result in a "highly concentrated industry dominated by huge companies." Read uncritically, this statement seems to say that competition will diminish. While it is true that consolidation will result in fewer and larger institutions, it does not follow that competition will be less. As discussed earlier, it is concentration in *relevant* markets that is critical, and, for reasons already discussed, the number of viable competitors in relevant markets will probably increase rather than decline. Further, even if this does not occur (or there are fewer "actual" competing institutions), competition is nevertheless likely to increase because entry barriers into these markets will be lower. Either way, the result is likely to be more, not less, competition.

Second, as indicated by his citing of statistics on the percentage of bank portfolios devoted to small business credit, Senator Proxmire confuses concentration with absolute bank size. He suggests that large banks may not serve the credit needs of small businesses as well as small banks do. His evidence is the lower percentage of a large bank's portfolio (13 percent) dedicated to small businesses. This is a misleading statistic: a smaller percentage of a larger pie may result in a larger (in absolute size) piece of pie than would a larger percentage of a smaller pie. Taken alone, the percentage of large versus small bank portfolios is meaningless. What matters is the *total* credit going to small businesses. It is easy to show that even if large banks were to devote a significantly lower percentage of their loan portfolios (the larger pie) to small businesses than small banks do, the total credit going to small businesses would increase, not decrease.

The concern about large banks sometimes stems from a belief that branch managers of large banks (or other financial firms) are not as responsive to local borrowers' needs as are local bankers. Local bankers, it is alleged, have a better understanding of local conditions and are better able to assess a borrower's credit worthiness. Further, they have the long-run interests of the community in mind.

Although it is difficult to evaluate this argument, a number of arguments can be made on the other side. First, branch banks may also have a long-run interest in a community. Why should they not? It is in their interest, just as it is for local bankers, to foster long-term, profitable banking relationships. Second, branch offices may be staffed by citizens of the local community, who possess the same knowledge about the community and its borrowers as do local, independent bankers. Third, it is at least conceivable that local bankers, because of their familiarity with local borrowers and their independence of action, may misjudge the ability of borrowers. They may not make objective assessments. Last, we have already had extensive experience with branching and with large branch banks. There is no evidence that local (or small) customers in branching states receive poorer financial service. It is, therefore, difficult to put much weight on the contention that large branch banks will not provide services of equal quality to local customers.

More important, the entire argument that we should be concerned about the effects of a revised financial structure on credit allocation is spurious. The new financial structure that will develop because of fewer regulatory restrictions will bring about a further integration of financial markets. Institutions will have offices in many locations and will quite naturally shift credit to areas and borrowers with the greatest need. Borrowers (of a given credit standing) who are willing to pay more for credit will receive the credit. Since borrowers who are willing and able to pay more presumably have more productive (or higher-yielding) uses for the credit, the result is a more efficient allocation of credit. Credit will flow to its most productive uses.

Credit should be priced and allocated like any other productive resource, such as labor. A more integrated financial structure will result in a more efficient allocation of credit and capital than we now have. If the result is a shift of credit away from one group of borrowers (say small businesses) toward another group (say households), this is probably welfare enhancing, just the opposite of what is suggested by Senator Proxmire's letter. There is nothing sacred about the existing distribution of credit. Credit allocation should depend upon the realities of market economics, not upon a financial structure that may be more reflective of historical accident than of sound economics.

There is, finally, one more argument against using a particular (or peculiar, depending on one's point of view) institutional structure to allocate credit to foster specified *real* economic objectives: it does not work.

Unless unacceptably severe restrictions are imposed, attempts to influence real investment or real spending on certain products or in certain areas of the country through credit allocation schemes are doomed to failure. Such efforts run counter to a key proposition in credit theory: the fungibility of credit. Credit fungibility permits investors to look beyond the superficial differences among securities in pursuit of high yields and low risk. Borrowers can transform an apparently designated loan into a source of general funds to be used for anything.

A home mortgage, for example, is merely a loan collateralized by a house. The house can be old or new. If the mortgage rate is lower because of an institutional structure that forcibly channels credit into mortgage lending, homeowners can refinance their homes. Home buyers can make smaller down payments to take advantage of the cheap credit too. In both cases lowering the cost of credit leads to increased mortgage lending, but in neither case need it affect housing construction. In other words, making more mortgage or small business credit available need not result in more housing or greater growth of small businesses; it may simply lead to more loans against existing houses or small business assets. This effect is certainly different from that which Senator Proxmire had in mind.

If there is a clear social goal to affect real economic activity in particular sectors of the economy, tampering with the institutional structure of financial markets is not the way to achieve it. A more direct tax or subsidy program is preferable. Such a program can work, and its costs can be made explicit.

Thus, fears that a new, more concentrated financial structure will alter credit flows in undesirable ways are misplaced and unfounded. We have, to the contrary, reason to believe that the resulting allocation of credit will be superior to that which we now have.

The Law and Policy Governing Competition

Policy governing both mergers and acquisitions (among banks and other financial institutions) and unfair competitive practices involves the complex application of several different bodies of law by several different regulatory authorities. This section discusses that policy as it applies to banks and thrifts.

Mergers and Acquisitions. Concern that a merger or acquisition between banks or thrift institutions will reduce competition can cause both the federal and thrift regulatory agencies and the Department of Justice to review the transaction and, if deemed necessary, intervene to prevent it from going forward.

There are several steps in this process.[31] First, the relevant bank and thrift regulatory agencies perform an initial competitive review. Under the Bank Merger Act of 1966, the Office of the Comptroller of the Currency (OCC) for national banks, the Federal Deposit Insurance Corporation (FDIC) for federally insured state-chartered banks that are not members of the Federal Reserve System, and the Federal Reserve Board of Governors (FRB) for state-chartered banks that are system members are required to conduct their own competitive analysis and to obtain competitive factor reports from each other and from the Department of Justice before approving a bank merger. (These transactions are exempt from Hart-Scott-Rodino Act premerger notification procedures.)

Under the Bank Holding Company Act the FRB must apply a competitive analysis before approving the acquisition of a bank (or bank holding company) by a bank holding company. Although competitive factor reports are not required, the FRB sends applications—exempt from Hart-Scott-Rodino premerger notification requirements—to the Department of Justice. Copies of applications for bank holding company acquisitions of nonbanks submitted must be filed with the antitrust agencies under Hart-Scott-Rodino at least thirty days before consummation, if the transaction is to be exempted from normal Hart-Scott-Rodino filing requirements. Thus, the Antitrust Division, like the FRB, reviews these transactions to assess their competitive effects.

The Federal Home Loan Bank Board (FHLBB) reviews mergers of savings and loan associations under regulations providing for analysis of competitive effects, as does the Federal Savings and Loan Insurance Corporation (FSLIC) for federally insured thrifts under its regulations. To satisfy the Hart-Scott-Rodino requirements, the parties seeking an exemption must file a copy of the application submitted to the thrift agency with the Department of Justice and the Federal Trade Commission.

For savings and loan holding company mergers and acquisitions, the FHLBB conducts competitive reviews and also requests competitive factor reports from the Department of Justice. No Hart-Scott-Rodino filing is required.

Second, the Antitrust Division of the Department of Justice screens all the applications it receives, whether from the agencies or through the Hart-Scott-Rodino process. Its objective is to identify those that exceed the standards of the Department of Justice Merger Guidelines as applied to depository institutions. Analysis under the guidelines centers on three factors: the product market, the geographic market, and the likely anticompetitive effects of the transaction within those markets. This analysis is similar to the legal elements considered under section 7 of the Clayton Act, which bars a merger or acquisition "where in any line of commerce in any section of the country, the effect of such acquisition may be substantially to lessen competition, or to tend to create a monopoly."

Next, after the screening and the initial analyses have been completed, the Antitrust Division decides whether the merger or acquisition should be opposed because it is "significantly adverse to competition." The standard used for this determination is that, unless other factors indicate an anticompetitive effect, the Antitrust Division will not oppose a bank or thrift merger unless the postmerger concentration ratio exceeds a prespecified level: unless the postmerger Herfindahl-Hirschman index (HHI) is 1,800 or greater and the HHI increase due to the transaction is at least 200 points.[32]

If the Antitrust Division concludes that a transaction is "significantly adverse to competition," it sends a full-blown competitive-factors report to the responsible agency. In all other instances where required by statue, the division sends only a short-form competitive-factors report, concluding that the transaction is "not significantly adverse to competition." If the regulatory agency nevertheless approves a transaction on which the Antitrust Division has submitted a "significantly adverse" letter, the division has thirty days after approval of a bank or bank holding company transaction to decide whether to sue. If the division does not sue, the transaction becomes immune from challenge except under section 2 of the Sherman Act. If suit is brought, the transaction is automatically stayed. Neither the time limit for an antitrust challenge nor the statutory stay, however, applies to savings and loan associations or savings and loan holding company transactions.

In determining whether a merger or acquisition is "significantly adverse to competition," the Antitrust Division undertakes a complex and sophisticated substantive analysis of its likely competitive effects. It defines and analyzes alternative product and geographic markets[33] and evaluates the potential structural effect of the transaction in these markets. Its structural analysis encompasses both direct competition (through the concentration-ratio tests noted above) and potential competition. With respect to potential competition, such factors as entry conditions (for example, branching restrictions), advantages that the acquiring firm may have as a possible entrant, and the market share of the acquired firm are considered.

The Antitrust Division is also willing to take account of other factors that may mitigate an inference of an anticompetitive effect.[34] For example, it will consider evidence that the transaction will enhance efficiency by achieving economies of scale, although this argument is customarily available only in the case of very small institutions. It will take into account evidence pertaining to the financial health of the firm to be acquired (under the "convenience and needs" clause). Such evidence is persuasive to the Antitrust Division and the courts, however, only when financial failure is a danger and when no less anticompetitive alternatives exist.[35]

In summary, with a few minor exceptions, which are more possibilities than likelihoods, the competitive standards applied by the Department of Justice to mergers and acquisitions among banking and thrift institutions are for all practical purposes identical to those imposed by the antitrust laws (in particular, section 7 of the Clayton Act). There seems to be little purpose to the cumbersome, bureaucratic, and costly screening procedures now employed by regulatory agencies and the Department of Justice. Further, as is evidenced by past developments of the law in this area, no convincing rationale has appeared for a competitive policy applicable to banks and financial institutions separate and distinct from that applied to mergers and acquisitions among nonfinancial firms.

Regional Compacts. Regional compacts, which have surfaced during recent years, are another regulatory aspect relevant to competition policy. These are arrangements among a relatively few states, often in a specific area of the country (such as New England), which permit mergers among depository institutions located within the specified region but prohibit mergers between depository institutions in the region and depository institutions outside the region.

While these compacts provide for some expansion of interstate competition, they are clearly designed to limit competition by excluding institutions outside the region as competitors. They should not, therefore, be permitted to become a permanent feature of our financial landscape. They are, at best, a short-run, transitional expedient.

Unfair Competitive Practices. Financial institutions engaging in unfair competitive practices are subject to section 1 of the Sherman Act.[36] In general, both tie-in sales and predatory pricing schemes that substantially lessen competition or tend to create a monopoly in any line of commerce are subject to attack under section 1.[37] *Fortner Enterprises, Inc.* v. *U.S. Steel Corp.* made it clear that the use of credit as a tying product is within the scope of the Sherman Act.[38] (In that case the defendant agreed to provide credit only on condition that the borrowers also purchase its prefabricated houses.)

In addition, with respect to mergers and acquisitions involving banks, section 4 (c)(8) of the Bank Holding Company Act[39] requires the Federal Reserve Board to consider whether the performance of the proposed activity by an affiliate of the holding company "can reasonably be expected to produce benefits to the public, such as greater convenience, increased competition, or gains in efficiency, that outweigh possible adverse effects, such as undue concentration of resources, decreased or unfair competition, conflicts of interests, or unsound banking practices."[40] Under this provision the Federal Reserve considers all unfair competitive practices, including predatory pricing[41] and tie-in sales.[42] Finally, explicitly coerced "joint sales" are expressly prohibited by the Bank Holding Company Act.[43]

The courts, in applying the antitrust laws, have condemned tying arrangements in cases where the tying seller is attempting to exploit its market power in the tying product to reduce competition in the tied-product market. For the arrangement to be considered a legal constraint of trade, however, the seller must have market power in the tying-product market, and there must be a substantial threat that the tying seller will be able to acquire additional market power in the tied-product market by harming existing competitors or creating barriers to entry.[44]

The Supreme Court's view of predatory pricing is best captured by the following comment in *Matsushita Electric Industrial Co., Ltd.*, where it concludes that predatory pricing schemes are unlikely to succeed in reducing competition.[45] The court's view is based upon the reasoning that, for a predatory pricing scheme to be rational, a predator must maintain monopoly power in the target market long enough both to recoup its (investment) losses and to harvest additional gain. There is no assurance, however, that the hoped-for monopoly power will materialize. Indeed, to recoup its losses and gain additional profits the predator will have to set and maintain supracompetitive prices, which will attract new entrants and competitors. Thus, unless rather special conditions prevent entry into the target market, the court is unlikely to find a predatory pricing scheme to be injurious of competition.[46]

Thus, the present antitrust laws are as applicable to unfair competitive practices perpetrated by banks and financial institutions as they are to nonfinancial firms. A comparison of the legal standards imposed by these laws with our economic analyses of tie-in sales and predatory pricing schemes also reveals that these standards are consistent with sound economic analysis. We have, therefore, no reason to develop a separate body of law applicable only to banks and financial institutions. The continued application of the antitrust laws to banks and financial institutions will amply protect the public welfare.

Summary and Recommendations

Recent structural changes in financial markets have raised some concern that the ultimate result of these changes will be fewer and larger financial institutions that operate in more concentrated and therefore less competitive markets. This study has evaluated the concerns commonly associated with concentrated financial markets and with either large financial institutions or large banks. In particular, it analyzes the likely effects of the envisioned structural changes on competition in financial markets and examines several issues associated with either concentrated markets or larger firm (or bank) size: conflicts of interest, soundness of the financial system, the political power of financial institutions, and the allocation of credit. Current competition policy, as represented by our various regulatory and antitrust standards, is also reviewed and evaluated.

My major conclusions are:

1. Concentration in *relevant* product and geographical markets is unlikely to increase. While there will be fewer total banks and financial institutions in the nation, the number of competitors may well increase in relevant markets.

2. Competition will increase, not decrease. Concentration will decline in relevant markets, and, most important, entry barriers will fall because of diminished regulatory constraints. As a result, competition in financial markets will be more vigorous than ever.

3. The fear that large, multiproduct financial institutions, especially banks, will use tie-in sales and predatory pricing strategies to constrain competition is unfounded. The market conditions under which such strategies can be effective will be eroded, not enhanced, by the current evolution in financial markets. Further, present anti-

trust laws and competitive standards provide a sufficient safeguard against abusive tying and predatory pricing strategies.

4. The present regulatory standards and antitrust laws applicable to mergers among financial institutions provide a sufficient safeguard against mergers that would significantly restrain competition. If anything, the acceptable concentration-ratio (or Herfindahl-Hirschman index) levels specified in the current Antitrust Guidelines are unnecessarily restrictive for the maintenance of competitive markets, and the importance attached to potential entry is too little.

5. The existence of large, multiproduct financial institutions will not exacerbate the conflict-of-interest problem. Indeed, with more competitive markets and better information, there will be less need for concern.

6. A financial system populated by large banks and financial institutions is likely to be more stable than the one we now have. There is no evidence to support the contrary view.

7. While the potential political power of large banks and financial institutions is of concern, no evidence suggests that large firms, or firms that operate in concentrated markets, have unusual political power. Existing empirical studies have not been able to discover a relationship between either firm size or concentration and political influence. Further, it is not clear why large financial institutions or large banks should be treated differently from other large firms. If there is a reason to impose restrictions on size or concentration out of a fear of excessive political power, such a policy should be extended to all firms and markets, not just to financial institutions or banks.

8. The argument that the development of large banks and financial institutions will have an adverse effect on the allocation of credit is without substance. We have, in the first place, no reason to think that the overall allocation of credit in the country is affected by the size of banks or financial institutions. Second, the development of large, multiproduct, multiregional institutions should make credit markets even more nearly perfect than they already are. If there is a reallocation of credit, therefore, it is likely to be market driven. Thus, if credit reallocation occurs, it should increase welfare, not reduce it.

9. Finally, no purpose seems to be served by continuing the bureaucratic and costly review process now used to evaluate the competitive effects of bank and thrift institution mergers. The process should be simplified so that such mergers need only meet the tests imposed by the antitrust laws.

Appendix A

TABLE A-1
Shares of Total Domestic Deposits and Assets of the Ten Largest Bank Holding Companies, 1984

	Domestic Deposit Rank	Domestic Deposits (billions of dollars)	Shares of Total (%)	Domestic Asset Rank	Domestic Assets (billions of dollars)	Shares of Total (%)
All commercial banks		1,727.1	100.0		1,956.9	100.0
Ten largest companies		286.3	16.6		449.1	22.9
BankAmerica Corp.	1	68.0	3.9	1	82.3	4.2
Citicorp	2	37.1	2.1	2	76.2	3.9
First Interstate Bancorp	3	31.8	1.8	4	40.8	2.1
Chase Manhattan Corp.	4	30.2	1.7	3	51.6	2.6
Security Pacific Corp.	5	24.1	1.4	8	32.7	1.7
Manufacturers Hanover	6	23.9	1.4	5	39.1	2.0
Chemical N.Y. Corp.	7	22.6	1.3	7	37.9	1.9
Wells Fargo & Co.	8	18.5	1.1			
J. P. Morgan & Co.	9	15.2	0.9	6	38.1	1.9
First Chicago Corp.	10	14.9	0.9	9	25.9	1.3
Bankers Trust N.Y. Corp.				10	24.5	1.3

Sources: Federal Reserve Board, BHC Financial Data, December 31, 1984, and flow of funds accounts as of December 31, 1984.

THE FUTURE FINANCIAL STRUCTURE

TABLE A–2
Assets of the Ten Largest U.S. Financial Enterprises,
Year-End 1985
(billions of U.S. dollars)

	Assets
Citicorp	173.6
BankAmerica Corp.	118.5
Federal National Mortgage Association	99.1
Prudential Insurance	91.1
Salomon Bros., Inc.	88.6
Chase Manhattan Corp.	87.7
Manufacturers Hanover	76.5
Metropolitan Life	76.5
GMAC	75.4
American Express	74.8

NOTE: Domestic assets of these companies are smaller than their total assets, and for bank holding companies domestic assets are relatively smaller than for the other firms.
SOURCE: *Fortune,* June 9, 1986, pp. 122–35.

TABLE A–3
Shares of Total Industry Capital of
the Ten Largest Securities Firms, 1984

	Capital (millions of dollars)	Share (%)
All firms	11,609.4	100.0
Ten largest firms	6,313.5	54.4
Merrill Lynch & Co., Inc.	1,685.3	14.5
Salomon Bros., Inc.	1,051.1	9.1
Shearson/American Express Inc.	836.6	7.2
E. F. Hutton Group Inc.	608.1	5.2
Goldman, Sachs & Co.	478.0	4.1
Prudential-Bache Securities Inc.	442.9	3.8
First Boston, Inc.	321.1	2.8
Paine Webber Incorporated	313.7	2.7
Dean Witter Reynolds Inc.	300.9	2.6
Bear, Stearns & Co.	275.8	2.4
Total number of firms	339	

SOURCE: *Institutional Investor* (April 1984), pp. 267–69.

TABLE A-4
Ten Largest U.S. Mutual Fund Managers, 1986

	Billions of Dollars	Percentage of Total Industry
Merrill Lynch Asset Management Inc.	64.7	10.0
Fidelity Investments	53.7	8.3
Federated Investors Corp.	38.8	6.0
Dreyfus Corp.	37.5	5.8
Franklin Resources	29.7	4.6
Shearson/Lehman Bros. Inc.	29.7	4.6
Dean Witter Reynolds	29.1	4.5
Vanguard Group	25.2	3.9
Kemper Financial Services	23.9	3.7
Putnam Management Co.	20.0	3.1

SOURCE: "The 1986 Annual Mutual Fund Survey," *Forbes*, September 8, 1986, pp. 104–226.

TABLE A-5
Shares of Total Industry Assets of the Ten Largest Life Insurance Companies, 1984

	Assets (billions of dollars)	Shares of Total (%)
All companies	723.9	100.0
Ten largest companies	352.7	48.7
Prudential	78.9	10.9
Metropolitan	67.4	9.3
Equitable	44.5	6.1
Aetna	34.0	4.7
New York Life	25.6	3.5
John Hancock	24.7	3.4
Travelers	23.3	3.2
Connecticut General	19.2	2.7
Teachers	19.2	2.7
Northwestern Mutual	15.9	2.2

SOURCES: *Life Insurance Fact Book*, 1985; *A. M. Best's Guide to Life Insurance Companies—1985 Edition*; and *Fortune*, June 10, 1986, pp. 188–89.

TABLE A–6
Shares of Total Industry Assets of the Ten Largest Property and Casualty Insurance Companies, 1984

	Assets (billions of dollars)	Shares of Total (%)
All companies	264.7	100.0
Ten largest companies	115.2	43.5
Travelers Group	31.7	11.9
State Farm Group	19.9	7.5
Aetna Life and Casualty Group	12.1	4.6
Allstate Insurance Group	11.9	4.5
CIGNA Group	10.1	3.8
Liberty Mutual Insurance Co.	8.2	3.1
Hartford Insurance Group	6.9	2.6
Continental Insurance Group	5.1	1.9
Farmers Insurance Group	4.9	1.9
Fireman's Fund (AMEX)	4.4	1.7

Sources: *1985–86 Property/Casualty Fact Book;* and *A. M. Best's Insurance Reports, P&C Companies—1985 Edition.*

TABLE A-7
Shares of Total Domestic Deposits and Assets of the Ten Largest Thrift Institutions, 1984

	Deposit Rank	Deposits (billions of dollars)	Shares of Total (%)	Asset Rank	Assets (billions of dollars)	Shares of Total (%)
All thrifts		965.1	100.0		1,181.3	100.0
Ten largest thrifts		120.7	12.5		158.1	13.4
American S&L Assn., Calif.	1	20.3	2.1	1	28.9	2.4
Home Savings of America, Calif.	2	18.6	1.9	2	23.7	2.0
Great Western Savings, Calif.	3	16.7	1.7	3	21.7	1.8
California FS&L, Calif.	4	14.3	1.5	4	17.7	1.5
PSFS, Philadelphia, Pa.	5	11.0	1.1	5	13.7	1.2
Goldome FSB, Buffalo, N.Y.	6	9.8	1.0	7	11.2	0.9
Glendale FS&L, Calif.	7	8.9	0.9	6	11.7	1.0
World Savings FS&L, Calif.	8	7.5	0.8	8	10.6	0.9
Empire of America FSB	9	6.9	0.7			
Home FS&L, Calif.	10	6.7	0.7			
First Federal of Michigan				9	9.5	0.8
First Nationwide S&L, Calif.				10	9.4	0.8

Sources: FHLB, Combined Financial Statements, December 31, 1984; National Council of Savings Institutions, *Economic Update*, December 31, 1984; and *American Banker*, February 28, 1985.

TABLE A–8: Share of Total Industry Base of
the Ten Largest Firms, by Rank of Concentration, 1984

Industry	Number of Firms	Top Ten Share of Total (percent)	Base	Total Base (billions of dollars)
Securities	339	54.4	Capital	11.6
Life insurance	2,134	48.7	Assets	723.9
Property and casualty insurance	3,468	43.5	Assets	264.7
Commercial banks	15,000	22.9	Assets	1,956.9
		16.6	Deposits	1,727.1
Thrift institutions	3,521	13.4	Assets	1,181.3
		12.5	Deposits	965.1

SOURCES: See sources for tables A–1, A–3, A–5, A–6, and A–7.

TABLE A–9

Ten Largest Commercial Banks in the World, 1970 and 1986
(by dollar value of assets)

Bank	Rank in 1986	Rank in 1970
Ten largest in 1986		
Citicorp, United States	1	2
Dai-Ichi Bank, Japan	2	38
Fuji Bank, Japan	3	13
Sumitomo Bank, Japan	4	17
Mitsubishi Bank, Japan	5	16
Banque Nationale de Paris, France	6	15
Sanwa Bank, Japan	7	18
Credit Agricole, France	8	
BankAmerica, United States	9	1
Credit Lyonnais, France	10	21
Ten largest in 1970		
Bank America, United States	9	1
Citicorp, United States	1	2
Chase Manhattan, United States	19	3
Barclays Group, United Kingdom	16	4
Manufacturers Hanover, United States	27	5
J. P. Morgan, United States	31	6
National Westminster Bank, United Kingdom	12	7
First Interstate Bancorp, United States	53	8
Banca Nationale Del Lavoro, Italy	39	9
Chemical New York, United States	43	10

SOURCE: *Banker* (August 1986), pp. 58–70.

FRANKLIN R. EDWARDS

Appendix B: Changes in Banking Concentration, 1966–1981

Trends in Local Market Concentration. The general tendency has been for concentration (defined by concentration ratio: the three-bank deposit ratio) to decline in most local banking markets. Tables B–1, B–2, and B–3 describe the changes in concentration over the period 1966–1976 in 152 standard metropolitan statistical areas (SMSAs) and in 129 counties. The concentration data are presented separately for SMSAs and counties according to whether they are in states classified as expansion or nonexpansion states. Expansion states are those considered more liberal with respect to either bank holding company affiliates or branch offices. Tables B–1 and B–2 show that in a large majority of local banking markets there have been decreases in concentration. Further, this tendency, surprisingly, is more pronounced in markets in nonexpansion states.

TABLE B–1

NUMBER OF SMSAs WITH CHANGES IN CONCENTRATION IN EXPANSION AND NONEXPANSION STATES, 1966–1976

	Number of SMSAs in Expansion States with Changes in Concentration Ratio			Number of SMSAs in Nonexpansion States with Changes in Concentration Ratio		
	Increases	Decreases	None	Increases	Decreases	None
1966–70	15	86	1	7	41	2
1970–76	22	79	1	5	45	0
1966–76	16	86	0	2	48	0

SOURCES: Steven A. Rhoades, "Geographic Expansion of Banks and Changes in Banking Structure," Staff Memorandum (Washington, D.C.: Board of Governors of the Federal Reserve System, 1979); and idem, "Size and Rank Stability of the 100 Largest Commercial Banks, 1925–1978," *Journal of Economics and Business*, vol. 34, no. 2 (1982), pp. 123–28.

Table B–3 shows the magnitude of changes in local market concentration that have occurred between 1966 and 1976. While the changes in expansion and nonexpansion states are quite similar, nonexpansion states show a somewhat larger decrease.

TABLE B–2
NUMBER OF COUNTIES WITH CHANGES IN CONCENTRATION IN
EXPANSION AND NONEXPANSION STATES, 1966–1976

	Number of Non-SMSA Counties in Expansion States with Changes in Concentration Ratio			*Number of Non-SMSA Counties in Nonexpansion States with Changes in Concentration Ratio*		
	Increases	Decreases	None	Increases	Decreases	None
1966–70	15	32	6	18	45	13
1970–76	13	32	8	11	57	8
1966–76	15	34	4	11	58	7

SOURCES: Same as sources for table B–1.

TABLE B–3
AVERAGE CHANGE IN CONCENTRATION IN SMSAs AND COUNTIES IN
EXPANSION AND NONEXPANSION STATES, 1966–1976

	Average Change in SMSA Concentration Ratio		*Average Change in Non-SMSA County Concentration Ratio*	
	Expansion states	Nonexpansion states	Expansion states	Nonexpansion states
1966–70	−2.37	−2.71	−1.12	−1.05
1970–76	−4.02	−4.88	−1.89	−2.63
1966–76	−6.39	−7.60	−3.01	−3.69

SOURCE: Rhoades, "Geographic Expansion."

Table B-4 shows the average percentage changes in local market concentration separately for all states for the period 1966–1981. The mean decrease in the concentration ratio is 10.28 percent. Thus concentration is clearly declining in local banking markets.

TABLE B-4
Average and Average Percentage Change in Concentration Ratio in SMSAs and Selected Counties, by State, 1966–1981
(commercial banks only)

	\multicolumn{3}{c}{Average Concentration}	\multicolumn{3}{c}{Average Percentage Change[a]}
	1966	1973	1981	1966–73	1973–81	1966–81
Alabama	83.5	77.3	72.5	−7.5	−6.2	−13.2
Alaska	96.6	89.8	71.7	−7.1	−20.1	−25.8
Arizona	91.9	89.9	86.4	−2.2	−3.9	−6.0
Arkansas	81.9	79.7	79.0	−2.6	−0.9	−3.5
California	79.2	73.4	68.3	−7.3	−6.9	−13.7
Colorado	76.9	71.7	67.1	−6.8	−6.4	−12.8
Connecticut	85.3	79.5	73.7	−6.8	−7.3	−13.6
District of Columbia	41.6	38.3	38.5	−8.0	0.4	−7.6
Florida	65.9	62.0	54.6	−5.9	−11.9	−17.1
Georgia	91.8	86.0	83.6	−6.4	−2.7	−9.0
Hawaii	78.0	74.5	77.2	−4.5	3.6	−1.1
Idaho	93.7	88.6	82.1	−5.4	−7.3	−12.3
Illinois	63.7	59.4	55.8	−6.7	−6.2	−12.4
Indiana	80.3	78.0	76.2	−2.8	−2.4	−5.1
Iowa	77.5	74.7	73.5	−3.7	−1.6	−5.2
Kansas	76.8	68.8	66.9	−10.4	−2.7	−12.9
Kentucky	84.4	82.9	81.2	−1.8	−2.1	−3.8
Louisiana	85.8	81.9	76.8	−4.5	−6.3	−10.5
Maine	95.9	92.9	95.5	−3.2	2.9	−0.4
Maryland	55.1	51.0	51.0	−7.4	0.1	−7.3
Massachusetts	82.6	80.5	77.2	−2.5	−4.2	−6.6
Michigan	82.2	78.6	76.3	−4.4	−2.8	−7.1
Minnesota	69.8	67.2	63.7	−3.7	−5.3	−8.8
Mississippi	96.0	93.2	87.9	−2.9	−5.7	−8.4
Missouri	67.9	64.3	63.8	−5.4	−0.8	−6.1
Montana	96.7	90.7	87.8	−6.2	−3.1	−9.1
Nebraska	89.8	84.0	76.2	−6.4	−9.3	−15.1
Nevada	93.7	90.0	84.9	−4.0	−5.7	−9.4
New Hampshire	92.3	89.9	75.9	−2.6	−15.5	−17.7
New Jersey	66.9	61.2	59.1	−8.5	−3.4	−11.6

(Table continues)

THE FUTURE FINANCIAL STRUCTURE

TABLE B–4 (continued)

	Average Concentration			Average Percentage Change[a]		
	1966	1973	1981	1966–73	1973–81	1966–81
New Mexico	99.0	96.6	87.8	−2.4	−9.0	−11.3
New York	80.8	77.8	71.1	−3.7	−8.6	−12.0
North Carolina	84.9	76.6	72.9	−9.7	−4.8	−14.0
North Dakota	79.8	77.2	73.3	−3.3	−5.1	−8.2
Ohio	74.4	72.1	72.5	−3.1	0.5	−2.6
Oklahoma	77.7	73.3	66.7	−5.7	−9.0	−14.2
Oregon	91.1	87.5	77.0	−4.0	−11.9	−15.4
Pennsylvania	64.2	65.3	64.8	1.7	−0.8	0.9
Rhode Island	97.0	93.2	79.5	−3.9	−14.7	−18.1
South Carolina	75.5	59.4	57.5	−21.3	−3.1	−23.8
South Dakota	85.7	84.4	74.5	−1.6	−11.6	−13.0
Tennesssee	76.7	71.6	64.5	−6.7	−9.9	−15.9
Texas	78.6	75.8	70.2	−3.5	−7.4	−10.6
Utah	58.8	62.2	54.6	5.9	−12.2	−7.0
Virginia	66.4	62.5	60.8	−5.9	−2.8	−8.5
Washington	83.8	81.2	77.6	−3.0	−4.5	−7.4
West Virginia	76.8	74.5	67.4	−2.9	−9.6	−12.2
Wisconsin	64.6	59.6	58.1	−7.8	−2.6	−10.2
Wyoming	96.5	95.9	90.0	−0.6	−6.2	−6.8

NOTE: Data for Delaware and Vermont were not available.
a. These percentage changes cannot be calculated from the data on the left side of the table. The changes shown are based on the average of the changes in individual markets.
SOURCE: Same as source for table B–3.

Trends in Statewide Concentration. The data summarized in table B–5 indicate a general tendency for statewide concentration to increase in expansion states. For the period 1960–1977, more than two-thirds (or fourteen) of the expansion states experienced an increase in statewide concentration as measured by the concentration ratio. Only twelve of twenty-eight nonexpansion states had increases in concentration during the same period.

TABLE B-5
Number of Expansion and Nonexpansion States with Changes in Concentration, 1960–1977

	Number of Expansion States with Changes in Concentration Ratio		Number of Nonexpansion States with Changes in Concentration Ratio	
	Increases	Decreases	Increases	Decreases
1960–70	11	9	10	18
1970–77	12	8	11	17
1960–77	14	6	12	16

Source: Rhoades, "Size and Rank Stability."

Trends in Nationwide Concentration. Analysis of trends in nationwide concentration indicates the following:

• Concentration of deposits in the largest 100 banks increased from 33.7 percent in 1925 to 51.4 percent in 1978 (see table B–6).
• Deposits have become increasingly concentrated *within* the top 100 banks (see table B–7).
• The pattern of changes and the absolute levels of concentration for the 100 largest banks are very similar to what has occurred for the 100 largest industrial firms over the same period.

TABLE B-6
Commercial Bank Deposits Accounted for by the 100 Largest Banks, 1925–1978
(percent)

	Deposits Held by 100 Largest[a]	Year	Deposits Held by 100 Largest[a]
1925	33.7	1953	45.1
1928	39.3	1958	46.3 (49.0)
1933	52.4	1963	47.4 (50.1)
1938	53.3	1968	48.2 (50.8)
1943	51.4	1973	49.6 (54.0)
1948	44.5	1978	51.4 (55.4)

a. Concentration ratios for 1925–1978 are based on foreign and domestic deposits for the 100 largest banks, *not* banking organizations. For the period 1958–1978 it was possible to construct deposit data for banking organizations, and the concentration ratios based on these data are shown in parentheses beginning with 1958.

Source: Same as source for table B–5.

TABLE B-7
Percentage of the Largest 100 Banks' Deposits Accounted for by Different Groups, 1925–1978

	Top 5	Top 6–10	Top 11–25	Top 26–50	Top 51–75	Top 76–100
1925	19	12	24	22	13	10
1928	23	14	23	20	12	8
1933	28	16	22	17	10	7
1938	30	15	23	15	10	7
1943	30	14	22	17	10	7
1948	30	13	22	16	11	8
1953	29	14	20	18	11	8
1958	31	13	20	17	11	8
1963	33	14	20	15	10	9
1968	33	14	20	16	10	7
1973	35	16	21	14	8	6
1978	36	15	18	13	7	6

Source: Same as source for table B-5.

Notes

1. See, for example, S. Peltzman, "Capital Investment in Commercial Banking and Its Relationship to Portfolio Regulation," *Journal of Political Economy* (1970), pp. 1–26; and F. Edwards, "Managerial Objectives in Regulated Industries: Expense Preference Behavior in Banking," *Journal of Political Economy*, vol. 85, no. 1 (February 1977), pp. 147–62.

2. There are several alternative measures of concentration used in the academic literature and in antitrust proceedings. While these can sometimes render different impressions of a particular market, they are not critical to the discussion in this paper.

3. This point has been amply discussed in the academic literature. The main papers are J. C. Panzar and R. D. Willig, "Free Entry and the Sustainability of Natural Monopoly," *Bell Journal of Economics*, vol. 67 (1977), pp. 1–22; W. J. Baumol, E. E. Bailey, and R. D. Willig, "Weak Invisible Hand Theorems on the Sustainability of Prices in a Multiproduct Natural Monopoly," *American Economic Review*, vol. 67 (1977), pp. 360–65; J. C. Panzar, and R. D. Willig, "Economies of Scale in Multi-Output Production," *Quarterly Journal of Economics* (1977), pp. 481–94.

4. W. J. Baumol, "On the Proper Cost Tests for Natural Monopoly in a Multiproduct Industry," *American Economic Review*, vol. 67 (1977), pp. 811–22; R. D. Willig, "Multiproduct Technology and Market Structure," *American Economic Review*, vol. 69 (1979), pp. 346–51; R. D. Willig and W. J. Baumol, "Intertemporal Unsustainability," ms., 1980; E. E. Bailey, "Contestability and the Design of Regulatory and Antitrust Policy," ms., 1980; and W. J. Baumol,

J. C. Panzar, and R. D. Willig, *Contestable Markets and the Theory of Industry Structure* (San Diego, Calif.: Harcourt Brace Jovanovich, 1982).

5. See appendix A, table A-1.
6. See appendix A, tables A-2 through A-8.
7. See appendix A, table A-9.
8. See appendix B, tables B-1 through B-7.
9. See note 3.
10. See, for example, the BankAmerica-Schwab decision by the Federal Reserve Board, January 7, 1983.
11. This was the view taken by the Federal Reserve Board in BankAmerica-Schwab, p. 111.
12. Jefferson Parish Hospital District No. 2 et al. v. Hyde, 466 U.S.2, at 33.
13. U.S. Congress, House of Representatives, Committee on Banking and Currency, "The Growth of Unregistered Bank Holding Companies—Problems and Prospects," Staff Report of the House Committee on Banking and Currency, 91st Congress, 1st session, February 11, 1969.
14. Testimony of W. Martin before House Committee on Banking and Currency on H.R. 9385 and H.R. 6778, *Federal Reserve Bulletin*, vol. 55, no. 4, p. 334.
15. 12 U.S.C. 1972-1978.
16. Northern Pacific R. Co., 356 U.S. at 6.
17. Ibid.
18. Cargill, Inc. et al. v. Monfort of Colorado, U.S. Court of Appeals, 10th Circuit, December 9, 1986, no. 85-473, at 12.
19. Matsushita Electric Industrial Co., Ltd. et al. v. Zenith Radio Corp. et al., U.S. Court of Appeals, 3rd Circuit, no. 83-2004, decided March 26, 1986, at 14.
20. For another analysis of conflicts of interest, see A. Saunders, "Conflicts of Interest: An Economic View," in I. Walter, ed., *Deregulating Wall Street: Commercial Bank Penetration of the Corporate Securities Market* (New York: John Wiley & Sons, 1985), pp. 207-30.
21. See G. Kaufman, "Implications of Large Bank Problems and Insolvencies for the Banking System and Economic Policy," Staff Memorandum, SM-85-3 (Chicago: Federal Reserve Bank of Chicago).
22. See George Benston and George Kaufman, "Regulating Bank Safety and Performance," Chapter 3 in this volume.
23. See Anna Schwartz, "Financial Stability and the Federal Safety Net," chap. 2 in this volume.
24. David Vogel, "A Case Study of Clean Air Legislation 1967-81," in B. Block, ed., *The Impact of the Modern Corporation* (New York: Columbia University Press, 1984).
25. L. E. Birdzell, "The Conglomerates: A Neighbor's View," vol. 44, *St. John's Law Review* (1970), p. 314.
26. Richard Posner, "Power in America: The Role of the Large Corporation," in J. F. Weston, ed., *Large Corporations in a Changing Society*, 1975, p. 99.
27. E. Epstein, "Firm Size and Structure, Market Power, and Business Political Influence: A Review of the Literature," in J. Siegfried, ed., *The*

THE FUTURE FINANCIAL STRUCTURE

Economics of Firm Size, Market Structure, and Social Performance (Washington, D.C.: Federal Trade Commission, 1980), pp. 240–81.

28. John T. Rose, "Industry Concentration and Political Leverage: An Empirical Test" (Washington, D.C.: Board of Governors of the Federal Reserve System, unpublished, 1976).

29. L. Edwards and F. Edwards, "Differential State Regulation of Consumer Credit Markets: Normative and Positive Theories of Statutory Interest Rate Ceilings," *Proceedings on Bank Structure and Competition*, Federal Reserve Bank of Chicago, April 22–28, 1978, pp. 202–36.

30. "The 'Nonbank' Threat Is Real," *Washington Post*, March 10, 1987.

31. In describing this process, I have relied extensively on a lucid exposition of the relevant issues by Robert Hauberg, Jr., assistant chief of the Antitrust Division, in a speech entitled "Mergers and Acquisitions of Depository Institutions," presented to the American Bar Association, May 23, 1985, Washington, D.C.

32. Letter from Charles F. Rule, acting assistant attorney general, to C. Todd Conover, comptroller of the currency, *First National Bank of Jackson Brookhaven Bank and Trust Company* (February 8, 1985); Letter from Charles F. Rule, acting assistant attorney general, to William M. Issac, chairman, Federal Deposit Insurance Corporation, *Indian Head Bank—Whitefield Savings Bank and Trust Company* (April 29, 1985); Letter from Charles F. Rule, acting assistant attorney general, to Paul A. Volcker, chairman, Board of Governors of the Federal Reserve System, *Savers Bancorp, Inc.—North Country Bank* (May 15, 1985).

33. See, for example, Rosenblum, DiClemente, and O'Brien, "On Banks, Nonbanks and Overlapping Markets: A Reassessment of Commercial Banking as a Line of Commerce," *Tennessee Law Review*, vol. 51(1984), p. 401; FRB decision in Bancorp Hawis, Inc January 24, 1985.

34. U.S. v. Marine Bancorporation, 418 U.S. 602, 631–32 (1974).

35. U.S. v. Third National Bank in Nashville, 390 U.S. 171, 187–89 (1968).

36. 26 Stat. 209 (1890), as amended, 15 U.S.C. 1 (1958). They may not be subject to section 3 of the Clayton Act, since this law covers only transactions involving "goods, wares, merchandise, machinery, supplies, or other commodities," 15 U.S.C. 14 (1958). Anticompetitive practices involving "services," therefore, may escape coverage. In U.S. v. Investors Diversified Services (102) F. Supp. 645, D. Minn., 1951), for example, a tie-in sale of loans with insurance was found to be beyond the reach of section 3.

37. See Jefferson Parish Hospital District No. 2 et al. v. Hyde, 466 U.S. 2 (1984); Cargill, Inc. et al. v. Monfort of Colorado, Inc., 761 F. 2d 570, reversed by S. Ct., December 9, 1986, No. 85–473; and Matsushita Electric Industrial Co. Ltd. et al. vs. Zenith Radio Corp., et al., 723 F. 2d 288, reversed by S.Ct. on March 26, 1986, No. 83–2004.

38. 394 U.S. para. 495 (1969).

39. 12 U.S.C. 1843 (c)(8) and section 225.4 (b)(2) of the Federal Reserve Board's Regulation Y (12 CFR 225.4 [b][2]).

40. Ibid.

41. See Citicorp (Citishare), *Federal Reserve Bulletin*, vol. 68, p. 505, para. 5112 (1982).
42. BankAmerica-Schwab, *Federal Reserve Bulletin*, vol. 105 p. 112 (1983).
43. 12 U.S.C. 1972–1978.
44. Jefferson Parish Hospital at 12–14; and Fortner I at 509.
45. See note 14.
46. See notes 15 and 16.

5
Bank Holding Companies: Structure, Performance, and Reform

Anthony Saunders

Until the passage of the Competitive Equality Bank Act of 1987 (P.L. 100-86), some progress had been made toward breaking down barriers limiting commercial bank affiliations with commercial firms, retailers, and other financial service firms. The main mechanism by which this was achieved was the establishment of nonbank banks, formed by exploiting a loophole in the Bank Holding Company Act. After opposition from the Federal Reserve,[1] this loophole was closed in the 1987 Bank Act.[2] At the same time the act placed a moratorium on bank holding companies' new securities, insurance, and real estate activities until March 1988.

Although this moratorium has now expired and the prospect that Congress will soon allow banks to engage in a full set of investment banking activities is good, a similar degree of optimism cannot be shared for the prospect of eliminating the barriers to affiliation among commercial banks and insurance companies on the one hand or among commercial banks and commercial firms on the other.

One of the central issues in this continuing debate over potential bank affiliations with firms such as Sears, J. C. Penney, American Express, and Prudential-Bache is the degree to which commercial banks provide a unique or special set of services to the economy and the extent to which this specialness would be endangered by a holding company dominated by commercial or retail activities. That is, would eliminating the post-1970 policy of constraining bank holding company activities to those "closely related to banking" weaken or enhance the specialness (if any) of bank services within a holding company framework? If, indeed, banks do provide socially valuable services that would be materially threatened by the commercial, retail, or other financial activities of holding company affiliates, a case could be made for continuing the traditional separation of banking and commerce. But if such a case cannot be adequately established, continuing this separation may well have greater costs than benefits. That is, there may be no valid public policy rationale for regulating the nonbanking activities of bank holding companies.

The next section discusses the question of bank uniqueness or specialness in the context of views expressed by representatives of the Federal Reserve as well as by academics. This chapter then examines the potential benefits and costs (risks) caused by bank affiliation with nonbank firms through a holding company structure and the special problems that might arise should some of these affiliates be firms engaged in commercial activities. Finally, it analyzes the corporate and banking organizational structures that might arise in a fully deregulated environment as alternatives to the one-bank holding company. These alternative structures include the universal bank and the 100 percent reserve bank.

The Unique or Special Functions of Banks

The Federal Reserve's thinking on the specialness of banks is summarized in works by Paul Volcker and E. Gerald Corrigan.[3] The issue of specialness concerns the special value of the banking system's and banking industry's aggregate supply of services (and the costs of interference with these services) compared with the social value of output and services of other sectors. Would, for example, a major destruction of the supply of bank services incur more social welfare costs than the destruction of the rail network? Corrigan identifies three services or characteristics that distinguish banks from other firms: (1) banks offer transaction accounts; (2) banks are the backup source of liquidity for all other economic institutions; and (3) banks are the transmission belt of monetary policy. Of the three, Corrigan argues, "the single characteristic of banks that distinguishes them from other classes of institution is that they issue transaction accounts: that is accounts that in law, in regulation, or in practice are payable on demand at par and are readily transferable to third parties."[4]

The special role of transaction account deposit contracts has generated considerable interest in the recent banking theory literature.[5] In these heavily stylized models, banks provide a market or institutional arrangement capable of dealing with the uninsurable liquidity risks facing endowment-constrained individuals by supplying instantaneously putable fixed-priced contracts instead of mutual fund shares that fluctuate with asset values. Tim Campbell, Charles Jacklin, and Joseph Haubrich and Robert King have emphasized, however, that the specialness of the insurance services provided by bank deposit contracts depends heavily on specific assumptions made for each model.[6] The social welfare improvement associated with deposit contracts is accomplished through a payoff structure that (1) is *expected* to return more than the illiquid investment-asset hoard choices available in a world without deposit contracts, such as cash or commodities, and (2) ensures that depositors without immediate liquidity needs find it advantageous not to engage in a bank "run" as long as confidence in the bank is maintained. This confidence factor is important since lack of confidence in uninsured bank deposit contracts can also cause bank runs. Runs can occur because the demand for deposit withdrawals derives not only from valid liquidity needs, but also from new information or fear of bank insolvency. In a run, even those depositors who rationally would prefer not to withdraw early (that is, those who have no liquidity need) find it optimal to withdraw. Depositors may be uncertain about a bank's asset quality or the withdrawal needs of others, about costs of early liquidation of security portfolios or of the interruption of real investment projects, or about the banks' practice of sequential servicing in honoring deposit redemption. Since the aggregate promised par value of deposits may exceed the liquidation value of the asset portfolio, runs may be privately rational since a depositor's place in line determines his payoff.[7] Because of the run, productive investment is interrupted, and the risk-sharing efficiencies of the deposit contract arrangement are destroyed. Thus, in contrast to the deposit contract that improves welfare with no run, the run makes everyone worse off.

Although these models provide some useful insights into the social value of transaction accounts, there is often an unfortunate tendency to extrapolate these findings on bank runs into positive policy implications. In particular, the social cost of a run on an individual bank is often viewed as being identical to the cost of a run on the banking system as a whole. One of the principal reasons for this is that these bank-run models usually assume a single representative bank, so that a run on an individual bank is a run on the whole system. Moreover, the alternative assets to "run to" are usually heavily circumscribed—largely being limited to real assets (the consumption good) or currency or both.[8] If one were to relax these assumptions and allow for a multibank system with a rich array of financial assets, then an individual bank run (barring any major contagion effect) might have very little effect on the aggregate supply of transaction accounts.

In a recent study, George Kaufman analyzed the effects of individual bank runs in such an economy.[9] He argues that most runs on individual banks would result in a simple process of redepositing from unsound to sound banks. More serious individual runs might also be met by a partial flight into quality assets such as Treasury bills with a resultant adjustment in yield spreads between deposit claims and such assets. Again, however, the aggregate stock of transaction accounts would not be significantly affected. Only in the extreme case of multiple or contagious bank runs where the public chooses to hold currency in open preference to bank deposits would there probably be a classic contraction in the aggregate quantity of transaction accounts. Yet even in this case, as long as the Federal Reserve provides sufficient funds through the discount window or open-market operations, the multiple contraction of transaction accounts can still be avoided. Thus, as Anna Schwartz notes, the ultimate cause of a major contraction in bank deposits is not multiple runs per se but rather inappropriate or ineffective Federal Reserve monetary policy.[10]

The growth of electronic funds transfer systems (EFTS) such as Fedwire, CHIPS, SWIFT, ACHs, and ATMs has accentuated the social welfare importance of the electronic settlement of transactions in the economy. (Fedwire is the Federal Reserve wire system; CHIPS is the Clearing House Interbank Payments System; SWIFT is the Society for Worldwide Interbank Financial Telecommunication; ACH is automated clearinghouse; and ATM is automated teller machine.) Hans Angermueller, extrapolating from the work of David Humphrey, reports, for example, estimates showing that the combined daily transaction volume on Fedwire and CHIPS was $860 billion in 1986, compared with $120 billion for checks.[11] The role of banks in supplying transaction account services that permit an efficient transfer of purchasing power is logically independent of the role of currency as the *numeraire* in the economy—a unit of account that can be exchanged or converted at par with bank deposits.[12] This independence is not clearly evident in the quotation from Corrigan above. Even in a hypothetical nonmonetary economic system, for example, where some commodity other than currency acts as the *numeraire*, "banks" may still play a role as transactions agents. As Fama argues, the only major difference is that debits and credits would be calculated in units of the new *numeraire*, and the ability of banks to maintain their transactions agency function would depend on the efficiency with which they transferred wealth between economic agents (whether electronically or otherwise) and the confidence these agents had in the integrity of banks in accomplishing this task.

Thus in a fully electronic or quasi-monetary economy, doubts or crises of confidence on the part of wealth holders regarding the integrity of the transactions mechanism as a whole may also have severe economic consequences beyond the banking system.[13]

While most academic research has evaluated bank specialness from the perspective of the liability or deposit side of the balance sheet, increasing attention is being paid to the specialness of banks as sources of liquidity (or, in Corrigan's terminology, as backup suppliers of credit to other sectors of the economy). Ben Bernanke has argued that, in a world of incomplete capital markets, bank failures may have serious effects on real investment and national income.[14] In particular, bank failures decrease the effective supply of credit intermediation services and increase the real cost of credit intermediation to firms. Moreover, asset portfolio adjustment policies pursued by surviving banks during periods of failure or crisis, such as increasing their share of low-risk liquid government securities at the expense of loans, exacerbate the effects of bank failures on credit supply and therefore on real investment. Bernanke, supported by empirical evidence, goes on to argue that it was not so much deposit or money supply contraction that was the cause of the Great Depression but rather the contraction in the supply of credit to the real sector of the economy.

Fama has also argued that bank loans are special.[15] Specifically, banks, by granting new loans or renewing lines of credit, are conveying important information to the market at large. In Fama's framework, banks are insiders while other investors and creditors are outsiders. As insiders, a status developed through long-term relationships and close monitoring of firms over time, banks have access to information that may be either unavailable to outsiders or too costly for them to obtain. Since loan defaults are costly, renewing a loan or granting a line of credit at market rates conveys a positive signal to outside investors regarding the riskiness of the firm and its attractiveness as an investment prospect. Fama presents empirical evidence showing that, on average, large bank certificates of deposit, which provide no transaction services, yield the same average rate as prime commercial paper issues.[16] Fama infers from this that borrowers, through the loan rate, are willing to pay the reserve tax on deposits on behalf of the bank (and its depositors) in return for a favorable loan renewal signal.

It might be argued that there is nothing unique in this bank function since insurance companies perform a similar signaling function through the private debt placement market. In a recent study Christopher James analyzed the response of the stock market and equity prices to commercial firm announcements of new bank loan agreements, new private placements, and publicly placed straight debt issues.[17] He found that public announcements of new loan agreements produced a significantly positive increase in equity prices (returns) for these firms at the time of the announcement, after adjustment for market risk. By comparison, he found a significant negative stock price response for his sample of private placements and an insignificant negative response for straight debt issues. These results are consistent with banks' providing a special service on the asset side of the balance sheet. Nevertheless, the apparent inconsistency of this evidence with the falling volume of loans relative to commercial paper and bonds in corporate capital structures is puzzling. That is, if loans provide such good signals, why has there been a decline in loan demand?

Even accepting the validity of the argument that loan information is a valuable signal, care has to be taken not to extrapolate major social welfare implications from individual bank and borrower activity. The failure of an individual bank today may have little effect on medium-sized and large borrowers with multiple lines of credit across banks and residual access to the commercial paper market. At worst, the borrowers most likely to be hurt would be relatively small and located in isolated towns or communities where regional monopoly power has been conferred on those banks by the state and federal chartering authorities. These circumstances suggest that restrictions on chartering (and branching) may be at least partly to blame for any social costs relating to local bank failures.

The logic behind Corrigan's description of banks as the transmission belt for monetary policy is that the government issues only a small proportion of the total money supply—namely, currency or notes and coin (so-called outside money)—which can be exchanged at par for deposits issued by commercial banks (so-called inside money). It is argued that the growth of the quantity of inside money needs to be constrained; otherwise, banks acting under competitive pressures could simply expand the supply of inside money to accommodate private sector demand. Unimpeded, this process might eventually result in price-level indeterminacy.

One mechanism by which the growth of inside money is typically constrained is the imposition of non-interest-bearing reserve requirements on banks in the form of vault cash or deposits at the central bank. Since reserve requirements create a clearly defined demand for reserves and since the aggregate supply of reserves can be determined by the Federal Reserve through open-market operations, the quantity of inside money and of the money supply itself can potentially be controlled by the monetary authorities. In theory, however, monetary policy does not have to be carried out in precisely this manner—that is, by using banks as the transmission belt for monetary policy.

Don Patinkin, Fama, and others have noted that the minimum conditions for price-level determinacy are that the monetary authorities control one price and one quantity—for example, the price of a currency unit and the quantity of currency outstanding.[18] In such a world, the public would have a real demand for currency because of its utility or convenience in transactions, and, since inside and outside money are instantaneously convertible through the banking system, banks would find it prudent to hold some quantity of outside money as a reserve asset.[19] Given a stable demand for currency, by changing its supply the authorities can affect the price of currency relative to the price of real goods (the price level) and achieve their price-level objectives. Moreover, many neo-Keynesians would argue that in addition to affecting the price level, changing monetary policy (that is, changing the stock of high-powered money without bank regulation) can have a powerful effect on real economic activity as well.[20]

In summary, the extent to which banks are special is clearly controversial. One problem has been the tendency to exaggerate the social costs of bank failures by loosely extrapolating the effects of an individual bank failure into a potential failure of the whole system. Only rarely, however, does an individual bank failure result in major contagions and panics.[21]

Indeed, the belief that bank failure produces special welfare costs has made the ownership of banks and regulation of the nonbanking activities of bank holding companies an imperative of Federal Reserve policy.[22] Corrigan argues, for example, that there are two essential criteria for nonbanking activity to be permissible—namely, such other activities should not entail excessive risk of loss (that is, they should pose no threat to the transactions mechanism), and they should not impair the impartiality of the process for allocation of loans and credit (that is, they should not result in conflicts of interest). Volcker raises similar issues in advocating the continued separation of banking from commerce.[23] Specifically, he argues that bank linkage with commercial firms may result in (1) increased risk to the transactions/payment mechanism and the indirect extension of the federal safety net (deposit insurance and discount window) to large commercial firms; (2) increased conflicts of interest in the credit-granting mechanism; and (3) increased conglomeration of real and financial services (the market structure–monopoly power argument).

The next section examines the arguments of Corrigan and Volcker relating to the potentially adverse effects on (1) bank insolvency risk, (2) deposit insurance subsidies, (3) payments system risk, (4) conflicts of interest, and (5) excessive conglomeration that may arise from bank holding company nonbank activity extensions. If such adverse effects are found to be either negligible or manageable through appropriate regulation, then overtly restrictive policies regarding the nonbank activities of bank holding companies cannot logically be supported given the relatively weak and tenuous nature of the argument in favor of bank specialness.

The Costs and Benefits of Bank Affiliation with Holding Companies

Insolvency Risk. Analyzing whether bank affiliation with nonbank firms (including commercial firms) increases or decreases the risk of bank insolvency requires a definition of insolvency risk. The work of John Boyd and Stanley Graham among others suggests that this can be done most easily by employing a risk-of-ruin framework.[24] If $\tilde{\pi}$ is the net income or profit of a bank as a proportion of assets (or asset return) and K/A the bank's ratio of capital to assets, then the probability (P) of the bank's becoming insolvent can be expressed as $P(\tilde{\pi} < -K/A)$. If, for simplicity, it is assumed that $\tilde{\pi}$ is normally distributed with a mean μ and a standard deviation σ, then the probability of insolvency can be written as

$$P(\tilde{\pi} < -K/A) = 1 - \phi\left[(K/A + \mu)/\sigma\right]$$

where $\phi(\bullet)$ is a cumulative distribution function of a standard normal variable.[25] Thus, the probability of insolvency is lower the larger the bank's capital-assets ratio (K/A), the larger its mean return (μ), and the lower its variance or standard deviation of returns (σ). In this framework, the question whether bank affiliation with nonbank firms in a holding company increases or reduces insolvency risk can be answered by determining how the three elements μ, K/A, and σ are affected by such bank affiliation. In what follows, I attempt to analyze the effects of bank holding company formation on each element in turn. It should be recognized, however, that these variables are, in general, related. Thus, for example, increased returns may be used to build up a bank's capital base (μ and K/A positively correlated), but increased returns may have been generated only by taking greater risk exposure (μ and σ positively correlated).

Bank holding company formation and bank returns. Early studies of the effects of holding company acquisition on return performance focused mostly on the multibank holding company (MBHC). These studies usually compared the mean accounting return on assets or capital for a group of MBHC banks with a population similar in size, region, and so on to that of independent banks. The general conclusion of these univariate studies was that banks associated with holding companies earned higher returns on average.[26] Later studies, however, criticized these findings as inadequate since they failed to control systematically for other independent variables affecting returns. These multivariate studies, which usually included a dummy variable to represent holding company affiliation within a multiple regression framework, tended to produce more disparate results. Specifically, Arthur Fraas and Jack Light found that banks affiliated with holding companies had worse return performance than independent banks; John Mingo found no difference, and Lucille Mayne found superior performance.[27]

In recent years increasing attention has been paid to the impact of the formation of one-bank holding companies and to analyzing stock market returns as well as accounting returns. The general idea underlying many of the stock market studies is that if the formation of bank holding companies is a net profitable activity, this should be reflected in the behavior of returns on these banks' stocks in the market. The general methodology followed is to compare returns around the time of the announcement of an event (such as the formation of the holding company) with returns generated on these banks' stocks before the formation of the holding company. John Martin and Arthur Keown's examination of equity prices after the announcement of the transformation of independent banks to one-bank holding company (OBHC) status found that the market reacted in a significantly positive fashion (that is, significantly positive returns were earned at the time of the announcement).[28] Joseph Aharony and Itzhak Swary, and Randall Billingsley and Robert Lamy, examined the announcement of OBHC status before and after the 1970 amendments to the Bank Holding Company Act.[29] Since the 1970 amendments restricted OBHCs to a range of activities "closely related to banking," holding company formation may have been perceived as being more profitable before rather than after 1970. Although Aharony and Swary found little effect of the 1970 amendments, Billingsley and Lamy found that the OBHC announcements before 1970 had positive abnormal return effects and those after 1970 had negative return effects.[30]

Further studies have analyzed the important question whether the return performance of holding company banks is superior or inferior to that of their nonbank affiliates—since, presumably, a major objective of nonbank affiliate expansion is to earn higher returns by avoiding regulations on bank interest rates, geographic expansion, and so on (although diversification and economies of scope are other reasons, which are discussed later). Donald Jacobs, Prescott Beighley, and John Boyd found higher accounting returns on nonbank assets than on bank assets while, surprisingly, Samuel Talley and Adi Karna found lower returns.[31] Using equity returns, Anand Desai and Roger Stover found that OBHC acquisitions of nonbank affiliates resulted in positive abnormal returns, while Swary, and Anthony Saunders and Michael Smirlock, analyzing the acquisition of, respectively, mortgage bank and discount house subsidiaries, could find no significant return effects.[32] On a similar theme, two other studies have examined how OBHC returns are affected as the proportion of nonbank activities increases. The studies were conducted by regressing OBHC asset returns on the ratio of nonbank assets to total holding company assets for a sample of firms. John Boyd and Pipat Pithyachariyakul found a significantly positive effect of nonbank activities on OBHC returns, while Boyd and Graham found an insignificant relationship for sixty-four holding companies over their whole sample period, 1971–1983, but a weak positive relationship for the most recent subperiod, 1978–1983.[33]

Although in general these results suggest that holding company affiliation may have a positive effect on returns, concerns have been expressed in the literature that a large proportion of bank returns (or profits) will be "upstreamed" to strengthen or benefit the parent holding company or its nonbank affiliates rather than being used to strengthen the bank and its capital base.[34] That is, higher gross return performance does not necessarily translate into higher retained earnings and, *ceteris paribus*, a reduced risk of insolvency.

The literature identifies four potential effects of return upstreaming or dissipation: (1) excessive fee payments to the holding company and its affiliates;[35] (2) excessive dividend payments to the holding company and its affiliates; (3) transfers of bank tax shelters to the holding company and its affiliates; and (4) transfers of assets from and credit extensions to the holding company and its affiliates.

Excessive fees might be paid by the bank to the holding company for management services provided to the bank. The difference between the true cost of services and the fees charged can be used to boost holding company profits and can be redirected to other uses such as aiding a weak nonbank affiliate. Both Roger Stover and Robert Kolb report evidence showing that banks affiliated with holding companies have higher noninterest operating expenses than independent banks.[36] Similarly, consolidated reporting of profits may allow tax shelters to be transferred from the bank to the holding company while the bank upstreams tax payments to the holding company as if it were an independent bank.[37] Nevertheless, it should be noted that fees and taxes are now covered by Section 23B regulations on inter-affiliate transactions (see below). Excessive dividends might also be paid to the holding company and then passed through to nonbank affiliates. Kolb, Stover, and Mayne all report evidence that holding company banks pay higher dividends than independent banks. Whether these are excessive is moot, however, given that the Federal Reserve closely monitors bank dividend payments to see that such payments do not dilute a bank's capital reserves. In addition, dividend payments are covered by bank regulation such as the National Bank Act.

Moreover, a major reason for upstreaming appears to be to help the holding company service debt issued to pay the purchase price of the acquired bank, rather than to subsidize the operations of nonbank affiliates.[38] Seen in this light, affiliated bank dividend payments are often strongly correlated with a holding company's repayment of the debt it incurred to acquire a bank, and the tax-free privilege of intercompany dividend transfers enables all dividends to go toward debt retirements.[39] Indeed, the tax-free provision reduces the aggregate amount of dividends a bank must pay to service a given amount of outstanding holding company debt.[40] Further, upstreaming funds (such as dividends and tax payments) from the bank and redirecting them to an affiliate makes economic sense only if the expected return on nonbank affiliate activities is greater than the returns on bank activities—that is, if the nonbank affiliate is a healthy institution. Assuming, for example, that holding company management wishes to maximize the value of the organization, redirecting earnings from the bank to a failing nonbank affiliate may result in replacing projects with high net present value (nonbank investments) with projects with a low net present value. Thus, generally, upstreaming of bank funds is more likely to be a reflection of higher holding company leverage and nonbank affiliate strength than of "subsidy" payments to failing nonbank affiliates of the holding company.

While the areas of fee, tax, and dividend transfers are subject to regulation, the fourth potential upstreaming device—banks' purchase of affiliate assets and credit extensions to affiliates—has also become increasingly regulated. One reason for new regulation was the belief of some that "mispriced" deposit insurance may create incentives for bank holding companies to transfer "bad" assets from nonbank affiliates to the bank—for example, by paying excessive prices for these assets. Given limited liability, any resulting increase in bank insolvency risk (fall in bank returns) after bad asset purchase would eventually be borne by the Federal Deposit Insurance Corporation (FDIC) or the Federal Reserve.

Another reason was the controversy surrounding the demise of the Hamilton National Bank of Chattanooga in 1976. As it transpired, the holding company transferred poor quality real estate loans from its troubled mortgage subsidiary (Hamilton Mortgage Corporation) to its banking subsidiaries—principally the Hamilton National Bank.

The failure of the Hamilton National Bank and these asset transfer–deposit insurance concerns eventually led (in 1982) to a strengthening of Federal Reserve Act Section 23A, which regulates the nature of bank–nonbank affiliate asset and credit transactions. Specifically, a bank is limited to a ceiling of 10 percent of capital on loans made to a single affiliate, with a 20 percent limit on loans to all affiliates combined. Moreover, all loans have to be collateralized at 100 percent or more of their face value. Indeed, in the recently passed Competitive Equality Banking Act of 1987, Section 23B added additional safeguards. These safeguards require that transactions with affiliates be undertaken on the same terms or pricing conditions as those with nonaffiliates, limit the cross-marketing of products and services by nonbank banks and affiliated companies, and restrict the ability of banks (and trust departments) to buy securities underwritten by an affiliate.

Given, however, that there is a potential for abuse through intercompany asset and credit transactions and for dissipation of bank earnings through bad loans and assets, what is the empirical evidence on the magnitude and direction of these transactions? The most extensive study to date is by John Rose and Samuel Talley, for 224 bank holding companies between 1976 and 1980, who concluded that the data pointed to a net downstreaming of funds from the parent and nonbank affiliates to the bank rather than the reverse.[41] In 1980, for example, 61 bank holding companies reported no interaffiliate extensions of credit, 128 extensions to subsidiary banks from nonbank affiliates (downstream), and 35 extensions from subsidiary banks to nonbanks (upstream); in dollar terms, $2,809 million was downstreamed and only $186.4 million upstreamed. Moreover, they found that the net tendency to downstream had increased over the sample period and, perhaps more important, "upstream extensions of credit have been quite small relative to the equity capital of banks involved, far below the quantitative limitations imposed by law."[42] Thus, in general, credit extensions were well below the regulatory maximum of 20 percent of capital. Nevertheless, despite this evidence the recent case of Continental Illinois and its First Options subsidiary has cast renewed doubts on the ability of 23A- and 23B-style restrictions to insulate a bank from its affiliates. Although in this case First Options was a direct subsidiary of the bank and not of the holding company and was not strictly subject to 23A and 23B restrictions, the bank had in effect agreed to similar lending restrictions with regulators at the time of acquisition of its First Options subsidiary. When on October 19 the options subsidiary got into financial difficulty, Continental Illinois, as the parent, extended loans to this affiliate beyond the agreed lending ceilings, thereby technically violating its agreement with the regulators.

In the case of intercompany asset flows, the Rose and Talley study showed that a large majority of holding companies (155 of 224) did not engage in such transactions in 1980. Of those that did, 34 reported downstreaming to banks ($517.9 million) and 35 upstreaming by banks ($269.1 million). As with credit extensions, there is little evidence to suggest that intercompany asset transactions have been systematically abused at the expense of the bank.

In sum, the higher dividend payments of affiliated banks can usually be explained by such things as the costs of servicing their acquisition debt. Similarly, while intercompany asset transactions and credit extensions may be abused, as in the Hamilton National Bank and the First Options cases, these seem to be exceptions. Indeed, Hamilton National Bank was the only one of the 120 bank failures occurring in the ten years before the strengthening of Section 23A that could be directly attributed to such abuses.[43] Further, the evidence of Rose and Talley suggests that credit extensions and asset transactions have been relatively small compared with bank capital and, if anything, funds have been downstreamed on a net basis. Even in lieu of the new Section 23B restrictions, these results are consistent with a view that the potential size and risks of upstreaming and downstreaming have been exaggerated.

Bank holding company formation and capital adequacy. The second component of the insolvency equation is the size of a bank's ratio of capital to assets *(K/A)*. Many studies have examined the effects of holding company affiliation on K/A.[44] The consensus appears to be that banks affiliated with holding companies have both lower capitalization levels (higher leverage) and slower rates of capital growth than independent banks. But to the extent that the Federal Reserve requires the holding company to be a source of strength to the affiliate, these differences are not surprising, since the holding company can use the double-leverage option to enhance a bank's capital. In particular, since 1983 the Federal Reserve has required the holding company to act as a source of strength to its banking affiliate—

although the policy existed unofficially for a long time before that. That is, the holding company can raise funds in the commercial paper and long-term bond markets that can be downstreamed as bank equity in times of need. Such a capital-raising option is not available to independent banks. Second, if the holding company can better diversify risks (see below), affiliated banks may need smaller capital ratios than independent banks of a similar size. Third, since in general banks affiliated with holding companies are larger than independent banks, the simple relationship between size and the potential for diversification of the bank balance sheet would argue for lower K/A ratios for holding company banks.

Bank holding company affiliation and return risk. The final and perhaps most controversial element in the insolvency equation is the effect of bank holding company affiliation on return risk (σ). The earliest studies tended to compare the asset composition of affiliated bank portfolios with those of independent banks.[45] The usual approach taken in these studies is to regress asset proportions on a vector of independent variables, including a dummy to signify holding company status. Most studies find that affiliated banks had larger amounts of loans and municipal securities and smaller amounts of U.S. government securities and cash than independent banks. Thus, it was generally concluded that affiliated banks adopt a more risky asset portfolio than independent banks. Michael Jesse and Steven Seelig took a less direct approach, regressing the coefficient of variation (σ/μ) of bank returns on a number of independent variables, including a bank holding company dummy and the proportion of nonbank business in the holding company. They did not find any significant association between holding company variables and bank risk.[46] Boyd and Graham regress the standard deviation of bank holding company returns on the proportion of nonbank assets in the holding company.[47] Like Jesse and Seelig, they find no significant relationship over the whole sample period, 1971–1983. But when they subdivide their sample they find a positive relationship in 1971–1977 and a weak negative relationship in 1978–1983.

Two studies have attempted to examine the effects on "nondiversifiable" or systematic risk (β) of a change from independent bank to one-bank holding company status.[48] Neither study found much impact on β. In particular, Billingsley and Lamy found no change in β in their sample, while Martin and Keown found that β for two banks increased and for two banks decreased out of a sample of twenty-five.

The effects of activity diversification. The great majority of studies of return risk have analyzed the effect of product or activity diversification on the risk of an affiliated bank in a "portfolio" or "mean-variance" framework. Essentially, the question is whether the bank indirectly benefits (and by how much) from affiliation with a diversified holding company. By engaging in activity diversification, the holding company may become less risky if the bank's net profits (returns) are imperfectly correlated with the activities undertaken by its nonbanking affiliates. As a result the bank may indirectly benefit from the lower risk and increased stability of the holding company's earnings:[49] in general, the lower the correlation between bank profits and profits from other potential activities (such as commercial and retail activities, leasing, securities underwriting), the greater will be the ability of the holding company to come to the aid of the bank should the bank itself get into trouble.[50]

Arnold Heggestad, using the IRS's *Corporate Source Book of Income*, derived profitability data for different industry groups that were at that time—or might in the future be—part of a bank holding company.[51] Apart from banks, thirteen other groups were investigated. Heggestad found that when looked at alone over the period 1953–1967 banking was one of the most risky activities. Six of the thirteen nonbank groups analyzed, however, had returns negatively correlated with commercial banking, including holding and investment companies, real estate agents, brokers, and managers, and insurance brokers and agents. Johnson and Meinster came to conclusions similar to Heggestad's, also using industry data.[52] But a later study by John Boyd, Gerald Hanweck, and Pipat Pithyachariyakul argued that using industry data tended to overstate diversification benefits and that when individual firm data were used these benefits were significantly reduced.[53]

Peter Eisemann considered the gains from diversification where the bank holding company is assumed to be (1) limited to diversifying into currently allowable activities only, (2) allowed to diversify into activities that have been neither permitted nor ruled nonallowable (so-called possible activities), and (3) allowed to diversify into activities that have been ruled nonallowable, such as investment banking.[54] Nine activities were viewed as permissible, seven as possible, and five as nonallowable. As a proxy for the profitability of these activities, however, average rates of return on the stocks of firms principally engaged in these various activities were calculated monthly from December 1961 to December 1968. Three "efficient activity frontiers" were calculated according to the set of activities viewed as being available to the bank. The major finding was that a holding company allowed to undertake both possible and nonallowable activities could earn a significantly higher return per unit of risk than when constrained to permissible activities only.

Meinster and Johnson use profit data from an existing bank holding company and its subsidiaries to compute an efficient set of company activities.[55] This efficient holding company structure can be compared with the actual profitability and risk of the existing holding company and the bank subsidiary, when viewed in isolation. The mean quarterly return and standard deviation of returns for the bank subsidiary from the first quarter of 1973 to the second quarter of 1977, viewed in isolation from the rest of the holding company, were .00527 and .00151 respectively, with an average return per unit of risk of 3.490. When other activities were considered and the efficient set of activities for the holding company was calculated, it was found that all existing subsidiaries were included in the efficient set—even those with higher profit variances and lower average profits than the bank itself, since these subsidiaries generated profits that were low or even negatively correlated with those of the bank. This efficient holding company was found to provide significant gains in reducing risk when compared with the weighting of activities in the existing holding company. Further, even the inefficiently diversified existing holding company was found to outperform the bank itself, with a return per unit of risk of 3.758 compared with 3.490 for the bank viewed in isolation.

The most recent and comprehensive study is by Larry Wall and Robert Eisenbeis, who updated the Heggestad study to cover the 1970–1980 period (that is, after the 1970 Bank Holding Company Act amendments).[56] Their results show that among nonallowable activities, operating food stores and holding companies (other than bank holding companies) was *less* risky than banking while some currently allowed activities such as consumer and commercial finance, small business investment corporations (SBICs), and savings and loans are more risky than banking. Interestingly, while general merchandise stores appeared to be quite risky as individual investment propositions, their return correlation with that of the banking group was negative (−.244), as were the returns on security brokers and dealers (−.178). These results are consistent with the potential diversification gains available from reducing the activity barriers between banking and commerce and banking and securities activities.

The methodology of these mean-variance studies can be criticized, however, since they implicitly assume that holding companies make optimal activity investment decisions as if they are "risk-averse" expected utility maximizers rather than risk-neutral value-maximizing agents, as is usual in the normative theory of the firm. To counter this criticism, Roger Stover considered the benefits of activity diversification in a model of holding company profit (value) maximization, under a leverage constraint, with relatively large-scale investment projects.[57] He found that diversification into nonallowable activities such as fire and casualty insurance, investment banking, and land development should be included in banking organization activities since they lowered the constraints (especially leverage constraints) on the firms' value-maximizing decisions.

Rather than look to equity returns to reflect risk changes, Wall and Eisenbeis also analyzed the effect on bond prices and implicitly on default risk premiums of (1) nonfinancial firms' acquiring financial firms (such as Sears Roebuck's acquiring Dean Witter Reynolds); (2) banks' acquiring discount brokerages (such as BankAmerica's acquiring Charles Schwab); (3) financial firms' acquiring other financial firms (such as American General's acquiring Credit Thrift Financial); and (4) financial firms' acquiring nonbank banks (such as Household International's acquiring Valley National Bank).[58] The initial premise was that if an acquisition increased perceptions of the risk of default, the market-adjusted bond returns of the acquiring firm would be adversely affected. Wall and Eisenbeis, however, found no evidence of any significant negative reaction to acquiring firm bond returns on acquisition.

Finally, Anthony Saunders and Pierre Yourougou, using multifactor market models to analyze the return-generating processes of existing bank holding company stocks and commercial firms' stocks, found that while the former were highly sensitive to nominal interest rates (such as shocks and variance changes), the latter were unaffected by such variables.[59] This finding suggests that combining banking and commercial activities within the same holding company may be one way to dilute the impact of interest rate risk on bank holding companies, thereby indirectly insulating the bank.[60]

The effects of geographic diversification. Under the 1927 McFadden Act and the 1956 Bank Holding Company Act, banks and bank holding companies face restrictions on their ability either to branch or to buy other banks across state lines. Although these restrictions have been partly eased through emergency purchase and assumptions of out-of-state banks, purchase of nonbank banks, the passage of reciprocal interstate banking laws and pacts, the growth of interstate automated teller machine (ATM) and automated clearinghouse (ACH) networks, the expansion of Edge Act corporations and loan production offices, and the purchase of S&Ls by out-of-state banks, remaining restrictions limit the ability of banks to diversify their earnings regionally either directly (through branching) or indirectly (through extensions of multibank holding companies).

Like activity diversification, however, regional or geographic diversification by the holding company in nonbank activities—for example, between the Sunbelt states and the old industrial states of the Northeast—also creates a potential for reduced risk exposure for the holding company, which indirectly benefits the bank.[61] That is, the bank holding company structure provides a substitute vehicle through which banks can indirectly enjoy some of the benefits of regional diversification (since nonbank activities are not directly subject to the McFadden Act) and at the same time bid down some of the discrepancies in regional rates of return, thereby providing a more efficient flow of capital between regions. Robert Eisenbeis presents evidence demonstrating that by far the largest number of one-bank holding companies exist in unit banking states, followed by limited branching and full branching states. In a more recent study, Robert Eisenbeis and others, using an event study framework, found that the gains from geographic diversification dominated those from pure activity diversification.[62]

In summary, the results from a large number of studies provide no strong evidence that banks affiliated with nonbanks in a holding company are any more risky than independent banks. Moreover, the potential of holding companies for activity and geographic diversification may be an indirect source of strength in reducing a bank's risk exposure, as long as diversification is used in an optimal fashion and a full range of financial and nonfinancial activities are available. Of course, to the extent that holding company management chooses such activities in a suboptimal fashion or invests excessively in high-risk activities to exploit any option value implicit in the federal safety net, these benefits may not be forthcoming. In large part, however, failure to exploit diversification opportunities fully may be directly blamed on existing regulation such as the Bank Holding Company Act and excessive risk taking on the maladministration of the deposit insurance safety net, which can create perverse risk-taking incentives.

Notwithstanding all this, and even assuming that an affiliated bank is not directly harmed by the investment activities of nonbank affiliates, there remain two indirect channels through which bank return risk may be adversely affected by the operations of the holding company and its affiliates. These are the *confidence or contagion risk effect* and the *corporate separateness risk effect*.

BANK HOLDING COMPANIES

The effects of loss of confidence. As argued by Mark Flannery and others, even if a bank affiliate has no direct investment or credit links with nonbank affiliates, adverse information regarding the performance of a nonbank affiliate may touch off a run on bank deposits.[63] This incentive to run has been extensively modeled (as discussed earlier in this chapter) because of the banks' practice of considering place in line when they issue fixed-face-value liabilities backed by assets of variable value. Aharony and Swary have divided information-induced contagion effects into two types: "noisy" signal contagion and pure contagion.[64] Noisy signal contagion might result if, for example, losses by an affiliate convey imprecise (noisy) but negative information to depositors and investors regarding the competency and quality of the bank and holding company management. Under such circumstances, depositors may revise downward their expectations regarding the value of bank assets, thereby creating an incentive to run. Pure contagion would result if some completely idiosyncratic news regarding a nonbank affiliate led investors to revise their expectations downward in a similar manner. In general, contagion effects can be divided into those internal to the banking organization (as above) and those external to the banking organization.

The most frequently cited example of a noisy signal causing internal contagion was that of Beverly Hills Bancorp. In 1974 losses by its real estate investment trust (REIT) attracted considerable media attention and exposure both in newspapers and on television, which led to a runoff of 15 percent in deposits of its affiliated bank. Ultimately, the affiliated bank was sold to Wells Fargo. Depositors, however, incurred no losses as a result of the run because of this prompt reorganization.

More recently the "failure" of Continental Illinois in April 1984 provides a good case study for analyzing external contagion caused by noisy signals among banks (and also provides evidence on whether failures of large individual financial firms can induce panics or runs on other nonaffiliated financial firms). At the time of its failure Continental was the eighth largest bank in the United States. It had assets of $42 billion, 85 percent of which were financed by rate-sensitive liabilities. More important, because of restrictions on branching in Illinois, Continental relied heavily on foreign interbank deposits and domestic interbank deposits, so that less than 40 percent of its deposits were liable to de jure FDIC insurance guarantees.

Two important dates for analyzing run and contagion effects were April 18, 1984, when Continental announced an increase of $400 million in its problem loan portfolio, and May 10, 1984, when the comptroller of the currency publicly denied rumors that Continental was in serious financial trouble. To analyze contagion effects in the United States, Swary tracked the impact these announcements had on other large U.S. banks' deposits—specifically, the large weekly (over $1.4 billion) reporting banks in the *Federal Reserve Bulletin*.[65] The announcement of April 18 had an imperceptible effect on large bank deposit flows—that is, the purchased funds of large banks increased by 1 percent that week. The announcement of May 10 appears at first to have had a more serious effect, with borrowed funds declining by 7 percent (or $13 billion) over the week of the announcement. Yet this decline was largely offset by an 8 percent increase in demand deposits in the same week. Thus, many depositors appear to have reacted to the crisis simply by switching funds into safer banks and more "secure" deposits rather than running per se[66]—or by switching into currency or Treasury securities—a result that is directly consistent with the Kaufman model (see the section in this chapter on the unique functions of banks).[67] Moreover, the very strong implicit guarantees provided by the Federal Reserve and the FDIC as to the safety of all domestic deposits, large and small, may have effectively defused the incentive to run. Although large depositors may have perceived that Federal Reserve guarantees applied to their deposits in the United States, it was not obvious that these guarantees extended to the overseas and offshore offices of U.S. banks operating in the Eurocurrency markets. Further, Continental was heavily engaged in borrowing on the London interbank market. In neither April nor May, though, was there a net negative effect on flows of nonsterling deposits to American banks in London. Indeed, in May overseas deposits (other than certificates of deposit) increased by 6.7 percent.[68] Nevertheless, while deposit flows were not directly affected, contagion did appear temporarily to affect risk premiums paid for large CDs and Eurodeposits over Treasury bill rates.[69] Hence, although a noisy signal contagion effect may not generate bank runs, it might result in an increase in a bank's cost of funds and, *ceteris paribus*, increase the risk of insolvency.[70]

The potential for noisy signal contagion for banks in holding companies affiliated with financial firms (as currently constituted) may be stronger than if they were affiliated with nonfinancial firms. To the extent that investment, financial, and operating decisions in nonfinancial firms are different from those in banks and other financial firms, the problems of a nonfinancial firm may convey much weaker information signals about the competence of holding company management vis-à-vis the bank than problems at a closely related financial firm.[71] Would, for example, difficulties at an affiliated steel-making plant convey negative information regarding the bank and its management and touch off a run? While the current separation of banking from commerce does not allow us to examine this question directly, commercial firms (such as steel companies) have been allowed to establish one-S&L holding companies. National Intergroup is a holding company that contained six business groups, one of which was National Steel (sold to what was then U.S. Steel on February 1, 1984), and another was a financial services group.

The financial services group included the Citizens Savings and Loan of San Francisco acquired by National Steel in 1980. In 1982 the S&L was expanded by further acquisitions and renamed the First Nationwide Savings & Loan. Currently, First Nationwide is one of the ten largest S&Ls in the country. In 1983 steel contributed to 69 percent of revenues of the holding company while other activities contributed 31 percent.

Because of the depression in the steel industry, the holding company experienced financial difficulties culminating in the sale of National Steel in February 1984. In 1982 the holding company suffered a net loss of $462.8 million and in 1983, $154.3 million. It is therefore interesting to examine the behavior of deposits and purchased funds at the affiliated S&L as adverse information regarding National Steel unfolded over the 1982–1983 period. First, total time and savings deposits grew from $2.185 billion to $4.480 billion (or by 105 percent) between the end of 1981 and the end of 1982 and to $5.851 billion (or by 30.5 percent over 1982) at the end of 1983. Hence, there appears to have been quite substantial growth in the deposit base over this period. Second, the more risk-sensitive "purchased funds"—funds that were not directly covered ex ante by the deposit insurance safety net—grew from $0.717 billion at the end of 1981 to $2.297 billion at the end of 1982 (or by 220 percent) but fell to $2.118 billion ($-7.78$ percent) at the end of 1983. Thus, there is evidence of a small erosion of purchased funds at the peak of the National Steel crisis, but it was more than offset by continued growth of the deposit base. Moreover, it is not at all clear that the decline in purchased funds was directly attributable to adverse information regarding the situation at National Steel. Specifically, First Nationwide, like all S&Ls in 1982 and 1983, was suffering from the general malaise in the thrift industry caused by high interest rates, a heavy proportion of fixed-interest-rate mortgages in their asset portfolios, low (book) ratios of capital to assets, and increased competition for funds.[72]

The risks of corporate separateness. A second indirect, or contingent, risk might arise should the legal wall or barrier separating subsidiary companies be breached after the failure of a nonbank affiliate. As has been discussed by Fisher Black, Merton Miller, and Richard Posner, the major question is the ability of unsatisfied creditors of a failing nonbank affiliate, or holding company, to lay claim to the capital or assets of the bank.[73] The general corporate separateness rule appears to stipulate that creditors of the affiliate have no claim on the bank's assets.[74] Nevertheless, through exceptions allowed under the principle of estoppel, creditors may be able to make a justifiable claim if they can show that the affiliate or bank holding company misled them into believing they were actually dealing with the bank. Elsewhere, this has been called "piercing the corporate veil."[75]

Black, Miller, and Posner suggest that if the following four circumstances are present, creditors of the affiliate may be able to make an estoppel argument: (1) the name of the affiliate providing the services is similar to the bank's, or the same services are undertaken by the bank; (2) the complaining creditor is a member of the general public rather than a "sophisticated" business person or investor; (3) the creditor is a contract creditor, such as a customer; and (4) the nonbanking activity is either a traditional banking service or is so closely related as to suggest to the customer that he is dealing with the bank rather than the holding company and its affiliate.

Most of these circumstances can be avoided or are unlikely to arise in the case of a failure of an affiliated commercial or retail firm rather than a financial firm. Specifically, the problem of similar names can always be avoided by ensuring that the nonbank affiliate and bank can be clearly distinguished (calling a bank "The Sears Bank" may pose potential problems). While the complaining creditor may be a member of the public, it would be difficult to argue, given recent regulatory history, that commercial and retail activities have been a traditional banking activity or that such activities are so closely related to banking as to induce the customer into believing that he is really dealing with the bank rather than the firm. Estoppel arguments may be more powerful, however, if the failing affiliate provided financial service products such as consumer finance.[76]

In summary, this section has analyzed the evidence relating to bank affiliation with a holding company and the potential effects such affiliation has on insolvency risk. Looking at the three elements in the "insolvency equation," it is far from clear that holding company affiliation increases risk. Specifically, the balance of the evidence suggests that, on average, banks affiliated with holding companies earn higher returns but maintain lower ratios of capital to assets. With respect to bank return risk, it is difficult to reach any firm conclusions because of its multidimensional direct and indirect aspects. On the one hand, affiliated banks appear to hold more risky portfolios and may or may not be subject to the internal contagion effects of information and breaches of corporate separateness; on the other hand, these risk-increasing effects may be offset fully or at least partly through the indirect benefits of activity and geographic diversification at the holding company level. Finally, after testing the relationship between the risk of insolvency (as measured here) and nonbank affiliation, Wall concludes, using equity data, that nonbank susidiaries have tended to reduce the risk of bank insolvency; Boyd and Graham, using accounting data, find no statistical impact on insolvency risk from nonbank affiliation over their whole sample period.[77]

Bank Holding Companies and Deposit Insurance Subsidies. Closely linked to the question of bank insolvency is the issue of deposit insurance and the potential extension of deposit insurance subsidies to nonbank firms through holding company affiliations. First, to the extent that banking is a competitive industry, any deposit insurance subsidies implicit in the provision of such insurance will be largely passed on to bank loan and deposit customers rather than to the holding company parent and its affiliates. Second, to the extent that an affiliated firm might indirectly borrow subsidized deposits by receiving loans from an affiliated bank, Section 23A limits such loans to 10 percent of the bank's capital. Thus a bank meeting capital adequacy requirements of 6 percent could allocate only up to 0.6 percent of its assets (or 0.64 percent of its noncapital liabilities or "deposits") to any affiliate, which is a very small amount of potential subsidy. Finally, the Federal Reserve, the Office of the Comptroller of the Currency (OCC), and the FDIC should make it absolutely clear that deposit insurance guarantees apply only to depositors of the bank affiliate and not to the debt holders and general creditors of the holding company. This policy appears to have been followed in the failures of such large banks as the First National Bank of Oklahoma City, the Bank of Oklahoma, and Banc Texas where creditors of the relevant holding company bore some of the losses.[78] Clearly, if these recent actions are construed as being credible signals of likely future actions by regulators, then nonbank affiliate and holding company debt will bear risk premiums different from bank debt (that is, deposit insurance cross-subsidization effects would be severely limited).

Bank Holding Companies and Transactions Mechanism Risk. A further concern closely related to the insolvency question is the possibility of an institutional contagion effect (as compared with the informational contagion discussed earlier), which might destroy the integrity of the wire transfer part of the payment system. This potential for contagion is fully discussed in the chapter by Mark Flannery in this volume. These systems now transmit, in dollar terms, a larger share of total payments than cash and checks combined (see the section on the unique functions of banks). Volcker and Corrigan argue that the risk of an institutional contagion effect would be enhanced should commercial firms be allowed to establish bank holding companies.[79] The scenario underlying this concern is a bankruptcy or a default by a commercial firm that is transmitted to other banks through its affiliated bank. Given the close interrelatedness of the bank settlement matrix, for example, the failure of the affiliated bank to settle net credit and debit claims with other banks at the end of the day may trigger other settlement failures. Such a failure would force the Federal Reserve to intervene and restore stability by rescuing the affiliated bank and indirectly (through upstreaming) the commercial firm and its holding company.[80] In doing so the federal government and its agencies would implicitly be extending the federal safety net (deposit insurance and lender of last resort) to the real sector of the economy. This practice, it is argued, would be contrary to the original intent of Congress in providing a safety net to depository institutions.

In evaluating this scenario, it is useful to identify first which payment mechanism might be subject to "institutionalized" systemic or contagion risk potential. Certainly Fedwire transfers, where all transactions are in "good funds"—that is, funds that are directly guaranteed by the appropriate Federal Reserve bank—appear to be free of contagion risk.[81] Presumably then, potential systemic settlement risk relates to private wire systems such as CHIPS—an electronically linked network of over 130 large banks that handles approximately 90 percent of all international interbank dollar transfers. Unlike Fedwire funds, funds transferred on CHIPS within any day are unguaranteed payments, which only become final at the end of the day.[82] Thus if a bank does not deliver promised funds at the end of the day, other banks may be pushed into a serious position as net debtors. Indeed, it is conceivable that for some banks this net debtor position may exceed capital and reserves, rendering them technically insolvent.[83] Currently such a disruption might be expected to occur only if a major fraud were discovered in a bank's books during the day and it was closed the same day by bank regulators. Alternatively, a bank might be transmitting funds that it does not have in the hope of "keeping its name in the market" so as to be able to raise funds later in the day. It is conceivable that other banks would revise their credit limits for this bank during the day, making it unable to deliver all the funds promised. If a bank cannot meet its settlement commitments,

CHIPS resolves this by completely unwinding all of that bank's transactions during the day with all other banks. The end-of-day net settlement matrix is recalculated for the remaining banks, excluding all transactions with the insolvent bank. As a result, banks that were net senders of funds to the insolvent bank, because they sent more than they received, will have their net settlement positions improved, while banks that were net receivers of funds from the insolvent bank will have their positions deteriorate further. Some banks that were originally in a net creditor position may be forced into a net debtor position, while others will have their net debtor position worsened in the revised settlement matrix. If some of these banks are then unable to meet their revised settlement requirements, a further rebalancing will be necessary by excluding them from the settlement matrix and so on until all banks left can meet their settlement obligations.

Although a CHIPS settlement failure of the intraday kind has yet to occur, Humphrey has simulated the contagion effect of a single large settlement failure on a random day in January 1983.[84] The settling participant selected had a net credit position of $321 million for the day. (This failure was viewed as being a "least worst" situation since realistically only net debtors are likely to default.) After deleting the transactions of this bank with all other banks and reestimating the transaction creditor-debtor matrix, he found that twenty-four banks had settlement obligations increased by more than the amount of their capital and ended up in a net debtor position. Of these, eight had been in a net creditor position before the removal of transactions with the nonsettling participant. It was then assumed that all banks whose net debtor positions deteriorated by an amount equal to or exceeding their capital were also unable to settle. Thus, another revised transactions matrix had to be constructed. This process was continued until no participant failed after a transactions matrix revision. It was found that six such iterations were required and that the number of "failed" banks was fifty. These fifty banks accounted for 39 percent of the total dollar value of messages sent for that day.

The Humphrey results, however, are contingent on banks' being unable to call in interbank loans, to borrow elsewhere (such as from the federal funds market), and to use the discount window, all of which would tend to curtail the unwinding process in the real world.[85] In addition, since under CHIPS the receiving bank controls for all the risk in the sending bank, including any risk to which the sending bank may be exposed through its affiliation with nonbank enterprises, the nonbank affiliate would find it extremely difficult to use its bank affiliate to put through an exceptionally large volume of wire transfers. Further, as noted earlier, a settlement failure contagion, while potentially disastrous, has yet to occur among CHIPS participating banks. If this is so, why would commercial firm participation through an affiliated bank increase the potential risk of systemic contagion and settlement failure? The only logical explanation would be a belief that commercial firms have a higher default or bankruptcy risk than financial firms, since the intraday risk of overdraft is really a problem of credit-risk assessment. In evaluating this question, the potential default risk of the largest commercial and retail firms is relevant, since only these firms are likely to be able to acquire or establish *de novo* a bank of sufficient scale to be a major participant in private wire systems such as CHIPS.

Useful insights into the probability of commercial firm settlement failures (defaults) can be gained by analyzing defaults on corporate bonds. Edward Altman has estimated that the total default rate on all issues of corporate debt between 1978 and 1985 was only one-tenth of 1 percent (compared with 3.2 percent between 1930 and 1939). Even for non-investment-grade (mostly small firm) high-yield bonds, the average default rate was 1.22 percent over the 1978–1985 period.[86]

It is also interesting to analyze the industries in which bond defaults occurred. Altman found that for the 1970–1985 period the percentage of defaults in dollar terms was largest for railroads (19.6 percent) and oil and gas firms (16.7 percent). Interestingly, the percentages of defaults in general manufacturing (8.7 percent), electronics, computers, and communications (8.6 percent), and retailers (10.2 percent) were similar to default losses in the financial services sector (8.8 percent). Moreover, defaults by real estate construction (3.2 percent), airlines/cargo (4.6 percent), sea lines (1.9 percent), and trucks and motor carriers (0.9 percent) were well below those for the financial sector. Based on these figures, it seems difficult to argue that commercial firms, with the exception of railroads and oil and gas firms, are likely to impose greater default and settlement risk potential than financial service firms currently linked to banking affiliates through holding companies.

Finally, even if banks affiliated with commercial firms were perceived to have greater settlement risk, this could be effectively dealt with by making it clear that Section 23A- and 23B-style limitations unambiguously apply to daylight overdrafts, by imposing bilateral and total caps on daylight overdrafts, by explicitly pricing them, and by requiring more frequent intraday settlements among participating banks.[87] This would seem both feasible and preferable to a policy of outright prohibition on participation, which could limit potential economies of scope for the commercial firm (for example, by preventing it from reducing its payments and transaction costs through vertical integration with a bank).

Conflicts of Interest. Potential conflicts of interest arise in any business organization (financial or commercial) that sells a spectrum of products to a diverse customer base. As multiproduct financial firms, bank holding companies and the potential conflicts of interest that may arise from their operations (especially in the allocation of credit) have become a major concern of bank regulators.[88] Indeed, concerns about conflict of interest were a primary reason for the passage of the Glass-Steagall Act of 1933 and the Bank Holding Company Act of 1956 (as well as its amendments in 1970), which limited commercial bank activities in, respectively, investment banking and commerce.[89]

As noted by Franklin Edwards, Stephen Halpert, and Anthony Saunders, the term "conflict of interest" has a number of different meanings and implications.[90] It may cover the potential for self-dealing at the expense of bank clients or for exploiting tying opportunities or may involve disincentives to transact with competitors of the bank and its nonbank affiliate. Whatever the potential conflict of concern, however, the economic conditions necessary for potential conflicts to be exploited are that either (1) contracting parties have imperfect (asymmetric) information regarding each other's actions (an imperfect information problem) or (2) one party has monopoly or monopsony power over another party (an imperfect market problem). Saunders has considered the potential for conflicts of interest should the Glass-Steagall Act be abolished and commercial banks be allowed to engage in investment banking activities.[91] Here we will consider potential conflicts should commercial firms be allowed to affiliate with commercial banks and vice versa.

It is important to observe, initially, that the range of potential conflicts that have raised concern in the commercial–investment banking context appear to be more extensive than those raised in the commercial bank–commercial firm context. The major potential conflicts of concern appear to be four: (1) restricting the supply of bank credit to the competitors of the commercial firm affiliate; (2) using a bank's monopoly power over bank products and services to tie customers to the commercial products of the holding company; (3) making bank loans to the commercial firm affiliate to keep it in business; and (4) disseminating inside or confidential information to the commercial affiliate regarding its competitors.

1. *Restricting the supply of bank credit to the competitors of the commercial affiliates.* The major concern is over equity in treatment in the provision of bank credit. In particular, the fear is that the affiliate bank may have an incentive to ration spot loans and restrict lines of credit to the commercial or financial affiliates of competitors. Although this con-

cern might have been realistic at the time of the 1970 Bank Holding Company Act amendments, the bank loan and securities markets have since undergone a remarkable transformation resulting in a dramatic decline in the relative importance of bank loans at both the short and long ends of the debt market and increased access to the capital market by small and medium-sized firms. Domestically, for large corporations,[92] the commercial paper market is now the primary source of short-term finance—with only 24 percent of short-term debt made up of bank loans in 1985 (compared with 59 percent in 1974).[93] In the long-term debt market the par value of straight and convertible debt outstanding was $459 billion in 1985 compared with total loans and leases of all commercial banks of $1,450 billion. In the international financial markets, financing in the form of securities made up over 80 percent of total funds raised in 1985 compared with 30 percent in 1980. These changes suggest that any monopoly power that banks had over large corporate customers through loan contracts has been significantly dissipated. Moreover, small and medium-sized firms as well as large firms have increased their access to the debt markets. New high-yield debt issues (so-called junk bonds), for example—increasingly the preserve of smaller companies—in 1985 numbered 188 (par value of $14.67 billion) compared with 32 issues in 1981 (par value of $1.65 billion). The direct access of both small and large firms to securities markets suggests, in turn, that with a declining market share and customer quality base commercial banks have an incentive to be as attractive as possible to all potential commercial and financial customers of reasonable credit rating, irrespective of whether they do or do not compete in the same product markets as an affiliate.

2. *Tie-ins of products.* Closely related to (1) above is the argument that market power over bank credit extensions implies the potential to tie the customer into products of the nonbank affiliates. Firms such as Sears, for example, might seek to use consumer loans to tie customers into products sold through the retail arm, or car manufacturers might link auto finance to purchase of their own models (as has happened recently). The key questions are to what extent the packaging of products in this fashion is feasible and, more important, whether the customer will be harmed. Studies by Posner and others have shown that the market conditions under which tie-in arrangements work to the benefit of the multiproduct firm are very restrictive.[94] In particular, if a firm has monopoly power in one market and attempts to tie a customer into a product sold in a competitive market (for example, by price cutting in the monopoly market), its overall revenue may well decrease. Thus, if low (below market) interest rates are offered by a car manufacturer for auto finance, any attempt by this manufacturer

to recoup the cost of the rate cut by attempting to tie the customer (in a product package) to a high-priced (or overpriced) model relative to its competitors is likely to be frustrated as customers switch to other models. At best, rational customers might view this arrangement as a package, allowing any lower cost of credit to be just offset by a rise in the auto's price. At worst, the customer gains an interest subsidy for credit and pays the same competitive price for the car.

3. *Bank loans to a failing affiliate.* This concern is similar to those about insolvency and transactions mechanism risk. As already noted, however, to the extent that the bank stays within the law, Sections 23A and 23B of the Federal Reserve Act require such loans to be at least 100 percent collateralized, to be no more than 10 percent of bank capital to an individual affiliate (20 percent in total), and to be made on market terms. Indeed, to the extent that the concern is over a "failing" commercial affiliate, there must be a strong possibility that such loans could not be made legally, since such firms would find it difficult to post acceptable collateral to back the loan in the first place.

To prevent the extension of loans in an "illegal" manner, when the bank is facing the extreme circumstances of a potential affiliate insolvency, Sections 23A and 23B may need to be buttressed by legal provisions allowing punitive financial (and even criminal) penalties to be imposed by regulators on managers and the corporation if these regulations are found to have been violated. If such penalties are set sufficiently high and managers know the penalties exist, then it would be "incentive compatible" for managers (and the corporation) never to violate these regulations. Indeed, proposals along these lines are contained in the bill recently introduced by Senators Cranston and D'Amato (S. 1905).

4. *Information advantages regarding current and future customers.* In the course of making deposit-loan transactions, a bank may become privy to confidential or inside information about its customers. A potential conflict of interest exists since there may be an incentive to pass on this information to an affiliate to help it gain a competitive advantage over commercial rivals. This type of information conflict already exists in investment banking, where Sears, American Express, and Prudential-Bache all have investment bank subsidiaries that underwrite corporate securities.[95] Similarly to commercial bank loan officers, investment bank underwriters acquire private information that may be of potential value to their nonbank affiliates. Of course, theoretically, "Chinese walls" or barriers limiting the transfer of information within the holding company should prevent abuse; nevertheless, recent scandals relating to insider trading suggest that a pervasive concern will remain.

It is of interest to consider analytically what general factors or incentives exist that mitigate against, or work in favor of, conflict exploitation. Saunders examined this question in the context of banks' securities activities.[96] Briefly, it was argued that a banking firm seeking to maximize its long-run profits must preserve its reputation as an asset. Exploiting conflicts by violating implicit and explicit contracts with customers for short-run gains would be suboptimal. Fear of civil and criminal penalties is also likely to discourage banking firms from exploiting conflicts (for example, by underpricing loans to a commercial affiliate).

Offsetting these conflict-mitigating factors is the possibility that "agency problems" may exist within the holding company. That is, managers may have objectives different from those of holding company stockholders (such as long-run profit or value maximization). Saunders argues that these problems may pose the most serious difficulties if managers have relatively short-run objectives and if managerial compensation schemes are structured to give managers in both the bank and the commercial affiliate a coalition of interests in exploiting potential conflicts. Such a case might arise if, for example, all managerial bonuses were linked to the combined profits of the holding company rather than to the profits of individual profit centers or subsidiaries. A second incentive to exploit conflicts (and to take excessive risks) might arise because of the maladministration of the deposit insurance scheme and other federal safety net subsidies. A third incentive reflects the potential for a holding company to shift bankruptcy risk from companies in which it has a high capital investment to those with a low capital investment. Interestingly, in existing OBHCs, banks are invariably the largest capital investments for the holding company. As such, this would appear to create an incentive to avoid transactions (conflicts) that put the bank at risk. Should commercial firms become part of OBHCs, however, the capital investment in the bank may become relatively small, which may create incentives to shift bankruptcy risk away from the firm to the bank. As already discussed, however, such a move would require contravention of Section 23A and 23B regulations and might harm the reputation of the parent as well as subject managers and the stockholders to potential penalties.

Market Structure Considerations. According to Halpert, one of the overriding reasons for the continued separation of banking and commerce is the fear of huge industry-banking conglomerations.[97] Indeed the Bank Holding Company Act imposes more restrictive limitations on corporate vertical integrations (bank–commercial firm) than is imposed on horizontal integrations (bank-bank, commercial firm–commercial firm) by the Sherman and Clayton acts. Moreover, these restrictions appear to be perverse when considered in light of the fact that individuals acquiring banks face very different rules and restrictions than corporations. Specifically, an individual, even if a major stockholder in a commercial operation, faces considerably lower barriers to acquisition than a corporation (bank or nonbank). Indeed, before 1978 there was very little control on individual changes of ownership at commercial banks not covered by the Bank Holding Company Act. The more stringent controls on individual ownership imposed by the Bank Control Act of 1978 require an acquirer to file a written notice of a proposed acquisition. If the agency responsible does not disapprove the application within sixty days, the acquisition goes through. Between 1978 and 1984 the three federal agencies received 2,390 change-of-control notifications and disapproved only thirty-four.

Fear of large bank and corporate conglomerates has been articulated in a number of ways. On the one hand, the fear emanates from a conventional wisdom that commercial banking is a protected and monopolistic industry, in which case the banking industry might use its monopoly rents to drive competition out of the commercial sector through predatory pricing and other methods, resulting in an undue concentration of economic resources in the hands of a few very large conglomerates. On the other hand, there appears to be a pervasive political mistrust of large money center banks among legislators, which was clearly evident in the proceedings leading up to the passage of both the Glass-Steagall and the bank holding company legislation. Even supposing these concerns had empirical validity (although the monopoly power of the banking industry is clearly contentious based on the loan market evidence already discussed above),[98] the crucial question is, What are the economic costs of the current market segmentation policy? At least five costs can be identified: (1) limits on economies of scale, (2) limits on economies of scope, (3) failure to internalize all relevant information through bank equity participations, (4) barriers to entry into the market for corporate control and perpetuation of agency problems, and (5) costs of international competition.

1. *Limits on economies of scale.* Although the conventional wisdom is that economies of scale are not terribly important in banking and that the optimal scale of a bank might be quite small,[99] the empirical evidence has generally been restricted to looking at relatively small

and medium-sized banks (those with under $400 million in assets) using functional cost analysis. Indeed Sherrill Shaffer and Edmond David have shown (using an alternative data set) the existence of economies of scale in very large regional and money center banks.[100] With respect to commercial firms, many studies have examined the relationship between size and unit costs in various industries. Frederic Sherer concludes, "If any single typical result can be identified . . . it is a cost curve showing definite economies of scale at relatively small plant sizes, a range of intermediate sizes over which unit costs did not vary perceptibly and (in a minority of cases) diseconomies of scale for large plants."[101] Based on the evidence of empirical cost curves discussed above, there seems to be limited potential for buying into economies of scale through conglomeration (commercial firms establishing banks *de novo* or buying existing banks, for example). Because of their vintage, however, many of these studies have inadequately reflected the potential influence of computers and information technology on cost functions, which one would expect to produce an increasing bias in favor of economies of scale. Further, to the extent that these studies concentrate on operating costs and pay only limited attention to borrowing and capital-raising costs, important economies of scale may be ignored. Notwithstanding the greater access of smaller firms to the debt and equity markets, transaction and issuing costs (per dollar) still remain considerably larger for small firms than for large firms.[102]

2. *Limits on economies of scope.* A second potential cost to separating banking from commerce concerns limits to economies of scope. Intercompany transactions in products, inputs, and management services, for example, may generate economies of scope—that is, savings in total holding company costs due to cost complementarities among the bank and its affiliates. Thomas Gilligan et al. have already shown, with a limited product set, that there may be quite large economies of scope within a banking firm.[103] Economies of scope, especially in joint production of information services, may also be generated from a commercial affiliation between a firm and a bank.[104] The commercial firm's cash management performance, for example, might be considerably enhanced through affiliation with a bank that has developed expertise in hardware and software in this area (such as real time cash portfolio management and lockboxes). The potential for such economies remains to be investigated, however.

3. *Internalizing relevant information (the internal capital market).* Many observers have argued that a major factor underlying the impressive performance of the German industrial sector in the post–World War II

period has been its universal banking system.[105] John Cable, building on the role of banks as information processors and capital suppliers, argues that for banks to exploit this advantage fully (in a world of asymmetric information) they need to become full insiders of the firm—equity owners rather than just creditors. Such full insider status internalizes information and creates an informal capital market within the firm. Moreover, as full insiders they can continue to monitor the real and financial decisions of the commercial firm and have incentives to resolve any agency problems that might arise. By separating banking from commerce, banks still have partial insider access to private information through lending contracts, but do not have an explicit equity (risk-sharing) contract.[106] This may limit their ability to resolve agency problems and increase the cost of capital, resulting in suboptimal investments by the firm.[107]

4. *Barriers to entry in the market for corporate control.* To the extent that managers of corporations fail (or are unwilling) to follow the long-run value-maximizing objectives of shareholders, the "market for corporate control" is a mechanism that may ultimately allow stockholders to achieve value-maximizing returns. The market for corporate control, which includes acquisitions, mergers, buyouts, greenmail, managerial reorganizations, and so on, disciplines those managerial teams that deviate too far from the value-maximizing goals of owners.[108] As managerial agency costs rise, so does the benefit to owners from seeking a resolution in the market for corporate control. Conceptually, at least, agency costs in the economy will be reduced, and resource allocation will more closely reflect stockholder valuation decisions the more active and efficient is the market for corporate control. Thus, to the extent that banking and commerce are separated, a false dichotomy is imposed on the market for corporate control. As a result, residual agency problems that might be reduced if banks were allowed to bid for and acquire commercial firms (and vice versa) will remain and impose a deadweight cost on the economy.

5. *International competitive costs.* An additional reason to be concerned about the separation of the U.S. banking and commercial sectors in what is now a global market for banking services is the limits separation imposes on the size of bank organizations and their capital bases. Recent reports have indicated that only two U.S. banking companies (Citicorp and BankAmerica) are ranked among the world's twenty-five largest. This compares with fourteen Japanese (including the world's four largest), four French, three British, and two German. Undoubtedly, the shrinking profits of U.S. banks

(aligned with their inability to tap the equity of commercial firms) have limited their ability to raise new funds and therefore to enlarge their capital bases—which appears to be a prerequisite to becoming, or to continuing to be, a major player in international financial services. One likely large benefit of eliminating the barriers between banking and commerce would be to reverse the long decline in the relative importance and market power of U.S. banking organizations in the world banking industry.

Summary and Policy Recommendations. Consideration of the costs and benefits of the current one-bank holding company structure suggests that although safety and soundness, conflict of interest, and market structure deserve attention, they do not make a strong case for continuing the current policy of barring holding company affiliations among commercial firms and banks. One might even argue that given subsidized deposit insurance as a policy "fact," allowing such affiliations within a holding company might have important net benefits as long as (1) Sections 23A and 23B restrictions on interaffiliate transactions (as well as existing restrictions on excessive dividend payments) were kept in place; (2) managers and firms that violated Sections 23A and 23B faced punitive financial (and possibly criminal) penalties; (3) such restrictions were extended to cover daylight overdraft transactions on CHIPS (which is essentially credit risk); and (4) holding company and nonbank affiliate debtors and creditors received a consistent and credible signal that bank deposit insurance guarantees do not extend to them. (This could be reinforced by using securities laws to prohibit the affiliates of banks from stating or implying that their debt is an obligation covered by deposit insurance.)

These recommendations are similar to those of the FDIC, Thomas Huertas, and the Cranston-D'Amato bill S. 1905 and its companion bill, H.R. 3799. Huertas, however, would go further to appease cautious legislators and regulators by adding (5) a "bear-down provision," which would empower regulators to force a bank owner either to add capital or to divest the bank should its capital adequacy fall below the regulatory minimum. If enforced, this would add very strong protection to the bank's depositors and thus insulation to the deposit insurance fund. He would also add (6) an extra-layer provision, which would require banks that are part of financial service holding companies to have higher capital adequacy ratios than independent banks; (7) a plenipotentiary provision enabling the bank's primary federal regulator to act flexibly in writing new rules and regulations regarding interaffiliate transactions when deemed necessary; and (8) an enforcement provision, which would allow a bank regulator access to the courts (through court injunctions) to dissuade banks from engaging in unsound transactions with affiliates.[109]

Regulatory restrictions 1, 2, 3, and 4 might be viewed as the minimum required if complete activity deregulation were to be allowed. The full set of regulations 1–8 would seem to provide an almost cast-iron protection to even the most risk-averse bank regulator. Indeed these provisions would appear to place sufficient tools in the hands of regulators to deal with most conceivable transaction abuses between banks and affiliates that threaten a bank. Should a bank fail it would be due more to inefficient regulation (monitoring, [dis]incentive systems, and enforcement) than to inherently unsound practices of the bank. Finally, since these restrictions require monitoring and enforcement effort to be concentrated on the bank rather than on the holding company and the nonbank affiliates, it is likely that the comptroller of the currency (in the case of national banks) and the FDIC would become more important in ensuring the integrity of the banking system.[110]

Alternative Bank Organizational Structures

One might ask whether the one-bank holding company structure would be the best organizational form for such a commercial-financial conglomerate in a fully deregulated environment without deposit insurance subsidies of any kind (that is, without deposit insurance or with fairly priced deposit insurance, including private insurance). In a world with no restrictions on the nonbank activities of banks, no geographic restrictions on branching, no mispriced deposit insurance, and no restrictions on the forms of external debt that could be raised by banks (such as commercial paper), many of the advantages of the OBHC form would disappear. Its remaining significant benefit would be its ability to use affiliates, and the principle of corporate separateness, to isolate relatively risky activities from more traditional banking activities. Such insulation might then be reflected in relatively "low" deposit insurance premiums and costs. In contrast, a corporation that sought to consolidate all activities within one firm would probably face a higher cost of capital and deposit insurance or be required by the market to maintain a lower leverage (higher capital adequacy) ratio. In selecting its optimal organizational form, a conglomerate might well trade net corporate separateness benefits and lower insurance and surveillance cost savings[111] for the benefits of forming a universal banking organization in which economies of scope and scale could be fully exploited and agency costs more fully controlled than in an OBHC.[112] Large conglomerates might find the universal bank more attractive, in a value-maximizing sense, than the OBHC.[113] Further, in a deregulated environment, it is not obvious that the OBHC is the only feasible structure to exploit corporate separateness so as to protect traditional banking activities such as transaction accounts. In recent years Jack Kareken and others have suggested an alternative bank holding company structure in which the commercial bank is insulated from the risk of other holding company activities by having its transaction accounts completely backed by short-term liquid assets (government bills).[114] This structure, it is argued, would provide full protection to the transactions or payment system from illiquidity, credit, and contagion effects and in effect eliminate the need for a residual federal safety net—that is, deposits would be virtually self-insuring. All other current bank activities such as purchased funds, long-term assets, and lending would take place at arm's length in separate subsidiaries of the holding company, along with nonbanking activities. Consequently, this 100 percent reserve bank would closely resemble existing money market mutual funds, which sell their shares in fixed dollar units.

Although at first glance this 100 percent reserve bank may appear attractive, it has some conceptual and institutional problems. First, it assumes that the unique aspect of banking is the provision of transactions accounts and the payments mechanism. To the extent that Fama and Bernanke are correct in arguing that bank loans are unique, the implementation of this plan might be costly if, as seems likely, the level of bank credit intermediation services falls with the removal of the federal safety net on the funds that back loans. Second, it is not clear that such a scheme is institutionally feasible. In particular, at the end of the second quarter of 1986 gross demand deposits of U.S. commercial banks were $322.4 billion, while the total government debt holdings (marketable and nonmarketable) of commercial banks were only $197.2 billion. Moreover, the total outstanding supply of all marketable government securities was $1,498 billion, comprising $397 billion in bills, $869 billion in notes, and $232 billion in bonds. Thus, assuming that banks wished to "match maturities" by using short-term bills as the reserve asset, this proposal would require commercial banks to hold over 81 percent of the stock of bills outstanding[115]—such a proportion would probably only be attained through significant asset price adjustments in the securities markets such as bidding up the relative prices of Treasury bills and producing a kink in the yield curve, or through a major alteration in Treasury debt management in which it would increase the relative supply of short-term to long-term debt maturities outstanding. Third, should the banks be unable to acquire sufficient amounts of bills and resort to using notes and bonds, they simply risk substituting the interest rate risk on marketable securities for the credit risk on loans, causing transaction accounts to become risky again.[116] Fourth, there is always the possibility that the nonbank subsidiaries of the holding company would try to develop close substitutes for the transaction balance accounts in the 100 percent reserve bank. This might be done by offering transaction account–like services such as check writing while paying higher interest rates than the maximum possible in the 100 percent reserve bank (which should closely approximate the risk-free Treasury bill rate). These higher rates may be offered in the ex ante expectation of higher returns from riskier investments. The obvious danger is that should these nonbank subsidiaries fail, presenting their investors and deposit holders with the risk of considerable losses, regulators may be strongly tempted to intervene and extend a safety net to these subsidiaries. Such a policy would simply tend to recreate the existing holding company and associated insurance and safety net structure. Hence, this scheme presumes a willingness of regulators to allow *all* holding company subsidiaries, with the exception of the 100 percent reserve bank, to fail.

Conclusion

This chapter has considered the question of bank uniqueness and whether this uniqueness can be protected in a bank holding company that engages in nonbanking activities including, potentially, commercial activities. In general it appears that even if a rather weak case can be made for believing that banks provide certain special transaction and credit intermediation services, there appears to be no overriding theoretical or empirical case for continuing the current policy of separating banking from commerce or banking from finance. Indeed, some strong arguments can be made for both bank safety and soundness and social welfare reasons for removing these artificial separations and allowing bank holding companies to choose their desired portfolio of commercial and financial activities freely (even under mispriced deposit insurance). This would be subject to Section 23A and Section 23B restrictions on interaffiliate transactions remaining in place and would be bolstered by similar restrictions on interaffiliate daylight overdraft transactions. Punitive penalties on managers and corporations for violating Section 23A and Section 23B restrictions could be enacted, along with enhanced restrictions on bank capital adequacy and increased enforcement powers of bank regulators.

It was also argued that in a fully deregulated environment, without deposit insurance subsidies, a number of alternative organizational forms for banking and commercial firm conglomerates might become feasible. In particular, the universal banking form might emerge as an alternative to the current OBHC form, especially if potential economies of scope and scale are large relative to the net benefits of corporate separateness. An alternative structure for a bank holding company was also considered whereby transaction accounts were segregated from the other activities of the holding company in the form of a self-insured 100 percent reserve bank. On the whole, this organizational structure was considered to be relatively unattractive. Nevertheless, in the absence of deposit insurance subsidies a banking organization should be allowed to choose any corporate, or even noncorporate, form it desires.

Notes

1. Paul A. Volcker, Statement before the Subcommittee on Commerce, Consumer and Monetary Affairs of the Committee on Government Operations, U.S. House of Representatives, June 11, 1986.

2. Specifically, the act defined "bank" for purposes of the Bank Holding Company Act to be any institution with Federal Deposit Insurance Corporation insurance or any institution that accepts demand deposits and makes commercial loans. Nonbank banks established before March 5, 1987, would be allowed to continue in business, but would be limited to a maximum growth in assets of 7 percent per year during any twelve-month period beginning one year after enactment. It also permitted nonbank banks that are allowed to remain in business to engage only in those activities in which they were engaged in March 1987 and limited the cross-marketing of products and services by nonbank banks and affiliated companies.

3. Paul A. Volcker, Statement before the Committee on Banking, Housing, and Urban Affairs, U.S. Senate, September 13, 1983; Volcker, Statement before the Subcommittee on Commerce, Consumer, and Monetary Affairs; E. Gerald Corrigan, "Are Banks Special?" *Federal Reserve Bank of Minneapolis Annual Report*, 1982; and Corrigan, "Financial Market Structure: A Longer View," Federal Reserve Bank of New York, January 1987.

4. Corrigan, "Are Banks Special?" p. 13.

5. See, for example, John H. Boyd and Edward Prescott, "Financial Intermediary Coalitions," *Journal of Economic Theory*, vol. 38, no. 2 (1986), pp. 211–32; and Douglas W. Diamond and Philip H. Dybvig, "Bank Runs, Deposit Insurance, and Liquidity," *Journal of Political Economy*, vol. 91, no. 3 (1983), pp. 401–19.

6. Tim S. Campbell, "Bank Deposit Contracts and the Demand for Liquidity" (Working Paper, Graduate School of Business Administration, University of Southern California, August 1984); Charles J. Jacklin, "Demand Deposits, Trading Restrictions, and Risk Sharing" (Working Paper, Graduate School of Business, Stanford University, 1983); and Joseph G. Haubrich and

Robert G. King, "Banking and Insurance" (National Bureau of Economic Research, Working Paper no. 1312, 1984).

7. It might be noted that during the pre–Federal Reserve period banks frequently resorted to suspensions of convertibility in an attempt to resolve panics. This effectively canceled the place-in-line servicing rule during these periods.

8. In addition, these models assume that the bank supplies only demand deposits. Introducing time-deposit contracts with withdrawal penalties would probably constrain the ability to run, although the degree of constraint would depend on the size of withdrawal penalties. To some extent, the loss of interest penalties currently in effect would not act as much of a disincentive for depositors to run from a "bad" bank.

9. George G. Kaufman, "The Truth about Bank Runs" (Paper presented at the Cato Conference, "The Financial Services Revolution: Policy Directions for the Future," February 26–27, 1987).

10. Anna J. Schwartz, "Financial Stability and the Federal Safety Net," chapter 2 in this volume.

11. See Hans H. Angermueller, Statement before the Commerce, Consumer and Monetary Affairs Subcommittee of the Committee on Government Operations, U.S. House of Representatives, Washington, D.C., December 17, 1986; and David B. Humphrey, *The U.S. Payments System: Costs, Pricing, Competition, and Risk,* Monograph Series in Finance and Economics, (New York: New York University, 1984).

12. Eugene F. Fama, "Banking in the Theory of Finance," *Journal of Monetary Economics,* vol. 6, no. 1 (1980), pp. 39–57.

13. Again, distinctions have to be drawn between problems for an individual bank and those encompassing all banks in the settlement system. This also invokes questions regarding optimal Federal Reserve policy on the integrity of electronic settlement systems.

14. Ben Bernanke, "Non-monetary Effects of the Financial Crisis in the Propagation of the Great Depression," *American Economic Review,* vol. 73, no. 3 (1983), pp. 257–76.

15. Eugene F. Fama, "What's Different about Banks?" *Journal of Monetary Economics,* vol. 15, no. 1 (1985), pp. 29–39.

16. Ibid. Fama's conclusions are supported by Christopher James, "Some Evidence on the Uniqueness of Bank Loans," *Journal of Financial Economics,* vol. 19, no. 2 (1987), pp. 217–36.

17. James, "Some Evidence on the Uniqueness of Bank Loans."

18. Don Patinkin, "Financial Intermediaries and the Logical Structure of Monetary Theory," *American Economic Review,* vol. 51, no. 1 (1961), pp. 95–116; Fama, "Banking in the Theory of Finance."

19. They would probably hold a smaller quantity of reserves than when non-interest-bearing reserve requirements are imposed. Thus reserve requirements create an involuntary demand for reserves that is similar in form to taxation.

20. See Marvin Goodfriend and Robert G. King, "Financial Deregulation, Monetary Policy, and Central Banking," chapter 6 in this volume.

21. See also Anna Schwartz's chapter in this volume for evidence on this.

22. As Edward Kane notes, virtually every firm, financial and nonfinancial, will affect some aspect of social-welfare-related specialness associated with its products and services. Even if banks are "extra" special, it is not clear why owners or affiliates of a bank have to be special. See Edward Kane, "How S and L's Are Special" (Federal Home Loan Bank of San Francisco, Conference on Thrift Performance and Capital Adequacy, December 1986).

23. Volcker, Statement before the Subcommittee on Monetary Affairs.

24. John Boyd and Stanley L. Graham, "Risk, Regulation, and Bank Holding Company Expansion into Nonbanking," *Federal Reserve Bank of Minneapolis Review* (Spring 1986), pp. 2–17.

25. This constraint specifies the economic determinants of insolvency probability and ignores exogenously determined regulatory decisions that may result in closure or reorganization before insolvency is reached.

26. Samuel H. Talley, "Bank Holding Company Performance in Consumer Finance and Mortgage Banking," *Magazine of Bank Administration* (July 1976), pp. 42–44; Robert F. Ware, "Characteristics of Banks Acquired by Multiple Bank Holding Companies in Ohio," *Federal Reserve Bank of Cleveland Economic Review* (August 1973), pp. 19–27; and Robert J. Lawrence, *The Performance of Bank Holding Companies* (Washington, D.C.: Board of Governors of the Federal Reserve System, 1971).

27. Arthur G. Fraas, "The Performance of Individual Bank Holding Companies" (Staff Economic Studies no. 84, Board of Governors of the Federal Reserve System, 1974); Jack S. Light, "The Effects of Holding Company Affiliation on De Novo Banks," in *Proceedings of a Conference on Bank Structure and Competition* (Chicago: Federal Reserve Bank of Chicago, 1976), pp. 83–106; Lucille S. Mayne, "A Comparative Study of Bank Holding Company Affiliates and Independent Banks, 1969–1972," *Journal of Finance*, vol. 32, no. 1 (1977), pp. 147–58; John J. Mingo, "Managerial Motives, Market Structures, and the Performance of Holding Company Banks," *Economic Inquiry*, vol. 14, no. 3 (1976), pp. 411–24. See also Timothy Hannan, "Safety, Soundness, and the Bank Holding Company: A Critical Review of the Literature" (Working Paper, Board of Governors of the Federal Reserve System, 1984); and Vincent Apilado and Larry Frieder, "Bank Holding Company Research: Classification, Synthesis, and New Direction," *Journal of Bank Research*, vol. 13, no. 2 (1982), pp. 78–95, for a more extensive review of these types of study.

28. John D. Martin and Arthur J. Keown, "Market Reaction to the Formation of One Banking Holding Companies," *Journal of Banking and Finance*, vol. 5, no. 3 (1981), pp. 383–93.

29. Joseph Aharony and Itzhak Swary, "Effects of the 1970 Bank Holding Company Act: Evidence from Capital Markets," *Journal of Finance*, vol. 36, no. 4 (1981), pp. 841–53; and Randall S. Billingsley and Robert E. Lamy, "Market Reaction to the Formation of One Bank Holding Companies and the 1970 Bank Holding Company Act Amendment," *Journal of Banking and Finance*, vol. 8, no. 1 (1984), pp. 21–33.

30. Returns on bank holding company stocks may give a slightly noisy picture of the returns on bank activities, given that the bank's share of holding

company assets is less than 100 percent. For virtually all existing one-bank holding companies, however, the share of bank assets exceeds 80 percent of total holding company assets.

31. Donald B. Jacobs, H. Prescott Beighley, and John H. Boyd, *The Financial Structure of Bank Holding Companies* (Chicago : Association of Reserve City Bankers, 1975); Samuel Talley, "Bank Holding Company Performance in Consumer Finance and Mortgage Banking"; and Adi Karna, "Bank Holding Company Profitability: Nonbanking Subsidiaries and Financial Leverage," *Journal of Bank Research*, vol. 10, no. 1 (1979), pp. 28–35.

32. Anand S. Desai and Roger D. Stover, "Bank Holding Company Acquisitions, Stockholder Returns, and Regulatory Uncertainty," *Journal of Financial Research*, vol. 8, no. 2 (1985), pp. 145–56; Itzhak Swary, "Bank Acquisition of Nonbank Firms: An Empirical Analysis of Administrative Decisions," *Journal of Banking and Finance*, vol. 7, no. 2 (1983), pp. 213–30; Anthony Saunders and Michael Smirlock, "Intra- and Inter-industry Effects of Bank Securities Market Activities: The Case of Discount Brokerage," *Journal of Financial and Quantitative Analysis*, vol. 22, no. 4 (1987), pp. 467–82.

33. John H. Boyd and Pipat Pithyachariyakul, "Bank Holding Company Diversification into Non-bank Lines of Business" (Unpublished manuscript, 1981); and Boyd and Graham, "Risk, Regulation, and Bank Holding Company Expansion."

34. See, for example, Lucille S. Mayne, "Bank Holding Company Characteristics and the Upstreaming of Bank Funds," *Journal of Money, Credit, and Banking*, vol. 12, no. 2 (1980), pp. 209–14.

35. The fee payments are excessive to the extent that they exceed the true economic value (marginal revenue product) of the services provided by the holding company's management.

36. Roger D. Stover, "The Single Subsidiary Bank Holding Company," *Journal of Bank Research*, vol. 11, no. 1 (1980), pp. 43–50; and Robert W. Kolb, "Affiliated and Independent Banks: Two Behavioral Regimes," *Journal of Banking and Finance*, vol. 5, no. 4 (1981), pp. 523–37.

37. See Stover, "The Single Subsidiary Bank Holding Company."

38. Anthony W. Cyrnak, "Chain Banks and Competition: The Effectiveness of Federal Reserve Policy since 1977," *Federal Reserve Bank of San Francisco Economic Review* (Spring 1986), pp. 5–16; and Stover, "The Single Subsidiary Bank Holding Company."

39. The dividend pay-out effect is also bounded by the fact that member banks must receive the Federal Reserve's approval to pay dividends greater than net profits for a given year and those retained in the previous two years.

40. Holding companies, however, tend to be more leveraged than their banking affiliates.

41. John T. Rose and Samuel H. Talley, "Financial Transactions within Bank Holding Companies," *Journal of Financial Research*, vol. 7, no. 3 (1984), pp. 209–17.

42. Ibid., p. 260.

43. See Morgan Guaranty, "An Investigation of Commercial Bank Failures," *Memorandum*, September 1, 1983.

44. Michael A. Jesse and Steven A. Seelig, *Bank Holding Companies and the Public Interest: An Economic Analysis* (Lexington, Mass.: D.C. Heath & Co., 1977); Mayne, "A Comparative Study of Bank Holding Company Affiliates"; Fraas, "The Performance of Individual Bank Holding Companies"; Mingo, "Managerial Motives"; Arnold A. Heggestad and John J. Mingo, "Capital Management by Bank Holding Company Banks," *Journal of Business*, vol. 48, no. 4 (1975), pp. 500–505; Dale S. Drum, "MBHC's: Evidence after Two Decades of Regulations," *Federal Reserve Bank of Chicago Business Conditions* (December 1976), pp. 3–15; Stover, "The Single Subsidiary Bank Holding Company"; and Kolb, "Affiliated and Independent Banks."

45. Light, "The Effects of Holding Company Affiliation"; Mayne, "A Comparative Study of Bank Holding Company Affiliates"; William Jackson, "Multibank Holding Company and Bank Behavior" (Working Paper, no. 75-1, Federal Reserve Bank of Richmond, 1975); Ronald D. Johnson and David R. Meinster, "Bank Holding Companies: Diversification Opportunities in Nonbank Activities," *Eastern Economic Journal*, vol. 1, no. 4 (1974), pp. 316–23; and Stover, "The Single Subsidiary Bank Holding Company."

46. Jesse and Seelig, *Bank Holding Companies and the Public Interest*.

47. Boyd and Graham, "Risk, Regulation."

48. The relationship between β and total return risk on bank stock i ($Var(R_i)$) is

$$Var(\tilde{R}_i) = \beta^2 Var(\tilde{R}_M) + Var((\tilde{\epsilon}_i)$$

where $Var(\tilde{R}_M)$ is the variance of returns on the market portfolio and ϵ_i is unsystematic or idiosyncratic risk of bank stock i. Thus, *ceteris paribus*, an increase in β increases $Var(\tilde{R}_i)$.

49. Again, the bank may benefit to the extent that the holding company is viewed by the Federal Reserve as a source of strength to the bank.

50. The mean return for a bank holding company will be

$$\sum_{i=1}^{n} x_i r_i$$

where x_i is the proportion of holding company assets invested in that activity and r_i is the rate of return (or profit) on capital invested in that activity. The standard deviation of holding company profit will be equal to

$$[\sum_{i=1}^{n} x_i^2 \sigma_i^2 + 2 \sum_{i=j}^{n} x_i x_j \rho_{ij} \sigma_i \sigma_j]^{1/2}$$

where σ_i, σ_j are the standard deviations of returns from individual activities and ρ_{ij} is the correlation between returns from different activities. As can be seen, as ρ_{ij} falls from $+1$ to -1, the standard deviation of holding company profits falls toward zero.

51. Arnold A. Heggestad, "Riskiness of Investments in Nonbank Activities by Bank Holding Companies," *Journal of Economics and Business*, vol. 27, no. 1 (1975), pp. 219–23.

52. Johnson and Meinster, "Bank Holding Companies."

53. John H. Boyd, Gerald A. Hanweck, and Pipat Pithyachariyakul, "Bank Holding Company Diversification," in *Proceedings of a Conference on Bank Structure and Competition* (Chicago: Federal Reserve Bank of Chicago, 1980), pp. 105–21.

54. Peter C. Eisemann, "Diversification and the Cogeneric Bank Holding Company," *Journal of Bank Research*, vol. 7, no. 1 (1976), pp. 68–77.

55. David R. Meinster and Ronald D. Johnson, "Bank Holding Company Diversification and the Risk of Capital Impairment," *Bell Journal of Economics*, vol. 10, no. 2 (1979), pp. 683–94.

56. Larry D. Wall and Robert A. Eisenbeis, "Risk Considerations in Deregulating Bank Activities," *Federal Reserve Bank of Atlanta Economic Review* (May 1984), pp. 6–19; and Heggestad, "Riskiness of Investments."

57. Roger D. Stover, "A Re-Examination of Bank Holding Company Acquisitions," *Journal of Bank Research*, vol. 13, no. 2 (1982), pp. 101–8.

58. Wall and Eisenbeis, "Risk Considerations."

59. Anthony Saunders and Pierre Yourougou, "Are Banks Special? Some Evidence from Stock Market Returns" (Working Paper, Graduate Business School, New York University, July 1987).

60. Of course, banks may use more direct means in the form of interest rate futures, options, and swaps.

61. Such geographic diversification may be particularly important today, given the problems of the oil and gas banks in the Southwest and the farm banks in the Midwest. Recent FDIC figures for bank failures between the first quarter of 1985 and the third quarter of 1986 show 108 farm banks failing against 117 nonfarm banks. The failure of many of these banks may be partially attributable to their inability to diversify regionally (in an optimal fashion) in the face of federal and state regulations on interstate banking.

62. Robert A. Eisenbeis, "Financial Innovation and the Growth of Bank Holding Companies," in *Proceedings of a Conference on Bank Structure and Competition* (Chicago: Federal Reserve Bank of Chicago, 1978), pp. 27–28; Robert A. Eisenbeis, Robert S. Harris, and Joseph Lakonishok, "Benefits of Bank Diversification: The Evidence from Shareholder Returns," *Journal of Finance*, vol. 39, no. 3 (1984), pp. 881–92.

63. Mark J. Flannery, "Contagious Bank Runs, Financial Structure, and Corporate Separateness within a Bank Holding Company," in *Proceedings of a Conference on Bank Structure and Competition* (Chicago: Federal Reserve Bank of Chicago, forthcoming).

64. Joseph Aharony and Itzhak Swary, "Contagion Effects of Bank Failures: Evidence from Capital Markets," *Journal of Business*, vol. 56, no. 2 (1983), pp. 213–30.

65. Ithzak Swary, "Stock Market Reaction to Regulatory Action in the Continental Illinois Crisis," *Journal of Business*, vol. 59, no. 3 (1986), pp. 451–74.

66. This seems to have been the behavior of small regional banks and their agents, the "deposits brokers." See also ibid.

67. George G. Kaufman, "The Truth about Bank Runs" (Paper presented at the Cato Conference, "The Financial Services Revolution: Policy Directions for the Future," February 26–27, 1987).

68. *Bank of England Quarterly Bulletin*, 1984, various issues.

69. A contagion effect is apparent in the effect on the spread between three-month CD rates and three-month T-bill rates in the secondary market. Between January and March 1984 (before the Continental announcements), the average monthly spread was 0.376 percent. It rose to 0.72 percent in April and to 1.28 percent in May. In the subsequent three months (June–August 1984), the average monthly spread was 1.30 percent. The average spread between three-month Eurodollar deposits and T-bills was 0.86 percent for January–March 1984. This rose to 1.14 percent in April and to 1.70 percent in May. In the three months June–August 1984, the average spread was 1.68 percent.

70. This result may not be much different from the effect of a major corporate bond default on other corporate bond rates.

71. This makes Corrigan's advocacy of bank holding companies that can undertake a full range of financial services (such as investment banking) but not commercial activities rather perplexing, given the Federal Reserve's pervasive fear of bank runs and contagion effects. See Corrigan, "Financial Market Structure."

72. At the end of 1982, First Nationwide's book value of capital to assets was 3.76 percent, and in 1983 it was 3.23 percent.

73. Fisher Black, Merton H. Miller, and Richard A. Posner, "An Approach to the Regulation of Bank Holding Companies," *Journal of Business*, vol. 51, no. 3 (1978), pp. 374–411.

74. Harry G. Henn, *Handbook of the Law of Corporations and Other Business Enterprises*, 2d ed. (St. Paul, Minn.: West Publishing Co., 1970).

75. Robert A. Eisenbeis, "How Should Bank Holding Companies Be Regulated?" *Federal Reserve Bank of Atlanta Economic Review* (January 1983), pp. 42–47; Paul M. Horvitz, "Bank Holding Company Regulation: Discussion," in *Proceedings of a Conference on Bank Structure and Competition* (Chicago: Federal Reserve Bank of Chicago, 1978), pp. 57–60.

76. Nevertheless, the new Section 23B restrictions placed on interaffiliate cross marketing and advertising should further weaken any estoppel arguments.

77. Boyd and Graham, "Risk, Regulation"; and Larry D. Wall, "Has BHCs' Diversification Affected Their Risk of Failure?" (Working Paper 85-2, Federal Reserve Bank of Atlanta, 1985).

78. Federal Deposit Insurance Corporation, "Mandate for Change: Restructuring the Banking Industry" (preliminary draft, Washington, D.C., August 18, 1987).

79. See Volcker, Statement before the Subcommittee on Commerce, Consumer and Monetary Affairs; and Corrigan, "Financial Market Structure." To some extent, the threat to transaction accounts, the primary concern of Corrigan in 1982, has now been superseded by concerns about the safety of

systems for the electronic transfer of funds. This change in emphasis directly reflects the growing size and importance of such mechanisms over traditional forms of payment such as checks and currency.

80. Although upstreaming is legally limited by Sections 23A and 23B of the Federal Reserve Act, it is unclear whether Section 23A applies to "off-balance-sheet" daylight overdrafts. See Mark J. Flannery, "Payments System Risk and Public Policy," chapter 7 in this volume.

81. In this case any settlement risk, such as the failure of a bank to settle its net debits in its reserve account at the end of the day, would be borne by the Federal Reserve, although such a failure to settle is still an important public policy concern.

82. David B. Humphrey, "Payments Finality and Risk of Settlement Failure," in A. Saunders and L. White, eds., *Technology and the Regulation of Financial Markets: Securities, Futures, and Banking* (Lexington, Mass.: Lexington Books, D.C. Heath & Co., 1986), pp. 97–120.

83. Even though one bank still retains a claim on another for funds, it cannot actually lay hands on these funds.

84. Humphrey, "Payments Finality."

85. It should be noted, though, that since "settlement failure" occurs at the end of the day these options are likely to be strictly limited.

86. Edward I. Altman, "Risks and Rewards in the High Yield Debt Market—Measurement and Performance" (Graduate School of Business, New York University, 1986, mimeo).

87. The imposition of cross-system caps, both bilateral and aggregate, appears to be the method currently being followed by the Federal Reserve to contain the daylight overdrafts in the system. For a thorough description of the Federal Reserve's policy, see Stevens, "Reducing Risk in Wire Transfer Systems," *Federal Reserve Bank of Cleveland Economic Review,* no. 2 (1986), pp. 17–22.

88. No similar level of concern has been apparent regarding potential conflicts in nonbank holding companies and commercial conglomerates, even though the necessary conditions for potential conflicts, such as information asymmetries and monopoly power, are often present in the real sector.

89. Stephen Halpert, "The Separation of Banking and Commerce Reconsidered" (University of Miami Law School, August 1986, mimeo).

90. Franklin R. Edwards, "Banks and Securities Activities: Legal and Economic Perspectives on the Glass-Steagall Act," in L. Goldberg and L. White, eds., *The Deregulation of the Banking and Securities Industries* (Lexington, Mass.: D.C. Heath & Co., 1979), pp. 273–94; Halpert, "The Separation of Banking and Commerce Reconsidered"; and Anthony Saunders, "Conflicts of Interest: An Economic View," in Ingo Walter, ed., *Deregulating Wall Street: Commercial Bank Penetration of the Corporate Securities Market* (New York: John Wiley & Sons, 1985), pp. 207–30.

91. Saunders, "Conflicts of Interest."

92. Jan Loeys, "Low Grade Bonds: A Growing Source of Corporate Funding," *Federal Reserve Bank of Philadelphia Business Review* (November/December 1986), pp. 3–12.

93. Jan Loeys, "Low Grade Bonds: A Growing Source of Corporate Funding."

94. Richard A. Posner, *Antitrust Law: An Economic Perspective* (Chicago: University of Chicago Press, 1976).

95. A recent example is Citicorp's problem in choosing underwriting syndicate lead-managers who would *not* also be participating in Manufacturers Hanover's new issue, for fear that there may be a potential conflict regarding the optimal timing of the new issue.

96. Saunders, "Conflicts of Interest."

97. Stephen Halpert, "The Separation of Banking and Commerce Reconsidered."

98. Further, Peltzman and others have argued that any monopoly rents in banking may be due largely to regulations that restrict the supply of new bank charters. See Sam Peltzman, "Capital Investment in Commercial Banking and Its Relationship to Portfolio Regulation," *Journal of Political Economy*, vol. 78, no. 1 (1970), pp. 1–26.

99. George Benston, Gerald Hanweck, and David Humphrey, "Scale Economies in Banking: A Restructuring and Reassessment," *Journal of Money, Credit, and Banking*, vol. 14, no. 1 (1982), pp. 435–56; and David B. Humphrey, "The U.S. Payments System."

100. Sherrill Shaffer and Edmond David, "Economies of Superscale and Interstate Expansion" (Research Paper no. 8612, Federal Reserve Bank of New York, 1986).

101. Frederic M. Sherer, *Industrial Market Structure and Economic Performance*, 2d ed. (Chicago: Rand-McNally, 1980), pp. 93–94.

102. Hans R. Stoll, "Small Firms' Access to Public Equity Financing," in P. Horvitz and R. R. Pettit, eds., *Sources of Financing for Small Business (Pt. B)* (Greenwich, Conn.: JAI Press, 1984), pp. 187–238.

103. Thomas Gilligan, Michael Smirlock, and William Marshall, "Scale and Scope Economies in the Multi-Product Banking Firm," *Journal of Monetary Economics*, vol. 13, no. 4 (1984), pp. 393–405.

104. Moreover, scope economies for information collection and use are potentially even larger for financial service firms. Consider, for example, the success of financial conglomerates such as American Express.

105. See John Cable, "Capital Market Information and Industrial Performance: The Role of West German Banks," *Economic Journal*, vol. 95, no. 1 (1985), pp. 118–32, for example.

106. Although it ought to be recognized that to the extent that deposit insurance is underpriced and bank managers are more risk averse than owners there may be decreased agency problems between the bank and the FDIC as well as between outside depositors and the bank.

107. See Halpert, "The Separation of Banking and Commerce," for arguments along similar lines. It should be noted that U.S. banks do have a limited ability to write loan contracts with equity kickers.

108. Michael C. Jensen and Richard S. Ruback, "The Market for Corporate Control: The Scientific Evidence," *Journal of Financial Economics*, vol. 11, nos. 1–4 (1983), pp. 5–50.

BANK HOLDING COMPANIES

109. See Thomas F. Huertas, "Redesigning Regulation—The Future of Finance in the United States," in *Restructuring the Financial System*, a symposium sponsored by the Federal Reserve Bank of Kansas City, Jackson Hole, Wyoming, August 1987).

110. One might even argue that there would be no bank regulatory role for the Federal Reserve under such a system.

111. One reason deposit insurance charges would probably be higher for a universal bank is that regulators in setting premiums would face the increased (examination) costs of collecting information and monitoring the commercial as well as financial activities of the organization. This would also require considerably more expertise and coordination among examining teams than at present. Such costs would presumably be paid by the insurees rather than the insurers.

112. In an OBHC, the management structure is likely to be more diffuse and therefore more difficult for stockholders to monitor and control than in a more centralized structure such as a universal bank.

113. A further institutional change required to enhance the relative attractiveness of the universal bank form would be to allow this bank to use the bankruptcy option available to commercial corporations and not be subject to exogenous closure rules and decisions of the chartering authorities. Conglomerates might find the universal bank more attractive particularly because an increased ability to integrate the technological side may have benefits of scope on the financial side. "Securitization," for example, which is intimately linked to a financial firm's ability to monitor, collect, and process information, in combining commercial and investment bank activities, crucially depends on the ability to integrate technology within the organization.

114. See John Kareken, "Federal Bank Regulatory Policy: A Description and Some Observations," *Journal of Business*, vol. 59, no. 1 (1986), pp. 3–48.

115. Admittedly, it is possible that investment bankers would have incentives to develop new securities such as T-bond maturity "strips" to augment the supply of short-term bills available to banks.

116. Although this effect would be mitigated if the new intermediary were allowed to take positions in financial futures, options, and swaps, such positions may also result in increased "off-balance-sheet" risk should they be used in a suboptimal fashion.

Commentary

Robert A. Eisenbeis

The papers by Professors Saunders and Edwards focus on different dimensions of the structural changes that have been taking place in banking. Tony Saunders looks at the micro implications of these changes for individual banking firms and how they organize their operations as powers and activities are expanded. He concentrates on the issue of whether banks are special and how our answer affects the approach to financial regulation and reform. Frank Edwards focuses on the macro effects of these changes and their effects on conduct and performance in financial markets. He is particularly concerned with debunking conventional wisdom about the anticompetitive nature of the changes that have been taking place and hence the need for more regulation to protect both customers and suppliers of services. Because of the different objectives of the papers, it is best to comment on them individually.

Bank Holding Companies: Structure, Performance, and Reform

Tony Saunders has four key conclusions about the need for financial reform in banking and its likely effects on banking organizational structure. First, although much of present banking regulation has been based on the premise that banks are special, there is now, at best, a weak case for that proposition. Second, there is no overriding theoretical or empirical case for continuing the separation between banking and commerce. Third, in a world without deposit insurance, a number of alternative organizational forms become economically feasible as vehicles for commingling banking and commerce. Finally, among the alternative ways for permitting expanded powers to banking organizations, the so-called fail-safe bank is an unattractive option.

Saunders begins his analysis by reviewing the now well-publicized reasons put forward by E. G. Corrigan why banks are special.[1] Corrigan argues that banks are special because they issue transaction accounts, because of their role as a transmission belt for monetary policy, and because they are the backup source of liquidity for the economy. After carefully reviewing the issues, Saunders concludes that the arguments do not stand up well, a view that is shared by others who have preceded him.[2] Here Saunders makes two important contributions. First is the integration of the recent literature on deposit contracting and bank runs into the debate. This work suggests that the costs of runs and the real effects of bank failure are high. Second, he points out, but not forcefully enough, the dangers of relying on the implications of that literature for policy purposes. The simplifying assumptions necessary to make the models tractable are abstractions that do not adequately capture the realities of the financial system. The literature on bank runs, for example (represented by Bryant and by Diamond and Dybvig), describes the consequences of runs on the banking system as a whole rather than the effects on a single bank within that system.[3] There is also a decided lack of richness in the assets available for individuals to hold, since the models usually contain only one financial asset (transaction accounts) and a consumption good. Saunders makes the useful point that this literature tends to encourage and facilitate loose extrapolation of the costs of bank failures from models in which there is only one bank and to assume that these same costs are relevant in a world with many banks and a much richer selection of financial assets. Here Saunders argues that academics may have clouded analysis of the policy issues rather than contributed to the debate.

Having raised, and then essentially rejected, the idea that banks are special, Saunders turns to a discussion of bank holding companies and the activities they should be permitted. He examines the effects of expanded bank holding company powers on (1) the solvency of subsidiary banks, (2) deposit insurance subsidies, (3) payments system risks, (4) conflicts of interest, and (5) conglomeration. The links between this second section of the paper and the first are a bit thin. Saunders points out that the rationale in the present policy debate for permitting expanded powers to banking organizations through a bank holding company rather than to bank subsidiaries rests on the view that banks are special in the sense that Corrigan described. Having essentially rejected the notion that banks are special, however, the main reason he holds out for caring whether activities are conducted within a holding company or within a subsidiary bank lies in the slim possibility they are special. This possibility is a thin reed upon which to conduct this policy debate.

There are, however, reasons other than the argument that banks are special why we might care where, within a banking organization, new activities are conducted. The most important is the distortion to risk-taking incentives under the present structure of the deposit insurance system.[4] These deposit insurance reform issues, however, are better addressed directly, as illustrated by the interesting policy proposals suggested by Benston and Kaufman in this volume, than by attempting to correct a structural defect in the deposit insurance system by imposing an additional set of regulations on banks restricting their activities.

At the end of the section on bank holding companies (BHCs), Saunders raises the most interesting and relevant question in the paper. He asks whether the BHC organizational form would be the optimal way for a commercial-financial conglomerate to conduct business in a fully deregulated world without deposit insurance. Is a BHC a desirable vehicle because of the implied option in the subsidiary structure to walk away from problem subsidiaries, or is the BHC form used primarily for its productivity in avoiding regulatory taxes, branching restrictions, and other regulatory constraints?[5] We need to understand better the behavior and motivation of financial (and nonfinancial) conglomerates before the benefits and costs of corporate separateness as a regulatory principle can be assessed adequately.[6] None of the existing banking or corporate finance literature addresses this issue, leaving open an interesting opportunity for theoretical research.

It is useful to point out some other interesting issues with regard to the drive for structural reform in banking. It was suggested in the discussion by Richard Herring (in this volume) that one of the motivations for new powers for BHCs is rooted in fundamental structural changes in the intermediation process.[7] This is illustrated by the growth of securitization, which unbundles the traditional lending process into its component functions of (1) credit evaluation, (2) guarantee, and (3) portfolio lending.[8] Reductions in information and transaction costs have narrowed spreads and reduced portfolio investment profits. The key to profitability today for many financial intermediaries may be in getting rid of portfolio investments—a strategy being followed by Bankers Trust, for example—and still capturing returns where banks have comparative advantages: in the credit evaluation, loan origination, and guarantee functions. Thus, banks may be pursuing securities powers as natural sources of potential scope economies. Realization of these economies may be necessary to the future production of credit services and the future viability of insured depository institutions. Without the ability to underwrite and distribute securities, it may not be possible to strip off the profits still available to banks.

To address the problem banks are perceived to face, two options have been proposed. The first is to give banks securities powers, but this is perceived as being too risky at the moment, despite the empirical evidence to the contrary.[9] The second alternative is to give new powers to bank holding companies, but with sufficient controls to ensure insulation by establishing a fire wall between the bank and its sister affiliates.

There are really two types of insulation—financial insulation and operational insulation.[10] Financial insulation restricts income flows and transactions between a bank and its sister subsidiaries through dividend restrictions, prohibitions, and limitations such as those contained in Section 23A of the Federal Reserve Act. Operational insulation would prohibit sharing and joint use of physical and productive resources, such as personnel. The Federal Reserve has imposed restrictions, for example, to enforce operational separation in permitting acquisition of S&Ls by bank holding companies. If both types of insulation were to be forced on a bank with respect to securities activities, for example, the bank would continue to be a less attractive alternative (as it allegedly is now). Operational insulation would make it uneconomical to offer credit services in their fully unbundled form, since it would be denied any synergies and scope economies that would come from having a sister broker-dealer affiliate. The only way for an affiliate to distribute securitized assets would be on an arm's length basis, which would mean that the only benefits to the holding company of engaging in securities activities would be the diversification benefits from earnings of the securities affiliate. But shareholders of the bank holding company should be able to achieve the same diversification benefits from owning shares in a completely insulated subsidiary in their own portfolios.

Most recent restructuring proposals have provided for less than complete insulation.[11] In particular, most attempt to preserve financial insulation while permitting operational integration. Can this be done successfully? Saunders starts by examining how much risk there really is. He summarizes the empirical work, which shows that BHC subsidiary banks have higher leverage and higher returns. What none of this work points out is that reported returns depend in large part on how the holding company chooses to allocate joint costs and what internal transfer pricing system is in use. Given the skills of accountants, the reported income figures can be almost anything the owners want them to be; hence, it is not clear how accurately the accounting numbers capture the underlying economic performance of subsidiaries.

It is possible to devise scenarios to illustrate the incentives that exist when operational integration is permitted. Suppose a bank holding company has a nonbank subsidiary that provides all the data processing services for its bank and nonbank subsidiaries. If this subsidiary gets into financial difficulty, will the bank (or holding company) be willing to incur the costs to walk away—to incur the embarrassment and to look for a new vendor to supply all data processing services? It might, but the disruption to service and the transfer costs would be large indeed, since the subsidiary would be servicing the operations of the company. A working hypothesis is that the more important an operationally integrated subsidiary is to the day-to-day business of the company, and the greater the extent to which it is a source of scale and scope economies, the larger the incentives would be to attempt to rescue the subsidiary.[12]

In the same way, would a bank be likely to walk away from a problem securities affiliate? The incentives and the ability to walk away are likely to be directly related to the operational necessity of the affiliate to the holding company. If the previous analysis is correct, and banks desire securities powers because of their importance in continuing to be able to offer credit services in a world with low transactions costs, then logically it would be very difficult for the bank to walk away. If the failure of the securities affiliate meant loss of the fees from credit investigation, origination services, and loan guarantees, the incentives to attempt to rescue the subsidiary would be very strong.

Because reform proposals have failed to deal adequately with the behavioral incentives and instead have rather mechanically sorted activities into categories that banks are and are not permitted to engage in, I am not enthusiastic about the present attempt to deal with the problems of devising effective insulation strategies. For this reason as well, I prefer the solution outlined by Benston and Kaufman in this volume that would permit a bank to engage in any activities it chooses. All that is required is the development of monitoring policies and procedures, much of which would be required anyway if insulation policies were adopted, to ensure that net worth did not go below zero.

The Future Financial Structure: Fears and Policies

Professor Edwards recently pointed out myths that were perversely affecting the debate on financial restructuring.[13] His paper in this volume follows in that same track by punctuating several fears that have been dredged up—mostly by those in the securities and insurance industries seeking to protect their turfs—concerning possible adverse effects associated with structural change in financial services. Specifically, in the new world that presumably would have fewer and bigger financial institutions, Edwards's analysis leads him to five general conclusions. First, competition would probably be greater not less. Second, larger institutions would pose less, rather than greater, financial system risks. Third, fewer institutions would not necessarily result in unfair competitive practices. Fourth, consolidation would not adversely affect the allocation of credit. Finally, larger institutions would not lead to undue concentration of political power.

Although there is really little new in this paper in terms of the data, arguments, or analysis provided, the points are well worth repeating at a time when the debate over financial restructuring is heating up. I tend to agree with these conclusions but believe Edwards could have made a more convincing case. Hence, my comments take the form of a few quibbles and observations.

In discussing the effects of recent structural changes, particularly with regard to interstate banking, Edwards argues that if markets are properly defined, concentration has declined. The data he uses from the early 1980s are not, however, appropriate for the case being made. Most of his data predate the recent interstate banking movement and thus do not provide any relevant evidence on the issues. To be convincing, evidence must hold up when concentration in 1986 and 1987 is examined.

Both Edwards and Saunders suggest, contrary to most widely known evidence, that economies of scale in banking may exist and that this explains why banks want to get bigger. Both state that studies implying the lack of scale economies rely on historical data and do not look at the largest banks. Neither cites more recent evidence using current data, which continue to show lack of evidence of scale and scope economies.[14] Only one study, by Shaffer and Edmond, seems to show economies for the very largest firms.[15] But these data do not take into account the levels of costs in comparing the efficiencies of different sized institutions. Evidence on low returns to assets and equity for the largest banks suggests that even if scale economies do exist, larger banks may have cost curves that lie above those for smaller firms. In general, this issue of the true nature of bank costs remains a major puzzle in the literature, and arguments for larger institutions based on efficiency grounds remain to be justified.

In another section, Edwards devotes some attention to the issue of fairness in competition. Here I have an observation rather than a criticism. Though it is difficult to rationalize treating individuals differently under the law, it is more difficult to be especially concerned about the principle of fairness when dealing with corporate regulatory burdens.[16] Differential regulation, for example, to the extent that regulation is a tax, has nothing to do with fairness. Rather, differential regulation is tax policy for the reallocation of resources, which has always been one function that government performs. Thus the cries for a level playing field and other arguments for fairness and equity in financial regulation are really cries for changes in tax policy to change resource allocation from one segment of the economy to another or from one set of shareholders to another.

I would particularly like to compliment Edwards on his treatment of the issues of predatory pricing, tie-ins, and conflicts of interest. He points out that these become significant policy problems when markets are not competitive. Such problems go away if competition is increased, heightening the need to show that the structural changes that have taken place are consistent with more and not less competition.

The last issue to be raised concerns the treatment of antitrust. First Edwards describes the process of antitrust enforcement and suggests there are few problems. There is need only for some tidying up. In particular, he says there is no need for an enforcement process for banks and bank holding companies separate from that for nonfinancial firms. I believe several important antitrust issues deserve more attention than they are given. First, Edwards makes the important point that the antitrust standards should be the same for banking as for other firms.[17] This I believe is consistent with judicial interpretation, but not necessarily with present enforcement policies. Second, he argues that since the Justice Department screens all mergers, there is no need for a separate agency review process. This argument ignores the rationale for imposing the review process, which was originally instituted because of the difficulty of requiring a divestiture of banking acquisitions should judicial review prove them to be anticompetitive. Moreover, it assumes that the Justice Department has been given adequate resources to screen proposed mergers and that these resources are evenly distributed across industries. Both assumptions are subject to serious question. Third, there is the problem of lack of consistency of enforcement policies over time. It is clear that enforcement policies changed significantly with the promulgation of the revised Justice Department guidelines, despite the fact that the underlying antitrust law did not change. Such unanticipated shifts in enforcement policies not only complicate the acquisition planning process but also raise questions about their legality. Finally, there is the particularly important issue of the adequacy of the antitrust laws to affect the evolution of banking markets when large discrete changes in financial structure accompany financial restructuring legislation. The antitrust laws were designed to deal with changes in structure on the margin as markets are transformed by mergers and acquisitions. Each case is treated sequentially on a case-by-case basis. The antitrust laws are not well designed to deal with issues of structural engineering when there are large discrete changes in structure. The Federal Reserve, for example, through its go-slow policies in Texas, attempted to use the applications process to affect the evolution of banking organizational structure. Mergers have been proscribed, even when they do not violate antitrust laws because they may imply the setting of a precedent. Whether engineering banking structure is an appropriate worry of the banking agencies is open to further debate, but it seems clear that the antitrust enforcement process is a poor vehicle for that end.

Notes

1. E. G. Corrigan, "Are Banks Special?" *Federal Reserve Bank of Minneapolis Annual Report*, 1982.

2. See, for example, James L. Pierce, "On the Expansion of Banking Powers," in Ingo Walter, ed., *Deregulating Wall Street* (New York: Wiley Interscience, 1985); and Richard C. Aspinwall, "On the 'Specialness' of Banking," *Issues in Bank Regulation* (Autumn 1983).

3. This results because the models contain effectively only one bank. See John Bryant, "A Model of Reserves, Bank Runs, and Deposit Insurance," *Journal of Banking and Finance*, vol. 4 (1980), pp. 335–44; and Douglas Diamond and Philip H. Dybvig, "Bank Runs, Deposit Insurance and Liquidity," *Journal of Political Economy* (1983), pp. 401–19.

4. See Edward J. Kane, *The Gathering Crisis in Federal Deposit Insurance* (Cambridge, Mass.: MIT Press, 1985); and George G. Benston, Robert A. Eisenbeis, Paul M. Horvitz, Edward J. Kane, and George G. Kaufman, *Perspectives on Safe and Sound Banking* (Cambridge, Mass.: MIT Press, 1986), for discussions.

5. See Edward J. Kane, "Accelerating Inflation, Technological Innovation, and the Decreasing Effectiveness of Bank Regulation," *Journal of Finance* (May 1981).

6. For reform proposals based on the idea of corporate separateness or insulation, see FDIC, *Mandate for Change: Restructuring the Banking Industry* (Washington, D.C., October 1987); Robert Litan, *What Should Banks Do?* (Washington, D.C.: Brookings Institution, 1987); Samuel Chase and Donn L. Waage, "Corporate Separateness as a Tool of Bank Regulation" (Washington, D.C.: Economic Advisory Committee of the American Bankers Association, 1983); and E. G. Corrigan, "Financial Market Structure: A Longer View," Federal Reserve Bank of New York, 1986.

7. For a full discussion, see Robert A. Eisenbeis, "Eroding Market Imperfections: Implications for Financial Intermediaries, the Payments System, and Regulatory Reform," in *Restructuring the Financial System*, a symposium sponsored by the Federal Reserve Bank of Kansas City, Jackson Hole, Wyoming, August 20–22, 1987.

8. Lawrence M. Benveniste, and Allen N. Berger, "Securitization with Recourse: An Instrument That Offers Uninsured Depositors Sequential

Claims," *Journal of Banking and Finance*, vol. 11 (1987), pp. 403–24; and Stuart I. Greenbaum and Anjan V. Thakor, "Bank Funding Modes, Securitization versus Deposits," *Journal of Banking and Finance*, vol. 11 (1987), pp. 379–401.

9. Arnold Heggestad, "Riskiness of Investments in Nonbank Activities by Bank Holding Companies," *Journal of Economics and Business* (Spring 1975), pp. 219–23; Myron L. Kwast, "The Impact of Underwriting and Dealing on Bank Returns and Risks," Financial Studies Section Working Paper, April 1987; and Larry Wall and Robert A. Eisenbeis, "Risk Considerations in Deregulating Bank Activities," *Federal Reserve Bank of Atlanta Economic Review* (May 1984), pp. 6–19.

10. Anthony Cornyn, Gerald Hanweck, Stephen A. Rhoades, and John T. Rose,"An Analysis of the Concept of Corporate Separateness in BHC Regulation from an Economic Perspective," Appendixes to the Statement by Paul A. Volcker before the Subcommittee on Commerce, Consumer, and Monetary Affairs of the Committee on Government Operations of the U.S. House of Representatives, Papers prepared by the Federal Reserve Board Staff, June 1986.

11. Thomas F. Huertas, "Redesigning Regulation: The Future of Finance in the United States," in *Restructuring the Financial System*.

12. Of course, at least one prominent banker has argued, "It's inconceivable that any major bank would walk away from any subsidiary of its holding company." See Walter Wriston, *Hearings before the Senate Committee on Banking, Housing, and Urban Affairs, Part 2*, 97th Congress, 1st session October 29, 1981, pp. 589–90.

13. Franklin Edwards, "Can Financial Reform Prevent the Impending Disaster in Financial Markets?" in *Restructuring the Financial System*.

14. David B. Humphrey, "Cost Dispersion and the Measurement of Economies in Banking," *Federal Reserve Bank of Richmond Economic Review* (May/June 1987).

15. Sherrill Shaffer and David Edmond, "Economies of Superscale and Interstate Expansion," Federal Reserve Bank of New York, Research Report 8612, November 1986.

16. The one exception may be in the area of taxation, where we subject individuals to differential taxes based on their incomes and the various sources of those incomes.

17. The only distinction is the override provision under the Bank Merger Acts to permit an anticompetitive merger if there are overriding considerations of convenience and need.

Thomas F. Huertas

This project is both timely and important: timely, because the Congress has begun to consider comprehensive reform of financial regulation, and important because the project provides guidance as to how regulation should be reformed.

In general, the project has taken a comprehensive look at major problems in financial regulation, including who should be able to own a depository institution, in which activities the affiliates or subsidiaries of a depository institution should be able to engage, and how an enterprise containing a depository institution within its corporate structure should be regulated.

To answer these questions the AEI study in general and the papers by Professors Saunders and Edwards in particular employed three criteria. The first was stability. Are restrictions on who can own a depository institution or on the activities in which a depository institution's affiliates or subsidiaries may engage necessary to ensure economic stability? Here the answer is quite simply no. Price stability through stable monetary policy is the prerequisite for a stable financial system.

The second criterion was safety. Are restrictions on who can own a depository institution and the activities in which a depository institution's affiliates or subsidiaries may engage necessary to ensure the safety of deposits or the soundness of depository institutions? Here, too, the answer is no. Deposit insurance ensures safety as far as the consumer is concerned. If restrictions on who may own a depository institution or on the activities in which a depository institution's affiliates or subsidiaries may engage are needed, then they are needed only insofar as it is necessary to limit excessive strain on the deposit insurance funds. Such restrictions are not necessary at all if the depository institution can be adequately insulated from its affiliates and subsidiaries. This study in general, and Professor Saunders's paper in particular, have suggested, along with recent reports of the House Committee on Government Operations, the FDIC, and the comptroller of the currency, that such insulation could be achieved largely by enforcing current requirements that depository institutions maintain adequate capital, that depository institutions conduct their transactions with affiliates on an arm's-length basis, and that failures of depository institutions be resolved in a manner that does not protect the creditors of the depository institution's affiliates or subsidiaries.[1]

More important, perhaps, recent events demonstrate that insulation is workable and that it is being enforced. In resolutions of bank failures since 1984 the FDIC has rigorously enforced the separation of insured banks from their affiliates. The former have been protected in full; the latter have not.[2] In general, restrictions on banks' transacting with their nonbank affiliates were rigorously observed during the stock market crash of October 1987 and its immediate aftermath. For example, insured bank subsidiaries of SEC-regulated securities firms did not make improper advances to their parents, subsidiaries, or affiliates. Nor, with one exception, did bank subsidiaries of bank holding companies. The one exception was the extension of credit by Continental Illinois Bank to an operating subsidiary conducting an activity (lending) that could have been conducted within the bank itself. In that case, enforcement was swift, and the insured bank was fully protected.[3]

In sum, the deposit insurance fund ensures safety as far as the consumer is concerned, and insulation adequately protects the deposit insurance fund. Consequently, there is no reason to restrict who may own a depository institution or the activities in which a depository institution's affiliates or subsidiaries may engage.

The third criterion employed in the studies related to the structure of the financial services industry. Are restrictions on who may own a depository institution or on the activities in which a depository institution's affiliates or subsidiaries may engage necessary to prevent conflicts of interest, to ensure the availability of credit, or to prevent economic concentration, harmful tie-ins, predatory pricing, or other anti-competitive practices? Again, the answer given in this volume, and in the Saunders and Edwards papers in particular, is no. Restrictions are not needed; indeed, removing those restrictions on affiliation between depository institutions and other enterprises would promote greater competition and reduce the chance that abuses could occur.

In sum, the conclusion to be drawn from these papers and from the study in general seems clear: there is no need for restrictions on who may own a depository institution or on the activities in which a depository institution's affiliates or subsidiaries may engage. There is a need to make sure that depository institutions are insulated from their affiliates and subsidiaries—but this is largely a matter of enforcing statutes and utilizing regulatory powers already on the books.

What then might be the rationale for keeping in place the restrictions on who may own a depository institution and on the activities in which a depository institution may engage? Implicit in the Saunders and Edwards papers is a rationale for putting reform on the back burner. Somewhat irreverently put, this rationale might be as follows.

One reason for not changing the current regulations might be to undermine the safety and soundness of today's banks. If banking organizations cannot offer what customers want, customers will go elsewhere. Banks will be less competitive and less sound, posing risk to the deposit insurance fund. Hardly anyone would suggest that prohibiting R&D would promote the health of drug companies or be good for the public. Yet current law limits, and the moratorium imposed by the Competitive Equality Banking Act of 1987 completely prohibits, certain types of new product development—products that customers want. If customers cannot get these products from banking organizations, they will get them elsewhere, albeit at higher cost, and banks will slowly but surely wither away.[4]

A second reason for doing nothing might be to maximize the cost of financial services or, more provocatively put, to fleece the public. Barriers to affiliation between banks and nonbank firms restrict competition and keep the prices of financial services higher than they need be. The barriers to affiliation contained in the Glass-Steagall Act, the Bank Holding Company Act, the Savings and Loan Holding Company Act, and various state laws keep potential entrants out of markets for financial services. Such barriers to entry convey market power to existing firms, and this tends to be translated into higher prices and higher costs. Eliminating barriers to entry would reduce prices to customers and force firms to become more efficient. For example, the Consumer Federation of America estimates that allowing the affiliation of commercial banks and insurance companies could save consumers some $5 billion per year, or approximately $50 per year for each household in the United States.[5]

A third reason for doing nothing might be to make life a bit more difficult for the FSLIC. Restrictions on affiliations between thrift institutions and other firms, such as investment banks and bank holding companies, help keep capital out of the thrift industry and thereby hamper the efforts of the bank board to resolve the thrift crisis.

A fourth reason to do nothing might be to raise the cost of capital to American business, especially to small, growing firms. Currently, these firms rely predominantly on commercial banks for financing, but neither banks nor their affiliates can raise funds for these companies in the public securities market. As a result, when the small, growing firms do go to the securities market, they tend to get taken to the cleaners. In fact, studies of initial public offerings show that underwriters tend to price deals so that significant amounts of money are left on the table, and this results in a higher cost of capital for the firm.[6]

A fifth reason for doing nothing might be to promote the development of London as the world's financial center. Over the past ten years U.S. firms have increasingly tended to raise funds in London, and foreign issuers have increasingly shied away from issuing securities in the United States, preferring the London market instead. Although many factors are at work, one of the reasons for this trend is that in London there are no barriers to affiliation between commercial banks and investment banks. Entry into investment banking is free, and affiliates of U.S. commercial banks have been active in underwriting and distributing securities for U.S. and foreign issuers. Their participation has resulted in lower spreads and a greater volume of business for the London market and a vast growth in employment in investment banking and ancillary services such as securities processing, custody, financial printing, and legal services—jobs that might otherwise be in the United States.

I could go on, but the point is clear. Doing nothing is risky. Indeed, in my opinion, doing nothing is riskier than redesigning regulation to permit depository institutions to be affiliated with a broader range of enterprises. And, according to the papers of Professors Saunders and Edwards and those of this volume generally, there is no rationale for limiting to financial enterprises the range of affiliations permissible for depository institutions. Any firm should be able to own a depository institution, and a depository institution's affiliates should be able to engage in any lawful activity.

Notes

1. House Committee on Government Operations, *Modernization of the Financial Services Industry: A Plan for Capital Mobility within a Framework of Safe and Sound Banking*, September 30, 1987 (House Report 100-234); Federal Deposit Insurance Corporation, *Mandate for Change* (Washington, D.C.: FDIC, 1987); Statement of Robert L. Clarke, Comptroller of the Currency, before the Subcommittee on Financial Institutions, Supervision, Regulation and Insurance of the Committee on Banking Finance and Urban Affairs, U.S. House of Representatives, October 28, 1987.

2. FDIC, *Mandate for Change*, pp. 71–74.

3. "Clarke Defends Agency's Role in Options Case," *American Banker*, October 29, 1987.

4. This moratorium expired March 1, 1988.

5. Consumer Federation of America, "The Potential Costs and Benefits of Allowing Banks to Sell Insurance" (Washington, D.C.: CFA, 1987, mimeo).

6. See Thomas A. Pugel and Lawrence J. White, "An Analysis of the Competitive Effects of Allowing Commercial Bank Affiliates to Underwrite Corporate Securities," in Ingo Walter, ed., *Deregulating Wall Street: Commercial Bank Penetration of the Corporate Securities Market* (New York: Wiley, 1985), pp. 116–23.

6
Financial Deregulation, Monetary Policy, and Central Banking

Marvin Goodfriend and Robert G. King

Financial deregulation is widely understood to have important economic benefits for microeconomic reasons. Since Adam Smith, economists have provided arguments and evidence that unfettered private markets yield outcomes superior to public sector alternatives. But financial regulations—specific rules and overall structures—are sometimes justified on macroeconomic grounds. This paper analyzes the need for financial regulations in the implementation of central bank policy. Dividing the actions of the Federal Reserve into monetary and banking policy, we find that financial regulation cannot readily be rationalized on the basis of macroeconomic benefits, especially those from monetary policy.

There is a consensus among professional economists that monetary policy can be executed without supporting financial regulations. This consensus reflects an understanding of the central role of open-market operations. Although economists disagree substantially on the nature and magnitude of monetary policy's influence on the price level and real activity, this disagreement should not mask agreement on the central role of open-market operations in the management of high-powered money. Nor should it obscure the general agreement that the public sector plays an important, even unique, role in the management of money.

Banking policy involves regular lending and emergency financial assistance to individual banks and other institutions. Many aspects of Federal Reserve lending resemble credit market relationships in the private sector. In particular, a useful analogy can be drawn between

---

The authors would like to thank Mark Flannery, Bennett McCallum, William Poole, Alan Stockman, and seminar participants at the Federal Reserve Bank of Richmond for valuable comments. Research support from the American Enterprise Institute and National Science Foundation is acknowledged. The views, however, are solely those of the authors and should not be attributed to any of the preceding institutions.

private lines of credit and Federal Reserve discount window lending. Its regulation and supervision support banking policy in much the same way as loan covenants and monitoring support private lending. The value of Federal Reserve regulation and supervision, then, depends on the need for banking policy. The Federal Reserve is only one of many competing entities in the credit market, however, and any rationale for intervention by the Federal Reserve must involve evidence of a relative advantage for the public sector or a market failure deriving from inappropriate private incentives. Moreover, banking policy may influence outcomes in banking and financial markets by subsidizing certain economic activities, eroding private arrangements for liquidity, and encouraging risk taking. On these grounds, we conclude that it is difficult to make a case for central bank lending policy and the public financial regulation that supports it.

We begin this chapter with definitions of monetary and banking policy. We then consider financial deregulation and monetary policy, beginning by considering monetary policy in a fully deregulated environment. We illustrate how a prominent feature of Federal Reserve monetary policy (interest rate smoothing) is undertaken in such an environment, pointing out the irrelevance for monetary policy of a well-known financial regulation, reserve requirements, given the Federal Reserve's preference for an interest rate as its monetary policy instrument.

We begin our discussion of deregulation and banking policy by considering a fully deregulated environment, outlining the character of private borrowing and lending transactions. Then we discuss the provision of line-of-credit services through the Federal Reserve discount window and go on to develop the distinction between illiquidity and insolvency as a means of judging the appropriateness of public line-of-credit services.

In our analysis of how monetary and banking policy could react to systemwide disturbances, including banking crises, we conclude that monetary policy can effectively and desirably limit crises arising from a widespread demand to convert deposits into currency. Illustrating our point, we interpret Walter Bagehot's "lender-of-last-resort" rule as an irregular interest rate smoothing policy. In contrast, banking policy can do little to influence such events. But we explore other potential roles for banking policy in response to systemwide disturbances.

Monetary and Banking Policy

Our investigation requires that we distinguish between central bank monetary policy and banking policy actions. By monetary policy, we mean changes in the total volume of high-powered money (currency plus non-interest-bearing bank reserves). Other central bank actions involve changes in the composition of the central bank's assets, holding the total fixed, or regulatory and supervisory actions of the central bank.[1] In general, the other actions might be described as commercial policies. In the United States, however, central bank commercial policies concentrate largely on the banking sector, so we term them banking policy.[2]

When the Federal Reserve was established, the major goals of central banking in the United States were, first, the provision of sufficient liquidity for the needs of enterprise so as to avoid banking crises and business fluctuations; second, the maintenance of liquid markets for bank assets; and, third, the public supervision of banking. These goals are reflected in the preamble to the Federal Reserve Act, which states that the purposes of the Federal Reserve were "to furnish an elastic currency, to afford a means of rediscounting commercial paper, and to establish a more effective supervision of banking in the U.S." Broadly, we take the Federal Reserve Act as mandating that the central bank manage society's provision of liquidity through its own actions and by influencing the choices of private agents.

These primary objectives involve a mixture of monetary policy and banking policy. The provision of an elastic currency is a monetary policy of sorts, since it implies that the stock of currency should be varied in response to economic conditions. The other objectives fall into the category of banking policy. For example, by allowing its inventory of government securities to vary, a central bank can accommodate variations in discounting without any change in the stock of high-powered money.

The primary objectives are of particular interest precisely because they are independent of the choice of monetary standard. In particular, these objectives were important under the gold standard, which was in force when the Federal Reserve was established. Other objectives for central banking such as management of the revenue from money creation and stabilization policy aimed at the price level are highly constrained under the gold standard. An additional rationale for central banking emerged with the Employment Act of 1946, which indirectly required the Federal Reserve to employ active monetary policy to stabilize business conditions.

Deregulation and Monetary Policy

Monetary policy involves the manipulation of high-powered money by the central bank to manage nominal variables like the price level, the inflation rate, and the nominal interest rate and possibly to influence outcomes for employment and output temporarily. We argue here that financial and banking regulations are not needed to conduct monetary policy, although their effects must be taken into account where they exist. We illustrate our point by discussing interest rate smoothing, an important feature of monetary policy in the United States, showing that such smoothing does not require financial regulation. Indeed, the practice of smoothing interest rates essentially eliminates the need for reserve requirements. We continue by considering the effect of financial deregulation on stabilization policy.

Why Regulations Are Not Necessary. There is a mainstream professional consensus that monetary policy can be accomplished without supporting financial regulations, although there is not a professional consensus on the efficacy of monetary policy or on desirable patterns of behavior for the monetary authority. For practical purposes most economists think of a fully deregulated environment as one in which the central bank has a monopoly on the issue of high-powered money but in which private markets are otherwise unregulated.

This view is based on the notion that currency and bank deposits are not perfect substitutes for transactions in which they are employed. For example, certain costs lead individuals to treat deposits and currency as distinct assets. Notably, when payments are made through bank deposits, costs are incurred to determine whether the payer has enough money to cover the transaction. Moreover, costs are incurred when securities are bought and sold to complete the desired wealth transfer. Bankers specialize in providing these transaction services. In a deregulated, competitive system banks have incentives to provide payment services at cost and to pay interest on deposits that reflects the net return on assets.

In contrast, when payments are made with currency, there is a relative saving on information and computation costs because the wealth value of currency is more easily verified than that of a check written against a bank deposit. Presumably, there is a substantial set of payments for which the verification cost saving from using currency more than offsets the interest forgone by using deposits. The privacy provided by currency is an advantage for some transactions, since currency does not leave a paper trail.

The implication that deposits are imperfect substitutes for currency is important for two reasons. First, the public has a determinate real stock demand for currency *(C/P)*, where *C* is the aggregate nominal stock of currency supplied by the central bank and *P* is the currency price of goods (the price level).[3] It follows that controlling the nominal stock of currency *(C)* and its growth rate is sufficient to control the price level *(P)*, the inflation rate, and the nominal interest rate (expected inflation plus the ex ante real rate).[4] Second, the banking system, then, can be completely deregulated without interfering with the ability of monetary policy to control nominal magnitudes. Open-market operations are sufficient to accomplish monetary objectives.[5]

To understand why banking regulations are not essential for monetary policy, consider the following two policy actions. In preventing a temporary increase in the real demand for currency from decreasing the price level, a central bank simply acquires securities temporarily in the open market, providing sufficient nominal currency to satisfy the higher real demand without a fall in prices. Alternatively, if a central bank wants to restore a lower price level after an inflationary period, it may do so by selling securities in the open market to reduce the stock of currency. The unchanged real demand for currency could be satisfied only at a lower price level; hence, prices would fall.

The view that financial and banking regulations—or even the structural details of the banking system—are not essential to understand the effectiveness of monetary policy is very widely held. This view is shared by major undergraduate and graduate macroeconomics texts.[6] Banking regulations in fact, however, influence the magnitude, timing, and targets of open-market operations necessary for a specific objective, such as changing the price level to some specified target. Banking regulations could influence policy implementation since they affect both the supply and the demand for currency. For instance, reserve requirements on bank deposits could absorb high-powered money made available through open-market operations, thereby influencing the effective quantity of currency supplied. Alternatively, by affecting the incentive to substitute currency for bank deposits and vice versa, a prohibition of interest on demand deposits would influence the magnitude of open-market operations necessary to minimize price effects of changes in market interest rates.[7] In short, although banking regulations are not needed for the execution of monetary policy, where they exist a central bank must take them into account in policy implementation.

Interest Rate Smoothing. We have emphasized that open-market operations are sufficient for a central bank to manage the price level, inflation, and nominal interest rates. Here we illustrate the point by describing how the Federal Reserve has employed monetary policy to smooth nominal interest rates against routine seasonal and cyclical variations in the demand for money and credit.

Evidence. One indicator of the Federal Reserve's success in changing the character of nominal interest rate movements is the behavior of short-term interest rates, measured by the monthly average call money rate on short-term broker loans in New York.[8] Before the advent of the Federal Reserve in 1914, the most notable characteristic of this short-term interest rate series was its irregular sharp, sudden, and temporary increases. In October 1867, for example, after remaining between 4.3 and 7.2 for the prior three years, the call money rate rose suddenly from 5.6 to 10.8 percent. Although this change seems large by postwar U.S. standards, similar episodes of at least this magnitude occurred twenty-six times between the end of the Civil War and the founding of the Federal Reserve. Moreover, sudden changes of over ten percentage points occurred with surprising frequency, on eight occasions during the same forty-nine-year period. In September 1873, the call money rate jumped from 4.6 percent in August to 61.2 percent, falling back to 14.9 percent in October and to 5.5 percent by January 1874. Accompanying these sudden upward jumps in call money rates were similar, though much less severe, movements in sixty- to ninety-day commercial paper rates. These episodes were distinctly temporary, ranging from one to four months, with many lasting no more than one month. Needless to say, such extreme temporary spikes have been absent from interest rate behavior since the founding of the Federal Reserve.

Another distinctive feature of the period before the Federal Reserve was the large seasonal movement in short-term interest rates. For example, the average seasonal variation for the call money rate from 1890 to 1908 ranged from a peak of +4.6 percent in January to a trough of −1.39 percent in June.[9] Generally, rates were at their annual mean in the spring, below it in summer, and at their highs in the fall and winter. By the 1920s the prominent seasonal movements of interest rates had virtually disappeared.

Definition and mechanics. Broadly speaking, then, the Federal Reserve may be said to have smoothed interest rates in two senses. First, it insulated nominal interest rates from regular seasonal movements in money and credit markets. Second, it removed temporary nominal interest rate spikes prompted by recurrent irregular tightness in money and credit markets. For purposes of this discussion, interest rate smoothing is a deliberate effort by the Federal Reserve to reduce or eliminate temporary nominal interest rate fluctuations.[10] We shall find the distinction between regular and irregular interest rate smoothing useful when we characterize Bagehot's lender-of-last-resort rule in the section on banking crises, monetary policy, and the Federal Reserve.

There has been considerable controversy about whether interest rate smoothing by the central bank is feasible when the public understands policy, that is, when the public has rational expectations. To illustrate its feasibility we consider the simplest possible model.[11] The model has three basic equations: (1) a money demand function; (2) a money supply function; and (3) an expression equating the expected real return on nominal securities (that is, the nominal interest rate minus expected inflation) to the expected real rate.

The model embodies two principles that are key to understanding nominal interest rate smoothing. First, because the price level is determined by a money supply rule, there is a nominal anchor in the system. Second, the nominal rate is affected by expected inflation, allowing a central bank to translate price level and inflation policy into interest rate policy.

Nominal interest rate smoothing works as follows. The money supply rule pins down the expected future nominal stock of money. Together with expected future real demand for money, this implies an anchor for the expected future price level. In practice, central banks have employed interest rate policy instruments to smooth interest rates.[12] This amounts to running an adjustable nominal interest rate peg; we therefore illustrate how a central bank smooths the nominal interest rate by pegging it. To see what happens, we consider the response to two disturbances. In each case we first ask what happens when the stock of high-powered money remains constant, and then we see how high-powered money must change to be consistent with a nominal rate peg.

- *A temporary rise in real money demand.* With high-powered money constant, the current price level would fall, raising both expected inflation and the nominal interest rate. By assumption, the required expected real yield on nominal securities is unchanged. Therefore, under a nominal rate peg expected inflation would remain unchanged, which means the current price level would remain equal to the expected future price level. The Federal Reserve would merely provide enough high-powered money, through open-market purchases, to satisfy the initial rise in money demand.

- *A temporary rise in the real rate.* With high-powered money constant, the nominal rate would rise, real money demand would fall, and the current price level would rise. Under a nominal rate peg the required increase in the expected real rate on nominal securities would be achieved by a matching expected deflation due to temporarily high prices. The Federal Reserve would merely provide enough nominal high-powered money to satisfy the unchanged demand for real money balances at the higher price level.[13]

A number of important points emerge from this theoretical discussion.

- First, nominal interest rate smoothing is monetary policy, because the power of the Federal Reserve to create or destroy high-powered money through open-market operations is necessary and sufficient for it to smooth nominal interest rates. In particular, no financial or banking regulations are necessary.
- Second, interest rate smoothing is clearly feasible when the public has rational expectations.
- Third, the mechanics of interest rate smoothing are the same regardless of whether the disturbances are seasonal or irregular.
- Fourth, since the nominal interest rate is the private opportunity cost of holding high-powered money (as currency for hand-to-hand transactions or as bank reserves), the change in the seasonal and irregular pattern of nominal interest rates produces a corresponding change in the pattern of real money balances held by individuals and banks. Thus, we interpret interest rate smoothing as the means by which the Federal Reserve satisfies its statutory mandate to provide liquidity for the U.S. economy by means of an elastic currency.
- Fifth, Federal Reserve interest rate smoothing has in practice made reserve requirements unnecessary for executing monetary policy. The conventional view, of course, is that reserve requirements help the Federal Reserve to control the stock of money. This is the view implicit in the 1980 Monetary Control Act, which extended reserve requirements to all depository institutions, whether Federal Reserve members or not. If the Federal Reserve were operating with a total reserve instrument, reserve requirements would help determine how a change in high-powered money would influence the price level and the nominal interest rate. The Federal Reserve, however, has chosen to operate with an interest rate instrument, that is, to run an adjustable rate peg. As should be clear from the examples discussed above, under even a temporary peg the current price level is determined by the chosen nominal interest rate, the real rate, and the expected future price level. The Federal Reserve simply uses open-market operations to satisfy current money demand at current prices. In such circumstances reserve requirements merely help determine the volume of open-market operations that the Federal Reserve must undertake to provide the accommodation; they do not help determine the money stock or prices.[14]

Financial Deregulation and Stabilization Policy. Since the Employment Act of 1946, the Federal Reserve has had a mandate to employ monetary policy to stabilize real economic activity. Thus, a major question about continuing and prospective financial deregulation concerns its influence on stabilization policy. While macroeconomic textbooks agree broadly on the nature of the demand for money, they do not show a similar agreement on a number of central issues concerning monetary policy.

Traditional monetarist arguments—originating with Milton Friedman and Karl Brunner, as developed in texts by Michael Darby and William Poole—hold that while monetary policy exerts a powerful influence over the course of the business cycle, in practice it has worked to exacerbate swings in economic activity.[15] From this perspective, monetary policy increases cyclical volatility for three reasons: (1) its effects are subject to long and variable lags, which make the timing of monetary policy actions difficult; (2) it is difficult for policy makers to assess the state of economic activity promptly, because of the complexity of the forces that drive the economy in a given period; and (3) policy makers' focus on smoothing nominal interest rates against cyclical changes in real rates generally leads monetary aggregates to be procyclical.

Rational expectations monetarist arguments—developed by Robert Lucas, Thomas Sargent, and Robert Barro, as summarized in Barro's text—stress the distinction between unpredictable policy actions (shocks), which are taken to exert a powerful influence on real economic activity, and predictable policy responses, which are taken to exert no real effects.[16] This group argues that systematic monetary policy cannot influence real activity, such as employment, real gross national product, and real interest rates, because private agents rationally anticipate the systematic component of monetary policy and take actions that neutralize its potential effects, leaving it to influence nominal variables only.

Analysts of real business cycles—according to theory developed by Edward Prescott, John Long, and Charles Plosser, as summarized in Barro's text—deny any major influence of money, anticipated or unanticipated, on real economic activity.[17] From the perspective of real business cycle analysis, variations in real activity (arising from changes in technology, sectoral reallocations, energy shocks, taxes, and government spending) drive the monetary sector, reversing the traditional macroeconomic view.

Modern Keynesian analysts—led by Stanley Fischer, Edmund Phelps, and John Taylor, as summarized in texts by Rudiger Dornbusch and Fischer and Robert Hall and Taylor—see a powerful role for monetary policy, even with rational private anticipations, because the Federal Reserve can act after private agents have entered into wage and price agreements. According to this view, monetary policy is a powerful stabilization tool, which can offset potentially inefficient economic fluctuations arising from variations in the demand for money, autonomous changes in private spending, and supply shocks.

The disagreement about the feasibility and desirability of stabilization policy, however, should not obscure a consensus on the operation of monetary policy apparent in all the current texts. Whether monetary policy influences real activity or only nominal variables, the prominent textbooks view it as the manipulation of the stock of high-powered money. The major professional debates concerning monetary policy accept as common ground the notion that open-market operations are a necessary and sufficient policy instrument. Financial market regulations are not necessary for the conduct of the Federal Reserve's attempts at stabilization policy irrespective of how it ultimately influences the cyclical component of economic activity.

Not only is this the point of view in the textbooks, it is also a central component of the modern Federal Reserve policy perspective. In its early years the Federal Reserve relied extensively on the discount window as a means of managing the high-powered money stock, but it rapidly came to view the method by which it managed high-powered money as a tactical consideration of little fundamental importance. For example, in the early 1920s the Federal Reserve largely substituted open-market security purchases for discount window loans as the primary means of adjusting high-powered money.

Deregulation and Banking Policy

Banking policy, as we defined it above, has three dimensions. It involves changing the composition of central bank assets holding their total (high-powered money) fixed, it involves financial regulation, and it involves bank supervision. When executing banking policy, a central bank functions like a private financial intermediary in the sense that its actions neither create nor destroy high-powered money. Banking policy merely involves making loans to individual banks with funds acquired by selling off other assets, usually government securities. The primary dimension of banking policy is provision by the central bank of line-of-credit services to private banks. Regulatory and supervisory components of banking policy may be understood in this regard. Private credit extension is accompanied by restrictions on the borrower to limit his ability to take risks and to protect the value of loan collateral. Private credit lines are accompanied by continuous monitoring of borrowers by lenders. Efficient central bank line-of-credit provision likewise requires regulation and supervision of potential credit recipients.

We have seen that banking and financial regulations are inessential for the execution of monetary policy. Here we ask whether banking policy needs supporting regulation and supervision. The analogy between private and central bank credit extension drawn above, however, suggests that our inquiry about banking policy will be somewhat different. If a central bank provides line-of-credit services, the analogy suggests that it must follow up with supervision and regulation to safeguard its funds and make sure its commitment is not abused. Ultimately we must ask, therefore, whether central bank line-of-credit services to banks are really necessary and desirable in the first place.

Our analysis follows the strategy employed earlier in the discussion of monetary policy, by initially considering a deregulated environment. After describing restrictions voluntarily agreed to by borrowers in private credit markets, we discuss the demand for line-of-credit services, emphasizing that by their very nature credit lines must be accompanied by continuous supervision by the banks. We then take up problems of central bank lending, particularly issues that arise for public lenders such as the Federal Reserve. To keep things concrete, we discuss this material in relation to Federal Reserve discount window lending practices. We emphasize how regulatory and supervisory actions taken by the Federal Reserve to safeguard its funds and ensure that its discount window facilities are not abused parallel those taken in private credit markets.

The Federal Reserve discount window functions most importantly as a source of, emergency credit assistance. It is a temporary source of funds, available on short notice, for financially troubled individual banks. No one argues that the discount window should be used to prevent insolvent banks from failing, only that the window be used to aid solvent banks. The distinction between illiquidity and insolvency is therefore crucial to the management of the discount window. First of all, the feasibility of such selective lending depends on the Federal Reserve's having an operational and timely means of distinguishing between insolvent and illiquid banks. Moreover, understanding the economic distinction between illiquidity and insolvency is necessary to decide whether discount window lending is desirable policy at all. We address these fundamental issues in the section on illiquidity and emergency credit assistance.

As was the case in our initial treatment of monetary policy, when we analyzed monetary responses to routine seasonal and cyclical macroeconomic disturbances, we confine our initial treatment of banking policy in this section to routine circumstances, that is, emergency credit assistance to individual troubled banks. In a later section we take up the feasibility and desirability of monetary and banking policy responses to systemwide banking and financial market crises.

Private Lending and Private Regulation. Lenders face many potential problems that arise from borrowers' ability to renege on loans. Thus, borrowers and lenders agree on sets of rules and restrictions to accompany loans. For example, in the case of a car loan the lender provides the borrower an initial amount of funds with which to purchase a car, and the borrower agrees to a regular pattern of loan repayments. But the car loan involves more than these financial flows. Typically, the car is collateral against the borrower's ability to pay back the loan. For this reason, as part of the contract the borrower gives up the right to sell the car for the duration of the loan.[18] Additional agreements may restrict other aspects of the borrower's behavior. For example, insurance against damage to the car may be required, or the borrower may be prohibited from renting the car to others. These additional restrictions further protect the lender against damage to the loan collateral.

It is important to note that restrictions on the borrower's range of actions are ultimately in his interest, since they lower the cost of the loan. For example, if someone wanted to borrow funds for a vacation and owned a debt-free car, then he could more cheaply borrow against the car, voluntarily accepting a set of restrictions on use or transfer of the car, than he could arrange an unsecured personal loan.

Issues concerning incentives for borrowers become far more important and sophisticated in corporate lending. For this reason, corporate loans typically require complex covenants (restrictive agreements) that limit the borrower's range of actions,[19] particularly covenants limiting risk taking. For example, it is naive to lend to a corporation engaged in a specific riskless line of business, using an appropriate rate of return for riskless loans, without any restrictions on how the funds are to be spent. Ultimately, the loan is a claim to the minimum of the stream of loan payments or the liquidation value of the corporation's assets if it fails. From the standpoint of its equity holders, the firm's taking on a risky project would thus be a good idea: if it is a success, the equity holders will get the rewards; if it is a failure, the losses will be the lender's, that is, the bondholder's. Thus, with managers of the corporation responsive to equity holders, the firm has incentive to use the borrowed funds to take on risky projects. This difficulty could be circumvented with a covenant restricting types of projects that the company could initiate.

Private Lines of Credit. Efficient loan design requires the costly accumulation of detailed information about borrowers, both to sort borrowers into risk classes and to design covenants. Like many other economic activities, information production is highly costly when undertaken quickly without development of systems and experience. For this reason, lending typically occurs in the context of long-term relationships, in which information can be produced less expensively.[20]

One sort of long-term lending arrangement is commonly known as a line of credit. The demand for line-of-credit services arises because firms often need funds suddenly, as a result of events that are difficult to predict. For example, a firm may discover a potentially lucrative investment opportunity that must be seized quickly to yield a high rate of return. The firm may not have a sufficient inventory of readily tradable assets such as U.S. Treasury bills from which to raise the necessary funds. Furthermore, the delay caused by making a public security offering may make that avenue of obtaining funds ineffective. In contrast, a line-of-credit arrangement is designed to make funds available on very short notice, possibly as a bridge loan until other arrangements can be made.

Alternatively, a firm might develop a sudden need for funds after suffering a bad shock. A decline in sales might force the firm to finance inventory accumulation, or the unexpected failure of a project might cause a sudden cutoff of revenue. Credit lines, of course, are specifically designed to make funds immediately available in such circumstances too.

The extension of credit in response to bad outcomes, however, is more troublesome for lenders. Bad outcomes might accompany information that a firm should be dissolved altogether, in which case the credit should not be extended. But credit lines are valuable precisely because they make funds immediately available. Thus lenders must protect themselves against such contingencies. For this reason, continual monitoring of potential borrowers is a particularly important feature of the provision of line-of-credit services.[21]

Lines of credit require the payment of a facility fee either on the full amount of the line or on the unused portion.[22] The fee is paid during normal periods to cover the cost of monitoring incurred by the bank. Often the fee is paid by holding a compensating balance, a bank deposit that pays a below-market rate of interest. Because the compensating balance allows a bank to observe the borrower's financial transactions, it helps reduce monitoring costs. In return for the fee, the line-of-credit recipient acquires an option to borrow funds, up to the amount of the line, at a predetermined interest rate spread above a market reference rate. The size of the fee and the rate spread are lowest for top borrowers, ranging higher for worse credit risks. For reasons discussed above, credit lines are also accompanied by restrictions and covenants, as well as specification of allowable collateral, if any is required, should a loan actually be taken down. Of course, since conditions affect the riskiness of the credit line from the lender's point of view, they will influence the fee and spread as well. More restrictions accepted by the borrower will, generally speaking, enable him to pay less. Finally, borrowers will differ according to the intrinsic ease of monitoring. Monitoring a mom-and-pop grocery store is relatively cheap compared with monitoring a firm with many employees, offices, and product lines. Higher monitoring costs would also be reflected in a higher fee or spread.[23]

Individual banks fund their credit lines by maintaining good credit ratings themselves so they can attract funds in the certificate-of-deposit market in a timely fashion and at relatively low cost.[24] To a lesser extent they hold inventories of readily marketable securities such as U.S. Treasury bills, which they can sell to acquire funds on short notice.[25] If the need for funds is expected to be particularly short-lived, borrowing federal funds may be most economical.[26]

Discount Window Lending. Discount window lending is the way central banks provide line-of-credit services.[27] There are thus important similarities between discount window operations and private lines of credit. There is, however, a potentially important difference because a central bank's liabilities are high-powered money. But while the discount window plays an essential role in the execution of banking policy, it is unnecessary for monetary policy. We develop these points below by describing discount window procedures actually followed by the Federal Reserve.

Discount window lending is the extension of credit, usually secured by collateral, from a central bank to a private institution. In the United States, Federal Reserve banks lend to individual banks or other depository institutions in their districts through their discount windows. Reserve banks can finance discount window credit with high-powered money or with funds obtained from securities sold in the open market. We define discount window lending that is deliberately allowed to create high-powered money as unsterilized. Under our definition, unsterilized discount window operations are, in part, monetary policy. We say that discount window lending is sterilized when it is accompanied by an open-market sale of equal value. Sterilized discount window operations are thus pure banking policy, with no monetary policy implications, since they leave high-powered money unchanged. In this case only a substitution of bank paper (that is, the loan collateral) for government paper on the books of the central bank has occurred, with no change in total central bank liabilities (that is, high-powered money).

As we made clear earlier, open-market operations are sufficient for the execution of monetary policy. It follows that unsterilized discount window lending is redundant as a monetary policy tool.[28] In contrast, sterilized discount window lending plays a distinctive role apart from monetary policy. It allows a central bank to lend selectively to individual banks without affecting aggregate monetary conditions. In other words, it enables a central bank to offer line-of-credit services to individual banks in much the same way as private banks provide credit lines to their customers.

The 1984 report of the Bush commission on financial regulation put the rationale for Federal Reserve provision of discount window services as follows:

> Operation of the FRB's discount window is a vital element in the public "safety net" supporting stability of the banking system. Particularly in the event of difficulties affecting a large financial institution, the FRB must remain available to provide potentially extremely large amounts of liquidity on extremely short notice, and it is the only government agency that is in a position to provide this type of support to the financial system.[29]

Earlier a 1971 Federal Reserve report reappraising the discount window stated:

> Under present conditions, sophisticated open market operations enable the System to head off general liquidity crises, but such operations are less appropriate when the System is confronted with serious financial strains among individual firms or specialized groups of institutions. At times such pressures may be inherent in the nature of monetary restraint, [which often has] excessively harsh impacts on particular sectors of the economy. At other times underlying economic conditions may change in unforeseen ways, to the detriment of a particular financial substructure. And, of course, the possibility of local calamities or management failure affecting individual institutions or small groups of institutions is ever-present. It is in connection with these limited crises that the discount window can play an effective role.[30]

The Federal Reserve discount window is understood and valued as a line-of-credit facility. Open-market operations are seen as capable of handling aggregate monetary conditions. Implicitly, this sterilized discount window lending is valued for its ability to direct potentially large quantities of funds, on very short notice, to individual troubled firms. Like private lenders, the Federal Reserve in its role as public provider of line-of-credit services would be expected to impose restrictions on potential borrowers and to engage in monitoring. It does. In the public sector, however, these activities are known as regulation and supervision.

As is the case for private lenders, the Federal Reserve too is concerned about pricing its loans according to risk.[31] According to Regulation A, the Federal Reserve classifies discount window loans into short-term adjustment credit, seasonal credit, and emergency credit assistance. Adjustment credit is, from time to time, temporarily employed by banks in basically good financial condition.[32] Seasonal credit is employed primarily by banks in agricultural areas. Its use is also rather routine. In contrast, emergency credit is the designation given to funds borrowed by troubled banks on what might be a rather protracted basis.[33] The discount rates on adjustment and seasonal credit are lower than for emergency credit because the riskiness of a loan is generally lower on adjustment and seasonal credit.

The riskiness of a discount window loan also depends critically on the collateral. The Federal Reserve has considerable latitude as to what it will accept and the "haircut" it will take.[34] Fully collateralizing a loan with prime paper such as U.S. Treasury bills, however, would make the value of the Federal Reserve's line of credit minimal. A bank could simply borrow privately on such collateral with no trouble. The Federal Reserve could still make its credit line attractive, however, by charging below-market rates or by taking less than a market haircut. At any rate, whatever the Federal Reserve might do in practice, our interest here is to analyze how a central bank that provides meaningful line-of-credit services, based on imperfect collateral, would operate.

In addition to setting the terms upon which a loan can be taken down, our discussion of private lines of credit emphasized the need for continuous monitoring of potential borrowers by the lender. This is no less necessary for public provision of line-of-credit services by the Federal Reserve. A 1983 Federal Reserve position paper on financial regulation stated:

> Central banking responsibilities for financial stability are supported by discount window facilities—historically a key function of a central bank—through which the banking system, and in a crisis, the economy more generally, can be supported. But effective use of that critically important tool of crisis management is itself dependent on intimate familiarity with operations of banks, and to a degree other finan-

cial institutions, of the kind that can only be derived from continuing operational supervisory responsibilities.[35]

Our interpretation of "effective use" in this quotation is that the Federal Reserve should, on short notice, be able to discern the financial position of a bank requesting funds. Especially with respect to emergency credit assistance, such information is necessary to price loans appropriately and, even more important, to be sure that the borrower is still viable. If the Federal Reserve is too lax, lending to excessively weak borrowers, then it will be taken advantage of, possibly supporting banks that should be dissolved. If the Federal Reserve is too stingy, it will fail to support temporarily troubled but fundamentally sound banks, possibly causing them to fail unnecessarily. Only by continually supervising banks to which it has credit commitments can the Federal Reserve hope to lend funds efficiently on short notice.[36]

Along with designating the terms upon which it is prepared to lend and the associated supervisory requirements, the Federal Reserve needs to set eligibility rules. Unlike a private firm, it is not completely free to choose whom it wishes to serve. The logic of the quotations presented above suggests that the Federal Reserve ought to provide line-of-credit services to the entire economy, nonfinancial as well as financial firms, to say nothing of banks. To do so, however, would require the devotion of resources for regulation and supervision on a scale society could not accept. Hence, the Federal Reserve has had to choose a rather arbitrary rule to limit its commitment. Currently, only Federal Reserve member banks or depository institutions holding transaction accounts or nonpersonal time deposits are entitled to basic discount window borrowing privileges. This group corresponds closely to those institutions holding reserves at Federal Reserve banks. Indeed, society's recognition of the need to limit the Federal Reserve's line-of-credit commitment is indicated by the choice of "central bank" rather than "credit market authority" to describe its functions.

If we take this logic one step further, we can better understand the concerns of policy makers for maintaining some form of separation between banking on one hand, and finance and commerce on the other, and for limiting access to the payments system.[37] We interpret their argument with regard to banking and commerce as recognizing the need to limit the Federal Reserve's line-of-credit commitments and the regulation and supervision that must accompany them to a manageable subset of the economy, namely, depository institutions. Blurring the line between banking and commerce, or banking and finance, would make it difficult for the Federal Reserve to do that. Without a reasonable limit, the Federal Reserve would tend to be drawn into additional implicit commitments that it could not keep. Even worse, without the regulatory and supervisory resources to safeguard its funds, the Federal Reserve might have to withdraw from providing line-of-credit services entirely.

The argument for limiting access to the payments system is similar. In the process of making payments over its electronic funds transfer network, Fedwire, the Federal Reserve grants same-day credit to depository institutions in the form of daylight overdrafts on their reserve accounts.[38] Because they are imperfectly collateralized, daylight overdrafts create problems for the Federal Reserve analogous to those associated with discount window lending. Although quantitatively much less significant, Federal Reserve float generated in the process of clearing checks creates similar problems.[39] Hence, the Federal Reserve needs to limit access to protect its funds. Of course, in principle it would be possible for the Federal Reserve to protect its funds by not granting credit in the process of making payments. That would be good policy only if any inefficiencies from completely eliminating or perfectly collateralizing daylight overdrafts and float did not offset the savings in regulatory and supervisory costs. Of course, the Federal Reserve could privatize the payments system entirely.

In summary, it is not because the Federal Reserve is selfish in wanting to protect its funds that banking policy must be accompanied by regulation and supervision. We saw for the case of private lines of credit that restrictions on borrowers were in their own interest because they lowered borrowing costs. That would be true here too. Efficient borrowing necessarily imposes restrictions, whether private or public in nature. If banking policy in the form of discount window lending and the production of payments system credit is necessary, then it should be accompanied by central bank regulation and supervision in both society's and the Federal Reserve's interest.

Illiquidity and Emergency Credit Assistance. The preceding discussion makes clear that the Federal Reserve discount window is most important as an immediately available source of emergency credit assistance for individual banks. As we noted above, no one argues that the discount window should be used to rescue insolvent banks, only that the window be used to aid temporarily illiquid banks. The familiar rule of thumb—lend only to illiquid but solvent banks—both protects public funds and safeguards the freedom to fail, which is vital to the efficiency of our economy.[40] The purpose of this section is to evaluate that rule of thumb in two senses: Can it be feasibly implemented, and does it provide a rationale for the public provision of line-of-credit services through the discount window? The value of central bank regulation and supervision of banking and financial markets hinges critically on the answer to the second question.

First, we require an operational means of distinguishing between illiquid and insolvent banks. This distinction appears meaningful only in the presence of incomplete and costly information about the character of bank assets. If information were freely available about these assets, then private markets would stand ready to lend any bank the present value of the income streams from its assets, discounted at a rate appropriate for the risk. Thus, any bank would always be fully liquid, able to pay all claimants, as long as it was also solvent, that is, it had nonnegative economic net worth.

If information is incomplete and costly to obtain, then it becomes possible to imagine an illiquid but solvent bank.[41] Suppose that a disturbance arises that adversely affects the returns to some existing bank loans. There are a large number of banks, some of which have made poor loans that will yield little revenue. If the private market cannot distinguish between good and bad banks, then it will lend to any individual bank at a rate appropriate for the pool of borrowing banks. For any good bank needing to borrow funds, then, the private market will charge a higher rate under incomplete information than under complete information, because the rate implies a probability that the bank is bad, even though it may not be. Faced with a need for funds, a good bank may find itself in difficulty: although its loans are capable of supporting a borrowing rate under full information, it cannot meet the higher market rate prevailing under incomplete information. That is, at the full information borrowing rate, the bank has positive economic net worth, but the private market is willing only to lend at a higher rate, at which the bank's net worth is negative. We would describe this bank as illiquid but solvent. The higher rate that prevails in the market is an outcome of costly information—it could be either a result of pooling diverse risk groups or a result of an actual cost of auditing the underlying assets of the firm. Timely auditing over very short periods could be quite costly, sufficiently so that individual banks would not find it feasible to engage in "last minute" auditing as part of a program for raising funds.

To avoid this situation, private line-of-credit arrangements provide banks with the option of borrowing funds on short notice, based on a continuing relationship, with periodic credit evaluation so that the lender can sort good risks from bad in the event of a request for funds. This relationship develops because the overall costs of evaluation are lower, as with many other economic activities, when they are distributed over time. A line of credit includes a commitment to lend funds at a fixed rate or a fixed rate spread; a bank then obtains funds on its own initiative if it is a good credit risk, with knowledge of its status made possible through continuing evaluation.

In operating a discount window, the government faces the same general problem as a private lender in the presence of incomplete and costly information. It has the same range of choices. If, for example, it lends to a pool of undifferentiated risks, then it must lend at a penalty rate equal to the private market pooled rate to break even. If the discount window has to compete with private lines of credit, however, such a pricing policy would attract only bad banks. In fact, whatever rate it set would tend to attract unprofitable risks, including insolvent banks. Hence, indiscriminate lending would be undesirable.

Alternatively, a central bank could supervise banks and lend selectively based on the information generated by that supervision, providing funds to banks facing pooled private market prices leaving them illiquid but solvent. Distinguishing between banks on this basis, a central bank selectively aids illiquid banks, but it incurs supervision costs to discriminate between types of banks. From this perspective, it is no accident that discount window lending and bank supervision are jointly included in the primary rationales for the Federal Reserve. If these supervision costs are taken into account, and they are at least as great as those of the private sector, then this banking policy breaks even or subsidizes illiquid banks. It could not penalize illiquid banks that have the option of using competitive private credit lines.

As with many other areas of government intervention, then, the efficacy of discount window lending turns on the relative efficiency of the government and the private sector in undertaking a productive activity. We know of no analyses that document the relative advantage of the Federal Reserve in this area. Plausibly, the private market is superior because it is difficult for the government to lend only to illiquid but not insolvent banks, rather than succumbing to political pressure to support powerful banks.[42] From this perspective, selective discount window lending and necessary supervision of banks fulfill the second objective of the framers of the Federal Reserve Act. It is unclear that this is an appropriate government intervention, however, in contrast to the provision of elastic currency.

We are finally in a position to answer more completely the question whether regulation and supervision are essential for central banking. We emphasized earlier that regulations were not essential for the execution of monetary policy. In sharp contrast, we showed that banking policy needed supporting regulation and supervision.[43]

The reason for the difference is that monetary policy can be carried out with open-market operations in riskless government securities. By its very nature, however, banking policy involves a swap of government securities for claims on individual banks. Just as private lenders must restrict and monitor individual borrowers, so must a central bank. Although we admit that more research needs to be done on it, we know of no compelling rationale for public provision of line-of-credit services to individual banks through a central bank discount window. The fiat monetary system we currently have requires central bank management of high-powered money. But today's financial markets provide a highly efficient means of allocating credit privately. Since central bank loan commitments do not appear to be necessary, neither do the supporting regulation and supervision.

We must, however, qualify our conclusion in two ways. First, this chapter does not analyze the benefits of Federal Reserve credit generated in the process of making payments. Provision of imperfectly collateralized daylight overdrafts and float requires regulation and supervision, too. Second, we have so far discussed banking policy only with respect to individual troubled banks. In the next section we ask whether banking policy has a useful role to play in response to systemwide disturbances.

Systemwide Banking and Financial Market Crises

Drawing a sharp distinction between monetary and banking policy, the previous two sections of this chapter have analyzed central bank policy in routine circumstances. Policy was analyzed as it might be undertaken in response to the normal course of macroeconomic seasonal and cyclical disturbances and in response to individual bank problems. Here we address questions concerning central bank policy with respect to systemwide banking and financial crises.

We begin our discussion by describing the nature of banking crises in the United States before the establishment of the Federal Reserve, paying particular attention to the measures taken privately by clearinghouses to protect the banking system. We then use the discussion to motivate the idea that monetary policy (provision of high-powered money), not banking policy (provision of sterilized discount window loans), is both necessary and sufficient for a central bank to protect the banking system against such crises. We proceed to characterize Walter Bagehot's famous lender-of-last-resort policy prescription as an irregular nominal interest rate smoothing policy. We show how Bagehot's rule could automatically trigger high-powered money responses to protect against the sort of banking system crises experienced before the establishment of the Federal Reserve. Finally, we compare Bagehot's proposed rule with regular interest rate smoothing procedures practiced by the Federal Reserve.

Having pointed out that monetary policy has an important role to play in response to systemwide banking or financial crises, we turn to the question of whether banking policy has a useful role to play in such circumstances. Here we reason by analogy. As we will illustrate below, monetary policy is valuable during potential banking crises because it can supply currency elastically to depositors who may doubt the banking system's ability to do so. Since banking policy does not change high-powered money, however, it cannot do that. Banking policy is a swap of one sort of credit for another, as when a central bank makes a discount window loan financed by a sale of U.S. Treasury debt. Hence, we ask what sort of systemwide disturbances in the credit market banking policy might address. We are particularly interested in assessing the costs and benefits of pursuing aggregate banking policy in comparison with those of monetary policy.

Banking Crises before the Federal Reserve. In his *History of Crises under the National Banking System*, O. M. W. Sprague identified five banking crises between the end of the Civil War and the advent of the Federal Reserve.[44] Sprague's crises occur in 1873, 1884, 1890, 1893, and 1907. Each of these crises was accompanied by interest rate spikes of the sort described above, although not all interest rate spikes were associated with banking crises.

All these banking crises included an incipient, widespread desire on the part of the public to convert bank liabilities into currency. They were also accompanied by a defensive effort on the part of banks by which they built up their reserve-deposit ratios.[45] Under the fractional reserve system without a central bank, this widespread demand for currency could not be satisfied. Organized around clearinghouses, the banking system responded in two ways.[46] First, clearinghouses, associations of commercial banks, were initially established to clear checks and settle accounts among member banks. Given their central position in the clearing process, they subsequently assumed responsibility for overseeing individual banks and protecting the banking system as a whole. In times of crises, clearinghouses did two things. First, they coordinated general restrictions on convertibility of deposits into currency, while maintaining banks' ability to settle deposit accounts among themselves and undertake lending. Second, clearinghouses issued temporary substitutes for cash, known as clearinghouse loan certificates. These notes were issued against acceptable collateral, as clearinghouse liabilities rather than as individual bank liabilities. In that way, clearinghouse certificates facilitated the settlement of accounts among banks mutually suspicious of one another. The clearinghouse certificates were issued in each of the crises discussed by Sprague and remained outstanding for as little as four months in 1890 and as long as six months in 1907. Restrictions, however, accompanied the issue of clearinghouse certificates only in 1873, 1893, and 1907.

Because restrictions thwarted an increased demand to convert deposits into currency at par value, they involved temporary periods in which currency sold at a premium relative to deposits. For example, during the restriction in 1907, the premium on currency over deposits ranged as high as 4 percent. Taken together, the actions of the clearinghouse allowed member banks both to accommodate a higher private demand for currency by using certificates in place of currency for clearing purposes and to frustrate the demand by temporarily increasing the relative price of currency to deposits. At unchanged relative prices and without accommodation, the increased private demand for currency would have resulted in larger outflows of reserves from banks than actually occurred.

How well did these measures contain the harmful effects of banking crises? As calculated from data reported in *Historical Statistics of the United States* for the period 1875 to 1914, the mean annual bank failure rate was less than 1 percent. Moreover, it was comparable to a nonbank business failure rate that was only slightly higher. The annual bank failure rate exceeded 2 percent in only three years, 1877, 1878, and 1893. It exceeded 4 percent only in 1893, when it was 5.8 percent. Notably, the failure rate was 1.7 percent in the 1884 crisis year and only 0.5 and 0.4 percent in the 1890 and 1907 crisis years respectively.

The 1940 *Annual Report* of the Federal Deposit Insurance Corporation reports data on losses to bank depositors over the period 1868 to 1940. The estimated average rate of loss on assets borne by depositors in closed banks was $0.06 from 1865 to 1920, $0.19 from 1865 to 1880, $0.12 from 1881 to 1900, and $0.04 from 1901 to 1920, per year per $100 of deposits.

The relatively small losses borne by depositors reflected, in part, the high capital-asset ratios of banks, which cushioned depositors against loss in the event of a bank failure. Wesley Lindow reports a ratio of total bank capital to risk assets from 1863 to 1963.[47] The ratio falls from a high of 60 percent in 1880 to approximately 20 percent at the turn of the century, then rises to about 30 percent in the 1930s and 1940s, and falls to under 10 percent by the 1960s.[48]

In summary, this discussion should not suggest that bank failures before the advent of the Federal Reserve were not potentially very harmful to those involved. It does suggest, however, that even at their worst they were roughly of the same order of magnitude as nonbank business failures. Their aggregate effects appear to have been reasonably well contained by the private provision of bank capital and, most of all, by the collective protective behavior of the banking system by clearinghouses.

Banking Crises, Monetary Policy, and the Lender of Last Resort. Our reading of the banking crises before the Federal Reserve and the response of the clearinghouses to them suggests these important lessons. From a systemwide point of view, banking crises were dangerous because they were accompanied by a widespread demand to convert deposits into currency that could not be satisfied under the fractional reserve system without a central bank. The clearinghouses responded in two ways. They made more currency available to the nonbank public by using certificates in place of currency for clearing purposes; and they organized restrictions on cash payments that reduced the quantity of currency demanded by temporarily raising its price in terms of deposits. These measures were clearly monetary in the sense that they responded to temporarily high real demands for currency with policy actions influencing conditions upon which currency was supplied to the nonbank public. We take the evidence documented above, that the systemwide effects of banking crises appear to have been relatively small, as supportive of the view that the aggregate difficulties were monetary in nature, since policies focusing on currency supply seem to have been sufficient to contain them.

The preceding remarks underlie our view that central bank monetary policy would have been both necessary and sufficient to prevent banking crises before the creation of the Federal Reserve; banking policy, in contrast, would have been neither necessary nor sufficient. Why? The policy problem was to satisfy a temporary increase in currency demand, and only monetary policy could do that. Significantly, the effectiveness of monetary policy in this regard does not depend on whether the Federal Reserve makes high-powered money available by accepting bank assets as collateral at the discount window or by purchasing securities in the open market. By extension, it is clear that the power of the Federal Reserve to create currency remains sufficient today to contain any aggregate disturbances due to sudden sharp increases in currency demand, whether they result from banking or other difficulties.

We can make this point more concrete by using it to interpret Walter Bagehot's famous recommendation that a central bank should behave as a lender of last resort.[49] Bagehot's policy prescription—summarized as "lend freely at a high rate"—advocates that the discount rate or simply a rate for buying designated classes of securities in the open market be kept fixed suitably above the normal range of market rates. That rate would provide an interest rate ceiling and therefore an asset price floor to allow banks, in the event of crises, to liquidate their assets while remaining solvent. The proposal amounts to providing a completely elastic supply of currency at the fixed ceiling rate. Put still another way, it amounts to a suggestion for irregular use of nominal interest rate smoothing, in the event that market rates reach a certain height.

An important point about lender-of-last-resort policy in banking crises is that in our nomenclature it is not banking policy at all: it is monetary policy because it works by providing an elastic supply of high-powered money to accommodate precautionary demands to convert deposits into currency. Furthermore, lending, in the sense of advancing funds to particular institutions, is not even essential to the policy since it can be executed by buying securities outright.

One aspect of Bagehot's rule deserves some additional comment. He argued that the last-resort lending rate should be kept fixed above normal market rates, making borrowing generally unprofitable to minimize any government subsidies that might accrue to individual banks. He counted on nominal interest rate spikes accompanying banking crises to hit the ceiling rate, thereby automatically triggering the injection of currency into the economy.

In this regard, Bagehot's advice has not been followed by the Federal Reserve. Rather, as discussed earlier, the Federal Reserve has regularly chosen to smooth interest rates. It has done so either by using a federal funds rate policy instrument directly or by using targets for unsterilized borrowed reserves together with discount rate adjustments to achieve a desired federal funds rate path.[50] It is important to point out, however, that regular interest rate smoothing could still satisfy Bagehot's concerns: first, it could be free of subsidies to individual banks if carried out by purchases and sales of securities in the open market; second, it provides lender-of-last-resort services that are automatically triggered at the current central bank interest rate. If an increased demand for currency were generated by an incipient banking crisis, we might want to think of the Federal Reserve's provision of currency as last-resort lending. But routine seasonal and cyclical increases in currency demand are also accommodated at the same rate.

Thus Federal Reserve practice makes particularly clear that lender-of-last-resort policy and the routine provision of an elastic currency are essentially the same. Both are directed at insulating the nominal interest rate from disturbances in the demand for currency. Both are executed by using open-market operations to create and destroy high-powered money. Since both are monetary policy, we may extend our conclusion from the section on interest rate smoothing to make the point that banking and financial regulations are neither necessary nor sufficient for a central bank to pursue effective last-resort lending.

Banking Policy and Credit Market Crises. In the section on illiquidity and emergency credit assistance we described how banking policy could provide line-of-credit services to enable illiquid but solvent banks to remain operating. Implicitly, we assumed that the source of the trouble was limited. At worst only a few banks were insolvent; so when line-of-credit services sorted the good banks from the bad, there was a negligible effect on the interest rate. During general credit market crises associated with aggregate economic activity, however, interest rates will rise. If banking policy is to have a role, it will be in response to real interest rates, since banking policy is clearly an inappropriate response to monetary disturbances, including nominal interest rate spikes. What can banking policy accomplish in response to real rate disturbances?

For purposes of this discussion, the important effects of credit market disturbances are summarized by changes in the real rate of interest applicable to bank assets. This real rate is determined in part by macroeconomic conditions, including anticipated changes in the state of the economy and uncertainty in future prospects. It adjusts to equate aggregate supply and demand for output or, what is the same thing, to equate the aggregate supply and demand for credit. For example, an increase in future prospects that raises current consumption demand will induce a rise in the real rate to induce consumers both to save more out of a given income and to produce more, thereby restoring equilibrium in the goods market. Likewise, an increase in investment resulting from a perceived increased profit opportunity would induce a real rate rise to cut back somewhat on desired investment and induce additional saving. Finally, if individuals become more uncertain about the outcomes of investment projects, they require greater expected returns from those investments.

To investigate whether banking policy has a role, consider an unexpected rise in the real interest rate. Even a temporarily high real rate could cause previously profitable investment projects to become unprofitable.[51] This, in turn, would generate a rise in nonperforming bank loans, which could create insolvencies. The role for banking market intervention in such circumstances is usually formulated as "lend only to illiquid but solvent banks," as we discussed earlier. But we argued then that illiquidity arises only when financial markets cannot readily determine the status of a particular financial institution. An interest rate rise is observable in financial markets, however, unlike firm or bank-specific shocks, which are costly to uncover. If firms were alike on one hand and banks alike on the other, the distinction between illiquidity and insolvency would surely be irrelevant for real interest rate shocks. A real interest rate spike per se could not make banks illiquid unless it also made them insolvent. Of course, insofar as its effects were distributed unevenly across firms and banks, a real rate rise could cause some individual banks to be illiquid but solvent.

Thus aggregate disturbances can affect individual bank liquidity in addition to factors specific to a bank. But the fact that an aggregate disturbance is the source of the trouble does not alter the relative advantages of the central bank and private markets in providing liquidity. Central banks and private markets continue to face problems of screening good from bad banks. In practice, the rule of thumb "lend only to illiquid but solvent banks" could preclude the use of banking policy entirely. If banking policy did not respect this rule, however, it could well have important negative effects by subsidizing risk taking. Our conclusion must be that to avoid producing greater incentives for crises to occur, banking policy should not attempt to mitigate credit market disturbances.

We feel a bit uneasy about the implications of our result. While we think the familiar rule of thumb makes sense, we wonder whether discount window lending could be rationalized under an additional criterion: to prevent the disruption costs of widespread insolvencies associated with temporary real interest rate spikes. If the disruption costs resulting from widespread temporary insolvencies were large enough, temporary transfers to the banking system to avoid such costs could be in society's interest. We should point out, however, that a similar argument could be made for avoiding disruption costs of temporary insolvencies anywhere in the economy. Therefore, acceptance of the criterion for banking policy alone would need to be based on a demonstration that disruption costs are much larger in the financial industry than elsewhere.

At any rate, without an effect on supply of or demand for goods, banking policy could not reverse a real rate rise. Of course, a central bank's interest income could change as a result of banking policy, that is, exchanging government securities for claims on private banks. But that fiscal effect per se would have no implications for the real interest rate.[52]

What banking policy could do is support otherwise insolvent banks by temporarily swapping government securities for nonperforming bank loans. If the disturbance were temporary and the loans earned nothing for the central bank, then the size of its subsidy would be the lost interest on government securities that now goes to bank depositors. Alternatively, if the loans proved to be permanently bad, the subsidy would be the entire face value of the loans purchased by the central bank. The Treasury, in turn, would have to finance the revenue loss by cutting back purchases of goods, raising current taxes, or borrowing, that is, raising future taxes. Banking policy of this sort is clearly redistributive in nature, a contingent tax-and-transfer fiscal policy. It need not represent a subsidy to the banking system as a whole, however, if banks are taxed during normal times to finance any transfers during periods of high real rates. Significantly, to reduce the risk of insolvency effectively, the tax-and-transfer policy needs supporting regulations. Otherwise banks might simply restore the risk of insolvency to its initially optimal level by reducing capital accordingly or by restructuring contingent liabilities to offset the transfers.[53] Thus we have another example of how banking policy needs supporting regulation and supervision to be effective.

By no means are we advocating the use of banking policy to rescue insolvent banks or, more generally, the use of tax-and-transfer policies to rescue insolvent firms in other industries. In fact, we think such a policy has serious problems: it requires costly regulation and supervision; it opens the door to bank rescues, which would be extremely difficult to limit in practice; it would not be easy to choose when to intervene; and there would be political pressure to abuse the policy. Moreover, it is far from clear that disruption costs associated with widespread temporary insolvencies are large. Last, we are worried about perverse incentive effects of systematic banking policies. Designed to promote financial market stability, they encourage risk taking and lead to the deterioration of private liquidity provision. Thus, they are likely to contribute to much more severe financial market crises, particularly if there are limits to the extent of central bank loans and guarantees or if political conditions arise under which anticipated public provision of financial support does not materialize.

Conclusion

This paper has analyzed the need for financial regulations in the implementation of central bank policy. To do so, it has emphasized that a central bank serves two very different functions. First, central banks function as monetary authorities, managing high-powered money to influence the price level and real activity. Second, central banks engage in regular and emergency lending to private banks and other financial institutions. We have termed these functions monetary and banking policies. Our analytical procedure was to investigate how a minimally regulated system would operate and then to consider the consequences of various forms of public intervention. The analysis drew on contemporary economic knowledge in finance, monetary economics, and macroeconomics.

Our conclusions regarding the need for supporting financial regulation were radically different for monetary and banking policy. We emphasized that regulations were not essential for the execution of monetary policy. The reason is that high-powered money can be managed with open-market operations in government bonds. By its very nature, however, banking policy involves a swap of government securities for claims on individual banks. Just as private lenders must restrict and monitor individual borrowers, a central bank must regulate and supervise the institutions that borrow from it.

Virtually all economists agree that there is an important role for public authority in managing the nation's high-powered money. In contrast, there is little evidence that public lending to particular institutions is either necessary or appropriate. Banking policy has been rationalized as a source of funds for temporarily illiquid but solvent banks. To assess that rationale, we developed the distinction between illiquidity and insolvency in some detail, showing the distinction to be meaningful precisely because information about the value of bank assets is incomplete and costly to obtain. Nevertheless, we saw that the costliness of information per se could not rationalize the public provision of line-of-credit services. Even if central bank lending served a useful purpose earlier in the century, today's financial markets provide a highly efficient means of allocating credit privately. On the basis of such considerations, we find it difficult to make a case for central bank lending, through either the discount window or the payments system, and the regulatory and supervisory activities that support it.

Consideration of the use of monetary and banking policy in response to systemwide crises led us to modify our conclusion only slightly. We saw that monetary policy, on the one hand, could play an important role in banking crises by managing the stock of high-powered money to smooth nominal interest rates. Moreover, it could do so without costly regulation and supervision. Banking policy, on the other hand, directly influences neither high-powered money nor the aggregate supply of and demand for goods. So banking policy could not influence either nominal or real interest rates. We recognized, however, that a role for banking policy in preventing banking crises might arise in response to real interest rate spikes, which could cause widespread insolvencies against which monetary policy would be ineffective. Such banking policy actions could have social value if the temporary disruption costs associated with widespread insolvencies were large. But central bank transfers to troubled financial institutions redistribute wealth between different classes of citizens at best. And inappropriate incentives for risk taking and liquidity management might lead to more severe and frequent financial crises at worst. Hence, it is by no means clear that there is a beneficial role for banking policy even in this case.

Notes

1. One can easily imagine central bank actions that combine both monetary and banking policy. An increase in bank reserve requirements, coupled with an increase in high-powered money sufficient for banks to finance it, is one important example. The possibility of combination policies in no way diminishes the usefulness of our distinction.

2. Donald R. Hodgman, *Selective Credit Controls in Western Europe* (Chicago: Association of Reserve City Bankers, 1976), is a good survey of commercial policies executed by foreign central banks. In the United States, commercial policies executed through the credit market are extensive. Federal deposit insurance, farm credit programs, and pension guarantees fall into this category. In contrast to the other credit market activities, Federal Reserve banking policy emphasizes availability on very short notice, through line-of-credit services at the discount window and through daylight overdrafts and float extended in the payments system.

3. A brief survey of money demand theory may be found in Bennett McCallum and Marvin Goodfriend, "Theoretical Analysis of the Demand for Money," in John Eatwell et al., eds., *The New Palgrave: A Dictionary of Economics* (London: Macmillan Press, 1987), vol. 1, pp. 775–81.

4. This argument is due to Don Patinkin, "Financial Intermediaries and the Logical Structure of Monetary Theory," *American Economic Review*, vol. 51 (March 1961), pp. 95–116. It was later emphasized by Eugene Fama, "Banking in a Theory of Finance," *Journal of Monetary Economics*, vol. 6 (January 1980), pp. 39–57.

Patinkin pointed out that a central bank must fix both a nominal interest rate and a nominal quantity to make the price level determinate. These conditions are met if a central bank pays no interest on currency and controls its aggregate nominal quantity. The price level is determined as follows: Because currency earns zero nominal interest, the opportunity cost of holding it is the nominal interest rate on securities. It is efficient for people to hold a real stock of currency for which the marginal service yield just equals the interest rate. For a diminishing marginal service yield on currency with a sufficiently high initial threshold, there is a determinate real stock demand for currency and a determinate price level, that is, for any given nominal interest rate on securities. The nominal interest rate on securities is the sum of expected inflation plus a real interest rate component. The central bank can control inflation and thereby expected inflation by choosing a desired rate of currency growth. For example, it can choose zero currency growth and zero inflation, so that the nominal interest rate is simply the real rate and the price level is constant.

5. Notably, this point has been emphasized in Milton Friedman, *A Program for Monetary Stability* (New York: Fordham University Press, 1960), and in Eugene Fama, "Financial Intermediation and Price Level Control," *Journal of Monetary Economics*, vol. 12 (July 1983), pp. 7–28.

6. See texts by Robert Barro, Michael Darby, Rudiger Dornbusch and Stanley Fischer, Robert Gordon, Robert Hall and John Taylor, and Thomas Sargent. A notable exception is the view emphasized in Neil Wallace, "A Legal Restrictions Theory of the Demand for 'Money' and the Role of Monetary Policy," *Federal Reserve Bank of Minneapolis Quarterly Review*, vol. 1 (1983), pp. 1–7. Bennett McCallum, "The Role of Overlapping Generations Models in Monetary Economics," in Karl Brunner and Allan H. Meltzer, eds., *Carnegie-Rochester Conference Series on Public Policy*, vol. 18 (Spring 1983), pp. 9–44, which emphasizes the medium-of-exchange services of money, and Robert G. King and Charles I. Plosser, "Money as the Mechanism of Exchange," *Journal of Monetary Economics*, vol. 17 (January 1986), pp. 93–115, which emphasizes verification costs, may be read as responses to the arguments of Wallace.

7. For an analysis of how recent financial deregulation has influenced the demand for money, see Yash Mehra, "Recent Financial Deregulation and the Interest Elasticity of M1 Demand," *Federal Reserve Bank of Richmond Economic Review* (July/August 1986), pp. 13–24.

8. This series is reported in Frederick R. Macaulay, *Bond Yields, Interest Rates, and Stock Prices* (New York: National Bureau of Economic Research, 1938).

9. These numbers come from Jeffrey A. Miron, "Financial Panics, the Seasonality of the Nominal Interest Rate, and the Founding of the Fed," *American Economic Review*, vol. 76 (March 1986), pp. 125–40.

10. There are actually a number of ways that one can define a nominal interest rate smoothing policy. It can mean eliminating deterministic seasonals, as emphasized by Miron, referenced in note 9. It can mean minimizing interest rate surprises, as studied by Marvin Goodfriend, "Interest Rate Smoothing and Price Level Trend-Stationarity," *Journal of Monetary Economics*, vol. 19 (May 1987), pp. 335–48. Or it can mean using monetary policy to maintain expected constancy in interest rates as studied by Robert Barro, "Interest Rate Smoothing," University of Rochester, February 1987. Regardless of what nominal interest rate policy is followed, however, the theoretical mechanism by which it works is basically as described in the text.

11. We are drawing on Goodfriend's article referenced in note 10 for this discussion.

12. The method by which the Federal Reserve smooths interest rates has varied over the years. In the 1920s the Federal Reserve forced the banking

system to be "in the window" for a portion of high-powered money demanded. Since there was relatively little nonprice rationing, the discount rate tended to provide a ceiling to interest rates. The discount rate was raised and lowered to adjust the level of interest rates, with appropriate adjustments to nonborrowed reserves to keep banks marginally borrowing reserves. In the 1930s nominal rates were near their floor at zero, and in the 1940s they were pegged. In the 1950s and 1960s the Federal Reserve used procedures similar to those it used in the 1920s. Explicit federal funds rate targeting was used in the 1970s. Likewise, the nonborrowed reserve operating procedure employed from October 1979 to the fall of 1982 was in effect a noisy week-by-week funds rate peg. See Marvin Goodfriend, *Monetary Policy in Practice* (Richmond, Va.: Federal Reserve Bank of Richmond, 1987), pp. 40–41. Since then the Federal Reserve has employed a mixture of borrowed reserve and federal funds rate targeting.

13. Empirical evidence on the high-powered money and inflation responses associated with the elimination of nominal interest rate seasonals around 1914 may be found in Barro's article referenced in note 10.

14. This was true even under the Federal Reserve's post–October 1979 nonborrowed reserve operating procedure. See "A Historical Assessment of the Rationales and Functions of Reserve Requirements," in Marvin Goodfriend, *Monetary Policy in Practice*.

15. See, for example, William Poole, *Money and the Economy: A Monetarist View* (Reading, Mass.: Addison-Wesley, 1978).

16. See Robert E. Lucas and Thomas J. Sargent, *Rational Expectations and Econometric Practice* (Minneapolis: University of Minnesota Press, 1980).

17. See Robert G. King and Charles I. Plosser, "Money, Credit, and Prices in a Real Business Cycle," *American Economic Review*, vol. 74 (June 1984), pp. 363–80.

18. If the individual could sell the car without permission from the lender, then there would be no effective difference between car loans and an unsecured personal loan to be used, for example, to finance a vacation. In general, without the security provided by the physical asset (car), there would need to be a higher interest rate, reflecting the lender's lessened probability of receiving loan payments or the resale value of the car.

19. See Clifford W. Smith, Jr., and Jerold B. Warner, "On Financial Contracting: An Analysis of Bond Covenants," *Journal of Financial Economics*, vol. 7 (1979), pp. 117–61.

20. For example, George Benston and Clifford Smith, "A Transactions Cost Approach to the Theory of Financial Intermediation," *Journal of Finance* (May 1976), pp. 215–31, discusses why bundling of financial products can be efficient in a world of costly information. Joseph Haubrich, "Financial Intermediation, Delegated Monitoring, and Long-Term Relationships" (Working Paper, Wharton School, October 1986), provides a recent formal description of one set of gains from long-term relationships in financial intermediation.

21. A number of authors in recent years have emphasized monitoring as a key function of banks. See, for example, Douglas Diamond, "Financial Inter-

mediation and Delegated Monitoring," *Review of Economic Studies*, vol. 51 (July 1984), pp. 393–414; and Eugene Fama, "What's Different about Banks?" *Journal of Monetary Economics*, vol. 15 (January 1985), pp. 29–39.

22. For descriptions of various aspects of lines of credit see Mitchell Berlin, "Loan Commitments: Insurance Contracts in a Risky World," *Federal Reserve Bank of Philadelphia Business Review* (May/June 1986), pp. 3–12; Dwight B. Crane, *Managing Credit Lines and Commitments* (Chicago: Association of Reserve City Bankers, 1973); Gerald Hanweck, "Bank Loan Commitments," in *Below the Bottom Line*, Staff Study, Board of Governors of the Federal Reserve System, January 1986, pp. 103–30; and Bruce Summers, "Loan Commitments to Business in United States Banking History," *Federal Reserve Bank of Richmond Economic Review* (September/October 1975), pp. 115–23.

23. Theoretical analysis of bank loan commitments is found in Gregory D. Hawkins, "An Analysis of Revolving Credit Arrangements," *Journal of Financial Economics*, vol. 10 (March 1982), pp. 59–81; and in Arie Melnik and Steven Plaut, "The Economics of Loan Commitment Contracts: Credit Pricing and Utilization," *Journal of Banking and Finance*, vol. 10 (June 1986), pp. 267–80.

24. See the chapter on certificates of deposit in Timothy Q. Cook and Timothy D. Rowe, eds., *Instruments of the Money Market*, 6th ed. (Richmond, Va.: Federal Reserve Bank of Richmond, 1986), as well as the chapter on repurchase agreements, a related bank funding source.

25. In recent years loan sales have apparently become more common. See Gary Gorton and Joseph Haubrich, "Loan Sales, Recourse, and Reputation: An Analysis of Secondary Loan Participations" (Working Paper, Wharton School, May 1987); and Christine Pavel, "Securitization," *Federal Reserve Bank of Chicago Economic Review* (July/August 1986), pp. 16–31. It is not clear, however, whether loan sales are being used as a funding source on short notice.

26. See the chapter on federal funds in Cook and Rowe, *Instruments of the Money Market*.

27. The name of the discount window arose from the following historical circumstances. In the eighteenth and nineteenth centuries, much of international and interregional trade was financed with bills of exchange, which were short-term securities without explicit interest. When sold or used as collateral, a security was discounted—or valued at less than its face value—to permit a return to its holder. The discount window thus took its name from the fact that its primary function was establishing a discount rate for securities purchased or used as collateral. Howard Hackley, *Lending Functions of the Federal Reserve Banks: A History* (Washington, D.C.: Board of Governors of the Federal Reserve System, 1973), contains a thorough discussion of the legal history of Federal Reserve lending. For many years virtually all Federal Reserve lending has taken the form of advances rather than discounts. Hackley describes the shift, as well as the evolution of other aspects of discounting such as eligible paper and the size of the basic borrowing privilege, that is, the amount of a temporary discount window loan that is permitted.

28. Nevertheless, over the years the Federal Reserve has extensively em-

ployed unsterilized discount window lending, together with discount rate adjustments, in the execution of monetary policy. See note 12. Though it remains puzzling, use of the discount window this way seems to be connected with the use of secrecy or ambiguity in monetary policy. See Alex Cukierman and Allan H. Meltzer, "A Theory of Ambiguity, Credibility, and Inflation under Discretion and Asymmetric Information," *Econometrica*, vol. 54 (September 1986), pp. 1099–1128; and Marvin Goodfriend, "Monetary Mystique: Secrecy and Central Banking," *Journal of Monetary Economics*, vol. 17 (January 1986), pp. 63–92. In a similar vein, Timothy Cook and Thomas Hahn, "The Information Content of Discount Rate Announcements and Their Effect on Market Interest Rates," *Journal of Money, Credit, and Banking*, vol. 20 (May 1988), pp. 167–80, provides extensive evidence that the discount rate has served as a monetary policy signal, signaling permanent changes in the federal funds rate.

29. Task Group on Regulation of Financial Services, *Blueprint for Reform* (Washington, D.C., 1984), p. 49.

30. *Reappraisal of the Federal Reserve Discount Mechanism* (Washington, D.C.: Board of Governors of the Federal Reserve, 1971), p. 19.

31. Notably, although the Monetary Control Act of 1980 directed the Federal Reserve to price many of its services, the discount window was exempted. There are some superficial similarities between Federal Reserve practices and private line-of-credit pricing. For instance, the non-interest-earning required reserves at the Federal Reserve are like compensating balances. But there is little evidence that the Federal Reserve prices line-of-credit services efficiently according to each bank's circumstances with respect to supervision cost, risk of insolvency, or collateral.

32. Since the early 1960s, the Federal Reserve has allowed the federal funds rate to move above the discount rate for long periods of time. To limit borrowing, the Federal Reserve has imposed a noninterest cost, which rises with the level and the duration of borrowing. In practice, higher and longer-duration borrowing increases the likelihood of triggering costly Federal Reserve consultations with bank officials. See Marvin Goodfriend, "Discount Window Borrowing, Monetary Policy, and the Post–October 1979 Federal Reserve Operating Procedure," *Journal of Monetary Economics*, vol. 12 (September 1983), pp. 343–56, for a discussion of how this means of administering the window has been employed in monetary policy.

33. For example, Continental Illinois Bank borrowed extensively at the Federal Reserve discount window from May 1984 to February 1985. It was in the window for over $4 billion during much of that period. See George Benston et al., *Perspectives on Safe and Sound Banking* (Cambridge, Mass.: MIT Press, 1986), pp. 120–24.

34. Hackley, *Lending Functions*, documents the history of legal collateral requirements in discount window lending. Although the Federal Reserve has wide discretion in what it can take, it has generally required very good collateral on its loans.

A "haircut" is a margin that is subtracted from the market or face value of a security for purposes of calculating its value as collateral in a loan transaction.

For example, a 10 percent haircut off face value of a $100 security would value it at $90 for purposes of collateral.

35. U.S. Congress, House of Representatives, Committee on Government Operations, *Federal Reserve Position on Restructuring of Financial Regulation Responsibilities*, 99th Congress, 1st session, 1985, p. 235.

36. In fact, although Federal Reserve regulations apply to all banks, the Federal Reserve directly supervises and examines only state-chartered Federal Reserve member banks and bank holding companies. The comptroller of the currency, for example, supervises and examines nationally chartered banks. The Federal Deposit Insurance Corporation does so for insured state-chartered nonmember banks. Other agencies, however, make information available to the Federal Reserve.

Committee on Banking, Finance, and Urban Affairs, Staff Report, *Continental Illinois National Bank: Report of an Inquiry into Its Federal Supervision and Assistance*, contains a good discussion of the difficulties of government supervision of banks.

37. See E. Gerald Corrigan, "Financial Market Structure: A Longer View," *Federal Reserve Bank of New York Annual Report* (February 1987).

38. David Mengle, David Humphrey, and Bruce Summers, "Intraday Credit: Risk, Value, and Pricing," *Federal Reserve Bank of Richmond Economic Review* (January/February 1987), pp. 3–14, describes the creation of daylight overdrafts as follows:

> On Fedwire, transfers take place by debiting the reserve account of the sending bank and crediting the reserve account of the receiving bank. However, the sending bank is not required to have funds in its reserve account sufficient to cover the transfer at the time it is made. Rather, the transfer must be covered by the end of the day. Allowing reserve balances to become negative during the day leads to "daylight overdrafts," and it is these overdrafts that are the major source of risk to Federal Reserve Banks from Fedwire. Since a Fedwire transfer becomes final when the receiving institution is notified of the transfer, the Federal Reserve could not revoke the transfer if the sending institution failed to cover its overdraft by the end of the day. Thus, the receiving institution would have its funds while the Fed would be left with the task of collecting the payment for the defaulting sending bank. Credit risk in this case is borne by the Reserve Banks and possibly by the public.

Mengle, Humphrey, and Summers, p. 12, report total funds transfer daylight overdrafts of $76 billion per day. This is an enormous number when one considers that total reserve balances with reserve banks are around $35 billion. Daylight overdrafts are currently not priced. They are interest-free loans. Therefore, depository institutions have little incentive to economize on their use. To limit somewhat the use of intraday credit, the Federal Reserve monitors depository institutions according to "caps" and relatively informal guidelines, resorting to consultations with bank officials when necessary. This is reminiscent of administration of the discount window. See note 32.

39. Checks sent to reserve banks for collection are credited to the deposit-

ing institution's reserve or clearing account automatically, according to a schedule that allows time for the checks to be presented to the depository institutions on which they are drawn. The maximum deferral is two business days. The depository institution's account is credited regardless of whether the checks have reached the banks on which they are drawn. Because it may take longer than two days to process and collect some checks presented for collection, depository institutions receive credit to their accounts for those checks before the institutions on which the checks are drawn lose reserves. This "extra" amount of reserves in the banking system is called Federal Reserve float. The effect of float on high-powered money is usually sterilized, however, by offsetting open-market operations.

The Monetary Control Act of 1980 mandated that the Federal Reserve charge fees to recover the cost of providing check clearing and other services. In particular, the Federal Reserve was directed to charge for Federal Reserve float at the federal funds rate. Consequently, check float has fallen from $7.4 billion in the first half of 1979 to under $1 billion today. See "The Tug-of-War over Float," *Morgan Guarantee Survey* (December 1983), pp. 11–14; U.S. Congress, *The Role of the Federal Reserve in Check Clearing and the Nation's Payments System*, 1983; and John Young, "The Rise and Fall of Federal Reserve Float," *Federal Reserve Bank of Kansas City Economic Review* (February 1986), pp. 28–38.

40. Walker Todd, "Outline of an Argument on Solvency" (Memorandum, Federal Reserve Bank of Cleveland, March 1987), documents in detail the establishment of the principle that the central bank should lend only to illiquid but not to insolvent institutions.

41. Our analysis here involves the substantial work on private information economies stimulated by Michael Rothschild and Joseph Stiglitz, "Equilibrium in Competitive Insurance Markets: An Essay on the Economics of Imperfect Information," *Quarterly Journal of Economics*, vol. 90 (November 1976), pp. 629–50. Since we consider costly evaluation, however, our treatment of private information economies is closer to John Boyd and Edward Prescott, "Financial Intermediary Coalitions," *Journal of Economic Theory* (April 1986), pp. 211–32.

42. Irvine Sprague, *Bailout: An Insider's Account of Bank Failures and Rescues* (New York: Basic Books, 1986), and Todd, "Argument on Solvency," report numerous instances of government support for insolvent institutions. The Federal Reserve minimizes the risk of supporting insolvent banks by making discount window loans only on the best collateral. By doing do, however, it greatly reduces the value of its line-of-credit services too. For example, it took the best collateral when lending to Continental Illinois in 1984–1985. See note 33.

There is an additional reason why government emergency credit assistance might be necessary. Private markets would make arrangements to protect themselves against liquidity problems only if they believed that the government would not offer such services. Yet it might be impossible for the government to make credible its intention not to intervene in future crises. To do so, the government would have to precommit itself not to provide emergency credit assistance. The worst possible case would be one where the government announced its intention not to provide emergency credit assistance in the future, but the banks believed that in fact it would. Then if a liquidity problem arose, banks would not have prepared for it by holding sufficient capital and by arranging lines of credit. If the government remained true to its policy, then widespread insolvency could prevail.

43. If the Federal Reserve always perfectly collateralized its banking policy loans, then in principle it could need very little supporting regulation and supervision. If it lent at below-market rates, however, it would still need regulation and supervision to see that its policy was not abused.

44. E. W. Kemmerer, *Seasonal Variations in the Relative Demand for Money and Credit in the United States* (Washington, D.C.: National Monetary Commission, 1910), pp. 222–23, contains a more extensive classification of financial panics including more moderate episodes.

45. See Phillip Cagan, *Determinants and Effects of Changes in the Stock of Money 1875–1960* (Washington, D.C.: National Bureau of Economic Research, 1965).

46. In addition to O. M. W. Sprague, *History of Crises under the National Banking System* (Washington, D.C.: National Monetary Commission, 1910), see James Cannon, *Clearing-Houses* (New York: D. Appleton and Company, 1908); Gary Gorton and Donald Mullineaux, "The Joint Production of Confidence: Endogenous Regulation and 19th Century Commercial-Bank Clearinghouses," *Journal of Money, Credit, and Banking* (forthcoming); Richard Timberlake, "The Central Banking Role of Clearing Associations," *Journal of Money, Credit, and Banking* (February 1984), pp. 1–15; and Timberlake, *The Origins of Central Banking in the United States* (Cambridge, Mass.: Harvard University Press, 1978).

47. Wesley Lindow, "Bank Capital and Risk Assets," *National Banking Review* (September 1963), pp. 29–46.

48. The measure of total capital here is generally defined to include total equity, reserves for losses on loans and securities, and subordinated notes and debentures. Risk assets are defined as total assets, less cash, less government securities issued by the U.S. Treasury Department.

49. Thomas Humphrey and Robert Keleher, "The Lender of Last Resort: A Historical Perspective," *Cato Journal*, vol. 4 (Spring/Summer 1984), pp. 275–318, provides a historical perspective on the concept of the lender of last resort.

50. See notes 12 and 28.

51. Many investment projects involve the purchase of inputs—fuel, intermediate goods, and labor—today, but yield output only in the future. Production is profitable if the current value of future output discounted back to the present at the real interest rate is greater than the current cost of inputs. By pushing the present discounted value of output below its cost of production, even a temporarily high real interest rate could cause a project to be shut down temporarily.

52. If a central bank's remittances to the government Treasury changed as well and the Treasury adjusted its goods purchases accordingly, then there

could be a goods market effect. But that would involve more than banking policy.

53. This argument is analagous to those that arise in consideration of the Ricardian equivalence proposition, which states that under certain situations a substitution of public debt for taxation will have no effects on prices or quantities. Robert Barro's *Macroeconomics* (New York: John Wiley, 1986) provides an accessible introduction to Ricardian analysis. Louis Chan, "Uncertainty and the Neutrality of Government Financing Policy," *Journal of Monetary Economics*, vol. 11 (May 1983), pp. 351–72, provides a proof of Ricardian neutrality under conditions of uncertainty, stressing the analogy to Modigliani-Miller propositions in finance.

The ineffectiveness of credit policy, of which banking policy is an example, is well illustrated by the student loan program. Student loans need not result in increased expenditure on education. A loan may reduce the extent to which families draw down their own financial savings or sacrifice expenditure on other goods and services to pay for a student's education. Because loan funds are fungible, they cannot ensure a net increase in expenditure in the targeted area. The targeted effect would require provisions in the program to prevent substitution for private outlays and to restrict access to other credit sources.

Commentary
Phillip Cagan

As continuing developments transform the financial system, our rickety regulatory apparatus no longer suffices. That generalization finds wide agreement. Although lack of consensus for the specifics of reform has paralyzed congressional action so far, eventually statutory changes will have to be made. To help guide those changes, Goodfriend and King analyze the basic issues of bank regulation. They question how much of our regulatory apparatus is needed. Their answer is, probably none. At the end of their analysis they admit some hesitancy in scrapping banking regulations entirely but are not very specific about why we might hesitate. Since I am generally sympathetic toward their point of view and also hesitant, let me try to clarify how far we should try to go with deregulation.

Goodfriend and King distinguish banking policy from monetary policy. This is a fruitful distinction, which we should follow. In their view monetary policy can pursue all our macroeconomic objectives through open-market operations. These provide full control of high-powered money and thereby provide the needed influence on aggregate demand and prices. Banking policies, in contrast, involve lending to individual banks, which can be done without changing high-powered money. A general liquidity crisis or any financial tightening calls for open-market operations to increase high-powered money, and that should suffice. Lending to individual banks that need special assistance is a kind of public service that could just as well be performed within the private sector if the aggregate economy is kept sufficiently liquid.

There is appeal in such a proposal to restrict banking policies severely. Once thought radical, it now receives wide and serious attention. There is much agreement outside the banking community that insolvent banks should not be kept alive. If they are solvent but illiquid, they should be able to find the needed credit in the private sector. Therefore, if we abolished reserve requirements and discounting, we could scrap the regulatory apparatus set up to enforce and police them.

This would *not* end all banking regulations, however, if present proposals to continue deposit insurance in some form prevail. Since deposit insurance is not in the purview of the topic for this session, let me put that issue aside and consider the abolition of reserve requirements and discounting.

Is there any benefit to reserve requirements and discounting that might justify keeping them? The answer also depends in part on the marginal social cost of the required supervision, which I consider below.

Goodfriend and King argue cogently that discounting is not needed, given an important assumption of their analysis, which I would characterize as the assumption that the market and policy makers possess all the information they need to identify the nature of shocks and adjust properly to them. Thus, while open-market operations take care of the market's liquidity needs, banks known to be solvent can always borrow in the private market. Insolvent banks, unable to borrow, would close down, as they should. There need be no panic and no general disruption of financial markets. I believe this argument is valid. If an argument is to be made in support of discounting, it has to emphasize *in*complete information. Let me sketch such an argument in order to evaluate it. Information becomes important in adjusting to shocks. Before considering the case of discounting, let me give a separate example from this paper of how imperfect information can be a problem for the dynamics of adjustment.

In discussing how control of high-powered money is sufficient to accomplish the Federal Reserve's preference for interest rate smoothing, Goodfriend and King consider what should happen when the aggregate demand for credit rises temporarily and starts to pull up the real rate of interest. Under the Federal Reserve's policy of pegging the nominal rate of interest, the *real* rate can rise if the *expected* rate of inflation declines. Given an assumption of accurate market expectations, the actual inflation rate must also decline. Thus a possible outcome of such a shock which does not disturb the equilibrium in the credit market would be a jump in prices (unanticipated by the market before the shock occurs). This price jump is supported as soon as it occurs by the provision of increased high-powered money by the central bank to satisfy the unchanged demand for *real* money balances. Then the price jump is followed by the needed decline in the inflation rate, produced by lower growth of high-powered money until the temporary rise in the real rate of interest has ended. According to Goodfriend and King, these adjustments in expectations and monetary policy allow the economy to adjust without disruption to this temporary shock in credit demand.

But now consider a similar rise in the equilibrium real rate of

COMMENTARY

interest that is *permanent*, which Goodfriend and King do not consider. Under interest rate targeting, a higher equilibrium real rate of interest can occur only with either a permanent rise in the nominal rate of interest or a permanent deflation or a combination of the two. Permanent deflation would require a permanent decline in the growth of high-powered money to the appropriate rate. Although such an equilibrium adjustment is possible, the dynamics of getting there are unclear without perfect foresight. No one can easily distinguish a temporary from a permanent change in the real rate of interest. If the credit market puts upward pressure on the rate, the usual response of the Federal Reserve under rate smoothing is to increase high-powered money. Under the circumstances this produces inflation and, given the pegged nominal rate of interest, *lowers* the ex post real rate, opposite to the needed increase. The upward pressure on the nominal interest rate then increases, and the dynamics begin an explosive inflation. Achieving a *non*inflationary equilibrium by the alternative route of raising the peg for the nominal rate of interest depends on correctly forecasting the rise in the equilibrium real rate, and such forecasts are notoriously unreliable. That, of course, is precisely why interest rate pegging is viewed as dangerous policy and why attention to a price level or monetary indicator is needed for long-run stability.

Goodfriend and King would concur, I am sure, in the dangers of blindly pegging the interest rate. It is the Federal Reserve's preference, not theirs. In their discussion they are careful to consider a policy of "smoothing" the rate, not targeting or pegging it, which implies that changes in the nominal rate should be made as needed. My point in this example is that the timing and direction of adjustments are often crucial to the effect of shocks on the monetary system.

With that red flag of caution raised, let us now consider the dynamic benefits of reserve requirements. Goodfriend and King see such requirements as unnecessary under interest rate targeting. I agree. But suppose we eschew rigid interest rate targeting for the reasons above. We may want to target monetary aggregates in order to achieve long-run price stability. If our chosen target is high-powered money growth, reserve requirements are not needed. But if, as seems likely, some other monetary aggregate will provide closer control over aggregate demand and prices, reserve requirements can help tighten the dynamic link from the high-powered money instrument to the monetary target. Even here I would not claim that reserve requirements are crucial. They may have a positive benefit, however, so their abolition is at least debatable and depends on the cost of imposing them.

By cost here I mean the social cost of regulatory supervision, to which I return below; I do not mean the seigniorage of required reserves that would be lost. By my rough calculation the seigniorage today from reserves is only $2 billion a year,[1] not important enough to determine such a major policy issue.

At one point Goodfriend and King argue that policy could simply target currency. There is indeed a determinant public demand for real currency balances, so the nominal quantity supplied controls the price level in the long run. On this line of argument based on equilibrium relationships, we could also claim that there is a determinant demand for $10 bills, so, as Jacob Viner once observed, we could just as well control the price level through the quantity of these bills. But the dynamics of these demands differ. Surely the public adjusts much sooner to changes in total monetary growth than to changes in growth of one of its components, owing to the different closeness of substitutes. And rapidity of response can be important in controlling the economy, given our imperfect information.

From the point of view of dynamic adjustments, let us now consider the more important issue of discounting. The Federal Reserve prefers that banks have such a cushion to alleviate the initial impact of open-market operations. The Federal Reserve settled on a nonborrowed reserves procedure in the 1980s with variable discounting. Is this procedure oversolicitous of bankers? Perhaps. The banking system could no doubt learn to live without discounting by being more liquid. But the issue concerns the benefit to monetary policy rather than to banks. The pros and cons are not clear-cut once we give up the unreality of possessing all the needed information. The Federal Reserve does not at any moment know accurately the state of credit demands and bank liquidity. It uses bank borrowing as a source of information and safety valve for mistakes. Under present conditions of discretionary monetary policy, weight should be given to the Federal Reserve's preference for targeting *non*borrowed reserves in pursuit of its long-run objectives, which implies easy access by banks to the discount window. Thus does monetary policy involve banking policy. The complaint about Federal Reserve policy is not how it conducts its short-run operating procedure but the long-run success of its monetary policies.

Goodfriend and King go on to discuss banking panics, which provided the proximate impetus for the founding of the Federal Reserve System. Their discussion downplays the seriousness of panics, on the argument that bank failures and deposit losses were in fact not extensive. But that does not mean that the founders of the Federal Reserve System had an irrational fear of panics. Panics partially closed down the payments system for periods of several months. The result was a stagnation of business. Banks survived by closing their doors during the storm while it ravaged the outside economy. We should not minimize the fear of panics as seen by contemporaries, which generated the political momentum to create a lender of last resort.

The old-fashioned panics in which the public withdrew currency from banks has been made harmless by the Federal Reserve's authority to print and issue unlimited quantities of Federal Reserve notes. The Aldrich-Vreeland Act of 1908 also solved the problem by authorizing the emergency issue of national bank notes, but because the authors of the Federal Reserve Act of 1913 thought more reform was needed, they gave us more. The only question today is whether there could be a panic shift from bank deposits, not to currency, but to Treasury bills or their equivalent. Ordinarily I would say impossible, but given the number of troubled banks, not to mention insolvent thrifts, and the limited resources of the Federal Deposit Insurance Corporation, I am not 100 percent sure. Moreover, after October 1987's Black Monday, we are now sure that market hysteria is not a thing of the past.

Of course, there is no danger to the banking system from a desired shift from deposits to anything except currency, for the deposits would remain in the system. The sellers of the desired assets would become the new owners of the deposits given up in the shift. But there could be a massive redistribution of deposits among banks, producing distress in certain sectors of the system and of the economy. No doubt the Federal Reserve would provide sufficient liquidity to the system, but the problem would be sectoral and not general. Possibly discounting would therefore allow the selective infusion of Federal Reserve credit at the core of the panic and thus nip it in the bud, before it gained momentum, and could prove more effective than a general rain of liquidity through open-market operations.

It is difficult to know how to weigh such a possibility, since it is so hypothetical. A similar episode was the storm that hit the commercial paper market when the Penn Central went bankrupt in June 1970. The Federal Reserve lent freely to major banks so they could lend liberally to businesses suddenly shut out of the commercial paper market, and the storm passed in a few weeks. The Federal Reserve insists on retaining such authority to act selectively in emergencies. We cannot categorically rule out all such contingencies.

But does that mean we should continue with the tangle of associated regulations? Twenty years ago most analysts probably would have answered yes, except for deposit rate ceilings. Today, given the spread of transactions accounts to nonbanking institutions and the heightened competition in financial markets, regulating banks no longer looks attractive or effective, and a forced extension of regulations to other institutions encroaching on the traditional preserve of banks looks even less attractive. We must weigh in the balance the associated social costs of regulation, which I alluded to earlier. I would argue that the *marginal* social costs of maintaining the two banking policies of concern to Goodfriend and King, reserve requirements and discounting, are low because they do not in fact require much supervision of banks. Reserve requirements are easily and cheaply enforced. If they are eliminated, it will be because they become irrelevant with the growth in importance of nonbank transactions balances. Discounting does not really require much supervision either. The Federal Reserve could return to the original discounting of acceptable collateral paper and rely on the present practice of making advances without collateral only when convenient. If troubled banks are low on acceptable collateral, then they could be advised to change their ways. Thus monitoring of bank solvency could be left to lenders in the federal funds market and thereby essentially privatized.

An argument for continued government supervision could be that it is a public service to private lenders. Goodfriend and King point out that the cost of supervision to maintain discounting is a subsidy to banks that use it. The seigniorage from reserve requirements can be viewed as a tax on banks to pay for this subsidy. If reserve requirements and the seigniorage were to be eliminated, any supervision that benefits banks should be charged for. As for same-day credit on Fedwire, surely that can be handled without supervision, which is not sufficiently up to date to be effective here anyway.

Nevertheless, these reforms could not yet satisfy Goodfriend and King's distaste for banking policy. The main need for supervision arises, of course, to back up deposit insurance and more generally to guarantee the safety of the payments system. Although it was not within the scope of their paper to be concerned with deposit insurance, it is relevant for our attitude toward banking policy that elimination of the insurance is so far politically out of the question. The recent Maryland and Ohio thrift episodes demonstrated this obvious political reality. For most practical proposals for reform under discussion, some form of supervision will remain. In that event the *marginal* social cost of monitoring banks for discounting and reserve requirements would be fairly low. Hence I tentatively conclude that, given the continuation of some form of banking supervision, we pay little and gain something for these two policies.

Note

1. High-powered bank reserves are about $40 billion (November 1987). If they grow in real terms at as much as 5 percent a year, the seigniorage is $2 billion a year. Most of the government's seigniorage comes instead from the currency outstanding of about $200 billion.

7
Payments System Risk and Public Policy

Mark J. Flannery

The U.S. payments system is a large, complex combination of institutional arrangements that daily transmit over $1.4 trillion among economic units. It includes currency, an extensive check collection system, automated clearinghouses (ACH), a growing number of interbank automatic teller machine (ATM) networks, and two large-dollar wire transfer systems. The wire transfer component—which includes the Federal Reserve's Fedwire and the New York Clearinghouse Association's Clearing House Interbank Payment System (CHIPS)—accounts for nearly 80 percent of the dollar volume of all transactions in the system, making it by far the most important segment. The volume and complexity of wire system transfers have raised both public and private concerns about their safety. The Federal Reserve has been particularly concerned about existing payments system risks and has argued that the kinds of transactions undertaken on wire transfer systems significantly influence the financial system's overall stability. These concerns have led the Federal Reserve to oppose potentially important reforms in bank holding company structure on the grounds that they would threaten the stability of the payments system. It is therefore important to evaluate the sources of payments system risk and its relation to the structure and functioning of private financial firms.

The relation between banking firms and payments system risk is a complex and far-reaching topic for analysis. A complete evaluation of payments system risks would require prior consideration of other, substantive issues, including the optimal means of providing settle-

---

I would like to thank (without implicating) Robert Eisenbeis, Edward Ettin, Marvin Goodfriend, Thomas Huertas, Jan Loeys, and especially David Humphrey for helpful comments on earlier drafts of this chapter. The opinions expressed are entirely my own.

ment for financial transactions, the Federal Reserve's role in providing daylight loans to payments system participants, possible public good aspects of an economy's payments system, and the desirability of private moneys as substitutes for nationally provided fiat money. These issues are described briefly later in this chapter. To focus on issues of more immediate policy concern, the chapter analyzes payments system risk under the existing set of regulations and technology. Federal Reserve involvement in the wire transfer system is taken as given, as is its guarantee of payments finality under Regulation J.

Three aspects of the U.S. payments system and its stability are evaluated here:

- Does settlement risk on the large-denomination wire transfer networks (CHIPS and Fedwire) threaten the stability of individual banking firms or of the financial system as a whole?
- What is the proper way to deal with daylight overdrafts on Fedwire?
- Are there any reasons related to the payments system why commercial firms should not be allowed to affiliate with banks?

The first section of the chapter describes the U.S. payments system, the sources of risk in wire transfers, and the existing means of controlling those risks.

The next section evaluates the potential for systemic instability associated with the massive daily flow of CHIPS and Fedwire payments. Because these two systems involve different kinds of risk exposure, systemic risks are limited to CHIPS, whose payments system risk is a particular kind of credit risk. Credit extensions associated with the payments mechanism must be evaluated and controlled in the same fashion as other credit risks, but few new regulatory tools are required to limit those risks to acceptable levels.

The following section addresses daylight overdrafts on Fedwire, concluding that, like all credit extensions, they should be priced to avoid market distortions. Fedwire technological capabilities, however, influence both the Federal Reserve's ability to price overdraft credit and the kind of payment and intraday credit arrangements that the private sector can implement.

The fourth section addresses the question of affiliation of commercial firms with banks and concludes that payments system risk has little to do with the social costs and benefits of such affiliations. A final section identifies some important and related policy questions that require further analysis elsewhere.

Risks in the Payments System

At its most basic level a payments system is a means of transferring claims on wealth among economic agents. Kenneth D. Garbade and William L. Silber point out that an efficient payments system encourages specialization in production and risk bearing by allowing traders to exchange value promptly, cheaply, and reliably.[1] Although such a system uses societal resources, it also provides real benefits through the efficiency gains of specialization.

Any combination of goods *could* be exchanged against one another, but Jurg Niehans and Karl Brunner and Allan Meltzer show how actual trading patterns will adjust to minimize total transaction costs.[2] Economic forces lead transactors to evolve toward a limited number of low-cost commodity moneys or other media of exchange. In the limit a pure fiat money may emerge, as it has in the United States. The existing, complex system of financial institutions and payment mechanisms thus provides alternative means of exchanging goods and securities against fiat money—or, more commonly, *claims* on fiat money in the form of reserve balances at the Federal Reserve.

Institutional Features of the U.S. Payments System. Table 7–1 provides basic information on the major components of our present payments system. Nonelectronic payments account for the vast majority of individual transactions, though only a minority of the dollar values transferred. The wire transfers category (that is, Fedwire and CHIPS) includes over 78 percent of all dollars transferred in the United States. For this reason payments system risks are almost exclusively associated with wire transfers, which have been the primary focus of Federal Reserve policy concerns about the payments mechanism.[3]

In evaluating the risks associated with the wire transfer systems, it is important to understand that U.S. payments activity has been expanding rapidly in recent years. Table 7–2 provides some information on this growth. From 1983 to February 1987 the deposit turnover ratio for New York City banks rose more than 50 percent—to an average of nine turnovers per business day. This phenomenon reflects an increasingly intensive use of the banks' Federal Reserve clearing balances: for example, the ratio of New York City debits to all bank reserve balances rose 22 percent during the same period.[4] These figures indicate that cash management practices are changing rapidly in major financial centers. One manifestation of change has been an increasing tendency of banks to run daylight overdrafts—that is, to

TABLE 7–1
VOLUME AND VALUE COMPOSITION OF U.S. PAYMENTS, 1983

Type of Payment Instrument	Volume Composition (percent)	Value Composition (percent)	Average Dollar Value per Transaction
Nonelectronic	99.50	21.50	247
Cash	70.41	1.54	25
Checks	25.14	19.80	910
Credit cards	3.13	0.11	42
Money orders	0.47	0.03	67
Traveler's checks	0.50	0.02	35
Electronic	0.35	78.50	258,993
Automated clearinghouses	0.25	0.39	1,800
Automated teller machines	0.05	0.00	70
Point of sale	0.01	0.00	30
Wire transfers	0.04	78.11	2,500,000

SOURCE: David Burras Humphrey, "Payments System Risk, Market Failure, and Public Policy," in Elinor Solomon, ed., *The Payments Revolution: The Emerging Public Policy Issues* (Boston: Kluwer-Nijhoff Publishing, 1987), p. 84.

initiate payments in excess of their collected balances at the time the payments are initiated. Although the payments system has always involved some credit extensions as a concomitant of transferring value among economic agents, recent institutional changes have increased the importance of the credit component. Analyzing the policy issues surrounding payments system risk in the United States requires an understanding of Fedwire and CHIPS.

Fedwire. The first Fedwire system was installed in 1917. Its successor system now effects settlement on the large majority of all U.S. payments. Fedwire has two distinct components: an interbank funds transfer mechanism and a system for exchanging book-entry government securities. The first component is used by banks to make and receive payments for loans and deposits, for their own account or on behalf of customers. These payments average approximately $570 billion daily in 214,000 individual transactions. In late 1986 book-entry securities transactions averaged $250 billion in daily volume, which was heavily concentrated in five major clearing banks in New York City.

Directly or indirectly the Federal Reserve's settlement function is employed in virtually all noncash payment transactions through its "net settlement" service. This service is provided to numerous private

TABLE 7-2
BANK DEBITS AND DEPOSIT TURNOVER, 1983–1987

	1983	1984	1985	1986	February 1987
	Annual Demand Deposit Turnover at U.S. Banks (not seasonally adjusted)				
All insured banks	379.9	433.5	497.4	564.0	550.0
Major New York City banks	1,510.0	1,838.6	2,191.1	2,494.3	2,273.2
Other banks	240.5	267.9	301.6	327.9	329.4
	Ratio of New York City Bank Debits to All Banks' Reserves				
Major New York City banks	1,320.7	1,411.9	1,503.0	1,597.2	1,616.3

NOTE: Turnover ratio for 1983–1986 is annual average of monthly figures. Ratio of New York City debits to bank reserves for 1983–1986 is ratio of average monthly debits to year-end total reserves of the banking system.
SOURCE: *Federal Reserve Bulletin* (June 1987), tables 1.20 and 1.22.

payments system participants, as explained by E. Gerald Corrigan in 1983 congressional testimony:

> In providing net settlement services the Federal Reserve enters into an agreement with each participating depository institution and its representative. On the basis of the agreements, the representative presents a daily settlement statement to the Federal Reserve that indicates each participant's net debit or credit balance resulting from all transactions processed during the day. Upon receipt, the Federal Reserve office posts the net debits and credits to the participating institutions' accounts. Through these entries, all the underlying transactions are settled.[5]

The CHIPS network is the most significant user of the net settlement service, using a special clearing account at the New York Federal Reserve Bank to settle daily net payment differences among its members. In addition, most interbank check clearing eventually involves a transfer of funds over Fedwire, often in the form of a net settlement transaction.[6]

In transferring funds among clearing accounts, the Federal Reserve (under Regulation J) provides irrevocable and immediate access to the transferred funds, a feature known as payments finality. Payments finality governs both interbank funds transfers and payments associated with book-entry securities transactions. By guaranteeing each transfer at the time it is made, the Federal Reserve becomes exposed to credit risk if the paying bank has overdrawn its reserve account. That risk is not priced in any way. If a net paying bank closes the day with a negative reserve account balance, the Federal Reserve has longstanding procedures, including a possible discount window loan, for resolving the situation. A phenomenon of growing importance, however, is the tendency of some banks to run substantial overdrafts in their reserve accounts *during the day*. These daylight overdrafts have grown to average $55 billion on the regular Fedwire network and an additional $55 to $60 billion in connection with book-entry securities. Payments finality means that, at least *under current operating procedures, the Federal Reserve bears considerable unpriced credit risk in connection with its settlement function.*

CHIPS. CHIPS is a wire transfer and message system serving approximately 140 member institutions. Most CHIPS traffic involves international payments or payments for foreign exchange transactions. On an average day in the first five months of 1987, CHIPS transferred $526 billion in 124,149 individual transactions. Its daily activity has peaked at more than $800 billion, and daylight overdrafts average about $45 billion daily.[7]

Unlike Fedwire payments, CHIPS payments are provisional. Although payment information is transferred throughout the day, claims to the medium of exchange are transferred only at the end of the day through a special net settlement account at the New York Federal Reserve Bank. If a CHIPS participant had insufficient resources to make settlement, all transactions for the day might be reversed ("unwound"). That is, all the failed bank's payments from *and* payments to other CHIPS participants would be removed from the day's transactions, and a new set of net settlement positions would be computed. Banks that had a net credit position vis-à-vis the failed institution might thus become unable to settle, raising the possibility of a systemic set of failures. This situation means that CHIPS participants that grant customers immediate access to funds transferred over the system are exposing themselves to credit risk.

The Risks Associated with Wire Transfers. Because the two wire transfer systems differ in payments finality, they differ significantly in the risks posed by daylight overdrafts. On CHIPS, provisional payments generate credit risk, which can become very substantial in relation to a bank's capital. By contrast, private sector participants in Fedwire bear no credit risk at all, because the Federal Reserve extends unpriced credit to institutions that overdraw their clearing accounts.[8] Note that intraday credit on both CHIPS and Fedwire involves a risk of default but has no pure time value.[9] For example, the market convention is that government securities are generally exchanged against good funds on the day after the trade. Whether the funds are received early or late in the day, the purchaser earns the full day's interest on the delivered securities. Similarly, the way bank reserve requirements are computed—both deposit and reserve balances are measured only at the close of business daily—provides no intraday value to collected balances.

Bankers and their customers have evolved a number of transactional arrangements to economize on non-interest-bearing demand deposit and reserve account balances. Because there is no explicit cost of intraday credit, many of these arrangements generate daylight overdrafts as a byproduct.

- Massive daily repayments of overnight federal fund loans and repurchase agreements occur early in the morning, and the paying banks refinance their liability positions only later in the day. With no price assigned to the resulting daylight overdrafts, bankers have no incentive to negotiate term federal funds or repurchase agreements rather than overnight transactions to minimize transaction flows and daylight overdrafts.[10]
- Government securities dealers routinely build their inventories throughout the day to avoid expensive delivery "failures." Consequently, their settling banks make large net payments on their behalf early in the day and receive offsetting credits only later in the day. Since government securities clearing over Fedwire is highly concentrated at five New York banks, this process generates very large overdrafts for a small number of banks.

Payment risks on CHIPS. The credit risk problem on CHIPS has two institutional causes. First, payments are arranged continuously by participants, but settlement occurs only at the close of business daily. Second, depository institutions frequently make payments for their customers in excess of the collected funds available in the payer's account. In other words, modern cash management practices link the payments system with substantial intradaily credit extensions.[11] It is important to emphasize that this is not a necessary feature of a payments system.

The combination of discrete settlement and provisional payments on CHIPS generates two broad kinds of payments system risk. First, a bank might advance funds on behalf of a customer that subsequently failed to make good on its obligation. The resulting credit loss might cause the bank to fail.[12] Edward J. Kane emphasizes that this "noncollection risk" is one of the few ways in which a large bank can quickly become insolvent.[13] Second, one bank's failure to settle its provisional CHIPS position might generate a wider, systemic shock, as CHIPS participants relying on payments from the failed institution to balance their overall cash flows might become unable to settle themselves after an unwind. This situation is more likely to occur if banks allow customers to overdraw their accounts.

Corrigan's recent evaluation of the financial system places great weight on the contagion effects of such a failure:

> The hard fact of the matter is that linkages created by the large-dollar payments systems are such that a serious credit problem at any of the large users of the systems has the potential to disrupt the *system as a whole*. . . . The large-dollar payments systems—because of their size, speed, and interconnections—have the potential *to trigger the feared chain reaction* whereby a problem at one major institution can all too quickly cascade to other institutions and markets.[14] (emphasis added)

Although it is difficult to find an explicit description of how one firm's failure endangers the banking or payments *system*, the fear appears to be that institutions undertake transitions that are large in relation to their capital without adequate information about their counterparties' financial condition. Any shock to the system might therefore induce a flight to quality that would generate self-fulfilling prophecies about the perceived weaker firms' impending failures. (Jack M. Guttentag and Richard J. Herring have suggested a similar kind of adverse systemic reaction to a single bank's failure in the Eurodollar market.)[15] Furthermore, if one bank's solvency were called into question, payment recipients might begin to discriminate among paying banks on the basis of their perceived ability to settle at day's end. Some nonfinancial entities would therefore become unable to transact and thus unable to undertake their primary business activities because an unrelated bank had failed.

Payment risk on CHIPS involves conceptually simple credit risk exposure for participating institutions. Although credit risk is not bad per se, it must be properly monitored and controlled. At least historically, however, individual banks have not properly monitored the credit risks associated with wire funds transactions. For example, in discussing intraday payment and collection procedures, Frederick Heldring reports that large institutions' payments system "operational controls are considerably more advanced than those on the credit policy side. . . . Bankers must understand that the loss potential in payment system activities is similar to that in other types of credit exposure, and that it must be underwritten and managed accordingly."[16] William C. Dudley explains this apparent lapse in management information:

> Because intraday exposures are generated as a result of payments, those banks typically have not focused on the issue from a credit perspective. One of the Federal Reserve's goals in this area is simply to force senior management to focus on the fact that they are extending credit to many institutions during the day.[17]

Whether these historical concerns remain valid should be a serious consideration for managers and regulators alike. No bank should make a daylight loan on terms it would be unwilling to accept after the sun sets. Payments system credit risks can be especially important because wire transfer exchanges are heavily concentrated among a relatively few large institutions.

Implications of credit risk on Fedwire. That Fedwire transactions involve no systemic risk does not mean that overdrafts on Fedwire generate no social costs. Because daylight overdrafts are not priced,[18] participating banks have inadequate incentives to monitor and control their use of daylight overdrafts.[19] Finance theory clearly indicates that underpricing daylight credits will lead banks to undertake (socially) excessive risks. The primary problem with mispriced Fedwire overdrafts, therefore, is that they may induce inefficient risk bearing or real resource use in the private sector. This situation is analogous to the effect of fixed-premium deposit insurance on private behavior, though more limited in scope.

As noted above, one important cause of daylight overdrafts on Fedwire is the extensive use of overnight federal funds transactions. These loans are repaid early in the morning, borrowing banks arrange new financing later in the morning, and the newly borrowed funds are generally transferred by midafternoon. The result is a substantial tendency for net funds purchasers to run daylight overdrafts at the Federal Reserve. This payment scheduling might allow lenders to run quickly from a troubled situation: late delivery of borrowed funds provides an opportunity to default on the lender's promise if adverse information about the borrower arrives during the day. As a consequence the Federal Reserve provides free intraday credit through overdrafts to net purchasers of federal funds, who would find it more expensive to borrow if lenders bore the full extent of interbank credit risk.

Another important cause of Fedwire daylight overdrafts is the practice of "position building" by securities dealers. The rules governing securities trades prohibit partial deliveries and impose a heavy burden on dealers who fail to deliver all the promised securities.[20] To minimize the probability of a large delivery failure, government securities dealers take delivery of securities throughout the day but wait until late in the afternoon to deliver on their sales and thus receive payment over Fedwire.[21] This procedure is known as position building. Since their banks' reserve accounts are debited immediately for the securities the dealers are receiving, the clearing banks run substantial daylight overdrafts. With underpriced daylight overdrafts, therefore, the Federal Reserve is bearing part of the cost of the dealers' risk control procedures. If its daylight credit were priced, the dealers would be forced to bear the entire cost of their position building, which would alter their optimal trading behavior.

Real resource allocations can also be affected by mispriced daylight credit. With free intraday credit, for example, banks will underinvest in backup computer systems for accessing Fedwire or CHIPS. A private operational failure of this sort can expose the Federal Reserve to unpriced credit risk if it continues making payments on behalf of the bank, or it could cause a CHIPS settlement failure.[22] Perhaps more significant, with the Federal Reserve providing underpriced payments finality on Fedwire, private firms offering competitive settlement services, such as CHIPS, will be disadvantaged. If the Federal Reserve's settlement services are more costly than those of actual or potential private suppliers, a deadweight social cost will be associated with mispriced daylight credit.

Offsetting these costs may be some social benefits if a fully reliable payments system is socially optimal and can be achieved most cheaply through daylight overdrafts. A full analysis of the proper pricing of daylight overdrafts must consider both the costs and the benefits of such a system.

Current Provisions for Controlling Payments System Risk. Current operating procedures on CHIPS allow each participant to control its exposure to each other participant, as it would any other kind of credit risk.[23] Since October 1984 CHIPS has required that all payments be consistent with the receiving bank's stated bilateral credit limit for the sending bank.[24] In addition, there is a systemwide CHIPS debit cap: no bank may have outstanding on the system a net debit balance exceeding 5 percent of the sum of its bilateral credit limits. If a bank tries to make a payment that would violate either of these constraints, the system will reject it.

The Federal Reserve has considered three means of controlling Fedwire daylight overdrafts: collateralization, debit caps, and, most recently, pricing. The method currently used is a net debit cap on Fedwire, which was implemented in March 1986.[25] Each institution wishing to be allowed daylight overdrafts on Fedwire must undertake an assessment of its own credit worthiness, its payments system operational procedures, and its general credit policies. A daily overdraft cap (applicable to both Fedwire and CHIPS positions) equal to some multiple of the bank's primary capital is then permitted, the multiple depending on self-assessed quality. A bank must delay any outgoing payments that would cause it to exceed its overdraft cap, perhaps inconveniencing itself or its customers. If the caps are binding, therefore, this arrangement can generate an intraday value for funds that was absent before March 1986. The economic merits of this system are discussed below.

Contagious Failures and Payments System Risk

The most subtle—and potentially the most important—issue associated with payments system risk is the possibility of contagious failures as a result of CHIPS daylight credit extensions. (Payments finality on Fedwire makes contagion there impossible.) The effect of a settlement failure on other CHIPS participants has been simulated by Humphrey.[26] The system "shock" was an assumed settlement failure by a randomly chosen bank with a net credit position. As the initial failure's payments were unwound, Humphrey assumed that any bank whose net CHIPS position fell by more than its equity capital would also fail to settle. Humphrey conducted four such experiments, which indicated that one initial failure might induce settlement failures at nearly half of all CHIPS members. He concluded "that systemic risk can be significant and that its possible effects on financial markets are substantial enough to constitute a serious problem."[27]

Equating an initial settlement failure with a contagious string of bank runs ignores the intended functioning of the Federal Reserve's discount window: the lender of last resort should provide liquidity to solvent firms. An institution that is unable to settle may be insolvent or merely illiquid. If a solvent bank is rendered illiquid by another bank's settlement failure, a discount window advance should be made freely available. If the bank is insolvent, however, Bagehot would advise that the lender of last resort allow it to fail, in which case its CHIPS counterparties will become general creditors in the bankruptcy proceedings.[28] Such payee banks can expect to collect some portion of their contractual payments from the bankrupt entity, though perhaps only after a lengthy judicial delay. Payee banks may also have a legal claim against customers for whom funds have been provisionally received from the failed bank. As long as the expected value of a bank's assets (including, of course, those claims on the failed institution) exceed the bank's liabilities, the discount window should be available as a source of liquidity.

Conceptually, then, provisional payments system risks are no different from any other credit risk. Whether a bank's illiquidity or insolvency derives from unfortunate interest rate bets, standard credit losses, operational inefficiency, or daylight overdrafts, the Federal Reserve's response should be the same: provide liquidity to solvent institutions and let the insolvent ones fail.

An operational problem with this prescription is that payments system risk may be quantitatively different from other credit risks, even if it is qualitatively similar. Daylight credit risk exposure can be large in relation to an institution's capital and concentrated; it can also change very quickly from day to day. Consequently, rapid solvency judgments may be very difficult to make. If the Federal Reserve must be involved in discount window lending, therefore, some prior regulatory constraints on intraday credit extensions may be appropriate.[29]

Since provisional payments system risk is merely a special kind of credit risk, regulators and managers should deal with it as such. One substantial regulatory gap exists in the treatment of payments system risk: intraday credit extensions are not subject to the limits on credit extensions that apply to overnight credits. Those limits take two forms. First, Section 23A of the Federal Reserve Act (as amended) prohibits unsecured overnight extensions of credit by a bank to its nonbank affiliates. Section 23A does not apply, however, to daylight credit positions. Second, national banks may not lend more than 10 percent of their net worth on an unsecured basis to any borrower overnight, but there is no corresponding limit on intraday credit extensions.[30] Regulators should not distinguish between daylight and overnight credit. If interaffiliate credits must be controlled and diversification of loan portfolios enforced, simple parity requires that these rules apply to daylight positions as well as those undertaken overnight. (Anthony Saunders and the Committee on Government Operations reach a similar conclusion about the need to control daylight overdraft credits.)[31]

Beyond these simple regulatory extensions, however, proper monitoring of daylight credit risks should require no new regulatory principles or powers. All banks are required to operate in a "safe and sound" manner, which should surely include safe extensions of intraday credit. Moreover, since payments system overdrafts are concentrated among a relatively few institutions, broad-gauge regulatory changes are not needed to address issues of payments system risk. The goal in regulating such risks should be to limit them to tolerable levels for the institutions most likely to be exposed.

Conclusion 1. Daylight overdrafts constitute one important kind of risk for at least some banks. Normal safety and soundness regulation therefore requires that such risks be properly monitored and controlled. A regulatory admonition that bankers continue to refine their technical ability to monitor intraday credit exposures is entirely consistent with private incentives: managers should be unwilling to make intraday loans that they would refuse overnight. Because such risks seem most concentrated in large banks, the cost of achieving a suitable monitoring capability should not be prohibitive for any institution.

Conclusion 2. Section 23A of the Federal Reserve Act should apply unambiguously to daylight overdrafts, as should other limitations on the proportion of net worth a bank may lend to a single borrower.

Controlling Daylight Overdrafts on Fedwire

Fedwire daylight overdrafts should be controlled to minimize the distorted risk incentives and real resource allocations associated with unpriced credit. The credit component of the payments system has expanded in recent years primarily because the existing system provides insufficient incentives to avoid daylight overdrafts, while there are private benefits to using them. Reliable estimates indicate that a small number of institutional changes, such as substituting term federal funds and repurchase agreements for overnight arrangements or eliminating position building by government securities dealers, would effectively eliminate the overdrafts.[32] Consequently, Fedwire overdrafts can probably be substantially reduced if transactors are given even a small incentive to improve the synchronization of payments. The question then is how the proper incentives can best be provided. Historically, the Federal Reserve has considered three options: collateralization of Fedwire overdrafts with a perfected security interest in government securities, debit caps, and pricing daylight credit extensions. It has implemented a system of debit caps.

In March 1986 the Federal Reserve introduced a new "payments system risk" policy under which each institution was assigned a daylight overdraft cap equal to a multiple of its primary capital.[33] That is, the Federal Reserve has established a specific line of credit for each bank, although use of the line entails no explicit cost. While this system does introduce some incentive to synchronize payments, it suffers from significant shortcomings. First, because overdraft positions are monitored only ex post, a bank that encountered serious financial difficulties would be able to obtain substantial unpriced overdraft credit from the Federal Reserve. Second, the administrative procedure for setting caps is too general to reflect the legitimate special situations of individual institutions, and no mechanism allows economically justifiable exceptions to the prearranged caps. As a result, the caps will sometimes force bankers to arrange payments in suboptimal ways. Because initial caps were deliberately made high, this has caused few problems so far, but the intention is to lower the caps gradually, making them a binding constraint for more and more institutions.[34] Third, the caps are not applicable to securities transfer transactions, which account for a large proportion of total overdrafts.[35] Finally, there is no immediate cost of overdrafts that do not violate the caps. In sum, debit caps constitute only an imperfect means of controlling Fedwire overdrafts. Risk incentives and resource allocations will still be influenced by free overdraft credit, even though their extent will be more limited.

Although the Federal Reserve rather quickly rejected the collateralization option as unduly burdensome for both banks and securities market participants, Corrigan has proposed a related idea.[36] He argues that systemic risk control requires payments finality for all large-dollar wire transfers, CHIPS as well as Fedwire. To provide such finality without substantial credit extensions, Corrigan would require large transactors to hold relatively large, interest-bearing clearing balances with the Federal Reserve. Those balances would be set so as to ensure that most banks would not run overdrafts. He estimates that the clearing balances would have to be approximately 250 percent of current reserves. (Note that this proposed collateralization could be applied to Fedwire alone, rather than paired with payments finality on CHIPS.) By paying a market interest rate on clearing balances, the Federal Reserve would eliminate one major reason to run overdrafts—the need to economize on sterile clearing balances. This reform would create no new incentive to increase the synchronization between a bank's inflows and outflows, but overdrafts would occur less frequently with the higher clearing balances. The difficult issue implied by Corrigan's proposal is whether the payments system (or Fedwire alone) should be constrained to operate without credit extensions. This subtle and central question deserves serious economic analysis.

Conclusion 3. The Federal Reserve should explicitly evaluate whether paying market interest rates on at least some clearing balances would be a socially efficient way of producing payments system reliability.

Even if Corrigan's reform were implemented, the question would remain of how to handle the overdrafts that inevitably occur. Setting Federal Reserve credit lines at zero seems unlikely to be optimal in all cases, but we need to maintain proper private incentives. Neither of the preceding solutions to the daylight overdraft situation—caps or higher clearing account balances—addresses the root cause of the problem: current institutional arrangements provide insufficient private benefits for avoiding overdrafts.

An intuitively appealing response to this situation is to price Fedwire daylight overdrafts explicitly. If the Federal Reserve could devise a pricing scheme that approximates the market cost of overdraft credit risks, private transactors would determine for themselves which overdrafts were worth having and which were unprofitable. Humphrey and others extensively discuss alternative means of pricing Fedwire overdrafts.[37] Essentially, they identify two potential means of pricing: price the credit risk alone, or price the intraday time value.

In setting credit risk premiums for individual banks' overdrafts, the Federal Reserve could either assign a different default premium to each bank (which would have most of the advantages and disadvantages of risk-based deposit insurance premiums) or charge all banks the same premium but vary their credit lines (which would share many of the characteristics of risk-based capital standards). Even a reasonably small risk premium would offer a new, private incentive to avoid overdrafts and would therefore considerably reduce their extent. Given the apparent ease with which bankers could avoid most overdrafts, such a risk premium seems the most efficacious means of reducing them.

The obvious problem with pricing overdrafts is how to assign appropriate risk premiums. Too low a premium would generate the same kinds of distortion we have under the present system, and an excessively high premium would cause banks to effect payments in a socially inefficient manner. An additional problem is whether Fedwire's technological capabilities can transmit proper private incentives, even assuming that prices are appropriately set. By mid-1988 all twelve Federal Reserve banks should have the technological ability to monitor all components of clearing account payments and receipts continuously, including Fedwire funds transfer, securities transfers, and cash items processing. Such extensive monitoring would be cumbersome and expensive if undertaken for all institutions, and the Federal Reserve intends to monitor only known problem institutions.[38] For most institutions, therefore, it would not provide real-time information on clearing balances, and banks would be charged for overdraft credit they were unaware of incurring.[39] With existing technological capabilities, pricing daylight overdraft credit would give bankers only imperfect incentives to rationalize their payment arrangements. For Fedwire credit to mimic rational private credit extensions fully, banks would have to know their clearing balances reliably at all times. This technology exists but is currently considered too expensive to apply to the universe of Fedwire transactors.

In addition to pricing Fedwire credit risk, the Federal Reserve could assign a pure time value to intraday funds. Suppose, for example, it charged for overdrafts at a rate proportional to the overnight federal funds rate. Three hours' credit would therefore cost one-eighth of the overnight rate. The out-of-pocket or opportunity cost of collected funds at the Federal Reserve would lead private traders to time-date their payments to one another in a way that is now unnecessary. Private incentives would arise to make a market in intraday federal funds, government securities would be priced according to the explicit time payment was to be received, and so forth.

The difficulty with assigning a pure time value to intraday funds is that the record-keeping requirements of such a settlement system would be immense, going beyond what is required for continuous monitoring of clearing balances. To allow an active intraday funds market, the Federal Reserve (or some other settlement agent) would need a computer system that reliably identified and time-dated every transfer into and out of each institution's clearing account.[40] Since present technology and reserve computation arrangements constrain private market incentives and abilities, a reliable time-dating system on Fedwire might generate substantial changes in private funds management techniques. With such a system private parties would be able to specify payment and delivery schedules more precisely than they now can, and pricing overdrafts would be an incentive to reduce their cost. The expense of the required technological revisions, however, raises the question whether the benefits are sufficient to justify the cost.

To summarize, Fedwire debt caps constitute one means of providing a private incentive to avoid overdrafts, but an incomplete and imperfect means. If the Federal Reserve is to continue providing daylight overdraft credit, it should supplement debit caps with an explicit pricing arrangement for the credit risks involved. Given the evidence that a small number of institutional changes would eliminate or substantially reduce most of today's overdrafts, even a small credit premium should significantly ameliorate the problem. The expense of continuously monitoring all institutions seems unlikely to be warranted.

Conclusion 4. The credit risk of daylight overdrafts on Fedwire should be priced to encourage transactors to synchronize their payment inflows and outflows more closely.

Commercial Firms' Access to the Payments System

The Federal Reserve has sought to preserve the separation of banking from commerce in the United States. It has recently taken the position that the payments system activities of banks constitute one important reason why banks should not be allowed to affiliate with commercial firms. This contention rests on two assertions:

- Affiliations between commercial and banking firms will increase the risk of a widespread payments system failure.
- A bank's participation in the payments system requires it to have access to the discount window and thus indirectly affords the commercial firm access to the discount window.

Affiliation and Bank Solvency. The issue of commercial bank affiliation with nonbanking firms was first addressed comprehensively in the Bank Holding Company Act of 1956. At that time the Congress limited permissible affiliations to activities that are "so closely related to banking as to be a proper incident thereto" (Bank Holding Company Act, 1970 Amendments, Section 4(c)(8)) and sought to insulate the bank from its affiliates by establishing strict corporate separateness. Proponents of expanded bank holding company powers frequently argue that new activities can be undertaken in separately capitalized, legally distinct subsidiaries without any substantial effect on the bank itself. An important component of this legal separation has been Sections 23A and 23B of the Federal Reserve Act (as amended), which effectively forbid a bank to make unsecured loans to affiliated nonbanking firms.

The Federal Reserve has not readily accepted the notion of corporate separateness, contending that it is virtually impossible to isolate a bank from its affiliates when substantial economic factors promote coordination of the firms' activities.[41] Purely statutory barriers to interactions between banks and affiliates are therefore viewed with skepticism:

Congress can of course legislate barriers between a bank and its affiliates, and has in fact done so by limiting inter-affiliate loans under section 23A of the Federal Reserve Act. But, under pressures to maintain the viability of their organization, management can and does find ways to support an affiliate that does not involve inter-corporate lending. Simply strengthening section 23A in the expectation that this would enforce true corporate separateness is *naive*, particularly where the parent and its affiliates are *unregulated* and unexamined so that *enforcement is much more difficult*.[42] (emphasis added)

The Federal Reserve fears that banks will undertake excessive, or at least uncompensated, risks in supporting troubled affiliates. The fact that banks fund themselves largely with insured deposits tends to support this view but only if one accepts the corporate separateness argument. In that case the holding company could benefit by concentrating all losses into the relatively uncapitalized banking subsidiary. If corporate separateness is inoperative, however, the holding company would back a failing subsidiary with all its available resources. It would then see no advantage in concentrating losses in a single subsidiary because that subsidiary's limited liability protection would not be used. Under this scenario a holding company has no incentive to exploit the bank for the benefit of other affiliates, either through the payments system or otherwise.

This historical concern becomes related to payments system risk because some commercial firms have acquired "nonbank banks" that have access to the payments system. Unitary thrift holding companies also allow affiliated commercial firms "indirect access" to the payments system. In addition, some investment banks have considered acquiring a bank to gain access to the Fedwire book-entry securities system directly.[43] These kinds of affiliation exacerbate the Federal Reserve's concern that "payments system risks may be increased by depository institutions' dealings with their affiliates."[44] Placing the payments system risk of daylight overdrafts to affiliates at center stage makes it appear that a bank can be exploited easily through this avenue.

Section 23A prohibits exploitation of a bank subsidiary through credits that extend overnight. It is illogical to exempt daylight overdrafts from Section 23A restrictions: if overnight loans to affiliates constitute improper public policy, so too should daylight loans. An extension of Section 23A to daylight loans would largely eliminate the likelihood that an affiliate would endanger its bank by using it as a conduit to the payments system. Regulators can also influence a bank's behavior to ensure that it is being operated in a safe and sound fashion. This requirement would sharply limit the ability of a large commercial firm to route immense daily payments—which generate similarly immense daylight overdrafts—through a tiny bank affiliate.

As Paul A. Volcker has noted, regulations and regulatory oversight are not guaranteed to be effective at all times.[45] But if banks were strictly prohibited from undertaking large daylight credit exposures to their affiliates and the law imposed stringent penalties on the surviving corporate entities and their principals, attempted evasions would be infrequent. Moreover, the Federal Reserve's emerging technological ability to monitor Fedwire overdrafts continuously could be applied to any bank with a large commercial or other affiliate, guaranteeing that the bank would never be endangered from this quarter. In short, it seems that commercial bank affiliation with nonfinancial firms involves no uncontrollable payments system risk that differs from the risks now associated with permissible kinds of affiliation. The public policy issues surrounding affiliations between banks and commercial entities need not significantly involve the payments system. The risks and benefits of such affiliations must be evaluated in the traditional fashion: by determining whether the social benefits outweigh their associated costs.[46]

Conclusion 5. If Section 23A clearly applied to daylight overdrafts, existing regulations governing corporate separateness within a bank holding company would be sufficient to protect payments system stability. The public policy issue of bank affiliations with commercial firms must be decided on grounds other than payments system risk.

Discount Window Access. The access of payments system participants to daylight overdrafts and discount window credit contributes significantly to the reliability of Fedwire payments. The operational rules are that solvent banks should be assured of the liquidity required to fulfill their payment obligations. The Federal Reserve has argued, however, that if commercial firms could affiliate with banks, they would, inappropriately, receive de facto access to the discount window.

> A loan to a depository institution to cover overdrafts of an affiliate, as might occur where a depository institution is established primarily to serve the payments needs of its affiliates, is in effect a loan to the nondepository institution affiliate. Under section 13 of the Federal Reserve Act, loans to nondepository institutions . . . on the security of collateral other than United States Government and agency securities

can only be made in unusual and exigent circumstances and require an affirmative vote of five members of the Board. Regulation A further specifies that such loans should only be made where failure to do so will adversely affect the economy.[47]

To avoid the possibility of such an improper discount window loan, the Federal Reserve opposes commercial firms' affiliation with banks.

In evaluating this argument, Bagehot's description of the lender of last resort is relevant: the central bank should provide liquidity only to solvent banks.[48] If an affiliate's failure to make good on funds transferred leaves the bank illiquid but solvent, a discount window advance fulfills a legitimate lender-of-last-resort obligation. If the affiliate-customer's default induces bank insolvency, however, the bank should be allowed to fail. If the Federal Reserve can reliably identify solvent banks, an "effective" extension of credit to the affiliate seems unlikely to occur very often, especially if the affiliate is large in relation to the bank and Section 23A limitations are made to apply.[49] It is also important to note that the failure of a financial affiliate would involve the same sort of potential access to discount window funds but such affiliations are now permitted. It is unclear why commercial affiliates present materially different risks from those the Federal Reserve willingly tolerates.

Conclusion 6. The Federal Reserve's opposition to the affiliation of commercial and banking firms cannot be credibly supported by concerns about access to the discount window.

Some Related Issues for Further Research

To derive specific policy recommendations that address contemporary issues, this analysis has taken certain important institutional characteristics of the existing payments system as fixed. A broader consideration of a socially optimal payments system would assess some of these institutional arrangements more fully. A list—doubtless incomplete—of topics that warrant further research follows.

The Social Value of a Payments System. John H. Kareken has maintained that regulatory influence over the banking system can be justified because a reliable payments mechanism exhibits important public good properties.[50] In other words, just as the government maintains a legal system and national defense, it should also ensure the safe operation of the payments system. An important issue therefore is whether a purely private system would entail any social inefficiency. Note two things about this topic. First, it is distinct from the question whether private moneys are preferable to public fiat money. Second, even if there were public good aspects of the payments mechanism, it would not necessarily follow that the government must operate the system. If payments system reliability is found to be a valuable social commodity, the following two issues must be further investigated.

Regulation J. Eliminating payments finality on Fedwire would avoid the problems associated with mispriced credit risk and potential access to the discount window by commercial affiliates of payments system participants. The question then arises whether Fedwire payments finality constitutes a necessary—or, more properly, a least-cost—means of providing the appropriate degree of payments system reliability.

Fedwire Overdrafts. Marvin Goodfriend and Robert King carefully establish the conditions under which Federal Reserve overnight lending to banks would or would not improve social welfare.[51] They do not claim, however, that their analysis is precisely applicable to daylight overdrafts on Fedwire, apparently because daylight overdrafts might contribute importantly to payments system reliability. A complete analysis of whether daylight Federal Reserve credit extensions are socially appropriate thus involves the same question as the treatment of Regulation J: Do Fedwire overdrafts constitute the most efficient means of providing payment reliability? In other words, is it cheaper for the Federal Reserve to provide controlled and properly priced daylight overdrafts than for payments system reliability to be achieved through more extensive use of private credit lines or collateralization?

The Federal Reserve as a Payments Processor. A related issue concerns the proper role of the Federal Reserve System in processing financial transactions. Through its twelve regional banks, twenty-five bank branches, eleven processing centers, and the Fedwire system, the Federal Reserve is the largest processor of checks and payment information in the country, handling more than 40 percent of all checks written and 60 percent of the dollar volume of wire transfers. Its private competitors in the processing business include correspondent banks, CHIPS, and a growing number of private service bureaus.[52] Before the Monetary Control Act of 1980 the Federal Reserve provided processing services free of explicit charge, to member banks only. The act required the Federal Reserve to provide payments system services on equal terms to all depository institutions. Section 107 of the act further required that virtually all such services be priced to reflect their fully allocated costs, including a private sector adjustment factor (PSAF) intended to reflect private competitors' tax liabilities and cost of equity capital. The question, of course, has been whether the Federal Reserve has actually priced its payments processing business properly.[53] The primary principle guiding public policy should be that the nation's payments be made efficiently, with minimal use of real resources. Applying this principle to payment processing is difficult, however, because the factors involved are numerous and technically complex.

Summary

Payments system risk is one kind of credit risk. As bankers generally evaluate and assume such risks, there is nothing qualitatively different about payments system risk that warrants special treatment. The extent to which such credit risks are concentrated in the nation's largest banks makes their effective control imperative for both managers and regulators. Careful risk control techniques and safety and soundness regulations should be applied to the credit risks associated with payments operations.

Given the Federal Reserve's role in guaranteeing Fedwire payments, it must take steps to price the risks it absorbs on behalf of the private sector. The situation is analogous to the problem of pricing federal deposit insurance: unless the Federal Reserve charges an appropriate risk premium on intraday overdrafts, its credit extensions will distort private risk-taking incentives and resource allocations.

Notes

1. See Kenneth D. Garbade and William L. Silber, "The Payment System and Domestic Exchange Rates: Technological versus Institutional Change," *Journal of Monetary Economics*, vol. 5 (1979), pp. 1–22.

2. See Jurg Niehans, "Money and Barter in General Equilibrium with Transactions Costs," *American Economic Review* (December 1971), pp. 773–83; and Karl Brunner and Allan Meltzer, "The Uses of Money: Money in a Theory of an Exchange Economy," *American Economic Review* (December 1971), pp. 784–805.

3. See David Burras Humphrey, "Payments System Risk, Market Failure, and Public Policy," in Elinor Solomon, ed., *The Payments Revolution: The Emerging Public Policy Issues* (Boston: Kluwer-Nijhoff Publishing, 1987), p. 85;

or E. Gerald Corrigan, *Financial Market Structure: A Longer View* (New York: Federal Reserve Bank of New York, 1987), p. 29.

4. The rise in bank debits may be attributable to the recent explosion in securities trading volume or to a cash management ratchet that accompanied the historically high interest rates of the early 1980s.

5. See U.S. Congress, House of Representatives, Committee on Government Operations and Committee on Banking, Finance, and Urban Affairs, *Joint Hearings before Certain Subcommittees on the Role of the Federal Reserve in Check Clearing and the Nation's Payment System*, 98th Congress, 1st session, June 15, 1983, pp. 412–13.

6. Because a paying bank has the right to inspect a check before making final payment on it, the collection process creates a need to transport and process physical checks. When a customer requests his bank to collect a check drawn on a distant institution, it can (1) present the check to the local Federal Reserve bank for collection; (2) present the check directly to the paying bank, perhaps via a private clearinghouse or nonbank processor; or (3) present the check to a (local or distant) correspondent bank for collection. Option 1 is used for approximately 40 percent of all checks written and explicitly uses the Federal Reserve's settlement mechanism. Option 2 frequently involves the Federal Reserve's net settlement service. Option 3 requires payment from the payer's bank to the payee's, perhaps with several correspondent banks involved. Some of these check collections occur through clearinghouses (and hence involve Federal Reserve net settlement); others involve debits and credits to private correspondent balances.

7. See Corrigan, *Financial Market Structure*, p. 16.

8. Although intraday credit on the wire transfer systems receives the most attention (because of the magnitudes involved), other means of payment also involve credit risks. Consider a restaurant meal. If I pay for the meal in cash, the restaurateur receives value without any risk (ignoring the possibility of counterfeit currency). If I pay with a check (which might bounce), the payee is exposed to credit risk until the check actually clears. By accepting a check as "payment," the payee has lent me the value of the meal until good funds are actually transferred to his account. With wire transfers the credit is usually extended for only a short time, but the amounts involved can be very large.

9. Humphrey, "Payments System Risk," provides one example of an intraday credit market: underwriters generally negotiate intraday loans with which to finance securities from the time they take delivery from the issuer until the ultimate purchasers have made payment. This arrangement appears to reflect the securities market convention that payment be made to the securities issuer with a certified check. Bankers will not certify a check on an overdrawn account and must therefore provide a daylight loan. The interest charge on these loans is almost always 1 percent (annualized), which must be viewed as a credit risk premium. The charges for these loans in many ways resemble fee payments for specific transaction services more than standard "interest" compensation.

10. See David L. Mengle, David B. Humphrey, and Bruce J. Summers, "Intraday Credit: Risk, Value, and Pricing," *Federal Reserve Bank of Richmond*

Economic Review (January/February 1987), pp. 8–9. Indeed, bankers have a positive incentive to shift credit risks to the Federal Reserve during daylight hours.

11. See E. J. Stevens, "Reducing Risk in Wire Transfer Systems," *Federal Reserve Bank of Cleveland Economic Review* (Quarter 2, 1986), pp. 17–22; Corrigan, *Financial Market Structure*; and Mengle, Humphrey, and Summers, "Intraday Credit," pp. 3–14. David Burras Humphrey, "Payments Finality and Risk of Settlement Failure," in Anthony Saunders and Lawrence J. White, eds., *Technology and Regulation of Financial Markets* (Lexington, Mass.: Lexington Books, 1986), identifies several reasons why a financial institution might be threatened by its involvement with the payments system: fraud, a technical failure of the systems that monitor and control the institutions' payments, and credit risk. Of these, he asserts that credit risk is the most important by far.

12. Because a customer is most likely to generate unreimbursed overdrafts as its financial condition deteriorates, this type of credit risk carries a substantial adverse selection component. Bankers should thus be especially anxious to monitor customer overdrafts.

13. See Edward J. Kane, *The Gathering Crisis in Federal Deposit Insurance* (Cambridge, Mass.: MIT Press, 1985), p. 139.

14. See Corrigan, *Financial Market Structure*, p. 16.

15. See Jack M. Guttentag and Richard J. Herring, "Uncertainty and Insolvency Exposure in International Banks" (Wharton Program in International Banking and Finance, December 1982, mimeographed), p. 25.

16. See Frederick Heldring, "Payment Systems Risk in the United States," *Journal of Bank Research* (1986), p. 211.

17. See William C. Dudley, "Controlling Risk on Large-Dollar Wire Transfer Systems," in Saunders and White, *Technology and Regulation of Financial Markets*, pp. 127–28. The monitoring problem involves not the bank's exposure on any single customer account but integrating across all of a large customer's accounts. Similarly, in the interbank market bank X might readily know its exposure to bank Y on federal funds transactions, though not on foreign exchange dealings.

18. Because there is no intraday pure time value of collected balances, this underpricing involves only a credit risk premium for possible defaults.

19. See Humphrey, "Payments System Risk."

20. Such failures are to be avoided because the recipient of the securities receives beneficial ownership without having to pay until full delivery is effected. Position building thus allows a dealer maximum freedom to substitute securities for one another and to avoid fails on large orders. The Association of Reserve City Bankers, *Report of the Working Group of the Association of Reserve City Bankers on Book-Entry Daylight Overdrafts* (Washington, D.C., June 1986), pp. 34–38, reports that one-half of all book-entry securities transfers occur after 2:00 P.M., while the wire's scheduled closing time for security deliveries is 2:30.

21. See Association of Reserve City Bankers, *Report of the Working Group*.

22. After the Bank of New York incident in November 1985, the Federal

Reserve imposed a 2 percent penalty fee on discount window advances resulting from private computer system failures.

23. Because members must access CHIPS from a business location in New York City, many participants route their CHIPS transactions through a subsidiary, such as an Edge Act corporation. For CHIPS members with less than $250 million in capital, the parent is required to submit a "comfort letter," which guarantees all the provisional payments made by its subsidiary.

24. See Kane, *The Gathering Crisis*.

25. See Matthew D. Gelfand, "Proposals for Daylight Overdraft Cap Reductions, De Minimis Caps, and Frequency of Self-Assessment Ratings" (Board of Governors of the Federal Reserve System, November 1986, mimeographed).

26. See Humphrey, "Payments Finality."

27. Ibid., p. 110.

28. See Walter Bagehot, *Lombard Street* (1873) (New York: Arno Press, 1978). Marvin Goodfriend and Robert King, in chapter 6 of this volume, discuss the information problem associated with distinguishing insolvent from illiquid institutions.

29. Goodfriend and King (ibid.) provide an exceptionally clear assessment of whether the Federal Reserve should be involved in overnight discount window lending. They indicate that the issue depends crucially on the extent to which private credit arrangements can substitute for discount window loans. If the discount window does not improve on private allocations, there is no reason for the Federal Reserve to extend any credit to the private sector. Whether this same argument applies precisely to daylight overdrafts is an important issue for further research. See section "Some Related Issues for Further Research."

30. Current regulations thus reflect the same shortsightedness attributed by Heldring, "Payment Systems Risk," pp. 209–13, and Dudley, "Controlling Risk," to private bankers' failure to recognize the credit implications of payments system operations. See also Humphrey, "Payments System Risk."

31. See Anthony Saunders, chapter 5 of this volume; and U.S. Congress, House of Representatives, Committee on Government Operations, *Modernization of the Financial Services Industry: A Plan for Capital Mobility within a Framework of Safe and Sound Banking* (Washington, D.C., 1987).

32. See Mengle, Humphrey, and Summers, "Intraday Credit," pp. 3–14.

33. This cap applies to the bank's net debit position on *all* wire transfer systems, not just Fedwire.

34. In December 1986 the Federal Reserve proposed a 25 percent reduction in permitted caps (*Federal Register*, December 16, 1986, pp. 45050–52).

35. The Federal Reserve has proposed a $25 million or $50 million transaction limit on Fedwire securities transfers, which would be intended (in conjunction with revisions in the delivery rules) to encourage partial deliveries and hence reduce the overdrafts associated with position building (ibid., pp. 45049–50). This would reduce daylight overdrafts by reducing the dealers' ability to build and hold positions during the day.

36. See Corrigan, *Financial Market Structure*.

37. See David Burras Humphrey, David Mengle, Oliver Ireland, and Alisa Morgenthaler, "Pricing Fedwire Daylight Overdrafts" (Federal Reserve Bank of Richmond, January 13, 1987, mimeographed).

38. David Humphrey of the Federal Reserve Bank of Richmond kindly provided the information in this paragraph during a telephone conversation on July 2, 1987.

39. Regular interbank Fedwire payments are initiated by the payer, who is therefore in a position to control overdrafts by timing outflows to correspond to inflows. By contrast, the *deliverer* of book-entry securities initiates a debit to the securities purchaser's clearing account by ordering that securities be transferred to the purchaser's name. A bank that has purchased book-entry securities thus has imperfect control over debits to its clearing account, which complicates its management of daylight overdrafts.

40. Such record keeping could be done ex post, provided that institutions can continuously monitor their account balances. The present Fedwire system produces a time-dated transactions log that could be the basic input for such a system.

41. See Anthony Cornyn, Gerald Hanweck, Stephen Rhoades, and John T. Rose, "An Analysis of the Concept of Corporate Separateness on BHC Regulation from an Economic Perspective," in Federal Reserve Bank of Chicago, *Proceedings of a Conference on Bank Structure and Competition*, Chicago, 1986, pp. 174–212, which was included as an appendix to Paul A. Volcker, "Statement" before Subcommittee on Commerce, Consumer, and Monetary Affairs of the Committee on Government Operations, U.S. House of Representatives, June 11, 1986. Mark J. Flannery, "Contagious Bank Runs, Financial Structure, and Corporate Separateness within a Bank Holding Company," in Federal Reserve Bank of Chicago, *Proceedings of a Conference*, pp. 213–30, and George J. Benston et al., *Perspectives on Safe and Sound Banking* (Cambridge, Mass.: MIT Press, 1986), offer a similar assessment.

42. See Volcker, "Statement," p. 24.

43. See Henny Sender, "The Day the Computer Went Down," *Institutional Investor* (March 1986), pp. 203–7.

44. See Volcker, "Statement," "App. E: Payment System Risk," p. E-4.

45. Ibid., p. 24.

46. Numerous studies have addressed these issues: for example, Benston et al., *Perspectives on Safe and Sound Banking*, chap. 6 and the references; or Larry D. Wall and Robert A. Eisenbeis, "Risk Considerations in Deregulating Bank Activities," *Federal Reserve Bank of Atlanta Economic Review* (May 1984), pp. 6–19.

47. See Volcker, "Statement," "App. E," p. E-5.

48. See Bagehot, *Lombard Street*.

49. In addition to the legal issue of discount window access, there is a possibility that a failed bank will impose credit losses on the Federal Reserve, which are ultimately borne by taxpayers. In receivership the failed bank retains a legal claim against the affiliate-customer firm. The Federal Reserve has a claim on the failed bank's assets, including the affiliate's obligation to its failed bank, and will suffer actual credit losses only if the affiliate itself fails.

50. See John H. Kareken, "Ensuring Financial Stability," in Federal Reserve Bank of San Francisco, *The Search for Financial Stability: The Past Fifty Years* (San Francisco, 1985).

51. See Goodfriend and King, chapter 6 of this volume.

52. See Martin Mayer, "General Electric Takes on the Fed," *Dun's Business Month* (February 1987), pp. 62–65.

53. Most of the issues involving Federal Reserve participation in payments information processing are addressed in the 1983 congressional hearings, *Role of the Federal Reserve*.

Commentary
Edward C. Ettin

At the outset of my comments on Professor Mark Flannery's excellent paper I should, of course, underline the standard disclaimer: my views are not necessarily those of the Board of Governors of the Federal Reserve System—although I wish that they were. In fact, the public policy issues associated with payments system risk are so complex that there are relatively wide-ranging views held among the board, the reserve bank presidents, and the staff as to what the next policy steps should be. Indeed, last summer the board asked Federal Reserve System staff and its private sector advisory group to review the issues again and present fresh options and recommendations for the board's consideration.

Though all good public servants must keep an open mind, my personal conclusions from review of the issues and evidence are virtually the same as those of Flannery—at least on the main issues: we need to develop further incentives to induce banks and their customers to behave in risk-reducing ways, and some form of pricing and continued regulatory admonition is likely to be the most productive approach. But, having declared my concurrence with Flannery's main conclusions, I want to suggest that some dimensions of the problem are both much more complex and at the same time simpler than his analysis suggests.

Let me address the complexities first.[1] The main public policy issue is risk, and it is important to be sure we understand the nature and sources of risk so that the incentives associated with pricing daylight overdrafts will be clear. The risk is of two types: direct and systemic. The Federal Reserve is subject to the direct risk that it will be unable to collect the irrevocable credit it extends on Fedwire to a bank that incurs daylight overdrafts and then fails before bringing its account into balance at the end of the day. The banking system as a

---

I want to thank my colleagues Matthew Gelfand, Jeffrey Marquardt, and Elliott McEntee at the Board of Governors and David Humphrey at the Federal Reserve Bank of Richmond for their observations on this commentary. The opinions (and errors) are mine alone.

whole is subject to systemic risk. When a bank receiving daylight credit from another bank on a private wire system, such as CHIPS, fails before covering its debit, it may cause the lending bank, and other banks to whom the lending bank owes funds, to suffer losses and possibly fail. Of course, systemic risk can be avoided if the Federal Reserve extends credit to any one or all of the failing banks.

On Fedwire a further distinction must be made between book-entry and funds transfers. Book-entry transfers result from the buying and selling of U.S. government securities. The securities receiver's account is debited to pay for the securities. A book-entry overdraft occurs when the receiving depository institution has insufficient cash in its account to take that debit.

One option for controlling risk caused by these transfers is to charge the bank receiving the securities a fee for the resulting overdrafts. The securities sender, whose account is credited, however, controls the timing of the transfer. Charging the bank that receives the securities for an overdraft beyond its direct control is unlikely to be very effective in controlling risk—in this case the risk to the Federal Reserve whose funds have been paid out to the bank sending securities on behalf of the bank paying for the securities. Alternatively, securities receivers could be required to carry larger balances or to give prior consent to a specific time for the transfer, presumably when they would have sufficient balances or collateral.

The first two options are expensive and likely to reduce the market liquidity of Treasury securities. The last option could also be expensive if it requires banks and their customers to segregate their eligible-to-pledge securities, securities not yet paid for by their customers, from other securities. Moreover, there are terribly complex problems of conflicting liens in the tiered structure of ownership of book-entry securities: customers may hold securities through successively higher "tiers," say, from their nonbank dealer, through several possible layers of clearing and custodial banks, to a Federal Reserve bank that maintains the book-entry record. All of these issues, and others, are behind the Federal Reserve's modest steps in the book-entry area, although I guess some form of collateralization to protect Federal Reserve risk will be developed that will minimize risk for buyers of Treasury securities—the customer and the customers' customers of clearing banks. I might add that collateralization for *funds* overdrafts on Fedwire was rejected earlier, not because of any burden but because it would not limit overdrafts for most banks. Most institutions could post collateral for funds overdrafts, but, while this would protect the Federal Reserve, it would be to the detriment of the FDIC without creating inducements for participants to adopt risk-reducing practices. Collateralization for book-entry overdrafts, as I

COMMENTARY

have just noted, is currently being reviewed because of the conflicting lien and the segregation of collateral issue. That is the burdensomeness Flannery refers to in his paper.

The other distinction regards funds transfers on the wire transfer systems—Fedwire and CHIPS. We can clarify the sources of risk but it is important to underline early on, as Flannery does, the basic differences between these two systems. Each message on Fedwire is cleared and settled as it occurs; that is, the payment information is exchanged between the payer and payee, and simultaneously a form of payment that satisfies the payee is effectuated—a credit to the payee's reserve account. Fedwire is often called a gross settlement system because it settles each transaction as it occurs. The continuous settlement still can create overdrafts because the payer may not have sufficient balances to cover the payment and, in such cases, the Federal Reserve extends intraday credit to the payer in anticipation of coverage before the end of the day. On CHIPS, payments are cleared throughout the day—that is, payment information is exchanged—but these payments are provisional and are settled net at the end of the day. Throughout the day, participants extend credit to one another and settle among themselves by having an agent, with whom they all maintain accounts, post the net of the payments exchanged to those accounts. It is, of course, the Federal Reserve with whom CHIPS participants currently maintain accounts, but it could just as well be a large correspondent bank. The correspondent and the Federal Reserve bear no *direct* net settlement risk since they agree to credit accounts only if there is another account with funds to debit. But, if the private network is large, a net settlement failure creates a very large indirect risk for the central bank—even if it is not a party to the settlement. More about that later. Note that the intraday credit extended to payers on Fedwire by the Federal Reserve and the intraday credit extended among participants on CHIPS are unrelated to the Federal Reserve and accounting conventions that reservability of deposits and holding of required reserves are measured only at the end of the day. Intraday exposures among the larger banks simply dwarf by multiples any reserve balances held, and the sheer mechanics of calculating deposit and reserve balances second by second make this approach impossible.

Returning to the effectiveness of pricing to reduce overdraft risk, the originating or sending bank faces a risk whenever it permits a customer to transfer uncollected balances, and this is just as much a risk for the sending bank on Fedwire as on CHIPS. (Flannery mentions it only in conjunction with CHIPS.) Several points are relevant about this risk to the originating bank. These overdrafts in a bank customer's account may or may not cause the bank to be in overdraft on Fedwire or in a net debit position on CHIPS. That will depend on other customers' positions and on transfers for the bank's own account. Be that as it may, it seems clear that either pricing of, or quantitative limits on, overdrafts on Fedwire or CHIPS will cause banks to adopt policies and strategies to limit customers' overdrafts. Explicit recognition of the daylight credit extension to customers will thus be increased, which is desirable, but, with the board's 1986 policy in effect, it is a rare bank that now is not at least aware of this risk—which exists with or without limits on banks' overdrafts.

When limits—including charges—are placed on overdrafts of banks' customers, those customers will have to reevaluate the underlying transactions. Some adjustments almost certainly will be made at trivial cost. We have already seen that payments that are high priority when there are no limits become less pressing when there are caps; that will happen with pricing too. But some of the underlying transactions, such as maturing commercial paper that will be refunded later in the day, can perhaps be less easily adjusted. This is not a reason to avoid pricing, but rather suggests imposing prices or tighter caps gradually with relatively long lead times, so that markets can adjust smoothly.

Still another source of risk is the sending bank. If that institution fails to meet its obligations by the end of the day on Fedwire, the Federal Reserve absorbs the risk by guaranteeing the payment—that is, by providing finality to the receiving bank on advice of crediting. Receiving banks can allow their customers immediate access to the transferred funds with no risk. But the direct risk of the Federal Reserve is not necessarily reduced by pricing of the overdraft since risky banks may find Federal Reserve daylight credit the cheapest available. Control of direct Federal Reserve risk thus requires at least continued supervisory admonitions and, I would argue, "debit caps" or quantitative restrictions. Thus, I think both pricing and caps—tariffs *and* quotas—may be necessary. I will return to direct Federal Reserve risk later.

On CHIPS, sender failure provides no difficulty for the banking system *if* the receiving banks have not already let their customers have access to the funds received; in that case, entries are reversed and the receiving customers try to get payment again from their counterparties. But, in reality, the customers of the receiving banks have almost certainly already used the proceeds credited to their accounts and, though the funds are perhaps contractually returnable to the receiving bank, most observers believe that resolution of the receiving banks' claims on their own customers will occur only after long legal battle. The risk is going to be absorbed by the receivers, and if they cannot absorb it all, systemic contagion will spread.

It is at this point that Flannery's analysis hits a rare air pocket. Not to worry, says Flannery. If the receiving bank is just illiquid, the Federal Reserve can lend and there will be no contagion; if the receiving bank is rendered insolvent, then, following Bagehot, the Federal Reserve should let it fail and all surviving participants will meet in court. This follows a citation of Humphrey's simulations, which suggest that random failures of senders will in fact cause many other participants on CHIPS to become insolvent; if they are permitted to fail, the contagion will spread. Moreover, after recognizing that the quantities involved are very large and that the rapidity of judgments required makes it difficult to make fine distinctions between illiquidity and insolvency, Flannery concludes that the Federal Reserve should continue to apply principles of safety and soundness to the few banks among which overdrafts are concentrated.

This is, I submit, not very helpful. Indeed, the problem with provisional payment systems, like CHIPS, is that the risks are not, as Flannery suggests, "conceptually . . . no different from any other type of credit risk," but are very different indeed. The problem with provisional payments system risks is that the risks are not assigned at all. All participants disown the risk and proceed as if it is not their problem; hence the risk of contagion.

That is among the major reasons why the Federal Reserve staff did not recommend pricing of Fedwire overdrafts in 1985 when the board's daylight overdraft policy was first adopted. After all, the Federal Reserve cannot impose pricing on a private network, and, consequently, a charge on Fedwire would probably induce a shift of payments to CHIPS. Such a shift would, for reasons discussed above, increase systemic risk.

Since 1985, however, conditions have changed. At the urging of the Federal Reserve, CHIPS has established bilateral credit limits among, and imposed debit caps on, its participants. More important, in 1987, it agreed in principle to impose settlement finality on the network—which means that if a sender fails, a prearranged, but yet to be worked out, loss-sharing formula will allocate the loss from the *net* position of the failed bank among all the participants. Settlement will occur, probably with secured Federal Reserve credit to some of the banks sharing the loss, but the loss is assigned in amounts that the surviving banks can absorb, and risk responsibility should make banks considerably more prudent. Loss-absorbing institutions after settlement can try to work out recovery of losses from customers, but in the meantime the financial system is not held hostage. All of this now makes more palatable the implications for systemic risk associated with the Federal Reserve's charging for overdrafts and a possible induced shift of volume to CHIPS. It is the reason I now support pricing.

But there is still a gnawing concern. Pricing of Fedwire overdrafts could tend to shift large dollar payments away from the Federal Reserve (and finality) to the private sector, a shift that may increase systemic risk—even with all the reforms on CHIPS. In principle, there is some combination of price on Fedwire overdrafts and operating procedures on CHIPS that minimizes systemic risk across the two systems. But a mistake on CHIPS—in terms of underevaluating its credit risks—could be extremely disruptive, while a mistake on Fedwire—in terms of underpricing overdrafts—will not spread to the banking system. On Fedwire, the risk (as now) will be contained. Moreover, Fedwire pricing will induce participants to look for other clearing and settlement procedures, including those offshore, where risks may be difficult to contain.

That is why I think the issue of pricing is so complex, but I suggested earlier that there is another reason why it may be simpler than Flannery proposes. The determination of price, in my view, should not become bogged down in issues of time-dating or pure time values or computer capabilities or risk-adjusted rates. Indeed, the steps that participants can take to reduce overdrafts have more to do with the costs of new funding and operational systems and the prices necessary to induce behaviorial changes than they do with the time value of money. The marginal costs of most banks and their customers of making adjustments that will significantly reduce their overdrafts are, I think, likely to be quite small—probably less than 50 basis points (annual rate), perhaps considerably less than that. These adjustments include all the ways to eliminate repayments early in the day and funding later in the day, which creates daylight overdrafts—for example, refunding only net amounts in the federal funds market each day, rather than repaying gross amounts in the morning and reborrowing gross amounts in the afternoon; relying more on term bank borrowing than on overnight borrowing; an intraday funds market; and better prioritizing of customer transfers. Rather than calculate some complex rate and devise a very sensitive pricing algorithm, there is much to be said for the simplicity of an arbitrary small price and a rather large overdraft amount—say 25 percent of bank capital—to which charges would not apply, with the deductible designed to account for average computer down times. A small price and a big deductible would, I think, address the institutions that account for most of the risk and induce significant risk-reducing behavior. It is, of course, the inducement to take some steps to avoid real or shadow prices that are missing from the current policy because caps are so high relative to actual overdrafts.

I do think that Flannery makes too much of the computer difficulties of pricing daylight overdrafts. As I noted, a deductible takes care of many problems, and the Federal Reserve can rather soon develop a system that permits participants to send or receive on specified payment and delivery schedules. Under current policy, because most banks are not significantly constrained, there is no demand for such services—a necessary part of an intraday funds market. All reserve banks now have the computer capability to monitor and control Fedwire funds overdrafts on a real-time basis for any institution in their district presenting unusual risks.

Time and space do not permit me to comment extensively on other issues raised by Flannery, but let me note briefly:

- I concur that Sections 23A (and B) of the Federal Reserve Act (which place constraints on loans to affiliates) and statutory loan limits to single borrowers (which place loan limits on nonaffiliated entities) should be applied to daylight overdrafts. And such limits should be in addition to such constraints now placed on overnight credits. (If limits are now constraining overnight credit extensions to a particular borrower, no additional daylight credit to that borrower should be permitted at all.) Development of accounting controls would be costly, however, and the concept of intraday accounting both novel and complex.
- A proposal to reduce daylight overdrafts by the payment of a market rate of interest on reserves must come to grips with the distribution of Fedwire funds and CHIPS overdrafts. Ten banks account for 35 percent of all such overdrafts and fifty banks for almost 75 percent. A rate of interest high enough to increase reserve balances for these institutions sufficient to limit their overdrafts measurably would create significant holding of excess reserves for other banks. To reduce overdrafts through clearing balances would mean *requiring* a clearing balance that is institution-specific with the total amount of interest paid on the clearing balances—out of Treasury coffers, I might add—thus dependent on the payments system business or funding pattern of each bank. Any interest paid, of course, must be linked to Federal Reserve pricing of either overdrafts or transactions.
- I think Flannery's analysis of the risk of affiliation of commerce and banking is wrong. It is exactly when firms are under duress that they will pay less heed to section 23A limits. Even if evasion is infrequent, the infrequent cases are the ones that cause Federal Re-

serve loss—and probably affiliated bank failure—because the bank will not, in fact, act as the independent evaluator of the risk of its commercial affiliate. Section 23A is desirable, but it is not enough of an insulation to permit affiliation with a type of entity that produces significantly more risk than virtually all financial affiliates.

Note

1. I ignore an interesting dimension of the daylight overdraft issue that my colleague, Jeff Marquardt, has pointed out to me: the conceptual difficulties of measuring an effective money supply if the central bank does not control the volume of daylight overdrafts. In effect, by focusing on money balances at the end of the day—those quantitatively limited by reserve balances and reserve requirements—we ignore the intraday money used for transactions as banks let their customers overdraft their accounts, and the Federal Reserve does the same for banks. I am reminded of an observation of, I think, Martin Mayer that demand deposits are those financial assets that banks have not succeeded in turning into nonreservable form by the end of the day.

8
The Future Structure of the Housing Finance System
John C. Weicher

The housing finance system has been coming apart for more than a decade, under the twin influences of volatile inflation and technological change. The system was not designed to withstand macroeconomic shocks of the magnitude experienced in the 1970s and early 1980s, and not surprisingly it has proved unable to withstand them. Public policy has reacted slowly, but policy issues are demanding attention. In 1987 Congress was forced to address the bankruptcy of the Federal Savings and Loan Insurance Corporation (FSLIC) and did so in a way that guarantees that the problem will have to be addressed again soon. A substantial minor fraction of the savings and loan associations (S&Ls) insured by the FSLIC are insolvent, and the policy issue is no longer just their future role in housing finance but their existence as distinct financial institutions. At the same time, there has been serious discussion of fundamental changes in the role of the federally sponsored secondary mortgage market agencies. Recent studies have raised the possibility of privatizing both the Federal National Mortgage Association (FNMA) and the Federal Home Loan Mortgage Corporation (Freddie Mac). The FNMA study was undertaken within the Reagan administration, the Freddie Mac study by a Freddie Mac advisory committee at the behest of some S&Ls. This issue has been obscured by the spectacular pyrotechnics of the FSLIC and S&L crises, but it is more fundamental: decisions about the future of the secondary market agencies will have a greater effect on the

---

I would like to thank James R. Barth, Frederick W. Deming, Bert Ely, Hilbert Fefferman, Michael J. Lea, Wilhelmina A. Leigh, John A. Tuccillo, and Susan E. Woodward for helpful comments on earlier drafts, in addition to my fellow authors and members of the advisory committee for the Financial Markets Project. I wrote this paper before accepting my present position at the Office of Management and Budget; the opinions expressed are my own and not necessarily those of the American Enterprise Institute or the Office of Management and Budget.

future structure of the housing finance system. This chapter discusses both the problems of the present system and the likely and desirable system of the future.

Like most other Western democracies, the United States has had a specialized housing finance system for a long time, in our case dating back to the Great Depression. The immediate rationale for creating the specialized system was to bring the housing industry out of the depression and perhaps to stimulate the economy as well. The long-term goals have been to promote housing construction and homeownership and to moderate housing construction cycles (the postwar equivalent of the macroeconomic concern during the 1930s). These goals have been justified partly by the claim that capital market imperfections have reduced the flow of funds to housing and partly by a political consensus that housing deserves special treatment.

Since the rationale for a specialized housing finance system is partly subjective, it is appropriate to state my own views at the outset. I believe there is some reason to subsidize housing consumption on externality grounds: the quality of an individual's housing affects the value of his neighbor's housing and the quality of the neighborhood, though the magnitude of the effect is probably not large. Social advantages of homeownership may exist, but have not been established. None of the rationales implies that the housing finance system is necessarily the best way to provide the appropriate subsidies; indeed, it is questionable whether the system can provide them at all.

The current policy debate about the future of the S&Ls and the FSLIC has occurred without much reference to these objectives; the issue has been whether the institutions can survive. Policy discussions about the federal secondary market agencies have devoted more attention to the public purposes of the agencies. This chapter follows a similar pattern, giving little attention to the social benefits of having separate specialized housing lenders and more to the arguments for secondary market agencies. I generally accept the rationales for the sake of analyzing the system and evaluating the extent to which it can achieve them, then broadly consider their validity in the concluding section.

The Development of the System

The New Deal System. The FSLIC and the federally chartered S&Ls are part of one set of housing finance institutions established during the depression, the federal secondary market agencies part of another one. In response to the wave of foreclosures on homes and failures of mortgage lending institutions (both S&Ls and banks), the administration of Herbert Hoover established a specialized housing finance system with preferential access to capital markets. The administration of Franklin D. Roosevelt immediately afterward chose a different strategy—broadening the base of housing finance—without reversing its predecessor's actions. The result, known loosely as the New Deal or depression-era housing finance system, was a bifurcated arrangement of complementary and competitive institutions.

President Hoover's policy was to strengthen the S&Ls, which were the most important and the most specialized mortgage lenders. In 1932 the Federal Home Loan Bank System was established as a regulatory and support structure for the S&Ls, with parallels to the Federal Reserve. The Federal Home Loan Bank Board (FHLBB) was empowered to charter and regulate federal S&Ls. Previously all S&Ls were chartered by the states, though state-chartered S&Ls could also belong to the federal system. Twelve regional Federal Home Loan Banks were created, owned by the member S&Ls in their district. The banks borrow in the capital markets and lend to S&Ls, accepting mortgages as security for their loans. These "advances" are intended to provide liquidity to S&Ls, particularly at cyclical peaks when interest rates are high and S&Ls have difficulty attracting funds at profitable rates. S&Ls also retained their exemption from federal income taxation.

In return for these privileges, the S&Ls were placed under both asset and liability restrictions. They made long-term home mortgage loans (ten to twelve years at that time, on average) financed by short-term time deposits. They were expected to attract the savings of workers and middle-income families—the "small saver." Their mortgage lending was restricted to their local market.

President Roosevelt's approach was in many respects the opposite. In 1934 the Federal Housing Administration was established to provide insurance against mortgage default for lenders. FHA insured a new kind of loan—a fixed-rate self-amortizing mortgage with a low down-payment requirement and a long term to maturity. The terms were much more liberal than any institution had offered before the depression.

The FHA was supposed to broaden the institutional base of housing finance, particularly by encouraging commercial banks to make mortgage loans.[1] Further inducement was to come from new secondary market institutions: private mortgage associations, chartered by the federal government, which were to issue bonds and buy mortgages from primary lenders. These associations were authorized as part of the 1934 National Housing Act. None were started, however; so in 1938 Congress created FNMA as a government-owned agency to provide a secondary market for FHA mortgages.[2]

Government mortgage insurance also stimulated the development of mortgage banking. Mortgage bankers originate and service mortgages, but sell them to other investors rather than hold them in their own portfolio. The institutional separation of the origination and servicing functions facilitated investment by other institutional lenders, mainly life insurance companies and mutual savings banks.

The S&Ls objected to the competition from FHA and opposed its creation. Federal deposit insurance was part of the political bargain to win their grudging acceptance of it;[3] it was to provide them with a "level playing field" to compete with the banks for funds to finance mortgages. The FSLIC was established under the FHLBB in 1934.

The fundamental difference between these systems is illustrated by their policies on the extent of the market area. The S&Ls were locally oriented. They started as neighborhood associations of individuals saving to buy their own homes, and they continued to operate within their local housing markets when the link between saving and borrowing was broken. Their trade association was created in the 1890s in reaction to the advent of "national" associations, which took deposits by mail and made loans through branch office networks. The traditional "local" associations vigorously opposed these competitors, lobbied for state supervision, and persuaded state regulators to impose limits on the national associations that effectively put them out of business by 1901. State laws typically limited an S&L's market area, and this practice was carried over to the Federal Home Loan Bank System; federally chartered S&Ls were limited to lending within a fifty-mile radius of their home offices.

The Roosevelt system, however, had a national focus. FNMA was expected to borrow in areas where credit was more available and lend where it was in short supply. The mortgage bankers served a similar function by selling mortgages to mutual savings banks, which operated primarily in the Northeast where the local demand for mortgages was relatively low.

The restrictions on S&L assets are analogous to the restrictions on banks imposed by the Glass-Steagall Act and other federal laws and regulations designed to limit competition between types of institutions. But the restrictions were not reciprocal; banks and insurance companies were not prohibited from holding mortgages. The S&Ls also had to compete with banks for deposits, which were their main source of funds.

The Postwar Period: Growth of the Specialized System. Each of these competing systems prospered as the economy recovered, the unprecedented postwar housing boom providing room for both. FHA mortgage and mortgage insurance proved to be successful; at the end of the war, the Veterans Administration (VA) drew on the FHA experience and began to guarantee mortgages for veterans. Effective mortgage interest rates declined, junior financing became less important, and the homeownership rate rose dramatically during the 1940s, from 43 to 55 percent of all households. Most informed contemporary observers assigned a significant share of the credit to the new institutions.[4] Data limitations make it impossible to evaluate this view in any rigorous way, and there was some dissent, but it is probably largely correct.[5] The record of the first two postwar decades has influenced many builders, mortgage bankers, and other market participants to favor restoring the original New Deal system by public policy.

The system was already changing by the early 1950s, however. The S&Ls began to gain market share. The success of the FHA mortgage had two demonstration effects. The S&Ls found it profitable to make long-term self-amortizing mortgage loans without government insurance, and private firms found it profitable to write mortgage insurance. Between 1957 and 1973, every state passed an enabling statute for private mortgage insurance, and the FHA's mortgage insurance monopoly ended. The private insurers were largely responsible for the decline in the FHA's market share during the 1960s and 1970s;[6] by the early 1970s, they were writing as much new coverage as the FHA and VA combined.

FNMA's activities were restricted by statute. From its inception to the end of World War II, it functioned as a dealer, buying and reselling a significant minor fraction of FHA-insured mortgages.[7] In the immediate postwar decade, however, it saw its mission as providing credit to ease the housing shortage and help veterans buy homes, and it became a portfolio lender, competing with the S&Ls. In 1954 Congress passed the FNMA Charter Act, directing the agency to become a dealer and liquidate its portfolio. It was expected to operate as a standby reserve facility in periods of unusual stress in the mortgage market.[8] At the same time, FNMA was given a new public purpose: it could be required to buy mortgages to support specific housing programs, mainly those providing low-income housing. During the next decade FNMA did function more or less as a dealer. It bought mortgages in more years than it sold them, but its total portfolio declined from about $2.5 billion in 1953 to $2.0 billion in 1965.

Finally, in 1970 the S&Ls were given a secondary market agency of their own, when Freddie Mac was established to deal in conventional mortgages. Freddie Mac is an agency within the Federal Home Loan Bank System; the bank board serves as its board of directors, its common stock is owned by the twelve home loan banks, and its preferred stock was distributed in 1984 to S&Ls belonging to the system.

With these changes, the thrift institutions (S&Ls and mutual savings banks) acquired a larger share of the mortgage market. In 1950, commercial banks and life insurance companies combined held about the same share of home mortgages as the thrifts (40 percent versus 39 percent). By 1965 the thrifts held more than twice as large a share (58 percent versus 27 percent).

Inflation and the Disintegration of the Specialized System

By the early 1970s, however, the specialized housing finance system was in trouble. Monetary policy became inflationary around 1965, as the federal government tried to fight both the War on Poverty and the Vietnam War without raising taxes. Since S&Ls borrowed short and lent long, unanticipated inflation drove up the rates they paid on all their deposits, but they could earn more only on new mortgages.

The first reaction to inflation was to extend Regulation Q (Reg Q) to S&Ls in 1966, imposing interest rate ceilings on their time deposits. The significance of the changes in Reg Q for financial institutions in general is discussed in more detail by Anna Schwartz in chapter 2. Extending it to S&Ls was supposed to prevent them from competing with commercial banks for time deposits and at the same time control their own cost of funds. During the first post-1966 housing cycle, in 1970, federal policy sought to help the S&Ls further by creating Freddie Mac and by allowing FNMA to buy conventional mortgages. During the second cycle, in the early 1970s, inflation reached double digits, and money market mutual funds (MMMFs) came into existence. S&L deposit inflows dropped precipitously in the face of this new competition. During the third cycle, in the late 1970s and early 1980s, with yet more severe inflation, interest rates reached unprecedented highs, S&Ls suffered net deposit outflows, and MMMF assets increased from $3.5 billion in 1977 to $180 billion in 1981.

Deposit rate ceilings survived the first two cycles, but they began to crumble and were phased out between 1981 and 1986. They may have held down the cost of funds temporarily, but at the cost of exacerbating housing cycles, drastically reducing the savings flow to S&Ls when interest rates were high, and creating a new competitor for household savings. The "small saver" proved to be unwilling to subsidize the homebuyer once market-rate, low-denomination alternatives were available.

As deposit rate ceilings resulted in disintermediation and new competition, expanded asset and liability powers for financial institutions became a major policy issue. At the beginning of the 1970s the Hunt Commission recommended broader powers for S&Ls as well as other institutions, and both the Nixon and the Ford administrations proposed legislation, but Congress reacted slowly. During the decade, the most effective impetus for new powers for S&Ls came from the state-chartered institutions, and then only on an ad hoc basis. Typically, the S&Ls in one or two states would win approval for new instruments from state regulators; then Congress would grudgingly grant the same authority first to federally chartered institutions in those states and finally to all S&Ls. Negotiable order of withdrawal (NOW) accounts and adjustable rate mortgages (ARMs) are cases in point.

Public policy also reacted slowly to the money market mutual fund; beginning in 1978, the bank board authorized a series of certificates, each offering some, but not all, of the attractive features of MMMFs.[9] The certificates quickly became the major sources of S&L funds, but they were not enough to prevent net outflows in 1981 and 1982 or to inhibit the growth of money market funds.

Broad expansion of powers finally came during the last, most severe, inflationary cycle. In 1981 the bank board allowed S&Ls to make almost any type of adjustable rate mortgage. The Depository Institutions Deregulation and Monetary Control Act (DIDMCA) of 1980 and the Garn–St Germain Act of 1982 allowed S&Ls to diversify out of mortgage lending. The Garn–St Germain Act also authorized a new savings account, the money market deposit account (MMDA), which is basically competitive with the MMMF.[10]

The Financial Situation of the S&Ls. The increase in interest rates pushed the entire S&L industry into insolvency. In 1980, two-thirds of the mortgages held by S&Ls carried interest rates under 10 percent,[11] while the effective conventional mortgage rate was over 12.5 percent. When these mortgages were valued at their market price, S&Ls as a whole had a negative net worth equal to about 12.5 percent of their assets.[12]

The S&Ls were not insolvent, however, according to generally accepted accounting principles (GAAP), because changes in the market value of mortgages do not have to be recognized until they are sold. By GAAP accounting, the industry had a net worth of just over 5 percent in 1980. The 5 percent figure was also the bank board's net worth requirement for individual institutions.

From 1980 to 1982, interest rates rose. The S&Ls managed to improve their position slightly on a market-value basis, but their GAAP net worth fell to just under 3 percent. Over this period, also, the number of insolvent S&Ls, on a GAAP basis, rose from 16 to 222—over 6 percent of the 3,300 S&Ls in existence, with over 9 percent of the assets ($63 billion out of $692 billion). The FSLIC might have been able to close all the GAAP-insolvent S&Ls if it could have limited its outlays to the amount required to restore them to solvency as measured by GAAP;[13] but it could not have begun to meet the costs of insolvency as measured by market values.

Public policy therefore chose to temporize, in the hope that a fall in interest rates would solve the problem. Congress passed a concurrent resolution in March 1982, placing the "full faith and credit" of the U.S. government behind the FSLIC and the Federal Deposit Insurance Corporation (FDIC), but otherwise took no action. The resolution did not have the force of law, and it expired with that Congress (it was not renewed until 1987 as part of the FSLIC recapitalization). Between 1980 and 1982, the bank board lowered its net worth requirement for S&Ls from 5 percent to 3 percent of liabilities—paralleling the actual decline in net worth for the industry—and it devised a number of accounting conventions to enable S&Ls to avoid technical insolvency.[14]

This strategy succeeded in postponing a formal collapse, and the market-value net worth of the industry improved as interest rates fell; by 1985 the industry as a whole was again solvent, though the number of insolvent S&Ls continued to grow and the financial situation of the FSLIC worsened. By 1985 the cost of closing all GAAP-insolvent S&Ls was estimated at $16 billion, more than double the FSLIC's reserves.[15] The most recent estimates range from $40 to $50 billion, and the FSLIC itself has been declared insolvent by the General Accounting Office.[16] Of the 222 GAAP-insolvent institutions in 1982, 65 achieved a positive net worth by 1986, 80 were still insolvent, and 77 had gone out of business through liquidation, merger, or acquisition. Meanwhile another 365 S&Ls had become insolvent, even though interest rates fell sharply. Twice as many institutions were insolvent in 1986, although the total number of insured S&Ls declined by 400.[17]

Several factors contributed to the growing number of insolvent S&Ls. Declines in energy and farm prices lowered the value of homes and other real estate in energy and farm states. Although geographic portfolio restrictions for S&Ls have been phased out since 1964, many S&Ls still lend primarily in their local markets. The decline in property values therefore translated into a decline in the assets of S&Ls in these states, particularly Texas, Louisiana, and Oklahoma. Geographic specialization, originally mandated by state and federal law, creates risks for the FSLIC.

The bank board has claimed that credit risk has become a more important explanation for losses than interest rate risk since the early 1980s.[18] Some analysts have questioned this claim;[19] others have argued that the bank board itself created credit risk problems. By allowing insolvent S&Ls to remain open, it gave them an incentive to take greater risks in order to recoup. If the gamble was successful, the management of the S&L would receive the benefit; if it failed, the cost would be borne by the FSLIC.[20]

This controversy is important not for resolving the current problems of the FSLIC, but because the bank board has used the problem of credit risk as the rationale for limiting S&L asset powers. The latter issue is discussed in the next section.

The Problem of the FSLIC and the S&Ls

The Recapitalization of the FSLIC. Four entities can pay for the FSLIC's losses: the savings and loan industry, the commercial banks as a whole (through a merger of the FSLIC with the FDIC), individual banks and other firms interested in expanding their markets, and the general taxpayer.

The FSLIC recapitalization plan passed in 1987 puts the initial cost on the S&Ls, but the amount is totally inadequate. Congress approved a recapitalization of $10 billion, to be spent over three years.[21] The amount is a compromise between $15 billion over five years, proposed by the Reagan administration, and $5 billion over two years, the preferred plan of the U.S. League of Savings Institutions. The funds will be raised by bond issues, backed by the assets of the twelve home loan banks and the future premium income of the FSLIC. All the proposals, as well as the final plan, fell far short of the $50 billion or so needed. Indeed, there are not enough resources in the Federal Home Loan Bank System to meet the costs. The combined total capital of the home loan banks is about $13.4 billion, and their annual net income is about $1.3 billion; annual deposit insurance premiums are about $1.9 billion. Public policy again is playing for time, in the hope that the problem will resolve itself, or at least that an explicitly expensive solution can be postponed.

Playing for time has not worked in the past and is not likely to work now. Estimates of the losses of insolvent S&Ls grew by about $10 billion during the time that it took policy makers to agree on a $10 billion recapitalization, and losses are growing from day to day about as fast as the FSLIC will be allowed to spend the recapitalization funds. The law requires the bank board to be lenient in deciding whether to close "well-managed but insolvent" thrifts in economically depressed regions. That might help in the energy states: the price of oil has risen sharply twice and fallen once since 1973, each time unexpectedly, and it might rise again if, for example, hostilities in the

Persian Gulf escalate. But the more likely outcome of leniency is that the FSLIC problem will get worse instead of better.

Merging the insurance funds is also likely to be inadequate. Paul Volcker, among others, has advocated a merger, but FDIC Chairman William Seidman has said that "insuring substantial amounts of deposits that are now FSLIC-insured certainly would stretch our reserves." Comptroller of the Currency Robert L. Clarke has been more pessimistic: "There isn't enough money in the FDIC to solve the [S&L] problem—even if you spend every penny."[22] This certainly seems to be the case. The assets of the FDIC are about $18 billion. They have not grown since 1985 and may decline in 1988 for the first time in the fund's history; outlays to help failing banks have been growing. The combined net worth of the two insurance funds is thus inadequate to meet the likely cost of closing the insolvent S&Ls alone. Both insurance funds have found it unexpectedly difficult and costly to resolve the problems of failing institutions. Merging them may be at best a way to buy time, using their resources for the S&Ls now instead of the commercial banks later. The possibility of a merger will receive further discussion; the General Accounting Office is studying it at the request of several members of Congress, and Representative Gerald Kleczka has said he will propose legislation to achieve a merger over a ten-year period. His plan, however, presupposes that the FSLIC is restored to solvency by stronger regulation and by the recapitalization, which is unlikely.

Some insolvent S&Ls still have a franchise value for banks, other S&Ls, and other financial firms that want to enter new markets. In the past the bank board has sometimes transferred failed thrifts to out-of-state firms as an "entry fee" into a new state, and the 1987 recapitalization plan allows nonbank banks and securities firms to buy failing thrifts. Some financial services firms and nonfinancial firms might also want an S&L as an expansion of their business; the S&L charter may be attractive to them. Interstate banking compacts are reducing the franchise value, but some S&Ls may still be attractive to some potential buyers. The franchise value of failed thrifts is far from enough to pay the FSLIC's losses, but it could help reduce them. This approach should also help remove some of the remaining regulatory barriers that limit the powers of different types of financial firms.

The most likely outcome is that the taxpayer, through the U.S. Treasury, will bear most of the cost, sooner or later. The small-scale recapitalization plan passed in 1987 could be the first installment in a series of biennial outlays, and it might prove more palatable politically to impose the later installments on the taxpayer if the industry has borne the first one.

A better alternative is to confront the problem in its entirety and close the insolvent institutions quickly. Bert Ely suggests allowing thrifts up to three years to transfer into the FDIC or find a buyer, giving the insolvent thrifts the shortest time.[23] In practice, closing the insolvent S&Ls might take longer; the bank board and the FDIC probably lack the resources to close 200 institutions in a short time. But on its current schedule the recapitalization plan will take fifteen years, assuming the losses get no worse. At this point, moving too quickly is better than moving too slowly.

The Effect on the S&Ls. Each of these options has implications for the future of the healthy S&Ls and the industry as a whole, but the consequences are not necessarily the obvious ones. Recapitalizing the FSLIC is often described as a way of preserving the S&Ls, and merging the insurance funds as the end of the industry, but neither is automatic.

The recapitalization plan imposes the cost of closing insolvent S&Ls on the remaining healthy ones, which must continue to pay deposit premiums and also suffer a loss in their earnings and net worth as the earnings and perhaps the assets of the home loan banks are drawn down.[24] The healthy S&Ls thus have an incentive to leave the system individually, convert to savings bank or commercial bank charters, and join the FDIC. A few have already left, and more will probably do so. To discourage conversions, the bank board has imposed exit fees on institutions leaving the Federal Home Loan Bank System. The recapitalization plan established an exit fee at twice the annual deposit insurance premium (including the special premium imposed in 1985), or about 20 basis points on assets. The S&L could recoup this amount in three years as a result of paying lower FDIC premiums, or less if FSLIC premiums have to be raised to pay the interest on the recapitalization bonds.[25] The law also imposes a one-year moratorium on S&Ls' leaving the FSLIC, but at least thirty-two associations, including four of the ten largest, are still eligible to leave because they started to do so before March 31, 1987.

An S&L would have to meet the more stringent capital requirements of the FDIC in order to convert its charter. The FDIC has stated that converting thrifts would have to meet a 6 percent minimum capital requirement, and additional capital could be required. Chairman Seidman has estimated that about one-third of the S&Ls could meet the 6 percent requirement.[26]

Other costs of shifting from S&L to commercial bank status may also inhibit conversions. The S&L would have to give up access to Federal Home Loan Bank System advances and repay its outstanding balance. It would have to sell off any investments that banks are unable to make; in practice this requirement would apply mainly to direct investments in real estate and would vary by state. A number of states allow the same investment powers to all state-chartered financial institutions, and others are considering doing so.[27] Corporations owning S&Ls, such as Sears Roebuck and Ford, could not own commercial banks, and presumably their S&Ls could be converted only if they were sold. The most serious problem is the loss of the bad debt allowance for S&Ls converting to commercial bank charters. Those S&Ls with $500 million or more in assets will have to count their accumulated bad debt allowance as income for tax purposes over a four-year period. In addition to these legal requirements, the converting S&Ls might face more vigorous and more stringent regulation. These legal and regulatory restrictions make it likely that most S&Ls would choose to become savings banks rather than commercial banks. The laws could of course be changed by Congress. The S&Ls that want to leave the FSLIC might be able to lobby successfully for changes in the tax treatment of the bad debt allowance. Alternatively, broader changes might occur as part of a merger of the two insurance funds.

Most S&Ls have feared that merging the funds would mean the end of their industry, and have traditionally opposed the plan. But that need not be the result. The mutual savings banks have remained distinct from commercial banks although they are insured by the FDIC. The S&Ls could still be chartered and regulated by the bank board or the states, while being insured by the FDIC, although the unsatisfactory regulatory record of the bank board makes this outcome unlikely. Even so, the problems of the S&Ls have led some industry leaders to change their opposition to a merger, among them James Cirona, president of the Federal Home Loan Bank of San Francisco; several of the large S&Ls that are considering conversion are located in California.

Closing the insolvent S&Ls and paying their losses quickly would permit the FSLIC and the Federal Home Loan Bank System to continue operating as a separate financial regulatory system, if it were combined with the Benston-Kaufman proposal outlined in this volume for timely reorganization of banks before their net worth becomes negative. Promptly closing institutions that fall below a minimum net worth, on a market-value accounting basis, should prevent a repetition of the current crisis. The Securities and Exchange Commission (SEC) follows this practice with respect to brokerage firms, and it is noteworthy that few firms had to close as a result of the stock market crash of October 19, 1987. Deposit insurance would continue for the much smaller number of S&Ls. The FSLIC and the Federal Home Loan Bank System would need to regulate and supervise more effectively than they have in the past. The bank board has already adopted this policy for one S&L in a recent acquisition case; if net worth falls below 3 percent, the board can replace the management and select new owners.[28]

This does not mean that the present system *should* continue. Whether a rationale exists for a separate regulatory system for the S&Ls depends on whether they have a separate purpose and whether that purpose can best be achieved by a separate system.

The Future of the S&Ls. Policy discussions of the problems of the S&Ls have generally ignored their role in housing finance, except incidentally, and have focused on their ability to survive.[29] This is consistent with their behavior. As their powers have expanded, they have steadily moved away from their traditional role, and as time goes on they will probably move further. Housing finance is now less important to them, and they are less important to housing finance.

The shift away from mortgage lending has been dramatic. From 1979 to 1986, mortgages and mortgage securities declined from 86 to 68 percent of S&L assets,[30] and the S&Ls' share of total nonfarm residential mortgages outstanding declined from 43 to 30 percent. Mutual savings banks show similar declines. In those years, thrift institutions accounted for less than one-third of the increase in outstanding mortgages and mortgage-related securities.[31]

Diversification. As the S&Ls diversify out of mortgage lending, they are becoming increasingly heterogeneous. George Hanc, executive vice-president of the National Council of Savings Institutions (the trade association for the large S&Ls and savings banks), recently summarized the changes:

> Some [savings institutions] operate, in effect, as commercial banks. Others are part mortgage portfolio lender and part mortgage banker, participating in all facets of the mortgage origination, servicing and investment process. Still others operate as integrated real estate financing companies. A few can best be described as diversified financial conglomerates. Many, however, remain mortgage portfolio lenders, engaged primarily in the business of making and holding residential mortgage loans, although usually on a basis that seeks to minimize interest rate risk in contrast with the borrow-short, lend-long syndrome of the past.
> Clearly, the thrift industry is anything but monolithic.[32]

Hanc, with other analysts, has identified four major lines of business: mortgage banking, portfolio lending on ARMs, real estate financing and investment, and consumer-oriented commercial banking. If he is correct, two conclusions seem warranted. First, sometime in the foreseeable future virtually no S&L will be operating in the same way that all S&Ls operated as recently as fifteen years ago, as unhedged portfolio lenders. Second, the S&L industry in effect is disappearing; the behavior of the industry is becoming the sum of the behaviors of individual associations. As the associations change, it is unclear whether they should still be regarded—or will still regard themselves—as part of the same industry. The S&L that increasingly functions as a mortgage banker, and certainly the S&L that operates as a commercial bank, is likely to reconsider its institutional identity.[33]

The evolution of the S&Ls vitiates the rationale for a separate regulatory system. Mortgage bankers and real estate developers are not regulated by the federal government. Commercial banks that started as S&Ls should not be regulated differently from other commercial banks. The issue of a separate system arises only for institutions that choose to continue as specialized housing lenders.

For these institutions, there is first the question of whether they can be profitable as specialized housing lenders. They have two possible strategies for avoiding the problems of the recent past if interest rates rise unexpectedly: they can make ARMs, or they can hedge the interest rate risk on fixed-rate loans. The problem with both strategies is that the spread between asset yields and deposit rates may be too small. Dwight Jaffee, who has recommended the hedging strategy in preference to ARM portfolio lending, has argued that it could work only if the S&L can obtain funds at below market rates, or if mortgage rates are high relative to other capital market rates.[34] Neither condition has held consistently since Jaffee wrote in 1981. The growing importance of the federal secondary mortgage market agencies, which are competing with the traditional portfolio lenders, has put downward pressure on the spread between mortgage and other rates; so has the continued integration of capital markets, as discussed by William Haraf in chapter 11. For these reasons, specialization as a portfolio lender is becoming harder.

Restrictions on diversification. Regulation and the tax laws limit institutional evolution; and though both have been changing, they still constrain the S&Ls. The original S&L tax exemption was changed in 1951 to a deduction for a bad-debt reserve, which still enabled most S&Ls to avoid paying taxes. The industry average effective tax rate was less than 2 percent on economic income.[35] Since 1982, however, the deduction has been steadily reduced: in 1986 the maximum tax rate was raised to 31 percent, just below the new 34 percent corporate rate.[36] Originally S&Ls had to keep 82 percent of their assets in home mortgages or U.S. government securities to qualify for the bad-debt deduction; the 1986 act reduced this to 60 percent. The S&Ls now have substantial leeway to reduce their mortgage holdings without tax penalty. If the new limits become binding constraints, they are likely to press for further reductions in the qualifying asset threshold and continue to diversify out of home mortgages.

Since the Garn–St Germain Act, the bank board has imposed some new restrictions on asset powers. In March 1985 it limited direct investments in real estate (as opposed to loans) to 10 percent of an S&L's net worth, arguing that direct investments were causing failures and increasing the cost to the FSLIC. After some controversy, a final regulation was issued in June 1987, placing limits on acquisition and development and on construction loans as well. The bank board's contention has not been borne out by independent research; several studies have concluded that direct investments do not affect the probability of failure (as measured by closure), but find some evidence that they do correlate positively with the cost to the FSLIC.[37]

This regulation does not by itself foreclose the possibility of an S&L's becoming a commercial bank, though it may raise problems for those wishing to operate as "integrated real estate financing companies," in Hanc's phrase. Viewed in the light of the evolution that has already occurred, any new regulation is likely to be a rearguard action rather than a reversal in policy. If it is part of an effort to reestablish the S&Ls in their pre-1978 specialized role, it is likely to be a costly failure.

The Secondary Market Agencies

The Growth of the Agencies after 1966. The problems of the S&Ls offered an opportunity for the other half of the New Deal housing finance system. Federally sponsored secondary market agencies were able to adapt to the new economic environment and take advantage of new technology. FNMA was split into two agencies, and Freddie Mac was created. FNMA's function of supporting federal housing subsidy programs was spun off to a new federally sponsored credit agency, the Government National Mortgage Association (GNMA or Ginnie Mae) in 1968. As FNMA was originally, GNMA is a government entity; it is located within the Department of Housing and Urban Development (HUD). The main reason for splitting FNMA was budgetary. The federal government adopted a unified budget in 1967, including formerly off-budget agencies such as FNMA. Agency loan purchases were counted as budget outlays. The new FNMA was not considered a federal agency and therefore was not subject to budget limits.

The restructuring of FNMA lessened its public purpose and created the potential for conflict. The president retained authority to appoint five directors (out of fifteen), and the government retained an oversight responsibility, but FNMA's private stockholders elected a majority of directors. The different ownership of the three secondary market agencies has affected their behavior.

FNMA. The 1966 credit crunch and accompanying disintermediation were the signal for FNMA to become an active mortgage investor. At first it purchased mortgages on a somewhat countercyclical basis, buying more during the housing cycle downturns in 1970 and 1973–1974. In the housing boom of the late 1970s, however, FNMA increased its purchases to record levels. It rarely sold mortgages. Its portfolio grew to $15 billion by 1970, $25 billion by 1975, $50 billion by 1979, and $78 billion by 1983.[38] In 1970, FNMA was allowed to buy conventional as well as government-backed mortgages; in 1976 more than half its purchases were conventional loans, and this has been the case in every year but two since then. It has become the largest mortgage portfolio lender in the country.

FNMA has several privileges as a federally chartered corporation. It is exempt from SEC registration and disclosure requirements, and its securities have special status as investments for several purposes. It has a $2.25 billion line of credit at the U.S. Treasury. Because of these privileges, it is widely perceived in the capital markets as having an implicit guarantee from the federal government that it will not be allowed to fail.

The line of credit and especially the implicit guarantee are FNMA's equivalent to deposit insurance for S&Ls and mutual savings banks. As a portfolio lender, FNMA has been a giant S&L and has accordingly experienced the problems of the S&Ls on a giant scale. In 1978 FNMA's market-value net worth became negative; by 1981, it had a negative net worth of almost $11 billion.[39] FNMA's agency status enabled it to continue as a portfolio lender and borrow at favorable rates in the capital markets; it also permitted public policy to delay dealing with FNMA's problems.

Like some S&Ls, FNMA chose to gamble that interest rates would come down. Its purchases doubled from 1981 to 1982 and rose further in 1983. It nearly stopped buying FHA and VA mortgages, concentrating on conventional fixed-rate loans and instituting new programs to buy ARMs and second mortgages. It began to issue mortgage-backed securities in 1981. FNMA was able to leverage its explicit and implicit federal guarantees to continue borrowing short term in the capital markets and buying long-term mortgages. Its stockholders had little to lose after the early 1980s, since its net worth was already negative.[40] The gamble paid off when interest rates did decline, and FNMA was able to regain solvency by 1985. By the end of 1986, its net worth was about $1 billion.[41] But it continues to function as a portfolio lender with a government guarantee, and it remains vulnerable to unexpected increases in interest rates, when the guarantee might have to be called into play.

FNMA took greater underwriting risks as part of its growth strategy in the early 1980s. Its foreclosures have increased steadily since 1981. The cost of these foreclosures has fallen partly on FHA and private mortgage insurers; their insurance payments to FNMA have increased steadily. Indeed, payments to FNMA by private mortgage insurers were larger than FNMA profits between 1984 and 1986; FNMA was profitable at the expense of the private insurers.[42] This suggests that FNMA has been a significant factor contributing to the losses experienced by the private mortgage insurance industry in recent years. Ironically, FNMA has now raised the possibility of establishing a mortgage insurance subsidiary itself, because of the problems faced by existing firms in that industry. A private insurer with significant federal support could drive competing firms out of the market.

GNMA. While FNMA increasingly functioned as an S&L, the new agencies assumed the original FHA role as a mortgage market innovator. In the early 1970s GNMA began to offer a new kind of mortgage market instrument: a security collateralized by a pool of FHA-insured mortgages (which it purchased under the Tandem Plan, a government mortgage market support program). GNMA guaranteed the timely payment of principal and interest, with the full backing of the government.

This new instrument, the GNMA pass-through security (PTS), was the first of the series of mortgage-backed securities that have proliferated through the 1970s and 1980s. Mortgage securitization is discussed in detail subsequently; here it is only important to note that securitization was a major step toward the integration of the mortgage market with other capital markets. The significance of the innovation can be seen in the changing pattern of security buyers. In 1971, two-thirds of PTSs were sold to S&Ls or savings banks; by 1979, half were being sold to pension funds and trusts.[43] The PTS was the first home mortgage instrument to appeal to pension funds.

Freddie Mac. Freddie Mac was established as a reaction to the problems that Reg Q created for S&Ls. When deposit inflows fell off, the S&Ls had to cut back on their mortgage lending. Freddie Mac was expected to buy their old mortgages and thereby provide funds for new ones. These purposes could also have been served by FNMA, which acquired the right to buy conventional loans in the same act that created Freddie Mac. The new agency did not in fact behave in an especially countercyclical fashion until the early 1980s.[44]

Freddie Mac operated differently from FNMA. It quickly became an issuer of mortgage-backed securities rather than a portfolio lender and has continued to function mainly as a secondary market maker. Its whole-loan portfolio is small compared with the value of its mortgage-backed securities. Freddie Mac has hedged its position by matching the maturities of its assets and liabilities; it is not subject to any substantial interest rate risk.

Like FNMA, Freddie Mac enjoys explicit and implicit federal subsidies. Its securities can be guaranteed by the Federal Home Loan Banks, which in turn have a $4 billion line of credit at the Treasury. Freddie Mac can also borrow from the home loan banks. It is exempt from SEC registration and state security laws and from state and local income taxation. As with FNMA, these explicit benefits are most important because they are viewed as implying further government support if necessary. Agency status enables both Freddie Mac and FNMA to compete with primary mortgage market investors, including the S&Ls that own Freddie Mac. The concern of some large S&Ls that continue to specialize in ARM portfolio lending was the impetus for the privatization task force; it has also led to calls for lower conforming limits on agency mortgage purchases.[45]

The revival of the secondary market agencies and the development of mortgage-related securities in the past two decades can be seen as a modern version of the original purpose of FHA and FNMA. They have brought new institutional investors into the mortgage market. This component of the New Deal housing finance system has flourished and taken new institutional forms. The growing role of the secondary market agencies raises important policy concerns, however. They receive explicit and implicit subsidies giving them an advantage over private competitors. The future role of the agencies is the most important long-term question about the housing finance system.

Public Purposes of the Federal Secondary Market Agencies. Secondary market agencies have three public purposes. First and currently most important is their demonstration effect. They are innovators of mortgage-backed securities. Because of their federal agency status, they are able to take risks that private firms cannot and to demonstrate the viability of mortgage securitization, as the FHA demonstrated the viability of long-term fixed-rate mortgages and mortgage insurance in the 1930s. The agencies also help to promote standardization in the mortgage market by deciding which types of mortgages to purchase. The second purpose is to provide countercyclical support to the mortgage and housing markets. The third is to help relatively low-income families become homebuyers. These rationales have been given more weight in the past than today, but they still deserve some discussion.

The agencies have two methods of meeting these objectives: as portfolio mortgage lender and as secondary market dealer through the origination of mortgage-backed securities. Freddie Mac and GNMA have functioned mainly as dealers; FNMA was almost entirely a portfolio lender until 1981, when it began to issue securities.

Demonstration effects in the secondary market. The development of mortgage-backed securities has consisted of finding ways to eliminate or minimize the disadvantages of mortgages compared with corporate bonds and other fixed-rate securities, from the investor's standpoint. Because of unforeseen changes in household circumstances such as divorce or death, the risk of default on mortgages is greater and less predictable. Mortgages also carry more interest rate or prepayment risk than bonds, because prepayment is typically at the option of the borrower. Prepayment patterns can be identified in the aggregate, but not for individual buyers, and the patterns are affected by changes in interest rates. If rates fall, buyers will prepay more rapidly and refinance at a lower rate; this happened on a large scale twice during the 1980s. Investors will therefore receive their principal sooner and receive lower returns than expected, because they will have to reinvest it at a lower rate. If rates rise, borrowers will delay repayment, and lenders will be forced to accept a below-market return.

Issuers of mortgage-backed securities have found ways to address prepayment risk through securities with multiple maturity classes, beginning with collateralized mortgage obligations (CMOs) in 1983 and continuing through real estate mortgage investment conduits (Remics) in the 1986 tax reform act. Innovations are continuing. So far, however, federal guarantees and agency sponsorship have been the only satisfactory method of reducing the default risk for the investor, by shifting it to the agency. Typically, either mortgage-backed securities carry a federal agency guarantee, or the underlying mortgages are insured or guaranteed by the government. Privately issued conventional mortgage-backed securities have been slow to win market acceptance,[46] and analysts have been continually overoptimistic about their prospects.[47]

Secondary market activities thus combine a demonstration effect with a subsidy, and it is difficult to separate the two. Some evidence suggests, however, that a market may be developing for securities without a government guarantee. Some $37 billion in fully private CMOs were issued between 1984 and 1986.[48] More significantly, Wall Street firms have shown a willingness to issue conventional mortgage Remics without a federal guarantee. The 1986 tax law permitted both FNMA and Freddie Mac to issue Remics, subject to the decision of their regulators, as well as private firms. Five major Wall Street securities issuers opposed agency issuance of Remics backed by conventional mortgages, claiming that they could enter this market if the agencies did not, but could not compete with the agencies. The bank board decided not to let Freddie Mac issue Remics, but FNMA received authorization from HUD Secretary Samuel Pierce after several months' deliberation, on an initially limited and temporary basis. The fact that Wall Street firms think they can successfully market conventional mortgage Remics indicates their belief that the default risk problem can be overcome.

The 1986 report of the Freddie Mac Advisory Committee Task Force on privatization argues that the secondary market for fixed-rate mortgages has been standardized and a federal role is no longer necessary, but the feasibility of a private secondary market for ARMs and other new instruments remains in question. The task force report acknowledges that the agencies themselves may be inhibiting the development of a private secondary market. The HUD report on FNMA concludes that investors probably place a relatively small value on the extra protection against default risk afforded by agency status—in the neighborhood of 20 basis points. If this is correct, a market for fully private securities should be feasible. The report also admits that its analysis may be wrong, noting, "there is no way to predict the actual reaction of investors without eliminating agency status."[49] A temporary prohibition of agency Remics might have provided a relatively costless test. The increasing sophistication of secondary market firms and investors suggests that markets for fully private ARMs securities and other innovations can be developed in a reasonable time period, albeit more slowly than if the agencies were involved.

Countercyclical market support. Countercyclical activities became a more important policy objective after Reg Q was imposed on S&Ls in 1966. Reg Q resulted in disintermediation when short-term interest rates went above the ceilings, as they did on several occasions, and housing construction suffered. The agencies were expected to mitigate the downturn, as was the Federal Home Loan Bank System through the advances mechanism. There is a substantial professional literature on the countercyclical effectiveness of the agencies, especially FNMA. The general though not universal conclusion is that they did operate in a modestly countercyclical manner through the late 1970s, though they were not aggressively countercyclical and were perhaps less effective than the home loan banks.[50] Cycles were, however, more severe after Reg Q was imposed than they were before 1966; the agencies could not offset the thrifts' loss of funds.

Financial deregulation raises the question of whether federal agencies could continue to have any countercyclical influence. If there are no deposit rate ceilings, disintermediation is not a problem; the cost of funds is. Homebuyers are rationed by price rather than by credit availability. Federal agencies have less ability to channel funds to housing in an integrated capital market.

Preliminary evidence indicates that this has been happening. Herbert Kaufman has found that FNMA purchases had no effect on mortgage rates, the volume of mortgage credit, or housing starts during the 1979–1982 recessions. His model is similar to that used by Jaffee and Kenneth Rosen; he attributes the difference in results to deregulation.[51]

Housing cycles occurred before Reg Q was imposed in 1966 and will certainly occur again. The demand for housing (as well as other durable goods) is sensitive to nominal interest rates. FNMA could still take advantage of its agency status to borrow short and lend long when interest rates are high, earn a profit if mortgage rates decline, and perhaps moderate housing fluctuations. The development of ARMs, however, limits this opportunity. When nominal rates have been high in recent years, borrowers have shifted to ARMs, reducing both the spread between initial mortgage rates and agency borrowing rates and the profitability of countercyclical lending. Whatever the effectiveness of the agencies in the past, they will probably have little in the future.

The "low-income homebuyer." FNMA and GNMA in particular are supposed to help relatively low-income families become homeowners. In the late 1960s and early 1970s FNMA bought mortgages under the Section 235 low- and moderate-income homeownership subsidy program; it has also bought mortgages for subsidized rental projects. Although most of these programs no longer exist, the objective still affects agency behavior. They cannot buy loans above a "conforming limit," a maximum amount established by the charter act and adjusted annually (and generously) for inflation. The limit ($168,700 in 1988) holds down the average amount of agency mortgages below the average for all mortgages. This does not mean that lower-income families benefit; it means that mortgages on high-priced homes are left to the S&Ls and other portfolio lenders. FNMA buys a less than proportionate share of mortgages for the lowest-income buyers.[52] The concept of the "low-income homebuyer" is rather a term of art; it usually means a family above the middle of the income distribution with income lower than the typical homebuyer's but higher than the typical family's. The basis for subsidizing these families is dubious to begin with. Insofar as there is a public purpose, because of the social benefits of homeownership, it is probably better fulfilled by channeling subsidies through GNMA, a government agency.[53]

Evaluation. The social benefits of the agencies depend on the extent to which the subsidies they receive are shifted forward to homebuyers—that is, whether they are marginal or inframarginal mortgage lenders. Some analysts have argued that FNMA at least is inframarginal: it holds a small share of outstanding mortgages, and innovations in securitization are making it less important.[54] If this is correct, the subsidies benefit FNMA stockholders. The political controversies about the agencies, however, arise because mortgage market participants believe that the agencies are in fact holding mortgage rates down. Recent estimates of the effect are about ¼ to ⅜ of one percentage point.[55] The housing market is generally regarded as competitive, and the supply is highly elastic over a period of perhaps five years.[56] The demands for housing and homeownership are sensitive to their prices.[57] If the agencies do lower the mortgage rate by this amount, they provide some incentive to homeownership and housing investment—less perhaps than they might like to claim, but enough to take seriously.

The social costs of the agencies must be weighed against these benefits. Are a more rapid development of the secondary market for ARMs and a reduction of ⅜ of a percentage point in the mortgage rate enough to justify the subsidies and implicit guarantees of the agencies? My opinion is that they are not, for reasons that are discussed in the conclusion. But even if they are, they imply a smaller and a different agency role. There is no need for FNMA to function as a large federally sponsored S&L. Other investors would be willing to hold most of its portfolio.[58]

The Future of the Agencies: Options and Issues. If Congress chooses to end federal subsidies to the secondary mortgage markets, there are two strategies: charging the agencies for the value of their agency status, or privatizing them.

Fees for subsidies. Charging the agency for the value of the subsidy, alone or in combination with tighter government regulation, has been proposed for FNMA and was considered in the HUD report.[59] The value of the government guarantee could be estimated periodically by marking the assets and liabilities to market and comparing them with the market value of the stock.[60] In the past, the value of the FNMA guarantee has varied with interest rates and the size of its portfolio.

Allowing the existing agencies to remain in business on an unsubsidized basis avoids disruptions during transition periods, lets them continue to use their accumulated mortgage market expertise, and should permit private firms to compete. But the political feasibility of this approach is questionable. Determining the value of the subsidies is not likely to be left to economists and technicians; it will become a political issue—if not immediately, then gradually. Setting the correct price will be difficult to begin with; preserving the market pricing will be harder still, because changing market conditions will make price adjustments necessary. There is a long record of government user fees becoming subsidies, and of subsidies becoming deeper subsidies, over time. Furthermore, the postwar history of FHA includes several programs that extended mortgage insurance to subsidized housing programs at the same rate charged to unsubsidized homebuyers as an implicit subsidy in addition to the explicit subsidies specified in the legislation.

The Reagan administration has in the past proposed charging a user fee on FNMA debt and FNMA and Freddie Mac mortgage-backed securities. The fee would be a flat charge (50 basis points per dollar of additional debt and 10 basis points per dollar of additional mortgage-backed securities by 1989, as proposed in the 1987 budget). The proposal can be regarded as a step toward charging the agencies for the value of agency status, but it is not likely to be effective. It is not directly related to the government's potential losses, and it probably strengthens the market perception of the guarantee, lowering agency borrowing costs. The HUD report on FNMA acknowledges that Congress might choose a lower, token fee; so might a future administration.

Privatization. The alternative is to privatize the agencies, in whole or in part, a possibility that was discussed in both the FNMA and the Freddie Mac studies. Both list a number of options, ranging from full and immediate privatization to partial privatization in stages over an extended period.

The simpler and more effective method of privatization would be for the federal government to buy the outstanding stock of an agency, liquidate the assets and liabilities, and resell the stock. The new firm would have no guarantees for its future business. The market value of FNMA stock in late 1987 was about $3 billion; since the agency probably has a positive net worth, the cost to the government would be less. Freddie Mac common stock is owned by the Federal Home Loan Banks and preferred stock is owned by the S&Ls; the government could either buy the stock or remove the restrictions on selling it.

Privatizing the agencies in this way leaves unsettled the status of current assets and liabilities. The mortgage-related securities of both agencies carry guarantees of timely payment of interest and (in the case of FNMA) principal. FNMA has been able to issue $100 billion of debt at favorable prices because of its agency status. Disavowal of federal support would impose capital losses on security owners and bondholders. One solution is for the government to make the federal guarantees explicit on the current securities and bonds while also making clear that there are no federal guarantees in the future, as the agencies are privatized.

The denial of future guarantees would have to be credible. It would need to become operational immediately, because about one-third of FNMA's debt matures within a year. Within a few years, the risk of loss from perfecting the current guarantees would be substantially lessened.[61]

Alternatively the federal government could buy FNMA's bonds rather than its stock. The government could then exchange the debt with FNMA for assets of equal value.[62] Finally, the government could sell the assets, without any additional guarantees. These transactions would be very large, but they should not be costly to the government. FNMA would be much smaller, except insofar as it chose to buy back its portfolio.

The Freddie Mac privatization task force recommends partial privatization. It proposes to split the agency in two, with one part (Freddie Mac I) continuing as a government agency and being responsible for fulfilling Freddie Mac's public purpose, and the other (Freddie Mac II) being fully private. The public agency would retain responsibility for helping low- and moderate-income homebuyers, providing countercyclical mortgage market support, serving smaller S&Ls that are inexperienced in the secondary market, and in particular helping to develop a secondary market for ARMs, which the task force believes would not exist without federal agency support, at least in the short run. The private agency, Freddie Mac II, would operate in the conventional secondary market for fixed-rate mortgages in competition with private issuers. It would lose its ties to the Federal Home Loan Bank System, and through the system to the Treasury. The current stockholders, S&Ls and home loan banks, could sell the stock on the open market and could probably realize a capital gain.[63]

The decision to divide Freddie Mac is a Solomonic judgment that perhaps reflects the division within the S&L industry between associations that mainly originate and sell mortgages to Freddie Mac and those that continue to operate as portfolio lenders with an ARM portfolio. It is reasonable to split the public and private purposes of Freddie Mac, but it is difficult to achieve the split in practice. The task force proposal is reminiscent of the 1968 FNMA split, which was supposed to lead to the privatization of FNMA, and it might have the same consequences. Freddie Mac I would duplicate FHA and GNMA to the extent that it subsidized relatively low-income homebuyers; there is no particular reason for two government agencies to buy these mortgages. In the deregulated mortgage market, Freddie Mac I would probably be no more successful as a countercyclical lender than FNMA has been, or than Freddie Mac itself was in the past. Splitting the mortgage securitization business between fixed- and adjustable-rate mortgages is unlikely to be a clean split in practice and would divide the agency's expertise as well. With this kind of functional division, especially, Freddie Mac II would probably retain some federal connection, as FNMA did after 1968, with the same subsequent confusion of public and private purpose, and the country would end up with four federally sponsored secondary market agencies instead of three.

Transitional issues. Privatization cannot be achieved cleanly without transitional problems and adjustments, but the temporary difficulties should not be allowed to prevent privatization permanently. There is a danger that a phased privatization will come to a halt midway and even be counterproductive. Some of the options discussed in the HUD report illustrate the risks.

One such option is full privatization after a transition period of unspecified length during which FNMA securities would have federal backing; but its mortgage purchases and debt issuances would have to have about the same duration—it could not borrow short and lend long. During that period, it would have a more perfect federal guarantee than it now has. During that period, it could also be required to support the mortgage market if rates rose. If that happened, FNMA would resume its role as an ostensibly countercyclical portfolio lender as well as a secondary market agency, but this time as a fully federal entity.

A second option is to turn FNMA into a holding company with fully private subsidiaries;[64] a third is to turn it into a subsidiary of a fully private holding company. As the HUD report acknowledges, these options are analogous to the 1968 split of FNMA, which did not result in the intended privatization. They reintroduce the problem of implicit guarantees for the nonagency subsidiaries or parent company.

FNMA has a special problem because a large minor fraction of its portfolio (between $30 billion and $40 billion at the end of 1987) consists of low-yield, fixed-rate, assumable FHA mortgages and mortgages on projects in various low-income housing programs. This was an acute problem in the early 1980s when the low-yield portfolio was much larger ($57 billion at the end of 1980), interest rates were high, and the agency was insolvent by market-value accounting. At this writing FNMA is again solvent, but interest rates are rising. FNMA could well have an interest-rate-spread problem whenever it is privatized, because of these mortgages.

A possible solution is to sell part or all of the low-yield portfolio to the Treasury. The HUD report raises this possibility in the context of immediate privatization. This could involve a large but not enormous one-time budget outlay, if Treasury resold the loans at market, or a series of smaller annual costs, if Treasury held them to maturity. The size of the outlays depends on interest rates at the time. FNMA does not make public the distribution of yields on its mortgage holdings, so any estimate of the cost is conjectural; my guess is that it is between $2 and $3 billion in early 1988. Buying out the low-yield portfolio is a simpler and more effective solution than continuing to manage it within a quasi-federal agency. It would be analogous to having the taxpayer bail out the FSLIC, but much less expensive under current conditions, and it should be a more effective way of privatizing FNMA and keeping it private. It could be the government's way of compensating FNMA for the loss of agency status, in lieu of buying either its stock or its debt.

This is not the only way to resolve the low-yield portfolio problem. The point is that this and other transitional problems can be resolved, and direct, expeditious solutions are preferable to gradual unwinding.

The viability of the agencies as private secondary market firms is a matter of conjecture. The Freddie Mac privatization task force, consisting of knowledgeable individuals within and close to the S&L industry, expresses confidence that privatization is feasible. The HUD report on FNMA also argues that privatization is possible for that agency, but at least one senior member of FNMA's management (Timothy Howard, senior vice-president and chief economist) has in the past stated that FNMA could not operate without its implicit federal guarantee.[65]

Privatization of both agencies should proceed simultaneously, for both economic and political reasons. Whichever is privatized first will be at a disadvantage to the other in the capital markets. The Freddie Mac task force report is replete with repeated assertions, on virtually every page, that Freddie Mac should not be privatized unless FNMA is too, and the HUD report assumes that both will be privatized at the same time.

The System of the Future

The housing finance system will look very different without specialized mortgage lenders and without federal secondary market agencies (or with their role limited to demonstrations and explicit subsidies). The system is already evolving in ways that are consistent with a diminished federal presence, and technological changes are pushing it further in that direction.

Institutional Changes. Functional specialization has been growing rapidly and is likely to continue. Mortgage origination, servicing, securitization, and investing are increasingly discrete functions, as communications technology permits continued unbundling. This market-driven functional specialization should be distinguished from the statutory specialization imposed by asset and liability restrictions; in fact, functional specialization and portfolio diversification have been occurring simultaneously. Institutions that specialize in holding assets are holding more diversified portfolios, while other institutions are moving away from portfolio lending into other activities. The new technology has enabled S&Ls to separate their mortgage banking from their portfolio lending and has contributed to the institutional evolution that has already occurred. It also allows firms with primary interests in many other aspects of the housing finance and housing delivery systems to set up mortgage banking subsidiaries. More than half of all mortgage bankers are subsidiaries of other firms. Some twenty-six of the 100 largest are subsidiaries of S&Ls;[66] several realtors, some Wall Street firms, and at least one large forest products company have also established large mortgage banking operations. As housing finance becomes less and less the province of specialized portfolio lenders, it is likely that commercial banks and other financial institutions will follow suit.

One continuing effect of these changes is to reduce the cost of originating and servicing mortgages, which in turn should reduce the spreads between mortgage and other interest rates.

The Extent of the Market. Technological progress is also creating a national mortgage market. With electronic mortgage networks, lenders can evaluate mortgage applications and borrowers can evaluate mortgage contracts over a wider geographic area, ultimately nationally. To date, the development of electronic networks has been slow, perhaps because borrowers prefer face-to-face contact, but they are likely to be increasingly important.[67]

Geographic differentials in mortgage rates are disappearing, as they have been for a century. The large regional rate spreads of the late nineteenth century were reduced substantially by 1940, from about three percentage points between the Northeast and the West to less than one point.[68] The creation of FHA and FNMA and the energies of mortgage bankers further reduced spreads; deregulation and mortgage securitization may have finally eliminated them.[69]

Improving the geographic allocation of mortgage credit has been a goal of public policy at least since the establishment of FNMA in 1938. Mortgage securitization has already expanded interregional credit flows substantially. Freddie Mac participation certificates, for example, probably were the vehicle for transferring over $5 billion from the Northeast and Midwest to the Southwest and West in the course of a decade.[70]

The development of a national market also should facilitate geographic portfolio diversification and eliminate the problem of institutions' becoming insolvent because of local economic problems, such as the collapse of the Florida land boom in the late 1920s, when 40 percent of Florida S&Ls, with 50 percent of the assets, disappeared while the industry prospered nationwide,[71] or the decline in farm and energy prices that has hurt S&Ls in the Southwest in the 1980s.

The Mortgage Instrument. Since the late 1970s new mortgage instruments have been devised at an extraordinary rate. Consumers formerly could choose only the term to maturity, usually within a range of twenty-five to thirty years, and some combination of loan-to-value ratio and fixed interest rate. Since the bank board deregulated the instrument in 1981, options have broadened. Rates are adjustable, by a variety of mechanisms; terms offered by conventional lenders now range from seven to thirty years; semimonthly payments are available. Patric Hendershott and Kevin Villani foresee the mortgage turning into a line of credit: the interest rate will vary with the market, the maximum principal balance will vary with the market value of the house, and the concept of a repayment schedule will disappear.[72] The home equity loan can be seen as a step in this direction. Even if evolution does not proceed that far, further innovation can be expected.

The changes that have already occurred have reduced the importance of once-controversial regulations. The due-on-sale clause was rendered nearly innocuous by the ARM at about the same time that it was upheld by the Supreme Court and Congress, although renewed interest rate volatility could revive the issue legislatively. Prepayment penalties will become less important as refinancing becomes a less common means of adjusting either the principal or the interest rate.

The main role for public policy in the future is a negative one: to avoid inhibiting further developments in a misguided concern for consumers. The policy of deregulation in the 1980s has been a vast improvement over the 1970s, when Congress first effectively prohibited federally chartered S&Ls from making variable-rate mortgages and then tried to design specific alternative mortgage instruments of its own. The legislators apparently believed that they or their staffs knew more about mortgages than either lenders or borrowers.[73] In the array of new instruments, those congressional initiatives have proved to be non-starters.

At the same time, there have been some consumer problems with ARMs. Buyers have been qualified for loans on the basis of the initial rate, without regard to whether they can meet the payments if rates rise. The problem has been compounded by initial-year buydowns and teaser rates. Consumer groups' concerns about ARMs, which delayed their development in the 1970s, have proved to be overstated but not totally unfounded. The problems, however, are likely to be resolved through further technological progress in the mortgage market. It should be possible to provide reliable consumer information about alternative mortgages, under a variety of economic scenarios, through appropriate computer software. Computerization is beginning to affect the services provided by *Consumer Reports* and similar organizations, and some are beginning to provide data and evaluation of financial products such as individual retirement accounts (IRAs) and NOW accounts. These developments should eventually reduce default risk on the new instruments.

Securitization. As technology makes it possible to separate and repackage the income streams, mortgage-backed securities and mortgage instruments will undoubtedly undergo further change. Again, the role of public policy is mainly to avoid substituting political for market judgment. There is also perhaps a short-term objective of preventing insolvent S&Ls from investing in new forms of securities until the risks are better understood. But this temporary concern should not be the rationale for inhibiting innovation.[74]

Housing and the New System

Will this system "work"—that is, will it provide enough resources to housing? The answer obviously depends on how much is "enough." It seems likely, however, that the new system will be at least as effective as the current system has been. The evidence indicates that the housing finance system since the 1950s has not channeled resources into housing to any great extent; if the outcome has been politically satisfactory, the new system should be about equally successful.

The Availability of Mortgage Credit. Concern about an "adequate" supply of mortgage credit has been a continuing brake on policy changes in the housing finance system. If the traditional sources—especially the thrifts—do not provide funds, who will fill the gap? This question has in fact been posed in the marketplace, as thrifts have diversified out of mortgage lending. Since the early 1970s, nearly all the increase in the annual volume of mortgage lending (including multifamily and nonresidential loans) has been provided by institutions other than thrifts. Between 1984 and 1987, thrift institution holdings of mortgages and mortgage-backed securities accounted for about one-quarter of the total increase in mortgages outstanding.[75]

Despite the growing importance of nontraditional investors, government has not abandoned its efforts to fill the gap. FNMA has been a portfolio lender, and state and local governments have used their tax-exempt borrowing status to offer below-market mortgages. Neither supplies a large share of mortgage credit. One common way of defining the mortgage gap is to begin with an estimate of the demand for credit and subtract the likely supply of funds by thrifts.[76] Between 1970 and 1987, purchases by FNMA and other agencies constituted less than 10 percent of the increase in mortgage holdings by institutions other than thrifts. From 1978, when state and local governments began to issue tax-exempt mortgage revenue bonds, to 1987 the bonds filled less than 5 percent of the gap. There is no reason to anticipate a shortage of credit if these government agencies were to terminate their lending activities.

Mortgage Rates. The obverse of availability is cost. A substantial body of econometric research on the housing finance system has evaluated the effects of the federal secondary market agencies and the Federal Home Loan Bank System. The evidence is conflicting, but the bulk of it suggests that neither FHLBB advances nor secondary market agency activities stimulated housing production in the long run.[77] Dwight Jaffee and Kenneth Rosen, for example, analyzing the housing boom of the late 1970s, conclude that the high level of FNMA purchases had very little effect; they attribute much more importance to the introduction of the money market certificate as an S&L deposit instrument in 1978.[78]

Spreads between mortgage and bond rates have fluctuated. They narrowed sharply in the 1960s. Several analysts have attributed the narrowing to federal agency activity.[79] Spreads apparently widened during the 1970s and early 1980s, though the pattern is less clear cut and depends on the choice of the comparable bond rate.[80] John Tuccillo, Robert Van Order, and Kevin Villani attribute this increase in part to the integration of mortgage and capital markets as the specialized housing finance system began to unravel, and other analysts have predicted that the breakdown of the system would result in higher mortgage rates and bigger spreads.[81] If this has happened, it has been obscured by the greater volatility in the mortgage market and the growth of ARMs. It is difficult to measure the spread properly because of the additional options incorporated within the new instruments, but it is certainly safe to say that spreads have not widened substantially, and they may have fallen. The structure of interest rates is likely to change as the mortgage and capital markets change; if the spreads of the mid-1980s are reasonable indicators of the future, homebuyers should find that mortgage rates are manageable.

Housing Cycles. The integration of mortgage and capital markets does not mean the end of housing production cycles. When nominal mortgage rates are high, families are likely to postpone buying homes, causing construction to decline. This pattern prevailed after World War II before Reg Q was extended to S&Ls in 1966, and it will probably be the pattern again.

Cycles are likely to be less severe in the future, however. Deregulation should reduce the fluctuations in the availability and cost of mortgage money. There has not yet been a cyclical downturn since Reg Q was phased out, and the housing finance system is certainly different from what it was before 1966; but if the cycles of the 1990s are similar to the cycles of the 1950s, they will seem mild by recent experience.

Homeownership. After a dramatic increase during the 1940s and 1950s, the homeownership rate has moved in a narrow range since

1960. It rose from 60 to 62 percent by 1970 and to 65 percent by 1980; during the 1980s it has come down to about 63 percent. Evidence suggests that the tenure choice decision is sensitive to the relative cost of owning and renting, and the housing finance system has certainly been intended to lower the cost of homeownership, but it is doubtful if the system has had much effect.[82] The relative cost of homeownership declined from the early 1960s to the late 1970s, but the main reason for the decline was the rising rate of inflation, which reduced the real after-tax cost of owning.[83] The high interest rates of 1979 to 1982 coincided with the downturn in the homeownership rate. From 1982 to 1986, however, the homeownership rate came down, even though nominal and real mortgage rates declined.

This pattern primarily reflects inflationary expectations. In the 1970s, owning a home was the best widely available hedge against inflation. In the 1980s, there has been much less need for a hedge, and homes have not been a good investment; homeownership patterns are readjusting to an economy with low inflation. The decline in homeownership may also reflect the tax-rate reductions passed in 1981, which reduced the tax benefits of homeownership at the same time. If the housing finance system has had an effect during this period, it has been dominated by inflation and demographic trends.

Is Housing Special?

This chapter has largely accepted the policy judgment that housing deserves special treatment. It is worth considering, though, whether housing is special and, if it is, whether the housing finance system is an appropriate vehicle for achieving social purposes.

The argument for housing preferences is twofold: (1) the private market will produce less than the optimal amount of housing; (2) homeownership is socially desirable.

Neighborhood Effects. The former argument is based on the concept of externality. Higher-quality housing increases the value of neighboring property, but the owner is not compensated for the benefit he or she confers upon the neighbors. Therefore less than the socially optimal amount of housing will be produced.

This is the classic argument for a subsidy on grounds of economic efficiency. It is not necessarily an argument for a specialized housing finance system, however, or for any other specific form of subsidy. Edwin Mills, for example, regards it as justification for the income tax treatment of owner-occupied homes, but not for the magnitude or distribution of the tax savings.[84] He offers a conjecture that the external benefits amount to perhaps 5 to 15 percent; that is, a dollar spent to improve one house will raise the value of adjacent houses by five to fifteen cents. This suggests a tax deduction proportionate to the value of the house, rather than to the income of the occupant. Other economists have advocated a tax credit rather than the present deduction system, on equity grounds and because relatively low-income homeowners may not be able to itemize. The 1986 tax law takes a long step in this direction by lowering and flattening the rate schedule. The tax benefits for rental housing are less generous, but the disparity is less than often presumed. Owner-occupants do not pay taxes on their imputed rent and can typically escape capital gains taxation; landlords are able to depreciate their investment at a rate much in excess of true economic depreciation.

The point is not to determine the appropriate tax treatment of housing, but to show that the social benefits can be provided through the tax system rather than the housing finance system. Much of the literature finds that the tax system has been more effective.

Homeownership. The social desirability of homeownership was asserted without contradiction as justification for establishing the housing finance system, and the extraordinary increase in the homeownership rate in the 1940s and 1950s was hailed as evidence of its success. The idea that homeownership promotes social cohesion and stability is plausible and has been advanced by many politicians and policy analysts, including the founder of the American Economic Association, Richard T. Ely, but it has received little serious study.[85] It is clear from international comparisons that widespread homeownership is not a necessary condition for stable democracy; Switzerland, the oldest democracy in the world, has the lowest ownership rate in Western Europe.[86]

In the United States, there is some evidence that homeowners are "better citizens" in that they vote in greater proportions than renters, particularly in local elections. The value of greater political participation has never been quantified, though Raymond Struyk, reviewing the literature, judges it to be "probably quite modest."[87] This judgment is necessarily subjective, but it seems reasonable.

Like the social benefits of better housing, the benefits of homeownership can be provided through the tax system as well as the housing financial system.

The Decline in the Social Preference for Housing. The integration of housing finance with other financial markets has gone part way toward abrogating the social preference that housing has enjoyed in the

United States since the 1930s. Given the durability of that preference, it is surprising that within a decade, far-reaching reform has occurred without much complaint.

Moreover, it has occurred without discernible negative consequences for housing. Homeownership affordability has steadily improved since 1982. In late 1987 and early 1988 the affordability index of the National Association of Realtors reached its highest level since the mid-1970s. The relative decline in mortgage rates is one major reason. Rental vacancy rates have risen during the 1980s to the highest levels in twenty years. This change is probably primarily a consequence of the generous depreciation schedules in the 1981 tax law, more than offsetting any effect from the change in the housing finance system. Since the feared negative consequences have failed to materialize, there has been no political backlash to militate against further reform.

The change in public policy may reflect a change in public attitudes. During the housing boom of the late 1970s, there was widespread concern over the low rate of growth in the stock of capital and its effects on the American economy,[88] and some housing analysts were concerned about overinvestment in housing.[89] Housing has not been an issue in the last two presidential campaigns. In 1980, candidate Ronald Reagan gave one speech on housing, which went almost unreported; but it was one more speech than President Carter made. In 1984 neither candidate and neither party platform did more than mention housing in passing—even after several years of decline in the homeownership rate, particularly for young families, who were the focus of many policy proposals in the 1970s. The 1981–1982 recession, the most severe since World War II, was the first since the 1950s in which no countercyclical housing subsidy program was enacted.

There is surely still a substantial social preference for housing. That preference, however, need not be, and perhaps cannot any longer be, achieved by channeling credit to housing. The apparent willingness of the public to accept changes in the housing finance system should make it easier for policy makers to improve the whole financial system.

Notes

1. Leo Grebler, David M. Blank, and Louis Winnick, *Capital Formation in Residential Real Estate* (Princeton, N.J.: Princeton University Press, 1956), pp. 245–50.

2. Milton H. Semer, Julian H. Zimmerman, Ashley Foard, and John M. Frantz, "Evolution of Federal Legislative Policy in Housing: Housing Credits," in National Housing Policy Review, *Housing in the Seventies, Working Papers*,

vol. 1 (Washington, D.C.: U.S. Department of Housing and Urban Development, 1976), pp. 29–30.

3. Marriner S. Eccles, *Beckoning Frontiers* (New York: Knopf, 1951); and George D. Green, "The Ideological Origins of the Revolution in American Financial Policies," in Karl Brunner, ed., *The Great Depression Revisited* (Boston: Nijhoff, 1981).

4. See, for example, J. E. Morton, *Urban Mortgage Lending: Comparative Markets and Experience* (Princeton, N.J.: Princeton University Press, 1956).

5. R. J. Saulnier, Harold G. Halcrow, and Neil H. Jacoby, *Federal Lending and Loan Insurance* (Princeton, N.J.: Princeton University Press, 1958).

6. David L. Kaserman, "An Econometric Analysis of the Decline in Federal Mortgage Default Insurance," in Robert M. Buckley, John A. Tuccillo, and Kevin E. Villani, eds., *Capital Markets and the Housing Sector* (Cambridge, Mass.: Ballinger Publishing Co., 1977).

7. Grebler, Blank, and Winnick, *Capital Formation*, chap. 16 and appendix Q.

8. U.S. Department of Housing and Urban Development, *1986 Report to the Congress on the Federal National Mortgage Association*, June 1987.

9. These included long-term certificates of deposit (CDs) with a fixed rate above the passbook rate but still below market; jumbo CDs offering a high rate but an extremely high minimum; money market certificates (MMCs), with a market rate for a short term but a high minimum; and small-saver certificates, with a market rate on a low minimum but a long term. Money market mutual funds offered market rates for low minimums and withdrawal on demand.

10. DIDMCA permitted savings associations to put 20 percent of their assets in consumer loans, long-term corporate debt, and commercial paper; to expand their investment in service corporations from 1 to 3 percent of their assets; and to invest in mutual funds, issue credit cards, and engage in trust operations. The latter two powers placed thrifts in competition with commercial banks, if they chose to enter those lines of business. The Garn–St Germain Act further expanded asset powers, allowing S&Ls to invest an additional 20 percent of their assets in corporate or government securities.

11. U.S. President's Commission on Housing, *The Report of the President's Commission on Housing* (Washington, D.C., 1982).

12. James R. Barth, R. Dan Brumbaugh, Jr., Daniel Sauerhaft, and George H. K. Wang, "Insolvency and Risk-Taking in the Thrift Industry: Implications for the Future," *Contemporary Policy Issues*, vol. 3 (Fall 1985), pp. 1–32.

13. Andrew S. Carron, *The Rescue of the Thrift Industry* (Washington, D.C.: Brookings Institution, 1983).

14. In 1981 the bank board began to allow S&Ls to defer losses from the sale of below-market-rate mortgages for accounting purposes. In 1982 it allowed S&Ls to count as part of their net worth the difference between the appraised value and the book value of their office buildings, equipment, and land (appraised equity capital). In the same year, it created new types of assets for S&Ls that were losing their net worth—the income capital certificate and the net worth certificate. These were issued under authority granted by

the Garn–St Germain Act; the bank board could issue promissory notes to an S&L with low net worth, in exchange for certificates, up to the value of the S&L's operating loss. The certificates could be counted as net worth for purposes of meeting the bank board's net worth requirement, even though the condition of the institution was unaffected.

15. Barth et al., "Insolvency and Risk-Taking."

16. Bert Ely, "The FSLIC Recap Plan Is Bad Medicine for Healthy Thrifts and for the American Taxpayer" (Alexandria, Va.: Ely & Company, September 1987); and "S&Ls' Bailout Could Cost $40 Billion, Study Shows," *Wall Street Journal*, July 16, 1987, p. 7.

17. U.S. General Accounting Office, *Thrift Industry: Forbearance for Troubled Institutions, 1982–1986* (GAO/GGD-87-78BR, May 1987).

18. Federal Savings and Loan Advisory Council, Committee III, "Recapitalization of the FSLIC and Variable Rate Deposit Insurance Premiums," December 1985.

19. George J. Benston, *An Analysis of the Causes of Savings and Loan Association Failures*, Monograph 1985-4/5 (New York: Salomon Brothers Center for the Study of Financial Institutions, New York University, 1986).

20. James R. Barth and Martin A. Regalia, "The Evolving Role of Regulation in the Savings and Loan Industry" (Paper presented at the Fifth Annual Monetary Conference, Cato Institute, Washington, D.C., February 1987).

21. The law also appropriates $800 million to restore the secondary reserve of the FSLIC. This reserve consists of funds owned by the S&Ls but held by the FSLIC. In the spring of 1987 the FSLIC claimed the reserve to meet its liabilities, over the protests of the S&Ls. The law in effect returns the funds to the S&Ls; the additional $800 million does not go to the FSLIC. The recap is often described as $10.8 billion, but the new resources for the FSLIC amount to $10 billion.

22. Margaret E. Kriz, "Band-Aid Banking Law?" *National Journal*, August 15, 1987, pp. 2082–86; and Jeff Bailey and G. Christian Hill, "Banks and S&Ls Face New Wave of Failures As Regulators Goof Up," *Wall Street Journal*, March 25, 1988, p. 1.

23. Bert Ely, "Bailing Out the Federal Savings and Loan Insurance Corporation" (Alexandria, Va.: Ely & Company, July 1986).

24. This problem already arose when the bank board attempted to preserve the FSLIC by increasing insurance premiums; a special but continuing assessment of 12.5 basis points on assets, amounting to over $800 million, was imposed in 1985. This is 150 percent of the regular premium (8.33 basis points, over $500 million). The special assessment cuts into the profits of the sound S&Ls—by one estimate, it cut industry earnings by 21 percent in 1985—and makes it harder for them to attract capital. The industry has objected vigorously. See also Ely, "Bailing Out the Federal Savings and Loan Insurance Corporation."

25. Victor L. Saulsbury, "S&Ls' Costs of Conversion to FDIC Insurance," *Regulatory Review* (May/June 1987), pp. 1–12.

26. Robert Trigaux, "Seidman Says FDIC Fund at Record Low," *American Banker*, May 7, 1987.

27. Saulsbury, "S&Ls' Cost of Conversion."

28. Lawrence J. White, "Facing the Issues," *Outlook of the Federal Home Loan Bank System*, vol. 3 (May/June 1987), pp. 24–28.

29. The first public speeches of new Federal Home Loan Bank Board Chairman M. Danny Wall and member Lawrence J. White are examples; the former makes only a brief reference to housing finance and the latter makes none. See M. Danny Wall, "An Address to the National Press Club" (speech presented August 1987, Washington, D.C.); and White, "Facing the Issues."

30. National Council of Savings Institutions, *1986 National Fact Book of Savings Institutions*, (Washington, D.C.).

31. These figures are taken from the "Database" Supplement to Freddie Mac's magazine, *Secondary Mortgage Markets*. They are admittedly rough and do not account for the ownership of a substantial volume of securities, but they are as good a measure of trends as is available. The data begin in 1982. See A. Thomas King and David Andrukonis, "Who Holds PCs?" *Secondary Mortgage Markets*, vol. 1 (February 1984), pp. 12–17.

32. George Hanc, "Is There a Future for Thrifts?" *Bottomline*, vol. 4 (March 1987).

33. In April 1987, Home Federal Savings of San Diego applied to the state of California for a charter as a commercial bank and simultaneously applied for deposit insurance from the FDIC. This action is apparently at least partly motivated by concern about an "exit fee" imposed by the bank board to protect the FSLIC, but Home Federal is already competing with California commercial banks in trust services, consumer finance, and corporate banking. Home Federal's president is quoted as saying, "We basically operate as a bank now." Michael Kinsman, "HomeFed Quitting FSLIC," *National Thrift News*, April 6, 1987.

34. Dwight M. Jaffee, "The Future Role of Thrift Institutions in Mortgage Lending," in *The Future of the Thrift Industry* (Federal Reserve Bank of Boston Conference Series no. 24, October 1981).

35. Raymond J. Struyk, Neil Mayer, and John A. Tuccillo, *Federal Housing Policy and President Reagan's Midterm* (Washington, D.C.: Urban Institute Press, 1983).

36. The increase in the thrifts' maximum tax rate to 31 percent had already occurred before tax reform, when the bad debt deduction was cut to 32 percent in 1984. The purpose of the changes in 1986 was to keep the thrifts' tax rate constant; the cut in the bad debt deduction from 32 to 8 percent exactly offset the reduction in the maximum corporate tax rate. For further discussion of the tax treatment of thrifts, see John A. Tuccillo with John L. Goodman, Jr., *Housing Finance: A Changing System in the Reagan Era* (Washington, D.C.: Urban Institute Press, 1983); and Barth and Regalia, "The Evolving Role of Regulation."

37. James R. Barth, R. Dan Brumbaugh, Jr., Daniel Sauerhaft, and George H. K. Wang, "Thrift-Institution Failures: Estimating the Regulator's Closure Rule" (Washington, D.C.: Federal Home Loan Bank Board Research Working Paper no. 125, January 1987); and Benston, *Analysis of the Causes of Failures*.

38. James J. Clarke, "An Interest Rate Risk Analysis of the Federal National

Mortgage Association," in U.S. General Accounting Office, *The Federal National Mortgage Association in a Changing Economic Environment* (GAO/RCED-85-102A, July 17, 1985).

39. U.S. Department of Housing and Urban Development, *1986 Report on FNMA*.

40. Edward J. Kane and Chester Foster, *Valuing and Eliminating Subsidies Associated with Conjectural Government Guarantees of FNMA Liabilities* (Working Paper 86-71, College of Administrative Science, Ohio State University, May 1986).

41. U.S. Department of Housing and Urban Development, *1986 Report on FNMA*.

42. U.S. General Accounting Office, *The Federal National Mortgage Association in a Changing Economic Environment*, chap. 4; and Leon T. Kendall, statement before the Senate Banking Committee, February 17, 1987, p. 4.

43. Tuccillo with Goodman, *Housing Finance*.

44. Federal Home Loan Bank of San Francisco, Economics Department, "The Historical and Contemporary Role of the Federal Home Loan Mortgage Corporation in Housing Finance" (Paper prepared for the Federal Savings and Loan Advisory Council, June 1986).

45. Dennis J. Jacobe, "Should the Restrictions on Freddie Mac Preferred Stock Trading Be Removed?" (Unpublished paper, June 1986).

46. Congressional Budget Office, *The Housing Finance System and Federal Policy: Recent Changes and Options for the Future*, October 1983; and Anthony Downs, *The Revolution in Real Estate Finance* (Washington, D.C.: Brookings Institution, 1985).

47. U.S. President's Commission on Housing, *Report*; and Tuccillo with Goodman, *Housing Finance*.

48. U.S. Department of Housing and Urban Development, *1986 Report on FNMA*.

49. Ibid., p. 150.

50. Leo Grebler, "An Assessment of the Performance of the Public Sector in the Residential Housing Market: 1955–1974," in Buckley, Tuccillo, and Villani, *Capital Markets and the Housing Sector*; and Dwight M. Jaffee and Kenneth T. Rosen, "Mortgage Credit Availability and Residential Construction," *Brookings Papers on Economic Activity*, no. 2 (1979), pp. 333–86.

51. Herbert M. Kaufman, "FNMA and the Housing Cycle: Its Recent Contribution and Its Future Role in a Deregulated Environment," in U.S. General Accounting Office, *The Federal National Mortgage Association in a Changing Economic Environment*, pp. 41–74. Kaufman's study covers only the period since 1979; he does not analyze earlier periods. His model is similar to Jaffee and Rosen's (see Jaffee and Rosen, "Mortgage Credit Availability"), but results for a longer period might have yielded a different conclusion.

52. Richard B. Clemmer, "Fannie Mae and Its Relationship to Low- and Moderate-Income Families," in *The Federal National Mortgage Association in a Changing Economic Environment*.

53. Downs, *The Revolution in Real Estate Finance*.

54. Kane and Foster, *Valuing and Eliminating Subsidies*.

THE FUTURE OF THE HOUSING FINANCE SYSTEM

55. Freddie Mac Advisory Committee Task Force, "Report,"October 1986; and Jacobe, "Should the Restrictions Be Removed?"
56. John M. Quigley, "What Have We Learned about Urban Housing Markets?" in Peter Mieszkowski and Mahlon Straszheim, eds., *Current Issues in Urban Economics* (Baltimore, Md.: Johns Hopkins University Press, 1979).
57. Patric H. Hendershott and James D. Shilling, "The Economics of Tenure Choice, 1955–1979," in C. F. Sirmans, ed., *Research in Real Estate,* vol. 1 (1982), pp. 105–33; and John C. Weicher, Susan M. Wachter, and William B. Shear, "Housing as an Asset in the 1980s and 1990s," *Housing Finance Review,* vol. 7 (Summer 1988), pp. 169–200.
58. A small part of FNMA's portfolio, about $6 billion, consists of mortgages on multifamily projects in federal low-income housing programs. See Downs, *The Revolution in Real Estate Finance.* FNMA was required to purchase them to support the programs. This form of subsidy is inefficient and complicates the agency's operations as a secondary market maker. The mortgages should be sold to the Treasury at a price compensating FNMA for the subsidy it has provided.
59. Edward J. Kane, "Discussion," in U.S. General Accounting Office, *The Federal National Mortgage Association in a Changing Economic Environment*; and U.S. Department of Housing and Urban Development, *1986 Report on FNMA.*
60. Kane and Foster, *Valuing and Eliminating Subsidies.*
61. U.S. Department of Housing and Urban Development, *1986 Report on FNMA.*
62. Kane and Foster, *Valuing and Eliminating Subsidies.*
63. Freddie Mac Advisory Committee Task Force, "Report,"appendix I, p. 10.
64. Downs, *The Revolution in Real Estate Finance.*
65. John C. Weicher, "Summary of Symposium Proceedings," in U.S. General Accounting Office, *The Federal National Mortgage Association in a Changing Economic Environment,* p. 25.
66. Federal Home Loan Bank of San Francisco, "Historical and Contemporary Role of the Federal Home Loan Mortgage Corporation."
67. James R. Follain, "The Experience of the U.S. Secondary Mortgage Market: Born in a Regulated Environment but Flourishing in a Competitive One" (Office of Real Estate Research Paper no. 50, University of Illinois, Urbana-Champaign, September 1987).
68. Grebler, Blank, and Winnick, *Capital Formation,* pp. 229–30.
69. Marvin J. Karson, Patricia M. Rudolph, and Leonard V. Zumpano, "Inter-Regional Differences in Conventional Mortgage Terms: A Test of the Efficiency of the Residential Mortgage Market" (Paper presented at the American Real Estate and Urban Economics Association meeting, December 1986).
70. King and Andrukonis, "Who Holds PCs?"
71. Morton Bodfish, *History of Building and Loan in the United States* (Chicago: United States Building and Loan League, 1931).
72. Patric H. Hendershott and Kevin E. Villani, "Housing Finance in America in the Year 2001," in George W. Gau and Michael A. Goldberg, eds., *North American Housing Markets into the Twenty-first Century* (Cambridge, Mass.: Ballinger Publishing Co., 1982). See also Edward J. Kane, "Change and

Progress in Contemporary Mortgage Markets," *Housing Finance Review*, vol. 3 (July 1984), pp. 257–84.

73. John C. Weicher, *Housing: Federal Policies and Programs* (Washington, D.C.: American Enterprise Institute, 1980).

74. White, "Facing the Issues."

75. Dennis E. Bennett, "The Impact of Government Sponsored Mortgage Agencies on Thrift Institutions" (Paper presented at the American Real Estate and Urban Economics Association annual meeting, Chicago, December 1987).

76. Dwight M. Jaffee and Kenneth T. Rosen, "The Demand for Housing and Mortgage Credit: The Mortgage Credit Gap Problem," in *Housing Finance in the Eighties: Issues and Options*, FNMA Symposium (Washington, D.C., 1981), pp. 6–19.

77. Grebler, "Assessment of the Performance of the Public Sector"; and Richard F. Muth, "The Supply of Mortgage Lending," *Urban Economics*, vol. 19 (January 1986), pp. 88–106.

78. Jaffee and Rosen, "Mortgage Credit Availability."

79. Timothy Q. Cook, "The Residential Mortgage Market in Recent Years," *Federal Reserve Bank of Richmond Economic Review* (September/October 1974), pp. 3–18; and Patric H. Hendershott, *Understanding Capital Markets*, vol. 1, *A Flow-of-Funds Financial Model* (Lexington, Mass.: Lexington Books, 1977).

80. The studies cited in the text use Moody's Aa bond rate and combine FNMA and FHLBS into a single variable. The spread between the effective conventional mortgage rate on new homes and Moody's Aaa bond rate declined until 1975, while the spread against the Aa bond rate fell more sharply in the 1960s but began rising after 1970. George Kaufman has argued that the corporate bond rate is not the relevant comparable rate. He compared the effective FHA rate with the ten-year Treasury rate, concluding that there was no downward trend in the spread during the 1960s or upward trend during the 1970s. (See George Kaufman, "Impact of Deregulation on the Mortgage Market," in *Housing Finance in the Eighties*, pp. 94–104.) If the conventional mortgage rate is compared with the Treasury rate, however, the spread declined, albeit erratically, into the 1970s. Hendershott, Shilling, and Villani calculate that spreads between Treasury bonds and secondary market securities rose from 1974 to 1982, partly because increased interest rate volatility increased the value of prepayment to borrowers. (See Patric H. Hendershott, James D. Shilling, and Kevin E. Villani, "Measurement of the Spreads between Yields on Various Mortgage Contracts and Treasury Securities," *AREUEA Journal*, vol. 11 [Winter 1984], pp. 476–89.)

81. John A. Tuccillo, Robert Van Order, and Kevin Villani, "Homeownership Policies and Mortgage Markets, 1960 to 1980," *Housing Finance Review*, vol. 1 (February 1982), pp. 1–21; Downs, *The Revolution in Real Estate Finance*; and Jaffee, "The Future Role of Thrift Institutions."

82. Hendershott and Shilling, "The Economics of Tenure Choice"; and Weicher, Wachter, and Shear, "Housing as an Asset."

83. Patric H. Hendershott, "Real User Costs and the Demand for Single-Family Housing," *Brookings Papers on Economic Activity*, no. 2 (1980), pp. 401–44.

84. Edwin S. Mills, "Housing Policy as a Means to Achieve National

Growth Policy," in National Housing Policy Review, *Housing in the Seventies: Working Papers* (Washington, D.C.: U.S. Department of Housing and Urban Development, 1976), vol. 1, pp. 202–14.

85. Marc A. Weiss, *Own Your Own Home: The American Real Estate Industry and National Housing Policy* (Cambridge, Mass.: Lincoln Institute of Land Policy, 1987), chap. 6.

86. Mark Boleat, *National Housing Finance Systems: A Comparative Study* (London: Croom Helm, 1985), pp. 460–63.

87. Raymond J. Struyk, *Should Government Encourage Homeownership?* (Washington, D.C.: Urban Institute, 1977), p. 27. There is also evidence that homeowners more often vote for Republican and conservative candidates and against tax increases. (See *Public Opinion* magazine, September/October 1986.) Whether this is a social benefit or not is for the reader to decide.

88. Herbert Stein, "Economic Fashions of the Times, 1977–1987," *AEI Economist*, October 1987.

89. Edward H. Ladd, "Discussion," in *The Future of the Thrift Industry* (Boston: Federal Reserve Bank of Boston Conference Series no. 24, October 1981); and Downs, *The Revolution in Real Estate Finance*.

Commentary
Bert Ely

Dr. Weicher's paper is excellent and well worth reading. It deals in depth with both sets of specialized housing finance lenders: thrift institutions, principally savings and loan associations, and the federally sponsored secondary mortgage market agencies. The paper weaves in various housing finance public policy issues as well. It also provides a valuable historical context for the issues it discusses and is laced with many cogent insights.

The paper poses three sequential questions that must be considered when addressing the structure of housing finance. Is housing special? If so, does its specialness warrant a government subsidy? If it does, is a specialized housing finance system the best way to deliver that subsidy, or would another mechanism, such as the tax system or needs-based cash grants, be a better way? While this paper does not provide hard and fast answers, the author's leanings are quite clear.

Specialized Housing Finance Lenders. The paper correctly identifies Federal Reserve System interest rate controls, or Regulation Q, as an early indicator that inflationary pressures eventually would materially weaken the economic foundations of savings and loan associations. Regulation Q signaled the susceptibility of thrifts to inflation by capping the cost of funds for savings and loan associations, thus lessening the impact of rising interest rates on thrift profitability. In effect, Regulation Q postponed the day of reckoning with the fundamental flaw of savings and loans—borrowing short to lend long. This flaw is greatly magnified when thrifts hold unhedged, thirty-year fixed-rate mortgages. Because of Regulation Q we are twenty years late in beginning to confront the structural problems of the thrift industry and of housing finance.

The paper should be expanded, however, to include more discussion about the recent problems of asset quality among many thrifts. These problems are causing the prospective insolvency losses of the Federal Savings and Loan Insurance Corporation (FSLIC) to skyrocket. Problems of asset quality have been driven in part by the regional and sectoral deflation of recent years, which has created pressures comparable to those of the deflation that was such a bank killer during the Great Depression. Other factors have contributed to the problems: regulatory failures, tax-driven overbuilding of commercial real estate, and mismanagement and fraud. Thrift mismanagement should not surprise anyone, however, for poor management has been endemic in almost all regulated industries.

Secondary Mortgage Market Agencies. The paper brings an appropriate skepticism to assessing each of the three purported public purposes of the three federally sponsored secondary mortgage market agencies—the Federal National Mortgage Association (Fannie Mae), the Federal Home Loan Mortgage Corporation (Freddie Mac), and the Government National Mortgage Association (Ginnie Mae).

The first public purpose, innovation and demonstration, is based on an interesting, unproven, and therefore presumptuous conceit: public agencies are better innovators than the private sector. The paper points out, however, that subsidies and wealth transfers so thoroughly infuse these agencies' innovations that it is difficult to assess their economic payoff. Moreover, we will never know what innovations the private sector would have developed in the absence of these agencies.

We must, then, ask, How beneficial have some of these innovations really been? Has the thirty-year fixed-rate mortgage benefited savings and loans institutions and their deposit insurer, FSLIC? Has the growth of Fannie Mae into America's largest savings and loan been desirable if, during the next period of high interest rates, it again becomes insolvent on the basis of the market value of its assets? Has the continuing dominance of the secondary mortgage markets by these agencies hindered or sidetracked needed refinements in the securitization process?

With regard to the second public purpose, countercyclical activities, the paper makes the excellent point that whatever countercyclical help these agencies provided in the past, it is largely impossible for them to render any such help today because of deregulation and the increasing integration of housing finance into the international capital markets. But even more basic questions must be raised about countercyclical activities of any kind: Do they merely exaggerate problems elsewhere in the economy? Do they distort capital flows? Do they cause unintended shifts in wealth?

With regard to the third public purpose, assisting the low-income home buyer, the paper makes this crucial, yet often ignored observation: While the low-income home buyer usually has a lower income than the typical home buyer, he or she usually has a higher income than the typical family. Thus this financial assistance goes right into the middle of the middle class. As America's dawning austerity forces a reexamination of heretofore sacrosanct subsidies for the middle class, this form of assistance should be among the first candidates for the guillotine.

This section of the paper could be strengthened with more discussion of the after-tax cost of financing a home purchase and the effect of tax law changes on this cost. For instance, the scheduled decline in the maximum personal income tax rate will probably have a greater effect on housing costs for many people than what is going on within the structure of housing finance.

Privatizing the Secondary Mortgage Market Agencies. The paper's discussion of the privatization of Fannie Mae and Freddie Mac makes two important but easily overlooked points: One, no matter how it is done, it is going to be a messy, complicated process. Two, it must be done quickly and with finality to avoid the later unwinding or compromise so common in the political process.

The paper suggests several ways to privatize the two agencies. I would like to suggest another alternative: immediately separate the old from the new. Here is how it would work. From a specified date place all new loans and guarantees made by an agency into a portfolio that would be a completely private sector activity operating without any implicit or explicit federal guarantees, access to the Treasury, agency status, and so on. All its funding would be raised in the private capital markets. Thus it would begin life as a private sector entity on both the asset and the liability sides of its balance sheet.

Meanwhile, a long-term liquidation of the old portfolio's assets and liabilities would commence. Existing assets would be run off, but no new ones would be added. Liabilities used to fund the old portfolio, including rollovers and refundings, would continue to carry whatever agency status they had in the past. The staff of the agency would serve both portfolios, obviously devoting increasing attention to the new, private sector activity. Stockholders in Fannie Mae and Freddie Mac would have equity interests in both their agency's portfolios. Housing subsidy programs now funded or run by these agencies would be shifted to the Department of Housing and Urban Development.

As we consider the privatization issue, we should be aware that innovations in financial technology may be making the secondary agencies obsolete as enhancers of credit. Senior/subordinated debt structures, for example, may be a more efficient way to minimize the credit risk premium that has to be incorporated in the interest rate on home mortgages.

The paper makes only brief mention of a fourth federal housing finance vehicle—the twelve federal home loan banks. These banks are able to provide relatively cheap financing to savings and loan institutions by virtue of having the status of federal agencies. As housing finance becomes increasingly integrated into the overall capital markets, a growing political question will become, Who gets access to these banks? Increasingly, large thrifts are the principal beneficiaries of the banks. At mid-1987 the banks funded $74.9 billion, or 10.1 percent, of the assets of the 224 FSLIC-insured thrifts with assets over $1 billion. In sharp contrast, the smallest 358 FSLIC-insured thrifts, with assets under $25 million, obtained only $94 million, or 1.7 percent, of their total funding from the banks.

Do big institutions, including the large thrifts, need funding help from the federal government? I doubt it. Moreover, using a quasi-governmental agency to provide what is effectively permanent funding for thrifts is very much at odds with the well-established policy of the Federal Reserve System *not* to provide discount window advances to banks on a continuing basis. Thus, if the need for specialized, federally prescribed housing finance agencies is drawing to a close, as appears to be the case, what future is there for the federal home loan banks? Very little, in my opinion. Furthermore, while there may be something to privatize at Fannie Mae and Freddie Mac, that does not appear to be the case with these twelve banks.

What the Future Holds. Weicher's paper offers some interesting visions for the future by discussing forces reshaping the marketplace for housing finance, forces that are increasingly beyond the control of the political marketplace.

The paper points out that financial and electronic technology is creating a national mortgage market. Of perhaps greater import, that technology increasingly provides worldwide funding for that marketplace. The paper also discusses how mortgage instruments are continuing to evolve. These instruments, for example, are increasingly shaped to meet securitization requirements. Of longer-term consequence, they may be evolving into a permanent line of credit, much like a home equity loan, with more flexible amortization requirements or perhaps none at all.

The paper draws some important conclusions regarding housing finance that have major implications for the future: One, the cost of housing credit, not its availability, now controls housing finance. Two, housing no longer has its own credit-driven cycles. Three, the housing ownership percentage today is primarily a function of demographics and overall income and wealth. Four—and most relevant to this volume—the rationale for a statutorily separate housing finance system is rapidly disappearing.

A key to the future of housing finance is the changing economics of the intermediation process. This change is the major force integrating housing finance into the overall capital markets. Specifically, securitization is narrowing lending spreads to the point that many thrifts will not survive very far into the 1990s. This loss of viability under almost any interest rate scenario will trigger the next and perhaps final crisis to strike the thrift industry. I call it the consolidation crisis. This crisis will strike hardest at the muddling middle: savings and loans solvent and profitable today but totally unprepared for the future.

The need for operating efficiencies will drive consolidation. The cost of operating institutions insured by the FSLIC and FDIC, now 2.6 percent of gross national product, will shrink. The $58 billion now invested in premises and equipment at banks and thrifts may also decline.

Consolidation will occur at three levels. First, the declining viability of branch offices will force their consolidation. Today we have over 85,000 bank and thrift offices. According to a recent Booz-Allen study, as many as half of them are unprofitable. The weakening capital bases of both the bank and the thrift industries cannot long tolerate these losses. Office closings and consolidations are inevitable as the total number of banking offices starts to shrink, much as the number of gasoline stations began to decline in the early 1970s after decades of growth.

Second, declining profitability and consolidation of branch offices will trigger consolidation at the organization level. Today's 14,000 bank and thrift organizations (banks, thrifts, and bank and thrift holding companies) will decline sharply in number as the weaker among them are merged or liquidated and as nationwide interstate banking becomes a reality.

Finally, marketplace forces will merge the commercial bank and thrift regulatory structures. Preceding this event may be some sort of merger of the FDIC and the FSLIC, although a sudden, crisis-driven merger will not be desirable for anyone.

The consolidation process will unfortunately have high transition costs as the going concern value of failing banks and thrifts evaporates. Stockholders will bear much of this cost, but so too will the deposit insurance funds. Consequently, consolidation will add billions more to the $50 billion of accumulated insolvency losses now confronting the FSLIC; it also will be very costly to the FDIC. The taxpayers' bailout of the FSLIC may become the catalyst for fundamental restructuring of the entire housing finance system.

Once the FSLIC bailout occurs, America may be ready to address the ultimate regulatory and structural issue for depository institutions: creating a true deposit insurance mechanism that constrains unwarranted risk taking by depository institutions. This mechanism will have to constrain risk taking through pricing rather than through regulatory processes that have long since exceeded their limits of effectiveness.

9
How Market Forces Influence the Structure of Financial Regulation
Edward J. Kane

This chapter analyzes the process of financial regulatory reform. The analysis asks and answers three central questions: Why does financial regulation exist? Why have government entities come to dominate the field? What changes in the framework of financial regulation would let private regulators compete on a more nearly equal footing with government regulators?

The chapter argues that a market for financial regulatory services exists precisely because the perceived quality of a financial services firm's products depends on the confidence and convenience that customers find in them. Because confidence and convenience are inherently system goods, they can be produced more efficiently (that is, at lower cost) with the help of a credible outside party.

Secular growth in government suppliers' share of the market for financial regulation is due not to greater productive efficiency but to reputational capital conferred by government sponsorship. Reputational capital adds weight both to government managers' explanatory statements and to their agencies' stated net worth positions. First, because the press and public trust the statements of government officials more than those of private regulators, the officials can undertake institutionally self-interested management of the flow of information about the costs and quality of their agencies' performance. Second, statutory provisions suggesting even tenuous government control create off-balance-sheet sources of contingent financial

---

Although the opinions expressed are my own, many parties have contributed criticisms that helped to shape this analysis. I want particularly to acknowledge extensive comments received from Ernest Bloch, Richard Herring, Robert Hetzel, and participants in the AEI Financial Markets Project.

strength that facilitate competitive strategies of offering regulatory clients long-lived subsidies that are predatory in their effects. Both advantages reflect agency problems that taxpayers as principals have inadvertently permitted to develop in their relations with jurisdiction-maximizing regulators and elected politicians.

These agency problems exist because misinformed taxpayers cannot appropriately constrain the economic deficits that government regulators run in competing with other regulators for potential clients. Defective profitability constraints permit government regulators to drive out marginal private regulators without facing up immediately or directly to the economic losses a predatory marketing strategy confers on their enterprise. After a long lag, losses from predation manifest themselves indirectly in the form of emerging policy crises. When such crises occur, government managers mine them for additional jurisdiction by claiming that they need new powers and larger budgets to bring the situation back under control

To allow private financial regulators to compete more nearly equally with government ones, we must constrain government regulators and politicians to play fair with one another and with taxpayers. A minimum first step is to force, under explicit penalties for fraud, a full accounting to taxpayers of all economic costs (implicit as well as explicit) generated by each agency's operations and commitments. The idea is to force government managers to calculate as competently as they can the true market value of any economic losses inherent in their operations. A further bureaucratic reform would be to assign the Office of Management and Budget the task of analyzing the appropriateness of the reported pattern of implicit and explicit expenditures.

The reforms promoted in this chapter focus on information systems and are generic rather than specific. This focus reflects the author's conviction that recommending and promoting a specific combination of reforms pushes a public policy economist to go beyond his or her narrow professional expertise in ways that distort the policy debate and narrow nonexperts' perception of the range of opportunities for reform. It is in identifying inefficient and inequitable policies and policy structures and in finding convincing ways to frame sources of inefficiency and inequity that a public policy economist can be socially most useful.

As in economic modeling generally, the distortion involved in advocating a specific set of reforms seldom embodies any sinister purpose to deceive. The object of most simplifications is expositional: to clear away what are presumed to be confusing second-order aspects of problems under examination. The polemical and distributional consequences of an uninvolved theorist's expositional assumptions are usually crystal clear to parties who have a concentrated stake in the outcome of the debate, who use or attack those assumptions as suits their purposes.

The following pages concentrate on explaining how interindustry, interregional, and international competition among alternative suppliers of financial regulatory services shapes the structure of financial regulation. The equilibrium industrial organization of these suppliers and secular changes in the framework of regulations are portrayed as resulting less from the personal intervention of influential decision makers than from the impersonal hand of market forces.

Regulatory Market Structure

Perhaps because of the economics profession's well-known preference for free markets, economists have typically viewed regulation as an *extramarket* activity. According to this view, regulation is created politically either to serve specific distributional interests or to correct a market failure. This chapter seeks to show that, at least in the financial sector, broad market forces drive the regulation process. Economic efficiency requires that financial services be produced jointly with external regulatory services designed to promote customer confidence and to superimpose and coordinate cooperative activity by competitors aimed at increasing customer convenience.

The analysis emphasizes, however, that regulatory services are not necessarily produced most efficiently by governmental bodies. Government's predominant role in the financial sector of modern economies flows from financial and marketing advantages that government sponsorship confers on an enterprise. At the same time the logically prior economic need for financial regulatory services creates political opportunities to develop governmentally sponsored enterprises to effect redistributions of income that interest groups in and out of government cannot help but recognize.

During the past year the *American Banker* has headlined three stories that juxtapose and integrate a political creationist and a market-driven evolutionist conception of regulatory structure. The first story tracks the financial community's response to a sweeping proposal by E. Gerald Corrigan, a leading Federal Reserve official and presumptive policy creator, to restructure the U.S. financial services industry and regulatory apparatus along what may be called European (and now Canadian) lines.[1] Corrigan's plan would permit financial services holding companies to operate all kinds of financial businesses but keep banking separate from nonfinancial commerce. To

HOW MARKET FORCES INFLUENCE REGULATION

nurture this separation, he proposes to limit access to the payments system and discount window by nondepository institutions and to expose any corporate entity that makes use of these facilities to consolidated supervision by the Federal Reserve. A counterproposal issued by the Federal Deposit Insurance Corporation (FDIC) six months later claims that it would be advantageous to locate new activities in bank subsidiaries rather than in holding company affiliates.[2] This controversy over the structural location of a bank's "nonbanking" business helps to clarify the dimensions of regulatory domain at stake in restructuring federal financial regulation.

The second story concerns the big role that state legislatures and banking departments have been playing in reshaping the nation's financial arena. Individual states have expanded the range of activities permissible for deposit institutions chartered by them to include such nontraditional lines of business as insurance and securities underwriting, real estate development, and equity investment.

The third story focuses on the growing stature of a lobbying coalition known originally as the Mayflower Group. This coalition, now named the Financial Services Council, combines major retailers, an automobile manufacturer, and various large banks. Its purpose is to work on behalf of firms in historically different industries to eliminate government restrictions on their ability to compete directly in banking, insurance, securities, and real estate markets. The diverse industrial origins of the coalition's members underscore how, when technological change makes the burdens generated by inherited regulatory structures increasingly less tolerable, regulated competitors can recognize common interests and band together politically to press on competing regulators mutually beneficial proposals designed to lessen their common regulatory burdens.

All three stories are framed as if governmental dominance of the financial regulatory process in the United States were inevitable. None of the stories, however, mentions that the Federal Reserve and the FDIC are in competition not only with each other but with foreign and state regulators or that state legislatures are in competition—with Congress and federal bureaucrats, with foreign regulators, and with one another—for the business of regulating the innovative financial activities of firms represented in the Financial Services Council. Nevertheless, a competitive perspective immediately organizes the three stories into a coherent pattern of regulatory market activity. Defining the relevant markets, the participants, and their motives is the first task of this chapter.

Some Definitions. Financial regulatory services consist of efforts to monitor, discipline, or coordinate the behavior of individual financial services firms to achieve some greater good. To analyze financial regulatory reform as a market-driven process, we must establish a correspondence between the concepts featured in theories of market behavior and the phenomena of regulatory activity. Although political analysis can be satisfied to depict regulators as altruistic persons selflessly performing community service, economics seeks to root such behavior in market incentives and satisfaction of individual wants.

Financial regulatory services are produced and delivered by private as well as governmental entities. Private regulators range from independent financial analysts, auditors, and credit-rating agencies to cooperative self-regulatory organizations such as clearinghouses, securities or commodities exchanges, accounting standards boards, and trade associations. Private regulators are supplemented, overseen, and sometimes superseded by specialized national, subnational, foreign, and even international governmental agencies.

If regulation is a business, each firm may be divided conceptually into production, marketing, and finance divisions. Similarly, alternative suppliers may be conceived as an industry, whose member firms battle one another for regulatory profit and market share. Competing firms operate on different levels (national, subnational, and supranational) and include elected politicians, governmental regulatory agencies, government-sponsored corporations, and various private regulators.

In most Western countries the fairness and legitimacy of private and governmental regulatory actions are subject to legislative oversight and judicial review. Although the regulatory jurisdictions of a country's financial regulators typically overlap to some degree, a dominant firm can usually be identified. In many countries this is the central bank. As a nation's most far-reaching financial regulator and stabilizer of last resort, the central bank's ability to enter any regulatory submarket in emergencies and to evoke top-level government support for its actions often permits it to impose a degree of cartel-like discipline on other members of its country's domestic financial regulatory industry. Every country's dominant domestic regulator must recognize, however, that it is constrained by its need to compete for regulatory business with regulators from other countries.

Changes in regulatory market structure often spring from supply-side innovations in regulatory pricing, production, financing, and marketing. Pricing innovations change the pattern of implicit or explicit charges or subsidies that a regulator establishes for its clients. Production innovations change the quality of the regulatory services a regulator produces or the services' explicit and implicit costs of production. Financing innovations reduce at least the explicit costs of financing an agency's unfunded expenditures. Marketing innovations seek to change public perceptions of the need for regulation and of the effectiveness of rival suppliers. To analyze regulatory innovations, it is helpful to conceive of individual regulatory entities as multiproduct firms and to employ the Baumol-Panzar-Willig paradigm of imperfectly contestable markets.[3]

A market may be defined as a body of persons carrying on extensive and at least partly voluntary transactions in a specific good or service. William Baumol, John C. Panzar, and Robert Willig define an individual market as perfectly contestable when the costs of entering or exiting that market are zero. In any such market the threat of hit-and-run entry by outside potential competitors can be counted on to hold the profit margin sought by incumbent firms to competitive levels, irrespective of the number of incumbents or of how highly concentrated the share of industry output produced by the few largest competitors happens to be.

Regulatory services are typically delivered in the context of a continuing client relationship rather than sold transaction by transaction. Much as medical patients do, regulated firms contract for a range of contingent services without haggling specifically over the prices at which individual services are obtained. Nevertheless, in an important sense, at least some of a regulator's clients are always shopping for better deals. Whenever a customer becomes concerned that its traditional supplier's prices stack up poorly against the competition, it must study its options for switching some or all of its business to a new supplier. In practice its doing so may be conceived primarily as a threat that puts pressure on its current principal supplier to negotiate more favorable prices or improved service.

Specifying Regulators' Goals and Constraints. Markets for regulatory services are demonstrably not *perfectly* contestable. Significant exit costs exist. Because they can conceal implicit losses, almost no matter how economically unprofitable their operations may become, government regulators can passionately resist exit. On the other side of the market, regulated firms that try to switch to a new supplier of regulatory services often incur substantial transition costs.

My purpose is to explain as endogenous variables what and whom various regulators control. The analysis focuses on the response of regulated entities and regulators to exogenous and endogenous decreases in the costs of entry into and exit from financial product markets. It portrays expansion by suppliers of financial regulatory services into new product lines and geographic markets as following and supporting rivalry between client firms within and across countries, regions, and administrative boundaries. Supplementing strictly bureaucratic theories of regulatory behavior (such as that of William Niskanen), my model takes as its motive force regulators' efforts—subject to a potentially defective long-run profitability constraint—to extend or to defend their share of the market for regulatory services in the face of exogenous and endogenous disturbances in the economic environment.[4]

In this contestable-markets conception the demand for a particular regulator's services is a derived demand. A regulator's market share is the proportion of total financial services business captured by firms that fall within its jurisdiction. To make this concept operational, it is necessary to define a way to adjust for the extent to which jurisdiction in particular markets is effectively shared with other regulators. Analytically, what is important is to employ a conception that permits each regulator's share to rise and fall with surplus and deficit spending units' worldwide consumption of the financial services produced by its regulatory clientele. A straightforward approach that I adopt provisionally here is to allocate the shared business according to the relative expenses the various regulators incur in overseeing the shared activities.

Promotional Strategies: Addictive Subsidization and Crisis Mining. In promoting the demand for its services, a government regulator possesses complementary marketing and financial advantages over competing private regulators. These advantages flow from its potential for co-opting the government and therefore the taxpayer into backing up its liabilities and public statements. Government regulators' conjectural support from rational politicians helps to explain both why private financial regulators tend secularly to lose market share to governmental ones and why government expenditure tends to grow secularly as a proportion of gross national product.

It is convenient to think of an agency's clientele as contributing a stream of explicit and implicit revenue (or sales) that the agency's managers seek to maximize. The deep pockets of sponsoring legislatures reinforce defects in sales-maximizing government agencies' profitability constraints that make it easier for their managers to bear the interim costs of following a strategy of "addictive subsidization." This strategy of using product giveaways as bait is exemplified in the private economy by the drug dealer who (promoting a kind of Faustian contract) deliberately gives away samples of his product to first-time users.[5] This strategy works because gifts are especially hard to turn down when they are offered repeatedly and in a seductive fashion. Because potential clients are encouraged to think that they are wise and strong enough to stop short of addiction, it is not enough for them to recognize that the short-run benefits of the good proffered tend to induce expensive long-run changes in the clients' patterns of consumption. At the same time, the high probability of these long-run changes and the difficulty of unwinding a developing addiction justify the drug dealer's initial investment. His purpose is to create and to sustain a large demand for his product.

The history of the Federal Reserve System offers a number of examples of this marketing strategy in action. This is partly because the flow of seigniorage into Federal Reserve accounts from the issue of currency and the creation of credit gives the system an enormous capacity to finance long-lived patterns of subsidization of specific activities and kinds of clients. Effectively, it receives from the government a series of monopolistic franchises and the right to choose each year its own effective tax rate.

To make membership attractive, the Federal Reserve provided subsidized check-clearing services to its member banks from the outset. In the 1970s Federal Reserve officials extended this basic subsidy by allowing a widening range of payments messages to be transmitted over the underpriced Fedwire. Years later problems and dangers for the payments system fostered by these subsidies (such as remote disbursement and high intraday volumes of electronic clearing) were transformed into justifications for expanding the Federal Reserve's jurisdiction over nonmember financial institutions and over emerging financial instruments and markets.[6] Check-clearing subsidies lessened the scope of private clearinghouses, and the valuable performance guarantees routinely given to users of the Fedwire drove the privately run Bankwire out of business.

A strategy of addictive subsidization is made even more effective by authorities' ability to engage in predatory news management. Exploiting the reputational capital conferred on them by their appointment to high government positions, authorities can and do control the short-run flow of information relevant to judging their performance. Self-serving public statements, press releases, personal interviews, and behind-the-scenes reprisals for unfavorable stories shape what amounts to a disinformation policy that resembles deceptive marketing practices in the private sector. Disinformation turns instances of poor agency performance into persuasive pleas for additional authority. Bureaucratic instincts to limit informational damage lead government regulators to suppress or sugarcoat information about failures in their decision making (for example, in deposit insurance) and to recast it as evidence of structural defects in the powers or dominion granted to them. In effect, crises are created in lagged fashion by regulators and legislators (most of whom do not expect to be around to suffer the consequences) and mined by their successors through scare tactics that distract the public and would-be critics from the underlying causes of policy failures. Metaphorically, legislators and government regulators dispense slow poisons, some of which are marketed as quick-acting remedies to what ought to be recognized as poisons administered some time before by these parties' predecessors in office.

For Federal Reserve officials, using scare tactics to mine macroeconomic and financial industry problems for new powers or jurisdiction has become reflex action. Whatever the problems—nonbank entry into banking activities; large interbank credit exposures in the electronic payments system; interstate, cross-industry, or off-balance-sheet activities of banking firms; decapitalized deposit institutions; or speculative activities in emerging new markets—their recommended solutions turn on giving new powers to the Federal Reserve. Corrigan's white paper is merely the latest manifestation of such crisis mining.[7] Corrigan habitually treats the existence of a public interest in external supervision and regulation of financial activity as if it were coextensive with a need for a governmental body, especially the Federal Reserve, to perform these tasks. Readers might as well believe that the stork delivers babies as regard Federal Reserve officials as unconflicted agents who merely monitor and report U.S. taxpayers' diffuse and changing interests in financial markets.

To clarify that creating and mining crises form an advantageous strategy for government regulatory bureaus that works to the disadvantage of taxpayers and private regulators, we may consider a medical metaphor. Let us view a pattern of regulatory subsidization as a treatment and a grant of new authority designed to alleviate problems caused by the subsidies as a form of countertreatment. Regulatory treatments and countertreatments impose costs on taxpayers. Because both actions have unintended side effects, it is unreasonable to presume that their simultaneous application is distributionally or allocationally neutral.

To put the problem vividly, let me recount as a parable an incident I witnessed while visiting a hospitalized friend. My friend was suffering from temporary kidney failure due to the failure of emergency room personnel to provide prompt treatment for a circulatory blockage and developing necrosis in his right leg. By the time the hospital staff recognized the urgency of his problem, the necrosis had become so extensive that his kidneys could not process the dead tissue entering his bloodstream, and he was forced into dialysis. As we talked, the dialysis machine began to malfunction spectacularly, inducing a massive clotting of his blood. Rather than fix the machine, the technicians set up a pair of intravenous tubes to inject an anticoagulant drug into his blood just before it entered the machine and a coagulating agent back into the blood on its way out. This arrangement permitted the machine to function in disrepair. Of course, my friend suffered the side effects of both drugs: nausea, headaches, and blurred vision. As if these side effects were not bad enough, this line of treatment authorized the hospital pharmacy to bill him for the unnecessary drugs the staff had administered. Excessive costs and multiplication of undesirable side effects are what happen when the convenience (that is, the generalized interest) of the regulators operating a treatment system is allowed to rank ahead of the needs of the parties under treatment.

In several places Corrigan roundly condemns the political efforts of regulated firms to lobby for their interests at the expense of what he sees as the common good.[8] But the chief problem blocking speedy reform of the U.S. financial regulatory system is not just private lobbying activity but, more important, the business for regulators and rents for elected politicians created by inherited patterns of federal subsidies. Politicians and regulators are unwilling either to surrender their existing job benefits or to stand up to the political and bureaucratic pressures that would be unleashed by those currently enjoying subsidies if authorities were to work effectively to rationalize the system.

Patterns of Adjustment in Regulatory Market Structure

During the past twenty years technological advances in information processing and telecommunications have regularly lowered the distance-related costs of entry and enterprise coordination confronting firms that operate in diverse and far-flung financial services markets. During the same interval increasing volumes of multinational production and world trade combined with temporarily massive balance-of-payments surpluses of the Organization of Petroleum Exporting Countries (OPEC) have greatly increased the rewards that financial services firms can expect to earn from adapting their operations to span and integrate financial markets multinationally.

Multimarket and multinational operation requires a firm to build and maintain confidence in every market in which it functions. The need for confidence associated with geographic and product line expansion created corresponding opportunities for market expansion by foreign and home country financial regulators.

In sorting out the ways in which individual regulators responded to these opportunities, the industrial organization perspective on regulatory competition supports a distinction between *active* and *passive* movements in a regulator's market share. Passive movements occur when a regulator's clients gain or lose market share on their own, without relation to prior or concurrent adjustments initiated by the regulator. Active movements are those brought about by regulators' efforts to realign the regulatory structure. Active adjustments may be either aggressive or defensive in intent.

In line with these distinctions, sequences of market share adjustments among regulators differ according to the nature of the initiating disturbance. In a defensive sequence the process begins when passive gains or losses in a regulator's market share alert its management team to opportunities for using reregulation as a way to defend the entity's traditional domain. Aggressive sequences begin with a regulator's direct pursuit of opportunities for gains in market share that are generated by exogenous changes in the economic environment. Passive sequences are marked by regulators' (possibly temporary) acquiescence in an observed gain or decline in the market shares of those they regulate.

Some Examples. Effects of the rapid growth of money market mutual funds (MMMFs) on U.S. regulators between 1974 and 1982 illustrate these distinctions. MMMFs offer customers low-denomination pro rata participation in a diversified portfolio of short-term securities and certificates of deposit. As investment firms MMMFs automatically fell under the jurisdiction of the Securities and Exchange Commission (SEC). Most of the funds that fueled their 1974–1982 growth were attracted away from banks and savings institutions, whose explicit deposit rates on accounts under $100,000 had been kept unrealistically low by specialized federal regulators of deposit institutions. In competing with deposit institutions, MMMFs were further assisted by being free from two longstanding regulatory burdens on deposit institutions: reserve requirements and restrictions on branch office locations that limited an institution's ability to raise funds outside its traditional geographic market areas by offering out-of-region customers the implicit interest of convenient office locations and first-class transactions services. Continuing advances in telecommunications (including toll-free telephone numbers) and declines in the cost of computer record keeping enabled centralized MMMFs to compete with local institutions as performers of transactions services. MMMFs found themselves able to raise small-denomination funds nationwide at transaction costs low enough to pass earnings from their uncomplicated asset portfolios through to customers at average yields far in excess of deposit-rate ceilings.

In 1974 and early 1975, as MMMFs grew in relation to deposit institutions, the SEC's market share expanded passively. Beginning with wild-card certificates in mid-1974, deposit institution regulators began actively to defend their jurisdiction. They could not merely assert jurisdiction over MMMFs, however. Before they could force MMMFs to submit to deposit-rate ceilings, they had to wrest from Congress a grant of new authority. Their request for this authority was channeled through the banking committees. MMMFs defeated their efforts with the help of the SEC, which pleaded its and its constituents' case through the commerce committees, which are specifically charged with overseeing the SEC's activities. The U.S. system of specialized regulators supported by specialized congressional oversight committees makes it hard to plug loopholes in the fabric of regulation that intensify rivalry among regulators. Because individual regulators and committee members extract various forms of tribute from actual and potential clients, negotiating adjustments in regulators' relative jurisdictions is a multisided and time-consuming business.

The growth of MMMFs demonstrates how technological changes that made deposit markets more contestable for securities firms unfavorably altered the opportunity sets of deposit institutions, their regulators, and banking committee members. The deposit institution deregulation acts of 1980 and 1982, which ultimately jettisoned explicit interest rate ceilings on household deposit accounts, were the invaded regulators' delayed defensive responses to incursions by MMMFs, the SEC, and the commerce committees.

Even as the commerce committees and the SEC were gaining market share from the banking committees and their client regulators, they were losing lesser amounts of market share to the Commodity Futures Trading Commission (CFTC) and the agricultural committees, to which the CFTC reports. Beginning in 1976 commodities exchanges supervised by the CFTC introduced a series of financial futures contracts and options on such contracts designed to function in part as substitutes for securities investments. Perhaps because the securities industry and its regulators were preoccupied with protecting the gains being made by MMMFs, the early incursions of the commodity exchanges were tolerated passively. Once MMMF gains had been politically secured, however, the SEC took on the CFTC in congressional hearings and in a settlement negotiated directly between the two agencies won back a substantial piece of the futures-contract action.[9]

Consequences of Imperfect Contestability. By entering and exiting specific product markets, individual regulatory players change the effective pattern of jurisdictional overlap. In a perfectly contestable set of markets, the equilibrium trajectory of this overlap may be conceived as an endogenous market structure whose adaptation over time would permit the "right" quantity and quality of regulatory services to be made available and would see that those services were produced by the most efficient suppliers.

As we have seen, however, the market for regulatory services is far from perfectly contestable. When regulatory services are produced predominantly by governmental enterprises, movements toward the equilibrium trajectory are slowed and constrained by the bureaucratic configurations within which these enterprises operate and by regulators' discretionary control over the ways in which they define their jobs and report their performance to elected politicians and the taxpayer. In *The Heretics of Dune* Frank Herbert observes: "Bureaucracy destroys initiative. There is little that bureaucrats hate more than innovations, especially innovation that produces better results than old routines. Improvements always make those at the top of the heap look inept. Who enjoys appearing inept?"[10]

Any model builder makes a series of deliberate simplifications that emphasize some ideas at the expense of others. In depicting regulators as sales maximizers, I do not mean to deny the strength of bureaucrats' interest, especially in the short run, in promoting job simplification and personal convenience. Governmental bodies' extremely secure hold on economic life and the short horizons of elected politicians and most agency heads permit bureaucrats to use their discretionary control over performance data to support a myopic overemphasis on the short-run transition costs to government officials of renovating the inherited regulatory structure. The resulting tendency of government regulators to see inaction as an optimal interim response to either technological change or pioneering kinds of regulatory avoidance increases the length of regulatory lags far beyond those that could be accepted by managers and stockholders of a profit-seeking enterprise that is subject to takeover discipline.

The ideal of perfect contestability entails zero entry costs and zero exit costs, a condition that facilitates hit-and-run entry. During the past twenty-five years technological change has greatly reduced entry costs into markets for financial services throughout the world.

Exit costs for high-technology plant and equipment are relatively low. This capital may easily be switched to other uses and depreciates rapidly because of obsolescence in any case. The relatively high current turnover rates for financial firms are consistent with this view.

The market structure for financial regulatory services is, in contrast, marked by dominant firms, influenced by market power conferred temporarily on elected politicians, and distorted by various subsidies these politicians deliberately or inadvertently permit to be transmitted to those who sign up for specific kinds of federal regulation. In the United States the Federal Reserve plays the role of dominant firm in the market for financial regulatory services. Nevertheless, except for the need for a prior accumulation of reputational capital, entry costs are relatively low even for state and cooperative self-regulators. What deters entry is that potential entrants know that exit costs for federal government regulators are so high that we seldom see any exit by them. Because regulatory recognition and action lags are longer than avoidance lags, clients' competition encourages long-run adaptation in the form of competitive reregulation that serves to validate efficient regulatory avoidance schemes. Clearly, however, adaptation is slowed by the lack of exits by federal regulators.

High exit costs and other constraints on competition among financial services regulators slow adaptations in the market structure of financial services providers. The U.S. Supreme Court is the dominant firm in antitrust regulation. Its adherence to outmoded concepts of banking as a single line of commerce and to the structure-performance paradigm of antitrust regulation has focused regulatory guidelines and targets for supervision away from assessments of entry and exit costs. The Court has concerned itself instead with the numbers of *actual* competitors in narrowly conceived geographic and product markets, an index whose relevance falls as entry and exit costs do.[11] To the disadvantage of domestic financial regulators, these narrow conceptions have mistakenly led the courts to view mergers of existing competitors into foreign financial firms as more procompetitive than parallel mergers into domestic competitors.

Regulatory Benefits, Costs, and Profits

In principle, financial regulators are given the right to restrain the activity of individual financial services firms to achieve benefits either for society or for the industry being regulated. We may distinguish five kinds of benefits: (1) certifying the integrity and competence of individual institutions and other contracting parties; (2) improving customers' convenience or productive efficiency by providing firms with coordinating services that lower transaction costs; (3) ensuring the continuing stability and orderliness of the system; (4) monitoring pricing arrangements for anticompetitive behavior; and (5) raising explicit and implicit revenue.

The first two sets of benefits enrich both society and individual financial services firms. They help financial intermediaries to transform risky and large-denomination corporate, government, and household assets into safer, low-denomination instruments such as deposits and mutual funds. That is why it is inefficient for society not to produce at least some forms of financial regulatory service. In contrast, pursuing the three other regulatory benefits tends to impose costs on at least some individual financial services firms by trying to prevent them either from setting their prices, product lines, and market territories as they see fit or from extracting unintended subsidies from regulatory arrangements.

Any good explanation of financial intermediation should also explain the demand for financial regulatory services. For indirect finance to make economic sense, the costs to a financial intermediary of contacting enough small surplus units and gathering their funds must be less than the costs of these units' directly financing deficit spending units. If networking economies exist, providing regulatory services that coordinate financial intermediaries' efforts to clear and settle financial transactions contributes to this end. Douglas Diamond emphasizes the high costs for deficit units of communicating to surplus units sufficient information on the changing state of their economic performance and of bonding their promised payments directly.[12] He conceives of surplus units as delegating the task of collecting reliable and confidential information to financial intermediaries, who are better able to design, enforce, and negotiate modifications in covenants (that is, bonding agreements) than a disorganized collection of deficit units would be. But for this system to work, deficit units and surplus units must have reason to trust financial intermediaries to execute this task faithfully and impartially. External regulators can help produce such confidence either by guaranteeing the performance of financial intermediaries or by committing their own reputations to overseeing the process. Hence the need to minimize generalized transactions costs also creates a demand for universally trusted parties to monitor financial intermediaries' performance as monitors.[13]

In exchange for explicit and implicit revenues, producers of regulatory services help individual financial services firms to bring about favorable movements in customers' confidence and convenience. Explicit regulatory revenue, R_R, consists of fees and other cash receipts (including seigniorage) that accrue from a regulator's operations. Implicit revenue, R'_R, consists of noncash benefits, such as improvements in an agency's prestige, size, effective autonomy, or market share. A regulator's profit or net budget deficit, π_R, may be defined as its implicit and explicit regulatory revenue, $R'_R + R_R$, minus the implicit and explicit costs, $C'_R + C_R$, of producing the services it supplies:

$$\pi_R = R'_R + R_R - C'_R - C_R \qquad (1)$$

The reader may have noted that, besides supplying a broad perspective on the evolution of regulatory structures, this chapter makes one critical and potentially falsifiable assumption that is thought to be a plausible characterization of at least the U.S. scene. The analysis assumes that, at least in the short run, regulatory profits are measured differently at stockholder-owned and government firms. Assuming efficient capital markets, at private firms stockholders and creditors or their equivalents monitor all evidence of *implicit* as well as *explicit* revenues and costs. When a private entity's regulatory profits prove repeatedly to be negative, its managers and economic activities fall increasingly under the whip of stockholder, creditor, and takeover discipline.

At government enterprises the equivalent of stockholder and creditor discipline is supplied by elected politicians, who are supposed to act as agents for the taxpayers, to whom a government firm's costs and revenues ultimately accrue. To perform this task properly, politicians need to monitor a regulator's performance carefully. But when the flow of information about that performance is managed for the short-run benefit of politicians and the employees of the regulatory entity, the sporadic and incomplete electoral discipline to which politicians are subject permits them to perform their monitoring tasks in a myopically self-serving way. These defects in the information flow and chain of accountability among regulated firms, regulators, and politicians also make it reasonable to distinguish between intended and unintended subsidies. Unintended subsidies arise when an imperfectly supervised agent pursues benefits that the principal either did not foresee and would not have allowed if it had or dislikes but accepts as a necessary evil so as to retain its options to conceal benefits it is extracting from its own principal.

To streamline the argument, I assume that, other things being equal, politicians consciously or unconsciously prefer to simplify their job assignments by granting the regulators they oversee an option to take less account of implicit costs than of implicit revenues. To make the analysis even sharper, I assume for expositional purposes that in any accounting period agencies may report implicit revenues and costs as they see fit.

This means that a government regulator can claim that its short-run profits are as high as $R'_R + R_R - C_R$ or as low as $R_R - C_R - C'_R$. Misrepresenting the firm's performance in the current period, however, has the unpleasant effect of reducing the flow of explicit and implicit profits to the firm's future managers. Overstating current profits *defers* losses rather than eliminates them. As the experience of the Federal Savings and Loan Insurance Corporation illustrates, hiding current losses creates unrecognized liabilities, the servicing of which reduces the present value of a regulatory firm's projected flows of future explicit and implicit income. Hiding losses by permitting economically insolvent firms to stay in operation had the further bad effect of increasing the flow of unintended subsidies to troubled savings institutions.[14] Because the immediate career prospects of heads of regulatory agencies appear to be affected principally by reported profits during their time in office, they face strong incentives to overreport earnings. To make a clean getaway back to the private sector or to a higher government position, they must hide current implicit losses and leave the consequences to be handled by their successors.

Politicians' concern for conserving explicit budget resources (which is enshrined in the Gramm-Rudman-Hollings Act) disinclines them to challenge what they know or ought to know are cosmetically doctored reports of agencies' net expenses. As long as political pressure focuses only on limiting the size of the government's explicit budget deficit, politicians will be interested in crediting a positive flow of reported regulatory profits to the national Treasury for possible transfer to assorted constituencies. This analysis assumes that congressional oversight committees require each government regulator to earn a (possibly negative) target level of reported regulatory profits (or to report a target profit margin) and to deliver a target pattern of implicit and explicit subsidies to selected constituents. Committee members do this in full knowledge that the selected constituents will often find it in their interest to pay tribute to members of their industry's oversight committees. This tribute takes the form, for example, of industry-distributed speaking and personal appearance fees and of campaign contributions that, if not fully expended, revert eventually to a committee member's own use.

Differences in Performance Criteria and Managerial Incentives between Private and Governmental Regulators

From the point of view of society as a whole, whether a governmental agency or a profit-making or cooperative private organization produces a given set of regulatory services is seldom a matter of indifference. Each kind of regulator confronts a different set of incentive conflicts. Private regulators have socially beneficial incentives to minimize the costs of confidence-building certification activity and to promote efficient coordinating arrangements. At the same time they have socially harmful incentives to monopolize critical information on their performance and to harbor cartel pricing. Although resulting problems tend to correct themselves in time, the adjustment process is far from costless to society. Information control and cartel pricing encourage the expansion of uncertified firms that operate outside the aegis of the private regulatory organization. Hence, under a purely private regulatory system, the adaptation of market structure to undo the effectiveness of informational monopolies and cartel pricing tends to expand the market share of unregulated firms. Where the categories of oversight being circumvented promote safe and sound operation, this process can undermine the soundness and integrity of the financial system.

When regulation is supplied by a governmental organization, the compatibility and conflict of incentives are partly reversed. Socially beneficial incentives exist to promote at least the appearance of stability and to restrain cartel pricing. But especially where regulators can distribute subsidies and distort the flow of information about performance, these incentives can be overwhelmed by myopia and distributional politics. Moreover, the more closely performance information is controlled, the weaker are bureaucratic incentives to minimize certification costs and to produce coordinating, guarantee, and regulatory services efficiently. Hence, when regulation is purely governmental, regulatory services tend to be produced at inefficiently high cost and to serve as vehicles for the redistribution of wealth.[15]

Much as other kinds of competition do, regulatory competition helps to resolve some of these incentive conflicts and produce the potential long-run benefits of slowly erasing short-run inefficiencies.[16] Even though regulatory overlaps impose avoidable short-run costs, on average and on balance they diversify against narrow or inflexible approaches to problem solving at individual agencies and facilitate the dynamic adaptations in market structure necessary to achieve a rough form of evolutionary optimality.

Opportunities for regulated firms to migrate to better regulators by relabeling their products, relocating their production, or adjusting their legal forms complement regulators' opportunities to enroll additional classes of regulated firms. Although these opportunities entail nonnegligible costs of transition, they constitute an important variety of social insurance. The possibility of regulatory migration protects financial firms and their customers from having to bear the excessive burdens that a cartel or monopoly supplier might be expected to impose.

Overlaps in regulatory jurisdictions encourage competing regulators and regulated firms to experiment with alternative patterns of coping with common problems. Moreover, alternative approaches are routinely tested against one another in the crucible of experience. This allows society's regulatory problems to be resolved with more creativity and without having to rely on the problem-solving ability of a narrow school of regulatory architects.

Duplicate regulatory functions and overlapping administrative boundaries that may seem inefficient from a purely static point of view provide dynamic opportunities for structural arbitrage that entails the adaptive affiliation and disaffiliation of individual regulated firms. I conceive of such behavior as arbitrage to clarify the close parallel that exists between differences in provisional net regulatory burdens and differences in prices on any service that are quoted by substitute suppliers. As long as regulatory profits are properly monitored, structural adaptation by regulated firms (especially by new entrants into markets for products and services that substitute for regulated ones) disciplines poor regulators and rewards good ones.

In an era in which rapid technological and regulation-induced changes in the operations of regulated firms require regulators continually to explore new ways of performing their tasks, regulatory competition induces more timely and economically better-adapted adjustments in regulatory structures than monopoly regulators would choose to make. The combined threats of legislative oversight, judicial review, and competition from other regulators encourage an agency's regulatory brain trust to produce its services more efficiently: to adopt regulatory strategies that serve the needs of new forms of business organization and would-be producers of new or improved products. In particular, rivalry among regulators tends to smooth out "bubbles" of oversevere regulation that would develop in response to intermittent financial market crises and scandals if financial regulation barriers to entry were more significant.

At the same time the periodic occurrence of regulatory scandals and crises testifies to the ability of both private and governmental regulators to conceal for long periods relevant information on the effects and quality of their performance. For this reason the most promising regulatory reforms are those that would improve the flow of timely information on regulators' performance or otherwise restrain the production of hidden regulatory subsidies and attendant agency losses.

Constraints on Effective Regulatory Burdens

From the point of view of those regulated, revenue losses imposed on them by regulators' explicit charges and various operational constraints reduce the value of the regulatory services they receive. The balance between the costs and the benefits that a given regulator succeeds in imposing on the firms it regulates is defined as their net regulatory burden. Because some of the costs imposed may not produce regulatory revenues and because the value of the benefits may exceed or fall short of the regulator's costs, this burden is far from being the mirror image of either the true regulatory net profits specified in equation 1 or the cosmetic regulatory profits a government firm chooses to report.

To explain how regulatory policy is constrained by the endogenous response of the regulated, it is convenient to conceive of the statutory tax system and industry regulators as setting a provisional pair of net burdens. These are the hypothetical burdens that would obtain if taxpayers, on the one hand, and regulated firms, their customers, and their competitors, on the other, were to make no creative, unanticipated efforts to adapt their organizational form or activities to minimize the net economic burdens that government operations place on them. With full information the adaptive capacity of taxpayers would reward governments that give fair value for their taxes and punish those that collect or expend their taxes inefficiently. Similarly, with full information on regulators' performance, the adaptive capacity of regulated firms would reward efficient regulators and punish inefficient ones.

Even with full information regulatory activities may temporarily be inefficient. First, the services a regulator offers may be produced at more than minimum cost. Second, the services offered may be maladapted to the evolving needs of producers and consumers. When subsidies may be hidden, a third kind of inefficiency may exist. Regulators may lack either the tools or the will to control the size of the implicit subsidies that aggressive regulated firms can extract from the system under the cover of inefficient regulatory arrangements.

Patterns of regulation that are inefficient in any of these senses impose excessively burdensome costs either on regulated firms or on taxpayers. Of course, neither party should be willing to finance what are known to be inefficient operations forever. Although opportunities for assessing and responding to regulatory inefficiencies are limited in the short run, effective avoidance options expand as long as a particular inefficiency remains in place. The speed with which more favorably regulated firms can gather customers from less favorably regulated ones varies with the difficulty of convincing their potential customers that their products are reliable substitutes for one or more traditional financial products. As financial services customers begin to move their business out of traditional channels, the regulated firms whose markets are being curtailed face an increasing incentive to transform their operations to permit them to migrate to the more favorable regulator as well. In the long run this double-barreled loss of regulatory market share alerts traditional regulators (including oversight committees in Congress) to a need to respond.

In both the short run and the long run, market adjustments to excessively costly or poorly adapted regulation is stabilizing, in that direct and indirect regulatory migration proceeds from socially high-cost producers to socially low-cost ones. As their jurisdictional domains become economically less significant, regulators whose production costs prove inefficiently high or whose response to the evolving needs of the marketplace proves consistently shortsighted or inflexible must eventually suffer declines in budget and employment.

In contrast, market response to socially unjustified subsidies is destabilizing in the short run. Until the migration has become substantial enough to persuade taxpayers to spend the resources necessary to build a coalition strong enough to extract the information needed to guard their economic interests, socially inefficient behavior patterns offer regulated firms extraordinarily high rates of return.

This analysis clarifies both what can go wrong in regulatory competition and why it is nevertheless a mistake to view rivalry among alternative regulators for clients and budgets merely as wasteful duplication. A monopoly supplier or regulatory cartel would tend in the long run to overregulation. When taxpayers and legislators are well informed, overlaps in regulatory missions among regulators promote long-run efficiency in the production and delivery of regulatory services, much as duplication of service functions among private institutions promotes efficiency in the provision of financial services. But when a regulator and its clients can exploit and perpetuate impediments in taxpayers' access to the information needed to judge the regulator's performance, this competition can temporarily promote inefficiency instead. Inappropriately monitored regulators can deliver unintended and economically inappropriate subsidies. Only as long as taxpayers enforce their interest in preventing subsidies from being hidden can we say that rivalry among regulators protects borrowers, depositors, and investors from the dangers of short-run underregulation as well.

Structural Arbitrage and Unintended Subsidies to Risk Bearing by Financial Institutions

By rearranging its activities and organizational form in prescribed ways, a regulated entity may change the regulatory climate within which it functions. The term "regulatory climate" serves as a useful shorthand expression for the set of laws and regulatory bodies by which an institution is governed. Structural arbitrage occurs when a firm improves its regulatory climate by substituting new or differently regulated products, processes, and organizational forms for its existing ones.[17] Over the past decade expansion in banks' use of off-balance-sheet activities constitutes a vivid example of structural arbitrage.

Structural arbitrage is importantly constrained by legal obstacles. But opportunities for regulators to extend their dominion to new kinds of institutions and instruments and the existence of even greatly constrained options for regulated firms to switch regulators create incentives for efficient adaptation by regulators. Without tough sunset laws it is almost prohibitively costly to force the complete exit of a government regulatory agency, particularly a national one. Nevertheless, declines either in an agency's share of regulatory activity or in its net regulatory profits tend to shrink the size of its budget and its political prestige. Because the unpleasant consequences of potential losses in regulatory domain undermine an agency's goals, they bring economic pressures on its management to lighten many of the burdens that in a changing marketplace an inherited system of regulation would otherwise impose on regulated firms and their customers.

In the increasingly global financial services industry of today, regulatory conflict is seldom driven by aggressive acts of bureaucratic expansion (the principal exception being the efforts of some countries to attract financial business to their shores as regulatory havens). Generally regulatory conflict develops as a delayed response to structural changes undertaken by financial services providers. The initiating structural changes reflect profit-seeking efforts by individual financial institutions either to invade nontraditional markets or to construct a more desirable regulatory climate for themselves. Such institutions are revising their organizational structures and extending their product lines and geographic reach to serve new markets and in the process selecting a set of regulatory microclimates that will minimize their burdens. As structural arbitrage disrupts the inherited regulatory equilibrium, the "law of one burden" forces even nonassertive regulators to struggle to defend or redefine the borders of their domains.

Structural arbitrage causes problems for society because of defective incentives for elected politicians to monitor and minimize the opportunity costs for government agencies of producing regulatory services. A good portion of the reductions in regulatory burdens that multinational and multipurpose financial firms win for themselves by structural arbitrage is generated by shifting real costs onto the taxpayer in hidden fashion. The most important of these hidden costs are unintended subsidies that flow from the improper pricing of explicit and implicit government and international financial guarantees. These guarantees dramatically lower individual firms' risks in extending product lines and geographic markets. They do so by imposing implicit and conjectural liabilities on governmental financial regulators. The unaccounted expense and unrecognized liabilities that governmental guarantors accept pass through to unwary taxpayers and conservatively run financial institutions that as a matter of practical politics bear the final responsibility for making good on contingent governmental commitments.

Democratic governments around the world respond to political pressure to bail out spectacularly insolvent debtors. The predictability of this response creates unpriced implicit guarantees. The desirability of limiting these guarantees and imposing user fees on their recipients provides a clear rationale for governments to construct and enforce explicit deposit insurance contracts.

Because of regulatory lags underpriced opportunities for shifting risk onto governmental guarantors are especially great for innovative activities. Market participants that put their own wealth on the line inevitably receive more timely and better-analyzed information on the risk implications of developing investment opportunities than governmental regulators do. Lags inherent in governmental information, monitoring, and regulatory response systems are exacerbated by self-interested management of information concerning the changing market value of government guarantees. Such information needs to be published in timely fashion for taxpayers to monitor. Mispricing governmental guarantees creates strong incentives for financial institutions to search out new forms of risk taking and for foreign financial firms and nonfinancial domestic institutions to devise inventive methods of folding government-guaranteed financial subsidiaries or affiliates into their operations. Because the resulting increase in a firm's anticipated earnings derives from increasing the risk that the firm may fail, defective regulatory incentives are secularly undermining the stability of the world's financial system.[18] Besides increasing the failure rates of deposit institutions, destabilizing structural arbitrage is also complicating the task of monetary policy targeting.

International Competition among Regulators

Competition for regulatory jurisdiction is inherent in the multinational organization of the world economy.[19] Restrictions on the entry and expansion of foreign financial firms and on domestic institutions' capital exports have long been common features of individual countries' regulatory architecture. Because they limit foreign regulators' access to the home country's markets and institutions, such regulations protect not just domestic financial services firms but domestic financial regulators as well.

In virtually all countries during recent years, competition from foreign regulators for domestic financial opportunities has become more intense. Macroeconomic events have made restrictions on international financial competition more burdensome to regulated firms while technological change has made them easier to circumvent. For both reasons, such restrictions are progressively losing force. In short, it has become harder and harder to keep out foreign financial services firms and to keep domestic firms from expanding their offshore activities.

To the extent that it improves a firm's regulatory climate, opening an international branch office or acquiring or forming an international banking or nonbanking subsidiary is an act of structural arbitrage. In particular, we may infer that forming a foreign subsidiary rather than a branch or divisional office lightens tax or regulatory burdens in some way. For U.S. corporations, potential benefits include these:

- Although this privilege is being phased out, under longstanding tax law firms could defer U.S. taxes on the subsidiary's foreign income until it was repatriated. The income of foreign branches is automatically consolidated with domestic income for tax purposes. It was, of course, particularly advantageous to accrue income in a wholly owned subsidiary located in a tax haven.
- They may be able to circumvent U.S. regulation of their foreign activities or pursue special privileges afforded certain kinds of subsidiaries, such as U.S. corporations chartered as international banking

facilities (IBFs) or Edge Act corporations to engage in international banking operations. Relevant restrictions include limitations on interstate operations; capital requirements, reserve requirements, deposit-rate ceilings, and explicit deposit insurance premiums; and prohibited activities, such as securities or insurance activities for banks.

• Their foreign financial subsidiaries often receive many of the same burdens and privileges that domestic firms enjoy in the host country. Locating specific lines of business in the host country's counterpart of an Edge Act corporation or an IBF creates opportunities to lessen the burden of regulation by the host country too.

As international patterns of activity change, efficient parallel adaptation of the market structure for financial services regulation is hampered by administrative entry barriers and by inflexible concepts of appropriate regulatory strategy and tactics. Corrigan argues that "much greater harmony in structural, supervisory, accounting, and tax policy as they apply in international banking and financial markets is needed and needed badly."[20]

This chapter's industrial organization perspective suggests that the difficulty of arranging durable patterns of international regulatory cooperation reflects difficulties inherent in forming and maintaining a worldwide cartel in any product or service. It is hard for national regulators to negotiate even bilateral rights to open offices in each other's regulatory territory, although the process is easier for close and longstanding allies such as the United States and the United Kingdom. Significant progress has recently occurred in two areas: arrangements to share flows of information across the global regulatory community and efforts to reduce differences in individual countries' capital requirements.

Because regulatory lags are longer than avoidance lags, the ability of regulated firms to shift selected parts of their operation to other nations or to other domestic regulators expands the scope of regulatory competition. Although the intensity of the competition is restrained by government regulators' need to operate largely from within national or administrative boundaries and by the infrequency of exits by national regulators, it is heightened by opportunities to regulate multinational and affiliated firms as a single entity.

Because tax and regulatory burdens vary substantially among countries, regulators and regulated firms must be aware of tax and regulatory incentives and the risk of future changes in those incentives. Financial evolution, flexible exchange rates, and higher and more volatile world interest rates have increased the burden of traditional regulatory structures based on liquidity requirements, capital standards, interest rate ceilings, and activity limitations. By developing a less burdensome tax and regulatory climate, an institution can increase net after-tax returns on its traditional business at the same time that it widens its sphere of activity.

A country's willingness to provide implicit regulatory subsidies to financial services firms affects the international division of labor and distribution of wealth. Such subsidies place a net burden for financing financial services export promotion on the general taxpayer and on the stockholders, managers, and customers of smaller institutions that do not participate in international financial transactions. Moreover, subsidy-seeking structural arbitrage tends to shift at least part of the subsidies from multinational institutions of the home country to depositors and borrowers of the host country. In this way another country's regulatory subsidies can squeeze the lending margins of intermediaries in their domestic markets. The existence of subsidies from the home country feeds political demands on its regulators to impose regulatory assessments against domestic banks' foreign deposits or loans and supports the efforts of institutions of the host country to push simultaneously for countervailing restrictions on foreign firms and for offsetting concessions from foreign regulators to ease reciprocal expansion into their competitors' home countries. Finally, the conjectural nature of incompletely financed government guarantees raises doubts about the reliability of conjectural home country guarantees of the debts of increasingly more highly leveraged structural arbitragers.

In large part the extent to which regulators of the home or host country gain or lose regulatory market share from structural arbitrage depends on the extent to which the services exported consist of truly new business for the relocating firm. From a single-entity view of the multinational financial services firm, new business (that is, trade creation) creates regulatory services in the home country by expanding the home regulator's jurisdiction over the new activity into foreign markets. Displacing business that was previously conducted domestically in the home country is experienced as a diversion of regulatory service. Whenever a regulated firm's traditionally domestic business is simply displaced to foreign locations, the home regulator is disadvantaged. It loses market share and regulatory revenue while continuing to absorb at least some of the costs of producing confidence-building and coordinating services that support the activity.

A spillover from domestic regulatory competition occurs when the regulator that loses volume in domestic markets differs from the regulator of the class of institution that is expanding abroad. For example, to circumvent Glass-Steagall restrictions that exclude U.S. commercial banks from domestic investment banking, the nation's major banks have established overseas investment banking networks. Because the SEC and individual state securities departments have jurisdiction over corporate underwriting and deal making in the United States, the ancillary foreign service volume that federal banking regulators gain unambiguously improves their market share. Although banking regulators may seek to recover any net costs that this activity imposes on them, they are apt to resist efforts by the SEC to close the associated loophole in domestic regulatory walls.

Picking up foreign clients does not always improve the market share of the host country regulator. A foreign client must always be shared in some proportion with regulators in its home country. Although sharing of offshore business tends to expand the host regulator's market share, any business absorbed from local firms entails at least a small diversion of traditional market share to foreign regulators. Moreover, governments and legislatures cannot ignore the plight of firms and workers in invaded industries. Foreign entry tends to lessen the autonomy of host regulators by putting downward pressure on domestic profit margins and increasing domestic demand for greater freedom for host country institutions to expand abroad reciprocally. Foreign institutions must be expected to discover ways to arbitrage differences in home and host regulatory burdens, and foreign entry into the domestic market creates incentives for their domestic competitors to study opportunities for expanding abroad.

Unless host country regulations comprehensively limit the rights and privileges of foreign institutions (something that expansion-minded subnational regulators exemplified by the state of Delaware may sometimes thwart), foreign institutions may find ways to enjoy regulatory freedoms that are not available to strictly domestic institutions. For example, although the International Banking Act of 1978 narrowed most of the differences, foreign bank operations in the United States enjoy lower capital requirements, fewer activity restrictions, more freedom to operate interstate, and advantages in surmounting the concentration-ratio tests the U.S. Supreme Court employs to assess takeovers of large domestic institutions. Foreign banks' exercise of their differential freedoms benefits consumers and creates and feeds a demand for compensatingly lighter burdens for domestic regulated firms. In Japan, for example, large domestic banks have welcomed the exercise of investment banking powers by foreign banks as a lever with which to pressure Japanese and foreign authorities to grant similar powers to Japanese institutions. Soon after the Japanese seated a few foreign firms on the Tokyo Stock Exchange, the Federal Reserve permitted Japan's Sumitomo Bank to purchase a substantial stake in Goldman, Sachs, and Company.

Efforts to persuade Japanese officials to join the United States and the United Kingdom in harmonizing capital standards temporarily foundered on the issue of how to treat so-called hidden reserves. Hidden reserves are off-balance-sheet sources of value (such as net unrealized capital gains on securities or real estate). These reserves are on average positive and substantial for Japanese banks (because of large amounts of unrealized gains on equity investments) and negative and substantial for large U.S. banks. Although Japanese authorities were willing to count 70 percent of a bank's hidden reserves as regulatory capital, American and British authorities are unwilling to acknowledge the relevance of market-value measures of bank capital. Such an acknowledgment would threaten in the long run to narrow these authorities' information-management options. Western officials' comical claim that the relatively low *book value* of Japanese banks' capital position gives them an advantage in competing for guarantee and deposit business with American banks turns economics on its ear. As table 9–1 documents, Japanese banks' advantage lies in their being more strongly capitalized on a market-value basis. Market values are the relevant measures of a bank's ability on its own to absorb losses or to withstand a run by depositors. Moreover, the sometimes expressed notion that hidden reserves may be "more vulnerable to market fluctuations" than other sources of bank capital is doubtful in principle. In any case, concerns about asset volatility apply symmetrically throughout an institution's entire balance sheet. While it might be reasonable for regulators to scale down the market value of some volatile items in assessing a client's financial strength, it makes no sense to assign a zero weight to hidden reserves. The compromise reached was to give a country's regulators the option of counting up to 55 percent of regulated firms' hidden reserves as capital.

I have emphasized that declines in market share tend to dispose home country regulators to engage in defensive regulation. Table 9–2 shows the geographic distribution of U.S. banks' foreign branch assets from 1973 to 1986. For U.S. banking regulators the observed secular expansion of these assets reflects a mixture of gains and losses. Over the fourteen years covered, United Kingdom banking regulators lost market share they used to enjoy in regulating the foreign activity of American banks.

Although regulatory havens in the Caribbean basin gained considerable ground in 1973–1976, their market share stabilized there-

TABLE 9–1
World's Leading Twenty-five Banking Institutions
in Market Capitalization, March 31, 1987
(millions of U.S. dollars)

Banking Company	Home Country	Market Capitalization
Sumitomo Bank	Japan	58,303.7
Dai-Ichi Kangyo Bank	Japan	55,569.0
Fuji Bank	Japan	51,185.2
Mitsubishi Bank	Japan	50,119.6
Industrial Bank of Japan	Japan	49,709.6
Sanwa Bank	Japan	46,050.7
Long-Term Credit Bank of Japan	Japan	23,972.6
Mitsui Bank	Japan	22,141.3
Tokai Bank	Japan	21,993.2
Bank of Tokyo	Japan	17,628.4
Daiwa Bank	Japan	16,093.2
Taiyo Kobe Bank	Japan	14,450.7
Union Bank of Switzerland	Switzerland	13,000.9
Deutsche Bank	West Germany	11,897.7
Nippon Credit Bank	Japan	11,183.6
Swiss Bank Corporation	Switzerland	9,595.0
Kyowa Bank	Japan	8,917.8
Bank of Yokohama	Japan	8,836.9
J. P. Morgan and Company	United States	7,696.7
National Westminster Bank	England	7,150.7
Citicorp	United States	6,984.0
Credit Suisse	Switzerland	6,297.8
Barclays Bank	England	5,539.2
Hokkaido Takushoku Bank	Japan	5,054.0
Hong Kong and Shanghai Banking Corporation	Hong Kong	5,022.6

Source: *American Banker,* July 6, 1987.

after. The relative fixity of the Caribbean share after 1976 suggests that reregulation by the United Kingdom, the United States, or competing regulatory havens (in Asia, for example) counteracted their differential burdens. Because regulators in other locations on the average gained market share and volume throughout the period examined, U.S. and British regulators may be said to have suffered a continuing decline. This decline helped to educate the London Stock Exchange to the need for its heralded October 27, 1986, "big bang" deregulation of British markets for equities and government securities.

TABLE 9-2
Geographic Distribution of U.S. Foreign Branch Assets, 1973–1986
(millions of U.S. dollars)

	United Kingdom Amount	Percent	Caribbean Basin Amount	Percent	Other Locations Amount	Percent	Total U.S. Foreign Branches Amount	Percent
1973	61,732	50	25,297	21	34,837	29	121,866	100
1974	69,804	46	34,424	23	47,677	31	151,905	100
1975	74,883	42	48,915	28	52,695	30	176,493	100
1976	81,466	37	70,603	32	67,351	31	219,420	100
1977	90,933	35	83,953	32	84,011	33	258,897	100
1978	106,593	35	99,402	32	100,800	33	306,795	100
1979	130,873	35	120,890	33	112,402	32	364,165	100
1980	144,717	36	123,837	31	132,581	33	401,135	100
1981	157,229	34	149,108	32	156,510	34	462,847	100
1982	161,067	34	145,156	31	163,209	35	469,432	100
1983	158,732	33	151,532	32	166,275	35	476,539	100
1984	144,385	32	146,811	32	161,009	36	452,205	100
1985	148,599	32	142,055	31	167,358	37	458,012	100
1986	140,917	31	142,592	31	173,119	38	456,628	100

NOTE: In May 1978 the exemption level for branches required to report their assets was increased, which lessened the comprehensiveness of the survey sample from which these data are constructed.

SOURCES: 1973–1984, Joseph F. Sinkey, Jr., *Commercial Bank Financial Management in the Financial Services Industry*, 2d ed. (New York: Macmillan, 1986), p. 659. 1985 and 1986, *Federal Reserve Bulletin* (June 1987).

Direct U.S. responses to its financial regulators' secularly declining market share, profits, and current-account position have lurched through several stages of reregulation. Notable developments include (1) loose capital controls and special reserve requirements on offshore deposits and borrowings; (2) redefinition by the International Banking Act of 1978 of the powers that foreign banks may exercise; (3) higher capital requirements for and closer supervision of U.S. multinational banks authorized by the International Lending Supervision Act of 1983; (4) expansion of opportunities for U.S. banks to set up subsidiary corporations whose onshore facilities are granted offshore privileges in transacting business with nonresidents; and (5) efforts to harmonize capital requirements with the United Kingdom and Japan.

Of these acts of reregulation, the fourth is theoretically the most interesting. For U.S. banks two main classes of onshore offshore offices exist: Edge Act corporations (first authorized in the 1920s and given expanded powers by the 1978 act) and IBFs (which have been allowed only since December 1981). The number of these institutions surged dramatically during the 1980s (see tables 9–3 and 9–4).

Edge Act and agreement corporations are bank subsidiaries chartered by the Board of Governors of the Federal Reserve System to conduct international banking business in U.S. and foreign locations.

TABLE 9–3

U.S. Banks with Foreign or Semiforeign Offices, 1950–1986

	Member Banks with Foreign Branches	Foreign Branch Offices	Domestically Owned Edge and Agreement Corporations and Branches[a]	International Banking Facilities[b]
1950	7	95		
1960	8	131		
1965	13	211		
1970	79	532		
1975	126	762	58	
1980	159	787	91	
1981	159	841	134	270
1982	162	900	164	430
1983	166	892	167	496
1984	163	905	162	524
1985	163	916	155	540
1986	158	952	129	540

NOTE: Data are year-end figures. Domestic nonmember banks have engaged in almost no foreign branching. Most of the twenty to thirty nonmember banks with foreign branches are foreign owned. In examining data from different sources for this table and the next, some minor but hard-to-reconcile differences emerged.
a. Data on these entities not available until after 1974.
b. International banking facilities were first authorized on December 3, 1981. The figures given include foreign-owned as well as domestic IBFs. On June 30, 1986, about 60 percent of the IBFs were foreign owned.
SOURCES: First two columns: 1950 from Sinkey, *Commercial Bank Management*, p. 653; 1960–1985 from telephone conversation with James Houpt, a staff member at the Board of Governors of the Federal Reserve System. Data on Edges come from Houpt and from computer runs supplied by Elizabeth Thorley of the Board of Governors staff. 1986 data and figures on IBFs come from the Board of Governors of the Federal Reserve System, *Annual Reports*.

TABLE 9-4
Foreign Banks in Domestic U.S. Banking Markets, 1972-1986

	Banking Families Operating U.S. Branches and Agencies	Uninsured Branches and Agencies	Insured Branches and Agencies	Foreign-owned Edge and Agreement Corporations (offices)	Foreign-owned Majority Positions in U.S. Banks	Percentage of U.S. Banking Assets Controlled
1972	53	82	—	0	25	4
1975	79	147	—	0	33	n.a.
1979	154	295	n.a.	2	42	n.a.
1980	153	322	n.a.	11	40	12
1981	193	410	24	16 (21)	55	14
1982	205	389	33	28 (36)	69	14
1983	225	416	34	31 (43)	67	14
1984	248	442	38	25 (41)	69	15
1985	255	451	51	22 (37)	71	17
1986	259	452	35	20 (34)	72	18

NOTE: n.a. = not available. Data are year-end figures. When known, the number of offices operated by foreign-owned Edge and agreement corporations is given in parentheses. I neglect Edges whose foreign control is indirect (eight in 1986) and foreign-owned New York investment companies (eleven in 1986). New York investment companies were permitted in all years covered by the table. The International Banking Act of 1978 authorized foreign banks to own Edge corporations and permitted all Edges to branch domestically. See James V. Houpt, "Performance and Characteristics of Edge Corporations," Staff Studies no. 110 (Washington, D.C.: Board of Governors of the Federal Reserve System, 1981).

SOURCES: 1981–1986, Board of Governors of the Federal Reserve System, *Annual Reports*. Figures on 1986 Edges and assets controlled are corrected figures supplied by James Houpt of the Board of Governors. 1972, 1975, 1979, and 1980, from telephone conversation with James Houpt, double-checked against computer runs on Edge corporations supplied by Elizabeth Thorley of the board's staff.

They may freely make investments in foreign financial organizations that would be impermissible for U.S. banks. Since 1978 they have been allowed to operate interstate branches. A large percentage of Edge assets are located in New York and Miami. An agreement corporation is a no longer consequential form of state-chartered national bank subsidiary that enters into an agreement with the board of governors not to exercise any power that is impermissible for an Edge corporation.

An IBF is essentially a set of accounts or ledger books segregated from the other accounts of its parent. Its parent can be a U.S. deposit institution, an Edge or agreement corporation, or a branch or agency of a foreign bank. Accounts are booked at these institutions *as if* they were located offshore. This means that IBFs are not subject to domestic reserve requirements, deposit-rate ceilings, or deposit insurance premiums. As long as capital standards are applied on a consolidated basis to U.S. banking corporations, however, U.S.-owned IBFs are subject to capital requirements. IBFs are designed to reduce the flight of banks competing for U.S.-connected international business to regulatory havens such as the Cayman Islands. Other countries are moving to introduce an IBF option into their regulatory structure. Early in 1986, for example, the Japanese Diet enacted legislation to set up similar corporations in Tokyo.

Data in tables 9–2 to 9–4 cover only U.S.-related components of the international market for banking regulation. Table 9–5, which compares the nationality of the leading banks in the world in 1964 and 1986, emphasizes the universality of pressures for competitive reregulation. Japanese banks and their regulators have made serious inroads into markets long dominated by North American, British, and continental regulators. In 1964 the four biggest banks in the world and six of the top ten, measured by the dollar value of their deposits, were American. The other members of the top ten were British or Canadian. These three countries dominated the scene, with only one Italian bank (eleventh) and one French bank (fourteenth) squeezing into the top nineteen positions. The largest Japanese banks held positions twenty through twenty-three. These four banks' total deposits barely exceeded those of the largest U.S. bank, the Bank of America.

By the end of 1986 a very different picture had emerged. Assisted by a sharp appreciation of the yen, Japanese banks had become the seven largest in the world. Other members of the top ten are two French banks and one German bank. In the next tier of fifteen banks are nine more Japanese, two British, two French, one German, and only one American bank. Now the largest Canadian bank (still the Royal Bank of Canada) ranks forty-first.

Allowing time for the passage of regulatory lags, a sustained redistribution of market share toward Japanese banks is creating pressure for defensive and aggressive reregulation in the world's other financial centers. Moreover, the near impossibility of exit for national regulators should serve to intensify the pressure they feel to respond. Foreign governments and trade associations of guest firms such as the Institute of Foreign Bankers in Japan are already placing considerable international political pressure on Japanese officials to improve for-

TABLE 9-5
WORLD'S TWENTY-FIVE LARGEST COMMERCIAL BANKS,
BY DOLLAR VALUE OF DEPOSITS, 1964 AND 1986

Rank in 1964	Bank[a]	Rank in 1986	Bank
1	Bank of America N.T. and S.A., San Francisco (29)	1	Dai-Ichi Kangyo Bank Ltd., Tokyo
2	Chase Manhattan Bank, New York (40)	2	Fuji Bank, Ltd., Tokyo
3	First National City Bank, New York (17)	3	Sumitomo Bank Ltd., Osaka
4	Manufacturers Hanover Trust Co., New York (55)	4	Mitsubishi Bank Ltd., Tokyo
5	Barclays Bank Ltd., London (21)	5	Sanwa Bank Ltd., Osaka
6	Midland Bank Ltd., London (36)	6	Norinchukin Bank, Tokyo
7	Chemical Bank New York Trust Co. (67)	7	Industrial Bank of Japan, Ltd., Tokyo
8	Royal Bank of Canada, Montreal (41)	8	Credit Agricole Mutuel, Paris
9	Morgan Guaranty Trust Co., New York (59)	9	Banque Nationale de Paris
10	Canadian Imperial Bank of Commerce, Toronto (53)	10	Deutsche Bank, Frankfurt
11	Banca Nazionale del Lavoro, Rome (37)	11	Credit Lyonnais, Paris
12	Lloyds Bank Ltd. (39)	12	Tokai Bank Ltd., Nagoya, Japan
13	Continental Illinois National Bank and Trust Co. of Chicago (112)	13	Mitsubishi Trust & Banking Corp., Tokyo

14	Credit Lyonnais, Paris (11)	14	Sumitomo Trust & Banking Co., Ltd., Osaka
15	Security-First National Bank, Los Angeles (72)	15	National Westminster Bank PLC, London
16	Bank of Montreal (47)	16	Mitsui Bank Ltd., Tokyo
17	National Provincial Bank Ltd., London (merged with Westminster)	17	Citibank NA, New York
18	Westminster Bank Ltd., London (15 for surviving corporation)	18	Société Générale, Paris
19	Bankers Trust Co., New York (73)	19	Mitsui Trust & Banking Co., Ltd., Tokyo
20	Fuji Bank, Ltd., Tokyo (2)	20	Long-Term Credit Bank of Japan, Ltd., Tokyo
21	Mitsubishi Bank Ltd., Tokyo (4)	21	Barclays PLC, London
22	Sanwa Bank Ltd., Osaka (5)	22	Dresdner Bank, Frankfurt
23	Sumitomo Bank Ltd., Osaka (3)	23	Taiyo Kobe Bank, Ltd., Kobe
24	First National Bank of Chicago (92)	24	Daiwa Bank, Ltd., Osaka
25	Société Générale, Paris (18)	25	Bank of Tokyo, Ltd., Tokyo

a. 1986 rank in parentheses.
SOURCES: 1964, Roger Orsingher, *Banks of the World: A History and Analysis* (London: Macmillan, 1967). 1986, *American Banker*, July 30, 1987.

eign access to their domestic financial markets. At the same time the U.S. Congress is considering legislation to bar Japanese securities firms from being recognized as primary dealers in U.S. government securities, a status that was first enjoyed by Daiwa Securities and Nomura Securities International. The strong secular outlook for the yen seems to have rendered Japanese regulators less resistant both to relaxing restrictions on foreign entry into Japanese financial markets (for example, into markets for bonds and commercial paper) and to permitting an increasing foreign demand for Euroyen instruments to be serviced. It would be a serious mistake, however, for Western financial services firms and U.S. regulators to believe that risk-based capital ratios and increased foreign entry into Japanese financial markets can significantly constrain future penetration of international financial markets by Japanese banks.

Summary and Policy Implications

Parallel structural arbitrage in international insurance, securities, currency, and banking markets is melting down longstanding geographic and functional barriers between financial activities. As institutional product lines fuse together across the globe, the activities of various financial regulators need to be reintegrated too.

Both in the United States and abroad, individual financial institutions are revising their organizational structures and extending their product lines and geographic reach to serve new markets and in the process selecting burden-minimizing regulatory microclimates for themselves. This structural arbitrage disrupts the inherited regulatory equilibrium, imposing a law of one burden on competing regulatory entities, who must struggle to defend and redefine the borders of their domains.

Drawing an analogy between operating a regulatory agency and operating an ordinary business, industrial organization concepts may be used to explain the evolution of regulatory structures. The analysis offered here emphasizes the growing intensity of competition from foreign regulators for opportunities to regulate domestic financial activities. The vigor of this competition has made it harder and harder for individual countries to keep foreign firms out of domestic financial markets and to keep domestic firms from expanding activities offshore.

U.S. officials have so far emphasized a political need to negotiate a formal harmonization of individual countries' approaches to financial regulation.[21] This chapter's industrial organization perspective suggests that the difficulty of arranging durable patterns of international regulatory cooperation reflects difficulties inherent in forming and maintaining a worldwide cartel in any product or service. Moreover, whatever effects U.S. regulatory reformers might intend to accomplish politically, reactive market forces will reshape the result.

In competing for clients, governmental regulators have two complementary advantages over private suppliers of regulatory services. Their governmental status confers reputational capital that makes it hard to force their exit when they are operating inefficiently. It permits them both to bear the financial strains of subsidizing critical elements in their service package for years on end and to manage self-interestedly the short-run flow of information concerning the effectiveness and cost-efficiency of their performance.

How to reintegrate financial regulatory services is a normative question. It is a difficult question because of incompletely financed and imperfectly monitored implicit subsidies to financial risk bearing that are hidden in the operations of government producers of financial regulatory services in the United States and other free-market countries. Reductions in regulatory burdens that structural arbitrage wins for multinational and multipurpose financial firms are often generated by surreptitiously shifting real costs onto various taxpayers. The most important of these hidden costs are unintended subsidies that flow from the improper pricing of explicit and implicit government and international financial guarantees. Concealing these subsidies from taxpayers makes their long-run effects destabilizing in that disinformation policies make it hard for taxpayers to fill the disciplinary role that stockholders and creditors play in a private firm.

A basic premise of economics is that in the long run, when transition costs are defined as negligible, bearers of unnecessary burdens will find ways to lay those burdens down. A basic premise of representative government is that when the public has accurate information, its representatives will make collectively rational choices. In the short run, pressure to make collectively rational choices is frequently overcome by counterpressure from side payments. The ability of powerful groups to extract government subsidies may be deemed to be part and parcel of the American system of free enterprise. No one should suppose that improving the flow of information about financial regulatory performance will end subsidies altogether. A more reasonable goal is merely to make the production of selective subsidies more painful to the agents that benefit from their creation. Evidence that a strong sense of shame underlies the production of subsidies may be found in the energies that givers and receivers of subsidies devote to packaging their dealings in forms that are hard to see and hard to measure even when seen. Perhaps because the need to obtain public esteem and approval is particularly great for those who seek political office, preserving at least the appearance of a public servant's personal honor and integrity appears to be an important goal, one that ranks above merely winning reelection or holding on to an agency job. Whether or not a better-informed electorate actually throws any regulatory rascals out of power, requiring authorities to provide appropriate evidence of how well public responsibilities are being handled greatly increases the odds that in their own lifetimes poor regulators will be censured rather than honored for compromising the common good.

The most stubborn issue in financial reform concerns the need to restructure government regulators' and politicians' incentives. These officials are engaged in a cyclical game of rescue, in which they are rewarded for solving problems that they first exacerbate by long-lived and addictive subsidies and for helping persons and institutions that they or their predecessors first victimize.

Designing financial regulatory structures that work *with* rather than *against* efficient adaptation by clients provides the best chance of achieving society's long-run regulatory goals. First and foremost, this means preventing regulators and regulated firms from continuing to distort the flow of information by which taxpayers assess their performance and finances.

Unless accounting reforms are adopted that enable the market value of regulatory subsidies to be credibly monitored and controlled by taxpayers, unfettered international competition among national regulators threatens to push global risk taking to unsustainable levels. Market-value accounting entails a double-entry system of records that would change government agency accounting in two ways.[22] First, it would completely eliminate the concept of an off-balance-sheet item. It would require agency managers to attach a current price to any and all sources of value: loan commitments, credit guarantees, fee-for-service business, and unrealized increases and decreases in the value of assets and liabilities of all kinds. Second, it would require agency officials to develop and publicize a system of calculating appraised market values for its explicit and implicit assets and liabilities. Much as in real estate appraisal, this implies assigning staff to the tasks of projecting contingent cash flows and analyzing current yields and prices in secondary markets for comparable financial contracts and instruments.

U.S. financial services firms face a painful choice. If they do not support the introduction of tough new constraints on the informational framework that regulators and those they regulate use to measure and report their economic performance and condition to each other and to taxpayers, they must acquiesce in the development of a cartel-like system of international regulatory coordination strong enough to limit the aggregate production of regulatory subsidies. What burdens this cartel would eventually seek to impose are uncertain and might depend on which agencies and nations lead the coordinating process.

Although accounting reform would be distributionally less arbitrary and economically more efficient than regulatory cartelization, it has powerful political enemies. It promises to be resisted by the recipients of hidden subsidies and by government officials because it imposes substantial transition costs on government regulatory enterprises. For society as a whole, the dangers of regulatory cartelization are that it is likely to support inefficient patterns of regulation and to break down at critical times. Limits on national sovereignty will tend to be least popular domestically when they are most beneficial internationally. So far the enemies of both approaches have been able to forestall effective action. Until this political stalemate is broken, the existing system of subsidized regulatory competition will continue. This forces all of us to live under a growing threat of global financial disruption.

Notes

1. E. Gerald Corrigan, "Financial Market Structure: A Longer View," in Federal Reserve Bank of New York, *Annual Report* (New York, 1987).

2. Federal Deposit Insurance Corporation, *Mandate for Change: Restructuring the Banking Industry*, preliminary draft (Washington, D.C., 1987).

3. William Baumol, John C. Panzar, and Robert Willig, "On the Theory of Contestable Markets," in G. Frank Matthewson and Joseph E. Stiglitz, eds., *New Developments in the Theory of Industrial Structure* (Cambridge, Mass.: MIT Press, 1986).

4. See William Niskanen, *Bureaucracy and Representative Government* (Chicago: Aldine, 1971).

5. The analogy to Faust was suggested by Ernest Bloch.

6. Mark Flannery, "Public Policy Aspects of the U.S. Payments System," University of North Carolina, 1987.

7. Corrigan, "Financial Market Structure."

8. Ibid.

9. Edward J. Kane, "Regulatory Structure in Futures Markets: Jurisdictional Competition between the SEC, the CFTC, and Other Agencies," *Journal of Futures Markets*, vol. 4 (September 1984), pp. 369–84.

10. Frank Herbert, *The Heretics of Dune* (New York: Berkley Books, 1984), p. 222.

11. Franklin R. Edwards, "Consolidation, Concentration, and Competition Policy in Financial Markets," Columbia University Graduate School of Business, 1987.

12. Douglas W. Diamond, "Financial Intermediation and Delegated Monitoring," *Review of Economic Studies,* vol. 51 (1984).

13. John F. Chant, "On the Rationale for the Regulation of Financial Institutions," Working Paper, Simon Fraser University, 1986.

14. James R. Barth, R. Dan Brumbaugh, Jr., and Daniel Sauerhaft, "Failure Costs of Government-regulated Financial Firms: The Case of Thrift Institutions," Federal Home Loan Bank Board, Washington, D.C., 1986.

15. George Stigler, "The Theory of Economic Regulation," *Bell Journal of Economics,* vol. 2 (Spring 1971), pp. 3–21; and Richard Posner, "Theories of Economic Regulation," *Bell Journal of Economics,* vol. 5 (Autumn 1974), pp. 335–58.

16. Ernest Bloch, "The Benefits of Multiple Regulators," New York University, Graduate School of Administration, 1984; Ian H. Giddy, "Domestic Regulation versus International Competition in Banking," *Kredit and Kapital,* vol. 8 (1984), pp. 195–209; Kane, "Regulatory Structure"; and Kenneth E. Scott, "The Dual Banking System: A Model of Competition in Regulation," *Stanford Law Review,* vol. 30 (1977), pp. 1–50.

17. Edward J. Kane, "Technological and Regulatory Forces in the Developing Fusion of Financial-Services Competition," *Journal of Finance,* vol. 39 (June 1984), pp. 759–72.

18. Edward J. Kane, *The Gathering Crisis in Federal Deposit Insurance* (Cambridge, Mass.: MIT Press, 1985).

19. This section draws on and extends Edward J. Kane, "Competitive Financial Reregulation: An International Perspective," in Richard Portes and Alexander Swoboda, eds., *Threats to International Financial Stability* (Cambridge: Cambridge University Press, 1987), pp. 111–45.

20. Corrigan, "Financial Market Structure."

21. Ibid.

22. George Benston, Robert Eisenbeis, Paul Horvitz, Edward Kane, and George Kaufman, *Perspectives on Safe and Sound Banking: Past, Present, and Future* (Cambridge, Mass.: MIT Press, 1986).

Commentary

Kenneth A. McLean

Professor Edward Kane has written a provocative and interesting paper that nonetheless seems to be at odds with itself. He cannot seem to make up his mind who is to blame for what he terms "a growing threat of global financial disruption." In the first half of the paper he fingers the regulators, whom he compares with drug dealers who push subsidized dope on an innocent and unsuspecting public. In his model, regulators push subsidies on a not too astute financial industry in order to expand their market share of the regulation business. Toward the end of the paper, however, he seems to hint that the subsidies are not so much given to as wrested away by financial firms aggressively seeking to avoid regulatory burdens while shifting costs to other parties.

Kane is equally ambivalent about the ability of financial firms to pick a friendlier regulator—a process he calls "structural arbitrage" and which Arthur Burns once termed "competition in laxity." At one point, Kane applauds competition among the regulators as necessary to prevent excessive regulation. According to Kane, a unified regulatory system—or, in his terminology, a regulatory cartel—will inevitably, over the long run, tend toward overregulation.

Having said this, Kane then goes on to deplore specific instances in which financial firms have used structural arbitrage to enhance their regulatory climate, including the growing use of off-balance-sheet liabilities by commercial banks. At the international level, he warns, "unfettered international competition among national regulators threatens to push global risk taking to unsustainable levels."

When Kane moves from the realm of theory to practice, he begins to sound more like Gerald Corrigan and less like Edward Kane. If we are indeed headed for a global financial collapse because of unfettered competition among the regulatory authorities, one would think that Kane would be joining with Corrigan and others in calling for better policy cooperation among the regulators. Alas, that is not the case. An international agreement among the regulators would constitute a regulatory cartel, and as we all know, cartels are bad. Or at the very least, they are unstable and ineffective.

Kane supports more disclosure instead of more international cooperation. He wants the regulatory agencies to calculate and disclose the economic value of all of the subsidies, explicit or implicit, that they provide to their clientele. He accuses the regulators of deliberately concealing these costs to hide the evidence of their own mismanagement.

Kane is somewhat vague about just how he expects these disclosures to reform our financial regulatory system. Presumably, his scenario runs something like this: If the "true" costs of the subsidies extended by financial regulators were known, the public would rise up in righteous indignation and, through their elected representatives, demand swift changes in the system.

As a model of the political process, this scenario is about as plausible as the notion that the good guys always win or that Washington, D.C., will soon get a major league baseball team. Since the days of Alexander Hamilton, subsidies have been an enduring feature of our political landscape. The relevant political issue is not whether subsidies do or do not exist, but who gets them and for what purpose. The ability of powerful groups to perpetuate questionable but nonetheless visible tax loopholes belies the public indignation model of political change implicit in Kane's paper.

Whatever the politics, there is one eminently predictable effect of the expanded regulatory disclosure system Kane calls for—it will raise the revenues of banking economists like Kane who have made the detection of implicit subsidies into a minor industry.

No matter what the banking agencies report as the cost of their hidden subsidies, a lot of controversy will be generated. Some economists will argue the costs are understated; some will say they are overstated; some will complain that not all of the corresponding implicit benefits have been measured; some will take no position on the numbers but complain about the methodology. Others will also offer their views. The accounting professionals are likely to say the economists who prepared the agency report are looking at the wrong numbers. Trade associations will argue both are wrong. All told, the reports will create a lot of revenue for banking economists in general and especially for those who are in the subsidy detection business. Whether any lasting reform results is problematical.

Another interesting feature of Kane's paper is the notion that financial regulation need not necessarily be a governmental function and that private firms might provide regulatory services more efficiently. The fact that the government has the dominant share of the market is not due to superior performance, according to Kane. Instead, it is due to the "reputational capital" possessed by governmental regulators and their ability to maintain that capital through predatory news management. These factors plus the inability of governmental agencies to exit the market account for the government's growing share of the financial regulation business.

In reading Kane's paper, one gets the idea that many potential Nicholas Biddles are waiting in the wings perfectly capable of acting as a central bank were it not for the predatory news management of the bad old Federal Reserve—or that several large insurance companies are straining to get into the deposit insurance business but are frustrated by the ability of the FDIC to conceal its losses.

There may indeed be some bank regulatory functions that can just as well be performed in the private sector. One good example is the check-clearing system operated by the Federal Reserve banks. Congress did mandate in 1980 that the Federal Reserve begin pricing its check-clearing services at their full economic cost. The General Accounting Office has reported that the Federal Reserve has by and large complied with this mandate. Incidentally, contrary to Kane's theory of regulators as jurisdiction maximizers, the Federal Reserve did not resist these reforms even though their intended effect was to cause the Federal Reserve banks to lose market share.

It is difficult, however, to see how most financial regulatory services can or should be performed by private firms. Kane's contrary conclusion may stem from his inappropriate model of financial regulation. He views financial regulation as a business with the same imperatives as any other business. The provision of financial regulatory services is essentially a contract between the producers of financial services and a regulator whose task it is to certify the competence and integrity of individual firms in order to maintain the confidence and trust of the public.

A good analogy would be the hiring of Pete Rozelle by the owners of professional football teams to "regulate" the NFL in order to maintain the confidence and trust of the football-watching public. The football commissioner's job is to rein in the occasional eccentric owner whose antics might undermine the profitability of the system as a whole. But there is no doubt in Rozelle's mind that he is working for the owners and not for the public.

The problem with Kane's model is that most financial regulation does not originate with the desire of the financial industry to be regulated. Virtually all of the major banking statutes were originally opposed by the American Bankers Association, including the Federal Reserve Act and the Federal Deposit Insurance Act. Rightly or wrongly, most financial regulation has been imposed on the financial industry by legislative bodies who made the judgment that the industry was not meeting the needs of important constituencies, including depositors and borrowers. Thus, if there is a social compact underlying financial regulation, it is between the regulator and the general public and not between the regulator and the industry it regulates.

This raises the issue of whether the conventional historical model of the regulatory process, for all of its faults, is not still a better model than the industrial organization framework adopted by Kane. According to the historical model, regulation represents a successful political victory by aggrieved parties to obtain redress from perceived injustices in the marketplace. A regulatory apparatus is set up to consolidate the gains and make them permanent. Over time, however, the agency begins to forget the reasons why it was created and becomes a captive of the very industry it is supposed to regulate. A new crisis then ensues, and if it is serious enough the agency is reborn or given a revised mission. Or if the original problems are believed to be no longer relevant, the agency is allowed to expire, as in the case of the Civil Aeronautics Board.

Under Kane's model, there is a long-run tendency toward over-regulation. The conventional historical model would suggest precisely the opposite: the long-run tendency is toward under-regulation.

Kane is right to be concerned about the potentially destabilizing effects of structural arbitrage among the regulators. The remedy, however, is not some elaborate new disclosure system, as he advocates. Instead, the national regulators should continue working on international agreements to provide for standard methods of regulation. And at the domestic level, we should end the competition in laxity among the three federal regulatory agencies by consolidating all of bank regulation into a single independent agency with a renewed sense of public purpose.

Kenneth E. Scott

Professor Kane's provocative paper is intended to present a positive economic analysis of the process of financial regulatory reform. His goal, in other words, is simply to account for the existence of a system of governmental regulation of financial firms and to understand how that system changes over time.

To do this, he applies the concepts and models of the field of industrial organization and stresses two organizing perspectives. First, financial regulatory agencies are viewed as supplying a valuable and desired product. Second, financial regulatory agencies compete among themselves for financial services firms as clientele.

These prove to be, I think, stimulating and productive points of view. But let me begin by relating his industrial organization approach to some other ways of explaining the existence of government regulation.

The traditional or public interest view of administrative agency regulation is that it is intended to promote the public good by requiring individuals and firms to change their preferred behavior in ways that will benefit others. To put it in more economic terminology, the coercive powers of government are used to correct market failures. That process might take a number of forms: external costs might be internalized by taxes or liability rules or regulatory schemes. In this view, for example, bank regulation might be explained as a justifiable attempt to deal with the externalities of bank panics.

Another public interest explanation would be that bank regulation is being used to redistribute wealth toward the poor. As compared with direct subventions, regulatory transfers are usually poorly targeted and inefficient, but they are thought to have the virtue (or defect) of not leaving expenditure choices up to the discretion of the poor.

The problem with these traditional views is that they do not seem to explain much of what we in fact observe. Regulation is used where there is little or no evidence of market failure or to create wealth transfers of little (or negative) benefit to the poor.

So another school of explanation has arisen—public choice theory—which views regulation as the outcome of the efforts of interest groups, politicians, and bureaucrats to use the political process for their own personal benefit. The rhetoric of the public interest is the language that all employ, but the various actors are assumed to be advancing their own self-interest. In this light, much of bank regulation (such as restraints on entry or price fixing through the late and unlamented Regulation Q) can be explained as successful efforts by banks to obtain monopoly rents through a cartel administered by the government.

Into which framework, if either, are we to fit Kane's analysis? His mind seems to belong to the public choice school, on the whole, but there are moments when his heart seems drawn to the public interest school. The two may prove to be incompatible, a point to which I shall return later on. Most of the time Kane's intention is to give us positive analysis—merely to explain the way things are. I shall begin with some comments on his positive model and its assumptions, therefore, and go on to develop some of the normative implications of his paper, to which he gives only passing attention.

The first theme of Kane's model is that the existence of financial regulation should be viewed as a response to the demand of financial service firms and their customers for certain products, such as certification of firm quality (soundness) and the coordination of certain interfirm transactions (administration of the payments system). In this view, the existence of financial regulatory agencies does not reflect the use of coercion to achieve the public good or the result of capture to serve the industry's private ends, but is just a market response to a customer demand.

A lot of actual bank regulation is difficult to explain in this manner. Where this perspective does seem applicable, however, the issue then becomes: Why do we observe a government response? Why could not private firms supply such services and products? Kane's answer is that private firms cannot compete with government firms, which deliver subsidies to their customers, as the Federal Reserve does in its payments system operation or the federal insurance corporations do in the deposit insurance system. That merely pushes the inquiry back another step: What is the explanation for the subsidies? Private firms are not in the business of delivering subsidies to their customers, so at this point we seem forced out of an industrial organization model and back to public interest or public choice explanations.

The second and major theme of Kane's paper is the importance of competition among alternative suppliers of financial regulation in understanding the content and trajectory of that regulation through time.[1] The significance of regulatory competition in no way depends on using an industrial organization model; it is equally relevant whether one views financial regulation as a demand-driven commodity, a quest for the public interest, or a covert grab for private gain. Competition among regulators will significantly affect the way they act, as Kane points out in many interesting insights. In this connection, it may be helpful to distinguish more clearly between two levels of competition—among regulators for firm clientele and among firms for customers. Firms can shift regulators, which is the essence of the dual banking system. Customers can shift among firms (under different regulatory systems) supplying close substitutes, which is the essence of international regulatory competition.

For the most part, Kane concentrates on description or positive analysis, without inferring the possible normative implications or drawing any policy conclusions. I would like to extend his analysis, therefore, by suggesting some of its normative implications, particularly with reference to the consequences of agency competition.

Under the traditional view that regulation is aimed at forcing the regulated firm to change its behavior, subjecting the regulatory agency to competitive pressures would be regarded as undesirable. The usual cliché is that such agency rivalry will result in "competition in laxity" and that the solution lies in centralizing regulation in a single federal banking commission.[2] The standard industry response is that the ability to shift between regulatory agencies provides "an escape from arbitrary supervision" and constitutes "a check on the abuse of discretionary power." There is some truth in both clichés, but neither captures the whole picture. Let us attempt, therefore, a less simplistic analysis, and consider the normative implications of agency competition in terms of the different roles played by financial regulation.

First, in accordance with Kane's paper, consider regulatory agencies as market producers of valuable services. Then it is easy to conclude that a competitive environment among agencies is desirable, for all the usual reasons; it will create pressures toward efficiency and innovation.

Admittedly, the assumptions of a profit-maximizing firm do not apply very well to a bureaucratic government agency, for which we have no fully satisfactory model. In determining agency behavior, is the maximand the agency's budget, the market share of its clientele, the generation of political contributions to the administration in power, the prestige or future income of the agency heads, or what? With an inadequately specified model, empirical testing of specific hypotheses becomes very difficult. But to some degree, all of these versions of the government firm point us in the same general direction, and perhaps that is enough for our present purposes. So, viewing the agency as a service producer, competition is to be encouraged, not prevented.

Second, I would argue that the same normative conclusion should be reached from the viewpoint of consumers if, under a capture theory, the regulatory agencies are seen as industry agents for cartel administration. Competition among regulators will tend to cause the cartel to break down, as each agency seeks to advance its own position.

As an example, take the case of the administration of entry controls in banking. Any cartel, to protect its monopoly rents, needs to prevent the entry of new competitors, and government regulation is an admirably effective way to achieve that objective. A classic case in point would be the record of the Civil Aeronautics Board in refusing to license any new trunk line air carriers for four decades after its creation.[3] In the banking field, however, charters could be obtained from either the comptroller of the currency or a state banking agency, and for a state bank the access to needed federal deposit insurance could be obtained through either the FDIC or the Federal Reserve. The result was that although entry into banking after 1933 was indeed restricted, many new charters were issued, and monopoly rents were far below the maximum attainable.[4]

But third, consider that regulatory agencies advance the public interest by coercing banks to change their behavior and internalize purported externalities. Competition, it is clear, will lessen the coercive powers of an agency, as regulated firms compare and shift between alternative legal environments to reduce the costs (including opportunity costs) of compliance.

Thus if activity restrictions on banks are really in the public interest, it is sensible that the Bank Holding Company Act be administered by one agency (the Federal Reserve) and not by several (as the Bush task force suggested); agency competition would lead to more liberal interpretations of just what activities are "so closely related to banking . . . as to be a proper incident thereto."[5] Conversely, of course, if those restrictions are not in the interests of consumers but merely in the interests of certain trade groups, the Federal Reserve's monopoly over the act's interpretation has been most regrettable. It might also be noted that the developing government support for "functional regulation" would preserve agency regulatory monopolies and prevent agency competition.

Fourth, what are the implications of agency competition for the role of regulatory agencies in effecting wealth transfers or cross-subsidies among firms or consumers? Kane argues plausibly that regulatory competition tends to inflate the subsidies beyond what they would otherwise be or what the legislature intended. Regulatory agencies are able to do this, in his view, by holding back or actually distorting information about the future costs of their policies and guarantees. He obviously has the FSLIC in mind, among others.

Kane's solution is to urge that more accurate and reliable information be demanded from the regulators. At this point, it seems possible that his public interest heart may be overpowering his public choice mind.

In what sense are these burgeoning subsidies "unintended" by the legislature? Lawyers are accustomed to the notion that people "intend" the natural and foreseeable consequences of their actions. Was it still news to Congress in 1987 that the deposit insurance guarantees were not properly priced? Does Congress really want more precise information about the financial condition of the FSLIC or the FDIC? If so, they could have obtained it years ago, through the General Accounting Office or in other ways.

But Congress seems to prefer as long as possible to say that everything is uncertain and nobody really knows. That position may be politically superior to better information, for the legislature as well as for the agency, since it aids in deferral of the presentation and payment of the bill for the subsidy program. In politics, a cost deferred to someone else's term of office is a cost avoided.

In short, improved cost information and greater public accountability are no doubt in the public interest, but Professor Kane does not give us much reason to believe that they will be the outcome of the political process in the near future.

Notes

1. It is hard for me to take issue with that proposition, since ten years ago in a paper on the dual banking system I tried to illustrate the same point at length. K. Scott, "The Dual Banking System: A Model of Competition in Regulation," *Stanford Law Review*, vol. 30 (1977), pp. 1–50.

2. A leading proponent was Federal Reserve Board Governor J. L. Robertson, "Federal Regulation of Banking: A Plea for Unification," *Law and Contemporary Problems*, vol. 31 (1966), pp. 673–95. See also Federal Bank Commission Act—1976: Hearings on S. 2298 before the Senate Committee on Banking, Housing, and Urban Affairs, 94th Cong., 2d sess., 1976.

3. Subcommittee on Administrative Practice and Procedure of the Senate Committee on the Judiciary, 94th Cong., 1st sess., *Civil Aeronautics Board Practices and Procedures*, vol. 6 (Comm. Print 1975).

4. Sam Peltzman, "Entry in Commercial Banking," *Journal of Law and Economics*, vol. 8 (1965), pp. 11–50; see also Franklin Edwards and Linda Edwards, "Measuring the Effectiveness of Regulation: The Case of Bank Entry Regulation," *Journal of Law and Economics*, vol. 17 (1974), pp. 445–60.

5. Section 4(c)(8) of the Bank Holding Company Act, 12 U.S.C. 1843(c)(8).

10
Innovation, Institutional Changes, and Regulatory Response in International Financial Markets
David F. I. Folkerts-Landau and Donald J. Mathieson

During the 1980s, international financial markets experienced rapid growth and major structural changes.[1] New instruments and issuance techniques emerged; extensive changes occurred in the role of financial institutions; regulations were liberalized; and supervisory practices were adapted to changing financial relationships. Many of these developments are a continuation of trends that have been evident since the 1970s but whose pace has accelerated in the 1980s.[2] The structural changes in these markets are responses to major macroeconomic disturbances and imbalances, to technological advances in telecommunications and data processing, and to arbitrage opportunities created by differences in financial structures (including regulations, tax codes, and portfolio preferences). Most major countries have increased the scope for international financial transactions by reducing their restrictions on both short- and long-term external capital flows. Liberalization has generally reduced restrictions on the products, activities, and location of financial institutions as well as on the interest rates that could be charged on loans or offered on liabilities. As these structural changes have taken place, integration between major domestic and offshore financial markets has increased. There is now, for example, a common set of debt and equity instruments that are issued and traded on most major markets.

The structural changes in financial markets have had important implications for the formulation and execution of regulatory and su-

---

The authors have benefited from the comments of other authors in the Financial Services Regulation Project and those of Richard Herring on an earlier draft. The views expressed here are those of the authors and should not be taken as reflecting the views of the International Monetary Fund.

pervisory policy in the major industrialized countries. In particular, new instruments and markets have combined with new telecommunications technology to make it easier for financial firms to relocate some of their activities to a regulatory or tax jurisdiction of their choice; at the same time, the growing integration of markets has meant that disturbances in one national market are transmitted swiftly to markets in other countries. The result has been a continuing feedback between changes in financial markets and regulatory and supervisory policies. Financial market regulatory policy, for example, which has stimulated innovations in financial products and influenced the location of new activities (especially in the offshore markets), has been forced to adapt to the expanding international activities of domestic financial institutions and to the possibility of spillovers of disturbances from other markets. In particular, the national authorities recognize the need for some cooperation in the design of national regulatory and supervisory policies, though a theoretical and political debate continues over the extent and nature of such cooperation.

To examine the implications of structural changes in international financial markets for the formulation of international regulatory and supervisory policies, this chapter is divided into three sections. The first section reviews the changes in international financial markets that have increased the interdependence between national regulatory policies in the major industrialized countries. This examination looks at the forces creating change in financial markets (including the role of regulatory policies and supervisory practices) and considers how these changes were transmitted across countries. The second section analyzes the response of supervisory and regulatory policies to these structural changes, especially the attempts to achieve a degree of international policy coordination. The last section examines current issues associated with formulating and implementing supervisory and regulatory policy in a world of increasingly integrated financial markets.

Structural Change, Regulatory Policy, and Supervisory Practices

The extensive changes in financial instruments, financial institutions, and regulatory structures from the late 1970s to the late 1980s are the competitive response of market participants (in both the private and public sectors) to macroeconomic disturbances and technological advances and to the arbitrage opportunities created by differences in financial structures. These trend changes in financial markets have reflected the continuing interaction between macroeconomic disturbances, technological advances, and official financial policies regarding capital controls, supervisory practices, and regulatory restrictions. This interaction between policies and financial market developments has provided much of the momentum for the extensive changes in financial markets. To illustrate, this section first considers the main forces for structural changes and then examines how changes in one market have been transmitted to other markets.

In the early 1970s the structures of the financial markets in the major industrialized countries were quite diverse. Although these countries experienced sustained growth and low inflation during much of the late 1950s and 1960s, each national financial market developed largely independently of others, reflecting both economic factors and government policies. Communications and transportation costs, differences in financial and legal arrangements, and even cultural and social traditions made it costly to undertake new financial operations in different national markets. In addition, capital and exchange controls on external financial transactions in France, Japan, and the United Kingdom discouraged financial integration. In this environment of relative macroeconomic stability and of incomplete cross-country links between financial markets, the structure of domestic financial institutions, and the attendant regulatory arrangements, primarily reflected domestic concerns.

Macroeconomic Disturbances. Financial systems in many countries have been forced since the early 1970s to adapt to increased uncertainty about macroeconomic conditions and to the need to finance large fiscal and current account imbalances. The abandonment of the Bretton Woods system of fixed exchange rates was accompanied by a sharp expansion of cross-border financial flows and by the increased variability of nominal and real exchange rates (figure 10–1). In addition, the 1970s and 1980s have witnessed an uneven pattern of growth and recession in economic activity[3] and higher and more variable inflation than in the 1960s.[4] Nominal and real interest rates reached levels during the early 1980s not experienced in most industrial countries during much of the post–World War II period.

In the 1970s the level of activity in international financial markets was sharply stimulated by sectoral imbalances associated with sharp changes in energy and commodity prices and the emergence of large fiscal imbalances in most industrialized countries. For example, the recycling of the current account surpluses of the oil-exporting countries associated with the oil price increases of 1973 and 1979 was accomplished primarily by private sector intermediaries. During this period, most of the reserves accumulated by oil-exporting countries

FIGURE 10–1
U.S. DOLLAR EXCHANGE RATES, 1974–1987
(monthly average of daily absolute percentage change)

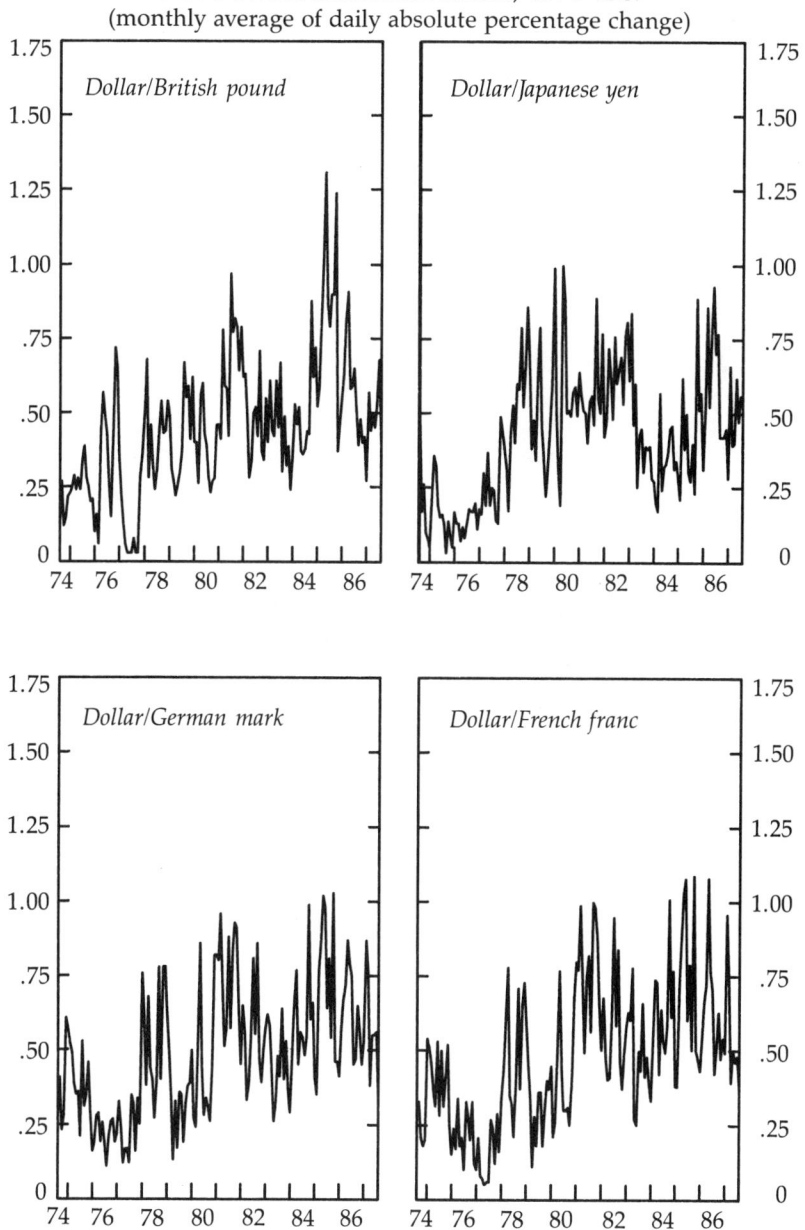

Dollar/British pound

Dollar/Japanese yen

Dollar/German mark

Dollar/French franc

SOURCE: International Monetary Fund, *International Financial Statistics*, various years.

395

were intially held as deposits in banks in offshore financial markets and in the major industrialized countries. As the current account deficit of industrialized and non-oil developing countries rose sharply, lending from banks and other private creditors financed nearly half the deficits of the non-oil developing countries.

Moreover, while developing countries with external payments difficulties during the 1980s were able to obtain only limited additional credits from private financial markets (generally through new money packages accompanied by adjustment programs supported by the International Monetary Fund), flows between borrowers and lenders in the industrialized countries accelerated sharply, with much of the growth in the securities markets rather than in bank lending. In addition, the emergence of large fiscal deficits in some major industrial countries in both the mid-1970s and early 1980s led over time to sharp increases in the stocks of government securities outstanding. To market those securities, governments removed restrictions on purchases by both the domestic nonfinancial sector (especially of short-term securities) and foreigners.

Technological Advances. The ability of financial institutions to adjust to these changes in macroeconomic conditions was influenced profoundly by innovations in telecommunications and data processing.[5] New developments in such areas as computer technology, computer software, and telecommunications permitted more rapid processing and transmission of information, completion of transactions, and less costly confirmation of payments. Such changes enlarged the set of markets in which financial institutions could provide intermediary services. With more institutions able to service the various markets efficiently, competitive pressures naturally increased.

Differences in Regulatory, Supervisory, and Tax Structures in the Mid-1970s. While macroeconomic shocks, payments imbalances, and technological changes provided the principal stimulus for the rapid expansion of activity in international financial markets during the 1970s and 1980s, attempts to arbitrage financial conditions (including regulatory and institutional differences) between the offshore and domestic markets of the major industrialized countries often played a role in determining the scale and composition of the flows between particular markets. In general, financial structures in the major industrialized countries differed most in (1) regulations concerning yields on financial instruments, the activities and location of financial institutions, and access to markets; (2) prudential supervision of the financial sector; and (3) tax and disclosure systems. The liberalizations of domestic financial markets were to play an important role in removing a number of these differences.

Regulations on yields, activities, and market access. In the mid-1970s interest rate ceilings were important constraints in France, Japan, and the United States, but were not present in the Federal Republic of Germany or in the United Kingdom. In Japan interest rates on most financial assets were closely linked to the official discount rate charged by the Bank of Japan on discounts of commercial bills and on loans secured by eligible paper. The ability of Japanese borrowers and lenders to evade those interest rate ceilings was constrained by the limited availability of short-term money market instruments and by a comprehensive system of exchange controls. But large bond-financed central government fiscal deficits, which emerged in the mid-1970s, created alternative portfolio instruments and exerted upward pressure on free-market interest rates, thereby creating strong incentives to shift away from assets with low fixed yields.

In the United States, Regulation Q prohibited the payment of interest on demand deposits and set interest rate ceilings on savings and time deposits at depository institutions. As inflation and market interest rates rose in the late 1960s and early 1970s, relative to the Regulation Q ceiling rates, there were repeated episodes of withdrawal of deposits (disintermediation) from financial institutions. Depositors sought higher yields through direct purchases of U.S. government securities and money market funds. In addition, large borrowers and lenders turned to the Eurocurrency market to obtain additional funds and to earn a market return on their financial assets.

Restrictions on the products, activities, and location of financial institutions differed significantly between financial systems with universal banks and those with more segmented markets and activities. In the Federal Republic of Germany and in Switzerland, banks were allowed to undertake both commercial and investment banking activities, and they developed extensive branch networks in their domestic economies. In contrast, commercial banks in the United States and Japan were more restricted, especially with respect to investment banking activities. Japanese banks, however, were legally permitted to branch nationwide; U.S. banks faced regulations that often limited their ability to branch both within a state and nationwide.

Such restrictions on activities and location at times limited the ability of certain types of financial institutions to attain a diversified portfolio, which made these institutions vulnerable to geographic or sector-specific shocks. Where restrictions on activities or branching existed, some financial institutions attempted to undertake restricted operations in the Eurocurrency markets (unless prevented by capital controls) or through domestic operations under alternative corporate forms.

During the early and mid-1970s, the maintenance of extensive capital controls and limitations on entry of foreign financial institutions into the domestic market were part of the effort to isolate domestic financial systems from external developments. In addition to controls on capital flows, the entry of foreign financial institutions was sometimes restricted through controls on chartering and licensing, through restrictions on the activities that these institutions could undertake, and through constraints on their access to certain markets. To the extent that these restrictions were effective, they helped create and maintain significant differences in financial market conditions across the major domestic markets.

Prudential regulation and supervision. Prudential regulations and the supervision of financial institutions differed sharply among countries in the mid-1970s. As noted earlier, exchange controls and transaction costs had limited the interdependence of the major financial markets during the 1950s and 1960s and thereby contributed to a diverse mix of disclosure and accounting standards, legal arrangements, and institutions in the major domestic financial systems. Prudential regulations and supervisory practices were primarily focused on domestic activities of national institutions. In particular, the oversight of banks' international operations lagged behind the growing integration of banking markets.

In this situation, prudential regulations at times created incentives for institutions to adjust the location or the types of their activities. Some financial institutions used off-balance-sheet activities (such as guarantees or currency swaps) or operations in the external markets to minimize the costs of satisfying capital requirements. In particular, to the extent that the operations of branches or subsidiaries in the Eurocurrency markets were not consolidated with the parent financial institutions, booking business offshore often reduced the effective level of capital needed for the firm as a whole.

Tax and disclosure systems. Differences in the taxation of financial transactions and income from financial assets often led to a situation where financial transactions would take place (be "booked") in a given market or country solely to reduce a tax liability. The withholding tax typically levied in domestic markets on payments of interest to foreign holders of domestic securities or deposits also stimulated the issuance of Eurobonds (not subject to any withholding tax) and acquisition of Eurocurrency deposits. In addition, transfer taxes on security transactions (such as existed in the Federal Republic of Germany and Switzerland) discouraged the use of domestic money market instruments and encouraged the use of external money markets.

Disclosure requirements were also diverse. In part, this difference reflected alternative philosophies about the types of borrowers that should be allowed access to financial markets. One view was that market participants should be allowed to take on whatever risks (at a market-related price) they desired as long as there was full disclosure of the relevant financial information about the borrower's condition. The alternative view was that market access should be limited to more credit-worthy borrowers (for example, through merit regulation often imposed by the market); with assurance about the quality of the borrower, less detailed disclosure could be required. In the mid-1970s, the disclosure requirements established by the U.S. Securities and Exchange Commission (SEC) came closest to the first view. In contrast, borrowers in the Eurobond markets were traditionally limited to the better-known firms, banks, and governments whose credit standing was considered sufficient. In line with the second view, that market therefore required less detailed disclosure, although to some degree additional disclosure existed when bonds were also issued in domestic markets. The combination of lower issuance cost and disclosure requirements made the offshore markets especially attractive for many major borrowers.

Given the structural differences in major domestic and offshore markets in the 1970s, three main elements appear to have influenced how rapidly the effects of structural changes and financial innovations moved across national boundaries or between domestic and offshore markets: the degree of competition in various financial markets; the method of regulatory enforcement; and the prevalence of restrictions on financial yields, the types of activities allowed for certain institutions, and international capital flows.

Perhaps the most important influence on the speed with which new innovations were transmitted was the degree of competition both within a domestic financial system and across financial markets. At the firm level, for example, an innovation by one firm in a competitive industry has, at times, led other firms to change their products to retain customers and market shares. At the industry level as well, such competition has meant that innovations in one sector of the financial system have led to new products in other sectors. At the regulator's level, the desire to avoid either sharp shifts in market shares of certain sectors of the domestic financial system or transfers of financial activity to external markets has at times induced significant regulatory changes.

An important force generating regulatory change through indirect competition among regulators has been the development of offshore markets. While capital controls at times inhibited the use of offshore markets, they proved difficult to enforce and, where effective, produced significant distortions. When such controls were ineffective or absent, the cost imposed by existing domestic regulatory requirements or taxes could frequently be lowered by moving an activity to an offshore market. The separation of commercial banking and investment banking, for example, was weakened by commercial bank ownership of investment banking subsidiaries in offshore locations. As will be discussed in the next section, the loss of financial activity to offshore markets has often resulted in modifications of domestic regulatory constraints.

The response of regulatory agencies to structural changes in financial markets was strongly influenced by the extent to which the regulatory structure and its legislative oversight have been concentrated or diffused. In the United States, the regulatory structure was specialized not only by industries such as securities (SEC), banking (Federal Reserve, Federal Deposit Insurance Corporation, and comptroller of the currency), and futures markets (Commodity Futures Trading Commission), but also along geographic lines (federal and state). Moreover, the federal legislative oversight was lodged with several congressional committees. This dispersed system of regulatory agencies and legislative oversight at times created incentives for institutions to switch from one regulatory domain to another and for regulators to take actions to maintain the competitive positions of the institutions they regulated. In contrast, the financial systems of continental Europe tended to have one or two main supervisory agencies and a single legislative group that provided regulatory structure. In such financial systems, financial firms had a more limited ability and incentive to shift their regulatory jurisdiction within the country by changing their product line, legal form, or domicile.

Evolution of International Financial Markets and Changes in Regulatory and Supervisory Policies

Although regulatory and supervisory policies in the major countries have been modified during the 1970s and 1980s in response to purely domestic developments (for example, problems with fraud or insider trading), structural changes in international financial markets (especially the progressive internationalization of financial activities and the securitization of international finance) have helped stimulate the liberalization of national financial markets and attempts to achieve a more coordinated approach to supervisory policies across countries. As noted in the previous section, these structural changes have reflected a continuing interaction between official policies toward financial markets and the attempts of the private sector to respond to macroeconomic developments, technological changes, and structural differences between markets. To examine the influence of these structural changes in international markets of supervisory and regulatory policies, we first review the aspects of the internationalization of financial activity and securitization that have created pressures on regulatory and supervisory policies and then consider the financial authorities' response to the growing integration of international financial markets.

Internationalization of Financial Activity. The internationalization of financial activity has been reflected in the more rapid expansion of international financial transactions relative to that of domestic markets.[6] The growth of international financial transactions has encompassed both (1) increased supply of traditional cross-border financial intermediary services (such as trade finance) and (2) increased external transactions between residents of the same country (designed to avoid domestic taxes and financial regulations).

During the past decade international bank lending (net of redepositing) and net bond issuance measured in U.S. dollars and deflated by the U.S. gross national product deflator grew 2½ times faster than real GNP in the industrialized countries (7 percent versus 3 percent per year, respectively) (see table 10–1).[7] Although domestic bond issuances climbed sharply in a number of major countries as large fiscal deficits arose in both the mid-1970s and the early 1980s, Eurocurrency bond issues grew even more rapidly. The rapid expansion of Eurocurrency bonds has been most notable in the Eurodollar sector, where Eurodollar bonds rose from roughly 4 percent of total (both public and private) domestic bonds issued in the United States in 1980 to nearly 10 percent in 1986 (table 10–2). Similarly, Eurobonds denominated in pounds sterling were about 12 percent of total domestic United Kingdom bonds in 1986.

The growing importance of external financial transactions for domestic banks in the major industrialized countries has been reflected in the rise in the proportion of total bank business accounted for by foreign loans or foreign security purchases. For example, the ratio of external assets to total assets of banking institutions in France, the Federal Republic of Germany, Japan, Switzerland, the United Kingdom, and the United States rose from 14 percent at the end of 1975 to 19 percent at the end of 1985.

401

TABLE 10-1
SIZE OF INTERNATIONAL FINANCIAL MARKETS, 1976–1986

	1976	1977	1978	1979	1980	1981	1982	1983	1984	1985	1986
					Billions of U.S. dollars						
Total international lending through banks and bond markets	96	95	114	148	179	194	144	131	152	181	245
International bond issues (net)[a]	26	27	24	23	19	29	49	46	62	75	85
International bank lending (net of redepositing)	70	68	90	125	160	165	95	85	90	105	160
International bond issues (net) deflated by U.S. GNP deflator	24	24	20	17	13	18	29	26	34	40	44
International bank lending (net) deflated by U.S. GNP deflator	66	60	74	94	111	105	56	49	50	56	83
						Percent					
Bond issues as ratio to world imports (U.S. dollars)	2.8	2.5	1.9	1.5	1.0	1.5	2.7	2.6	3.3	4.0	4.1
International bank lending (net) as ratio to world imports (U.S. dollars)	7.5	4.6	7.2	7.8	8.6	8.7	5.2	4.9	4.9	5.6	7.8
International bond issues (net) as ratio to international bank lending (net)	37.1	39.7	26.7	18.4	11.9	17.6	51.6	54.1	68.9	71.4	53.1

a. New international bond issues less redemptions, repurchases, and bank purchases of bonds.
SOURCES: International Monetary Fund, *World Economic Outlook* and *International Financial Statistics*, various years; Organization for Economic Cooperation and Development, *Financial Market Trends*, various years; and Bank for International Settlements.

The internationalization of financial activity was also evident in the greater participation of foreign financial entities in domestic markets in most major markets. The number of foreign banking firms in the major industrial countries increased sharply and accounted for a considerably greater share of total bank assets (table 10–3). The introduction of foreign securities firms into domestic markets also proceeded at a rapid pace. Several stock exchanges (in Japan and the United Kingdom, for example) expanded their membership in 1986 and 1987 to include foreign firms. Moreover, the standardization of market practices such as bond ratings, settlement procedures, and codes of conduct facilitated cross-border transactions.

Securitization. The internationalization of financial activity has been accompanied by increased securitization of international finance, which has involved a greater use of international direct debt markets and a shift away from international finance through financial intermediaries. In particular, syndicated loans have been increasingly displaced by issues of international bonds or, more recently, by the use of note issuance facilities or nonunderwritten Euro–commercial paper. Syndicated lending (excluding reschedulings) declined from its peak of $98 billion in 1982 to $58 billion in 1986, while the international bond market grew from $76 billion to $226 billion over the same period and the volume of Euronote borrowing facilities (including nonunderwritten Euro–commercial paper) grew from $5 billion in 1982 to $84 billion in 1986 (see table 10–4). Moreover, the structure of borrowing in the Euronote market has shifted significantly away from underwritten note issuance facilities toward the nonunderwritten Euro–commercial paper market. Part of the decline in the note facilities appears to be associated with the proposal to apply capital requirements against facilities arranged by banks in the United States and the United Kingdom. In 1984 underwritten facilities amounted to $29 billion, while Euro–commercial paper was not yet significant; by 1986 the importance of the two sources of funds had been reversed—underwritten facilities amounted to $27 billion and Eurocommercial paper had grown to $57 billion. In all major countries, the funds raised in the bank loan market as a percentage of GNP declined from 1980 to 1986 (except in Japan), while funds raised through securities markets increased.

Regulatory and Supervisory Response. The changes in international financial markets had a number of implications for existing regulatory and supervisory policies. As the share of financial activity taking place in the offshore markets increased, the authorities were unable to

TABLE 10–2
Size of Major Bond Markets, 1980–1986
(billions of local currency units at end of period; and percent)

	1980 Amount	1980 Percent	1981 Amount	1981 Percent	1982 Amount	1982 Percent
France (French francs)						
Public sector	376.9	77.1	437.3	78.4	565.9	80.2
Corporate sector	108.1	22.1	116.6	20.9	134.4	19.1
Foreign bonds[a]	3.9	0.8	4.1	0.7	5.3	0.7
Total	488.9	100.0	558.0	100.0	705.6	100.0
Eurobonds[b]	8.7	1.8	11.1	2.0	10.5	1.5
Federal Republic of Germany (deutsche marks)						
Public sector	130.8	13.2	127.9	11.3	156.6	12.5
Promissory notes[c]	360.6	36.5	439.1	38.7	480.1	38.3
Corporate sector	417.9	42.3	488.0	43.0	533.7	42.5
International bonds	79.2	8.0	80.3	7.0	83.6	6.7
Total	988.5	100.0	1,135.3	100.0	1,254.0	100.0
Japan (yen)						
Public sector	109,893	74.5	127,013	75.7	144,670	76.2
Corporate sector	35,867	24.3	38,590	23.0	42,312	22.3
Foreign bonds	1,784	1.2	2,251	1.3	2,874	1.5
Total	147,544	100.0	167,854	100.0	189,856	100.0
Eurobonds	125	0.1	205	0.1	322	0.2
United Kingdom (pounds sterling)						
Public sector	82.7	93.9	90.4	93.8	96.3	92.8
Corporate sector	5.3	6.0	5.4	5.6	6.2	6.0
Foreign bonds	0.1	0.1	0.6	0.6	1.3	1.2
Total	88.1	100.0	96.4	100.0	103.8	100.0
Eurobonds	0.7	0.8	0.8	0.8	1.2	1.2
United States (dollars)						
Public sector	1,043.3	67.0	1,171.5	68.6	1,377.5	70.5
Corporate sector	465.4	29.9	483.7	28.3	516.1	26.4
Foreign bonds	47.8	3.1	53.2	3.1	59.9	3.1
Total	1,556.5	100.0	1,708.4	100.0	1,953.5	100.0
Eurobonds	63.8	4.1	80.3	4.7	113.4	5.8

TABLE 10–2 (continued)

	1983		1984		1985		1986	
	Amount	Percent	Amount	Percent	Amount	Percent	Amount	Percent
	690.0	80.4	852.9	80.9	1,034.7	79.7	1,282.8	81.2
	161.5	18.8	194.4	18.4	251.7	19.4	285.2	18.0
	6.4	0.8	7.3	0.7	11.8	0.9	13.0	0.8
	857.9	100.0	1,054.6	100.0	1,298.2	100.0	1,581.0	100.0
	10.1	1.2	9.0	0.9	11.0	0.9	32.2	2.0
	191.0	14.0	228.0	15.5	272.4	17.3	329.7	19.6
	504.2	36.8	520.1	35.5	527.5	33.5	514.5	30.6
	586.6	42.8	622.0	42.4	657.0	41.7	688.1	41.0
	87.6	6.4	96.3	6.6	117.4	7.5	147.2	8.8
	1,369.4	100.0	1,466.4	100.0	1,574.3	100.0	1,679.5	100.0
	163,979	76.7	178,996	76.3	196,528	76.6	208,231	75.3
	46,503	21.7	51,346	21.9	54,930	21.4	62,846	22.8
	3,427	1.6	4,171	1.8	5,174	2.0	5,337	1.9
	213,909	100.0	234,513	100.0	256,632	100.0	276,414	100.0
	365	0.2	749	0.3	1,855	0.7	4,890	1.8
	105.5	92.9	114.9	91.4	124.6	91.7	131.9	90.8
	6.2	5.4	7.9	6.3	7.6	5.6	9.5	6.6
	1.9	1.7	2.9	2.3	3.7	2.7	3.8	2.6
	113.6	100.0	125.7	100.0	135.9	100.0	145.2	100.0
	2.6	2.3	5.4	4.3	10.0	7.4	16.8	11.6
	1,624.0	72.2	1,920.2	73.0	2,301.3	73.5	2,670.3	74.4
	562.3	25.0	643.0	24.4	756.9	24.2	867.3	24.2
	63.7	2.8	67.6	2.6	72.7	2.3	51.5	1.4
	2,250.0	100.0	2,630.8	100.0	3,130.9	100.0	3,589.1	100.0
	145.1	6.5	195.9	7.5	267.2	8.5	350.6	9.8

(*Table continues*)

TABLE 10–2 (continued)

	1980 Amount	1980 Percent	1981 Amount	1981 Percent	1982 Amount	1982 Percent
Switzerland (Swiss francs)						
Public sector	23.4	24.6	23.6	22.3	23.8	19.4
Corporate sector	45.8	48.1	51.0	48.3	56.3	45.9
Foreign bonds	26.0	27.3	31.1	29.4	42.6	34.7
Foreign notes (private placements)	n.a.	n.a.	n.a.	n.a.	n.a.	n.a.
Total	95.2	100.0	105.7	100.0	122.7	100.0

NOTE: n.a. = not available.
a. Foreign bonds are issued by a borrower who is of a nationality different from the country is which the bonds are issued. Such issues are usually underwritten and sold by a group of banks of the market country and are denominated in that country's currency.

attain as comprehensive a view of the activities of major financial institutions as in the past. This situation was accentuated by the growing use by many financial institutions of off-balance-sheet business (such as the provision of guarantees and swaps) that was often not fully incorporated into such supervisory measures as minimum capital-asset ratios. In response to these developments the authorities have removed some of the incentives for using offshore markets by liberalizing the regulatory structures in domestic markets; they have broadened the supervisory net to include more of the external and off-balance-sheet activities and have attempted better coordination of changes in regulatory and supervisory policies with other countries.

Three major changes in the institutional and regulatory environment of international financial markets have been evident. First, the authorities are relying more on measures to promote competition within and across major markets as a means of obtaining greater efficiency within financial systems. Competition has been enhanced by the weakening of capital controls and restrictions on the entry of foreign firms into domestic markets.[8] In addition, most industrialized countries have liberalized their domestic financial structures by removing or weakening restrictions on interest rates that could be paid on financial institution deposit liabilities, the use of instruments, and access to markets.[9]

The reductions in these restrictions have enabled domestic financial institutions to compete more readily in nontraditional markets

TABLE 10–2 (continued)

1983		1984		1985		1986	
Amount	Percent	Amount	Percent	Amount	Percent	Amount	Percent
23.5	17.8	24.5	16.8	25.0	10.9	24.8	9.3
59.1	44.6	63.3	43.6	66.7	29.1	77.5	28.9
49.7	37.6	57.5	39.6	67.4	29.4	90.6	33.8
n.a.	n.a	n.a.	n.a.	70.0	30.6	75.0	28.0
132.3	100.0	145.3	100.0	229.1	100.0	267.9	100.0

b. Eurobonds are those underwritten and sold in various national markets simultaneously, usually through international syndicates of banks.
c. These include certain public sector issues.
SOURCE: Salomon Brothers, *How Big Is the World Bond Market?* (New York: Salomon Brothers, 1987).

and have allowed the emergence of more universal financial institutions. These institutions have had the ability to diversify their activities better and to broaden their range of financial services and funding options. Though important specialized or sector-specific financial institutions still exist, their viability increasingly depends on economic factors (such as the market and economies of scale) rather than official restrictions on entry or competition.

A second major change in the regulatory environment has been to remove restrictions on the use of financial instruments. One aspect of competitive behavior in the Eurocurrency market has been a willingness to try a variety of novel techniques and instruments (syndicated loans, floating rate notes, Euro–commercial paper, and interest rate and exchange rate swaps) that have had characteristics closely tailored to the portfolio preferences of borrowers and lenders and have been introduced in other domestic markets. Many of those new instruments can now be used in the major domestic markets (see Appendix).

A third major change in the evolution of supervisory policies has been the response to the increased internationalization of financial transactions. Some of the most significant changes in this area, especially as they have related to the cross-country agreements, have occurred in periods after major crises. The disturbances surrounding the failures of Bankhaus I. D. Herstatt in the Federal Republic of

INTERNATIONAL FINANCIAL MARKETS

TABLE 10–3
POSITION OF FOREIGN BANKS IN SELECTED COUNTRIES,
1960–FIRST HALF OF 1985

	1960			1970	
Host Country	Number of institutions	Number of banking offices[a]	Foreign bank assets as percentage of total bank assets	Number of institutions	Number of banking offices[a]
Belgium	14[b]	n.a.	8.2[c]	26	n.a.
Canada	n.a.	n.a.	n.a.	n.a.	n.a.
France	n.a.	33	7.2	n.a.	58
Germany, Federal Republic of[e]	n.a.	24	0.5	n.a.	77
Italy[g]	1	n.a.	n.a.	4	n.a.
Japan[h]	n.a.	34	n.a.	n.a.	38
Luxembourg[i]	n.a.	3	8.0	n.a.	23
Netherlands[j]	n.a.	n.a.	n.a.	23	n.a.
Switzerland	8	n.a.	n.a.	97	n.a.
United Kingdom	51[k]	n.a.	6.7	95	n.a.
United States[m]	n.a.	n.a.	n.a.	n.a.	n.a.[n]

NOTE: Foreign banks defined as foreign banking institutions ("families") operating in the country through branches or majority-owned subsidiaries unless otherwise specified. Numbers given are taken from end-of-year data. n.a. = not available.
a. Foreign banking organizations represented by more than one entity are double-counted.
b. 1958.
c. End of 1958.
d. End of 1984.
e. Assets are for branches only.
f. At the end of June 1985 these offices represented ninety-five different banking organizations.
g. Branches only; at the end of June 1985 there were five foreign-owned subsidiaries.

Germany and Franklin National Bank in the United States in 1974, for example, led to the formation of the Committee on Banking Regulation and Supervisory Practices (Cooke Committee), under the auspices of the Bank for International Settlements. The committee's stated objective has been to establish comprehensive prudential practices including, notably, practices designed to ensure that banks' foreign operations do not "escape supervision." In December 1975 the

TABLE 10–3 (continued)

	1980			First Half of 1985		
Foreign bank assets as percentage of total bank assets	Number of institutions	Number of banking offices[a]	Foreign bank assets as percentage of total bank assets	Number of institutions	Number of banking offices[a]	Foreign bank assets as percentage of total bank assets
22.5	51	n.a.	41.5	57	n.a.	51.0
n.a.	n.a.	n.a.	n.a.	57	n.a.	6.3
12.3	n.a.	122	15.0	n.a.	147	18.2[d]
1.4	n.a.	213	1.9	n.a.	287[f]	2.4
n.a.	26	n.a.	0.9	36	n.a.	2.4
1.3	n.a.	85	3.4	n.a.	112	3.6
57.8	n.a.	96	85.4	n.a.	106	85.4
n.a.	39	n.a.	17.4	40	n.a.	23.6
10.3	99	n.a.	11.1	119	n.a.	12.2
37.5	214	n.a.	55.6	293[l]	n.a.	62.6
5.8[o]	n.a.	579	8.7	n.a.	783[p]	12.0

h. Branches only; at the end of June 1985 there were seventy-six different foreign banks operating in Japan.
i. Belgian-owned banks are not considered foreign banks.
j. Universal branches only.
k. 1962.
l. At the end of June 1985, there were 357 if joint ventures and consortium banks are included.
m. Assets are for foreign agencies and branches only.
n. In the early 1970s there were about fifty foreign banking offices.
o. End of 1976.
p. At the end of June 1985, these offices represented approximately 350 institutions.
SOURCE: Bank for International Settlements, *Recent Innovations in International Banking*, 1986.

Cooke Committee endorsed a concordat on international bank supervisory cooperation, indicating the division of supervisory responsibilities between parent and host country supervisors.

In 1978, the governors of the Bank for International Settlements endorsed the Cooke Committee's proposal that banks' capital adequacy should be monitored on a consolidated basis, inclusive of foreign branches and of majority-owned subsidiaries and, where pos-

TABLE 10-4
EUROMARKETS FINANCIAL ACTIVITIES, 1973–1987
(billions of U.S. dollars)

	1973	1975	1980	1981	1982	1983	1984	1985	1986	First Half of 1987
Eurobonds	4.2	8.7	20.4	31.3	50.3	50.1	81.7	135.4	187.0	86.3
International bank loans[a]	20.8	20.6	81.0	144.4	96.0	73.5	108.5	110.3	82.8	43.6[b]
Issuance facilities[c]						9.5	28.8	68.6	92.2	28.8[b]
Note issuance facilities						3.5	17.4	36.3	21.4	7.2[b]
Other						6.0	11.4	32.3	70.8	21.6[b]
Other committed facilities						n.a.	(11.4)	(10.5)	(5.6)	(1.2)[b]
Euro-commercial paper programs						n.a.	n.a.	(11.2)	(56.7)	(17.4)[b]
Other nonunderwritten facilities						n.a.	n.a.	(10.6)	(8.5)	(3.0)[b]
Equity-related bonds						8.0	10.9	11.5	22.3	10.2[b]

n.a. = not available.
a. Defined here as credits extended by commercial banks wholly or in part out of Eurocurrency funds.
b. Estimated.
c. Excludes merger-related standbys.
SOURCE: Organization for Economic Cooperation and Development, *Financial Statistics Monthly* and *Financial Market Trends*, various issues.

sible, minority holdings and joint ventures.[10] Nonetheless, events such as the problems of Banco Ambrosiano Holding in Luxembourg in 1982 indicated that there were still gaps in the supervisory net.[11] In 1983 a revised version of the concordat was published,[12] which examined ways of avoiding gaps in supervision caused by inadequately supervised centers or by the existence of intermediate holding companies within banking groups. By the end of 1986, consolidated supervision for purposes of capital adequacy of foreign branches and majority-owned subsidiaries for capital adequacy purposes had been established among the Group of Five countries and Switzerland.[13]

Since the emergence of widespread debt-servicing difficulties among developing countries and weaknesses in certain sectors of industrial economies during recessions in the early 1980s, there has been a coordinated effort to strengthen banks' balance sheets, reversing the downward trend that prevailed during the 1970s and early 1980s. Banks in industrialized countries, except Japan, have increased their capital relative to total assets (table 10–5). But because of accounting differences these measures are not strictly comparable across countries. Nonetheless, although the composition of assets and definitions of capital differ, supervisors in major industrialized countries have increasingly agreed that capital adequacy requirements should be strengthened and should converge internationally.

Two principal supervisory techniques are used for assessing capital adequacy—a gearing ratio, which is the unweighted total of all on-balance-sheet items divided by capital, or a risk-asset ratio, which is a risk-weighted total of on- and off-balance-sheet items relative to capital. During this period supervisors agreed on the advantages of the risk-asset approach, especially for coping with off-balance-sheet risks. At the end of 1986, France, the Federal Republic of Germany, Switzerland, and the United Kingdom used a risk-asset approach, and Japan applied this approach to overseas activities of Japanese banks with foreign branches. In 1986 U.S. federal regulators circulated a proposal for a risk-asset ratio approach. Despite this progress, substantial differences remain among major industrial countries in the risk weights assigned and in the definition of capital.

In 1986 the Cooke Committee published a report outlining a framework for supervisory reporting systems that sought to integrate off- and on-balance-sheet risks.[14] It was argued that risks associated with most off-balance-sheet activities—market risk, credit risk, and management risk—are not different in principle from the risks arising from on-balance-sheet business. In order to develop an integrated approach to assessing a bank's risk exposure, the report suggested

TABLE 10–5
CAPITAL-ASSET RATIOS OF BANKS IN SELECTED INDUSTRIALIZED COUNTRIES, 1978–1986
(percent)

	1978	1979	1980	1981	1982	1983	1984	1985	1986
Canada[a]	3.3	3.2	3.0	3.5[b]	3.7	4.1	4.4	4.6	5.0
France[c]	2.3	2.6	2.4	2.2	2.1	2.0	1.9	2.2	2.6
Germany, Federal Republic of[d]	3.3	3.3	3.3	3.3	3.3	3.3	3.4	3.5	3.6
Japan[e]	5.1	5.1	5.3	5.3	5.0	5.2	5.2	4.8	4.8
Luxembourg[f]	—	—	3.5	3.5	3.5	3.6	3.8	4.0	4.1
Netherlands[g]	3.9	4.3	4.2	4.3	4.6	4.7	4.8	5.0	5.2
Switzerland[h]									
Five largest banks	7.8	7.6	7.6	7.4	7.3	7.1	7.1	7.8	7.8
All banks	7.8	7.6	7.6	7.5	7.5	7.3	7.4	7.8	7.9
United Kingdom									
Four largest banks[i]	7.5	7.2	6.9	6.5	6.4	6.7	6.3	7.9	8.4
All banks[j]	5.2	5.1	5.0	4.5	4.1	4.4	4.5	5.5	5.4
United States									
Nine money center banks[k]	4.7	4.5	4.5	4.6	4.9	5.4	6.2	6.8	7.3
Next fifteen banks[l]	5.4	5.4	5.5	5.2	5.3	5.7	6.6	7.2	7.5
All country reporting banks[k,l]	5.5	5.3	5.4	5.4	5.6	5.9	6.5	6.9	7.2

NOTE: Aggregate figures such as the ones in this table must be interpreted with caution because of differences across national groups of banks and over time in the accounting of bank assets and capital. In particular, provisioning practices vary considerably across these countries as do the definitions of capital. Therefore, cross-country comparisons may be less appropriate than developments over time within a single country.

a. Ratio of equity plus accumulated appropriations for contingencies (before 1981, accumulated appropriations for losses) to total assets (*Bank of Canada Review*).

b. The changeover to consolidated reporting from November 1, 1981, had the statistical effect of increasing the aggregate capital-asset ratio by about 7 percent.

c. Ratio of capital, reserves, and general provisions to total assets. Data exclude cooperative and mutual banks. This ratio is not the official one (ratio of risk coverage), which includes loan capital and subordinate loans in the numerator and in the denominator weights according to quality. This ratio provides the groundwork for the control of the banking activities by the Commission Bancaire (Commission de Contrôle des Banques, *Rapport*).

d. Ratio of capital including published reserves to total assets. From December 1985, the Bundesbank data incorporate credit cooperatives (Deutsche Bundesbank, *Monthly Report*).

e. Ratio of reserves for possible loan losses, specified reserves, share capital, legal reserves plus surplus and profits and losses for the term to total assets (Bank of Japan, *Economic Statistics Monthly*).

f. Ratio of capital resources (share capital, reserves excluding current-year profits, general provisions, and eligible subordinated loans) to total payables. Eligible subordinated loans are subject to prior authorization by the Institut Monétaire Luxembourgeois and may not exceed 50 percent of a bank's share capital and reserves. Data in the table are compiled on a nonconsolidated basis and as a weighted average of all banks (excluding foreign bank branches). An arithmetic mean for 1986 would show a ratio of 7.7 percent. Inclusion of current-year profits in banks' capital resources would result in a weighted average of 4.3 percent for 1986. Provisions for country risks, which are excluded from capital resources, increased considerably in 1986. The 1986 level of provision is almost five times the level of 1982.

g. Ratio of capital, disclosed free reserves, and subordinated loans to total assets. Eligible liabilities of business members of the agricultural credit institutions are not included (De Nederlandsche Bank, N.V., *Annual Report*).

h. Ratio of capital plus published reserves, a part of hidden reserves, and certain subordinated loans to total assets (Swiss National Bank, *Monthly Report*).

i. Ratio of share capital and reserves, plus minority interests and loan capital, to total assets (Bank of England).

j. Ratio of capital and other funds (sterling and other currency liabilities) to total assets (Bank of England). Note that these figures include British branches of foreign banks, which normally have little capital in the United Kingdom.

k. Ratio of total capital (including equity, subordinated debentures, and reserves for loan losses) to total assets.

l. Reporting banks are all banks that report their country exposure for publication in the *Country Exposure Lending Survey* of the Federal Financial Institutions Examination Council.

SOURCES: Data provided by official sources; and IMF staff estimates.

methods for translating the various types of off-balance-sheet instruments into their roughly equivalent on-balance-sheet credit risks.

The issuance by the United Kingdom and the United States in March 1987 of a joint convergence proposal for monitoring capital adequacy marked a significant step toward a common supervisory framework for credit risk. In June 1987, Japanese authorities announced their support, in principle, for the British-U.S. proposals. A common supervisory framework for monitoring capital adequacy would significantly diminish the opportunities for regulatory arbitrage by banks among the three largest international financial centers.

In December 1987 the Basel Committee on Bank Regulation and Supervisory Practices published a proposal for international convergence of capital measures and capital standards.[15] The committee proposes to include ordinary paid-up share capital and disclosed reserves as well as some proportion of hidden reserves, property, equity holdings, and subordinated debt. In addition, it would assign different fixed weights for different types of on- and off- balance-sheet items used in calculating overall risk exposure and establish an overall ratio of bank capital to risk-weighted bank assets of 8 percent.[16]

Issues Raised by Recent Developments

Recent developments in international financial markets have affected the objectives of the financial authorities (especially as they relate to the regulation of domestic financial activity) and have introduced new complexities into the formulation and implementation of domestic macroprudential policies. While no central bank provides a detailed description of the circumstances under which it will provide emergency liquidity assistance, the growing integration of financial markets and the blurring of the distinctions between banks and other financial institutions have raised questions about which institutions or markets may have to be supported during a crisis and by whom. In particular, it has been argued that the close links between major short-term money markets (especially the interbank markets) may make it more difficult to confine the effects of a major domestic bank or nonbank financial institution failure solely to the domestic market. Moreover, the extensive growth of international financial markets has led some to conclude that the scale of emergency assistance needed (such as in the period surrounding the difficulties of the Continental Illinois Bank) could be significantly larger than in earlier periods.

One of the key issues in the formulation of these macroprudential policies has been what should be the extent and nature of the safety net provided for the major countries' financial systems. This issue has been discussed extensively in the other chapters in this volume, and an alternative to the traditional view of the appropriate safety net in the case of the United States has been presented. Other recent proposals, however, reflecting either the traditional or the alternative view on the appropriate nature of the safety net, have generally stressed the importance of strengthened supervision, especially with regard to achieving capital adequacy. This section examines the implication of the growing integration of international financial markets for the implementation of macroprudential policies that focus on strengthening capital adequacy. After a brief review of the perceived rationale for strengthened capital adequacy under the various proposals, we consider the problems of implementing such policies when financial institutions have the capability to undertake activity in a variety of corporate forms in a variety of international markets.

Concerns about the stability of the financial system, including maintenance of the payments system and protection of depositors and investors, have provided the traditional rationale for macroprudential policies that include not only the central bank's lender-of-last-resort function and public sector deposit insurance guarantees, but also the supervision and regulation of financial institutions. It has been argued that the absence of lender-of-last-resort assistance or deposit insurance could mean that even rational economic agents would rapidly withdraw their funds from financial intermediaries during a crisis.[17]

The use of supervision to prevent or limit fraud, insider trading, and self-dealing has traditionally been viewed as a complement to lender-of-last-resort assistance. In part, this practice reflects the fact that the availability of lender-of-last-resort assistance (or in some countries of public sector deposit insurance guarantees) might encourage less prudent policies on the part of banks or other financial institutions (the problem of moral hazard).[18] In particular, troubled institutions could engage in high-return and high-risk activities in the hope of earning sufficient profits to avoid closure (a double-or-nothing strategy).

In addition to concerns about fraud and moral hazard problems, some have also argued that macroprudential policies should reflect the possibility that recent changes in financial markets have not given financial institutions sufficient time to adjust their risk management techniques to the new environment, perhaps leading financial institutions to assume excessive risks. Views differ, however, about whether the liquidity and credit risks in newly liberalized financial markets have increased and what the sources of any increased risks are.

Though the volatility of some asset prices (including exchange rates and equity prices) has increased in recent years, it has been difficult to identify the degree to which this greater volatility has been a response to unstable macroeconomic conditions or whether it reflects the activities of financial market participants. In particular, financial arrangements, institutions, and prices may show some evidence of instability as long as major macroeconomic imbalances remain.

Other chapters in this volume argue that the traditional approach to macroprudential policies has resulted in a safety net that leads to inefficiencies and may encourage some financial institutions to take risks. When public sector guarantees of financial sector liabilities and lender-of-last-resort assistance are part of the system and cannot be appropriately priced, it has been noted that, in order to limit any exploitation of such guarantees and improve efficiency, some minimum restriction would have to be imposed on the financial institutions' decisions regarding some aspects of their asset selection, the composition of their liabilities, the level of their required capital, and closure rules defining when the institution can remain in business.[19] These restrictions would be accompanied by supervision of the asset side of the financial institutions, which in effect would mark assets to market and, in combination with capital requirements, determine whether the institution could remain open. A key issue is what constitutes the optimal level of such restrictions.[20]

Despite differences between the traditional and alternative approaches to designing a safety net for the financial system, most of the current proposals for improving the financial system support strengthening capital adequacy requirements. As already noted, the Basel committee proposal for capital adequacy has emphasized the use of a common risk-asset ratio to measure an institution's capital position and to inhibit regulatory arbitrage and provide a "level playing field."[21] This proposal focused on establishing a uniform risk-adjusted capital-asset ratio of 8 percent for internationally active banks. Though the risk weighting attached to bank loans to those governments apparently will be zero and certain types of hidden reserves will be included in measured capital, this could potentially require additional capital for banks in some countries, especially since risk-adjusted off-balance-sheet business would reportedly be included in the definition of assets. This proposal would also presumably involve the continued consolidation of foreign branches and majority-owned subsidiaries with the parent bank for purposes of assessing capital adequacy. Such harmonization and consolidation would be necessary if regulatory arbitrage were not to be encouraged. Similarly, although the proposals discussed in this volume generally regard the risk-asset ratio approach as providing an inadequate measure of capital adequacy, they also envision some potential increases in required capital in a system where assets are marked to market and capital could include subordinated debt.

Recent developments in international financial markets raise the issue of whether these minimum capital-asset ratios (or other supervisory restrictions) can be effectively enforced. Even if supervisory and regulatory policies are to be coordinated across countries, a number of obstacles to their successful implementation could remain. First, depending on the extent to which higher capital-asset ratios raise the cost of funding for banks, there still may be an incentive to relocate activity under alternative corporate forms. Though consolidation of branches and majority-owned subsidiaries currently helps limit this problem, a sharp rise in funding costs could induce the expanded use of minority-owned subsidiaries or affiliates in offshore markets. A key issue in this situation would be the nature of the guarantees offered by the parent bank to depositors in the minority-owned subsidiaries or affiliates.[22] If a domestic institution guaranteed the activities of its foreign affiliates, for example, then those affiliates would have to be consolidated with their parent for supervisory and regulatory purposes. If a domestic institution had an interest in a foreign affiliate but was not obligated to stand by the affiliate, then its position in the affiliate could be treated for supervisory and regulatory purposes like any asset on its domestic balance sheet. Monitoring the nature of the guarantees offered through affiliates may be no easy task, however. Moreover, if domestic institutions do provide guarantees to the activities of their minority-owned subsidiaries or affiliates, then consolidation may well have to be extended significantly beyond current practices.

A second potential issue in applying higher capital-asset ratios and enhanced supervision for banks is whether comparable treatment should be applied to other financial institutions such as securities houses. If the objective of these supervisory and regulatory policies is principally to limit any potential exploitation of lender-of-last-resort assistance or public sector deposit insurance guarantees by those institutions benefiting from these services, then it has been argued that this requires consideration of the extent to which the benefits of the guarantees provided to one set of financial institutions (banks, for example) also accrue to other sectors of the financial system. This involves considering how wide and explicit safety net guarantees should be and the direct and indirect costs (as measured by potential moral hazard problems) of extending safety net guarantees to a broader class of financial market participants. Although expanding the safety net guarantees could create moral hazard problems, it may prove difficult for the authorities to avoid extending these guarantees during a major crisis when potential spillover effects on the money markets or clearing systems are viewed as especially important. Some have argued, for example, that during the collapse of equity market prices in October 1987, the Federal Reserve effectively extended a form of lender-of-last-resort assistance to some of the major securities houses. If a broad system of safety net guarantees exists, or is perceived to exist by market participants, then enhanced supervision of the financial institutions protected by the safety net may be necessary. A decision to extend enhanced supervision to financial institutions other than banks, however, could be difficult to achieve, since there has been relatively little international coordination of supervisory policies relating to investment houses or other financial institutions (especially as it pertains to the monitoring of the consolidated positions of domestic securities houses and their foreign affiliates).

Finally, since the extent of lender-of-last-resort assistance and public sector deposit insurance guarantees differs significantly from country to country (for example, the Federal Republic of Germany and Switzerland have private but not public sector deposit insurance), it is not clear that a common capital-asset ratio would provide the most appropriate constraint. Since significant differences between tax, legal, accounting, and disclosure requirements continue to affect the location of financial activity, the harmonization of capital-asset ratios would most likely be sustainable only if the other remaining structural differences between markets were also eliminated over time.

In considering future efforts at coordinating financial regulatory and supervisory policies, much of what is likely to occur depends on whether the current efforts at liberalizing domestic financial markets are sustained. It could be difficult, for example, to reconcile further liberalization of international financial transactions if there should be a major expansion of protectionism in the major industrial countries. Moreover, a combination of protectionism and efforts to restrict external financial transactions would clearly be a "worst case" scenario, especially since it would be difficult to envision an effective set of capital controls that would not severely affect financial market efficiency. If recent financial liberalization measures are sustained or expanded, the pressures for further coordination not only of prudential regulatory and supervisory policies but also of accounting, tax, and disclosure systems are likely to continue to grow. Any growth, however, will require solving the analytical problem of what common standards should prevail across still relatively diverse economic systems.

Appendix: Liberalization and Innovation

The liberalization of financial markets during the past decade has proceeded along four avenues: the liberalization of cross-border financial flows, the growing foreign participation in domestic markets, the introduction of new instruments, and the removal of domestic price and quantity restrictions.[23]

An early but significant step toward the liberalization of capital flows came with the removal of controls on capital outflows from the United States. The Interest Equalization Tax had discouraged foreign borrowers from issuing securities in U.S. financial markets, and the Voluntary Foreign Credit Restraint Program may have inhibited U.S. banks and financial institutions from increasing the level of loans to foreign entities. By 1974, these measures and various other administrative guidelines had been removed. Foreign banks and other financial entities have generally had access to U.S. domestic markets, and the access for banks has been on the basis of national treatment (that is, they faced the same regulatory and supervisory requirements as domestically chartered banks) since the International Banking Act of 1978. In 1984 the U.S. authorities also abolished the withholding tax levied on nonresident holders of bonds issued by U.S. residents.

The United Kingdom liberalized sterling cross-border transactions by removing exchange controls in 1979. The controls were designed to prevent capital outflows; their removal, along with the lifting of lending restrictions on banks (the so-called corset), opened the sterling banking and securities markets to foreign borrowers.

The German authorities also have significantly reduced restrictions on capital inflows. In the 1970s these restrictions were principally authorization requirements for nonresident purchases of domestic bonds and money market instruments and, for a few years, restrictions on payments of interest on bank deposits held by foreigners. Such restrictions were gradually removed in the 1980s. Access to the German capital markets was further liberalized with the recent replacement of the calendar for issues in securites markets with a simple notification system and with the removal of a 25 percent withholding tax on interest payments on domestic bonds to nonresidents. In 1988, however, a 10 percent withholding tax on income from bonds issued on German markets was reimposed.

Since the early 1980s in Japan, the authorities have undertaken an extensive liberalization of cross-border financial activities. The number of foreign institutions allowed to borrow from Japanese banks, or to issue in the Japanese securities markets, has been gradually expanded. In addition, the Euroyen bond market was opened to foreign corporations in 1984, and access to this market was further extended to foreign banks in 1986.

In the mid-1980s, the French authorities undertook an extensive liberalization of cross-border financial flows. The Euro–French franc bond market was reopened and exempted from a 10 percent withholding tax applied in domestic markets, and foreign exchange repatriation and hedging restrictions were reduced.

Over the past decade—and particularly since the early 1980s—the range of instruments used in international and domestic financial transactions has expanded significantly. Many of these innovations originated either in the domestic U.S. market or in the Eurodollar markets and then spread to domestic financial markets in other countries. The introduction of the floating rate note in the early 1970s was one of the first major innovations. Over time, the volume of international lending through this instrument grew to exceed the volume of lending through the syndicated loan market. The introduction in 1981 of note-issuance facilities—medium-term arrangements that allow borrowers to issue short-term notes in the Euromarkets backed by underwriting commitments of commercial banks—constituted another important broadening of the choice of instruments. Currency and interest rate swaps—first undertaken in 1981 and amounting to over $500 billion by 1986—are particularly significant, because of both their scale and their apparent availability.

In France, the volume of mutual fund assets quadrupled between 1982 and 1986. French banks started issuing negotiable certificates of deposit in 1985. In addition, the government made short-term Treasury securities available to nonbanks and banks.

In Germany, the range of new instruments was extended by granting permission for zero-coupon bonds with debt warrants, floating rate notes, certificates of deposit, dual currency bonds, and currency and interest rate swaps. In Japan, the liberalization effort centered on the creation of money market instruments. The authorities legalized negotiable certificates of deposits, removed restrictions on the interbank call and bill discount markets, and permitted repurchasing of bonds and growth of certificates of deposit. The maturity spectrum of money market instruments was broadened further with the introduction of money market certificates and of auctioned, discount, short-term government refinancing bonds. In the United Kingdom, commercial paper was introduced into domestic financial markets, while in the United States the introduction of exchange-traded financial futures and options was noteworthy.

The removal of restrictions on interest rates has been most notable in Japan and the United States. Although ceilings on the interest rates offered on the liabilities of financial institutions in Japan have been removed gradually, most large deposits now carry market-related interest rates. In the United States, Regulation Q ceiling interest rates were removed.

Notes

1. In this chapter, international financial markets are viewed as comprising the major domestic and offshore financial markets. A domestic market includes those financial centers in each country that provide financial intermediary services principally to domestic residents and whose operations are subject to a set of regulatory, supervisory, tax, accounting, and disclosure requirements established or supported by the national authorities. The offshore markets include those financial centers that provide financial intermediary services primarily for nonresident borrowers and lenders, usually in a currency other than that of the country in which they are located. In general, institutions in such markets are not subject to direct national regulations, including interest rate ceilings, reserve requirements, controls over portfolio decisions, or certain taxes. The distinctions between domestic and offshore markets have diminished over time as a result of the liberalization of domestic financial markets and innovations in financial instruments.

2. See Haraf and Kushmeider, "Redefining Financial Markets," in this volume for a general review of recent innovations in financial instruments and structural changes in U.S. markets.

3. The average rate of growth in the industrial countries fell from 4.8 percent per year in the 1960s to 3.3 percent and 2.3 percent in the 1970s and the period 1980–1986, respectively. In contrast, the variability of GNP growth rates (as measured by the variance) was ten times as high in the 1970s and 1980s (4.1 percent) as in the 1960s (0.4 percent).

4. The average rate of inflation in the industrial countries in the 1960s was 3.1 percent per year but rose to 7.9 percent in the 1970s before declining to 5.0 percent in the period 1980–1986. The variance of inflation rates also increased from 0.6 percent in the 1960s to 6.7 percent in the 1970s, before declining to 5.5 percent in the 1980s.

5. For a detailed discussion of the implications of these technological changes for financial markets, see Anthony Saunders and L. White, eds., *Technology and the Regulation of Financial Markets* (Lexington, Mass.: Lexington Books, 1986).

6. See footnote 1 for the definitions of domestic and offshore markets used in this chapter.

7. International bank lending and net bond issuance also rose from 10.3 percent of the value of world imports in 1976 to 11.9 percent in 1986. More-

over, between 1981 and 1986 the stock of Eurocurrency bank loans rose from $1.5 trillion to $2.1 trillion (an annual real rate of 7 percent); whereas the outstanding stock of Eurocurrency bonds increased from $134 billion to $369 billion (an annual rate of growth of 22 percent).

8. See Appendix for a more detailed discussion of these changes.

9. During these reforms, tax policies have also been modified to some extent to avoid creating incentives for undertaking offshore activities. All major industrialized countries have removed withholding taxes on foreign-held domestic securities in order to reduce the tax advantage associated with using Eurobonds as opposed to domestic bonds.

10. For a more detailed discussion of international coordination of bank supervision see G. Johnson and R. Abrams, "Aspects of the International Banking Safety Net," Occasional Paper no. 17, International Monetary Fund, Washington, D.C., 1983.

11. Since Banco Ambrosiano Holding was a bank holding company—a 65 percent controlled subsidiary—and not a bank, under Luxembourg law, the Luxembourg authorities did not have supervisory powers. The Italian authorities felt limited responsibility for foreign subsidiaries whose activities they were unable to supervise. Subsequently, consolidated supervision was required by the Italian authorities of foreign banking and financial companies controlled, either directly or indirectly, through the possession of more than 50 percent of capital.

12. This document ("Principles for the Supervision of Banks' Foreign Establishments") was published in appendix I of R. Williams, P. Heller, J. Lipsky, and D. Mathieson, "International Capital Markets, Developments and Prospects, 1983," Occasional Paper no. 23, International Monetary Fund, Washington, D.C., March 1983.

13. There has also been consideration of the ways in which central banks could cooperate to provide official emergency assistance for temporary liquidity shortages in the Euromarkets. A communiqué of the governors of the Bank for International Settlements issued in 1974 stated:

> The Governors . . . had an exchange of views on the lender of last resort in the Euromarkets. They recognized that it would not be practical to lay down in advance detailed rules and procedures for the provision of temporary liquidity. But they were satisfied that means are available for that purpose and will be used if and when necessary.

This statement, which has been reaffirmed on a number of occasions, remains the major policy statement on the lender-of-last-resort function for international markets. For a detailed discussion of the issues surrounding the provision of lender-of-last-resort assistance in an international setting, see J. Guttentag and R. Herring, *The Lender of Last Resort Function in an International Context*, Essays in International Finance, no. 151 (Princeton, N.J.: Princeton University Press, 1983).

14. "The Management of Banks' Off Balance Sheet Exposures: A Super-

visory Perspective," Committee on Banking Regulations and Supervisory Practices (Basel, March 1986).

15. The committee comprises representatives of the central banks and supervisory authorities of the Group of Ten (G-10) countries.

16. Bank loans to any of the G-10 countries would apparently carry a zero weight.

17. See E. Fama, "Banking in the Theory of Finance," *Journal of Monetary Economics*, vol. 6. no. 1 (January 1980), pp. 39–57 ; Fama, "What's Different about Banks?" *Journal of Monetary Economics*, vol. 15, no. 1 (January 1985), pp. 29–39; and D. Diamond and P. Dybvig, "Bank Runs, Deposit Insurance, and Liquidity," *Journal of Political Economy*, no. 91 (June 1984), pp. 401–19, for a discussion of the conditions under which such runs are likely to occur. For a critique of the relevance of these models, see George Benston and George Kaufman, "Regulating Bank Safety and Performance," in this volume.

18. The nature of this problem was stated clearly by Governor Henry Wallich of the Federal Reserve in testimony to the U.S. Congress:

> There are dangers in trying to define and publicize specific rules for emergency assistance to troubled banks, notably the possibility of causing undue reliance on such facilities and possible relaxation of needed caution on the part of all market participants. Therefore, the Federal Reserve has always avoided comprehensive statements of conditions for its assistance to members banks. Emergency assistance is inherently a process of negotiation and judgment, with a range of possible actions varying with circumstances and need.

19. This discussion also applies to the mispricing of other services provided by the public sector such as access to the clearing system (Fedwire).

20. For a discussion of the policy options in the United States, see Benston and Kaufman, "Regulating Bank Safety and Performance."

21. For a discussion of the view that such cooperation is designed principally to support regulatory cartels, see Edward Kane, "How Market Forces Influence the Structure of Financial Regulation," in this volume.

22. It has been argued in another chapter in this volume that the extension of such guarantees should be prohibited. See chapter 3 by Benston and Kaufman.

23. These changes have been discussed in detail in M. Watson, R. Kincaid, C. Atkinson, E. Kalter, and D. Folkerts-Landau, *International Capital Markets, Developments and Prospects* (Washington, D.C.: International Monetary Fund, 1986).

Commentary
Richard J. Herring

David Folkerts-Landau and Donald Mathieson have provided an excellent overview of the process of innovation and the trend toward securitization of international financial flows—the displacement of bank loans by marketable securities. Their account raises three important questions for regulatory and supervisory policy that I would like to consider. (1) Does the trend mainly reflect irreversible technological and institutional factors that are beyond policy control, or is it partly the consequence of regulatory constraints? (2) Is the trend toward securitization of international credit flows a good thing? (3) Is the international regulatory response to this trend—the proposal for a common approach to regulating capital adequacy issued by the Bank for International Settlements Committee on Banking Regulations and Supervisory Practices (BIS proposal)—likely to improve the safety and soundness of the financial system?

Folkerts-Landau and Mathieson make a persuasive case that technological and institutional factors have been important. Advances in telecommunications and computer technology have led to reductions in the cost of collecting, processing, analyzing, and distributing information regarding credit worthiness and market conditions. And increases in the volume of financial transactions and the shift to electronic clearing have produced dramatic declines in transactions costs in many markets. It is now possible for a well-trained undergraduate to use current international financial data to construct and implement complicated international hedge positions virtually instantaneously, often using sophisticated mathematical models that were not even available in the academic literature a decade ago.

A more puzzling (and perhaps more transitory) factor that has facilitated securitization is an increased willingness of investors to accept significant credit risk. This phenomenon is not well understood. The growth of markets in what are euphemistically known as high-yield securities may reflect an increased capacity of institutional investors to analyze and diversify credit risks. But it also may be the result of an excessively optimistic extrapolation of experience that until October 19, 1987, had been largely favorable.

In addition, regulatory and supervisory initiatives to enhance the safety of the banking system may have contributed to the trend by increasing the cost of intermediated credit relative to the cost of securitized credit. I think that Folkerts-Landau and Mathieson place too little emphasis on this factor, even though it is at least partly a response to international events.

Their data show that 1982 was the turning point in the securitization of international credit flows. Before 1982, most international credit flows were intermediated by banks; but after 1982, direct issues of bonds, floating rate notes, Euronotes, Euro–commercial paper, and other securities began to surpass new bank lending, so that by 1986 direct issues of securities were a large multiple of new bank loans.

Why did securitization accelerate after 1982? One key factor was the eruption of the external debt crisis. In August 1982, when Mexico announced that it could not service its bank debt, market participants abruptly lowered their estimates of the earnings prospects of banks that held heavy concentrations of claims on Mexico and other Latin American borrowers, a category that included most of the largest U.S. commercial banks. The market responded by increasing the cost of funds to such institutions. This was particularly apparent in the market for long-term debt. The ratings agencies lowered their assessment of the credit worthiness of most money center banks, and banks were obliged to pay more for long-term funds than some of their traditional clients. This, of course, has had a devastating effect on the ability of banks to fund loans to high-quality borrowers. When investors hold nonbank borrowers in higher esteem than banks, profitable intermediation is simply not feasible.

The regulatory authorities also reacted to the perceived decline in the credit standing of banks. As Folkerts-Landau and Mathieson document, banks have been required to raise capital-asset ratios in most major countries. In the United States the link between increases in minimum capital-asset ratios and the debt crisis was quite explicit. A routine bill to increase the U.S. quota in the International Monetary Fund became a vehicle for disciplining banks. What emerged from Congress in 1983 was the International Lending Supervision Act, which (among other provisions) mandated that the supervisory authorities increase standards of capital adequacy. Subsequently capital-asset ratios have increased by nearly 50 percent at most money center banks. This has reduced the extent to which banks can take advantage of conjectural deposit guarantees and sharply increased the spread over the cost of funds that U.S. banks must earn to yield a competitive rate of return for shareholders. This has further diminished the profitability of funding loans to high-quality borrowers.

COMMENTARY

The debt crisis thus confronted U.S. banks with a difficult problem: how to continue to do profitable business with prime customers even though it was no longer profitable to hold claims on those customers. One solution was to unbundle the traditional loan package so that the bank could earn compensation for some of the services traditionally included in the loan package (such as origination and the acceptance of credit, liquidity, interest rate, and exchange rate risk) without actually holding the claim on the borrower. Thus to some extent securitization was simply a shift in credit flows from regulated channels—where the costs of holding claims on the borrower had increased—to the securities markets where the regulatory burden was lower, a dynamic process that Edward Kane describes authoritatively elsewhere in this volume.

Is securitization of international credit a good thing? This question is difficult to answer—and, if you believe that securitization is largely the result of irreversible technological and institutional developments—it is largely irrelevant. But if you believe that regulatory policy has had an important effect, then it warrants closer scrutiny.

Optimists view securitization as an improvement in market efficiency: borrowers obtain funding at lower costs, investors earn higher returns, and all financial market participants have a broader range of choice for managing their economic and financial exposures. Optimists would argue that since securitization involves voluntary transactions among sophisticated, well-informed market participants, it will tend to redistribute risks to investors who are more willing and better able to manage them. In short, securitization is a phenomenon we should applaud.

Pessimists, however, are more likely to wring their hands than to clap. They are concerned that securitization makes it difficult for supervisors—and for managers—to monitor and manage credit exposures. For example, when a conventional loan is replaced by the issuance of a fixed-rate bond denominated in New Zealand dollars, which is then swapped into fixed-rate sterling and then again into floating-rate dollars, it becomes very difficult to anticipate what may happen if the borrower is unable to honor his commitments. Pessimists are concerned that much of the liquidity generated through the securitization process may prove illusory—that investors may not fully appreciate that a *marketable* instrument is not necessarily a *liquid* instrument. (From this perspective, the difficulties in the perpetual floating-rate note market and the breakdown of several organized markets in the wake of Black Monday are viewed as a warning of much graver problems ahead.)

Pessimists also worry that securitization may simply redistribute risk from carefully supervised, conservatively managed institutions to less sophisticated or less well supervised investors. And they are concerned that separation of the origination function from the rest of the traditional loan package may weaken the quality of credit decisions. An institution that originates a credit but does not hold it to maturity may be less likely to take a long, careful view of credit quality, may have less incentive to monitor the borrower's performance and initiate corrective action when necessary. Moreover, if trouble occurs, it may be much more difficult to rehabilitate a borrower in distress when claims on that borrower have been securitized and are widely held. Indeed, this concern is sometimes expressed with regard to the current LDC debt problem. Since the debt problem is at least a proximate cause of the current difficulties of large U.S. banks, it provides a useful context to explore whether the optimists or the pessimists have a stronger case.

If all bank loans to developing countries had been displaced by securities, would borrowers, lenders, and the world economy be better off? This is a highly speculative question that can be answered more easily by posing three simpler questions. First, if the debt had been securitized, would it have been as heavily concentrated in the portfolios of major banks? I think that the answer to this is almost certainly no—partly because it is less costly to diversify a portfolio of marketable assets and partly because publicly visible fluctuations in the market value of individual assets would provide a powerful incentive to diversify.

Second, would the *quantity* of debt have been as large? Although I am less confident of this answer, I suspect the answer is no. If these claims had been traded in active markets, the market discipline on both lenders and borrowers would have been greater. Lending to less-developed countries seems to have been a case where the banking system did not perform the traditional "watchdog" function. The prospect of visible capital losses on outstanding exposure might have provided lenders with a better incentive to monitor the borrowers' policies. Moreover, continuous market surveillance might well have improved the policy process in debtor countries since proponents of imprudent policies would have been subject to swift market sanctions that would have made it very difficult to finance such policies.

But suppose that my intuition about the second answer is wrong. Suppose that despite increased market discipline, borrowers would have pursued equally imprudent policies and borrowed the same amount. Would borrowing countries and the world economy be in worse condition today if the workout process had been conducted by loosely organized investor committees? Conjecture regarding this third question approaches the metaphysical, but it is plausible that the situation might not have been much worse. After all, the workout process so far has not restored the major debtors to credit worthiness. Indeed, most major debtors have higher ratios of debt to exports and lower per capita GNPs now than in 1982.[1]

In short I think it unlikely that securitized lending to developing countries *would have* generated a worse outcome than traditional bank lending *actually* produced. Indeed, rather than weakening the quality of credit decisions, securitization might have improved the allocation of credit. With regard to sovereign lending, the optimists may have a stronger case than the pessimists.

Nonetheless, bank regulatory and supervisory authorities are professional pessimists, and they have responded to the international trend toward securitization by attempting to expand the supervisory and regulatory framework to encompass the activities of banks in the securitization process. The most ambitious initiative is the BIS committee proposal for risk-based capital adequacy standards which (at this writing, November 1987) seem likely to be adopted in a modified form by all the countries participating in the Cooke Committee. The proposal sets out a common definition of capital in book-value terms and a classification system separating assets into five categories, each with a different risk weighting.[2] The innovative feature of the proposal is that it also specifies a technique for incorporating off-balance-sheet activities in the capital adequacy standard: each off-balance-sheet transaction is converted into an on-balance-sheet loan equivalent and then classified in one of the five risk categories for aggregation in the risk-adjusted asset total. This approach permits the authorities to supervise and regulate the participation of banks in the securitization process (and other fee-generating activities) just as they supervise traditional, on-balance-sheet activities.

Will this ambitious international attempt to regulate off-balance-sheet activity enhance the safety and soundness of the financial system? If the proposal is adopted, it will reduce some of the perverse incentives that have led U.S. banks to shift business off their balance sheets and reduce their holdings of safe, liquid assets. Yet the BIS committee proposal is more impressive as a feat of international financial diplomacy than as a mechanism for controlling risk. The risk classification scheme is really a standardized accounting format rather than a practical technique for evaluating an institution's risk of failure. The financial instrument-by-instrument approach and emphasis on the book value of capital is conceptually flawed. What ultimately matters for safety and soundness of a bank is not the characteristics of particular assets or off-balance-sheet commitments, but rather the market value of the portfolio of all the bank's activities.

In addition to this fundamental defect, the approach has several other questionable features. The highest risk weighting is applied to all claims on the private (nonbank) sector and foreign governments. This is an extremely broad category that includes not only loans to IBM, but also loans to Nicaragua. It takes no account of obvious differences in credit risk and transfer risk and thus perpetuates some of the perverse incentives of the current system in the United States. Neither is there an attempt to take account of the bank's liquidity position in assessing capital adequacy. And the attempt to incorporate interest rate risk focuses inappropriately on the interest sensitivity of individual assets rather than on the institution's aggregate exposure to a change in interest rates.

The proposal also gives interbank claims a peculiarly privileged position. The risk weight applied to short-term claims on foreign and domestic banks is one quarter of that applied to claims on all other private sector borrowers. This optimistic view of the relative credit standing of banks is clearly not shared by the rating agencies or the market. And it seems incompatible with the rhetoric of the regulatory authorities who argue that "the freedom to fail" must accompany liberalized financial powers. Unfortunately the BIS committee proposal perpetuates the notion that banks should be exempt from the usual standards of credit analysis because they have access to the safety net.

Notwithstanding Folkerts-Landau and Mathieson's important reservations about the remaining differences between countries in taxation, accounting practices, disclosure policies, deposit insurance, and lender-of-last-resort facilities, the proposed convergence in capital adequacy requirements should help to level the international playing field among banks. But this is not the only uneven part of the terrain that concerns U.S. banks. The fact that nonbank domestic competitors will be able to compete under different rules will continue to be a source of irritation. Securitization has contributed to the blurring of traditional distinctions among commercial banks and other financial institutions and further undermines the rationale for institutionally based regulation.

Notes

1. The pre–World War II era in which most external debt was securitized provides some basis for speculating on what might have happened. Indeed, it featured many of the same borrowers. See Barry Eichengreen and Richard

COMMENTARY

Portes, "Debt and Default in the 1930s: Causes and Consequences," *European Economic Review,* vol. 30 (1986), pp. 559–640; and Jeffrey Sachs, "LDC Debt in the 1980s: Risk and Reforms," in Paul Wachtel, ed., *Crises in the Economics and Financial Structure* (Lexington, Mass.: D.C. Heath, 1982).

2. The lengthy footnotes to Folkerts-Landau and Mathieson's table 10–5 indicate some of the difficulties in comparing capital-asset ratios across countries in today's very heterogeneous supervisory system.

11
Principal Policy Conclusions and Recommendations of the Financial Services Regulation Project

William S. Haraf

Our system of financial regulation has evolved in response to a number of economic and political objectives. Regulations have not always accomplished these objectives, and they have often had unintended and unexpected consequences. The studies in this volume illustrate the many parallels between financial regulatory issues and regulatory issues in other areas. Price controls, barriers to entry, and a variety of hidden taxes and subsidies have raised the cost of services, reduced the options available to consumers, and shifted costs and risks to taxpayers.

Nonetheless, there is a widespread belief that financial regulation is special. To a great extent, the current system was shaped by the macroeconomic catacylsm of the 1930s. The Great Depression convinced lawmakers that unregulated and competitive financial markets posed serious risks to economic stability. Congress embarked on a far-reaching program of government involvement in the financial sector. It established a complex regulatory framework intended to restrain competition and a deposit insurance system intended to protect small depositors and to enhance financial stability.

Today there is broad agreement that the depression of the 1930s was unrelated to practices in private financial markets. Macroeconomic causes were responsible, not too much competition. There is also growing recognition of the corrupting influence of the present deposit insurance system and a greater appreciation of the positive role of competition in financial markets. Nonetheless, the barriers to competition, efficiency costs, and moral hazards of the present reg-

---

This chapter reflects my own judgments about the principal policy conclusions and recommendations of the AEI study. Although I have tried to be faithful to the analysis in the preceding chapters, the authors may not agree with all of my conclusions.

ulatory system are, in large part, a legacy of that painful episode. The regulatory system has not contributed to macroeconomic stability. Indeed, by encouraging risk taking and by limiting opportunities for diversification, it may have made the goal of a stable financial system more difficult to achieve.

In recent years, volatile economic conditions, technology, and market innovations have subjected the financial system to new pressures. These pressures have exacerbated problems with existing regulations. The social costs of restrictions on competition and the integration of financial services have increased. Important market disciplines have eroded. Government agencies, and ultimately federal taxpayers, have assumed increasingly greater financial risk through a range of credit, contingent credit, and insurance programs.

The present regulatory system is rife with implicit taxes, subsidies, and entry barriers that have reduced the efficiency of the financial system and shifted risks to taxpayers. Viewed together, the studies point toward reducing these distortions insofar as possible. Their main message is that the goal of a safe, efficient, and fair financial system is achievable with regulations that are less intrusive to the functioning of free markets.

The principal policy conclusions and recommendations can be grouped into five categories: (1) competition and financial structure; (2) deposit insurance reform; (3) monetary policy, central banking, and the payments system; (4) the housing finance system; and (5) the regulatory structure and international coordination.

Competition and Financial Structure

An efficient financial system that is responsive to changing consumer demands provides great public benefits. Promoting competition is the best means to this end.

Depository firms differ from most other financial services firms in that their ownership, the activities of their affiliates and subsidiaries, and the geographic markets they can serve are restricted by law. On balance, these restrictions on competition have been detrimental to the financial system. They are important obstacles to an efficient financial system.

Eliminating barriers to geographic expansion and to the integration of banking services with other lines of business could lower the cost and improve the quality of financial services in several ways. Doing so would limit the ability of some suppliers to exercise market power. It would allow the most efficient producers, those providing the most desirable products and services at the best prices, to enter markets from which they are currently excluded. It would provide new opportunities to achieve economies of scale and scope from joint production, distribution, and information management. Finally, it would allow consumers the convenience of purchasing from a single supplier combinations of services that are now available only from separate suppliers.

Those who favor restrictions on the ownership of depository firms and the activities of their affiliates and subsidiaries cite concerns about safety and soundness, concentrations of power, abusive tie-ins, and conflicts of interest. Public policy must balance these concerns against the social costs of regulations designed to address them. Blanket restrictions on affiliations are not the best means to address such concerns. They do not contribute to financial stability, and they have large efficiency costs.

Depository firms can be adequately insulated from risks posed by affiliates and subsidiaries without destroying desirable synergies in the joint production, distribution, and marketing of financial services. Indeed, present law already provides substantial insulation through tight restrictions on intercompany transactions. Our objective should not be to devise a framework in which no competitive abuses ever occur or in which no depository firm ever fails because of activities of nonbank affiliates. Even if some abuses do occur from financial integration, consumers would still be better off, and losses to the deposit insurance agencies would still be reduced.

The potential for abusive tie-in arrangements, predatory pricing, and conflicts of interest is greatest when barriers to competition are present. Eliminating barriers to product and geographic expansion will make it less likely that such strategies can be effective. Existing antitrust laws and competitive standards provide adequate safeguards against such abuses. There is no convincing reason to have a competitive policy applicable to banks and other financial firms that is different from that applied under present laws to nonfinancial firms.

In sum, financial services firms, including depository firms, should be allowed to affiliate freely with other firms, including those engaging in commercial activities. The line between commercial and financial activities can be fuzzy. As long as insulating safeguards are in place, it is best to let the market determine the activities that can be profitably conducted within a single organization. For that reason, broader enforcement powers and strict penalties against noncompliance with insulating safeguards are preferable to outright prohibitions on affiliations.

Deposit Insurance Reform

The social costs of individual bank failures have been exaggerated. Historically, bank failures have not generally led to losses of confidence in the banking system. True banking panics have been rare. The chances of their occurring in the future can be minimized with sound monetary policy.

Deposit insurance was a response to the financial collapse of the 1930s. For better or worse, the public now expects its deposits to be protected by government. That commitment, however, need not be open-ended. It is widely acknowledged that deposit insurance encourages risk taking. This problem has been exacerbated in recent years as the degree of protection has expanded. What began as a program to protect small depositors and prevent them from running has developed into a system of guarantees that regularly protects large depositors and often other creditors, managers, and shareholders of depository firms and their holding companies. As a result, the incentives of financially sophisticated investors to monitor and discipline the practices and balance sheets of depository firms have diminished. In addition, Congress and the regulators have chosen to forbear on capital standards, allowing very troubled banks and thrifts to continue operating with little or no economic capital at stake.

Under generally accepted accounting principles (GAAP), loans and investments can generally be carried at acquisition cost, or book value. Experience has shown that capital value as measured by GAAP can differ substantially from true economic value and can be manipulated to meet capital standards or to preserve the appearance of solvency. As a result, GAAP rules allow depository firms to operate with very high leverage and to survive well after their true net worth is exhausted. Although implementing market-value accounting would pose important practical problems, the distortions under GAAP are great enough that developing a workable system is warranted. If market-value accounting were applied to depository firms and their subsidiaries, gains and losses would quickly show up on balance sheets, providing a powerful disincentive to adopt risky strategies. Over time, it would induce beneficial adjustments to balance sheets.

A policy of strictly enforcing capital standards based on market values will substantially enhance market discipline and reduce the cost of reorganization to the deposit insurance funds, large depositors, and other creditors. Permitting subordinated debt to fulfill some of those capital requirements has advantages. Debt holders would be inclined toward conservative operations since they would, in effect, be "insuring" deposits up to the amount of their investment. The rating and pricing of such debt would also provide a market signal of asset quality to regulators.

When capital standards are violated, regulators should have

powers to suspend interest on subordinated debt, dividends, and other payments to a parent or affiliates. In most instances, this suspension would lead debt holders to force timely reorganization or recapitalization. If owners of capital-impaired firms elect not to recapitalize on their own, the deposit insurance agencies should also have the right to take them over for sale, merger, or liquidation before their capital is exhausted. These rules can safely apply to depository firms of all sizes without significant disruptions of financial markets. No bank is too big to be reorganized.

These accounting and reorganization rules differ substantially from those that apply to nondepository firms. Deposit insurance justifies stringent standards. With such rules in place, permissible activities for depository firms could be expanded. Indeed, organizations could be granted greater latitude in determining where to locate activities within the corporate structure based on the accounting and reorganization rules that apply to depository firms and their subsidiaries as compared with their nondepository affiliates.

In sum, deposit insurance was intended to protect small depositors and to support a stable financial structure, not to protect all individuals and firms from loss. The more regulators rely on meaningful capital standards and prompt reorganization of capital-impaired depository firms, the less regulation is needed to protect the deposit insurance funds. Greater freedom from regulation would, in turn, contribute to a more efficient, adaptable, and safe financial system.

Monetary Policy, Central Banking, and the Payments System

To a great extent, the safety and soundness of the financial system depends on factors beyond the control of financial intermediaries, either individually or as a class. A basic prerequisite for financial stability is macroeconmic stability, in particular price stability. This requires sound monetary policy focused on limiting the growth of the monetary base over time. Price level instability induces interest rate instability and distorts perceptions of credit risk. The rising number of failed and weakened depository firms in recent years is, in part, a result of the cycle of inflation and disinflation and the accompanying volatility of interest rates, assets values, and real returns that began in the 1970s. Historically, both in the United States and elsewhere, periods of price level instability have been accompanied by high rates of bank failures.

Conducting monetary policy to achieve macroeconomic stability can be done without supporting financial market regulations. Open-market operations are a necessary and sufficient policy instrument. A related responsibility of the Federal Reserve is to provide liquidity during financial crises in order to limit the effects of financial failures to insolvent firms. Open-market operations are also sufficient to stabilize markets when a financial crisis develops.

In addition to its monetary responsibilities, the Federal Reserve regulates, supervises, and conducts a wide range of operations with depository firms. These activities, which include discount window lending, payments system operations, and establishing reserve requirements, can be termed banking policies. The banking policies of the Federal Reserve cannot be readily justified in terms of macroeconomic benefits. Reserve requirements, in particular, are unnecessary for the conduct of monetary policy.

Today's financial markets are highly efficient in allocating credit privately. The Federal Reserve discount window is a public line-of-credit service that is similar in many respects to private lines of credit. The discount window is most importantly a source of emergency credit assistance to banks that the Federal Reserve perceives to be illiquid but solvent. The Federal Reserve faces the same problem as private lenders in distinguishing insolvent from illiquid banks. There is little reason to believe that it is superior to private lenders in determining the solvency of potential borrowers. Under normal circumstances, discount window lending, collateralized by Treasury securities, involves minimal subsidies. A potentially larger implicit subsidy arises from the Federal Reserve's discretionary power to lend on less than perfect collateral. The availability of this public line of credit may have hidden economic costs. It may encourage some forms of risk taking and lead to the erosion of private arrangements for liquidity. For these reasons it is difficult to justify routine discount window lending as an appropriate government intervention.

Responsibility for preserving financial stability has also come to include protecting the payments system. Rapid growth in the volume of payments and an expansion in the range of firms that have access to the payments system, either directly or through affiliates, has raised new concerns about the vulnerability of the payments system. The main risks are associated with the electronic transfer systems, the operation of which currently involves substantial intraday credit, or daylight overdrafts.

The risk exposure from daylight overdrafts to payments system participants is no different from other types of credit exposure. Safe and sound management requires monitoring and limiting exposures. Historically, however, overdrafts have not been carefully monitored, and incentives to limit overdrafts remain small. If overdrafts bore a market rate of interest, their volume would shrink and lenders would be compensated for the risk they bear. An intraday market for federal funds can be encouraged in several ways. In addition, regulatory changes, such as substituting term federal funds for overnight funds, would substantially reduce their volume. With these changes, payments system risks can be reduced to tolerable levels.

Daylight overdrafts over Fedwire create problems analogous to those of discount window lending. These mechanisms for extending credit justify Federal Reserve regulation and supervision in the same way that private suppliers of credit monitor and supervise borrowers to protect their funds. If discount window lending and daylight overdrafts on Fedwire were substantially curtailed, the costly regulatory and supervisory responsibilities of the Federal Reserve might also potentially be curtailed. A thorough review of Federal Reserve banking policies is necessary to explore these issues further.

The goal of protecting the payments system does not justify limitations on affiliations between banks and other firms. Daylight overdrafts granted to nonbank affiliates of banks should be subject to the same restrictions as other extensions of credit by a bank to its affiliate. These restrictions can adequately protect a bank from excessive credit exposure to its affiliates.

The Housing Finance System

The federal government is extensively involved in the operation and regulation of the housing finance system through the Federal Home Loan Bank System and the federally sponsored secondary mortgage market agencies. The evidence indicates that these institutions have not channeled resources into housing to any great extent since the 1950s.

A separate institutional framework to provide preferential treatment for housing finance is becoming increasingly anachronistic. Moreover, it is now unraveling under the pressures of inflation and technological change. As savings and loans have been granted broader asset and liability powers, housing finance has become less important to them. In turn, as alternative sources of mortgage finance have emerged, S&Ls have become less important to housing finance. The role of S&Ls in housing finance no longer justifies the regulatory advantages they have, if it ever did.

In today's financial markets, there is little public policy justification for government agencies to function as mortgage lenders, securities issuers, and secondary market makers in competition with private firms. Over time, the Federal National Mortgage Association and the Federal Home Loan Mortgage Corporation should be privatized. Government involvement can be decreased in a variety of ways.

The recent recapitalization of the Federal Savings and Loan Insurance Corporation is totally inadequate. Congress will soon be forced to address this problem again. Merging the FSLIC with the Federal Deposit Insurance Corporation will not be an adequate solution to the problem. Ultimately, taxpayers will bear most of the cost. Forbearance and leniency will lead to a further deterioration in the FSLIC's situation as insolvent firms continue to pursue go-for-broke strategies. For that reason, every effort should be made to close insolvent firms as quickly as possible.

The Regulatory Structure and International Coordination

Competition in financial services is taking place not only among private firms, but also among overlapping regulatory systems both nationally and internationally.

The effects of regulatory competition have generally been healthy within the United States and can be healthy worldwide, but competition can also have undesirable dimensions to be guarded against. It is beneficial when regulators are pressed into establishing a regulatory climate in which financial services can be efficiently and safely provided. Regulatory competition reduces the risk of adopting narrow and inflexible approaches to problems, fosters experimentation, and facilitates timely and efficient adaptation to changing market conditions. Just as private firms routinely face potential conflicts of interest, so do financial regulators, who not only represent the public interest but also have incentives to maximize their own jurisdiction and authority. Regulatory competition helps to resolve these incentive conflicts.

Regulators also compete by providing hidden subsidies. The most significant subsidies come from implicit or explicit protections extended to financial firms through deposit insurance, the discount window, the payments system, and other mechanisms governments may use to bail out private financial firms. As noted earlier, these protections create incentives for financial firms to take on greater risk. Over time, they can undermine financial stability. Clearly, this type of competition is undesirable. Taxpayers must be able to assess the costs and risks of such policies. This will require fundamental reporting and accounting reforms and clearly defined rules governing reorganizations of capital-impaired firms.

Although efforts to achieve greater international coordination of regulatory policies are well-intentioned, the potential problems with coordination are illustrated by the recent efforts to achieve an international agreement establishing uniform risk-based capital standards. This plan has major flaws and should not become a uniform international standard at this stage.

In sum, for regulatory reform to have a lasting positive effect, it must deal constructively with the highly competitive environment within which both financial firms and their regulators operate. It can best do so by improving incentive structures and information systems applying to both private firms and their regulators.

Conclusions

A fundamental restructuring of our laws and regulations is now imperative. Sweeping reforms are long overdue. Policy makers have been paralyzed by battles over turf among competing industry segments and battles to preserve public subsidies and protections. Private lobbying activity is not the only obstacle to regulatory reform. The subsidies provided by the regulatory system create business for regulators and rents for elected politicians, which they too have incentives to protect.

If Congress and the regulators fail to act, taxpayers will be left to underwrite an increasing amount of financial risk that is now being loaded on the system. In addition, significant public benefits in the form of lower prices for services, an improved allocation of resources, and a broader range of choices will be lost.

Ideally, financial markets channel savings to their highest valued uses, facilitate payments, provide liquidity, and allocate risks to those willing and best able to bear them. Desired financial services are supplied at minimum resource cost. The government's objectives should be to ensure that these functons are undertaken efficiently and fairly, that financial market participants are not themselves a source of disturbances to the economy, and that the financially unsophisticated are protected. These studies clearly indicate that these objectives can be accomplished with a much less intrusive and more focused body of regulation than now exists.

The Policy Proposals in the AEI Studies

Allan H. Meltzer

William Haraf and the American Enterprise Institute deserve praise for bringing together a group of eminent scholars to survey our knowledge of the financial services industry, to comment on its problems and prospects, and to recommend changes. Though we have not suffered from a dearth of proposals or remained unaware of the growing problems of the financial services industry, a comprehensive review by many of the leading scholars in the field is welcome.

In the past, we have relied on the recommendations of groups such as the Commission on Money and Credit, or of government-appointed committees like the famed Macmillan and Radcliffe committees in England or the Aldrich and Hunt commissions in the United States. AEI has taken the useful step of bringing together scholars with longstanding interest and expertise in various aspects of the problem to propose a more or less compatible set of recommendations for financial reform. We are in their debt, not only for undertaking to provide this public good but for producing a set of generally thoughtful papers and many useful suggestions for reform.

I have been asked to comment on the policy recommendations and to provide an overview of the studies as a group. It is a formidable task. Many are rich in detail; they are full of references to historical experience and cover a wide range of topics. I must be selective.

The role of a discussant is to criticize and suggest improvements. My negative remarks should not be misinterpreted. This is a valuable set of studies that shows a considerable amount of thought directed to major problems. There is a comprehensive set of recommendations, and there are many additional suggestions by the individual authors. There are also differences of opinion. Edward Kane and David Folkerts-Landau and Donald Mathieson have very different ap-

---

The author received helpful comments from Marvin Goodfriend, George G. Kaufman, and Robert King.

proaches to regulation. There are even disagreements, for example, about the desirability of having a lender of last resort or preserving deposit insurance, and even about whether financial firms should be regulated at all. These are not simple issues, and reasonable people can disagree, as they have in the AEI studies.

General Comments

Three general issues relevant to several of the studies are, I believe, basic to an analysis of financial structure and proposals for reform.

First are the issues of failure, financial fragility, and banking crises. Anna Schwartz touches on these issues in presenting comparative data on years of crisis and pointing out that, since 1866, there has not been a crisis in the United Kingdom banking system. None of the studies explains why banking crises were more common in the United States than in other countries.[1] Or, perhaps more important for understanding our current position, why are U.S. financial firms more prone to failure than financial firms in other developed countries? The U.S. economy is not subject to greater risk or more variability than many other countries. Inflation, disinflation, and oil shocks contributed to the current problems of the U.S. financial system, but these shocks are common to many countries that do not have similar problems.

I stress this issue because I suspect that part of the difference between the United States and other countries is that regulation has failed in the United States. Two examples illustrate the point. First, Regulation Q was extended to all financial institutions in the mid-1960s and allowed to continue in effect throughout the 1970s despite the enormous cost imposed on the public and the negative effects on the safety and soundness of financial firms. Second, John Weicher reports an estimate of the costs of delaying the insolvency of many thrift institutions. He suggests that in 1983 all GAAP-insolvent thrifts could have been closed at a cost of $2.5 to $6.5 billion. Today, he estimates the cost at $40 to $50 billion. Many of the losses, which may someday be shifted to the taxpayers, could have been avoided if failed firms had been closed promptly.

Similar bad management, neglect, and delay in the private sector would properly be regarded as scandalous. Yet the scandalous regulatory failures that maintained Regulation Q, substituted accounting gimmicks for responsible action to close insolvent banks and thrift institutions, and bankrupted the FSLIC and some of the government credit agencies receive little attention from the Congress, the administration, the press, and the AEI studies.

Quis custet custodes?—Who will guard the guardians? Perhaps no one. I recommend that AEI undertake a study of the politics and economics of regulatory behavior as a companion to these studies to help us understand how and why this failure occurred. Do we have in the thrift industry an example of capture theory, according to which the regulated become the regulators and use the agency for their own purposes? A proper reform proposal must go beyond a statement of the problem to an analysis of why the problem occurred, whether the problem arose as a result of regulatory failure and, if so, what changes in regulatory structure would provide incentives to prevent small problems from becoming large. In addition, we must be concerned about the incentives in the political and regulatory environment. Without such incentives, proposals for reform are not likely to succeed.

Second, how do we get from where we are to where we want to be? These studies are not clear about the problems of transition. Who pays the cost of closing the insolvent thrift institutions? John Weicher suggests that the most likely outcome is that the costs will be borne by the taxpayers, but the study does not take a position on this issue. Should we instead treat the thrift industry, or the banking and thrift industries, as a risk class that must pay, ex post, for the mistakes or faults of members of the class? All sixteen- to twenty-five-year-old boys pay automobile insurance premiums to cover the costs imposed by the more reckless members of their age group. All buyers of health insurance pay premiums to cover the costs of treating cancer patients. These are ex ante differences. Here the failures are a fact. What is optimal in present circumstances? Should surviving banks and thrifts pay the costs of the failures? Or should these costs be shifted to the taxpayers? The implications for the future are important. Imposing the costs on surviving banks and thrifts creates an incentive for improved future self-regulation. Imposing the costs on the taxpayers maintains business as usual, or as it has become.

Third, not much is said explicitly about the goal of public policy. Judgments about the proper degree of regulation or deregulation can be found in several of the studies, but none offers a standard by which to decide whether there is too much or too little regulation. Much of the public discussion of risk either ignores the risks inherent in nature and in institutional arrangements or tries to redistribute these risks by shifting the costs to others while retaining the benefits for one's own group.

The proper standard is to reduce the risks to the minimum inherent in nature and other institutional arrangements. It is not easy to apply this standard in practice. But it is a standard against which to judge whether there is too much or too little regulation, whether there are too many failures or, as in the past, perhaps too few. I believe that the contribution of these studies would have been increased if they had proposed a risk standard for regulation and had attempted to apply it by considering explicitly where there are problems of moral hazard, adverse selection, or other types of risk that can be avoided by choice of institutional arrangement. Though some individual studies implicitly use the proper standard, the studies as a whole do not. A case in point is the suggestion in one of them to restore double liability on bank capital. I believe that this standard, if applied, would produce a suboptimal supply of banking services.

Regulation of banking and finance is one of the oldest forms of regulation. It is unlikely that unregulated competitive banking will be found to be economically efficient or politically attractive. A main reason is that information about safety and soundness is not a free good. An important issue is whether the benefits that consumers receive from the use of banking services and the increased efficiency of the payments mechanism exceed the cost of providing these services. Part of the cost is the risk of bank failures. Deposit insurance shifts this cost from the individual to the group and perhaps to society and provides incentives to increase the risk imposed on society by financial institutions with low or negative net worth.[2]

The AEI recommendations correctly emphasize the roles of competition between institutions and of new entry in achieving a social optimum. They are less clear about the means of lowering the risk of a near universal system of deposit banking. The recommendations go part of the way toward accepting a comprehensive system of voluntary deposit insurance and reliance on owners of capital and subordinated debt proposed by George Benston and George Kaufman. The recommendations do not emphasize a key feature of the Benston-Kaufman argument: banks decide whether to offer deposit insurance. If a bank joins the deposit insurance system, management must maintain capital. If capital falls below some positive minimum, the proposal allows the insurer to close the bank if the owners do not provide additional capital.

I believe the recommendations would be improved if the explicit recommendations of the Benston and Kaufman study were incorporated, with some amendments or extensions.[3] Deposit insurance does not have to shift from 100 percent to zero at $100,000. More thought might be given to determining the point at which individuals or firms would co-insure. More attention could be given to determining the optimal failure rate. Much more attention should be given to the difficult problem of valuing consumer loans or small business loans that are behind in their payments. I believe that success or failure in the business of being a banker depends on how these judgments are made and that it is misleading to suggest that accountants can make the judgments for us. Nor do I believe much will be gained from having small banks issue debentures, since market valuation requires that the debentures be traded frequently, and this is unlikely for debentures issued by small banks.

The Specific Recommendations

I have drifted from general issues into concern for a specific proposal to balance social and private interest in the regulation of financial institutions. Let me return to the specific recommendations of William Haraf in chapter 11.

The study locates the problems of the banking and financial industry in four main areas. These are (1) restrictions on competition; (2) mismanagement of deposit insurance, particularly the improper incentives in the deposit insurance system and its relation to capital requirements; (3) monetary policy, particularly the policies of persistent inflation and rapid disinflation; and (4) the mistaken attempts to use the financial system to subsidize housing, homeowners, and perhaps home builders. Two additional areas are discussed, international coordination of regulation and the system for transferring payments and overdrafts.

I have little to say about the last two topics. The recommendations might have suggested that more consideration be given to privatizing wire transfers as a desirable end and as a means of eliminating potential costs of defaults to the taxpayers. On international coordination of regulation, I agree with the general approach. The record of financial regulators in the United States is a brief against an international agreement to coordinate regulation. Before proceeding to international regulation, it would be interesting to see the results of a study of the net costs or benefits of the banking and financial regulations of the past fifty years. It would also be useful to consider why uniform regulation of banking and finance is more appropriate or socially desirable than uniform international regulation of the automobile industry, the chemical industry, electrical utilities, or other industries where social costs arise in the production process. Before opting for a regulatory cartel, one should recognize that several states have acted as a constructive force pushing the U.S. Congress toward financial deregulation. And one should not forget that it was Comptroller of the Currency James Saxon in the 1960s who began or encouraged the deregulation process at the national level.

Haraf's recommendations to reform the financial system are steps in the right direction. In effect, he asks how market forces can be used to foster a responsible, competitive financial system. In this respect, the proposals are an improvement over the present arrangements as well as over many alternative proposals that rely less on incentives and market forces to regulate or that seek, perversely in my view, to set out a rigid structure within which firms must operate.

An additional, commendable feature of the AEI studies and of Haraf's recommendations is the recognition of the importance of stable, predictable prices. I would prefer to see that recognition phrased as reducing variability to the minimum inherent in nature and institutional arrangements, and I believe emphasis should be on the stability of expected prices, but those are small points in this context. The main point is the implied recognition that many of the problems in real estate, farm lending, federal credit agencies, and international debt are the heritage of policies of first chasing the evanescent Phillips curve followed by rapid disinflation.

I disagree with some conclusions of the studies. I will focus on three issues. First is the role of lender of last resort and its relation to deposit insurance. Second is the financing of housing. Third is the issue of political incentives. I have written on two issues earlier, so I will make explicit the predilections that I bring to these issues.

Many years ago, I pointed out that the public provision of deposit insurance was based on a confusion between individual bank failure and system failure.[4] I proposed private deposit insurance and a public lender of last resort. Later, I urged that the public lender of last resort follow a rule similar but not identical to Bagehot's famous rule.[5] I want the lender to be required to lend always—borrowing should be a right, not a privilege, for any bank offering to discount standard banking assets at a penalty rate. Even a small penalty rate would ensure that the lender of last resort would do no lending except in a severe banking crisis when (or if) markets do not function. As Marvin Goodfriend and Robert King propose, central bank operations would be limited to open-market operations. Lending activity would be limited to times when the market malfunctions, specifically when there is a premium on cash and no one wishes to lend. If this type of malfunction does not occur, central bank lending will remain at zero.

Though I agree with the general position taken by Goodfriend and King, I think they are wrong to claim that supervision and regulation are a necessary part of central bank lending to financial institutions. Their discussion applies much more to publicly supplied deposit insurance than to a properly restricted lender of last resort. A rule that all loans are at a penalty rate is a contingent rule that separates borrowers into those who do not borrow and those who have acceptable collateral that cannot be sold in the market at less of a sacrifice than the central bank penalty.[6] A rule of this kind does not require regulation or supervision.

The reason for insisting on retaining the lender-of-last-resort function is to avoid catastrophes like that of 1931–1933 when the lender refused to lend. Having penalty-rate loans as an option means that banks have access to base money even if the central bank repeats its major error of the 1930s. It is useful to recall, in this regard, that Bagehot did not criticize the Bank of England for failing to lend. He criticized it for allowing panics to spread before they decided to lend. Bagehot's main criticism is *not* that the Bank of England failed to act. It is that uncertainty and panic increased because no one knew in advance what the bank would do. The solution he proposed was precommitment to a rule—in fact, to his rule.[7] As Anna Schwartz points out, after the bank accepted responsibility as lender of last resort, there were no further panics. There were bank failures.

In our time, the rule provides an additional safeguard. Central banks and governments are prone to too much rather than too little activism. A rule setting a penalty rate is helpful for this problem also.

How does my earlier proposal for private deposit insurance compare with the Benston-Kaufman proposal? Both face at least one common problem—valuing the banks' assets when, as is true of many assets, these assets are not traded. The Benston-Kaufman proposal avoids two problems of private deposit insurance: (1) the responsibility of the auditor to make judgments about the risks undertaken by banks that have sufficient capital and that accept sizable interest rate risk; and (2) the cancellation of insurance in periods of turbulence, as recently occurred with directors' and officers' insurance. On the other side, Benston and Kaufman rely on the regulators to take charge of problem banks. Why would the regulators under their system function more effectively than current regulators? Would they find ways to redefine capital, obfuscate, and delay?

John Weicher's chapter on housing finance has much interesting material. Weicher reaches the right conclusion—eliminate the government's mortgage operations. He errs, I believe, on two main points.

First, he claims that the social preference for housing can no longer be secured by financing arrangements. Subsidy elements aside, this has always been true.[8] Selling a bond and issuing a mortgage might change the way the public borrows, but mortgages are nominal instruments and housing is a real asset. Supplying more mortgages does not create more housing, and I know of no evidence that it ever has. This issue is important because protection of housing has long been an excuse for wrong-headed financial policies offered to assist housing.

Second, I am skeptical about his argument that specialized mortgage lenders will disappear in the future. Costs of information are important in appraising or valuing real property; so specialized entities arise to fulfill these functions. A more likely development is that the specialized lenders will be part of a diversified institution as suggested, indirectly, by Franklin Edwards.

Finally, I comment briefly on the political economy of reform. Only Edward Kane's chapter recognizes that regulators do not act solely to achieve a social optimum. Industries, unions, regulators, and other parties have interests that may include, but are not limited to, social welfare or economic efficiency. Haraf accepts many of Kane's strictures when discussing international regulation, but neither he nor the others see the relevance of what Kane discusses for other reform proposals. The authors should have devoted more attention to the political economy aspects of regulatory reform. That most financial reforms of the past decade have come from the piecemeal actions of the states, not from comprehensive reform, is not an accident and not a consequence of a shortage of proposals.

Notes

1. Schwartz suggests in passing that after 1866 the Bank of England accepted the role of lender of last resort.
2. As is well known, such institutions face asymmetric risks and returns. Losses are borne by the insurer; gains go to the owners. Hence the owners take excessive risk.
3. I note, however, that there are potential problems of dissident stockholders and of the protection of minority stockholders in the event of recapitalization.
4. Allan H. Meltzer, "Major Issues in the Regulation of Financial Institutions," *Journal of Political Economy*, vol. 75 (August suppl. 1967), pp. 482–501.
5. Allan H. Meltzer, "Financial Failures and Financial Policies," in George Kaufman and Roger C. Kormendi, eds., *Deregulating Financial Services* (Cambridge, Mass.: Ballinger Publishing Co., for the Mid-America Institute of Public Policy, 1986), pp. 79–96.
6. The penalty rate should float with the market rate. If there is no private demand, so the market does not function, there must be a rule fixing the penalty in relation to market rates in the recent past. This is a detail. The main point is the importance of a rule to prevent nonfeasance by the central bank.
7. Walter Bagehot, *Lombard Street* (New York: Scribner, Armstrong, 1873; reprinted with introduction by F. Genovese, Homewood, Ill.: Irwin, 1962).
8. Allan H. Meltzer, "Credit Availability and Economic Decisions: Evidence from the Mortgage and Housing Markets," *Journal of Finance* (June 1974).

Bibliography

Aharony, Joseph, and Itzhak Swary. "Contagion Effects of Bank Failures: Evidence from Capital Markets." *Journal of Business* (March 1983): 213–30.

———. "Effects of the 1970 Bank Holding Company Act: Evidence from Capital Markets." *Journal of Finance* (September 1981): 841–53.

Aliber, Robert Z. "International Banking: A Survey." *Journal of Money, Credit, and Banking* 16 (November 1984, pt. 2): 661–78.

Allen, Linda, and Anthony Saunders. "The Large-Small Dichotomy in the Federal Funds Market." *Journal of Banking and Finance* (June 1986): 219–30.

Altman, Edward I. "Risks and Rewards in the High Yield Debt Market—Measurement and Performance." Graduate School of Business: New York University, 1986. Mimeo.

Altman, Edward I., and Scott A. Nammacher. *Investing in Junk Bonds.* New York: John Wiley, 1987.

American Banker, various issues.

American Bankers Association. "Expanded Products and Services for Banking: Customer Benefits." Washington, D.C., September 1986.

———. "Expanded Products and Services for Banking: The Public Policy Perspective." Washington, D.C., September 1986.

———. *Statistical Information on the Financial Services Industry.* Washington, D.C., 1987.

Angermueller, Hans H. Statement before the U.S. Congress, House of Representatives, Commerce, Consumer, and Monetary Affairs Subcommittee of the Committee on Government Operations, 99th Congress, 2d session, December 17 and 18, 1986.

Apilado, Vincent, and Larry Freider. "Bank Holding Company Research: Classification, Synthesis, and New Direction." *Journal of Bank Research*, no. 2 (1982): 78–95.

Aspinwall, Richard C. and Robert A. Eisenbeis, eds. *Handbook for Banking Strategy.* New York: John Wiley and Sons, 1985.

Association of Reserve City Bankers. *Report of the Working Group of the Association of Reserve City Bankers on Book-Entry Daylight Overdrafts.* Chicago, 1986.

———. *Report on the Payments System.* Chicago, 1982.

Bagehot, Walter. *Lombard Street.* New York: Arno Press, 1978. Originally published 1873.

———. *The Works of Walter Bagehot,* Vol. 5: *Economic Studies,* edited by Forrest Morgan. Hartford, Conn.: The Travellers Insurance Company, 1889. Originally published 1876.

Bailey, Elizabeth E. "Contestability and the Design of Regulatory and Antitrust Policy." 1980. Manuscript.

Balazsy, James J. "The Government Securities Market and Proposed Regulation." *Federal Reserve Bank of Cleveland Economic Commentary* (April 1, 1986): 1–4.

BankAmerica v. Schwab. Board of Governors of the Federal Reserve System. Decision, January 7, 1983.

Banker, various issues.

Bankers Magazine, various issues.

Bank for International Settlements. *Annual Report.* Basel, various years.

———. *Recent Developments in the Economic Analysis of the Euro-Markets.* Basel, September 1982.

———. *Recent Innovations in International Banking.* Basel, 1986.

Banking Report, various issues. Formerly *Washington Financial Reports.*

Bank of Canada. *Annual Report.* 1965.

Bank of England Quarterly Bulletin. 1984.

Baring, Sir Francis. *Observations on the Establishment of the Bank of England and on the Paper Circulation of the Currency.* New York: August M. Kelley, 1967. Originally published 1797.

Barro, Robert J. "Interest Rate Smoothing." University of Rochester, February 1987.

———. *Macroeconomics,* 2d ed. New York: John Wiley and Sons, 1986.

Barsky, Robert, Greg Mankiw, Jeffrey Miron, and David Weil. "The Worldwide Change in the Behavior of Interest Rates and Prices in 1914." University of Michigan, May 1987.

Barth, James R., Dan Brumbaugh, and Daniel Sauerhaft. "Failure Costs of Government-regulated Financial Firms: The Case of Thrift Institutions." Research Working Paper no. 123. Washington, D.C.: Federal Home Loan Bank Board, October 1986.

Barth, James R., Dan Brumbaugh, Daniel Sauerhaft, and George H. K. Wang. "Insolvency and Risk-Taking in the Thrift Industry: Implications for the Future." *Contemporary Policy Issues* (Fall 1985): 1–32.

———. "Thrift-Institution Failures: Estimating the Regulator's Closure Rule." Research Working Paper no. 125. Washington, D.C.: Federal Home Loan Bank Board, January 1987.

Barth, James R. and Martin A. Regalia. "The Evolving Role of Regulation in the Savings and Loan Industry." In *The Financial Services Revolution: Policy Directions for the Future*, edited by Catherine England and Thomas Huertas. Boston: Kluwer Academic, 1988.

Baumol, William J. "On the Proper Cost Tests for Natural Monopoly in a Multiproduct Industry." *American Economic Review* (December 1977): 809–22.

Baumol, William J., Elizabeth Bailey, and Robert D. Willig. "Weak Invisible Hand Theorems on the Sustainability of Prices in a Multiproduct Natural Monopoly." *American Economic Review* (June 1977): 350–65.

Baumol, William J., John C. Panzar, and Robert D. Willig. *Contestable Markets and the Theory of Industry Structure*. New York: Harcourt Brace Jovanovich, 1982.

———. "On the Theory of Contestable Markets." In *New Developments in the Theory of Industrial Structure*, edited by G. F. Matthavson and Joseph E. Stiglitz. Cambridge, Mass.: MIT Press, 1986.

Becketti, Sean, and Charles S. Morris. "Loan Sales: Another Step in the Evolution of the Short Term Credit Market." *Federal Reserve Bank of Kansas City Economic Review* (November 1987): 22–31.

Bennett, Barbara. "Bank Regulation and Deposit Insurance: Controlling the FDIC's Losses." *Federal Reserve Bank of San Francisco Economic Review* (Spring 1984): 16–30.

Bennett, Dennis E. "The Impact of Government Sponsored Mortgage Agencies on Thrift Institutions." Paper presented at the American Real Estate and Urban Economics Association annual meeting, Chicago, December 1987.

Bennett, James, and Thomas DiLorenzo. *The Underground Government: The Off Budget Public Sector*. Washington, D.C.: Cato Institute, 1983.

Bennett, Veronica. "Consumer Demand for Product Deregulation." *Federal Reserve Bank of Atlanta Economic Review* (May 1984): 28–41.

Benston, George J. "Accounting Numbers and Economic Values." *Antitrust Bulletin* (Spring 1982): 161–215.

———. "An Analysis of the Causes of Savings and Loan Failures." *Monograph Series in Finance and Economics*, 1985-4/5. New York: Salomon Brothers Center for the Study of Financial Institutions, New York University, 1986.

———. "An Analysis of the Evidence Supporting the Separation of Commercial and Investment Banking Mandated by the Glass-Steagall Act." 1987. Manuscript.

———. "Bank Examination." *Bulletin* (Institute of Finance, New York University), no. 89–90 (May 1973).

———. "Deposit Insurance and Bank Failures." *Federal Reserve Bank of Atlanta Economic Review* (March 1983): 4–17.

———. "The Effects of Regulation." In *Payments in the Financial Services*

Industry in the 1980s, Federal Reserve Bank of Atlanta. Westport, Conn.: Quorum Books, 1984.

———. *The Evidence on the Passage and Continuation of the Glass-Steagall Act Separation of Commercial and Investment Banking: An Analysis of a Hoax*. Chicago: Association of Reserve City Bankers, 1988.

———. "Federal Regulation of Banking: Analysis and Policy Recommendations." *Journal of Bank Research* (Winter 1983): 216–44.

———. "Interest Payments on Demand Deposits and Bank Investment Behavior." *Journal of Political Economy* (October 1974): 431–49.

———. "The Market for Public Accounting Services: Demand, Supply, and Regulation." *Journal of Accounting and Public Policy* (Spring 1985): 33–79.

Benston, George J., ed. *Financial Services: The Changing Institutions and Government Policy*. Englewood Cliffs, N.J.: Prentice-Hall, 1983.

Benston, George J., Robert A. Eisenbeis, Paul M. Horvitz, Edward J. Kane, and George G. Kaufman. *Perspectives on Safe and Sound Banking: Past, Present, and Future*. Cambridge, Mass.: MIT Press, 1986.

Benston, George J., Gerald Hanweck, and David B. Humphrey. "Scale Economies in Banking: A Restructuring and Reassessment." *Journal of Money, Credit and Banking* (1982): 435–56.

Benston, George J., and George G. Kaufman. "Risk and Solvency Regulation of Depository Institutions: Past Policies and Current Options." *Monograph Series in Finance and Economics*, Salomon Brothers Center for the Study of Financial Institutions, New York University, 1988.

Benston, George J., and Clifford Smith. "A Transaction Cost Approach to the Theory of Financial Intermediation." *Journal of Finance* (May 1976): 215–31.

Benveniste, Lawrence M., and Allen N. Berger. "Securitization with Recourse: An Instrument that Offers Uninsured Depositors Sequential Claims." *Journal of Banking and Finance* (1987): 403–24.

Berger, Allen N., and David B. Humphrey. "The Role of Interstate Banking in the Diffusion of Electronic Payments Technology." In *Technological Innovation, Regulation, and the Monetary Economy*, edited by Colin Lawrence and Robert Shay. Cambridge, Mass.: Ballinger, 1986.

Berlin, Mitchell. "Loan Commitments: Insurance Contracts in a Risky World." *Federal Reserve Bank of Philadelphia Business Review* (May/June 1986): 3–12.

Bernanke, Ben S. "Non-monetary Effects of the Financial Crisis in the Propagation of the Great Depression." *American Economic Review* (June 1983): 257–76.

Bierwag, Gerald O., and George G. Kaufman. "A Proposal for Federal Deposit Insurance with Risk-sensitive Premiums." *Staff Memoranda* 83-3. Chicago: Federal Reserve Bank of Chicago, March 1986.

Billingsley, Randall S. and Robert E. Lamy. "Market Reaction to the Formation of One Bank Holding Companies and the 1970 Bank Holding Company Act Amendment." *Journal of Banking and Finance* (March 1984): 21–33.

Birdzell, L. E. "The Conglomerates: A Neighbor's View." *St. John's Law Letter*, no. 44.

Black, Fisher, Merton H. Miller, and Richard A. Posner. "An Approach to the Regulation of Bank Holding Companies." *Journal of Business* (July 1978): 379–412.

Bloch, Ernest. "The Benefits of Multiple Regulators." Graduate School of Business Administration, New York University, 1986.

Board of Governors of the Federal Reserve System. *Annual Report*. Washington, D.C., various years.

———. "Book-Entry Daylight Overdrafts." Washington, D.C., November 1986.

———. "Capital Maintenance: Supplemental Adjusted Capital Guidelines." Press Release. Washington, D.C., January 24, 1986.

———. "Consolidated Daylight Overdraft Monitoring of Affiliated Depository Institutions." Washington, D.C., November 1986.

———. *Federal Reserve Board Rules and Regulations*. Regulation A (as adopted effective September 1, 1980).

———. *Flow of Funds Reports*. Washington, D.C., various issues.

———. "Pricing Fedwire Daylight Overdrafts." Washington, D.C., November 1986.

———. *Reappraisal of the Federal Reserve Discount Mechanism*. Washington, D.C., 1971.

———. *A Review and Evaluation of Federal Margin Requirements*. Washington, D.C., December 1984.

———. "Risk Associated with the Automated Clearing House Mechanism." Washington, D.C., November 1986.

Bodfish, Morton. *History of Building and Loan in the United States*. Chicago: U.S. Building and Loan League, 1931.

Boleat, Mark. *National Housing Finance Systems: A Comparative Study*. London: Croom, Helm, 1985.

Boyd, John H., and S. L. Graham. "Risk, Regulation, and Bank Holding Company Expansion into Nonbanking." *Federal Reserve Bank of Minneapolis Review* (Spring 1986): 2–17.

Boyd, John H., Gerald A. Hanweck, and Pipat Pithyachariyakul. "Bank Holding Company Diversification." In *Proceedings of a Conference on Bank Structure and Competition*. Chicago: Federal Reserve Bank of Chicago, 1980.

Boyd, John H., and Pipat Pithyachariyakul. "Bank Holding Company Diversification into Non-Bank Lines of Business." 1981. Manuscript.

Boyd, John H., and Edward C. Prescott. "Financial Intermediary Coalitions." *Journal of Economic Theory* (April 1986): 211–32.

Brady, Thomas F. "Changes in Loan Pricing and Business Lending at Commercial Banks." *Federal Reserve Bulletin* (January 1985): 1–13.

Brandt, L., and Thomas J. Sargent. "Interpreting New Evidence about China and U.S. Silver Purchases." 1986. Processed.

Broaddus, Alfred. "Financial Innovation in the United States—Background, Current Status, and Prospects." *Federal Reserve Bank of Richmond Economic Review* (January/February 1985): 2–22.

Brunner, Karl, and Allan H. Meltzer. *Some General Features of the Federal Reserve's Approach to Policy.* Washington, D.C., 1964.

———. "The Uses of Money: Money in a Theory of an Exchange Economy." *American Economic Review* (December 1971): 781–805.

Bryant, John. "Bank Collapse and Depression." *Journal of Money, Credit, and Banking* (November 1981): 454–64.

———. "A Model of Reserves, Bank Runs, and Deposit Insurance." *Journal of Banking and Finance* (1980): 335–44.

Bryant, Ralph C. *International Financial Intermediation: Issues for Analysis and Public Policy.* Washington, D.C.: Brookings Institution, 1987.

Bulow, Jeremy I., and Kenneth Rogoff. "A Constant Recontracting Model of Sovereign Debt." Hoover Institution, Stanford University, December 1986.

Buser, Stephen A., Andrew H. Chen, and Edward J. Kane. "Federal Deposit Insurance Regulatory Policy, and Optimal Bank Capital." *Journal of Finance* (March 1981): 51–60.

Business Week, various issues.

Cable, John. "Capital Market Information and Industrial Performance: The Role of West German Banks." *Economic Journal* (March 1985): 118–32.

Cagan, Phillip. *Determinants and Effects of Changes in the Stock of Money, 1875–1960.* New York: National Bureau of Economic Research, 1965.

Calem, Paul. "Interstate Bank Mergers and Competition in Banking." *Federal Reserve Bank of Philadelphia Business Review* (January/February 1987): 3–14.

Campbell, Timothy S. "Bank Deposit Contracts and the Demand for Liquidity." Working Paper. Graduate School of Business, University of Southern California, August 1984.

Canada. *Commons Debates.* February 3, 1967.

Cannon, James G. *Clearing-Houses.* New York: D. Appleton and Company, 1908.

Cargill, Inc. et al. v. Monfort of Colorado. U.S. Court of Appeals, 10th Circuit, December 9, 1986, No. 85-473, at 12.

Carron, Andrew S. *The Rescue of the Thrift Industry.* Washington, D.C.: Brookings Institution, 1983.

Chan, Louis. "Uncertainty and the Neutrality of Government Financing Policy." *Journal of Monetary Economics* (May 1983): 351–72.

Chancellor of the Exchequer. *Banking Supervision.* London: Her Majesty's Stationery Office, 1985.

Chant, John F. "On the Rationale for the Regulation of Financial Institutions." Working Paper. Burnaby, B.C.: Simon Fraser University, 1986.

Charwat, W., T. Cornyn, E. Hancock, M. Holloy, and M. Wolfsen. "Performance of Bank Holding Companies in Non Bank Activities." Board of Governors of the Federal Reserve System, 1984.

Chase, Laub & Co. *Insulating Banks from Risks Run by Nonbank Affiliates.* Washington, D.C., 1987.

Chase, Samuel, and Donald L. Waage. "Corporate Separateness as a Tool of Bank Regulation." Washington, D.C.: American Bankers Association, 1983.

Chessen, James. "Feeling the Heat of Risk-based Capital: The Case of Off-Balance-Sheet Activity." *Federal Deposit Insurance Corporation Regulatory Review* (August 1987): 1–18.

———. "Off-Balance-Sheet Activity: A Growing Concern?" *Federal Deposit Insurance Corporation Regulatory Review* (May 1986): 1–15.

———. "Regulatory Proposals for a Supplemental-Adjusted-Capital Measure." *Federal Deposit Insurance Corporation Banking and Economic Review* (March 1986): 11–17.

———. "Risk-based Capital Comes to the Fore." *Issues in Bank Regulation* (Spring 1987): 3–15.

———. "Standby Letters of Credit." *Federal Deposit Insurance Corporation Economic Outlook* (November 1985): 13–25.

———. "Third-Quarter Update: Bank Off-Balance-Sheet Activity." *Federal Deposit Insurance Corporation Regulatory Review* (November/December 1987): 1–8.

Clark, Truman A. "Interest Rate Seasonals and the Federal Reserve." *Journal of Political Economy* (February 1986): 76–125.

Clarke, James J. "An Interest Rate Risk Analysis of the Federal National Mortgage Association." In *The Federal National Mortgage Association in a Changing Economic Environment.* GAO/RCED-85-102A. Washington, D.C.: U.S. General Accounting Office, July 1985.

Clarke, Robert L. Statement before U.S. Congress, House of Representatives, Subcommittee on Financial Institutions Supervision, Regulation, and Insurance of the Committee on Banking, Finance, and Urban Affairs, 100th Congress, 1st session, October 28, 1987.

Clarke, Stephen V. O. American Banks in the International Interbank Market. *Monograph Series in Finance and Economics,* no. 1983-4. New York: New York University, 1983.

Clemmer, Richard B. "Fannie Mae and Its Relationship to Low- and

BIBLIOGRAPHY

Moderate-Income Families." In *The Federal National Mortgage Association in a Changing Economic Environment*. GAO/RCED-85-102A. Washington, D.C.: U.S. General Accounting Office, July 1985.

Comptroller of the Currency. *Annual Report*. Washington, D.C., 1922–1930, 1932–1937.

———. "Capital Forbearance Policies." News Release. March 28, 1986.

———. *An Evaluation of the Factors Contributing to the Failure of National Banks*. Washington, D.C., January 1988.

———. "Minimum Capital Ratios: Risk-based Capital Ratios." News Release. March 25, 1986.

———. News Release, 88-14. March 1, 1988.

Congressional Budget Office. *The Housing Finance System and Federal Policy: Recent Changes and Options for the Future*. Washington, D.C.: October 1983.

Consumer Federation of America. "The Potential Costs and Benefits of Allowing Banks to Sell Insurance." Washington, D.C., 1987. Mimeo.

Cook, Timothy Q. "The Residential Mortgage Market in Recent Years."*Federal Reserve Bank of Richmond Economic Review* (September/October 1974): 3–18.

Cook, Timothy Q., and Jeremy G. Duffield. "Short-Term Investment Pools." *Federal Reserve Bank of Richmond Economic Review* (September/October 1980): 3–23.

Cook, Timothy, and Thomas Hahn. "The Information Content of Discount Rate Announcements and Their Effect on Market Interest Rates." *Journal of Money, Credit, and Banking* (forthcoming).

Cook, Timothy, and Timothy D. Rowe, eds. *Instruments of the Money Market*, 6th ed. Richmond, Va.: Federal Reserve Bank of Richmond, 1986.

Cornyn, Anthony, Gerald Hanweck, Stephen Rhoades, and John T. Rose. "An Analysis of the Concept of Corporate Separateness on BHC Regulation from an Economic Perspective." In *Proceedings of a Conference on Bank Structure and Competition*. Chicago: Federal Reserve Bank of Chicago, 1986.

Corrigan, E. Gerald. "Are Banks Special?" *Federal Reserve Bank of Minneapolis Annual Report* (1982).

———. "Financial Market Structure: A Longer View." *Federal Reserve Bank of New York Annual Report* (1987): 3–54.

———. "A Framework for Reform of the Financial System." *Federal Reserve Bank of New York Quarterly Review* (Summer 1987): 1–8.

———. Statement before the U.S. Congress, House of Representatives, Subcommittee on Commerce, Consumer, and Monetary Affairs of the Committee on Government Operations, May 15, 1985. *Federal Reserve Bulletin* (July 1985): 524–28.

———. Statement before the U.S. Congress, Senate, Subcommittee on Securities of the Committee on Banking, Housing, and Urban Affairs, May 9, 1985. *Federal Reserve Bulletin* (July 1985): 520–24.

Cox, Albert. *Regulation of Interest Rates on Bank Deposits.* Michigan Business Studies 17. Ann Arbor: University of Michigan Press, 1966.

Cox, William H. "Southeastern Credit Unions: From Delicatessen to Supermarket." *Federal Reserve Bank of Atlanta Economic Review* (June 1983): 40–43.

Cramer, T. P., Jr. "Double Liability (A Nationwide Survey)." *Banking* (May 1936): 84–87.

Crane, Dwight B. *Managing Credit Lines and Commitments.* Chicago: Association of Reserve City Bankers, 1973.

Crane, Dwight B., and Samuel L. Hayes. "The Evolution of International Banking Competition and Its Implications for Regulation." *Journal of Bank Research* (Spring 1983): 39–58.

Cukierman, Alex, and Allan H. Meltzer. "A Theory of Ambiguity, Credibility, and Inflation under Discretion and Asymmetric Information." *Econometrica* (September 1986): 1099–1128.

Curry, Timothy, and Mark Warshawsky. "Life Insurance Companies in a Changing Environment." *Federal Reserve Bulletin* (July 1986): 449–60.

Cyrnak, Anthony W. "Chain Banks and Competition: The Effectiveness of Federal Reserve Policy since 1977." *Federal Reserve Bank of San Francisco Economic Review* (Spring 1986): 5–16.

Danker, Deborah J., and Mary M. McLaughlin. "The Profitability of U.S. Chartered Insured Commercial Banks in 1986." *Federal Reserve Bulletin* (July 1987): 537–46.

Darby, Michael R. "The Internationalization of American Banking and Finance: Structure, Risk, and World Interest Rates." *Journal of International Money and Finance* (December 1986): 403–28.

———. *Macroeconomics: Theory of Income, Employment, and the Price Level.* New York: McGraw-Hill, 1976.

Desai, Anand S., and Roger D. Stover. "Bank Holding Company Acquisitions, Stockholder Returns, and Regulatory Uncertainty." *Journal of Financial Research* (1985): 145–56.

Dewey, Davis R. *State Banking before the Civil War.* Washington, D.C.: National Monetary Commission, 1910.

Diamond, Douglas. "Financial Intermediation and Delegated Monitoring." *Review of Economic Studies* (July 1984): 393–414.

Diamond, Douglas W., and Philip H. Dybvig. "Bank Runs, Deposit Insurance, and Liquidity." *Journal of Political Economy* (June 1983): 401–19.

Domberger, S. "Relative Price Variability and Inflation." *Journal of Political Economy* (June 1987): 547–66.

Dornbusch, Rudiger, and Stanley Fischer. *Macroeconomics*. New York: McGraw-Hill, 1984.

Dowd, Kevin. "Some Lessons from the Recent Canadian Failures." In *Research in Financial Services: Private and Public Policy*, edited by George G. Kaufman. Greenwich, Conn.: JAI Press, forthcoming.

Downs, Anthony. *The Revolution in Real Estate Finance*. Washington, D.C.: Brookings Institution, 1985.

Drum, Dale S. "MBHC's: Evidence after Two Decades of Regulations." *Federal Reserve Bank of Chicago Business Conditions* (December 1976): 3–15.

Dun's Business Month, various issues.

Eccles, Marriner S. *Beckoning Frontiers*. New York: Knopf, 1951.

Economic Report of the President. Washington, D.C., various years.

Economist, various issues.

Edwards, Franklin R. "Banks and Securities Activities: Legal and Economic Perspectives on the Glass-Steagall Act." In *The Deregulation of the Banking and Securities Industries*, edited by L. Goldberg and L. White. Lexington, Mass.: D.C. Heath, 1979.

———. "Can Financial Reform Prevent the Impending Disaster in Financial Markets?" In *Restructuring the Financial System*, a symposium sponsored by the Federal Reserve Bank of Kansas City. Jackson Hole, Wyoming, August 20–22, 1987.

———. "Managerial Objectives in Regulated Industries: Expense Preference Behavior in Banking." *Journal of Political Economy* (February 1977): 147–62.

Edwards, Franklin R., and Linda Edwards. "Differential State Regulation of Consumer Credit Markets: Normative and Positive Theories of Statutory Interest Rate Ceilings." In *Proceedings of a Conference on Bank Structure and Competition*. Chicago: Federal Reserve Bank of Chicago, 1978.

Eichengreen, Barry, and Richard Portes. "Debt and Default in the 1930s: Causes and Consequences." *European Economic Review* (1986): 559–640.

Eisemann, Peter C. "Diversification and the Cogeneric Bank Holding Companies." *Journal of Bank Research* (Spring 1976): 68–77.

Eisenbeis, Robert A. "Eroding Market Imperfections: Implications for Financial Intermediaries, the Payments System, and Regulatory Reform." In *Restructuring the Financial System*, a symposium sponsored by the Federal Reserve Bank of Kansas City, Jackson Hole, Wyoming, August 20–22, 1987.

———. "Financial Innovation and the Growth of Bank Holding Companies." In *Proceedings of a Conference on Bank Structure and Competition*. Chicago: Federal Reserve Bank of Chicago, 1978.

———. "How Should Bank Holding Companies Be Regulated?" *Federal Reserve Bank of Atlanta Economic Review* (January 1983): 42–47.

———. "New Investment Powers for S&Ls: Diversification or Specialization?" *Federal Reserve Bank of Atlanta Economic Review* (July 1983): 53–62.

Eisenbeis, Robert A., Robert S. Harris, and Josef Lakonishok. "Benefits of Bank Diversification: The Evidence from Shareholder Returns." *Journal of Finance* (July 1984): 881–92.

Ely, Bert. "Bailing Out the Federal Savings and Loan Insurance Corporation." Alexandria, Va.: Ely & Company, July 1986. Manuscript.

———. "The FSLIC Recap Plan Is Bad Medicine for Healthy Thrifts and for the American Taxpayer." Alexandria, Va.: Ely & Company, September 1987. Manuscript.

———. "Yes—Private Sector Depositor Protection Is a Viable Alternative to Federal Deposit Insurance." In *Proceedings of a Conference on Bank Structure and Competition*. Chicago: Federal Reserve Bank of Chicago, 1985.

England, Catherine. "Agency Problems and the Banking Firm: A Theory of Unregulated Banking." In *The Financial Services Revolution: Policy Directions for the Future*, edited by Catherine England and Thomas Huertas. Boston: Kluwer Academic, 1988.

———. "A Proposal for Introducing Private Deposit Insurance." In *Proceedings of a Conference on Bank Structure and Competition*. Chicago: Federal Reserve Bank of Chicago, 1985.

Epstein, E. "Firm Size and Structure, Market Power and Business Political Influence: A Review of the Literature." In *The Economics of Firm Size, Market Structure, and Social Performance*, edited by J. Siegfried. Washington, D.C.: Federal Trade Commission, 1980.

Ettin, Edward C., Elliott C. McEntee, and Oliver Ireland. "Further Steps to Reduce Payments System Risk: An Overview of Staff Proposals." Washington, D.C.: Board of Governors of the Federal Reserve System, November 1986. Mimeo.

Euromoney, various issues.

Fama, Eugene F. "Banking in the Theory of Finance." *Journal of Monetary Economics* (January 1980): 39–57.

———. "Financial Intermediation and Price Level Control." *Journal of Monetary Economics* (July 1983): 7–28.

———. "What's Different about Banks?" *Journal of Monetary Economics* (January 1985): 29–39.

Federal Deposit Insurance Corporation. *Annual Report*. Washington, D.C., 1941.

———. *Deposit Insurance in a Changing Environment*. Washington, D.C., April 1983.

———. *The First Fifty Years*. Washington, D.C., 1984.

———. "Mandate for Change: Restructuring the Banking Industry." Washington, D.C., August 1987.

BIBLIOGRAPHY

———. "Statement of Policy on Principles of Capital Forbearance for Banks with Concentrations in Agriculture and Oil and Gas." March 27, 1986.

Federal Home Loan Bank Board. *Agenda for Reform*. Washington, D.C., March 1983.

Federal Home Loan Bank of San Francisco. "The Historical and Contemporary Role of the Federal Home Loan Mortgage Corporation in Housing Finance." Paper prepared for the Federal Savings and Loan Advisory Council, June 1986.

Federal Home Loan Mortgage Corporation. *The Secondary Market in Residential Mortgages*. Washington, D.C., December 1984.

Federal Reserve Bank of Cleveland. *Annual Report*. 1985.

Federal Reserve Bank of New York. *Recent Trends in Commercial Bank Performance: A Staff Study*. 1986.

Federal Reserve Bank of San Francisco. *The Search for Financial Stability: The Past Fifty Years*. Asilomar, Calif., 1985.

Federal Reserve Bulletin, various issues.

Federal Savings and Loan Advisory Council, Committee III. "Recapitalization of the FSLIC and Variable Rate Deposit Insurance Premiums." December 1985.

Fed Fortnightly, various issues.

Felgran, Stephen D. "Bank Entry into Securities Brokerage: Competitive and Legal Aspects." *New England Economic Review* (November/December 1984): 12–33.

———. "Banks as Insurance Agencies: Legal Constraints and Competitive Advances." *New England Economic Review* (September/October 1985): 34–49.

Financier, various issues.

Flannery, Mark J. "Contagious Bank Runs, Financial Structure and Corporate Separateness within a Bank Holding Company." In *Proceedings of a Conference on Bank Structure and Competition*. Chicago: Federal Reserve Bank of Chicago, 1986.

———. "Deposit Insurance Creates a Need for Bank Regulation." *Federal Reserve Bank of Philadelphia Business Review* (February 1982): 17–27.

Flannery, Mark J., and Jack M. Guttentag. "Problem Banks: Examination, Identification, and Supervision." In *State and Federal Regulation of Commercial Banks*, edited by L. Lapidus et al. Vol. 2, *Appraising the System: Significant Activities and Issues, Examination Studies*. Washington, D.C.: FDIC Task Force on State and Federal Regulation of Commercial Banks, 1980.

Follain, James R. "The Experience of the U.S. Secondary Mortgage Market: Born in a Regulated Environment but Flourishing in a Competitive One." Research Paper no. 50. Office of Real Estate, University of Illinois, Urbana-Champaign, September 1987.

Forrestal, Robert P. "Competitive Forces in Financial Services: Signals for Southeastern Thrifts." *Federal Reserve Bank of Atlanta Economic Review* (September 1984): 4–7.

Fortner Enterprises, Inc. v. U.S. Steel Corp. 394 U.S. 495 (1969).

Fortune, various issues.

Fraas, Arthur G. "The Performance of Individual Bank Holding Companies." *Staff Economic Studies*, no. 84. Washington, D.C.: Board of Governors of the Federal Reserve System, 1974.

Frankel, Allen B., and Catherine L. Mann. "A Framework for Analyzing the Process of Financial Innovation." International Finance Discussion Paper no. 283. Washington, D.C.: Board of Governors of the Federal Reserve System, June 1986.

Freddie Mac Advisory Committee Task Force. "Report." October 1986.

Freund, William C. "The Securities Industry in the Financial Services Marketplace: A Review of Dynamic Trends." Working Paper, no. 61. Center for Applied Research, Pace University, September 1986.

Friedman, Milton. *A Program for Monetary Stability*. New York: Fordham University Press, 1960.

Friedman, Milton, and Anna J. Schwartz. *A Monetary History of the United States, 1867–1960*. New York: National Bureau of Economic Research, 1963.

Frodin, Joanna H. "Fed Pricing and the Check Collection Business: The Private Sector Response." *Federal Reserve Bank of Philadelphia Business Review* (January/February 1984): 13–22.

Frydl, Edward J. "The Challenge of Financial Change." Federal Reserve Bank of New York. *Annual Report* (1985): 3–27.

Furlong, Frederick T. "New Deposit Instruments." *Federal Reserve Bulletin* (May 1983): 319–26.

Furlong, Frederick T., and Michael C. Keeley. "Bank Capital Regulation and Asset Risk." *Federal Reserve Bank of San Francisco Economic Review* (Spring 1987): 20–40.

Gabriel, Stuart A. "Housing and Mortgage Markets: The Post-1982 Expansion." *Federal Reserve Bulletin* (December 1987): 893–903.

Gajewski, Gregory, and Deano Hagermand. "Should the Feds Prop Up Ailing Banks and S&Ls?" *Rural Development* (October 1987): 29–34.

Garbade, Kenneth D., and William L. Silber. "The Payment System and Domestic Exchange Rates: Technological versus Institutional Change." *Journal of Monetary Economics* (1979): 1–22.

Gart, Alan. *Banks, Thrifts, and Insurance Companies*. Lexington, Mass.: Lexington Books, 1985.

———. *The Insider's Guide to the Financial Services Revolution*. New York: McGraw-Hill, 1984.

Geis, Thomas G., and Lucy J. Reuben. "Impact of Bank Failures on

Local Economies." Paper presented at the Annual Meeting of Midwest Finance Association, March 31, 1977.

Gelfand, Matthew D. "Proposals for Daylight Overdraft Cap Reductions, De Minimis Caps, and Frequency of Self-Assessment Ratings." Washington, D.C.: Board of Governors of the Federal Reserve System, November 1986. Mimeo.

George, A., and Ian Giddy, eds. *International Finance Handbook*, Vols. 1 and 2. New York: John Wiley, 1983.

Germany, J. David, and John E. Morton. "Financial Innovation and Deregulation in Foreign Industrial Countries." *Federal Reserve Bulletin* (October 1985): 743–53.

Giddy, Ian H. "Domestic Regulation versus International Competition in Banking." *Kredit and Kapital* (1984): 195–209.

Gilbert, R. Alton, and Levis A. Kochin. "Local Economic Effects of Bank Failures." In *Proceedings of a Conference on Bank Structure and Competition*. Chicago: Federal Reserve Bank of Chicago, 1987.

Gilligan, Thomas, Michael Smirlock, and William Marshall. "Scale and Scope Economies in the Multiproduct Banking Firm." *Journal of Monetary Economics* (May 1984): 393–406.

Globecon Group. *Cash Management and the Payments System: Ground Rules, Costs, and Risks*. Morristown, N.J.: Financial Executives Research Foundation, 1986.

Goldsmith, Raymond W. *The Flow of Capital Funds in the Postwar Economy*. New York: National Bureau of Economic Research, 1965.

Golembe, Carter H., and David S. Holland. *Federal Regulation of Banking, 1986–87*. Washington, D.C.: Golembe Associates, 1986.

Goodfriend, Marvin. "Discount Window Borrowing, Monetary Policy, and the Post-October 1979 Federal Reserve Operating Procedure." *Journal of Monetary Economics* (September 1983): 343–56.

———. "Interest Rate Smoothing and Price Level Trend-Stationarity." *Journal of Monetary Economics* (May 1987): 335–48.

———. "Monetary Mystique: Secrecy and Central Banking." *Journal of Monetary Economics* (January 1986): 63–92.

———. *Monetary Policy in Practice*. Richmond, Va.: Federal Reserve Bank of Richmond, 1987.

Goodhart, Charles. *The Evolution of Central Banks*. London: London School of Economics and Political Science, October 1985.

———. "Why Do We Need a Central Bank?" n.d. Processed.

Gordon, Robert J. *Macroeconomics*. Boston: Little, Brown and Co., 1987.

Gorton, Gary. "Clearing Houses and the Origin of Central Banking in the United States." *Journal of Economic History* (June 1985): 277–83.

Gorton, Gary, and Joseph Haubrich. "Bank Deregulation, Credit Markets, and the Control of Capital." *Carnegie-Rochester Series on Public Policy* (Spring 1987): 289–333.

———. "Loan Sales, Recourse, and Reputation: An Analysis of Secondary Loan Participations." Department of Finance, University of Pennsylvania, May 1987.

Gorton, Gary, and Donald J. Mullineaux. "The Joint Production of Confidence: Endogenous Regulation and Nineteenth Century Commercial-Bank Clearinghouses." *Journal of Money, Credit, and Banking* (November 1987): 457–68.

Goudreau, Robert E., and Harold D. Ford. "Changing Thrifts: What Makes Them Choose Commercial Lending?" *Federal Reserve Bank of Atlanta Economic Review* (June/July 1986): 24–39.

Government Credit Allocation: Where Do We Go from Here? Rochester, N.Y.: Center for Research in Government Policy and Business, Graduate School of Management, University of Rochester, 1975.

Grebler, Leo. "An Assessment of the Performance of the Public Sector in the Residential Housing Market: 1955–1974." In *Capital Markets and the Housing Sector: Perspectives on Financial Reform*, edited by Robert M. Buckley, John A. Tuccillo, and Kevin E. Villani. Cambridge, Mass.: Ballinger, 1977.

Grebler, Leo, David M. Blank, and Louis Winnick. *Capital Formation in Residential Real Estate*. Princeton, N.J.: Princeton University Press, 1956.

Green, George D. "The Ideological Origins of the Revolution in American Financial Policies." In *The Great Depression Revisited*, edited by Karl Brunner. Boston: Nijhoff, 1981.

Greenbaum, Stuart I., and Anjan V. Thakor. "Bank Funding Modes, Securitization versus Deposits." *Journal of Banking and Finance* (1987): 379–401.

Guttentag, Jack, and Richard Herring. *Disaster Myopia in International Banking*. Essays in International Finance, no. 164. Princeton, N.J.: Princeton University Press, 1983.

———. "Emergency Liquidity Assistance for International Banks." Working Paper. University of Pennsylvania, September 1986.

———. *The Lender of Last Resort Function in an International Context*. Essays in International Finance, no. 151. Princeton, N.J.: Princeton University Press, 1983.

———. "Uncertainty and Insolvency Exposure in International Banks." The Wharton Program in International Banking and Finance, University of Pennsylvania, December 1982. Mimeo.

Hackley, Howard H. *Lending Functions of the Federal Reserve Banks: A History*. Washington, D.C.: Board of Governors of the Federal Reserve System, 1973.

Hagermand, Deano, and Gregory Gajewski. "Patterns of Financial Institution Failures: Some Thoughts on Policy Implications." *Federal*

Deposit Insurance Corportion Banking and Economic Review (May/June 1987): 5–10

Hall, Robert E., and John B. Taylor. *Macroeconomics: Theory, Performance, and Policy.* New York: Norton, 1985.

Halpert, Stephen. "The Separation of Banking and Commerce Reconsidered." University of Miami Law School, August 1986. Mimeo.

Hanc, George. "Is There a Future for Thrifts?" *Bottomline* 4 (March 1987).

Hannan, Timothy. "Safety, Soundness, and the Bank Holding Company: A Critical Review of the Literature." Working Paper. Board of Governors of the Federal Reserve System, 1984.

Hanweck, Gerald A. "Bank Loan Commitments." In *Below the Bottom Line*. Washington, D.C.: Board of Governors of the Federal Reserve System, January 1986.

Haraf, William S. "Maintaining Financial Stability: Financial Strains and Public Policy." In *Contemporary Economic Problems: Deficits, Taxes, and Economic Adjustments*, edited by Phillip Cagan. Washington, D.C.: American Enterprise Institute, 1987.

———. "Nonbanks and Nonproblems." *Regulation* (September/October 1986): 8–11.

Hauberg, R., Jr. "Mergers and Acquisitions of the Depository Institutions." Speech delivered to the American Bar Association, Washington, D.C., May 23, 1985.

Haubrich, Joseph. "Financial Intermediation, Delegated Monitoring, and Long Term Relationships." Wharton School, University of Pennsylvania, October 1986.

Haubrich, Joseph G., and Robert G. King. "Banking and Insurance." Working Paper no. 1312. National Bureau of Economic Research, 1984.

Havrilesky, Thomas M., et al., eds. *Dynamics of Banking.* Arlington Heights, Ill.: Harlan Davidson, 1985.

Hawkins, Gregory D. "An Analysis of Revolving Credit Agreements." *Journal of Financial Economics* (March 1982): 59–91.

Hawtrey, R.G. *The Art of Central Banking.* London: Frank Cass, 1962. Originally published 1932.

Hayes, Samuel L. "Investment Banking: Commercial Banks' Inroads." *Federal Reserve Bank of Atlanta Economic Review* (May 1984): 50–59.

Heggestad, Arnold A. "Riskiness of Investments in Nonbank Activities by Bank Holding Companies." *Journal of Economics and Business* (Spring 1975): 219–23.

Heggestad, Arnold A., ed. *Regulation of Consumer Financial Services.* Cambridge, Mass.: Abt Books, 1981.

Heggestad, Arnold A., and John J. Mingo. "Capital Management by Bank Holding Company Banks." *Journal of Business* (October 1975): 500–505.

Heimann, John G. "Financial Innovation: The Issues and Risks." Paper presented at the Institutional Investor Conference on Innovation in the Capital Markets, New York, June 1986.

———. "Market-driven Deregulation of Financial Services." *Federal Reserve Bank of Atlanta Economic Review* (December 1984): 36–41.

Heldring, Frederick. "Payment Systems Risk in the United States." *Journal of Bank Research*, no. 4 (1986): 209–13.

Hendershott, Patric H. "Real User Costs and the Demand for Single-Family Housing." *Brookings Papers on Economic Activity*, no. 2 (1980): 401–44.

———. *Understanding Capital Markets*. Vol. 1, *A Flow-of-Funds Financial Model*. Lexington, Mass.: Lexington Books, 1977.

Hendershott, Patric H., and James D. Shilling. "The Economics of Tenure Choice, 1955–1979." *Research in Real Estate* 1 (1982): 105–33.

Hendershott, Patric H., James D. Shilling, and Kevin E. Villani. "Measurement of the Spreads between Yields on Various Mortgage Contracts and Treasury Securities." *AREUEA Journal* 11 (Winter 1984): 476–89.

Hendershott, Patric H., and Kevin E. Villani. "Housing Finance in America in the Year 2001." In *North American Housing Markets into the Twenty-first Century*, edited by George W. Gau and Michael A. Goldberg. Cambridge, Mass.: Ballinger, 1982.

———. *Regulation and Reform of the Housing Finance System*. Washington, D.C.: American Enterprise Institute, 1978.

Henn, Harry G. *Handbook of the Law of Corporations and Other Business Enterprises*. St. Paul, Minn.: West Publishing, 1970.

Herbert, Frank. *The Heretics of Dune*. New York: Berkley Books, 1984.

Hickman, W. Braddock. *Bond Quality and Investor Experience*. Princeton, N.J.: Princeton University Press, 1958.

Hodgman, Donald R. *Selective Credit Controls in Western Europe*. Chicago: Association of Reserve City Bankers, 1976.

Horvitz, Paul M. "Bank Holding Company Regulation: Discussion." In *Proceedings of a Conference on Bank Structure and Competition*. Chicago: Federal Reserve Bank of Chicago, 1978.

———. "The Case against Risk-related Deposit Insurance Premiums." *Housing Finance Review* (July 1983): 253–63.

Horvitz, Paul M., et al. "A Reconsideration of the Role of Bank Examination." *Journal of Money, Credit, and Banking* 12 (November 1980, pt. 1): 654–59.

———. "Research on Federal Deposit Insurance." In *Proceedings of a Conference on Bank Structure and Competition*. Chicago: Federal Reserve Bank of Chicago, 1983.

Houpt, James V. "Performance and Characteristics of Edge Corporations." *Staff Economic Studies*, no. 110. Washington, D.C.: Board of Governors of the Federal Reserve System, 1981.

Huertas, Thomas F. "The Protection of Deposits from Risks Assumed by Non-Bank Affiliates." Appendix C to Hans H. Angermueller testimony before U.S. Congress, House of Representatives, Subcommittee of the Committee on Government Operations, 99th Congress, 2d session, December 17–18, 1986.

———. "Redesigning Regulation: The Future of Finance in the United States." In *Restructuring the Financial System*, a symposium sponsored by the Federal Reserve Bank of Kansas City, Jackson Hole, Wyoming, August 20–22, 1987.

———. "Risk in the Payments System." Appendix D. To Hans H. Angermueller testimony before U.S. Congress, House of Representatives, Subcommittee of the Committee on Government Operations, 99th Congress, 2d session, December 17–18, 1986.

Huertas, Thomas F., and Rachel Strauber. "An Analysis of Alternative Proposals for Deposit Insurance Reform." Appendix E to Hans H. Angermueller testimony before U.S. Congress, House of Representatives, Subcommittee of the Committee on Government Operations, 99th Congress, 2d session, December 17–18, 1986.

Humphrey, David B. "Cost Dispersion and the Measurement of Economies in Banking." *Federal Reserve Bank of Richmond Economic Review* (May/June 1987): 24–38.

———. "Electronic Payments System Links and Risks." In *Electronic Funds Transfers and Payments: The Public Policy Issues*, edited by Elinor H. Solomon. Boston: Kluwer-Nijhoff, 1987.

———. "Payments System Risk, Market Failure, and Public Policy." In *The Payments Revolution: The Emerging Public Policy Issues*, edited by Elinor H. Solomon. Boston: Kluwer-Nijhoff, 1987.

———. *The U.S. Payments System: Costs, Pricing, Competition, and Risks*. Monograph Series in Finance and Economics. New York: Salomon Brothers Center for the Study of Financial Institutions, New York University, 1984.

Humphrey, David B., David Mengle, Oliver Ireland, and Alisa Morgenthaler. "Pricing Fedwire Daylight Overdrafts." Federal Reserve Bank of Richmond, January 13, 1987. Mimeo.

Humphrey, Thomas M., and Robert E. Keleher. "The Lender of Last Resort: A Historical Perspective." *Cato Journal* (Spring/Summer 1984): 275–318.

Hurley, Evelyn M. "The Commercial Paper Market since the Mid-Seventies." *Federal Reserve Bulletin* (June 1982): 327–34.

Huyser, Daniel. "Problem Banks: The Phoenix Factor." In *Proceedings of a Conference on Bank Structure and Competition*. Chicago: Federal Reserve Bank of Chicago, 1987.

Institutional Investor, various issues.

Investor's Daily, various issues.

Jacklin, Charles J. "Demand Deposits, Trading Restrictions, and Risk

Sharing." Working Paper. Graduate School of Business, Stanford University, 1983.

Jackson, William. "Multibank Holding Company and Bank Behavior." Working Paper no. 75-1. Federal Reserve Bank of Richmond, 1975.

Jacobe, Dennis J. "Should the Restrictions on Freddie Mac Preferred Stock Trading Be Removed?" June 1986.

Jacobs, Donald B., H. Prescott Beighley, and John H. Boyd. *The Financial Structure of Bank Holding Companies*. Chicago: Association of Reserve City Bankers, 1975.

Jaffee, Dwight M. "The Future Role of Thrift Institutions in Mortgage Lending." In *The Future of the Thrift Industry*. Federal Reserve Bank of Boston Conference Series no. 24, October 1981.

Jaffee, Dwight M., and Kenneth T. Rosen. "The Demand for Housing and Mortgage Credit: The Mortgage Credit Gap Problem." *Housing Finance in the Eighties: Issues and Options*. Washington, D.C.: FNMA, 1981.

———. "Mortgage Credit Availability and Residential Construction." *Brookings Papers on Economic Activity*, no. 2 (1979): 333–86.

James, Christopher. "Some Evidence on the Uniqueness of Bank Loans." *Journal of Financial Economics* no. 2 (1987): 217–36.

Jefferson Parish Hospital District no. 2 et al. v. *Hyde*, U.S. 2 at 33.

Jensen, Frederick H. "Recent Developments in Corporate Finance." *Federal Reserve Bulletin* (November 1986): 745–56.

Jensen, Frederick H., and Patrick M. Parkinson. "Recent Developments in the Bankers Acceptance Market." *Federal Reserve Bulletin* (January 1986): 1–12.

Jensen, Michael C., and William H. Meckling. "The Theory of the Firm: Managerial Behavior, Agency Costs, and Ownership Structure." *Journal of Financial Economics* (October 1976): 305–60.

Jensen, Michael C., and Richard S. Ruback. "The Market for Corporate Control: The Scientific Evidence." *Journal of Financial Economics* (1983): 5–50.

Jesse, Michael A., and Stephen A. Seelig. *Bank Holding Companies and the Public Interest: An Economic Analysis*. Lexington, Mass.: D. C. Heath, 1977.

Johnson, G., and R. Abrams. *Aspects of the International Banking Safety Net*. Occasional Paper no. 17. Washington, D.C.: International Monetary Fund, March 1983.

Johnson, Ronald D., and David R. Meinster. "Bank Holding Companies: Diversification Opportunities in Nonbank Activities." *Eastern Economic Journal* no. 4 (1974): 316–23.

Kane, Edward J. "Accelerating Inflation, Technological Innovation, and the Decreasing Effectiveness of Banking Regulation." *Journal of Finance* (May 1981): 355–67.

BIBLIOGRAPHY

―――. "Appearance and Reality in Deposit Insurance." *Journal of Banking and Finance* (June 1986): 175–88.

―――. "Change and Progress in Contemporary Mortgage Markets." *Housing Finance Review* (July 1984): 257–84.

―――. "Changes in the Provision of Correspondent-Banking Services, and the Role of Federal Reserve Banks under the DIDMC Act." *Carnegie-Rochester Conference Series on Public Policy* (1982): 93–126.

―――. "Competitive Financial Reregulation: An International Perspective." In *Threats to International Financial Stability*, edited by Richard Portes and Alexander Swoboda. Cambridge: Cambridge University Press, 1987.

―――. "Dangers of Capital Forbearance: The Case of the FSLIC and 'Zombie' S&Ls." *Contemporary Policy Issues* (January 1987): 77–83.

―――. "Discussion." In *The Federal National Mortgage Association in a Changing Economic Environment*. GAO/RCED-85-102A. Washington, D.C.: U.S. General Accounting Office, July 1985.

―――. *The Gathering Crisis in Federal Deposit Insurance*. Cambridge, Mass.: MIT Press, 1985.

―――. "How S and L's Are Special." Conference on Thrift Performance and Capital Adequacy, Federal Home Loan Bank of San Francisco, December 1986.

―――. "Microeconomic and Macroeconomic Origins of Financial Innovation." In *Federal Reserve Bank of St. Louis Financial Innovations: Their Impact on Monetary Policy and Financial Markets*. Boston, Mass.: Kluwer-Nijhoff, 1984.

―――. "No Room for Weak Links in the Chain of Deposit Insurance Reform." *Journal of Financial Services Research* 1 (1987): 77–111.

―――. "Policy Implications of Structural Changes in Financial Markets." *American Economic Review* (May 1983): 96–100.

―――. "Regulatory Structure in Futures Markets: Jurisdictional Competition between the SEC, the CFTC, and Other Agencies." *Journal of Futures Markets* (September 1984): 369–84.

―――. "Technological and Regulatory Forces in the Developing Fusion of Financial Services Competition." *Journal of Finance* (July 1984): 759–72.

―――. "Who Should Learn What from the Failure and Delayed Bailout of the ODGF?" Working Paper 2260. National Bureau of Economic Research, 1987.

Kane, Edward J., and Chester Foster. "Valuing and Eliminating Subsidies Associated with Conjectural Government Guarantees of FNMA Liabilities." Working Paper 86-71. College of Administrative Science, Ohio State University, May 1986.

Kareken, John. "Federal Bank Regulatory Policy: A Description and Some Observations." *Journal of Business* (January 1986): 3–48.

Kareken, John, and Neil Wallace. "Deposit Insurance and Bank Regulation." *Journal of Business* (July 1978): 413–38.

Karna, Adi. "Bank Holding Company Profitability: Nonbanking Subsidiaries and Financial Leverage." *Journal of Bank Research* (Spring 1979): 28–35.

Karson, Marvin J., Patricia M. Rudolph, and Leonard V. Zumpano. "Inter-regional Differences in Conventional Mortgage Terms: A Test of the Efficiency of the Residential Mortgage Market." Paper presented at the American Real Estate and Urban Economics Association Meeting, December 1986.

Kaserman, David L. "An Econometric Analysis of the Decline in Federal Mortgage Default Insurance." In *Capital Markets and the Housing Sector: Perspectives on Financial Reform*, edited by Robert M. Buckley, John A. Tuccillo, and Kevin E. Villani. Cambridge, Mass.: Ballinger, 1977.

Kaufman, George G. "Bank Capital Forbearance and Public Policy." *Contemporary Policy Issues* (January 1987): 84–91.

———. "Banking Risk in Historical Perspective." In *Proceedings of a Conference on Bank Structure and Competition*. Chicago: Federal Reserve Bank of Chicago, 1986.

———. "Bank Runs: Causes, Benefits, and Costs." *Cato Journal*, forthcoming.

———. "Federal Bank Regulatory Policy." *Journal of Business* (January 1986): 69–78.

———. "Impact of Deregulation on the Mortgage Market." In *Housing Finance in the Eighties: Issues and Options*. Washington, D.C.: FNMA, 1981.

———. "Implications of Large Bank Problems and Insolvencies for the Banking Industry and Economic Policy." *Issues in Bank Regulation* (Winter 1985): 35–42.

———. "Implications of Large Bank Problems and Insolvencies for the Banking System and Economic Policy." Staff Memorandum SM-85-3. Federal Reserve Bank of Chicago, 1985.

———. "Public Policies towards Failing Institutions: The Lessons from the Thrift Industry." In *Proceedings of a Conference on Bank Structure and Competition*. Chicago: Federal Reserve Bank of Chicago, forthcoming.

———. "The Truth about Bank Runs." In *The Financial Services Revolution: Policy Directions for the Future*, edited by Catherine England and Thomas Huertas. Boston: Kluwer Academic, 1988.

Kaufman, George G., and Roger C. Kormendi, eds. *Deregulating Financial Services: Public Policy in Flux*. Cambridge, Mass.: Ballinger, 1986.

Kaufman, Herbert M. "FNMA and the Housing Cycle: Its Recent Contribution and Its Future Role in a Deregulated Environment." In

The Federal National Mortgage Association in a Changing Economic Environment. GAO/RCED-85-102A. Washington, D.C.: U.S. General Accounting Office, July 1985.

Keeley, Michael C., and Frederick T. Furlong. "A Deposit Insurance Puzzle." *Federal Reserve Bank of San Francisco Weekly Letter,* July 3, 1987.

Kelly, Edward J. "Conflicts of Interest: A Legal View." In *Deregulating Wall Street: Commercial Bank Penetration of the Corporate Securities Market,* edited by Ingo Walter. New York: John Wiley, 1985.

Kemmerer, E. W. *Seasonal Variations in the Relative Demand for Money and Capital in the United States.* Washington, D.C.: National Monetary Commission, 1910.

King, A. Thomas, and David Andrukonis. "Who Holds PCs?" *Secondary Mortgage Markets* 1 (February 1984): 12–17.

King, B. Frank. "Depository Institutions: Trends Show Major Shifts." *Federal Reserve Bank of Atlanta Economic Review* (June 1983): 47–54.

———. "Upstate New York: Tough Market for City Banks." *Federal Reserve Bank of Atlanta Economic Review* (June/July 1985): 30–34.

King, Robert G., and Charles I. Plosser. "Money as the Mechanism of Exchange." *Journal of Monetary Economics* (January 1986): 93–115.

———. "Money, Credit, and Prices in a Real Business Cycle." *American Economic Review* (June 1984): 363–80.

Kinsman, Michael. "HomeFed Quitting FSLIC." *National Thrift News,* April 6, 1987.

Koch, Donald L. "The Emerging Financial Services Industry: Challenge and Innovation." *Federal Reserve Bank of Atlanta Economic Review* (April 1984): 25–30.

Koehn, Michael, and Anthony M. Santomero. "Regulation of Bank Capital and Portfolio Risk." *Journal of Finance* (December 1980): 1235–44.

Kolb, Robert W. "Affiliated and Independent Banks: Two Behavioral Regimes." *Journal of Banking and Finance* 4 (1981): 523–37.

Kriz, Margaret E. "Band-Aid Banking Law?" *National Journal* (August 15, 1987): 2082–86.

Kwast, Myron L. "The Impact of Underwriting and Dealing on Bank Returns and Risks." Working Paper. Board of Governors of the Federal Reserve System, April 1987.

Ladd, Edward H. "Discussion." In *The Future of the Thrift Industry.* Federal Reserve Bank of Boston Conference Series no. 24, October 1981.

Lawrence, Colin, and Robert P. Shay. "Technology and Financial Intermediation in a Multiproduct Banking Firm: An Econometric Study of U.S. Banks, 1979–1982." In *Technological Innovation, Regulation and the Monetary Economy,* edited by Colin Lawrence and Robert Shay. Cambridge, Mass.: Ballinger, 1986.

Lawrence, Joseph S. "What Is the Average Recovery of Depositors?" *American Bankers Association Journal* (February 1931): 655ff.

Lawrence, Robert J. "Minimizing Regulation of the Financial Services Industry." *Issues in Bank Regulation* (Summer 1985): 22–30.

———. *The Performance of Bank Holding Companies*. Washington, D.C.: Board of Governors of the Federal Reserve System, June 1971.

Light, Jack S. "The Effects of Holding Company Affiliation on De Novo Banks." In *Proceedings of a Conference on Bank Structure and Competition*. Chicago: Federal Reserve Bank of Chicago, 1976.

Lindow, Wesley. "Bank Capital and Risk Assets." *National Banking Review* (Comptroller of the Currency) (September 1963).

Litan, Robert E. "Evaluating and Controlling the Risks of Financial Product Deregulation." *Yale Journal on Regulation* (Fall 1985): 51–52.

———. "Reuniting Investment and Commercial Banking." In *The Financial Services Revolution: Policy Directions for the Future*, edited by Catherine England and Thomas Huertas. Boston: Kluwer Academic, 1988.

———. "Taking the Dangers out of Bank Deregulation." *Brookings Review* (Fall 1986): 3–12.

———. *What Should Banks Do?* Washington, D.C.: Brookings Institution, 1987.

Loeys, Jan G. "Interest Rate Swaps: A New Tool for Managing Risk." *Federal Reserve Bank of Philadelphia Business Review* (May/June 1985): 17–25.

———. "Low-Grade Bonds: A Growing Source of Corporate Funding." *Federal Reserve Bank of Philadelphia Business Review* (November/December 1986): 3–12.

Lucas, Robert E., and Thomas J. Sargent. *Rational Expectations and Econometric Practice*. Minneapolis: University of Minnesota Press, 1980.

Luckett, Charles. "Recent Developments in Automobile Finance." *Federal Reserve Bulletin* (June 1986): 355–65.

Macaulay, Frederick R. *Bond Yields, Interest Rates, and Stock Prices*. New York: National Bureau of Economic Research, 1938.

Mahoney, Patrick I., and Alice P. White. "The Thrift Industry in Transition." *Federal Reserve Bulletin* (March 1985): 137–58.

Makin, John. "The Third World Debt Crisis and the American Banking System." *AEI Economist* (May 1987).

Martin, John D., and Arthur J. Keown. "Market Reaction to the Formation of One Bank Holding Companies." *Journal of Banking and Finance* (1981): 383–93.

Martin, Preston. Statement before the U.S. Congress, House of Representatives, Subcommittee on Telecommunications, Consumer Protection, and Finance of the Committee on Energy and Commerce, May 2, 1985. *Federal Reserve Bulletin* (July 1985): 508–13.

Martin, William. Testimony before the U.S. Congress, House of Representatives, Committee on Banking and Currency. *Federal Reserve Bulletin* 55 (1969): 334.

Matsushita Electric Industrial Co., Ltd. et al. v. Zenith Radio Corp. et al. U.S. Court of Appeals, 3d Circuit, no. 83-2004, decided March 26, 1986, at 14.

Mayne, Lucille S. "Bank Dividend Policy and Holding Company Affiliation." *Journal of Financial and Quantitative Analysis* (Spring 1980): 469–80.

———. "Bank Holding Company Characteristics and the Upstreaming of Bank Funds." *Journal of Money, Credit, and Banking* 12 (May 1980, pt. 1): 209–14.

———. "A Comparative Study of Bank Holding Company Affiliates and Independent Banks, 1969–1972." *Journal of Finance* (March 1977): 147–58.

———. "Funds Transfer between Bank Holding Companies and Their Affiliates." *Journal of Bank Research* (1980): 20–27.

McCall, Alan S., and Victor L. Saulsbury. "The Changing Role of Banks and Other Private Financial Institutions." *Federal Deposit Insurance Corporation Regulatory Review* (April 1986): 1–5.

McCallum, Bennett. "Bank Deregulation, Accounting Systems of Exchange, and the Unit of Account: A Critical Review." *Carnegie-Rochester Conference Series on Public Policy* (Autumn 1985): 13–45.

———. "Price Level Determinacy with an Interest Rate Policy Rule and Rational Expectations." *Journal of Monetary Economics* (November 1981): 319–29.

———. "The Role of Overlapping Generations Models in Monetary Economics." *Carnegie-Rochester Conference Series on Public Policy* (Spring 1983): 9–44.

McCallum, Bennett, and Marvin Goodfriend. "Money: Theoretical Analysis of the Demand for Money." In *The New Palgrave: A Dictionary of Economics,* edited by S. Eatwell, P. Newman, and M. Milgate. London: Macmillan, 1987.

McCarthy, I. S. "Deposit Insurance: A Survey." Washington, D.C.: International Monetary Fund. 1979. Mimeo.

Mehra, Yash. "Recent Financial Deregulation and the Interest Elasticity of M1 Demand." *Federal Reserve Bank of Richmond Economic Review* (July/August 1986): 13–24.

Meinster, David R., and Ronald D. Johnson. "Bank Holding Company Diversification and the Risk of Capital Impairment." *Bell Journal of Economics* (Autumn 1979): 683–94.

Melnik, Arie, and Steven E. Plaut. "The Economics of Loan Commitment Contracts: Credit Pricing and Utilization." *Journal of Banking and Finance* (June 1986): 267–80.

———. "Loan Commitment Contracts, Terms of Lending, and Credit Allocations." *Journal of Finance* (June 1986): 425–35.

Mengle, David L., David B. Humphrey, and Bruce J. Summers. "Intraday Credit: Risk, Value, and Pricing." *Federal Reserve Bank of Richmond Economic Review* (January/February 1987): 3–14.

Mester, Loretta J. "Efficient Production of Financial Services: Scale and Scope Economies." *Federal Reserve Bank of Philadelphia Business Review* (January/February 1987): 15–25.

Miller, M. "Financial Innovation: The Last Twenty Years and the Next." *Journal of Financial and Quantitative Analysis* (December 1986): 459–71.

Mills, Edwin S. "Housing Policy as a Means to Achieve National Growth Policy." In *Housing in the Seventies: Working Papers*. Vol. 1, *National Housing Policy Review*. Washington, D.C.: U.S. Department of Housing and Urban Development, 1976.

Mingo, John J. "Managerial Motives, Market Structures, and the Performance of Holding Company Banks." *Economic Inquiry* (1976): 411–24.

Miron, Jeffrey A. "Financial Panics, the Seasonality of the Nominal Interest Rate, and the Founding of the Fed." *American Economic Review* (March 1986): 125–40.

Moran, Michael J. "Recent Financing Activity of Nonfinancial Corporations." *Federal Reserve Bulletin* (May 1984): 401–10.

Morgan Guaranty. "An Investigation of Commercial Bank Failures." Memorandum. September 1, 1983.

Morton, James E. *Urban Mortgage Lending: Comparative Markets and Experience*. Princeton, N.J.: Princeton University Press, 1956.

Moulton, Janice. "New Guidelines for Bank Capital: An Attempt to Regulate Risk." *Federal Reserve Bank of Philadelphia Business Review* (July/August 1987): 19–33.

Muth, Richard F. "The Supply of Mortgage Lending." *Urban Economics* (January 1986): 88–106.

Myers, Stuart C. "Determinants of Corporate Borrowing." *Journal of Financial Economics* (November 1977): 147–75.

National Council of Savings Institutions. *1986 National Fact Book of Savings Institutions*. Washington, D.C., 1986.

New York Times, various issues.

Niehans, Jurg. "Money and Barter in General Equilibrium with Transaction Costs." *American Economic Review* (December 1971): 773–83.

Niskanen, William. *Bureaucracy and Representative Government*. Chicago: Aldine, 1971.

Nomura Research Institute. *The World Economy and Financial Markets in 1995: Japan's Role and Challenges*. Tokyo, 1986.

Northern Pacific R. Co. v. U.S., 356 U.S. 1 (1958).

Orsingher, Roger. *Banks of the World: A History and Analysis.* London: Macmillan, 1967.

Panzar, John C., and Robert D. Willig. "Economies of Scale in Multi-Output Production." *Quarterly Journal of Economics* (August 1977): 481–94.

———. "Free Entry and the Sustainability of Natural Monopoly." *Bell Journal of Economics* 67 (Spring 1977): 1–22.

Parham, Linda. "Signals from the Future: The Emerging Financial Services Industry." *Federal Reserve Bank of Atlanta Economic Review* (September 1983): 20–32.

Patinkin, Don. "Financial Intermediaries and the Logical Structure of Monetary Theory." *American Economic Review* (March 1961): 95–116.

"The Pattern of Growth in Consumer Credit." *Federal Reserve Bulletin* (March 1974): 175–88.

Pavel, Christine. "Securitization." *Federal Reserve Bank of Chicago Economic Review* (July/August 1986): 16–31.

Pavel, Christine, and David Phillis. "To Sell or Not to Sell: Loan Sales by Commercial Banks." Paper presented at a conference, "Asset Securitization and Off–Balance Sheet Banking," Chicago, January 1987.

Pavel, Christine, and Harvey Rosenblum. "Financial Darwinism: Nonbanks—and Banks—Are Surviving." Staff Memoranda SM-85-5. Federal Reserve Bank of Chicago, 1985.

Pecchioli, R. *The Internationalization of Banking: The Policy Issues.* Paris: Organization for Economic Cooperation and Development, 1983.

Peltzman, Samuel. "Capital Investment in Commercial Banking and Its Relationship to Portfolio Regulation." *Journal of Political Economy* (January/February 1970): 1–26.

———. "Entry into Banking." *Journal of Law and Economics* (October 1965): 11–50.

Pennacchi, George. "Loan Sales and the Cost of Bank Capital." Department of Economics, University of Pennsylvania, January 1987.

———. "Market Discipline, Information Disclosure, and Uninsured Deposits." *Proceedings of a Conference on Bank Structure and Competition.* Chicago: Federal Reserve Bank of Chicago, forthcoming.

Pierce, James L. "On the Expansion of Banking Powers." In *Deregulating Wall Street: Commercial Bank Penetration of the Corporate Securities Market*, edited by Ingo Walter. New York: John Wiley, 1985.

Poole, William. *Money and the Economy: A Monetarist View.* Reading, Mass.: Addison-Wesley, 1978.

Posner, Richard A. *Antitrust Law: An Economic Perspective.* Chicago: University of Chicago Press, 1976.

———. "Power in America: The Role of the Large Corporation." In *Large Corporations in a Changing Society*, edited by F. Weston. New York: New York University Press, 1975.

---. "Theories of Economic Regulation." *Bell Journal of Economics* (Autumn 1974): 335–58.

Pozdena, Randall J. "Securitization and Banking." *Federal Reserve Bank of San Francisco Weekly Letter*, July 4, 1986.

Pugel, Thomas A., and Lawrence J. White. "An Analysis of the Competitive Effects of Allowing Commercial Bank Affiliates to Underwrite Corporate Securities." In *Deregulating Wall Street: Commercial Bank Penetration of the Corporate Securities Market*, edited by Ingo Walter. New York: John Wiley, 1985.

Pyle, David H. "Capital Regulation and Deposit Insurance." *Journal of Banking and Finance* (June 1986): 189–201.

---. "Deregulation and Deposit Insurance Reform." *Federal Reserve Bank of San Francisco Economic Review* (Spring 1984): 5–15.

Quigley, John M. "What Have We Learned about the Urban Housing Market?" In *Current Issues in Urban Economics*, edited by Peter Mieszkowski and Mahlon Straszheim. Baltimore: Johns Hopkins University Press, 1979.

Reid, M. I. *The Secondary Banking Crisis, 1973–75: The Inside Story of Britain's Biggest Banking Upheaval*. London: Macmillan, 1982.

Robinson, Roland I., and Dwayne Wrightsman. *Financial Markets: The Accumulation and Allocation of Wealth*. New York: McGraw-Hill, 1980.

Rose, John T. "Industry Concentration and Political Leverage: An Empirical Test." Board of Governors of the Federal Reserve System, 1976.

Rose, John T., and Roger D. Rutz. "Organizational Form and Risk in Bank Affiliated Mortgage Companies." *Journal of Money, Credit, and Banking* (August 1981): 375–80.

Rose, John T., and Samuel H. Talley. "Financial Transactions within Bank Holding Companies." *Journal of Financial Research* (1984): 209–17.

Rosenblum, H., J. DiClemente, and K. O'Brien. "On Banks, Nonbanks, and Overlapping Markets: A Reassessment of Commercial Banking as a Line of Commerce." *Tennessee Law Review*, no. 401 (1984).

Rothschild, Michael, and Joseph Stiglitz. "Equilibrium in Competitive Insurance Markets: An Essay on the Economics of Imperfect Information." *Quarterly Journal of Economics* (November 1976): 629–50.

Rule, C. F. Letter to C. Todd Conover. "First National Bank of Jackson-Brookhaven Bank and Trust Company." February 8, 1985. Letter to William M. Issac. "Indian Head Bank—Whitefield Savings Bank and Trust Company." April 29, 1985. Letter to Paul A. Volcker. "Savers Bancorp, Inc.—North Country Bank." May 15, 1985.

Sachs, Jeffrey. "LDC Debt in the 1980s: Risk and Reforms." In *Crises in the Economics and Financial Structure*, edited by Paul Wachtel. Lexington, Mass.: D.C. Heath, 1982.

BIBLIOGRAPHY

Samuel Chase & Co. *A Financial Services Industry Handbook.* Washington, D.C.: Association of Bank Holding Companies, March 1987.

Sargent, Thomas J. *Dynamic Macroeconomic Theory.* Cambridge, Mass.: Harvard University Press, 1987.

———. *Macroeconomic Theory.* New York: Academic Press, 1979.

Sargent, Thomas J., and Bruce D. Smith. "Irrelevance of Open Market Operations in Some Economies with Government Currency Being Dominated in Rate of Return." *American Economic Review* (March 1987): 78–92.

Saulnier, R. J., Harold G. Halcrow, and Neil J. Jacoby. *Federal Lending and Loan Insurance.* Princeton, N.J.: Princeton University Press, 1958.

Saulsbury, Victor L. "Commercial Banks: An Endangered Species?" *Federal Deposit Insurance Corporation Regulatory Review* (March 1986): 1–24.

———. "S&Ls' Costs of Conversion to FDIC Insurance." *Federal Deposit Insurance Corporation Regulatory Review* (May/June 1987): 1–12.

Saunders, Anthony. "Conflicts of Interest: An Economic View." In *Deregulating Wall Street: Commercial Bank Penetration of the Corporate Securities Market,* edited by Ingo Walter. New York: John Wiley, 1985.

Saunders, Anthony, and Michael Smirlock. "Intra- and Interindustry Effects of Bank Securities Market Activities: The Case of Discount Brokerage." *Journal of Financial and Quantitative Analysis,* no. 4 (1987): 467–82.

Saunders, Anthony, and Lawrence J. White, eds. *Technology and the Regulation of Financial Markets.* Lexington, Mass.: Lexington Books, 1986.

Saunders, Anthony, and P. Yourougou. "Are Banks Special? Some Evidence from Stock Market Returns." Working Paper. Graduate School of Business, New York University, December 1986.

Savage, Donald T. "Interstate Banking Developments." *Federal Reserve Bulletin* (February 1987): 79–92.

Scherer, Frederick M. *Industrial Market Structure and Economic Performance.* Chicago: Rand-McNally, 1980.

Schwartz, Anna J. "The Lender of Last Resort and the Federal Safety Net." *Journal of Financial Services Research* 1 (1978): 1–17.

Scott, Kenneth E. "The Dual Banking System: A Model of Competition in Regulation." *Stanford Law Review* (1977): 1–50.

Selby, H. Joe. Statement before U.S. Congress, Senate, Committee on Banking, Housing, and Urban Affairs, July 23, 1985.

Semer, Milton H., Julian H. Zimmerman, Ashley Foard, and John M. Frantz. "Evolution of Federal Legislative Policy in Housing: Housing Credits." In *Housing in the Seventies,* Working Papers, National

Housing Policy Review, Department of Housing and Urban Development, 1976.

Shad, John S. R. Statement to U.S. Congress, House of Representatives, Subcommittee on Commerce, Consumer, and Monetary Affairs of the Committee on Government Operations, April 3, 1985.

Shadow Financial Regulatory Committee. "Statements on Regulatory Proposals for Risk-related Capital Standards." March 31 and May 18, 1987.

Shaffer, Sherill, and Edmond David. "Economies of Superscale and Interstate Expansion." Research Paper no. 8612. Federal Reserve Bank of New York, 1986.

Silber, William. "The Process of Financial Innovation." *American Economic Review* (May 1983): 89–95.

Singer, Mark. *Funny Money.* New York: Alfred Knopf, 1985.

Sinkey, Joseph F., Jr. *Commercial Bank Financial Management in the Financial Services Industry.* New York: Macmillan, 1986.

Smith, Clifford W., and Jarold B. Warner. "On Financial Contracts: An Analysis of Bond Covenants." *Journal of Financial Economics* 7 (1979): 117–61.

Smoot, Richard L. "Billion-Dollar Overdrafts: A Payments Risk Challenge." *Federal Reserve Bank of Philadelphia Business Review* (January/February 1985): 3–13.

Solomon, Elinor H. "Bank Product Deregulation: Some Antitrust Tradeoffs." *Federal Reserve Bank of Atlanta Economic Review* (May 1984): 20–27.

Spero, J. *The Failure of the Franklin National Bank: Challenge to the International Banking System.* New York: Columbia University Press, 1980.

Sprague, Irvine H. *Bailout: An Insider's Account of Bank Failures and Rescues.* New York: Basic Books, 1986.

Sprague, O. M. W. *History of Crises under the National Banking System.* Washington, D.C.: National Monetary Commission, 1910.

Stein, Herbert. "Economic Fashions of the Times." *AEI Economist* (October 1987).

Stevens, Edward J. "Reducing Risk in Wire Transfer Systems." *Federal Reserve Bank of Cleveland Economic Review* (Quarter 2, 1986): 17–22.

Stigler, George. "The Theory of Economic Regulation." *Bell Journal of Economics* (Spring 1971): 3–21.

Stoll, Hans. "Small Firms' Access to Public Equity Financing." In *Sources of Financing for Small Business* (pt. B), edited by Paul Horvitz and R. R. Pettit. Greenwich, Conn.: JAI Press, 1984.

Stone, Bernell K. "Business and Bank Reactions to New Securities Powers." *Federal Reserve Bank of Atlanta Economic Review* (May 1984): 41–48.

Stover, Roger D. "A Re-Examination of Bank Holding Company Acquisitions." *Journal of Bank Research* (Summer 1982): 101–8.

———. "The Single Subsidiary Bank Holding Company." *Journal of Bank Research* (Spring 1980): 43–50.

Struyk, Raymond J. *Should Government Encourage Homeownership?* Washington, D.C.: Urban Institute, 1977.

Struyk, Raymond J., Neil Mayer, and John A. Tuccillo. *Federal Housing Policy and President Reagan's Midterm.* Washington, D.C.: Urban Institute, 1983.

Summers, Bruce J. "Loan Commitments to Business in United States Banking History." *Federal Reserve Bank of Richmond Economic Review* (September/October 1975): 115–23.

Swary, Itzhak. "Bank Acquisition of Nonbank Firms: An Empirical Analysis of Administrative Decisions." *Journal of Banking and Finance* (1983): 213–30.

———. "Stock Market Reaction to Regulatory Action in the Continental Illinois Crisis." *Journal of Business*, no. 3 (1986): 451–74.

Symons, Edward L., Jr., and James J. White. *Banking Law.* St. Paul, Minn.: West Publishing, 1984.

Talley, Samuel H. "Bank Holding Company Performance in Consumer Finance and Mortgage Banking." *Magazine of Bank Administration* (July 1976): 42–44.

———. "The Effect of Holding Company Acquisitions on Bank Performance." *Staff Economic Studies*, no. 69. Washington, D.C.: Board of Governors of the Federal Reserve System, February 1972.

Taoka, G. M. "The Role of the Bank of Japan in the Administration of the Economic and Financial Controls of the Government during National Emergencies with Special Emphasis on the Sino-Japanese War and the World War II Periods." Ph.D. dissertation. Columbia University, 1955.

Task Group on Regulation of Financial Services. *Blueprint for Reform.* Washington, D.C., 1984.

Taylor, William. Statement before U.S. Congress, House of Representatives, Subcommittee on Commerce, Consumer, and Monetary Affairs of the Committee on Government Operations, May 15, 1985. In *Federal Reserve Bulletin* (July 1985): 528–32.

Thornton, Henry. *An Enquiry into the Nature and Effects of the Paper Credit of Great Britain*, edited by F. A. Hayek. London: Allen & Unwin, 1939. Originally published 1802.

Thorp, W. L. *Business Annals.* New York: National Bureau of Economic Research, 1926.

Timberlake, Richard H. "The Central Banking Role of Clearing Associations." *Journal of Money, Credit, and Banking* (February 1984): 1–15.

———. *The Origins of Central Banking in the United States.* Cambridge, Mass.: Harvard University Press, 1978.

Tobin, James. "Financial Innovation and Deregulation in Perspective." In *Financial Innovation and Monetary Policy: Asia and the West*, edited by Y. Suzuki and H. Yomo. Tokyo: University of Tokyo Press, 1986.

Todd, Walker F. "Outline of an Argument on Solvency." Federal Reserve Bank of Cleveland, March 1987.

Tuccillo, John A., with John L. Goodman. *Housing Finance: A Changing System in the Reagan Era*. Washington, D.C.: Urban Institute, 1983.

Tuccillo, John A., Robert Van Order, and Kevin Villani. "Homeownership Policies and Mortgage Markets, 1960 to 1980." *Housing Finance Review* (February 1982): 1–21.

Tucker, James F. "Investments for Small Savers at Commercial Banks." *Federal Reserve Bank of Richmond Economic Review* (September/October 1980): 24–27.

"The Tug-of-War over Float." *The Morgan Guaranty Survey* (December 1983): 11–14.

U.S. Congress. *The Role of the Federal Reserve in Check Clearing and the Nation's Payment System*. 1983.

———. House of Representatives. Committee on Banking and Currency. "The Growth of Unregistered Bank Holding Companies—Problems and Prospects." Staff Report. 91st Congress, 1st session, February 11, 1969, p. 2.

———. Committee on Banking, Finance, and Urban Affairs, Subcommittee on Financial Institutions Supervision, Regulation, and Insurance. *Inquiry into Continental Illinois Corporation and Continental Illinois National Bank: Hearings*. 98th Congress, 2d session, September 18–19 and October 4, 1984.

———. Committee on Government Operations. *Federal Reserve Position on Restructuring of Financial Regulation Responsibilities*. 99th Congress, 1st session, 1985.

———. *Modernization of the Financial Services Industry: A Plan for Capital Mobility within a Framework of Safe and Sound Banking*. 100th Congress, 1st session, September 1987.

———. Joint hearings before certain subcommittees of the Committee on Government Operations and the Committee on Banking, Finance, and Urban Affairs, "The Role of the Federal Reserve in Check Clearing and the Nation's Payments System." 98th Congress, 1st session, June 15–16, 1983.

———. Subcommittee on Economic Stabilization of the Committee on Banking, Finance, and Urban Affairs. *Hearings on Federal Credit Activities*. 98th Congress, 2d session, 1984.

———. Subcommittee of the Committee on Government Operations. *Bush Task Group Report on Regulation of Financial Services Blueprint for Reform (Part 1): Hearings*. 99th Congress, 1st session, 1985.

U.S. Department of Commerce. *Historical Statistics of the United States*. Washington, D.C., 1975.

BIBLIOGRAPHY

──────. *Statistical Abstract of the United States*, various issues.

U.S. Department of Housing and Urban Development. *1986 Report to the Congress on the Federal National Mortgage Association*. June 1987.

U.S. General Accounting Office. *The Federal National Mortgage Association in a Changing Economic Environment*. GAO/RCED-85-102A. Washington, D.C., July 1985.

──────. *Thrift Industry: Forbearance for Troubled Institutions, 1982–1986.* GAO/GGD-87-78BR. Washington, D.C., May 1987.

──────. *Thrift Industry: The Management Consignment Program.* Washington, D.C., September 1987.

U.S. President's Commission on Housing. *The Report of the President's Commission on Housing*. Washington, D.C., 1982.

U.S. v. Investors Diversified Services, 102 F. Supp. 645, D. Minn., 1951.

U.S. v. Marine Bancorporation, 418 U.S. 602, 631–32.

U.S. v. Third National Bank in Nashville, 390 U.S. 171, 187–89 (1968).

Upham, Cyril B., and Edward Lamke. *Closed and Distressed Banks*. Washington, D.C.: Brookings Institution, 1934.

Vogel, David. "A Case Study of Clean Air Legislation, 1967–1981." In *The Impact of the Modern Corporation*, edited by Betty Block. New York: Columbia University Press, 1984.

Volcker, Paul A. "Statement." *Federal Reserve Bulletin* (February 1986): 115–25.

──────. Statement before the U.S. Congress, Senate, Committee on Banking, Housing and Urban Affairs, September 13, 1983.

──────. Testimony before the U.S. Congress, House of Representatives, Subcommittee on Commerce, Consumer, and Monetary Affairs of the Committee on Government Operations, 99th Congress, 2d session, June 11, 1986.

Waldrop, Ross. "Commercial Bank Performance in 1986." *Federal Deposit Insurance Corporation Banking and Economic Review* (March/April 1987): 11–18.

Wall, Larry D. "Has BHCs' Diversification Affected Their Risk of Failure?" Working Paper 85-2. Federal Reserve Bank of Atlanta, 1985.

──────. "Insulating Banks from Nonbank Affiliates." *Federal Reserve Bank of Atlanta Economic Review* (September 1984): 18–28.

Wall, Larry D., and Robert A. Eisenbeis. "Risk Considerations in Deregulating Bank Activities." *Federal Reserve Bank of Atlanta Economic Review* (May 1984): 6–19.

Wall, M. Danny. "An Address to the National Press Club." August 1987.

Wallace, Neil. "A Legal Restrictions Theory of the Demand for 'Money' and the Role of Monetary Policy." *Federal Reserve Bank of Minneapolis Quarterly Review*, no. 1 (1983): 1–7.

Wall Street Journal, various issues.

Ware, Robert F. "Characteristics of Banks Acquired by Multiple Bank Holding Companies in Ohio." *Federal Reserve Bank of Cleveland Economic Review* (August 1971): 19–27.

Washington Post, various issues.

Watson, M., R. Kincaid, C. Atkinson, E. Kalter, and D. Folkerts-Landau. *International Capital Markets, Developments and Prospects*. Washington, D.C.: International Monetary Fund, 1986.

Weicher, John C. *Housing: Federal Policies and Programs*. Washington, D.C.: American Enterprise Institute, 1980.

———. "Summary of Symposium Proceedings." In *The Federal National Mortgage Association in a Changing Economic Environment*. GAO/RCED-85-102A. Washington, D.C.: U.S. General Accounting Office, July 1985.

Weicher, John C., Susan M. Wachter, and William B. Shear. "Housing as an Asset in the 1980s and 1990s." *Housing Finance Review* 7 (Summer 1988): 169–200.

Weintraub, Benjamin, and Alan N. Resnick. *Bankruptcy Law Manual*. Boston: Warren, Gorham, and Lamont, 1986.

Weiss, Marc A. *Own Your Own Home: The American Real Estate Industry and National Housing Policy*. Cambridge, Mass.: Lincoln Institute of Land Policy, 1987.

Welldon, S. A. *Digest of State Banking Statutes*. Washington, D.C.: National Monetary Commission, 1910.

Weston, R. *Domestic and Multinational Banking*. London: Croom Helm, 1980.

White, Eugene A. "Before the Glass-Steagall Act: An Analysis of the Investment Banking Activities of National Banks." *Explorations in Economic History* (1986): 33–55.

———. "State-sponsored Insurance of Bank Deposits in the United States, 1907–1929." *Journal of Economic History* (September 1981): 537–57.

White, Lawrence J. "Facing the Issues." *Outlook of the Federal Home Loan Bank System* (May/June 1987): 24–28.

———. "Mark-to-Market Accounting for Thrifts: Vital to the FSLIC and Valuable to Well-managed Thrifts." *Outlook of the Federal Home Loan Bank System* (forthcoming).

———. "Opinion Roundup: Owners and Renters." *Public Opinion* (September/October 1986): 21–29.

Whitehead, David D. "The Sixth District Survey of Small Business Credit." *Federal Reserve Bank of Atlanta Economic Review* (April 1982): 42–47.

Wigmore, B. "Was the Bank Holiday of 1933 a Run on the Dollar Rather Than the Banks?" *Journal of Economic History* (September 1987): 739–55.

Williams, R., P. Heller, J. Lipinsky, and D. Mathieson. *International Capital Markets, Developments and Prospects, 1983.* Occasional Paper no. 23. Washington, D.C.: International Monetary Fund, 1983.

Willig, Robert D. "Multiproduct Technology and Market Structure." *American Economic Review* 69 (1979): 346–51.

Willig, Robert D., and William J. Baumol. "Intertemporal Unsustainability." 1980. Manuscript.

Willis, H. P., and B. H. Beckhart, eds. *Foreign Banking Systems.* New York: Holt, 1929.

Wilson, J. *Banking Policy and Structure.* New York: New York University Press, 1986.

Wilson, John F., Elizabeth M. Folger, James L. Freund, and Guido E. vanderVen. "Major Borrowing and Lending Trends for the U.S. Economy, 1981–1985." *Federal Reserve Bulletin* (August 1986): 511–24.

Woerheide, Walter J. *The Savings and Loan Industry: Current Problems and Possible Solutions.* Westport, Conn.: Quorum Books, 1984.

Wojnilower, Albert "The Central Role of Credit Crunches in Recent Financial History." *Brookings Paper on Economic Activity,* no. 2 (1980): 277–340.

Wriston, Walter. Testimony before the U.S. Congress, Senate, Committee on Banking, Housing, and Urban Affairs, 97th Congress, 1st session, October 29, 1981.

Young, John E. "The Rise and Fall of Federal Reserve Float." *Federal Reserve Bank of Kansas City Economic Review* (February 1986): 28–38.

Zweig, Philip L. *Belly Up: The Collapse of the Penn Square Bank.* New York: Crown, 1985.

Index

Accounting, bank
    assets, 80–83, 85–86, 88, 93
    book-value, 69, 78–79, 90–91
    debt, 86–87
    generally accepted accounting principles (GAAP), 78, 81, 88, 302, 434
    liabilities, 79–80, 88
    market-value, 69, 78–79, 82, 90–91, 103, 302, 380
    monitoring, 83, 103, 108
    off-balance-sheet activity, 8–9, 10, 88, 364, 370, 380, 398, 406, 411, 414, 428
    reform, 381
    regulatory accounting principles (RAP), 78
ACH. *See* Automated clearinghouse
Acquisitions. *See* Mergers and acquisitions
Affiliations. *See* Banking industry, affiliations/subsidiaries
Aldrich-Vreeland Act of 1908, 258
Antitrust issues, 209
    Department of Justice, 135–37, 209
    mergers and acquisitions, 135, 209–10
    tying arrangements, 138, 182, 183–84
ATM. *See* Automated teller machine
Automated clearinghouse (ACH), 159, 172
Automated teller machine, 10, 45, 47, 119, 159, 172

Bank Control Act of 1978, 186
Bank failure
    causes of, 24–25, 34, 35–36, 41, 60n.29, 78, 107–8, 268
    consequences of, 25, 64, 75, 77, 93, 94, 160, 161, 162, 286n.49, 305
    federal deposit insurance system, 23, 305, 306
    forbearance programs, 77
    history of, 35–36, 39–47, 72
    panics, 34, 35, 36, 38–40, 41, 49,
55n.1, 106, 194n.7, 257–58
    regulations and, 5, 12, 137, 198n.61
    reorganization and, 75–96, 112, 306
    runs. *See* Runs
    settlement, 22, 179–81, 194n.13, 200n.81
    social costs, 19, 162
    thrifts, 23, 305–6
    wire transfers and, 22, 271–73
Bank failures
    Banc Texas, 178
    Bankhouse I. D. Herstatt (Germany), 407
    Bank of Oklahoma, 178
    Beverly Hills Bancorp, 174
    Continental Illinois, 24, 40, 42, 49, 51–52, 167–68, 174, 199n.69, 213, 249n.33
    First National Bank of Oklahoma City, 178
    First Republic Bank Corporation (Texas), 24
    Franklin National Bank (U.S.), 407
    Hamilton National Bank of Chattanooga (Tenn.), 167, 168
    Home State Savings Bank of Cincinnati (Ohio), 51, 66
    Penn Square Bank of Oklahoma, 13
Bank for International Settlements, 408–9
Bank holding companies, 156. *See also* Banking industry; Financial structure
    affiliations/subsidiaries, 18, 89–90, 167, 168, 169–72, 175–78, 206, 212
    capital ratios, 78–79, 89, 168–69, 177
    conflicts of interest, 162, 182–85, 206–7
    costs, 186–89, 208, 219
    deposit insurance, 178, 205
    dividends, 166, 168, 196n.39
    geographic expansion, 172–73, 198n.61
    nonbank activities, 162–63, 164–68, 181–86, 204
    performance, 6, 74, 213–15

483

INDEX

profitability, 165–66, 170–71, 172, 196n.35, 197n.50
reform, 20, 115, 156–57, 186–93, 203–15
regulations, 157, 166–67, 168, 172, 186, 189–90, 206
returns, 163–68, 169, 177–78, 195n.30, 197n.50, 200n.80
risks, 163–81, 185, 197n.48, 277–79
securities transactions, 6, 205–6
structure, 17, 47, 89, 163–64, 187–89, 190–92, 202n.112, 205
universal bank, 192–93, 202nn.111, 113, 397
Bank Holding Company Act (BHCA)
1843, 390
1956, 172, 182, 193n.2, 214, 277
1970, 5, 11, 17, 123, 135, 138, 156, 171, 173, 183, 185–86, 277
Banking, international. *See also* Financial services, international; Regulation, financial; Regulators; Structural arbitrage
capitalization, 371
commercial banks, 376
expansion, 14
financial activities, 410
foreign banks in U.S. markets, 374
foreign branch assets (U.S.), 372
foreign branches (U.S. banks), 373
onshore offshore offices (U.S.), 372–73
regulations, 15, 366–78
securitization, 14–15
Banking Act of 1933, 5, 11, 25, 47, 61n.30
Banking Act of 1935, 61n.30
Banking Act of 1987, 89, 92, 156
Banking industry. *See also* Bank holding companies; Bank safety and soundness; Central banks; Financial structure; Payments system
affiliations/subsidiaries, 16–20, 22, 81, 88, 89–90, 214, 262, 346, 366
chartering, 43–44, 57n.9, 161
consolidation, 5, 30n.40, 115, 117, 120, 208, 341–42
expansion, 14, 47, 366
"free banking," 71
functions, 157–63, 203–4
interstate, 12, 47
limited-service banks, 6–7, 17
mergers and acquisitions. *See* Mergers and acquisitions
price level stability and, 48, 55
reform recommendations, 444–47
regulations, 9–11, 12, 17, 26, 47, 161, 198n.61, 219

risk. *See* Risk
safety and soundness of, 19, 47–48, 54–55, 100–101. *See also* Bank failures; Bank safety and soundness
social welfare implications, 157, 161, 162
Bank Merger Act of 1966, 135, 211n.17
Bank reorganization. *See* Reorganization, bank
Bankruptcy. *See also* Bank failures
bank, 86, 93
nonbank, 92, 93
Banks, 1, 37, 65, 118–19, 146. *See also* Money center banks
capital ratios. *See* Capital, ratios
capital requirements. *See* Capital, requirements
definition of, 17, 193n.2
double liability (shareholders) for, 61n.30, 71, 103–4
illiquid/insolvent, 23, 25, 75–76, 91, 108, 234, 235, 242, 243, 244, 251n.42. *See also* Bank failures; Regulation, forbearance; Reorganization, bank
international finance, 15
limited-service ("nonbank banks"), 6–7, 17, 117, 118, 193n.2, 278
money supply and, 161
narrow "fail-safe," 74–75, 203
New Deal and, 34
"nonbank." *See* Banks, limited-service
off-balance-sheet activity, 8–9
regulations, 44, 182, 186. *See also* Regulation, banking; Regulation, financial
reorganization. *See* Reorganization, bank
reserve requirements, 161, 162, 191, 194n.19, 223
securitization and, 4–7
shareholders, 54, 61n.30, 71, 78, 79, 92, 95, 110
zero-balance accounts, 21
Bank safety and soundness. *See also* Bank failure
capital standards regulation, 72, 434–35
crises, 217, 236–43
deposit insurance and, 47–48, 64–71, 127, 158, 173
institutional size and, 127, 208
price level environment and, 54–55, 105, 435–36, 445
Basel Committee on Bank Regulation and Supervisory Practices, 414, 416, 424

484

INDEX

Benston, George J., xix
BHCA. *See* Bank Holding Company Act
Borrowing, 4. *See also* Loans
Bretton Woods system, 40, 394

Cagan, Philip, xix
Canada, 40, 66, 375
C&I loans. *See* Loans, commercial and industrial
Capital
    definition, 88
    deposit insurance and, 71, 86, 90–92, 103
    measurement of, 78–79, 88–89, 109–10
    ratios, 238, 252n.48, 412–13, 414, 416–17, 425
    reorganization and, 78–83, 85–91
    requirements, 71–74, 85–96, 99n.32, 103, 411, 414, 416
    risk, 10–11, 71–73, 75, 79, 411–13
    standards, 10–11, 71–73, 85, 87–88, 370, 372, 414
Central banks, 52, 161. *See also* Discount window; Federal Reserve System
    banking policy, 218, 225, 226, 229, 233, 235–36, 239, 241, 242, 244–45, 245n.1, 254, 257
    discounting, 218
    goals, 218
    interest rate smoothing, 219, 220–23, 246n.12
    lender of last resort, 240, 241, 415, 422n.13
    line-of-credit services, 225, 229–33, 236, 241
    monetary policy, 217–23, 229, 235–36, 239, 243–44, 254, 257
    regulations/supervision, 219–20, 233, 235, 241, 242, 243, 244, 250n.36, 255, 257, 445–46, 447n.6
CFTC. *See* Commodity Futures Trading Commission
Charters. *See* Banking industry, chartering
CHIPS. *See* Payments system, Clearing House Interbank Payments System
Clayton Act, 136, 137, 154n.36, 186
Clearing House Interbank Payments System. *See* Payments system, Clearing House Interbank Payments System
Clearinghouses, 237–39, 350
Commercial paper, 27n.1, 75, 119, 183, 221
    market, growth of, 2–3, 10, 183
Committee on Banking Regulation and Supervisory Practices (Cooke Committee), 408–9, 411, 414, 416, 424
Commodity Futures Trading Commission (CFTC), 354, 400
Compacts, regional, 137
Competition
    banking, 12–13, 24, 43–45, 208–9
    financial services, 13, 15, 19
    international, 14–15, 16, 26
    regional compacts, 137
    regulations and, 15–16, 44, 134–39
    regulatory, 349–52, 438–39
    unfair practices, 20, 122–25, 138–39, 209, 433
Competitive Equality Banking Act of 1987, 12, 17, 20, 23, 25, 156, 167, 214
Conflict of interest. *See also* Competition, unfair practices
    bank holding companies, 19, 182–85
    financial markets and, 125–27
Cooke Committee, 408–9, 411
Corporate finance
    debt, 14, 181
    product innovation and, 10
    securitization and, 2–3, 4
Corrigan, E. Gerald, 157, 345–46, 367
Cranston-D'Amato bill, 189
Credit. *See also* Central banks, banking policy; Loans
    allocation, 132–34, 182, 236, 244
    demand for, 10
    exposure, 269
    fungibility, 134, 253n.53
    policy, 253n.53
    restrictions/supervision, 225
    risks, 21–23, 250n.38, 268–69, 303, 424
    services, 225
Crises. *See* Financial markets, crises
Currency
    creation of, 239
    demand for, 257
    deposits, compared with, 219–20
    elastic, 218, 223, 235, 240–41
    price level and, 220
    regulation and, 220

Daylight overdrafts, 22, 181, 192, 233, 250n.38, 267, 269, 289
    CHIPS, 189, 266, 271–73, 294
    commercial firms, 277–79
    Fedwire, 262, 266, 269–70, 273–77, 281, 286n.39, 292, 294, 437
    reforms, 270–77, 294
Debt, subordinated, 85–87, 98n.29, 103, 110–11
Debt instruments
    asset-backed obligations, 3

485

INDEX

mortgages, 3
Department of Justice, Antitrust Division, 135–37
Deposit insurance, federal
   bank failures and, 23, 24, 112, 179
   bank reorganization and, 76, 78, 92–94
   bank runs/panics and, 48, 58n.19, 84, 93, 101
   capital and, 71, 86, 90–92, 103
   co-insurance and, 66–67
   costs of, 85
   coverage, 67–68, 104, 112
   establishment of, 64
   "fail-safe" banks and, 74–75, 101–2
   financial stability and, 34, 35, 49, 418
   fraud and, 89
   New Deal and, 36, 47–48, 100
   price level instability and, 36, 48, 58n.21, 105–6
   reform, 36, 47–50, 64–71, 84, 86, 90–96, 101–2, 205, 255, 305, 433–35
   risk-based, 68–71, 72, 73, 74, 84–85, 104, 107
   as subsidy, 20, 49, 76, 178, 185
Deposit insurance, private, 65–66, 69, 84, 94, 418
Depository firms. *See also* Banking industry; Financial products; Financial services; Securities firms
   accounts of, 8
   competitors, 12
   daylight overdrafts, 267
   discount window lending to, 229, 232
   expansion of, 12
   government and, 34, 84
   insolvencies, 36, 75–76
   intermediaries, 35, 36, 45, 46
   regulation, 16, 17, 54, 432–33
   reserve requirements, 223, 255, 256–57, 259, 267
Depository Institutions Deregulation and Monetary Control Act of 1980, 7, 21, 46, 302, 330n.10
Depression, Great, xiv, 43, 95, 160, 297, 431
Deregulation. *See also* Regulation
   banking policies and, 225–36, 316
   financial stability model and, 35, 37, 223–24
   monetary policies and, 218–25
Discount rate, 240, 249n.32
Discount window. *See also* Federal Reserve System; Lender of last resort; Payments system
   collateral, 231

emergency credit assistance, 233, 242, 251n.42, 266, 271–72, 280, 423n.18
   functions, 226, 257
   history, 225, 248n.27
   lending, 229–33, 235–36, 242, 251n.42, 285n.29
   line-of-credit facility, 230–31, 232
   reform/recommendations, 346
   regulation/supervision, 231–32, 234–35, 259
   sterilized/unsterilized operations, 229, 230, 240, 248n.28
Downstreaming. *See* Bank holding companies, returns

Economy
   monetary policy and, 223–25
   securitization and, 3
   stabilization policy, 223–25
Edge Act of 1978, 172, 285n.23, 367, 373, 374, 375
Edwards, Franklin R., xix
EFTS. *See* Electronic funds transfer systems
Eisenbeis, Robert A., xix–xx
Electronic funds transfer systems (EFTS), 159–60, 194n.13, 393, 396, 424. *See also* Automated clearinghouse; Automated teller machine; Payments system, Clearing House Interbank Payments System; Payments system, Fedwire
Electronic mortgage network, 323, 340
Ely, Bert, xx
Employment Act of 1946, 50, 218, 223
Ettin, Edward C., xx
Eurocurrency, 14, 30n.45, 407
Exchange rates, 40, 50, 394–95

Failure, commercial firm, 181, 184
   Penn Central, 258
Fannie Mae. *See* Federal National Mortgage Association
FDIC. *See* Federal Deposit Insurance Corporation
Federal Deposit Insurance Act, 46–47
Federal Deposit Insurance Corporation (FDIC), 17, 23–24, 47, 64, 65, 96, 258, 303, 305, 306, 341, 400
   FSLIC and, 102, 305
Federal deposit insurance system. *See* Deposit insurance, federal
Federal Home Loan Bank Board, 17, 23, 25, 47, 78, 95–96, 135–36, 298, 326
Federal Home Loan Bank System, 298, 299, 300, 316, 319, 326
Federal Home Loan Mortgage Corpora-

486

INDEX

tion (Freddie Mac), 4, 300, 301, 311–12, 313, 314, 318, 319–20
Federal Housing Administration (FHA), 298, 299–300, 316
Federal National Mortgage Association (Fannie Mae), 4, 298, 299, 300, 301, 311–12, 313, 314, 316–22, 315, 334n.58
Federal National Mortgage Association (FNMA) Charter Act of 1954, 300
Federal Reserve Act of 1913, 25, 61n.30, 89, 218, 235, 258
   Regulation A, 280
   Regulation Q, 301, 313, 315–16, 326, 337, 387, 397, 420, 441
   section 13, 279–80
   Section 23, 166, 167, 168, 178, 181, 184, 185, 189, 192, 200n.80, 206, 272, 273, 277–78, 279, 294–95
Federal Reserve Board of Governors, 135
Federal Reserve System. *See also* Central banks; Payments system
   credit market and, 217
   credit risk and, 265–66
   development, 43, 64, 350–51
   discount window, 65, 159, 217. *See also* Discount window
   effectiveness, 43, 50, 64–65, 104, 159
   float, 233, 251n.39
   interest rate smoothing. *See* Interest rates, smoothing
   open-market operations, 220, 223, 230, 255, 436
   policies, 16, 50–51, 162, 216–17, 233, 250n.36, 251n.42, 257, 261, 275
   regulation and, 217, 233, 350–51, 400
   securities activities and, 6
   services, 65, 94, 106, 135, 161–62, 179, 249n.31
   settlement services, 264–65, 270
   stock market crisis (October 1987), 52, 212–13, 258
Federal Savings and Loan Insurance Corporation (FSLIC), 65, 359
   FDIC, compared with, 102
   functions, 135
   housing finance system and, 296, 299, 302–3, 304–8, 331nn.21, 24, 337, 341
   recapitalization, 23, 304–8, 441
   savings and loan industry, 23, 47. *See also* Housing finance system; Savings and loans (S&Ls)
Federal Share Insurance, 47
Federal Trade Commission, 135
Fedwire. *See* Payments system, Fedwire
Finance companies, 1
Financial firms. *See also* Bank holding companies; Banks; Depository firms; Finance companies; Insurance companies; Investment banking
   expansion, 13–14, 15, 114
   industrial-based firms, 18
   insurance companies, 143, 144
   international, 19
   mutual fund managers, 143
   regulation, 358
   retail-based firms, 17–18
   securities and, 2
   securities firms, 17, 142
   services/products, 1–2, 119–20
   thrift institutions, 145, 214. *See also* Savings and loans (S&Ls)
Financial markets
   credit, 241
   crises, 237–43, 244, 436, 441
   defining, 1, 439
   entry costs, 117, 118, 214
   Euroequities, 14
   payments system. *See* Payments system
   regulation, effects on, 115–16
   securitization and, 4–5, 400, 403
Financial markets, international. *See also* Banking, international; Regulation, financial; Regulators
   arbitrage. *See* Structural arbitrage
   bond markets, 403, 404–6
   competition, 114, 393, 396, 399, 406, 407
   debt crisis, 425–26
   domestic, 398, 400, 401, 403, 406–7, 421n.1
   expansion, 13–16, 401, 402
   innovation, 392–93, 419–21
   institutional/structural changes, 393–94, 414–19, 424–25
   integration, 392, 393, 398
   internationalization, 401–3, 407
   macroeconomic disturbances, 394, 396, 401
   offshore, 372–73, 393, 396, 400, 406, 421n.1
   regulation, 366–78, 392, 393, 394, 396–98, 399–400, 403, 406–7, 411, 414, 415, 416, 418–19, 424, 428
   risk management, 415–16
   securitization, 403, 424–29, 429n.1
   structure, 394, 396–97, 400–401
   tax and disclosure systems, 398–99
Financial products. *See also* Financial services
   adjustable rate mortgages (ARMs), 302, 309, 315, 316, 324
   automated teller machines (ATMs),

INDEX

10, 45, 47, 119, 159
bonds, 7, 10, 27nn.2, 3, 119, 181
certificates of deposit (CDs), 7, 10, 330n.9
commercial paper, 2–3, 10, 14, 27n.1, 75, 119, 160, 183, 221, 258
deposit accounts, 21
Eurobonds, 14, 398, 401
Euro–commercial paper, 14, 407
Eurocurrency, 398, 401, 407
Eurodollars, 7, 8, 15, 199n.69, 268, 397, 401
floating-rate notes (FRNs), 14, 420
innovation of, 8–11, 24
money market deposit accounts (MMDAs), 8, 302
money market mutual funds (MMMFs), 7, 21, 301, 302, 330n.9, 353–55
money market securities, 46
note issuance facilities (NIFs), 14, 31n.52
NOW accounts, 8, 45, 302
repurchase agreements (RPs), 7, 45, 267
swaps, 8, 14, 45, 243, 244, 406
sweep accounts, 7, 45
Financial services. *See also* Banking industry, functions
credit cards, 119
definition, 1–2
deposit accounts, 21, 119
financial advice, 1
geographic expansion of, 11–16, 114
innovation in, 7–11, 23–25, 118
integration, 16–20
intermediation/disintermediation, 1, 5, 160, 301, 311, 315, 316, 341, 397
international, 188–89, 368–78
payments system, 20–23, 104
risk management, 1
securitization and, 2–7
transactions services, 1, 3, 157–59, 191, 192, 219
wire transfer, 20–22, 45
Financial stability. *See also* Deposit insurance, federal
incentives and, 24–25
lender of last resort, 35, 37, 51–53, 106, 179, 221, 239–40, 415, 418, 445, 446
models, 34, 35, 37, 49, 52, 53, 56n.1
price level stability and, 35, 41, 48, 53, 55, 105
relative price change, 41
safety net, 34–35, 49, 175, 185, 192, 213, 230, 414–15, 416–18

Financial structure
antitrust activities and, 135–37
branching, 115, 118, 132
competition, 113, 116, 120, 121–25, 127, 132, 136, 139
competition, unfair, 124–25, 139–40, 182–85
concentration, 114, 116–20, 128–30, 131, 139, 140, 147–52, 208
conflicts of interest, 126, 182–85
consolidation, 115, 117, 120, 208
credit allocation, 132–34, 139, 140
failures, 116
federal guarantees, 121
institutional size, 114, 116, 120, 126–29, 130, 131, 132, 140, 141–46, 186–87, 208
market entry/exit, 116–17, 118, 123–24, 130, 132, 389–90
mergers, 116, 135–38, 140
monopoly power, 116, 117, 123, 129, 136, 138, 182, 183–84
political power, 128–32, 140
regulations, 114, 115–16, 121, 134–39, 140, 212–15
services/products, 121, 131
Financial theory
banking, 157–59, 161–62, 203–6, 269
concentration, 116–17
credit, 134
debt and equity, 86, 87
interest rate, 222–23
law of large numbers, 127–28
monetary policy, 216, 223–25
regulatory, 348–49, 355–56, 358–59, 362–64, 388–90
securitization and, 4
stability, 34, 35, 37, 49, 223–25
Flannery, Mark J., xx
Folkerts-Landau, David F. I., xx
Foreign banking. *See* Banking, international; Financial markets, international
Fraud
bank failures and, 78, 110, 111
deposit insurance and, 70, 74, 83–84, 85
occurrence of, 89, 179
prevention of, 83–84, 85
Freddie Mac. *See* Federal Home Loan Mortgage Corporation; Housing finance system
FSLIC. *See* Federal Savings and Loan Insurance Corporation

Garn-St Germain Act of 1982, 7–8, 12, 21, 47, 302, 310
Germany

INDEX

banking system, 48, 187–88, 375, 399, 419, 420–21
deposit insurance, 418
interest rates, 397
Ginnie Mae. *See* Government National Mortgage Association
Glass-Steagall Act of 1933, 5, 6, 7, 44, 182, 186, 214, 299, 369. *See also* Banking Act of 1933
Goodfriend, Marvin, xx–xxi
Government National Mortgage Association (GNMA, Ginnie Mae), 310, 312–13, 314, 320
Gramm-Rudman-Hollings Act, 359

Haraf, William S., xxi
Hart-Scott-Rodino Act, 135, 136
Herfindahl-Hirschman index (HHI), 136, 140
Herring, Richard J., xxi
HHI. *See* Herfindahl-Hirschman index
Hoover, Herbert, 298
Horvitz, Paul M., xxi
Housing
 cycles, 326
 homeownership, 326–29, 446
Housing finance system, 296–97, 329, 437–38. *See also* Mortgage loans
 development, 297–302, 322–27, 340–42
 inflation and, 301–2
 interest rates and, 302–4
 mortgage banking, 299
 mortgage insurance, government, 298–99
 mortgage loans, 300, 308
 mortgage securities, 308
 privatization, 320–22, 339–40, 446–47
 Regulation Q, 301, 313, 315–16, 326, 337, 387, 420, 441
 regulations, 309–10
 savings and loan associations (S&Ls), 297–98, 299, 300–302, 304–10
 secondary market agencies, 298, 299, 300, 310–11, 313–22, 338–40, 447
 taxes, 298
Housing finance system, agencies
 Federal Deposit Insurance Corporation (FDIC), 303, 305, 306, 341
 Federal Home Loan Bank Board (FHLBB), 298, 326
 Federal Home Loan Bank System, 298, 299, 300, 316, 319, 326
 Federal Home Loan Mortgage Corporation (Freddie Mac), 300, 301, 313, 314, 318, 319–20
 Federal Housing Administration (FHA), 298, 299–300, 316
 Federal National Mortgage Association (FNMA), 298, 299, 300, 301, 311–12, 313, 314, 316–22, 325, 334n.58
 Federal Savings and Loan Insurance Corporation (FSLIC), 296, 299, 302–3, 304–8, 331nn.21, 24, 337, 341
 Government National Mortgage Association (GNMA), 310, 312–13, 314, 320
 Veterans Administration, 300
Huertas, Thomas F., xxi
Humphrey-Hawkins Full Employment and Balanced Growth Act of 1978, 50

IBF. *See* International banking facility
Inflation
 currency and, 219–20, 256
 financial strain and, 24, 26, 41
Insider trading, 184. *See also* Conflict of interest
Insurance, 7, 127–28. *See also* Deposit insurance, federal; Deposit insurance, private
Insurance companies, 1, 156
Interest rates. *See also* Savings and loans (S&Ls)
 banking policy and, 241
 ceilings, 7, 45–46, 131, 240, 301, 315–16, 337, 354, 397, 421
 financial strain and, 24, 26
 nominal, 220, 223, 246n.4, 256
 pegging, 222, 223, 255–56
 price level instability and, 36, 41, 223
 regulation/deregulation of, 21, 44–46, 337
 risk, 72, 172
 smoothing, 217, 220–23, 240, 244, 246nn.10, 12, 255
Intermediation services
 bank failures and, 160
 commercial banking and, 5
 definition, 1
 disintermediation, 15, 301, 311, 315, 316, 397
 housing finance and, 341
 price level instability and, 41
International Banking Act of 1978, 369, 372, 419
International banking facility (IBF), 366–67, 373, 374–75
International financial services. *See* Banking, international; Financial markets,

489

INDEX

international; Financial services, international
International Lending Supervision Act of 1983, 72, 372, 425
International Monetary Fund, 396, 425
Investment banking, 1, 4, 5–7, 14

Japan
   banks, 375
   capital standards, 370, 372, 414
   expansion, 378
   financial firms, 14–15
   interest rates, 397, 421
   international banking facilities (IBFs), 375
   regulations, 16, 369–70, 378, 419–20
   securities firms, 378
   stock exchange, 403
Justice, Department of. See Department of Justice, Antitrust Division

Kane, Edward J., xxi–xxii
Kareken, John H., xxii
Kaufman, George G., xxii
King, Robert G., xxii
Kushmeider, Rose Marie, xxii

Lender of last resort. See also Discount window; Federal Reserve System; Financial stability
   bank panics and, 42, 106
   bank runs and, 36, 52–53, 271
   financial stability and, 34–35, 59n.27
Line of credit. See Loans, line-of-credit services
Loan certificates, 42
Loans. See also Mortgage loans
   as assets, 80–81
   bank holding companies, 184
   commercial and industrial (C&I), 4
   Federal Home Loan Mortgage Corporation (Freddie Mac). See Federal Home Loan Mortgage Corporation
   Federal National Mortgage Association (Fannie Mae). See Federal National Mortgage Association
   line-of-credit services, 225, 228, 229–36, 241
   loan certificates, 42
   nonperforming, 109–10
   price level stability and, 48

Markets. See Financial markets
Mathieson, Donald J., xxii–xxiii

McFadden Act of 1927, 11, 172, 173
McLean, Kenneth A., xxiii
Meltzer, Allan H., xxiii
Merchant banking, 5–6
Mergers and acquisitions
   commercial bank, 13
   competition and, 135–37
   good will and, 82
   and integration of financial services, 16–20
   regional compacts, 137
   regulations, 135–37
Mexico, 425
Monetary Control Act of 1980, 223, 249n.31, 251n.39, 281
Money center banks, 3, 186. See also Banks
   credit worthiness, 425
   income, 29n.28
   off-balance-sheet activities, 8
   securitization and, 4
   wire transfer systems, 21
Money demand. See Money supply/demand
Money supply/demand. See also Currency
   deposit insurance and, 65
   high-powered money, 218, 219, 222, 225, 229, 240, 243, 244, 255–56
   inside/outside money, 161–62
   interest rates and, 222, 223
   measuring, 295n.1
Mortgage loans. See also Housing finance system, mortgage loans
   adjustable rate (ARMs), 302, 309, 313, 315, 316, 324
   default, 314, 315
   fixed-rate, 315
   instruments, 323–24
   rates, 316, 317, 325–26, 329, 335n.80
Mortgage market
   collateralized mortgage obligations (CMOs), 314, 315
   geographic differentials, 323
   mortgage banking, 299
   mortgage insurance, government, 298–99
   mortgage investing, 311
   mortgage securities, 308, 313, 314, 315, 319
   mortgage securitization, 312, 324–25
   Remics, 314, 315
   secondary agencies. See Housing finance system, secondary market agencies
   securitization and, 3, 4–5
Mutual funds, 7, 10, 21

INDEX

National Bank Act of 1864, 61n.30, 71, 95, 166
National Credit Union Administration, 47
New Deal
 banks and, 43
 deposit insurance and, 47
 financial stability model, 34
 housing finance system, 297–99, 313
 regulations, 43–47
"Nonbank" banks. *See* Banks, limited-service

Off-balance-sheet activities, 8–9, 10, 364, 370, 380, 398, 406, 411, 414, 428

Panics, banking, 42–43. *See also* Bank failure; Deposit insurance, federal; Lender of last resort
 bank failures and, 34, 35, 36, 38–40
 causes, 41
 definition, 55n.1
 prevention of, 41–43, 53
Payments finality, 265–66
Payments system
 access to, 233
 bank affiliations and, 22, 277–79
 bank panics and, 53
 commercial firms and, 277–80
 costs (pricing), 263, 270, 275–76, 282, 293
 credit, 264, 269, 272, 273, 274
 daylight overdrafts, 263–64, 271–73, 275, 276–77, 436–37. *See also* Daylight overdrafts
 definition, 263
 discount window and, 279–80
 evolution of, 21, 263–64
 Federal Reserve and, 263, 269–77, 281–82, 284n.17
 nonelectric payments, 263
 reforms/recommendations, 274–75, 292–95, 346
 safety of, 259, 436
 social value, 280–81
 stability, 262, 279
Payments system, Clearing House Interbank Payments System
 activities, 22, 159, 266, 285n.23
 daylight overdrafts, 189, 266, 271–73, 289
 debit cap, 270, 271, 291, 292–93
 Federal Reserve and, 265, 291–92
 risks, 179–81, 266, 267–69, 290–91
 unwinding, 180, 266, 268, 271
Payments system, Fedwire, 22, 157, 179, 233, 250n.38, 350
 activities, 264–65, 286n.39

 daylight overdrafts, 262, 269–70, 273–77, 281, 286n.39, 292, 437
 debit cap, 271, 273–74, 276, 291
 Federal Reserve and, 264, 266–67, 273–74, 281, 282, 285n.35, 291
 monitoring, 286n.40
 position building (securities), 270, 289
 risks, 266–67, 269–70, 290
Payments system, risks, 288–89, 292, 293
 contagious failures and, 271–73
 controlling, 270–71, 289–92
 credit, 21–22, 268–69, 272, 282, 283nn.8, 9, 284n.11
 Federal Reserve and, 261, 288–89
 risk premiums, 275
 settlement, 262
 wire transfer, 263, 266
Payments system, wire transfer, 20–22, 178–81, 261, 263, 266–77, 285n.33
Political power, 128–32, 140
Predatory pricing, 124–25, 138–39
Price level
 currency and, 220
 deposit insurance and, 36
 determinacy, 161, 162, 245n.4
 effects of, 41
 environment, 54–55, 105, 435–36, 445
 interest rates and, 223
 monetary policy and, 222, 223
 relative price change and, 41
 stability, 35, 36, 41, 48, 53, 55, 58n.21, 105–6, 223
Products. *See* Financial products
Proxmire, William, 132

Rates. *See* Interest rates
Regulation. *See also* Deregulation
 competition and, 15–16, 27, 44, 45, 134–39
 daylight overdrafts, 22, 200n.80
 expansion, 11–12, 47
 financial services, 11, 366
 financial stability, 34–35, 49, 104, 365–66
 forbearance, 25
 innovation and, 10–11
 interest rates, 21
 international banking, 15
 market forces and, 45
 reform, 254–59
 securities deregulation (United Kingdom), 16
 securitization and, 4
Regulation, banking, *See also* Reorganization, bank

491

INDEX

bank activities, 44, 94, 104, 111, 212
bank affiliations, 19–20
banking policy and, 226, 259
bank risk, 49, 54–55, 68, 71, 74, 76, 212, 365–66
capital standards, 10–11, 71–73, 85, 87–88
mergers/acquisitions, 135–37
monetary policy and, 220, 223–25, 226
New Deal, 34
interest rates, 45–46
interstate banking, 12
savings and loans, 25, 309
services, 17
Regulation, financial, 343–44, 431–32. See also Financial theory, regulatory; Structural arbitrage; Subsidies, regulatory
Baumol-Panzar-Willig paradigm, 348
competition in, 347, 356, 360–61, 363–64, 366–78, 369, 379, 387, 388, 390, 400, 432–33, 443
contestability, 355–56
costs, 344, 348, 351, 355–56, 357, 362–63, 365, 379, 391, 400
expansion, 348–49, 352, 364–65, 369, 378, 432
government, 345, 346, 358, 359, 379, 384–86, 387
historical model, 386, 387, 389
information, 344, 357, 358, 360, 362, 365, 367, 370, 380–81, 390–91
international, 366–81, 397–98, 399
market structure, 345–48, 352–55, 356, 363, 368, 432–33
pricing, 347
profits, 358, 359, 361, 362
promotional strategies, 349–52, 368, 369, 372
reform, 345–46, 380, 433–35, 442–47
regulatory burden, 362, 365, 367–68, 369, 370–71, 379–80, 383
regulatory climate, 364, 383
services, 346–47, 348, 365, 389, 390
Regulators
benefits/goals, 356–57, 360, 362, 364, 447
competition, international, 366–78, 383–84, 399–400
constraints, 356, 364, 365
disclosure, 384
Federal Reserve, 350–51, 373, 385
governmental, 348, 358, 360–62, 364, 365, 379
market share, 349, 355, 363, 369, 370, 372, 375, 378
private, 347, 358, 360–62, 385

Securities and Exchange Commission, 354, 369, 399
U.S. Supreme Court, 356, 369
Reorganization, bank
advantages of, 94–96
capital and, 78–83, 85–91
legality of, 106–7, 108
plan for, 85–96, 106–9, 110
rules, 90–94, 103
timely, 75–78, 85, 93–94, 102, 110, 111–12
Risk. See also Payments system, risks
bank, 47–49, 53, 64, 74, 76, 95, 170, 180–81, 243, 268, 411, 414
capital and, 10–11, 71–73, 75, 79, 411–13
confidence risk (contagion) effect, 173–76, 178, 199n.69, 268, 271–73, 292
corporate separateness risk effect, 173, 176–78, 190
cost monitoring and, 69–70, 71
credit, 21–23, 250n.38, 268–69, 303, 424
deposit insurance and, 64, 68–71, 108
inflation, 7
insolvency, 163–78
insurance premiums and, 68–71
interest rate, 7, 72, 74, 303
price, 9–10
risk-of-ruin framework, 163
Risk exposure, 4, 11, 24, 25, 74, 127, 173, 411, 414
Roosevelt, Franklin D., 298
Runs, 34, 52, 55n.1, 77, 84, 93, 101–2, 158–59, 174–75, 194n.8. See also Bank failure
definition, 55n.1
history, 40, 41, 42, 43
Maryland, 51
occurrence of, 54
Ohio, 51
stability models and, 52

Safety net, 34–35, 49, 175, 185, 192, 213, 230, 414–15, 416–18
S&Ls. See Savings and loans
Saunders, Anthony, xxiii
Savings and Loan Holding Company Act (SLHCA), 17, 214
Savings and loan industry. See also Housing finance system
regulations, 309–10
regulatory forbearance, 25, 111
reorganization, 111, 340–42. See also Reorganization, bank

492

INDEX

securitization and, 4–5
taxes, 309–10, 332n.36
Savings and loans (S&Ls). *See also* Housing finance system, savings and loan associations
  adjustable rate mortgages (ARMs), 302, 309, 313
  asset powers, 304, 337
  consolidation, 30n.40, 341–42
  conversion, 306–7, 310, 332n.33
  diversification, 308–10
  financial situation, 302–4, 330n.14
  ownership of, 17
  securitization and, 4–5
Schwartz, Anna J., xxiii
Scott, Kenneth E., xxiv
SEC. *See* Securities and Exchange Commission
Secondary market agencies. *See* Housing finance system, secondary market agencies
Securities
  as assets, 80
  "haircut," 231, 249n.34
  pass-through (PTSs), 312
  Treasury, 65, 74, 75
  wire transfer and, 264, 267, 270, 289–90
Securities and Exchange Commission (SEC)
  money market mutual funds and, 354
  Rule 415, 4
Securities firms, 5, 17
Securities markets, 2–7, 28n.8
Securitization
  banking, commercial and investment, 5–7
  causes, 3–4
  consequences of, 4–5
  corporate finance and, 2–3
  definition, 2
  international finance, 403
  of loans, 80–81
  mortgage markets and, 3
Seigniorage, 257, 259, 260n.1, 350, 358
Selby, H. Joe, 95
Services. *See* Financial services
Sherman Act, 136, 138, 186
Silverberg, Stanley C., xxiv
Stability. *See* Financial stability
Standard, monetary, 218
Standby letter of credit (SLC), 8, 20n.30
Stock brokerages, 47
Stock market
  bank functions and, 160–61
  crisis (October 1987), 52, 83

Structural arbitrage, 364–66, 368, 369, 378, 379, 383, 386, 393, 396, 416
Subsidies. *See also* Deposit insurance, federal
  banking policy and, 243
  interest, 184
  lender of last resort and, 240, 436
  regulatory, 362, 365, 368, 379, 380, 384, 390
  secondary mortgage market, 310, 312–13, 317, 327
  unfair competition and, 20

Tax, Interest Equalization, 419
Taxes, 243, 298, 327, 366, 398–99, 422n.9
Tax Reform Act of 1986, 314, 315, 328
Telecommunications. *See* Electronic funds transfer systems
Thrifts. *See also* Financial firms, thrift institutions; Savings and loans (S&Ls)
  definition, 28n.12
Transactions services. *See* Financial services, transactions services
Tying arrangements, 122–23, 138, 182, 183–84

United Kingdom
  as banking center, 214–15
  banking panics, 42, 441
  capital standards, 72, 370, 372, 414
  deposit insurance, 58n.20
  interest rates, 397
  Johnson Matthey, 66
  leading banks, 375
  London interbank market, 175
  regulators, 370, 371
  securities deregulation ("big bang"), 16, 371, 419
United States
  banking panics, 42, 441
  capital standards, 370, 414
  credit market activities, 245n.2
  deposit insurance, 50
  financial system, 37, 47, 441
  interest rates, 397. *See also* Interest rates
  leading banks, 375
  regulation, 441–42
  regulators, 370, 371
Unwinding. *See* Payments system, Clearing House Interbank Payments System, unwinding
Upstreaming. *See* Bank holding companies, returns

Volcker, Paul, 22, 157, 162, 279, 305

493

INDEX

Weicher, John C., xxiv
Wire transfer systems, 20–23
    Bankwire, 350
    CHIPS. *See* Payments system, Clearing House Interbank Payment System
    Fedwire. *See* Payments system, Fedwire

The American Enterprise Institute for Public Policy Research

Founded in 1943, AEI is a nonpartisan, nonprofit, research and educational organization based in Washington, D.C. The Institute sponsors research, conducts seminars and conferences, and publishes books and periodicals.

AEI's research is carried out under three major programs: Economic Policy Studies; Foreign Policy and National Security Studies; and Social and Political Studies. The resident scholars and fellows listed in these pages are part of a network that also includes ninety adjunct scholars at leading universities throughout the United States and in several foreign countries.

The views expressed in AEI publications are those of the authors and do not necessarily reflect the views of the staff, advisory panels, officers, or trustees. AEI itself takes no positions on public policy issues.

Board of Trustees

Willard C. Butcher, *Chairman*
Chm. and CEO
Chase Manhattan Bank

Paul F. Oreffice, *Vice-Chm.*
Chairman
Dow Chemical Co.

Robert Anderson
Chm. and CEO
Rockwell International Corp.

Warren L. Batts
Chm. and CEO
Premark International

Winton M. Blount
Chm. and CEO
Blount, Inc.

Edwin L. Cox
Chairman
Cox Oil & Gas, Inc.

John J. Creedon
Pres. and CEO
Metropolitan Life Insurance Co.

Christopher C. DeMuth
President
American Enterprise Institute

Charles T. Fisher III
Chm. and Pres.
National Bank of Detroit

D. Gale Johnson
Chairman
AEI Council of Academic Advisers

Richard B. Madden
Chm. and CEO
Potlatch Corp.

Robert H. Malott
Chm. and CEO
FMC Corp.

Paul W. McCracken
Edmund Ezra Day University Professor Emeritus
University of Michigan

Randall Meyer
Former President
Exxon Co., U.S.A.

Paul A. Miller
Chm. and CEO
Pacific Lighting Corp.

Richard M. Morrow
Chm. and CEO
Amoco Corp.

David Packard
Chairman
Hewlett-Packard Co.

Edmund T. Pratt, Jr.
Chm. and CEO
Pfizer, Inc.

Mark Shepherd, Jr.
Chairman
Texas Instruments, Inc.

Roger B. Smith
Chm. and CEO
General Motors Corp.

Richard D. Wood
Chairman of the Board
Eli Lilly and Co.

Walter B. Wriston
Former Chairman
Citicorp

Officers

Christopher C. DeMuth
President

David B. Gerson
Executive Vice President

James F. Hicks
Vice President, Finance and Administration; Treasurer; and Secretary

Patrick Ford
Vice President, Public Affairs

Council of Academic Advisers

D. Gale Johnson, *Chairman*
Eliakim Hastings Moore
 Distinguished Service Professor
 of Economics
University of Chicago

Paul M. Bator
John P. Wilson Professor of Law
University of Chicago

Gary S. Becker
University Professor of Economics
 and Sociology
University of Chicago

Donald C. Hellmann
Professor of Political Science and
 International Studies
University of Washington

Gertrude Himmelfarb
Distinguished Professor of
 History
City University of New York

Nelson W. Polsby
Professor of Political Science
University of California at
 Berkeley

Herbert Stein
A. Willis Robertson
 Professor of Economics
 Emeritus
University of Virginia

Murray L. Weidenbaum
Mallinckrodt Distinguished
 University Professor
Washington University

James Q. Wilson
James Collins Professor of
 Management
University of California at
 Los Angeles

Research Staff

Claude E. Barfield
Resident Fellow; Director,
 Science and Technology

Walter Berns
Adjunct Scholar

Douglas J. Besharov
Resident Scholar; Director,
 Social Responsibility Project

Robert H. Bork
John M. Olin Scholar in Legal
 Studies

Nicholas N. Eberstadt
Visiting Scholar

Mark Falcoff
Resident Scholar

Gerald R. Ford
Distinguished Fellow

Murray F. Foss
Visiting Scholar

Suzanne Garment
Resident Scholar

Allan Gerson
Resident Scholar

Robert A. Goldwin
Resident Scholar; Codirector,
 Constitution Project

Gottfried Haberler
Resident Scholar

William S. Haraf
J. Edward Lundy Visiting Scholar;
 Director, Financial Markets
 Regulation Project

Karlyn H. Keene
Resident Fellow; Managing
 Editor, *Public Opinion*

Alan L. Keyes
Resident Scholar

Jeane J. Kirkpatrick
Senior Fellow
Counselor to the President for
 Foreign Policy Studies

Marvin H. Kosters
Resident Scholar; Director,
 Economic Policy Studies

Irving Kristol
Senior Fellow

Robert Licht
Visiting Scholar;
 Associate Director,
 Constitution Project

S. Robert Lichter
DeWitt Wallace Fellow

Chong-Pin Lin
Associate Director,
 China Studies Program

John H. Makin
Resident Scholar; Director,
 Fiscal Policy Studies

Brian F. Mannix
Resident Fellow; Managing
 Editor, *Regulation*

Constantine C. Menges
Resident Scholar

Joshua Muravchik
Resident Scholar

Michael Novak
George F. Jewett Scholar;
 Director, Social and Political
 Studies

Norman J. Ornstein
Resident Scholar

Richard N. Perle
Resident Fellow

Thomas Robinson
Director, China
 Studies Program

William Schneider
Resident Fellow

Peter Skerry
Research Fellow

Herbert Stein
Senior Fellow;
 Editor, *AEI Economist*

Edward Styles
Director, Publications

Sir Alan Walters
Senior Fellow

Kazuhito Wantanabe
Visiting Fellow

Ben J. Wattenberg
Senior Fellow;
 Coeditor, *Public Opinion*

Carolyn L. Weaver
Resident Scholar; Editor,
 Regulation

*John C. Weicher
F.K. Weyerhaeuser Scholar

Makoto Yokoyama
Visiting Fellow

*On leave for government service.

A Note on the Book

*This book was edited by Janet Schilling, Trudy Kaplan,
and Dana Lane of the publications staff of
the American Enterprise Institute.
The figure was drawn by Hördur Karlsson,
and the index was prepared by Julia Petrakis.
The text was set in Palatino, a typeface designed by Hermann Zapf.
Coghill Book Typesetting Company, of Richmond, Virginia,
set the type, and Edwards Brothers Incorporated,
of Ann Arbor, Michigan, printed and bound the book,
using permanent, acid-free paper.*